Regional Innovation Systems

Second Edition

The role of governance in a globalized world

Edited by
Philip Cooke, Martin Heidenreich and
Hans-Joachim Braczyk

Routledge
Taylor & Francis Group

LONDON AND NEW YORK

First published in 1998
Second edition published 2004
by Routledge
11 New Fetter Lane, London EC4P 4EE

Simultaneously published in the USA and Canada
by Routledge
29 West 35th Street, New York, NY 10001

Routledge is an imprint of the Taylor & Francis Group

© 2004 Philip Cooke, Martin Heidenreich and
Hans-Joachim Braczyk, selection and editorial matter; individual
chapters, the contributors

Typeset in Galliard by
HWA Text and Data Management Ltd, Tunbridge Wells
Printed and bound in Great Britain by
The Cromwell Press, Trowbridge, Wiltshire

British Library Cataloguing in Publication Data
A catalogue record for this book is available from the British Library

Library of Congress Cataloging in Publication Data
Regional innovation systems : the role of governance in a globalized
world / edited by Philip Cooke, Martin Heidenreich and Hans-
Joachim Braczyk. – 2nd ed.
    p. cm.
Includes bibliographical references and index.
    1. Regional planning. 2. Technological innovations–Economic
aspects. 3. Regional economics. I. Cooke, Philip (Philip N.) II.
Heidenreich, Martin. III. Braczyk, Hans-Joachim, 1942–
    HT391 .R3355 2004
    307.1' 2–dc22
                                                    2003017057
ISBN 0–415–30368–0 (hb)
ISBN 0–415–30369–9 (pb)

Regional Innovation Systems

In the most comprehensive and detailed way yet attempted, this second edition of *Regional Innovation Systems* re-examines key theoretical and empirical elements of contemporary regional economic development and provides an interesting test of the robustness of the original arguments in the book. Since the first edition, more industrial policy-making is influenced by the RIS analysis, and many national and regional governments have adopted RIS approaches, along with related instruments such as promotion of industry clusters, academic entrepreneurship, regional venture capital and science-led development strategies.

Set within a broadly evolutionary economics perspective, accounts are given of the systems interactions occurring between firms and the innovation support infrastructure. Case studies include 'high road' instances such as Baden-Württemberg, Brabant and Singapore, and reconversion regions which emphasize 'upstream' innovation such as Tampere (Finland) with close university–industry links or 'downstream' near-market innovation such as Catalonia. Some have quite *dirigiste* systems, as in Singapore, Slovenia and Gyeonggi (Korea), others are more localist, as in the cases of Tohoku (Japan) or Tuscany. Policy implications of the analyses offered and variation explored are set in a context where regional administrations have limited access to the full scale of innovation policy instruments.

Students and researchers will welcome this comprehensive treatment of regional innovation systems, a key concept in understanding regional and industrial development, which is a topic widely studied by geographers, economists and planners. Regional administrations, intermediaries and firms will also benefit from reading the analysis and accounts presented in this volume.

Philip Cooke is Director of the Centre for Advanced Studies at the University of Wales, Cardiff. **Martin Heidenreich** is Professor of European Studies in Social Sciences at the University of Bamberg. **Hans-Joachim Braczyk** (1942–99) was a member of the Board of the Centre of Technology Assessment in Baden-Württemberg and head of the Technology, Organization, Work department.

Other titles available from Routledge

Geographies of Labour Market Inequality
Edited by Ron Martin and Philip S. Morrison

Metropolitan Governance and Spatial Planning
Comparative Case Studies of European City-Regions
Edited by Willem Salet, Andy Thornley and Anton Kreukels

Social Exclusion in European Cities
Processes, Experiences and Responses
Edited by Ali Madanipour, Goran Cars and Judith Allen

Regional Innovation Strategies
The Challenge for Less-Favoured Regions
Edited by Kevin Morgan and Claire Nauwelaers

Restructuring Industry and Territory
The Experience of Europe's Regions
Edited by Anna Giunta, Arnoud Lagendijk and Andy Pike

Community Economic Development
Edited by Graham Haughton

For further information and to order from our online catalogue visit our website at www.routledge.com

Contents

Contributors

Shiro Abe is Professor of Sociopolitical Information Science, Graduate School of Information Sciences at Tohoku University, Sendai, Japan, and General Director, Intelligent Cosmos Academic Society. His research subjects are the study of political behaviour and regional policy.

Jordi Bacaria is Professor of Economics at the University Autònoma de Barcelona, researcher at the Institut Universitari d'Estudis Europeus (IUEE), and European Co-director at the Instituto de Estudios para la Integración Europea, in Mexico on behalf of the European Commission. He is author and co-author of several publications on regional innovation, monetary union, jurisdictional cooperation and competition in Europe, Euro-Mediterranean trade and European and Latin American relations.

Patricia Boekholt works in the field of science, technology and economic development as a director of Technopolis, a British-Dutch research and consultancy organization specializing in innovation policy. She was previously a senior researcher at the TNO Centre for Technology and Policy Studies. Her current work focuses on regional technology policies, with research projects such as regional innovation systems for the European Commission, the targeted socio-economic research programme and involvement in several EU regional innovation and technology transfer strategy projects. She has also published on comparative studies in RTD policies, the competitiveness of industrial clusters and interfirm networks.

Susana Borràs Alomar is Associate Professor in the Department of Social Sciences, Roskilde University, Denmark. Her current research interests are centred on EU policy-making and governance patterns, together with the political economy of the EU's technology policy and cohesion policy. She is currently co-ordinating a research project on the European system of innovation (www.segera.ruc.dk).

Hans-Joachim Braczyk Died in 1999. He worked at the Freie University of Berlin, at the Technological University of Berlin, at the Institute for Social Research in Dortmund, at the University of Bielefeld and as Director of the ASIF-Institute of Bielefeld founded by him. Since 1992 he was a member of the board of the Centre of Technology Assessment in Baden-Württemberg and head of the Technology, Organization, Work department. His work focused on changes in industry, and transformations to a service and information society. He was Chair of Industrial Sociology at the University of Stuttgart.

Philip Cooke is Professor of Regional Development at the University of Wales, Cardiff, and Director of its Centre for Advanced Studies. His principal research interest is in knowledge economies and regional innovation systems. His main current focus is Life Sciences and he is part of Cardiff University's ESRC-funded CESAGen, the UK's first dedicated research centre in the economics and ethics of genomics. He is author or editor of ten books on aspects of regional development and innovation, most recently *Knowledge Economies* (Routledge, 2000). He has published more than a hundred articles on this and related subjects and is editor of the journal *European Planning Studies*.

Dick de Jager works as a senior consultant at Technopolis in Amsterdam, specializing in the analysis and implementation of national and regional innovation systems, currently in the Netherlands, the UK, Belgium, Estonia and Croatia. Before joining Technopolis he was the project manager for the RITTS project (Regional Innovation and Technology Transfer Strategies and Infrastructures) in North-Brabant.

Gabi Dei Ottati is Professor of Industrial Economics at the University of Florence (Faculty of Economics). Her principal research interest is in industrial districts. She is the author of many articles on various aspects of local development, among them 'Trust, interlinking transactions and credit in the industrial district' (*Cambridge Journal of Economics*, 18(6) 1994), 'Exit, voice and the evolution of inudstrial districts: the case of the post World War II economic development of Prato', (*Cambridge Journal of Economics*, 27(4), 2003), 'Social concertation and local development: the case of industrial districts' (*European Planning Studies*, 10(4), 2002). Recently she was co-editor (with Becattini, Bellandi and Sforzi) of the volume *From Industrial Districts to Local Development: An Itinerary of Research*, Edward Elgar, 2003.

Andrea Fernàndez-Ribas is an economist researcher at the Universitat Autònoma de Barcelona at the Institut Universitari d'Estudis Europeus (IUEE). . Her research and publications have focused largely on industrial location in urban areas, regional innovation systems and evaluation of innovation and technology policies. Her PhD thesis was on cooperative innovation and the role of public policies.

Meric S. Gertler is Professor of Geography and Planning, and Goldring Chair in Canadian Studies at the University of Toronto. He co-directs (with David Wolfe) the Program on Globalization and Regional Innovation Systems (PROGRIS) at Toronto's Munk Centre for International Studies. His current research interests include: the role of regional and national institutions in shaping industrial knowledge and practices; the emergence and evolution of Toronto's biomedical cluster; and the role of creativity and diversity in determining the ability of cities to attract and retain highly educated workers in North America. He is co-investigator (with David Wolfe) on a major five-year national study 'Innovation systems and economic development: the role of local and regional clusters in Canada'. His recent publications include *Innovation and Social Learning* (with David Wolfe, Palgrave/Macmillan, 2002), *The Oxford Handbook of Economic Geography* (with Gordon Clark and Maryann Feldman, Oxford University Press, 2000), and *The New Industrial Geography: Regions, Regulation and Institutions* (with Trevor Barnes, Routledge, 1999). He is Associate Editor of *The Journal of Economic Geography* and is also a member of the Canadian Institute of Planners.

Robert Hassink is a Lecturer at the University of Bonn, Department of Geography, Socio-Economics of Space. His research interests include economic geography, evolutionary regional economics, industrial restructuring and regional economic development, and regional innovation policies. His PhD thesis was on regional innovation policy: case studies from the Ruhr Area, Baden-Württemberg and the North East of England.

Martin Heidenreich studied economics and social sciences at the universities of Bielefeld, Bologna and Paris VII. Previously senior researcher at the Centre for Technology Assessment in Baden-Württemberg, since 2000 he has been Professor of European Studies in Social Sciences at the University of Bamberg. His research interests are regional and national patterns of work, management and innovation.

Rolf G. Heinze is Professor of Sociology at the Ruhr-University of Bochum (Germany). His research activities focus on sociology of work, employment policy and political sociology. He is a consultant for national and regional authorities on these issues.

Josef Hilbert is head of the Research Group on Health and Quality of Life Businesses at the Institute for Work and Technology (Science Centre North Rhine-Westphalia), Gelsenkirchen, Germany. His research activities focus on innovation, training, re-engineering and growth strategies in health and social services.

Hing Ai Yun teaches in the Department of Sociology, the National University of Singapore, and is currently doing research on the restructuring of financial institutions and new forms of work and production relations. Another area of her research examines the interaction between home and work.

Mika Kautonen is a Research Fellow at the Work Research Centre's Research Unit for Science, Technology and Innovation Studies and at the Research Unit for Urban and Regional Development Studies, both at the University of Tampere, Finland. Recently he was in charge of a large research project Networks, Innovation Milieus and Regions, (1998–2001), which was funded by the National Technology Agency of Finland (Tekes) and which investigated firms' innovation environments and regional innovation policies in Finland. He has participated in several international comparative research projects, among which are Regional Innovation Systems: Designing for the Future, under the TSER Programme of the European Commission, and a newly started City-Regions as Intelligent Territories: Inclusion, Competitiveness and Learning. He has published more than thirty articles related to his research interests in regional innovation systems, innovation processes and networks, and innovation policies. He has also consulted several national and regional authorities on these issues.

Knut Koschatzky studied geography and economics at Berlin's Free University and at Hanover University and gained his PhD in economic geography in 1986. He served as assistant in the Department of Economic Geography and to the President of Hanover University. He began work in the Fraunhofer Institute for Systems and Innovation Research in 1988. During the same year scientific administration at the Bavarian Ministry of Economic Affairs. Since 1995 he has been head of the Department of Innovation Services and Regional Development. He has been a Reader in Economic Geography at Hanover University since 2001. His research and publication activities focus on new economic geography, regional innovation systems and innovation networks, technology and innovation indicators, knowledge and technology transfer, innovative services, firm foundations, and regional technology policy.

Pasi Koski is a Research Fellow at the Work Research Centre's Research Unit for Science, Technology and Innovation Studies at the University of Tampere, Finland. His current research includes the internationalization of science and technology systems, innovation policies and workplace development. He is also preparing his doctoral dissertation on teamworking and organizational learning in a tyre manufacturing firm.

Gerhard Krauss is Associate Professor in Sociology at the University of Lille I and researcher at the Centre Lillois d'Études et de Recherches Sociologiques et

Économiques (Clersé). Previously he worked at the University of Stuttgart and at the Centre for Technology Assessment in Baden-Württemberg; he was also a visiting scholar at the University of California, Los Angeles (UCLA) and at the Centre de Sociologie de l'Innovation of the Ecole des Mines, Paris. He is currently running a comparative research project on the failure of start-up founders and their companies in emerging knowledge-based fields.

Peter Maskell initially trained as an economic geographer (Master's degree) and regional economist (PhD) but was conferred a doctorate (Dr. mere.) in business economics before being offered a chair at Copenhagen Business School in 1993. He is a former chairman of Denmark's Social Science Research Council (SSF) and of the Standing Committee of Social Sciences at the European Science Foundation as well as a number of other international scientific bodies. His work includes books on regional development, industrial restructuring, new firm formations, spatial competitiveness and related policy questions. He is presently Research Director for DRUID – the Danish Research Unit on Industrial Dynamics (www.druid.dk).

Jürgen Nordhause-Janz is a social scientist and senior researcher at the Research Group Development Trends of the Employment System at the Institute of Work and Technology (Science Centre, North Rhine-Westphalia), Gelsenkirchen, Germany. His research activities focus on structural change, innovation, qualifications and regional labour market analysis.

Dieter Rehfeld is director of the research department of Innovative Spaces at the Institute of Work and Technology (Science Centre, North Rhine-Westphalia), Gelsenkirchen, Germany. His research activities focus on regional and sectoral innovation systems, production clusters and regional change.

Gerd Schienstock is Professor of Social Sciences at the University of Tampere and Scientific Director of its Work Research Centre in Finland. He has recently co-ordinated the National Research Programme on the Finnish Innovation System funded by the Finnish National Fund for Research and Development Sitra. His research focuses on regional innovation systems, work organization and management systems, technology assessment, and the information society.

David A. Wolfe is Professor of Political Science at the University of Toronto and Co-Director (with Meric Gertler) of the Program on Globalization and Regional Innovation Systems (PROGRIS) at the Centre for International Studies. He is National Co-ordinator of the ISRN and the Principal Investigator on its recently awarded Major Collaborative Research Initiative on Innovation Systems and Economic Development: The Role of Local and Regional Clusters in Canada.

His recent publications include *Innovation, Institutions and Territory: Regional Innovation Systems in Canada*, and *Knowledge, Clusters and Regional Innovation: Economic Development in Canada*, both co-edited with J. Adam Holbrook, *Innovation and Social Learning: Institutional Adaptation in an Era of Technological Change*, co-edited with Meric S. Gertler, and *Clusters Old and New: The Transition to a Knowledge Economy in Canada's Regions*.

Preface

This is the second edition of *Regional Innovation Systems*, a book whose first edition experienced an extended gestation period due to publishing industry takeover turmoil in the mid-1990s. The first edition nevertheless sold out and the new owners of the title, Taylor & Francis, kindly invited us to consider writing a new edition. Helen Ibbotson has been our invaluable guide in this challenging task. Phil Cooke and, especially, Martin Heidenreich shouldered the logistical burden of commissioning new work and encouraging original authors to reprise and revise their work of nearly ten years ago. Sadly, in November 1999, the death occurred of Hans-Joachim Braczyk, key animator of the original conference in Stuttgart and co-editor of the first edition. All who knew him personally or by his works will be pleased that his influence in this burgeoning academic and policy field lives on.

As a further sign of change in the context of intellectual production, the Centre for Technology Assessment (CTA) in Stuttgart will close at the end of 2003. Funded by the Baden-Württemberg government in the optimism of the mid-1990s, it closes due to re-prioritization of expenditure in the troubled early 2000s. The first volume was the fruit of a collaborative effort of the Centre for Advanced Studies (CASS), University of Wales, Cardiff, and the Centre for Technology Assessment in Baden-Württemberg (CTA). In March 1995, Phil Cooke (CASS) and Gerd Schienstock (CTA, subsequently Professor at the Work Research Centre at the University of Tampere, Finland) wrote a position paper on 'Regional innovation systems – designing for the future'. The authors stated:

> Today, the number one factor for competitive advantage is innovation. With the changes brought about in global economic relations by the rise to prominence of the East Asian economies and the demise of Fordism as a model of industrial and wider societal regulation, new approaches to fashioning competitive advantage from innovative capacities have emerged. Amongst the most challenging of these are the efforts to forge systems of innovation in support of business competitiveness on a regional scale. These complement more established systems of innovation that operate at the national level by seeking, as appropriate and with local sensitivity, to integrate

the whole industrial fabric within a given regionally administered space. Evidence of such systems began to emerge in the 1980s as a consequence of studies showing the existence of networked innovation architectures linking firms, intermediaries, research institutes, government agencies and technology bureaux, especially in regions with many small sub-contracting firms.

Inspired by this paper, the Centre for Technology Assessment in Baden-Württemberg asked experts from thirteen regions all over the world to describe their regional innovation systems, and the Centre invited them to participate in an international conference on the subject, which was held in Stuttgart in Autumn 1995. On the basis of the discussions held during the conference, the editors asked all the authors to rewrite their papers and to adjust them to the plan of this book. We were very grateful that the contributors to the present volume accepted this task.

For this second edition all the original authors were invited to update their chapters. All but four of them were in a position to do so. Accordingly, the second edition offers a unique longitudinal study of innovation system evolution over some ten years during which *globalization* has become entrenched, *innovation* has become key to increases in productivity and competitiveness, and scientific as well as creative *knowledge* has become a key economic asset. The original studies dealt with regional innovation in Asian, European and North American settings. The second edition strengthens representation of the first two continents with commissioned chapters on Slovenia and South Korean regional innovation models.

In compiling this second edition, the editors wish to thank all contributors, our publisher, especially Helen Ibbotson, and readers and purchasers of the first edition who showed their interest in the subject of regional innovation systems even though, or probably because, it was a new and challenging field linking distant disciplines of regional science, policy studies and innovation economics in interesting ways.

For this edition, the publishers invited us to choose a cover design. We chose a lighthouse motif for a number of reasons. Lighthouses illuminate routeways and guide voyagers away from darkness and uncertainty. Their beams reach out beyond the region in which they are set and they act as an international network of such beacons. But, mostly, as Ronald Coase[1] stated in his famous paper, 'The Lighthouse in Economics':

> The lighthouse appears in the writings of economists because of the light it is supposed to throw on the question of the economic functions of government. It is often used as an example of something which has to be provided by government rather than private enterprise. What economists usually seem to have in mind is that the impossibility of securing payment from the owners

of the ships that benefit from the existence of the lighthouse makes it
unprofitable for any private individual or firm to build and maintain a
lighthouse.

What Coase goes on to show, of course, is that historically they were privately
supplied though subsequently managed subnationally (at least in the UK and
Ireland) and paid for by a levy on shipowners at the port. They function efficiently
without national administration. This seems to us a good metaphor for a book
that sees virtue in *regional* innovation systems.

Philip Cooke
Martin Heidenreich
March 2003

Note

1   R. Coase (1974) 'The lighthouse in economics', *Journal of Law and Economics*,
     17, 357–76, reprinted in R. Coase (1988) *The Firm, the Market and the Law*,
     Chicago: University of Chicago Press.

Abbreviations

3M	3 Metropolitan
APMA	Automotive Parts Manufacturers' Association
ASEAN	Association of Southeast Asian Nations
AUR	Administration of University Research grants
BERD	Business R&D Expenditure
CAS	collective agreements
CASA	Higher Education and the Assessment and Monitoring Council
CASS	Centre for Advanced Studies
CEEC	central and eastern European countries
CFI	Canada Foundation for Innovation
CIC	Council of Catalonia
CIDEM	Centre of Entrepreneurial Information and Development
CIRIT	Commission for Research and Technology Innovation
CIS	Community Innovation Survey
CRITTS	centres of research, innovation and technology transfer
CSIC	Spanish National Public Research Centre
CST	Council for Science and Technology
CTA	Centre for Technology Assessment
CTID	Centre for Technological and Industrial Development
DURSI	Department of Universities, Research and Information Society
EDB	Economic Development Board
EEDC	Employment and Economical Development Centres
EOI	export-orientated industrialization
EPA˙	Economic Planning Agency
EPE	electronics and precision engineering
EPO	European Patent Office
ERDF	European Regional Development Fund
ERIS	Entrepreneurial Regional Innovation System
FDI	Foreign Direct Investment
FEDER	Fonds européen de développement régional (European Regional Development Fund)
FORCEM	Foundation for Continuous Training

FTA	Free Trade Agreement
FTN	Fomento del Trabajo Nacional
GDP	Gross Domestic Product
GERD	gross expenditure on R&D
GSBF	Gyeonggi Small Business Foundation
HDA*	Hokkaido Development Agency
HEI	higher education institute
ICO	Official Credit Organization
ICR	Intelligent Cosmos Research K K
ICREA	Catalan Institute for Research and Advanced Studies
ICT	Information and communication technology
IPO	initial public offering
IRAP	Industrial Research Assistance Program
IRIS	Institutional Regional Innovation System
ISR	International Survey Research Corporation
ITA	Industrial Technology Advisors
ITE	Institute of Technical Education
JST	Japan Science and Technology Corporation
KEF	Knowledge Exploitation Fund
KIBS	knowledge-intensive business services
KIC	Knowledge-intensive Clustering
KISTEP	Korea Institute of Science and Technology Evaluation and Planning
LGAI	General Laboratory of Experiments and Investigation
MAFF*	Ministry of Agriculture, Forestry and Fisheries
MAS	Monetary Authority of Singapore
MC*	Ministry of Construction
MCA*	Management and Co-ordination Agency
ME*	Ministry of Education
MEST	Ministry of Education, Culture, Sports, Science and Technology
METI	Ministry of Economy, Trade and Industry
MHA*	Ministry of Home Affairs
MITI*	Ministry of International Trade and Industry
MLIT	Ministry of Land, Infrastructure and Transport
MNCS	multinational corporations
MOCIE	Ministry of Commerce, Industry and Energy
MOE	Ministry of Environment
MOST	Ministry of Science and Technology
MPM	Ministry of Public Management, Home Affairs, Posts and Telecommunications
MPT*	Ministry of Posts and telecommunications

MT*	Ministry of Transport
MVA	Medicon Valley Academy
NAFTA	North American Free Trade Agreement
NCD	National Comprehensive Development
NCDP	National Comprehensive Development Plan
NIC	New Industrial City
NICP	New Industrial Cities Promotion
NIEs	Newly Industrialized Economies
NIRA	National Institute for Research Advancement
NLA*	National Land Agency
NPB	National Productivity Board
NRC	National Research Council
NSI	National Systems of Innovation
NSTB	National Science and Technology Board
NTUC	National Trade Union Council
OCRI	Ottawa Centre for Research
OEM	Original Equipment Manufacturers
PCD	Pollution Control Department
PMO	Prime Minister's Office
PRE	public research establishment
PSI	Pollutant Standards Index
R&D	Research and development
RIS	Regional Innovation Systems
RITTS	Regional Innovation and Technology Transfer Strategies
ROI	return on investment
RRC	Regional Research Center
RTD	Research and Technology Development
RTP	Regional Technology Plans
S&T	science and technology
SEP	Strategic Economic Plan
SMBA	Small and Medium Business Administration
SME	small and medium-sized enterprises
SMIPC	Small and Medium Industry Promotion Corporation
SPM	strategic planning meeting
SRE	Samenwerkingsverband Regio Eindhoven (Eindhoven Regional Government
STA*	Science and Technology Agency
STEPI	Science and Technology Policy Institute
TFP	total factor productivity
TI	Technology Institute
TIC	Technology Information Centres, Japan

TIC	Tohoku Intelligent Cosmos, Japan
TQM	Total quality management
TSER	Targeted Socio-Economic Research
TUT	Tampere University of Technology
UNIDO	United Nations Industrial Development Organisation
USEPA	US Environmental Protection Agency
UTA	University of Tampere
WDA	Welsh Development Agency
WDR	Westdeutscher Rundfunk
WEFO	Welsh European Funding Organisation

Note: * Name of Japanese entities prior to central government reorganization in January 2001.

Introduction
Regional innovation systems – an evolutionary approach

Philip Cooke

> At the threshold of a new century we are operating with models and policies which apply to the last one. There is no doubt whatsoever that in the next century the capability to produce and use knowledge will be the key to success for countries as well as firms and individuals. Being good at allocating tangible resources will be only of secondary importance; what will matter is how well one succeeds in developing organisations, which promote learning and the wise use of knowledge. Countries which are successful in upgrading skills and in creating knowledge intensive jobs – that is countries with strong systems of innovation – will be most successful in avoiding unemployment and the development of bad jobs.
>
> (Lundvall, 1994).

Introduction: into the knowledge economy

This book re-introduces, in the most comprehensive and detailed way yet attempted, the theoretical and empirical construct we call regional innovation systems.[1] The title of this chapter, and particularly the quotation from Lundvall, were part of the original introduction for the first edition. The old title, oddly cryptic as it must have seemed, has been widely cited, signifying the interest in and usefulness of the first edition. So much has this been the case that the first edition sold out and we were approached by the current publisher to edit a second, revised edition. Accordingly, virtually all the chapters have been updated and partly or wholly rewritten. Two new chapters, on Slovenia and a South Korean region, were commissioned. Much has changed since 1995 when these chapters were first commissioned by and for the initial Centre for Technology Assessment (CTA) conference in Stuttgart. CTA itself is, in 2003, in the throes of closure as the resources of its sponsor, the government of Baden-Württemberg, have shrunk with the economic downturn of the early tenty-first century. Hence the importance of Lundvall's (1994) prescient words even today. Notice the robustness of the conviction 'that in the next century the capability to produce and use *knowledge* will be the key to success for countries as well as firms and individuals' (my emphasis).

The present economic downturn mimics the timing of the last one (early 1990s) but the cause of the present malaise is different. Then it was 'debt overhang', over-investment in unproductive assets like land and property, and for manu-facturers the drying up of demand after the initial economic upturn associated with the liberalisation of Central and Eastern Europe and the EU Single Market. 'Innovation' was the injunction from academe and governance entities alike as competitiveness gaps between the main trading blocs were becoming exposed. Innovation duly occurred, so much so that by the end of the 1990s normally sober financial experts like Alan Greenspan, Chairman of the US Federal Reserve Bank, were observing that GDP had suddenly become 'lighter' and hinting that full-spread features in *Business Week* trumpeting the birth of a 'new economy' might be worth taking seriously. Later, his reference to the perils of 'irrational exuberance' heralded the end of the longest stock market boom and the onset of what may yet be the longest slump. Without wishing to individualise history, Greenspan's observations between 1998 and 2000 are emblematic of the apogee of what can already be seen as an exceptional feeding frenzy for innovators, particularly but not only in the USA.

Innovation, much of which historically had followed a 'chance discovery' model where occasional 'breakthroughs' punctuated lengthy periods of relative quiescence, had become – as the textbooks advocated – systemic. It also became distinctively regional, concentrating where pools of 'talent' in entrepreneurship, investment, science and technology coincided. As Florida (2002) later showed us, these spaces also coincided with 'the Geography of Bohemia', in the creative arts rather than the Czech regional sense. Certain cities and their regional hinterlands became carriers of this 'new economy' rooted in telecommunications, information technology, biotechnology and both old and new media. To these can be added, though not always geographically overlapping, advanced financial services such as futures, options and derivatives, and creative arts giving rise to cultural industries. Together these account, for the most part, for what has come to be called the *knowledge economy* (Cooke, 2002). This is what Lundvall's quotation refers to and this is the phenomenon that now exercises the minds of academics, firms and governance entities for which *innovation* became a mantra in the 1990s. It is the 'new kid on the block' and it holds out vast opportunities, but also major obstacles and difficulties, as regions and cities that led the 'new economy' surge, reel back in the face of major industrial wreckage of the Internet-invoked dot.com 'bubble', and try to work out how to 're-think science' (Nowotny *et al.*, 2001).

Thus, a model of innovation that propelled the business boom of the 1990s arose regionally in Massachusetts centred on Greater Boston, California north at San Francisco–San Jose, California south at Los Angeles–San Diego, and New York. Lesser upsurges were found by Norton (2000) in Seattle, Denver and Austin. These were, and remain, locations where interaction among scientists, engineers, entrepreneurs and venture capitalists freely occurs. This is of the essence, for the regional innovation model was simply one where largely publicly-funded research organisations with high financial absorptive capacity and numerous research 'stars' housed in specialist research centres (Gibbons, 2000) generated knowledge, and venture capitalists scoured the laboratories for knowledge to exploit commercially by arranging patenting, licensing, spinout, incubation, financing and, in successful cases, swift stock market flotation through an initial public offering (IPO). As Mark Granovetter and colleagues showed, such interactions were highly embedded, exclusive, localised and heavily reliant on network modulation in a milieu characterised by vibrant and active social capital (Castilla *et al.*, 2000).

Varieties of regional innovation system

Now that regional innovation systems thinking has grown in prominence to the point where, including the studies represented in this book, over 200 (Carlson, 2004) have been conducted in often exemplary empirical detail, initially in Europe (including the East, see Cooke *et al.* 2000) but also in Asia (Abe, 1998; Hing, 1998; Hassink, 2000) and North America (Latouche, 1998; Wolfe and Gertler, 1998; Bergman and Feser, 2001), it is diversifying. The initial position, arising from the European experience, was very different from that just outlined as having risen in regions in the USA. A widely understood definition was: 'a regional innovation system consists of interacting knowledge generation and exploitation sub-systems linked to global, national and other regional systems for commercialising new knowledge' (see, for example, Cooke *et al.*, 2000 for a graphic representation). The European perspective was conditioned by three problems to which a regional innovation systems approach was thought a likely antidote. First, excellent science remained in dusty journals and laboratories rather than being exploited commercially. Worse, excellent published science originating from Europe was being commercially exploited in the USA by excellent technologists and investors. Second, Europe was assailed, as had been the USA, by innovations in mature manufacturing sectors like automotive and consumer electronic engineering, and was responding by placing responsibility and stress upon the supply chain through lean production and business process re-engineering. This also ritualistically cut costs by making core workers redundant. For the supply-chain incumbents, innovation was often an indigestible novelty. So innovation effort was expended overwhelmingly on incremental improvements in mature manufacturing firms. Third, there was massive market failure in advanced business services of the kind discussed that managed knowledge exploitation in Silicon Valley and such places. This meant that state intervention was necessary to substitute for what ordinarily would have been market transactions. Though many regional governances (meaning private associations, chambers of industry and commerce and governments – thus private and public entities) proved to be smarter than the market, their executives were ill-attuned to innovation support, being under-trained, risk-averse and used to facilitating 'rent-seeking' by grant-hungry businesses rather than more innovative financial packages.

We may refer to the latter kind of regional innovation system as an Institutional Regional Innovation System (IRIS) since it is heavily based on public knowledge generation and exploitation institutions such as public laboratories, universities, technology transfer organisations, incubators, investors, trainers and other intermediaries. A good, but salutary example of an IRIS is Wales, with which this author is very familiar as the appropriate chapter in this and the previous edition show, where almost every innovation-promoting actor is public but in which innovation capability has declined very rapidly since approximately 1998. While the private sector was leading the innovation effort, especially in the shape of inward investors from Japan, Wales was the only UK region in which manufacturing employment continued to grow and a good innovation profile was registered (see Cooke *et al.*, 2000). But in 1998–2002, 44,000 manufacturing jobs disappeared as these innovators shifted production to Central and Eastern Europe and elsewhere while other firms went under. Although public agencies had worked closely with such firms – even assisting in the building of supply-chain clusters in electronic and automotive engineering – they seem to have learned little. Now, even an innovative public venture capital entity, established to compensate for market failure, is inducing 'rent-seeking' from interested equity-hunting innovators by requiring them to raise half the required amount from grant-aid first.

In an attempt to get to grips with the abiding gap in innovation performance between Europe and the USA, contrasts were made with what have elsewhere been referred to as 'new economy innovation systems' and 'private innovation systems' (see, for example, Cooke, 2001). Critics of that position (see, for instance, Asheim, 2002) see, not incorrectly, danger if European regions move too swiftly away from their IRIS traditions towards what, pulling together the two prefigurative concepts above, is more appropriately termed an Entrepreneurial Regional Innovation System (ERIS).[2] The first policy danger is that ERISs 'do not have the same long-term stable and systemic support of historical technological trajectories, which … have represented the most important growth factor' (ibid., 120). This is a respectable, not untypical European position, one for which the present author was upbraided, after criticising the US regional boom-and-bust innovation model, with the following comment: 'Ah, I see, you want a plane that never crashes' to which I responded in the affirmative (Isaacs, 2002). But, of course that is easier said than done. Europe needs ERISs that can escape 'lock-in' of the kind implied above and minimise wasteful 'scrapping' of jobs, firms and investments in ways in which the US model seems incapable. In the chapters from the Nordic countries of Denmark and Finland, a possible alternative may be found.

The second, more intellectual, objection to ERIS as compared to IRIS is that it appears to give the lead in innovation to venture capitalists rather than scientists or governments, in any case to actors driven by money-making rather than higher ethical or democratic ideals. This is a profound and complex point that will come more and more to the forefront as the knowledge economy becomes a more thoroughgoing aspect of life in the future. Three points only can be made here. First, there is a feeling of the danger that ERIS lacks the system-like characteristics of IRIS identified in the quotation from Asheim (2002) and venture capital-driven market forces alone will determine innovation trajectories. That is, no checks and balances such as those implied in the interactive systems model of innovation promulgated especially by the early proponents of national systems of innovation (Lundvall, 1992; Nelson, 1993; Edquist, 1997). But this is to miss a key point, which is that most research is publicly funded. Without governments and foundations, there would be less and less research as companies and whole sectors cut back on what can too easily be perceived by shareholders as wasteful R&D expenditure (Stewart, 2001). Accordingly, venture capital is symbiotic (some would say parasitic) upon government. Second, the advocacy of IRIS as a source of long-term stability and path-dependent development trajectory relies on a comparable economic context. But globalisation, capital flight to cheap labour zones and the onset of a knowledge-driven economy have shattered such comfortable equilibrium notions. The new context has been captured with *élan* in the following quotation:

> Science is certainty; research is uncertainty. Science is supposed to be cold, straight and detached; research is warm, involving and risky. Science puts an end to the vagaries of human disputes; research creates controversies. Science produces objectivity by escaping as much as possible from the shackles of ideology, passions and emotions; research feeds on all of those to render objects of inquiry familiar.
>
> (Latour, 1998)

If we connect Latour's observation to the identified weaknesses of IRIS, then it is clear that the European way (including the UK, despite perceptions that those Anglo-Celtic islands share the same 'Anglo-Saxon' variety of capitalism as the USA) is still quite fully immersed in a scientific rather than a research-driven institutional culture and manner of conceiving of innovation. However, under knowledge economy conditions it is those regional innovation set-ups that accommodate to the economic dynamism that can be associated with 'research' that will prosper most. Finally and briefly, it is important not to forget that democratic and inclusive (to citizens) as states may be, a great deal of science and research upon which modern high technology economies rest is derived from the 'crusade against communism' in its various forms from military to space expenditure. Death still motivates the newer post-Cold War 'crusade against cancer' research budgets, albeit with preventative rather than destructive intent in mind.

Regional innovation systems and clusters

We have seen that there are distinctive generic types of regional innovation system, but the conceptual and empirical diversification associated with the concept has at least two further variations. Both are influenced by the meteoric rise up the policy and intellectual agendas during the 1990s and early 2000s of the concept of clusters. In the Introduction to the first edition this was, of course noted as a factor affecting broader thinking about systems of innovation. However, then, vertical clusters centred upon supply chains were more to the forefront in the still-useful thinking of authors such as Sabel (1992) and others reprised below. Where lateral relationships among firms were in question, the idea of inter-firm and inter-organisational *networks* was then more pronounced. However, two influences brought new intellectual respectability to both the concept of the *region* and its equally spatial micro-variant *cluster*. The authors of this rise up the popularity stakes for economic geography were two economists, Paul Krugman and Michael Porter, both of whose intellectual influence may have already passed its zenith for reasons to be discussed later, but whose legacy upon policy lingers for the foreseeable future.

Why did this interest in regions and clusters burgeon at the same time among thinkers for whom their subject had for decades 'revolved as if on the head of a pin'? Three brief reasons can be advanced. First, the spatial dimension of social and economic life had not in itself disappeared, rather, the lenses through which economists of all stripes looked at the world were, if not rose-tinted, blurred by scale. That is, economies of scale from bulk production yielding constant returns under conditions of modest stability and predictability ruled the roost as both analytical and policy model. This applied, to repeat, to the whole spectrum of economists from neoclassical to Marxist.

Second, this old-fashioned view, inherited from the 'bad' Marshall (1890/ 1961) incorporating mechanistic, marginalist economic models that he himself knew to be based on poor analogies, but mathematically representable techniques, de-socialised humanity. Neoclassical theorems finished the job, transforming economics into a sub-species of applied mathematics. Much of the task of writers from an evolutionary economics and social economy perspective has been concerned to re-socialise economic thought and policy. Hence the popularity of such elements of study as innovation, interactive learning, trust, proximity, embeddedness, cognition, tacit and codified knowledge exchange, traded and untraded interdependencies and the ways co-operation and collaboration have always underlain successful competitiveness in economies. These are susceptible to and articulate modalities of socio-spatial interaction in economic affairs. Finally, recognition of the failure of the old ocular instrumentation led to rediscovery of the 'good' Marshall (1919) whose work on 'industrial districts' was grounded in precisely the evolutionary elements listed above. Much of the praise for this rehabilitation goes to heterodox Italian economists like Becattini (1989) and Brusco (1990), political economists like Piore and Sabel (1984) and economic geographers like Scott (1988).

As economies of scale in giant corporations characterised by sourcing internally, researching and innovating internally and competing on a stand-alone basis with little concern for the 'soft infrastructure' of the host location, ceased to be the exemplar of modernity they once were, interest in scope and space economies mushroomed. The following section from the first edition of this book still rings true. Collaborative manufacturing (Sabel *et al.*, 1989) requires 'medium-term relationships based on trust' (Towill, 1993). It requires 'faith in the absence of opportunistic behaviour' (Sako, 1989) and above all:

> [It] begins when the flow of knowledge from key suppliers to the customer is such that the latter could not in reasonable time teach itself what its subcontractors are currently teaching it. That knowledge could be technical in the narrow sense; but it might as well be, and typically is, an indissoluble mixture of process/design and technological expertise. Whether or not any major firm has crossed that line, many have begun to reorganise themselves to limit the risks to which they would be exposed if they do.
>
> (Sabel *et al.*, 1989: 13)

That quotation betrays only the early 1990s, tendency to see value chains as the principal driver of new, more collaborative relationships between customers and suppliers. This is now, of course commonplace, to the point where supply chains are globalised in value networks (Gereffi, 1999; Dicken, 2001) capable of being re-jigged as customers spot competitive cost advantage from shifting production to, for example, low labour cost Romania (Cappellin, 1998), Morocco (Cooke *et al.*, 2003) or, dauntingly, China (UNIDO, 2002).

But this apparently Pavlovian stimulus-response is contingent upon one key resource that demonstrates that it is not merely a mindless roaming of global low-cost labour spot-markets. As UNIDO's (2002) authoritative analysis shows, *globalisation* integrates knowledge flows through value chains to local and regional clusters. That is, multinational firms source from locations that combine cost and skills advantages since advanced economy markets have increasingly exacting quality requirements. This means the presence of talent pools from agglomeration in specific industry sectors, and elements of 'soft infrastructure' to upgrade the clusters. 'Upgrading' by regional innovation entities is both observed and advocated as policy for regional agglomerations in developing countries as an alternative to upgrading of skills and quality being left at the behest of multinationals addicted to hyperactive international competitive tendering (Gereffi, 1999; Schmitz, 1999). Hassink's Chapter 12 shows how this process has evolved with newly imposed regional emphasis to re-energise the waning innovation impulse in South Korea, one of the successful newly industrialising countries of the 1980s that faltered in the 1990s.

Hence, it is UNIDO policy to assist the elaboration of regional innovation systems in developing countries as its signature conference in Shenzen, China, in 2002 testified. This is one of the ways in which knowledge transfer of regional innovation systems insights and policy assessments from, especially, Europe is proceeding. As indicated above, among the knowledge being transferred are the following three elaborations on the themes explored in this book's first edition. The first is that regional, *sectoral* innovation systems are powerful forces in the new economic geography. In the Nordic countries, for example, specialisation in relatively narrow segments of, for instance, ICT or biotechnology, aligned with 'Triple Helix' interactions among universities, industry and governance in proximity explain the continuing success of performance engineering at Jaeren, Norway (Asheim and Isaksen, 2002), wireless telephony innovation in Aalborg, Denmark (Dalum, 1995; Bruun, 2002), telecom software at redundant naval dockyards centre Karlskrona and many others in Sweden (Lundequist and Power, 2002), biotechnologically derived lactobacters and other nutraceuticals like Benecol in Turku region, Finland (Bruun, 2001; Tulkki *et al.*, 2002) and new media in former textiles town, Tampere, in Finland, as shown in Chapter 5. As Dalum and Bruun, in particular, make abundantly clear, the sixty small university spinouts in the Aalborg region, primarily in the university Science Park, are completely globalised through having attracted acquisition from the likes of Analog Devices, Motorola, Flextronics, BellSouth, Ameritech and Texas Instruments from the USA, and Cambridge Silicon Radio, Infineon, Siemens and STN-Atlas from elsewhere in Europe.

The second elaboration to the basic regional innovation systems idea that has occurred since the first edition and is implicit in the content of the previous paragraph, is that regional innovation systems are driven in important ways by their key cities. However, the regional systems dimension gains prominence in this by virtue of the networks linking city-focused assets such as universities, innovation support entities and clusters of businesses to remoter incubators, colleges, research stations and firms located in more rural parts of the region. In a recent survey (Simmie and Wood, 2002) global, primate cities were shown to be strong in basic research but weak in commercial exploitation of innovations. This is because the rarefied air of leading-edge research prioritises international knowledge interchange among 'communities of practice' or 'epistemic communities' in other primates (Revilla Diez, 2000). Contrariwise, such centres lack incubators, Science Parks, academic entrepreneurship and innovation, as distinct from innovation *inputs* like R&D expenditure and patents (Audretsch, 2002). These variables score lower than might be expected. Many of the following chapters, most obviously that of Hing on Singapore and Gertler and Wolfe on Ontario, place due emphasis on the city as an innovation (sub-) system. But the latter are also clear that despite Toronto's primacy in Canada, it is an industrial as well as financial cluster, strongly integrated to other cities in its region for innovation. And this is the second new finding from research on city innovation systems, which is that the more a city is a regional capital and the region is industrial, the more the city innovation system is integrated with the regional, in some cases more than the national, and much more than the global levels (Strambach, 2002).

Finally, and newest of all, is the limited evidence of how a few 'ahead of the curve' regional entities are reinventing themselves as regional knowledge economy systems. There is not yet a satisfactory term for this, though *Lighthouse Regions* captures important elements combining information beacon, collectively sustained, scanning horizons, transceiving locally valuable knowledge (hence the cover design of this book). The phraseology comes from Bruun's (2002) account of the Digital North Jutland regional innovation system. Thus in February 2000 the Danish Ministry of Research and Information Technology designated North Jutland as one of two 'IT Lighthouses' (ibid.). This was part of their 'Digital Denmark' initiative to make the country a 'network society'. A key measure involved perceiving the region as a 'developmental knowledge laboratory'. This meant conducting a large-scale regional experiment in North Jutland, one-third paid by the Ministry and two-thirds paid by regional authorities, local government and business to the tune of some 50 million Euro. The lighthouse experiment operates as a technology programme that funds specific applications projects. Significantly, these projects have four streams: (1) IT infrastructure; (2) E-Science; (3) E-Learning and Skills; and (4) E-Administration. It thus involves not only the techno-economic networks of the university and IT firms, but the community networks of consumers of health, local government, retail, transport, etc. This means that, instead of 'knowledge networking' being confined to the political and policy arenas as a means of engaging with the knowledge economy, the regional community 'contextuates' the policy and technology arenas (Nowotny *et al.*, 2001), accessing their tacit knowledge to build a market for innovative products and services. Thus, there are 'Lighthouse' projects on wireless services for delivery of healthcare, administration, local government services and project-based e-learning. The first round of funding brought forth fifty-five projects in these and more technology-focused fields, the second round raised this number to ninety-four.

A different initiative is found in an economy assailed by 'high-tech capital flight', namely Scotland. An early act of the post-devolution Scottish Executive was to commission Scotland's Science Strategy. This reviewed basic scientific research, costed it, assessed it in relation to world-class benchmarks, and prioritised three fields for which extra resources and attention would be forthcoming. The fields are Biosciences, Medical Science and E-Science. Activities to develop closer networking among public and private research laboratories, to stimulate technology transfer from the Scottish health system and to promote a science-based economy were begun.

Regarding the latter, the Scottish Executive then produced an economic strategy document charging Scottish Enterprise and economic actors generally, to espouse their vision of a 'Smart, Successful Scotland'. This was predicated on the knowledge economy and proposed more actions to develop a new strategy aimed at strengthening Scotland's position as a science-based economy. Key to this is Scottish Enterprise's new approach to try to turn Scotland and the governance system of Scottish Enterprise itself into a globally networked knowledge management system. Three policies, Global Connections, Growing Business, and Learning & Skills are meant to enhance knowledge inputs and outputs among global businesses in or relevant to Scotland; to hasten the rate of spin-outs from scientific research; and to make Scotland's 'talent' base more 'sticky' while augmenting it by stimulating a more cosmopolitan image. Among the instruments deployed to further these ambitions are those that incentivise potential translocating multinationals to replace production jobs with R&D, the establishment of intermediary technology institutes to improve research-intensive spin-out firms, and the construction of intranet- and extranet-based knowledge management systems to integrate both the Scottish business 'diaspora' and assist the global recruitment and retention of scientific and technological talent (see Hood *et al.*, 2002).

Regions as developmental knowledge laboratories: what has changed since 1995?

Research on regional innovation was in its infancy when this book was first conceived in 1995. Epistemological issues as well as theoretical innovations to regional science had to be discussed at length, and the reader interested in an early statement of the importance of evolutionary theory for regional science is referred to Braczyk *et al.* (1998) for a full exposition. Crucial to the configuration of understanding in the first edition was the graphic representing the two-dimensional structure of innovation activity, in which the *governance* infrastructure and the *business* superstructure are constitutive. The original Introduction promised a 'productive iteration' between the conceptual and real regional innovation systems ideas based on successive approximations to specific 'ideal' categories.[3] These will not be changed; hence previous readers will find familiarity in some of what follows. What is now of real urgency is to inquire about the evolution of the systems categorised in the first edition in light of the monumental economic shifts and uncertainties that have characterised the past decade. Rather than re-design the analytic tool, commentaries based on the new accounts are inserted as appropriate.

The governance dimension

In thinking more specifically of modes of regional innovation Cooke (1992) proposed three modalities: (1) grassroots; (2) network; and (3) *dirigiste*. These were further elaborated, by inclusion of modes of business inter-relationship, into three kinds of innovative milieu in Cooke and Morgan (1994). For the purposes of this discussion, as before, the categorisations will be described and compared, drawing on textured case material from the first cut, and now the second examination a decade later.

Grassroots RIS

In terms of technology transfer action the *initiation* process in this modality is locally organised, at town or district level. *Funding* will be diffuse in origin, comprising a mix of local banking, local government, possibly local Chamber of Commerce capital, grants and loans. The *research* competence is likely to be highly applied or near-market. The level of technical *specialisation* will be low and generic problem-solving is more likely than significant, finely honed, technological expertise. Finally, the degree of supra-local *co-ordination* will be low because of the localised nature of the initiation. To some extent the multimedia cluster in Southern California (Scott, 1994) was 'grassroots' in its governance structure with initiation for systemic co-ordination coming from within the technology districts themselves rather than from state or federal level. But the governance power of the Hollywood studios was then burgeoning in this direction and is, by 2003, globally hegemonic, integrating tightly with other new media nodes in Canada (Brail and Gertler, 1999), the UK (Cooke and Hughes, 1999) and Asia as well as elsewhere in the USA. So Hollywood has become more globalised since 1995, though innovation is still controlled in the sub-contracting new media specialists concentrated in Los Angeles.

The North-central Italian industrial districts were of great academic and policy fascination as localised innovation systems a decade ago. Now, as noted, clusters – their genotype – are everywhere in policy documents and journal articles, even if elusive on the ground. In Tuscany, the business innovation infrastructure was locally initiated, funded, researched, co-ordinated and focused because the Tuscan regional government had no innovation policy. Hence, within the region there were distinctive types of localised system both in terms of governance and business inter-relationships, as Dei Ottati's chapter in the first edition made clear. How has that changed and has the region become more of a 'developmental knowledge laboratory'? Three things are signalled in Dei Ottati's new chapter in this book. First, a relentless rise in innovativeness in clothing ('washed silk'), furniture (modular bathrooms) and shoes (fashion). Second the replacement of manufacturing by services and the formation of multiple knowledge 'enterprise groups' of micro-firms, and acquisition by Tuscan leather firms of Latin American tanneries. The challenge is for wider institutional innovation support and 'constructive co-operation' of the kind that a 'developmental knowledge laboratory' at regional level might entail. Business innovation remains 'localist' but there is a slight shift towards a more networked governance of innovation support.

Network RIS

Initiation of technology transfer action in a network modality is multi-level, meaning it can encompass local, regional, federal and supranational levels, as appropriate. In consequence, *funding* is more likely to be guided by agreement amongst banks, government agencies and firms. The *research* competence in a networked innovation architecture is likely to be mixed, with both pure and applied, 'blue-skies' and near-market activities geared to the needs of large and small firms. System *co-ordination* is likely to be high because of the large number of stakeholders and the presence of associations, fora, industry clubs and the like. *Specialisation* within such a system is likely to be flexible rather than dedicated because of the wide range of system demands from global to small-firm scale.

This, from Heidenreich and Krauss' chapter in the first edition, was a stylised picture of Baden-Württemberg In its crisis periods, such as 1993–4 and, earlier in 1984, the *Land* established Commissions involving experts from the research, governance and industry communities to exercise foresight on future needs and chart a new course to meet them. This exercise was repeated, albeit by consultant Roland Berger, in 2000. There, new sectors like health and life sciences, ICT and sensors/photonics were earmarked for support. Yet, even though the region has pockets of these knowledge-intensive industries, its strength lies in advanced engineering, particularly automotive, and its influence, through Daimler-Benz, Porsche and Audi but particularly the first-named, now has global reach in control as well as purchase of inputs in ways that were less prevalent in 1995 (see Chapter 7 in this book for details). The latter also makes clear that the region maintains its strong networking culture, albeit a degree of 'privatisation' could be detected compared to more interactive modes of regional foresight practised hitherto.

Dirigiste RIS

Technology transfer activities in a *dirigiste* innovation model are animated mainly from outside and above the region itself. *Initiation* of actions is typically a product of central government policies. *Funding* is largely centrally determined although the agencies in question may have decentralised locations in the regions. The kind of *research* conducted in *dirigiste* systems is often rather basic or fundamental and it may be expected to relate to the needs of larger, possibly state-owned, firms in or beyond the region in question. The level of *co-ordination* in such a RIS is very high, at least potentially, since it is state-run, and the level of *specialisation* is also likely to be high.

The paradigm example here is, of course, France, the government of which has, over the past thirty years, implanted metropolitan research laboratories in regions such as Rhône-Alpes, Midi-Pyrénées and Brittany and followed this up with a technopole policy which was certainly initiated centrally though the funding regime involves local stakeholders. Later when this approach began to reveal some weaknesses, central government established the regionalised centres of research, innovation and technology transfer (CRITTS). Even venture capital is dominated by the devolved central funding agency ANVAR. Local interaction and 'systemness' are not high, one of the reasons for establishing the CRITTs. Also, large firms were anchors of such technopole architectures. Two highly significant developments have occurred that remove the governance of innovation from its earlier position. The first is the increased *animateur* role in innovation facilitation by the Regional Council. Second is the belated implementation of *regional* 'Triple Helix' policies integrating universities and industry. France lags behind the USA and the UK in this and recent regulatory changes have sought to bring regional innovation systems up to speed. Thus, Midi-Pyrénée for example, has evolved towards the 'Network' mode of innovation governance as its leading product – Airbus – challenges Boeing for supremacy in the global aircraft market. Slovenia's innovation was *dirigiste* but fragmented, now liberalisation is coinciding with network-building, as Koschatzky indicates, in Chapter 13.

The business innovation dimension

Complementing the governance dimension, important for providing the soft infrastructure of enterprise innovation support, is the posture of firms in the regional economy both towards each other and the outside world as well in relations with producers and consumers in the market place. Clearly, firms can range from possessing global to merely local reach. But we are also interested, to the extent relevant, in the disposition of industries and, indeed networked industrial clusters towards innovation. What is the role of lead firms? What advantage does a private or in-house activity have over public research activity? And what is the nature of the innovation milieu within which firms operate? Figure 0.1 shows the typology and evolution of the RIS discussed in the chapters in this book.

Localist RIS

If we approach the business innovation dimension in terms first of the extent of its *domination* by large enterprise, either indigenous in origin or inward investment, then a localist RIS will tend to have few or no large indigenous firms and relatively few large branches of externally-controlled firms. A localist business innovation culture is one in which the research *reach* of firms is not very great, though there may be local research organisations capable of combining with industry clusters within the region. A localist set-up will probably have few major *public* innovation or R&D resources but may have smaller *private* ones. Finally, there will be a reasonably high degree of *associationalism* amongst entrepreneurs and between them and local or regional policy-makers.

Of the chapters in this book, that on Tuscany by Dei Ottati still captures most of these features, while to varying degrees the Scandinavian arrangements were relatively localist, even becoming more so in Maskell's account of Denmark and Schienstock *et al.*'s analysis of the Finnish region of Pirkanmaa centred on Tampere. The most striking evolutions in innovation action since 1995 are, in Tampere, the firmer regional entrenchment of business networking, as the economy has more fully embraced the knowledge economy. ICT employment shot up by 125 per cent and Nokia, for example, is firmly embedded in Triple Helix networking with government-funded Centres of Expertise in the university Science Park. We can say that stronger regional interaction for innovation is the key move made in Tampere during the past decade. In Denmark, tighter embrace of the knowledge economy and Triple Helix interactions are well exemplified by North Jutland's wireless telephony cluster, as we have seen, and the remarkable Medicon Valley life sciences R&D complex, which ranks third in Europe and now extends interaction across the Øresund bridge to Sweden and Lund, aspiring to evolve one of the first cross-border regional innovation systems. Japan's economy has stagnated over the past decade. The Japanese region of Tohoku combined small and medium-sized enterprises (SMEs) in disconnect with branch-plants. Shiro Abe showed the region to have been relatively more proactive than most in over-centralised Japan in accessing central government instruments like Technopolis. In Abe's update much has changed. The engine of post-war economic growth policy, MITI is no more, Technopolis policy has been abandoned as a failure and more of Tohoku and Japan's ICT industry has been hollowed out by translocation of investment to China and other East Asian economies. In place of this, a new regionalisation of innovation has occurred, including official adoption of regional innovation systems thinking, supported

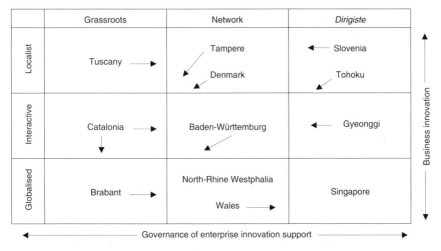

	Grassroots	Network	*Dirigiste*
Localist	Tuscany →	Tampere Denmark	← Slovenia Tohoku
Interactive	Catalonia →	Baden-Württemburg	← Gyeonggi
Globalised	Brabant →	North-Rhine Westphalia Wales →	Singapore

Governance of enterprise innovation support

Business innovation

Note: Arrow indicates direction of RIS movement 1995–2005

0.1 Regional innovation systems: typology and evolution

also with regional cluster policy. Slowly, Japan's innovation strategy, like that of South Korea, is becoming a regional innovation systems strategy. Slovenia shows comparable signs of evolving from centralised determination of policy to a more networked and open modality.

Interactive RIS

Here, the economy is neither particularly *dominated* by large nor small firms but rather by a reasonable balance between them, whether indigenous or FDI in origin. The *reach* of this combination will vary between widespread access of regional research resources to foreign innovation sourcing as and when required. There will be a reasonably balanced mix of *public* and *private* research institutes and laboratories, reflecting the presence of larger firms with regional headquarters and a regional government keen to promote the innovation base of the economy. Such regions will be highly *associative* vertically and laterally as evidenced by abundant industry networks, fora and clubs.

Baden-Württemberg remains the exemplar of this kind of RIS, but Catalonia has an associative and interactive culture in business, labour and civic organizations, good representation between these and the regional government and an 'entrepreneurial culture' of 'industrial networks' to which Bacaria and Borrás alluded. Since 1995, Catalan innovation has developed a stronger regional identity, being more international in outlook, stronger in basic R&D and improving on a historically low level of patenting. It is shifting both towards globalisation and enhanced regional institutionalisation. Quebec (Noisi, 2002) is also interesting for its retention of many indigenous public innovation institutions as part of its corporatist political culture and, industrially, strong networking and cluster-building predilections, though within a quite strongly state (Province)-led system overall. Knowledge economy clusters such as ICT, aerospace and biotechnology have become stronger, but the lead in formulation of science and technology strategy seems to have been lost.

Globalised RIS

In a globalised RIS there is *domination* by global corporations, often supported by clustered supply-chains of rather dependent SMEs, meeting some of the requirements of indigenous or inward investor multinationals. The research *reach* in such systems will be largely internal and highly *privatistic* rather than *public*, though a more public innovation infrastructure aimed at helping SMEs may have developed more recently. To the extent firms are *associative* it will be under tutelage of larger firms and conducted, accordingly, on their terms.

In California (Kenney, 2000), high-tech clusters are illustrative of this modality with firms that have displayed rapid and high rates of growth dominating the local supply industries and, in the form of organisations such as Sematech, creating their own inter-firm collaboration arrangements. Ontario is dominated by large firms, especially US automotive companies, though some indigenous ones such as Nortel are also important. The downturn in 2000 hit the region hard as Gertler and Wolfe show in Chapter 4, and the faint glow of regional government proactivity in the 1990s has been almost extinguished, flickering somewhat in 2002 with new Federal programmes. Much the same may be said for Brabant in the Netherlands as described by Boekholt and de Jager in Chapter 2, dominated as it is by Philips and DAF.

Wales and North Rhine-Westphalia are reconversion economies, learning to network and aiming to building clusters from the ashes of the old. Hilbert *et al.*'s account in Chapter 9 of the endogenous emergence of the environmental technology industry and Cooke's in Chapter 8 of the exogenous stimulation of engineering clusters bore witness to this in the mid-1990s. However, as hinted, Wales has suffered major reverses with the slimming down of Asian transplants. Its new, devolved Welsh Assembly Government is, in brief, engaged in *neo-dirigisme* but without the advantage of guiding vision or informed leadership. North Rhine-Westphalia is hamstrung by Germany's Japan-like economic stagnation. Knowledge clusters like media, software and healthcare seem the only bright spots. Finally, in strong *dirigiste* political systems, Singapore, with its high-tech FDI and indigenous clusters is testimony to Andrew Carnegie's famous recipe for economic success: 'put all the eggs in one basket – but *watch the basket*'.

Conclusion

The original Introduction to the book and this reprise were exercises in defining and exemplifying and now studying longitudinally actual instances of variably integrated regional innovation systems (RIS). The most striking new features concern the shadows cast by globalisation, economic downturn, the emergence of knowledge economies and cluster-led entrepreneurship upon innovation. Either regions have stagnated or otherwise remained comparably positioned to that of a decade ago, or they have tended to converge towards a more knowledge-intensive, interactive and networked posture, or, in admittedly few cases, moved laterally towards a more managed governance of innovation. For regions performing relatively well in these uncertain times, deeper engagement with knowledge-intensive industry and firmer institutional founding for systemic innovation are common elements. They have engaged successfully in evolving *constructed advantage* (Foray and Freeman, 1993; de la Mothe, 2003).

In the first edition, the question of systemic innovation had been posed for regions because of certain dissatisfaction with the broad-brush national systems approach. That volume and this vindicate that critique as everywhere regional innovation infrastructures are being strengthened because of the failure of centralised, national champions and 'picking winners' approaches. For those interested in innovation as an interactive process, time shows it to be increasingly a broad framework, the details of which are being filled in more and more by regions operating as 'developmental knowledge laboratories'. The National Systems of Innovation (NSI) literature made enormous strides in defining innovation, correcting the perceived wisdom about innovation processes by showing them to be interactive not linear, and introducing the important concept of 'institutional learning' into this more systemic analysis of innovation. But as a policy arena, it is arguable that its day has passed.

What this research has done is to integrate evolutionary economic and regional development theory the better to understand innovation. Regional innovation systems are evolving as their contextualisation elements shift with globalisation, the rise of knowledge-intensive industry and the hollowing-out of 'Industrial Age' industries. Such are the powers arraigned against adequate national responses to these forces that the experimentation of greatest intellectual and policy interest now occurs sub-nationally. We may say that regional innovation systems are coming of age, that some are grasping the opportunities offered by globalisation, the knowledge economy and clustering – evolving towards the condition of regions as 'developmental knowledge laboratories' – while others that were leading governance and policy formulation a decade ago, such as Ontario, Tohoku, Singapore, North Rhine-Westphalia and Wales seem to be battening down the hatches in a forlorn attempt to ride out the 'gales of creative destruction' as Schumpeter (1975) once memorably put it.

Notes

1 The specific concept was new in 1995 when the original 'Introduction: Origins of the Concept' was written, having been deployed only since 1992 (see, for example, Cooke, 1992). There was no mention of the terminology even as late as Hilpert (1991) one of the few collections on the substantive matter in question. As in the discourse of the late 1980s and early 1990s more generally, there was there and in other publications (e.g. Malecki, 1991; Bergman *et al.*, 1991) reference to 'regional innovation policies' (Antonelli and Momigliano, 1981; Cooke, 1985), 'innovative milieux' (Aydalot, 1986; Maillat and Vasserot, 1986; Maillat, 1991) 'regional technology policies' (Rothwell and Dodgson, 1991), 'regional innovation potential' (Meyer-Krahmer, 1985) and 'innovation networks' (Camagni, 1991) as well as 'high technology complexes', 'technopoles' and 'new technology industries' upon which very large amounts had been written during the period.

2 For a comparable categorisation, but referring to technological regimes, see Sidney Winter (1984).

3 It remains necessary to distinguish between 'operational' and 'conceptual' systems. An operational system refers to a real phenomenon; a conceptual system represents a logical abstraction, a theoretical construct which consists of principles or laws that explain relationships between and among variables. In the latter meaning the term system is related to a specific methodological approach, it is an analytical framework. Using the system approach we construct entities but they do not represent the totality of a real phenomenon. The scientific approach is to look for the constituent elements and their specific characteristics, the relationships between these elements, the boundaries of this system and the interaction with its environment. Defining the system concept as an analytical tool requires no assumption that innovation systems always consist of closely linked actors or that they have clear-cut boundaries. Nor need it be anticipated that innovation systems consist of similar actors performing comparable functions.

Part One
Informal and Market-driven Co-ordination
Grassroots Between Local and Global Reach

Chapter 1

The remarkable resilience of the industrial districts of Tuscany

Gabi Dei Ottati

Introduction

Since the mid-1980s, the Italian industrial districts have become internationally renowned for their remarkable success.[1] Their achievements have been seen as particularly surprising because of the small size of the firms located in the districts, and their engagement in 'traditional sectors', such as textiles, clothing and furniture. Yet, during the 1980s, after several decades of continuous development through the proliferation of specialized industrial units, most Italian districts started a period of change and restructuring. Consequently, the decline of the Italian districts was declared and, further, it was even argued that the 'industrial district', as a form of socio-economic development, could no longer be viable due to its 'underlying contingency and ultimate instability' (Harrison, 1994a: 3, n. 1; also Blim, 1992; Harrison, 1994b).

As in other regions of the central and north-eastern parts of Italy, the predominant form of post-war development of Tuscany has been that of the 'industrial district', i.e. 'an integrated industrial area, which produces economies external to the firm, and even to the industrial sector defined by technology, but internal to the "sectoral–social–territorial" network' (Becattini, 1978: 114).[2]

Therefore, it seems that an analysis of the changes that have occurred in the Tuscan districts in the two past decades is of particular interest, not only in order to help Tuscan districts to construct their own future, but also to assess whether the industrial district model *can* be a viable form of socio-economic development.

Although the industrial growth of post-war Tuscany was and still is driven by the districts, not all the industrial areas of the region are production systems of small specialized firms. Along the coast, for example, there are mixed tourism and industrial areas where large plants operating in steel (in Piombino) or chemicals (in Livorno) dominate the local landscape (ibid.: 113). Such areas are not considered here.

In addition, there are some local production systems, such as that of the marble and building stone industry of Carrara, or that of the precious metal jewellers industry of Arezzo, which initially were not identified as industrial districts, because they differ in some respect from the canonical ideal type. The

Carrara production system, for example, is located in a tourist area, whereas the jewellers production system of Arezzo is in an urban centre; nevertheless, they are similar to industrial districts, both from the point of view of their organization of production and that of their export performance in goods typical of 'made in Italy' products (Porter, 1990: 421–435). Consequently, a complete study of the developments in the districts of Tuscany should also include such local systems.[3]

However, this chapter will focus only on five well-established industrial districts of Tuscany: the clothing system of Empoli, the Santa Croce sull'Arno leather tanning district, the textile district of Prato, the Poggibonsi furniture system and the footwear system of Monsummano (see Figure 1.1 and Table 1.1).[4]

Material for the chapter comes from different sources. As far as statistical data are concerned, the main sources are the general census of population and the

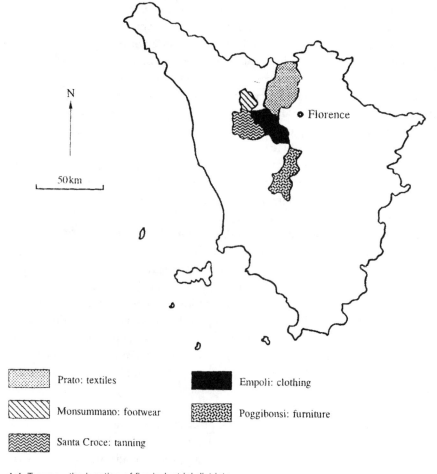

N

50 km

● Florence

Prato: textiles

Monsummano: footwear

Santa Croce: tanning

Empoli: clothing

Poggibonsi: furniture

1.1 Tuscany: the location of five industrial districts

Table 1.1 Area and population in five industrial districts of Tuscany and in Italy, 1991 and 2001

Districts	Area	Resident population		Var. %
	(km²)	1991	2001	1991–2001
Empoli	341	90,855	95,816	5.46
Santa Croce	301	88,314	91,822	3.97
Prato	694	319,623	334,616	4.69
Poggibonsi	377	49,514	53,460	7.97
Monsummano	125	68,801	71,830	4.40
Tuscany	22,997	3,529,946	3,460,835	–1.96
Italy	301,309	56,778,031	56,305,568	–0.83

Sources: Istat (1991a) and Istat (2001a).

general census of industries and services of 1981, 1991, 1996 and 2001. For the interpretation of restructuring, however, I have used most of the studies that exist on each of the districts considered. In addition, in the case of Prato, I have been able to use the results of surveys in which I have participated, as well as a large fund of information built up during years of personal research on that district (Dei Ottati, 1993, 1994b, 1996). For the other districts, the information drawn from the census and the available studies have been supplemented by interviews with representatives of local government, with officers of local industrialist and artisan associations, with entrepreneurs, and with staff from service centres.

In what follows, I first outline the changes in the external context and then the main adjustment strategies adopted by local firms. Afterwards I move on to look on the transformations that have occurred in the industrial districts of Tuscany, in respect of both employment changes and industrial restructuring. Some final comments follow.

Changes in the external context

Since the 1950s, most of the industrial districts of Tuscany have experienced a long period of practically uninterrupted industrial growth, in terms of both the numbers of firms and the level of employment. Thanks to a combination of factors, including a large local supply of labour and the formation and the thickening of those 'sectoral–social–territorial networks' mentioned earlier, the industrial districts of Tuscany were able, first, to take advantage of the long phase of consumption growth in the Western countries during the 1950s and the 1960s and, then, to continue to prosper, even during the 1970s, when the demand for consumer goods became more differentiated and variable.

During the 1980s, however, the international and national competitive context of the sectors typical of the Tuscan districts changed (including, for example, textiles, clothing, leather goods, and shoes). Competition from countries with low labour costs emerged in some industries, particularly in clothing and in footwear, competition that was accentuated by the sharp reduction in the value of the US dollar in 1985 and by the revaluation of Italian lira (in real terms) during the second half of the 1980s (Graziani, 1994).

Further, the reorganization of large firms (introduction of information technologies and outsourcing) increased their capacity to compete on production flexibility with district firms. Moreover, the demand for some products in which the districts of Tuscany had specialized drastically declined, because of changes in people's tastes and lifestyles. That is the case, for example, of carded woollen fabrics from Prato,[5] tubular moccasins from Monsummano, and bedroom suites from Poggibonsi.

Adjustment strategies of local firms

The importance of the changes in the external context was possibly at first undervalued by many of the 'final firms', that is, those who specialize in the design and the sale of the products of the district.[6] After all, their entrepreneurial recipe had a long record of success, and the ever-increasing variability and fragmentation of consumer demand made it more difficult to interpret the changes taking place. Nevertheless, in general, local firms have been capable of reacting to the new conditions and, often, by emulation, new strategies have spread rapidly throughout the district.

The variety of specific situations and of decisions taken to meet external challenges notwithstanding, the enterprises in the districts of Tuscany have mainly responded in one or more of the following three ways:

- product differentiation and innovation;
- quality upgrading;
- commercial specialization.

Among the adjustment strategies most widely followed by firms in the districts has been that of differentiation and innovation of products (i.e. switching to different products and markets), usually by broadening the range of items offered. So, for example, some 'final firms' in Prato have added to traditional carded woollen fabrics worsted wool and especially summer fabrics made of linen, silk, viscose, or cotton, others have shifted from producing fabrics to knitwear or clothing; Poggibonsi firms have moved on from producing complete lounge and bedroom suites to bathroom furniture, modular kitchens, chairs and components; Monsummano footwear firms changed from producing moccasins to fashion shoes; and Santa Croce tanneries compensated for the decline in demand from the domestic shoe industry by increasing exports and by selling their products also to clothing and furniture industries.

Once a new strategy has been identified and pursued successfully by one or a few firms in the district, it is normally imitated, with small variations, by other local firms, so that the process of product and market diversification diffuses rapidly in the system. Such a process sometimes leads to real innovations (products which are either completely new, or simply new to the district), thanks to the increased variety of materials and technologies used, and consequently the enlarged possi-bilities for their recombinations.[7] In Prato, for example, the introduction of silk in the local production cycle, gave rise to the creation of the so-called 'washed silk', a new kind of fabric with a special finishing, which was well received by consumers.

A second strategy that has been followed by firms of the Tuscan districts is quality upgrading: moving to higher market segments, both in the sense of better intrinsic quality and/or higher fashion content,[8] or even of meeting particular technical standards or delivery terms requested by customers. Often, this strategy was adopted by firms that maintained a specialization in the traditional products of the district, for the manufacturing of which they could take advantage of the remarkable amount of skills accumulated locally.

A third strategy that has been adopted by the firms of the districts of Tuscany is increased commercial specialization. In the face of the decline in the demand for products typical of the district and, partially because of the heightened price competition, some firms, in order to recover profitability, began to buy goods produced elsewhere, often imported from countries with lower labour costs, instead of having them made by local subcontractors. Intermediate products manufactured outside the district have been bought in order to have them finished locally and then marketed, but also finished products have been bought in order to resell them directly to customers in Italy and abroad.[9]

Changes in the industrial districts

The shift from industrial to service employment

The clearest effect of the changes in the external context, and of the adjustment strategies adopted by the firms in the districts of Tuscany has been a drop in industrial employment, especially during the 1980s (see Tables 1.2 and 1.3).

The international trend towards a reduction in industrial jobs was reflected in Italy during the 1970s by falls in employment in the large firms of the so-called modern sectors (such as vehicles, chemicals and steel), which then continued and became more general in the 1980s. In fact, during the 1980s, manufacturing employment for the whole country declined by more than 10 per cent, reaching

Table 1.2 Percentage distribution of workforce* by sector in five industrial districts of Tuscany and in Italy, 1981 and 1991

Districts	Agriculture		Industry		Services	
	1981	*1991*	*1981*	*1991*	*1981*	*1991*
Empoli	7.3	4.3	57.8	50.5	34.9	45.2
Santa Croce	4.9	2.6	66.5	61.0	28.6	36.4
Prato	2.2	1.3	65.0	54.7	32.8	44.0
Poggibonsi	8.2	5.8	53.6	46.1	38.2	48.1
Monsummano	5.0	3.4	49.1	41.5	45.9	55.1
Italy	11.1	7.6	39.5	35.7	49.4	56.7

Note: All the people working or available to work
Sources: Istat (1981a) and Istat (1991a)

Table 1.3 Employment in industry and services in five districts of Tuscany, 1981, 1991 and 2001

Districts	Industry			Services		
	1981	*1991*	*2001*	*1981*	*1991*	*2001*
Empoli	22,322	19,847	16,422	13,032	16,872	16,203
Santa Croce	25,116	23,063	21,745	12,037	15,122	14,572
Prato	95,164	81,180	75,542	45,583	59,481	56,130
Poggibonsi	11,017	10,116	10,285	6,876	9,179	8,235
Monsummano	13,372	9,752	10,037	13,063	15,708	14,928

Sources: Istat (1981b), Istat (1991b) and Istat (2001b).

a rate of 30 per cent in large firms (those employing more than 100 people), and by 20 per cent in Piedmont, one of the older industrialized regions of Italy (Istat, 1991b). Thus, the fall in industrial employment in the districts of Tuscany appears to be part of a more general trend.

Data from the general census of industries and services of 1981, 1991 and 2001 (Table 1.3) demonstrate the importance of the phenomenon for each of the districts considered in this chapter. So, during the 1980s, the Santa Croce and the Poggibonsi districts experienced a reduction of industrial employment of about 8 per cent, and the Empoli and the Prato districts lost respectively 11 and 14 per cent, whereas in Monsummano the drop reached 27 per cent. The industrial employment continued to shrink also during the 1990s, albeit generally at a reduced rate in Santa Croce, Prato and Empoli, whereas it slightly increased in Poggibonsi and Monsummano.

On the other hand, Table 1.3 also shows that during the 1980s the reduction in industrial employment has, for all districts except Monsummano, been counterbalanced by a parallel increase in the service sector. During the 1990s, however, also the latter lost employment, in particular due to a significant restructuring of traditional commerce and because of the decrease in the putting out of service functions by local manufacturing firms (Bacci, 2002: 189–96).

Despite the remarkable shift to services experienced during the 1980s (Table 1.2), the figures demonstrate also the persistent importance of industry in the local economy. In fact, in all the districts considered – with the exception of Monsummano, which includes the tourist area of Montecatini Terme (thermal waters), covering three municipalities out of the six that comprise the district – the industrial employment figures outweigh those in the service sector.

Moreover, apart from Poggibonsi, which is not a monosectoral district,[10] local manufacturing occupation is predominantly concentrated in the main local industry and in activities auxiliary to it (Table 1.4). In the district of Santa Croce, for example, in 1996 leather and tanning jobs covered about 81 per cent of total manufacturing employment, and in the district of Prato, in spite of the severe contraction of the local textile industry, about 70 per cent of the manufacturing jobs were still in textiles (Table 1.5).

It is worth noting, however, that in the recent process of restructuring some auxiliary activities, both in related industries (such as the manufacture of machine tools for the localized industry) and services, have grown considerably. Indeed, much of the increase in the service sector, especially during the 1980s, was attributable to an extraordinary development in producer services.[11]

Industrial restructuring

Changes in the division of labour among firms

The changes in the external context and the reactions of the firms did not result in a mere reduction of industrial employment. Rather, they generated a broad restructuring of the local production system that, usually, involved a shortening of the established production cycle and a differentiation of the manufacturing processes carried out in the district.

Changes in the division of labour inside the districts

Before considering the changes in the division of labour that occurred in most of the Tuscan districts, a brief mention should be made of the restructuring that took place in the Poggibonsi furniture system, since it differs from the other cases and calls to mind similar changes that took place in other districts of Tuscany in

Table 1.4 Businesses in manufacturing industry and in the main local industry in five industrial districts of Tuscany, 1991 and 1996

Districts	Manufacturing industry		Main local industry		
	1991	1996	1991	1996	
Empoli	2,185	1,992	1,167	946	Clothing and leather
Santa Croce	2,580	2,595	1,847	1,808	Tanning and leather
Prato	13,942	12,599	10,666	9,101	Textiles and clothing
Poggibonsi	1,023	991	360	359	Wood and furniture
Monsummano	1,238	1,182	495	450	Footwear and leather

Sources: Istat (1991b) and Istat (1996).

Table 1.5 Employment in manufacturing industry and in the main local industry in five industrial districts of Tuscany, 1991 and 1996

Districts	Manufacturing industry		Main local industry		
	1991	1996	1991	1996	
Empoli	17,041	15,236	8,615	6,794	Clothing and leather
Santa Croce	20,689	21,621	16,795	17,502	Tanning and leather
Prato	71,230	73,128	50,777	50,900	Textiles and clothing
Poggibonsi	8,659	8,648	2,410	2,062	Wood and furniture
Monsummano	7,945	7,474	3,350	3,246	Footwear and leather

Source: Istat (1991b) and Istat (1996)

the 1950s.[12] At Poggibonsi, in the early 1980s, the local furniture firms underwent a process of vertical disintegration and specialization, which followed a period of difficulties, mainly because of the already mentioned changes in demand. Until then, most of the Poggibonsi furniture firms were complete-cycle factories: that is, they undertook internally all the stages necessary to produce the furniture that they sold on the market. However, the fundamental change that occurred in the type of furniture produced led to a radical transformation.

As a consequence of the restructuring, some of the complete-cycle furniture firms began specializing in finishing and selling the final products, and put out the other phases of production. Others, instead, specialized in a few phases of the furniture production process, hence becoming 'phase-firms' or subcontractors. Further, many of the workers who lost their jobs, because of the complete-cycle factories' restructuring, bought second-hand machinery and started up on their own as small subcontractors.

The new division of labour among local firms was particularly suited to the changes in products manufactured: modular kitchen and bathroom furniture, instead of complete lounge and bedroom suites. In fact, the new products, together with an appropriate new division of labour, provided the possibility of standardizing the manufacture of component parts, *and* also the opportunity to assemble them in a variety of different ways, thus facilitating the ability to adapt final goods to changes in design or consumer requirements.

Apart from Poggibonsi, in the other districts at the end of the 1970s there was already a well-developed division of labour among local firms, with some enterprises specializing in the marketing and design of goods made in the district ('final firms'), while many others were specialized in a few phases or just one phase of the production process ('phase-firms'). The restructuring that occurred during the 1980s, and partially continued in the 1990s, gave rise to a complex redefinition of the division of labour and of specialization, both inside the firms and among the firms of the district. In order to understand the rationale of such a redefinition, it is useful to distinguish between the manufacturing cycle of the product typical of the district, and the cycle of the new items introduced by the firms that adopted a differentiation and innovation strategy.

As far as the cycle of the products typical of the district is concerned, in some stages (often the initial stages with lower value-added) the restructuring brought about a reduction in the number of local firms and employment; by contrast, in other stages (frequently the finishing ones) it resulted in their increase. Thus, for example, in the Prato district the sorting of rags,[13] the carbonizing of fibres and carding went through a severe reduction that, during the 1980s, was associated with an increase in fabric finishing operations. Or, to give an other example, in the Monsummano footwear system the production of uppers decreased, but the finishing of shoes continued to be made locally and the activities related to shoe design and to the preparation of sample collections grew, giving rise also to new firms specialized in design and marketing advisory services.

Also, the differentiation strategy adopted by many firms to meet the changes in demand altered the division of labour, both inside the enterprises and among them in the local system. In fact, the introduction of new products favoured the development of new specialized activities. In the Prato district, for example, the contraction of employment in producing winter woollen fabrics was partly countered by an increase in employment in manufacturing summer fabrics, made from other fibres, as well as by the growth of completely new products, such as imitation fur and imitation leather, non-woven fabrics, and technical textiles.[14] In the Santa Croce district there was a partial substitution of bovine leather with ovine, pig and reptile hides.

The new division of labour between inside and outside the districts

The broad industrial restructuring that occurred during the past two decades also involved important changes in the division of labour between inside and outside the districts. In fact, the contraction in the initial stages of the productive cycle of the localized industry was accompanied by sourcing outside the district for the output of those very stages. This was a break with the past, when the districts had a remarkable degree of productive self-sufficiency; that is, the 'final firms' acquired (often abroad) raw materials which were entirely transformed by local specialized subcontractors. As a consequence of the restructuring, however, some intermediate production is being subcontracted to, or bought from, areas outside the districts, and a part of this bought-in production is being imported from countries with lower labour costs.

Although it is difficult to assess for each district the level of significance that the outsourcing has now reached, the import pattern of some intermediate and semi-finished products provides an indirect insight into the phenomenon. During the period 1986–93, for example, the quantity of woollen yarn imported into the Prato district grew by 185 per cent (reaching approximately 6,000 tons in 1993), and the amount of woollen semi-finished fabric imported into the area during the same period increased by 262 per cent (reaching about 1,700 tons in 1993).[15] The import of vegetable fibres for clothing in the province of Florence (which includes the Empoli system) grew by 130 per cent (achieving approximately 22,000 tons in 1993). By contrast, the increase of imports of semi-tanned leather (wet-blue) experienced by the Santa Croce district was much less (only 23 per cent between 1986 and 1993),[16] because of the difficulties of ensuring the necessary standards both of raw material and labour in the initial processing of the Santa Croce top-quality tanned leather.

Even more since the 1980s, 'final firms' not only bought components made outside the district but also increased the subcontracting out of the local system, albeit usually for limited quantities of production and for special items. Surveys conducted in various districts of Tuscany confirm such an interpretation. Both in the Monsummano footwear system and in the Prato textile district, for example, most of the production is still made locally: about 70 per cent of the total value of the production subcontracted by the Monsummano footwear firms is manufactured by local subcontractors (Cee-Force, 1993: 157), whereas, 73 per cent of the Prato 'final firms' subcontract more than half of their production within the district, and 40 per cent of them have up to more than 90 per cent of their production made locally (Iris, 1994: 106).

However, subcontracting out of the local system is a reality in most of the districts. This has been confirmed by field research. In the Empoli clothing system, about 30 per cent of the production value is manufactured outside the region and

17 per cent of it is made abroad (Promomoda, 1993: 18), whereas 16 per cent of the production subcontracted by the Monsummano footwear firms comes from enterprises external to the region (Cee-Force, 1993: 157). In the Prato district too about half of the 'final firms' subcontract a small part of their production (usually less than 30 per cent) to firms located in northern Italy and about 25 per cent of them have established subcontracting relations with foreign companies (Iris, 1994: 117).

Also, for a better understanding of outsourcing, it is useful to distinguish between the productive cycle of the goods typical of the district and the cycle of the new products introduced to face the changes in the external context. As far as the output of the initial stages of the productive cycle typical of the district is concerned, the outsourcing from regions of lower labour cost allows local firms to maintain price competitiveness, and encourages the district as a system to specialize in those activities that require higher skills and are more profitable. Thus, this kind of outsourcing is to be regarded positively.

A different form of outsourcing occurs when firms are searching for the components needed to manufacture new products as part of a differentiation strategy. Thus, for example, linen and silk yarns are being bought in by Prato 'final firms',[17] and Poggibonsi firms are sourcing semi-finished panels and furniture made in solid wood from Veneto. Again, such outsourcing has a positive function to the extent that it permits a rapid and often successful adjustment to changes in demand, through the adoption of an innovation strategy that requires the quick acquisition of new specialized resources (especially skills) that are not readily available locally.

It is complex and difficult to evaluate the effects of this second type of outsourcing on the future vitality of the district as a system. This is because, at least in the short run, it reduces the '*localized* thickening of intra- and inter-industrial relationships' among firms (Becattini, 1989: 132), and it tends to accelerate the obsolescence of the contextual knowledge that has accumulated in the district. Traditionally, this localized intensifying of industrial relationships and skills has provided much of the basis for the districts' competitive advantage. However, in the longer run the introduction of new industrial and service activities by innovative firms should promote a local development of the specialized resources required by new products and processes. If such a development occurs, then it is also likely that the localized thickening of intra- and inter-industrial relationships among the firms, which is so important for the co-ordination of their different activities (Dei Ottati, 1994c: 465–466), and for the reproduction of contextual knowledge (Becattini and Rullani, 1996) will be maintained.

A further note is that also local subcontractors have started to produce for firms external to the district. Some furniture subcontractors of Poggibonsi, for example, receive orders from firms located in Pesaro (Marche) and in Brianza

(Lombardy). Empoli and Prato specialist subcontractors receive orders also from firms outside the district.[18]

Thus, the empirical evidence collected with reference to the Tuscan districts leads us to think that they are capable of renewal, thereby reproducing themselves as viable local systems.

Further changes in relationships among firms, both inside and outside the districts

The broad changes in the division of labour outlined in the previous section also brought about an organizational restructuring which involved a redefinition of relationships among firms, both inside and outside the districts.

Inter-firm relationships within the district

In respect of the rearrangement of inter-firm relationships within the local system, a significant type of restructuring that took place in most of the Tuscan districts was the development of *enterprise groups*. By 'enterprise group' I mean a *stable* collection of firms bound together by economic and social ties (such as subcontracting relations and kinship ties amongst entrepreneurs), which create an atmosphere of loyalty between persons working in them. Enterprise groups can be distinguished between *formal* groups whose firms are connected by some form of ownership relation, and *informal* groups, or teams, whose firms not only are legally independent, but among which there are no ownership control.[19]

The emergence of small formal groups of enterprises controlled by one or more local families for the most part goes back to the 1970s. At this time some of the more successful firms found it useful for various reasons[20] to divide off their commercial and manufacturing operations from their financial activities, setting up for the latter a suitable holding or real estate company, owned by various members of the family.[21]

However, it was during the 1980s and the 1990s that this initial nucleus really developed, both through the formation of new groups of firms and through the consolidation of those groups already in existence. The latter extended both by the creation of new units (as was usual in the past) and by the acquisition of companies that were already operational.

Typically these formal enterprise groups comprise firms specializing in different products and/or in different stages of the production cycle. Usually, they include a parent company, a holding company, a real estate company, one or more production units according to the number of products made, and various 'phase firms' specializing in some production phases that are strategic for the specific business of the group. (See Figure 1.2). The parent company is primarily

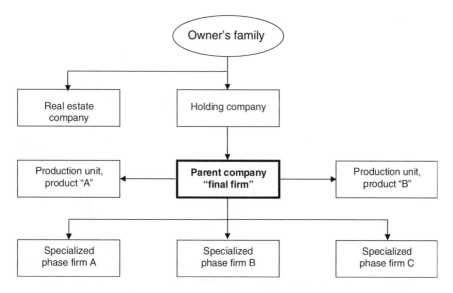

1.2 Typical configuration of a district enterprise group

engaged in carrying out the design of samples, the marketing of final products, often the purchase of raw materials or intermediate products, and the co-ordination of production. Production itself normally occurs in several different 'phase firms', only a small proportion of which are part of the formal group, or of the team of enterprises. Moreover, even specialized 'phase firms' that are totally or part-owned by a parent firm usually work for other customers as well, so allowing the parent company to remain flexible, and the 'phase firms' to obtain economies of scale and be driven to efficiency by competition in the local market.[22]

The evidence about the enterprise groups existing in the districts of Tuscany is very scanty, because even formal groups are not easily detectable, as the ownership relations among companies are often established through personal investments by different members of the same family without any official recording in the balance sheet of the parent company. So, an accurate estimation of their number is very difficult.[23]

From a study mentioned earlier, it emerged that in the Prato district about 10 per cent of the 'final firms' have shareholdings in other companies, which are usually local specialized 'phase firms'. The latter, in their turn, are jointly owned by other companies in 14 per cent of cases, and the co-owner is normally a holding company or a parent company of a local formal group (Iris, 1994: 122, 129). However, the information available leads us to believe that the absolute number of formal enterprise groups in each district is not large.[24]

Nevertheless, since the formal groups are led by local families with a relatively long entrepreneurial tradition, and because the formal groups often include firms which are among the most innovative ones, they tend to be influential in the local system. But their influence derives mainly from the fact that their successful innovations are promptly followed by other firms in the district, thus amplifying their effect, rather than by financial concentration and hierarchical relations.

The organizational restructuring that took place within the districts of Tuscany during the 1980s and the 1990s entailed also the spread of informal groups, or teams of enterprises, that is, relatively stable collections of firms bound together mainly by social and cultural ties built up over time by means of frequent personal contacts, exchanges of information, and repeated transactions. Unfortunately, there is even less information available on informal enterprise groups, since they are almost invisible organizations, despite the fact that their importance is clearly seen by those belonging to them. Nonetheless, various studies and our interviews have brought to light that during the restructuring the relations between 'final firms' and 'phase firms' have become more stable and, at the same time, more selective than in the past. For example, a survey of 289 Prato textile firms found that subcontracting relations have become more stable for 77 per cent of the 'final firms' and for 75 per cent of the 'phase firms' (Iris, 1994: 114). A similar tendency has also appeared in other districts, where preferential economic relations among circles of local entrepreneurs have expanded.[25]

Another study has found that 'final firms' now tend to share with their stable subcontractors (which are often independent enterprises), market information, production planning and, on occasion, investments (Forlai, 1993: 76). Indeed, firms in district teams are connected by strong social ties that have sprung forth from repeated common work experience, during which a shared language and mutual personal trust developed.

So, even if also informal groups are not new to Tuscan districts, the evidence collected leads us to conclude that they developed strongly during the 1980s and the 1990s. This begs the question as to why the groups and teams formation has grown recently. The reasons for that are related both to the strategies adopted by local firms in the face of the new market conditions, and to the changes they brought about in the division of labour among firms.

In fact, the successful implementation of product innovation and quality upgrading strategies calls for a closer co-ordination amongst the differently specialized phase firms than was necessary in the past, when product ranges were limited to the traditional articles, quality requirements less cogent and delivery terms less strict.

In addition, the substitution of traditional and lower value-added activities by new ones, related to product differentiation and quality upgrading, requires considerable investments in new plants and skills that are different from the ones necessary for products and processes that are already established locally. Hence, they are highly risky, particularly for specialized subcontractors that have little contact with the increasingly changing final demand.

It is therefore logical that the relationships between 'final firms' and 'phase firms' have tended towards greater stability and tighter integration, so giving rise to the spreading of informal and formal enterprise groups. The characteristics of the new products and processes have required a less 'automatic' and more 'planned' co-ordination between the various specialized firms.[26] Moreover, the heightened riskiness of the investments involved has called for some form of risk-sharing device among the different partners engaged in the new business.

Formal enterprise groups bring about a quasi-integration inside the group and clearly meet both the above-mentioned needs. But, in the industrial district, informal groups too can be sufficient for the purpose. In fact, the socio-economic environment typical of the district favours the conclusion of special contractual arrangements, such as interlinking transactions.[27] In addition, the district environment promotes investments in personal reputation.[28] All that leads easily to the formation of teams and groups of enterprises. Indeed, arrangements such as interlinking transactions and investment in reputation create an economic and social incentive to reciprocal co-operation and mutual adjustment among partners. This is because of the increased cost of defection for each participant in the group and because of the development of a sense of loyalty among its members.

Evolution of relationships between local and external firms

Clearly, the changes in the division of labour between the inside and the outside of the district discussed above have also entailed an evolution of the relationships between local firms and companies external to the district.

Before considering such an evolution, however, it is worth noting that in the districts of Tuscany here examined, I found no evidence of important cases of takeovers by external large corporations. By contrast to what has occurred in other regions of northern Italy,[29] the only notable example of ownership transfer of local firms to an external large company has been the acquisition of some Prato spinning enterprises by the Benetton group, in 1991. But in the Prato district there are hundreds of spinning mills and this takeover did not significantly alter the functioning of the local market for spinning. Moreover, the acquisition of a local firm by an external large enterprise may even have positive consequences on the vitality of the district. If, for example, the local purchased firm maintains the management of its production and the acquisition brings about innovative investments, especially in new skills, that were otherwise impossible, external acquisition can even contribute to the regeneration of the district competitiveness.

More significant, although not widespread, is the evidence of the opposite phenomenon (i.e. the purchase of external companies by firms in the districts). From a study of 35 enterprise groups of Prato, for example, it emerged that some of them owned shares of companies located in other Italian textile systems, such as the ones in Carpi, Biella and Vicenza (Costi, 1993). In addition, a few of these groups also have investments abroad, especially in marketing companies that promote the sale of their products in countries like Japan or the USA. Also, some medium-sized firms and groups in Santa Croce have bought shares in tanneries in Southern and Central America, as well as elsewhere. Foreign investments, however, remained very limited and essentially due to the purpose of overcoming shortages in the supply of raw skins and hides, and of avoiding the costs and difficulties arising from the observance of environmental laws in Italy (Bartolini, 1994; Caporale, 1995).

Interesting information on the acquisitions of external firms by the local enterprises is found in a study on the productive internationalization of districts in Tuscany (Cavalieri, 1995). Such a study confirms that the purchase of shares of foreign companies is often coupled with subcontracting relations with the external firms. It proves also that international subcontracting often involves labour-intensive and low value-added stages, in order to cut production costs. However, there are also many investments in foreign companies that instead have the aim of gaining access either to a supply of raw materials or to new final markets.[30]

This study also reveals that Tuscan firms acquiring shares of foreign companies are on average very small, with fewer than eight employees each. In addition, it brings to light the crucial role often played by local intermediaries in establishing contacts with foreign enterprises, especially in international subcontracting. Indeed, because of their knowledge of producers in some foreign country and their personal reputation of trustworthiness among entrepreneurs in the district, these inter-mediaries are in the position to provide a kind of guarantee about the performance of the foreign company they introduce to local firms. Thus, in the industrial district, investments in personal reputation are essential, not only for the co-ordination of transactions inside the local system (Dei Ottati, 1994c), but, possibly, also for the co-ordination of transactions with external partners.

Conclusions

There is no doubt that during the past two decades Tuscany's industrial districts have been transformed under pressure from external challenges such as, for example, reductions in the level of demand for the products they typically produced. On the whole, however, the districts have demonstrated a remarkable resilience and an ability to adjust to a competitive context, which is increasingly global and changing. It is true that, after several decades of growth, particularly in the 1980s, there was a drop in industrial employment but it was largely compensated for by an expansion of the service sector, especially in respect of producer services. In fact, it is a general trend for services to grow and for producer services to play an increasingly strategic role in manufacturing production. Thus, the shift from industrial employment could be seen as an indicator of the ability of the districts to restructure and adapt.

The reduction of the districts' productive self-sufficiency through the acquisition of components made elsewhere and the partial use of subcontractors external to the local system has also been a break with the past. On a closer examination, however, outsourcing should not necessarily be interpreted as a sign of decline. On the contrary, we have seen that it usually allowed local firms to focus on strategic activities, such as design, preparing sample collections, marketing, or specializing on high value-added production stages, such as finishing. Moreover, we have also seen that often sourcing outside the district speeded up the process of product differentiation and innovation, which was essential for a successful adaptation to the new market conditions.

There is the issue of the formation of business groups. At first sight, this tendency seems to imply that a shift is occurring towards a more hierarchical organization. If so, this would mean a change in the relations among local firms which, in an industrial district, are typically characterized by a mix of both competition and co-operation (Becattini, 1990: 45–6; Dei Ottati, 1991; Brusco, 1995). However, in this case also, a closer examination reveals that the kind of 'grouping' developed in the districts of Tuscany should be interpreted more as an outcome of the district logic of evolution through the dual process of increasing division of labour among firms on the one hand, and, on the other, of more complex forms of integration between them (Loasby, 1998). Actually, that dual process leads to a peculiar way of consolidation of district firms, that is through the formation of teams and groups of enterprises according to whether the prevailing connecting element is trust or ownership relations (Dei Ottati, 2002).

Consequently, the restructuring that has occurred in the districts of Tuscany seems to have caused a shift from an 'almost-automatic co-ordination' (Marshall, 1919: 599) to a more conscious and 'planned' form of integration, among complementary specialized firms. As we have seen, a closer co-ordination was needed, both in order to meet the new quality and time delivery requirements and to support new risky investments. What should be noted here, however, is that such a need in the districts of Tuscany tended to be satisfied more through investments in personal reputation and through special contractual alliances, which encourage the continuity of the relationship among parties, rather than through ownership control and hierarchical monitoring. Moreover, to a large extent, such a restructuring retains both the autonomy of the individual firms and the flexibility of the local production system.[31]

The evidence, therefore, leads to the conclusion that, all in all, Tuscany's industrial districts have been able to preserve their basic identity despite of, or paradoxically because of, having changed (Becattini, 1989: 132). A sign of the continuing economic viability of the districts is their persistent export significance: for example, Santa Croce in 2000 accounted for 20 per cent of all Italy's exports of tanned skins and hides; in the same year, Prato made up around 23 per cent of all Italy's exports of textiles; whereas Empoli accounted for more than 6 per cent of the Italian exports of clothing.

Further, in spite of the difficulties of the restructuring during the 1980s, the Tuscan districts have been able to maintain a relatively good standard of living. The rate of employment in Tuscan districts is generally higher that for Italy as a whole.[32] Also blue-collar wages usually stay higher than the national average (see Table 1.6),[33] and the proportion of people living in houses they own is around 75 per cent in most districts of Tuscany, whereas in Florence is only 60 per cent (Istat, 1991a).

Thus, these indicators sustain the view that the kind of adjustment that has occurred in Tuscany's districts is closer to a 'high road' model than to a 'low road' one: it is more in line with a search for competitiveness through innovation, quality upgrading and the creation of new market niches, rather than through the exploitation of low labour standards (Sengenberger and Pyke, 1992: 11–13).[34]

Taken together, the preceding considerations could lead to the conclusion that the districts of Tuscany, or even all local systems organized according to the industrial district model, will automatically continue to reproduce both themselves and their successes over time. In fact, such a conclusion is not only false (as demonstrated, for example, by the decline of nineteenth-century English industrial

Table 1.6 Average blue-collar annual wages in five industrial districts of Tuscany and comparison with the Italian average in the same industry, 1993 and 1998

Districts	1993		1998		Main local industry
	Average wage (€)	Percentage of Italian average	Average wage (€)	Percentage of Italian average	
Empoli	10,020	101.0	14,760	105.1	Clothing and leather
Santa Croce	14,359	121.9	18,249	113.2	Tanning and leather
Prato	15,185	126.4	18,247	115.6	Textiles and clothing
Poggibonsi	12,138	101.3	15,144	98.9	Wood and furniture
Monsummano	10,330	104.1	14,473	103.8	Footwear and leather

Source: Inps (Istituto Nazionale Previdenza Sociale) database, our elaboration (data by province).

districts), but, worse, it is misleading and dangerous. Indeed, if, as I have argued elsewhere (Dei Ottati, 1994c), the support by local appropriate institutions has been necessary for the reproduction of industrial districts in the past, now that production has become globalized, and that the pace of market and technological changes has increased, the need for institutional intervention has heightened. In particular, effective collective action is required for the accelerated renewal and upgrading of localized knowledge,[35] and to ensure a more conscious and pre-determined co-operation among the many actors (individual and collective) that populate the district.

In fact, the increased speed and variety of innovations call for the injection and wide diffusion of new, partially heterogeneous, skills but such a need, especially in a system of small and medium-sized firms, can be met only by some form of collective provision.[36] By the same token, the reduced productive self-sufficiency of the districts, and the introduction of substantial innovations, entail costs and benefits that must not be distributed too unfairly among the main local categories, if 'constructive co-operation' (Marshall, 1919: 598) is to continue among them.[37] Therefore, perhaps a primary objective for institutional intervention could be the provision of forums for regular exchange and debate among representatives of the various interest groups (e.g. representatives of employers, workers, local government, banks, research and training institutions, etc.), in order to develop a shared understanding of local problems and to come to commonly agreed programmes of action.[38]

To be sure, the growth of localized knowledge and the promotion of effective progressive coalitions are not easy tasks, but they are urgent requirements for the very survival of the industrial districts, because, as recognized by Alfred Marshall, 'even a little obstinacy or inertia may ruin an old home of industry whose conditions are changing' (1919: 287).

Acknowledgement

The previous version of this chapter was originally prepared for publication in F. Cossentino, F. Pyke and W. Sengenberger (eds) (1996) *Local and Regional Response to Global Pressure: The Case of Italy and its Industrial Districts*, Geneva: International Institute for Labour Studies.

Notes

1   Among the collections of essays in English dealing with Italian industrial districts, see Piore and Sabel (1984), Goodman and Bamford (1989), Best (1990), Pyke *et al.* (1990), Pyke and Sengenberger (1992), Benko and Lipietz (1992), Storper and Scott (1992), Becattini *et al.* (2003).

2   On the economic development of Tuscany, see also Irpet (1975) and Becattini (1999).

3   According to the method of spatial identification adopted by Fabio Sforzi, in Tuscany there are as many as eight canonical industrial districts (Sforzi, 1994: 101–102).

4   The *Empoli* district includes the following six municipalities in province of Florence: Capraia e Limite, Cerreto Guidi, Empoli, Montelupo Fiorentino, Montespertoli, Vinci. The *Santa Croce sull'Arno* district includes the following six municipalities, five of which are in the province of Pisa and Fucecchio in the province of Florence: Castelfranco di sotto, Montopoli, San Miniato, Santa Croce, Santa Maria a Monte, Fucecchio. The *Prato* district includes the following thirteen municipalities, ten of which are in the province of Florence and three (Agliana, Montale and Quarrrata) in the province of Pistoia: Barberino di Mugello, Calenzano, Campi Bisenzio, Cantagallo, Carmignano, Montemurlo, Poggio a Caiano, Prato, Vaiano, Vernio, Agliana, Montale, Quarrata. The *Poggibonsi* district includes the following four municipalities, three of which are in the province of Florence and one (Casole d'Elsa) in the province of Siena: Casole d'Elsa, Colle Val d'Elsa, Poggibonsi, Barberino Val d'Elsa. The *Monsummano* district includes the following six municipalities in the province of Pistoia: Buggiano, Massa e Cozzile, Monsummano, Montecatini Terme, Pieve a Nievole, Ponte Buggianese.

5   Between 1985 and 1990 the production of carded woollen textiles declined by about 40 per cent in Prato and by about 30 per cent in Italy (Uip, 1990).

6   Because of the marked division of labour existing among firms in industrial districts, it is important to distinguish different kinds of firms: 'final firms' which have direct connection with final markets, 'phase firms' or subcontractors, that specialize in one or a few production stages, and 'service firms', which specialize in activities like producer services that are auxiliary to the local industry.

7   On the industrial district as a creative milieu, see Becattini (1991) and Bellandi (1992). On the patterns of economic change in the 'industrial district', see Bellandi (1996).

8   By way of example, consider that the models presented by the Monsummano footwear firms in their collections increased from an average number of 87 in 1980 to 221 in 1992 (Cee-Force, 1993: 133).

9   Usually, however, the acquisition of fully finished goods is limited to some special article, which is aimed at completing the range of products offered to the customers. For evidence in respect of Monsummano footwear system, see Cee-Force (1993: 152–153).

10   In the Poggibonsi district both the glassware industry (at Colle Val d'Elsa) and the mechanical industry are traditionally important. In particular, the latter

(which also includes the manufacture of woodworking machinery) have developed significantly in recent years.

11   The employment growth in producer services in the districts of Tuscany, calculated from the census data of 1981 and 1991, ranges from an increase of 100 per cent in Santa Croce and Monsummano to a boost of 184 per cent in Poggibonsi. Moreover, in all the districts considered, the new employment in producer services accounts for more than 30 per cent of all the new jobs in the services, public sector included. In appreciating the amount of producer services provided in industrial districts, however, we should include all the services here usually supplied by the local industrialist and artisan associations that are not included in the census data, and all the services supplied by special real service centres. On service centres in Tuscany, see Freschi (1992).

12   In Prato, for example, disintegration of complete-cycle woollen mills took place between 1949 and 1952 (see Dei Ottati, 1994b).

13   A measure of the decline in the use of rags by the Prato textile industry is that, between 1985 and 1993, the quantity of rags imported in the district dropped by a half, from approximately 93,000 to 45,000 tons.

14   On the diversification strategy of Prato firms specializing in products completely new to the district, see Zagnoli (1993).

15   In 1999 the yarn of all kinds of fibres imported into Prato reached 78,000 tons, but only 5,800 were of woollen yarn. In the same year the quantity of fabric imported was about 28,000 tons, but only 2,000 were woollen fabric.

16   Figures on the import of woollen intermediate products and of wet-blue refer to Tuscany (see Cavalieri, 1995). However, they are almost totally bought by firms in the Prato and Santa Croce districts respectively.

17   Figures for imports show how new patterns of outsourcing are facilitating product differentiation. For example, in the Prato district the imports of silk yarn, which was only 1 ton in 1985, reached 126 tons in 1992; and the imports of linen yarn increased from about 2,000 tons in 1985 to more than 5,000 tons in 1993.

18   Surveys done at the beginning of the 1990s found that Empoli subcontractors sold 23 per cent of their production (in terms of turnover) to firms located in northern Italy and 4 per cent abroad (Romagnoli, 1995); 17 per cent of Prato subcontractors received orders from firms in northern Italy (Iris, 1994: 117).

19   On district teams of enterprises, see Becattini (2001), and Dei Ottati (2002: 453).

20   Among the reasons for the formation of formal enterprise groups are: (a) the possibility of bringing relatives and skilled employees into the ownership structure; (b) the decision to introduce product differentiation; (c) the need to enhance quality and hence of getting closer integration among the different

production stages; and (d) the possibility of attaining larger economies of scale in functions such as finance and marketing.

21 For evidence on the early formation of formal groups in respect of the Prato district, see Pdup (1975); and in respect of Santa Croce, see Arpes (1982).

22 The tendency towards the grouping of firms concerns not only the development of enterprise groups led by 'final firms'. On the contrary, it encompasses also cases of consortia and other aggregations among 'phase firms' specialized in the same operation. Examples of that are two consortia among some Prato weaving firms called Gruppo tessile Gulliver and Grantessuto.

23 According to a recent analysis carried out by the Research Department of the Confederation of the Chambers of Commerce, in Tuscany, there are about 3,000 business groups, 98 per cent of which are small and medium-sized groups (less than 500 employees). These groups include more than 8,500 firms which represent 2.6 per cent of all business (but about 23 per cent of joint stock companies) present in Tuscany.

24 Some evidence about the presence of enterprise groups in Tuscan districts can be found in Cappiello (1992), concerning the Tuscan footwear local systems; Amin (1994), Bartolini (1994), and Bortolotti and Casai (1994), in respect of the Santa Croce district; and Iris (1994), concerning the Prato district.

25 On informal enterprise groups in Tuscan districts see, for example, Cappiello (1992) and Mariani (1992).

26 On the 'semi-automatic' co-ordination of relatively homogeneous industrial districts, see Dei Ottati (1991).

27 On interlinking transactions see Bell (1988); on interlinking transactions in the industrial district and particularly on interlinking transactions of subcontracting and credit, see Dei Ottati (1994a). As far as evidence about interlinking transactions is concerned, a study in the Prato district found that interlinking transactions of subcontracting and credit are twice as frequent than ownership relations among local firms: in fact, about 20 per cent of 'final firms' declared having recently financed either new machines or buildings of their subcontractors (cf. Iris, 1994: 134).

28 On investments in personal reputation and the co-ordination of risky transactions in the industrial district, see Dei Ottati (1994a; 1994c).

29 In Emilia Romagna, for example, about 24 per cent of the major takeovers of local firms that occurred from 1983 to 1988 were by foreign multinational business groups (see Bianchi and Gualtieri, 1990: 98). On the presence of multinational business groups in the Italian local systems of small and medium-sized enterprises, see Tessieri (2000).

30 Often, foreign investments in commercial units have the further purpose of facilitating a quicker response and generally offering a better service to customers.

31   We have seen that even jointly owned firms do not have exclusive subcontracting relationships with their parent company.

32   In 1999, the rate of employment in Tuscan districts was more than 60 per cent of the resident population (15–64 years old), when the average for Italy was 52 per cent.

33   For evidence on the higher per-capita labour costs in the district of Prato (and Biella) than for the Italian woollen industry as a whole, see Signorini (1994).

34   On the role of labour standards in economic development and industrial restructuring, see Sengenberger (1994: 3–41).

35   On the importance of the permanent recombination of localized contextual knowledge with globalized codified knowledge for the reproduction of viable local systems, see Becattini and Rullani (1996).

36   Examples of institutions (like service centres) that can promote the growth of competence in industrial districts are found in Brusco (1995).

37   On the need of institutional support for 'constructive co-operation', see Wilkinson and You (1994).

38   On the critical role of collective action and policy-making to the maintenance of dynamic local systems, and on the radically different policy approach that it requires, see Scott (1995). On concerted collective action as governance device for the successful reproduction of the industrial district, particularly when coping with external major changes, see Dei Ottati (2002).

Chapter 2
South-East Brabant
A regional innovation system in transition

Patricia Boekholt and Dick de Jager

Introduction

Can open regions overcome the challenges of globalisation? Paradoxically, heightened globalisation and ongoing European integration go hand in hand with the increasing significance of regional economies as entities of competitive rivalry. Internationally oriented enterprises are more likely to move their business functions, whether this is production, research, distribution or administration, to those locations that best fit their market needs or where added value is highest. The process of global sourcing has made firms more aware of the competitive advantages of particular nations or regions. At the same time, firms that have built up collaborative links in a particular region, with other firms, knowledge centres, education institutes or government funding agencies, could choose to stay (partly) located in that area, to utilise these networks. Networks in this sense are an important source of innovative ideas, not only in terms of transfer of scientific and technological expertise, but also in terms of inter- and intra-firm organisation. But are they strong enough to embed globally operating firms?

This chapter discusses the region of South-East Brabant which has a number of indigenous global firms and a large network of smaller suppliers that are closely linked to them. In the past two decades the region has seen both growth and depression, directly related to the global performance of the small number of international firms. We discuss how this has affected the region and the response of policy-makers.

The case of the region of South-East Brabant presented in this chapter also illustrates the role of these networks in the 'regional innovation system'. The argument put forward here is that historically developed strong networks could, on the one hand, hamper innovation in a regional system, if these networks cannot adapt to the dynamic of globalisation. 'The weakness of strong ties' as Grabher (1993: 255) put it, could mean that once booming regions become industrial districts of the past. But if the institutional and business infrastructures are able to adapt their strategies to the new challenges, this weakness can also be turned into a real strength.

The region of South-East Brabant is a particularly good example of a region that shows two sides of the coin, on the one hand it has been able (and is still able) to use and adapt its strong internal networks to react in a dedicated and flexible way to the changing economic challenges of the region. On the other, the strong industrial supplier networks mean that economic problems in the firms at the core of these networks are immediately felt throughout the whole regional economic system.

The rise of regional innovation policy

Regional governments in industrialised countries have realised that their economic development policy requires more than attracting new firms through industrial estates, investment grants or tax reliefs. Furthermore, indigenous firms are facing tough global competition and those that are operating internationally threaten to become footloose. Building up an innovation support system is seen as the key to recover, sustain or improve the economic performance of an area. After developing an investment acquisition strategy, regional governments have discovered the growth potential of emerging technologies and high-technology industries as a potential source of work and wealth. For instance, many science parks have been set up with the hope of creating new firms that spin off from university research or locate in the science park to be near to research expertise. Nevertheless this needs to be combined with a strategy to keep existing firms innovative and competitive. South-East Brabant is trying to do both: facilitate new ventures and support existing industries to remain strong.

The European Union has helped to trigger this heightened activity: many European innovation support activities are implemented on the regional level. In 1993 the European Commission DG Regio launched a pilot initiative called Regional Technology Plans (RTP) which aimed to initiate the development of a Regional Strategy for Research, Technology and Development Policy. The projects in this initiative were to be undertaken in so-called 'less favoured regions' which had an Objective 1 and 2 status. The initiative was made possible under Article 10 of the European Regional Development Fund (ERDF), which stated that part of the Structural Funds should be allocated to studies and pilot projects to promote innovation in regional development. The initiative proved a success and the philosophy was perpetuated in a number of successor programmes. Since this initiative, many other EU programmes have followed, of which the most important ones have been the Regional Innovation Strategy (RIS and RIS+) and Regional Innovation and Technology Transfer Strategy (RITTS) programmes. The province of North Brabant, which includes South-East Brabant, also entered the RITTS programme with the aim to boost innovation. This EU support has helped widen and deepen the understanding of innovation policy for a number of key actors.

New insights into how innovation processes work also helped to give the regions a greater role in this matter. Current thinking on innovation has moved away from the linear approach, which assumed that efforts in research and development are the source of innovation and commercialisation and, subsequently, better economic performance. Innovation is an interactive process in which its key actors, e.g. firms, interact with many other actors in their environment (research organisations, customers, regulators), influencing this innovation process. Innovation is therefore understood as a very complex process with intricate causal links. The set of institutions and actors, which influence the innovation process, is referred to in the literature as *national innovation systems*. National policies have to adapt to the specific dynamics and composition of these systems. Regional innovation systems are not simply national systems on a smaller scale. The scope of regional innovation systems varies greatly from country to country, depending on issues such as empowerment of these regions, size and so on (Cooke *et al.*, 2000).

In the past ten years or so, there has been a revolution – a 'paradigm shift' – in the way we understand the relationship between research, innovation and socioeconomic development

As one would expect with such a new concept, a precise definition of a 'national innovation system' is still emerging. Nelson and Rosenberg (1993) use a rather narrow definition, namely the 'set of institutions whose interaction determine the innovative performance of national firms'. Metcalfe (1995) says:

> A system of innovation is that set of distinct institutions which jointly and individually contributes to the development and diffusion of new technologies and which provides the framework within which governments form and implement policies to influence the innovation process. As such it is a system of interconnected institutions to create, store and transfer the knowledge, skills and artefacts which define new technologies.

Freeman who introduced the concept 'national system of innovation' (NSI) defined it as 'the network of institutions in the public and private sectors whose activities and interactions initiate, import, modify and diffuse new technologies' (1987: 1). Freeman's approach centres around the actors involved in the NSI. These could include a wide variety of organisations such as firms, research centres, government innovation bodies, intermediaries, and so on.

This NSI approach is subsequently used as a framework for analyses in the comparison of nations. Contributions such as Lundvall's (1992) and Nelson's (1993) integrate several elements of the integrative innovation theory into the NSI concept. The role of institutional learning, user–producer relations, networking, scientific institutions, finance, and so on, are all discussed in these studies, but not integrated into a systemic analysis. The study of regional innovation systems could shed more light on the dynamics of these systems. Empirical study at that level can show more clearly the interconnectedness of the elements of the innovation system.

When thinking in terms of national innovation systems, the links between actors in the system are necessary to maintain flows of knowledge throughout the system. 'Networking' as an important mechanism for innovation is yet another force behind the emergence of the regional dimension. Networking becomes easier with proximity. The vast amount of literature on the subject illustrates this (see, for instance, Håkansson, 1989; Camagni, 1991; Grabher, 1993; Morgan, 1996; Cooke *et al.*, 2000).

One important kind of networking takes place in clusters of firms. Clusters can be characterised as networks of production, of strongly interdependent firms (including specialised suppliers), knowledge-producing agents (universities, research institutes, engineering companies), bridging institutions (brokers, consultants) and customers, linked to each other in a value-adding production chain (see, for instance, OECD, 1999).

With the increasing globalisation of markets and technology, the reduction of product life cycles, more demanding customers for suppliers, many small and medium-size enterprises (SME) face increasing difficulties dealing with the challenges brought by these changes. They are most often rooted in a local market and global sourcing is not an available option for them. Isolated, their resource base is too limited to find and implement the solution to the increasing demands of the market. Networking with other firms with common problems or working in a similar field of technology or market, can give them the scope to find new opportunities. Therefore, initiatives to support the networking of firms can be vital for innovative SMEs to expand their possibilities, or even to survive. Many networks of firms are strongly rooted in one particular region. A study into the competitiveness of the Dutch industries showed that those sectors with a relatively high share in the world market have a strong regional or national production and institutional base, combined with a international market orientation. The best example of such a regional-based cluster is the cut flower industry with a wide and well-knit production, research and technology transfer network (see Boekholt, 1997). In industrialised regions such as South-East Brabant, large firms are important actors in existing networks. They have built up supplier networks, established contacts with knowledge centres and very often they form a source of technology transfer themselves, through spin-offs, tacit knowledge transfer, and so on.

The success stories of Silicon Valley, Baden-Württemberg and Emilia Romagna have inspired policy-makers, authorities engaged in regional development, and technology transfer experts to try to copy the network model in other locations. There is a trend for these types of actor to operate as 'brokers' between potential partners. In South-East Brabant, the region under investigation, these publicly supported networking or cluster initiatives are playing an increasing role in innovation policy.

Greater awareness of both regions and nations as entities of competitive advantage and the role of strong clusters within them came from Michael Porter's (1990) book *The Competitiveness of Nations*. It drew attention to the importance of mainly national factors determining the competitiveness of industrial sectors. It put the concepts of (regional) clusters of related industries back on the agenda of both policy-makers and academics. In Porter's view, industries in a particular nation or region have competitive advantage if they are embedded in a wide and deep network. A well-developed and dense network consists not only of inter-firm links within a particular industry, but also with related industries, specialised knowledge centres, education facilities, innovation support agencies and direct links with clients. In an institutional context where co-operative public and private relations can create an environment in which firms find stimuli to upgrade their activities through access to training, finance, business services and sources of knowledge, they are likely to perform better.

Clusters are not created overnight, it is often a long-term historical process. They are gradually expanded to involve related industries, suppliers, knowledge sources, distribution channels, and so on. Initiatives, whether public or private, aimed at establishing new clusters from scratch will be very difficult to implement.

We can define clusters in a very broad manner: a group of firms, knowledge centres and innovation support organisations with a functional affinity which co-operate to achieve new market strategies, product or process innovations (see Jacobs *et al.*, 1995). Co-operation can be formal, i.e. with an explicit contract (e.g. a supplier contract, a joint venture), or informal. In the latter case we may think of kinds of informal knowledge transfer, connections with 'related' industries (i.e. industries which have no direct horizontal or vertical relationships, but which may share some 'economies of scope', e.g. similar technologies, similar markets).

The following text will discuss the role of clusters in a regional innovation system for the case of South-East Brabant. The role of vertical clusters around a few large Original Equipment Manufacturers (OEM) is the dominant networking pattern in the regional economy. Two sets of effects have had a great influence on these networks in recent years. The first is the emergence of management practices such as 'lean production', flexible specialisation and just-in-time delivery among the larger companies under pressure of globalisation. The second is the sudden crisis and downsizing of the two most important OEMs in the region, i.e. Philips and DAF, in the early 1990s. Both sets of effects have considerable consequences for the relationships between the main contractor and its supply chain. The question is, how does the region manage to cope with these effects? What is the effect on the regional economy and its long-established networks? Is there an adequate institutional response?

South-East Brabant as a system of innovation

One could argue that we can hardly speak of regions in a small country such as the Netherlands. The country can be seen as one 'urban region' within the Western European economic core area. In many political respects the Netherlands is highly centralised, in particular in the areas of science and technology policy. However, even within this small country, there are strong regional features, in economic terms (highly industrialised areas and service sector areas versus rural areas), in cultural terms (for instance with difference in languages), and in administrative terms.

Even a small geographical area such as South-East Brabant can be analysed as a system of innovation, due to the presence of a wide range of local actors whose activities and interactions initiate, import, modify and diffuse new technologies. One has to be careful, however, to look at this system in its national and international context.

South-East Brabant, situated in the south of the Netherlands, is a sub-region of the province of North-Brabant.[1] The region is centrally located between various industrial areas: Rotterdam and Antwerp in the west and the German Ruhrgebiet in the east. The region has economic links with the Flemish-speaking part of Belgium on its south border and in particular to the northern part of the province of Limburg on its west border.

South-East Brabant is an area with great diversity: it is at the same time the most industrialised region in the Netherlands and a rural area with strong agriculture, albeit in a quite radical transition.

The city of Eindhoven is the industrial and innovative heart of South-East Brabant. It is the fifth largest city in the Netherlands and the home-base of the multinationals Philips and DAF and high tech companies such as ASM Lithography (producer of wafer steppers). Some 10 miles from Eindhoven lies Helmond, a city with a history in textile and metal industries.

The administrative status of South-East Brabant is a layer in between the provinces and local governments (SRE, Eindhoven Regional Government). The scope of political responsibilities of these kinds of sub-region, particularly in urban and industrialised areas, *vis-à-vis* the provinces is still under debate in Dutch politics, although it seems that the advocates of stronger formalised urban regions have lost their momentum. The issue of upscaling local authorities is also causing great debate. In general, the large city areas claim more authority whereas the sur-rounding towns and rural areas wish to remain independent.

The actors in South-East Brabant have a clear regional identity. Contrary to other parts of the Brabant province, the South-East has developed a strong specialisation in high-level manufacturing, in particular in the areas of electronics, ICT, metalworking (equipment and instruments) and the automotive industry. The institutional set-up of this region in terms of education, research and public and private business services has followed this specialisation pattern. Furthermore, the local authorities in and around the industrial heart of South-East Brabant see it as a distinctive area with a strong high-technology potential. However, the existing inter-firm networks, mainly supplier links, do not let institutional borders deter them from close collaboration outside the region or country.

Some key indicators on population, size and economic structure are shown in Table 2.1. It shows that in size the region is small, but has a relatively higher than average population and labour force. Unemployment has dropped over a period of ten years from figures higher than average in the Netherlands to figures lower than average. Although a small region in size, it is considered one of the most dynamic modern industrial parts of the country. Some major problems in the region started in the early 1990s: downsizing of large firms, fall in employment and a feeling of acute crisis. But the region has recovered impressively from this crisis, although the current ICT crisis has led to new problems.

The business perspective: innovative firms and clusters

It is a testimony to the positive changes in the past ten years that the labels which the region invented for itself ('Industrial Mainport' and 'Leading in Technology') are now widely recognised and acknowledged within the Dutch mindset. Together with the Twente region, South-East Brabant is now seen as the high tech hotspot within the Netherlands. Between 1995 and 2000 there was a growth of 7,100 firms and almost 45,000 new jobs in the region (ETIN, 2002). This growth has been concentrated in professional and financial services and communication and ICT. Whilst the biggest growth has been in services, the industrial base is still strong: 1 in every 5 jobs is industrial, compared with 1 in 7 in the Netherlands as a whole.

The industrial structure of the region is influenced by the following characteristics:

- The location of Philips, the electronics multinational, with several production plants (i.e. Philips Medical Equipment in Best) and research facilities (Philips NAT Lab and high-tech campus) and a supplier network.
- The relatively large presence of mostly indigenous 'high-tech' firms in electronics and mechatronics: ASM-Lithography (production equipment for ICs), Origin (measuring and testing instruments), NedCar Pd&E (automotive), Te Strake (weaving machines), Stork (textile and printing

Table 2.1 Some key indicators about South-East Brabant

Indicator	Statistic		
Population (2000)	714,160 (4.5% of Netherlands)		
Labour force (2000)	335,280 (4.6% of Netherlands)		
Unemployment in 2001 (definition Central Statistics Office)	1.6% (Netherlands 1.9 %)		
Size	1441 km² (4.3% of Netherlands)		
Employment structure (2000)	agriculture	4.2%	
	industry	21.8%	
	services	74%	
Number of firms (2000)	44,000		
(of which foreign)	(278)		

Source: *Facts and Figures Eindhoven Region*, NV REDE Regional Economic Development Corporation, May 2002

machines), ODME (optical instruments), and many others. Two other influential firms, located just outside South-East Brabant's borders in the province of Limburg, but with a supplier network in South-East Brabant, are the manufacturers of office copiers Océ (with product development) and Rank Xerox (assembly and distribution). All these firms are OEMs and most of them are not solely assembly plants, but with product development capacities.

• The large presence of firms in the automotive sector, transport and logistics (DAF, several coach and truck building companies, road transport companies). As a result of this clustering of firms, regional actors in business and (public) support agencies are aiming to develop the region into an 'indistribution' centre: the combination of assembly, packaging, labelling, stocking, distribution and physical transport of goods.

South-East Brabant relies heavily on the growth of these internationally oriented manufacturers of end products. Around and alongside these firms we can distinguish clusters of firms, partly spin-offs from the larger companies and from the university, partly suppliers or firms attracted to the region because of its reputation.

The industrial distribution of employment shows the importance of the electronics industry in South-East Brabant (see Table 2.2). Other important sectors are the food and beverages industry (strongly related to agricultural production, i.e. dairy, meat and poultry), metalworking, machines/equipment/instruments and automotive industries. Data on the production of these sectors confirm this picture.

The location of several OEMs has created several industrial clusters in which SMEs also play a large role. These clusters were already highly developed in the last decades of the twentieth century. A study into innovative networks in South-East Brabant concluded that inter-firm links are crucial for innovation in local firms (see Bosman *et al.*, 1993).[2]

These findings have recently been confirmed by a survey that was executed within the framework of the RITTS programme. The results of this survey stated that public sources of knowledge and support are hardly used, but that partnerships with clients and suppliers are regular innovation mechanisms (North-Brabant Development Agency, 2000).

The 1993 survey found that of those suppliers that made an important contribution to the respondent's innovation, more than 20 per cent came from the Eindhoven district and almost 40 per cent came from the South part of the Netherlands, within a circle of approximately 100 kilometres around Eindhoven. Clients that made a contribution to innovation were 37 per cent from the Eindhoven locality and 51 per cent from South Netherlands. A more recent survey (2002) by the Boston Consulting Group showed that 40 per cent of total turnover of regional industrial suppliers in the South of the Netherlands still depends on regional OEMs.

For a regional innovation system to be dynamic, it is important to have sophisticated industrial clients, i.e. manufacturers of end products, demanding

Table 2.2 Sectoral division of employees in North Brabant, 2000

Activity	Employees	Growth (1996–2000) (%)	Region (%)	The Netherlands (%)
Food	7,156	– 3.2	9.9	13.4
Textiles	3,362	– 10.6	4.6	3.3
Wood	1,771	+ 17.1	2.4	2.5
Paper/graphical	4,515	– 0.7	6.2	12.2
Chemicals	4,046	+ 22.6	5.6	12.1
Building materials	1,978	+ 20.1	2.7	3.6
Metal products	10,771	+ 5.3	14.8	13.4
Equipm./instrum.	7,624	+ 30.7	10.5	9.2
Electronics/optics	18,058	+ 6.2	24.9	10.4
Automotive	6,097	+ 10.9	8.4	5.8
Furniture and rest	7,192	+ 14.2	9.9	14.1
Total industry	72,597	+ 8.3	100	100

Source: Company register North-Brabant, processed by ETIN (2002)

high quality from their local suppliers. South-East Brabant has these types of industrial client, but on several occasions in the past decades, they have faced great problems, leading to reorganisations and downsizing, with profound implications for the total regional economic system.

In the late 1980s the problems of the region's two largest employers (Philips and DAF) began to manifest themselves clearly. Philips' poor results, especially in the computer and consumer electronics division, led to a 'shock therapy' type of reorganisation. The so-called Operation Centurion which took place in 1990 meant the loss of approximately 65,000 jobs worldwide.

Only a year later a similar crisis occurred with DAF manufacturers of trucks and vans. Due to the collapse of the European market for trucks and vans, the already highly concentrated industry had to close down factories and lay off many of its employees. The position of DAF in the automotive sector was not as dominant as that of Philips in the electronics sector: even before its crisis, truck manufacturer DAF used the supplier networks of Mercedes in Baden-Württemberg for many vital parts (see Jacobs *et al.*, 1990). Regional and national policy-makers feared that DAF would become 'footloose' in the regional economy. Little did they know that due to the collapse of truck markets, DAF had nearly disappeared altogether. DAF Trucks went bankrupt but got the chance to restart as a 'leaner and meaner' company. Emergency funding from national and regional governments and from a public fund raising action, in the region, helped enable the company to make this new start.

Nevertheless, the whole network around the automotive sector underwent severe reorganisations and downsizing. SMEs in particular were worst hit. Those that survived developed into main suppliers, producing complete systems with higher quality standards (see Beek *et al.*, 1994). In this downsizing the region lost many highly qualified jobs both in production, middle management and R&D.

The problems with DAF triggered discussion on the relevance of 'clusters' in the Netherlands. Policy-makers stated their concerns that with the closing down of DAF, a whole cluster of suppliers would have to close down as well. This was put forward as a key argument for government support to rescue the company.

Policy since then has been strongly focused on reducing the dependence of the region on a limited number of OEMs. Although there has been a strong growth of innovative SMEs in the region, some fundamental characteristics of the regions have proven to be quite persistent. In a recent study by the Boston Consulting Group (2002) the main characteristics of the present situation are described as follows:

- Together with professional services, high level manufacturing industries are the most important with regard to economic value added for the province, especially for South-East Brabant, which is still the focal point of manufacturing industries in the Netherlands.

- The regional economic situation is still very much dependent on six large OEMs: Philips, NedCar, DAF, ASML, Océ and Rank Xerox.
- Although the OEMs enable the region to focus on high-level technological design and production, this also leads to the fact that the positive and negative developments of the OEMs are strongly felt throughout the region.

This can be illustrated by the recent problems for the regional suppliers of ASM Lithography, which lowered its production of wafer steppers due to the global ICT crisis, this has led to a new period of job losses which started in the second half of 2001.

The further development since the mid-1990s of the strong Mechatronics cluster, which combines elements of several 'traditional' clusters (especially mechanics and electronics) has been interesting. South-East Brabant is by far the number one region in the Netherlands in the field of mechatronics, with 1,552 companies providing almost 40,000 jobs in 2000. The major player in this field is ASM Lithography, to the point that the old dependence of suppliers upon Philips, Océ and DAF has in part been replaced by a fairly large dependence on ASML, as has been argued in the Regional Innovation Profile made in the course of the RITTS programme.

Historical changes in the supplier networks: from purchasing to subcontracting

Although the industrial clusters in South-East Brabant have a long history and seem to be quite stable in the long run, apart from periodic economic crises, there have been some important qualitative changes in past decades.

Two networks studied in the 1992 survey showed differences in the strategic position of the firms around Philips and Océ respectively. In 1987 the firms around Philips were in their early growth stage while those around Océ were in a stable phase. Five years later, the firms around Philips were also in a stable phase. The study concluded that the position of the firms in the Philips network had deteriorated (see Bosman *et al.*, 1993: 113–116). However one could also argue that the relatively younger network had stabilised itself in those five years. A significant difference found between the firms within the Océ and Philips networks, compared to those outside, was that among the former group, a smaller number of respondents stated that innovation came from a specific request from their client. In addition, the former group was more oriented towards process innovation. Improvement of production capacity and delivery time were more frequently mentioned as a result of their innovative efforts, compared to the latter group of companies. An earlier study into the networks of Océ showed that local suppliers manufactured the 'low-tech' components of copiers, whilst more sophisticated components were purchased in South-East Asia (electronics, motor parts) or Eastern Europe (optical parts) (see Jacobs *et al.*, 1990). These results indicate that the local supplier network of Philips and Océ had at that moment in time the function of extending capacity in less value-added components. A relationship of co-makership where suppliers are (partly) responsible for the development of their products was not clearly visible among the SME suppliers.

Looking at the major original OEMs in the South-East Brabant region (Philips, DAF and NedCar), a tardy but lasting shift in their supply strategy has laid the foundation for more recent developments. When we take a closer look at the strategy of the OEMs, the recent attention to cluster building is a result of an evolution in subcontracting activities. We can describe the history from research into the supplier networks of Philips, but the story can be applied in a wider sense.

We can distinguish three phases in these supplier networks:

1   In the 1950s to 1960s supplies came mainly from developing integrated divisions within the OEMs. These companies expanded through growth and acquisitions. External contracting was limited and mainly concerned standard products or components.
2   In the second period, in the 1970s and 1980s, the OEMs developed a strategy of establishing a large external supply industry. The large firms started to focus on their core business. Doubts about the efficiency of internal suppliers, fierce international competition and globalisation of production led to cost awareness and a policy of decentralisation, resulting in an enormous number of external suppliers.
3   In the most recent period from the early 1990s, the OEMs started to realise that they could benefit from the use of the specialised knowledge and experience of their suppliers. Instead of singular parts or components, more complex sub-assemblies were contracted out to main suppliers with engineering and logistical capacities. These main suppliers often consist of a group of co-operating companies with different specialisations. A second layer of suppliers, mostly less knowledge-intensive 'jobbers', delivers to the main suppliers and only rarely direct to the OEMs. A network with different layers evolves.

Thus we can distinguish two types of suppliers in the regional networks. The first are highly specialised firms that can provide value-added products due to their technological, development, design or organisational related expertise. The other group consists of suppliers who can produce standard products or components either on the basis of detailed instructions by their clients or on the basis of cost competition. The challenges of globalisation are different for both types of suppliers.

The network around Philips is a good example of this. In the 1980s an important change in the mutual relations and dependencies between Philips and its suppliers arose. A first tier of suppliers had been very successful in adopting modern production technology such as CNC production equipment. Through modernisation and specialisation in production techniques, which they originally learnt from Philips, a proportion of the supply companies equalled or even surpassed the master from a technological point of view.

In the mid-1980s Philips had a total of 3,902 suppliers in the South-East Brabant region only. In view of the enormous amount of transaction costs involved, it is not surprising that from the early 1990s Philips aimed to cut back its number of suppliers. This trend, not only at Philips but also present at other major OEMs (see Praat, 1992; Boston Consulting Group, 2002), was reinforced by the sudden economic problems around 1992. The changes in supplier relations have had major implications for the companies involved. In order to reduce the number of supplier relations, large companies began contracting out more complex sub-systems (see Praat *et al.*, 1994). Some suppliers now fulfil the role of main contractors or main suppliers. Rival companies have to be involved, networks have to be formed, in order to get access to complementary processing techniques and expertise. Through this network system, temporary combinations are formed to integrate all the required specialisations and create the capacity to carry out complex and sizeable assignments (see Praat *et al.*, 1995; Boston Consulting Group, 2002). Networking capabilities become essential skills to keep competitive advantage. Around this first tier of suppliers, those who have managed to upgrade to the status of main suppliers, we can distinguish a second tier of suppliers, whose direct relations to the OEMs are cut off. The second tier companies, producing specialised components in large quantities, have the main suppliers as their clients. Very often their competitive advantage depends on price and/or logistics.

To conclude: since the mid-1990s, a number of trends have dominated and will continue to dominate the further development of the regional industrial networks[3] in the southern part of the Netherlands and especially South-East Brabant:

- The relocation of production to low cost countries has not ended. Consumer electronics is a good example (further relocations to Mexico and South-East Asia). ICT developments also influence areas that were thought to be relatively immune until recently.
- There is an ongoing trend for OEMs to increase the intensity of subcontracting their design and production, concentrating their own activities on

product development, marketing and sales. Hence they are developing into 'head–tail' companies. This increases their interaction with a limited number of trusted and highly qualified main suppliers.

- OEMs are increasing their forward integration by developing services for their end customers. Océ, DAF and Philips Medical Systems are examples of firms that are increasingly active in service development.
- Supply to OEMs is an increasingly globalising business. The OEMs in the region will buy more supplies on the global market in the future.
- OEMs are in a process of further consolidation by mergers and take-overs. This trend is also visible for main suppliers, especially in the automotive sector.
- Modular production is still increasingly important (especially in consumer electronics and the automotive sector). This leads to a pressure on suppliers, forcing them into a more intensive co-operation within supplier networks, in order to be able to produce complex modules instead of simple parts.
- This shift towards complex modules puts pressure on the suppliers with regard to their own product development capabilities. Suppliers in the region expect their expenditures on product development to rise by 20 per cent in the next five years.
- The risk of product development investments shifts from OEMs to suppliers, as 'pay-on-production' concepts spread from automotive to other industries (such as Xerox in the Southern Netherlands region).
- These greater responsibilities for suppliers put pressure on their ability to have a good understanding of market trends and market developments.
- These developments lead to a new position of main suppliers in the regional networks. Their position is increasingly important as they become focal points for product development and knowledge creation in the production chain.

The question for the region is thus whether the industrial networks and the firms within these networks will be able to make the most of these trends. Are the companies in the region on the one hand able to form high quality partnerships with the main OEMs, while at the same time decreasing their too great dependence on the six main players in the region?

A survey executed within the framework of the RITTS programme in 1998 among some of the main suppliers in the region led to the conclusion that the production skills of these companies are on a high level, while their networking and market development skills are sub-optimal and below the level needed to be excellent all-round innovators in the future (North-Brabant Development Agency, 2000).

Both RITTS and the study on the future prospects of the regional manufacturing industries point towards a number of policy options for the future:

- Improve the networking and market development capabilities of the regional supplier firms.
- Intensify the further development of technology-based and knowledge-intensive clusters (i.e. Intelligent Systems) and the further development of an 'open' knowledge infrastructure, with more possibilities for spin-offs, spin-outs and other new business arrangements.

To sum up the key elements of the innovation system from the firm perspective:

- There are tightly networked clusters in the region in 'high-tech and 'medium-tech' industries. However, the success of these clusters is dependent on a limited number of powerful OEMs. Recent changes in supplier–contractor relations give new challenges for the smaller firms in the region. There is likely to develop further a two-tier system of interfirm networks. Firms in the first tier can upgrade their activities and manage to create horizontal collaborations based on complementary assets. Firms in the second tier will operate in hierarchical and vertical supply chains and are more and more under pressure from low-cost competition from abroad.
- The crises in some of the OEMs has revealed the vulnerability of the RIS, illustrated by sudden drops in employment.

The policy dimension: strengthening the organisational capabilities of the region

So far we have only described the predominant inter-firm relations in the South-East Brabant region. The regional innovation system also consists of an institutional context that shapes innovation in the business sector. The system of innovation support is a combination of European, national, provincial and sub-regional initiatives.

Public innovation support in the region relies in part on national policy instruments such as R&D subsidy schemes, funding of the knowledge infrastructure, and support for technology transfer. Regional institutions and regional and European support programmes exist alongside national activities.

Regional policy instruments were strengthened in the wake of the Philips/DAF crisis in the beginning of the 1990s. Acting on the 'sense of urgency', some regional key players like the Mayor of Eindhoven, the University Chairman, the Chairman of the Chamber of Commerce and captains of industry combined forces and tried to find new development possibilities for the region.

The region obtained European Objective-2 status (currently Phasing Out) and developed the Objective-2 Stimulus Programme. This Programme focused upon the improvement of regional economic infrastructures (hard and soft) and on creating new employment and opportunities for growth in existing and start-up companies.

Stimulus has been important for the region as a focal point for regional development capabilities. The region has been quite successful in the past decade with regard to its organisational capabilities and flexible responses to the regional situation and opportunities.

A number of success factors are:

- The existing knowledge infrastructure and industrial infrastructure of the region.
- Excellent co-operation between the main regional actors from government, the knowledge infrastructure and industry, focusing their efforts on a common goal, summarised in two 'labels' for regional development: 'Industrial Mainport' and 'Leading in Technology'.
- Strong informal linkages between organisations and a willingness to combine forces to seize opportunities.
- A keen eye for these opportunities. The region has been successful in attracting TNO Industry, a main industrial R&D organisation, a Twinning Centre (an incubator for high-level ICT start-ups) and 'Knowledge City', a large-scale ICT programme to promote the implementation of 'e-solutions' in society.
- The availability of European Structural Funds money, acting as a focal point and as lubricating oil for co-operation.

One specific action that has been successful and acts nowadays as an explicit model for further clustering initiatives, is called *Knowledge-Intensive Clustering* (KIC) and is a typical example of public network involvement in the Netherlands. In the KIC initiative, a cluster of suppliers with complementary assets has been set up around one large or medium-sized manufacturing company. The supported projects had to involve joint development of a new product. The aim was to increase the capability of local suppliers for high quality product development, to turn them into strategic partners for the OEM and to involve them in the production of the newly developed products. Although the KIC project was an initiative of the central government, regional actors were made responsible for its implementation. The most prestigious project has been developed around the photocopier company Océ. This company developed a new type of colour copier and printer. For modules of the new products, joint development projects with groups of local suppliers were formed. The development of the network was predominantly the job of the Regional Development Agencies and Syntens which acted as a broker in conjunction with Océ. The most appropriate local suppliers were selected to co-develop some of the components supplied to Océ.

The early involvement and combination of expertise from different types of supplier speeded up the development process. Océ is very positive about the project and is now contracting out more of its product development than before. At the same time, one of its leading executives has stated in the press that the local suppliers still cannot reach the required quality and Océ cannot afford to have more patience with the local suppliers compared to global ones. It remains to be seen what the long-term effect on the network will be and if the local suppliers will also be successful in acquiring production contracts for these new products.

Although it can be argued that the region still has a long way to go in reducing its dependency on a limited number of OEMs, it has done quite an outstanding job in the past decade. The region has managed to increase high-level employment, develop new knowledge-intensive businesses (especially ICT) and improve the technological infrastructure (i.e. TNO Industry, the Science Park, a couple of Incubators).

The awareness that the recent success of the region goes hand in hand with some persistent structural weaknesses was heightened by the results of a number of recent surveys and studies. A survey executed within the framework of the RITTS programme pointed towards the sub-optimal networking and market development capabilities of suppliers in the region. A study commissioned by the Regional Development Agencies of Brabant and Limburg (BOM and LIOF) on the future of regional manufacturing industries pointed towards dependence on a limited number of OEMs and indicated some important trends (mentioned earlier in this article).

These surveys and studies led to several action programmes. A recent example of the regional organisational capabilities and willingness to act is the *Horizon Programme*, implementing the results of the regional study on the future for manufacturing industries, also taking the RITTS results into account. Hence, Horizon is complementary to the *Innovative Actions Brabant*, which is the RITTS follow-up at the provincial level.

The Horizon Programme has been drawn up by the new 'Committee for Regional Opportunities' (in which the government, knowledge centres, intermediaries and the business community participate) and is a strategic action plan that has to contribute to the reinforcement of the economic structure in a mid-term perspective. 'Technology and knowledge' and 'Entrepreneurship and marketing' are the unifying elements that ensure the Programme's coherence.

The mission of the Horizon Programme is to do the following:

- To support the transformation from manufacturing industry to a national and international design industry and design services. Part of manufacturing industry will switch to commercial services. An increase in productivity and capabilities is vital. Product development, production technology and marketing are important core competencies.

* To pay more attention to market development and innovation management capabilities in SMEs. SMEs also need to undertake more independent innovation and must become owners of their own knowledge input in the supply chain.

In the case of South-East Brabant, there has been a high degree of formal and informal co-operation since the Philips/DAF crisis, centred upon the ambition to make the region 'leading in technology'. Certainly, there are still overlaps and fragmentation of efforts and the region still has a long way to go to realise its potential and overcome its weaknesses. But South-East-Brabant shows that a combination of 'urgent threats', dedicated actors, clear policy goals, (European) money and a willingness to act and seize opportunities can transform traditional regional networks and linkages into a more dynamic system of flexible adaptation.

Conclusion: is there a regional innovation system to cope with the transition?

South-East Brabant has a well-developed system of innovation, with R&D-intensive clusters, some world-class companies, several knowledge centres and various technology transfer agencies. In addition, the proximity to other Dutch, Belgian and German systems of innovation increases the scope of firms to obtain the necessary external incentives for institutional learning. There is a strong awareness that clustering of existing strengths gives opportunities to create value-added products and services. The economic recession of the early 1990s and crises within some major firms increased awareness of the importance of strong networks. At the same time the central role of a few large companies as the 'spiders in the network' showed the vulnerability of these clusters and eventually the regional economy. The main threat to the system comes from relocation or downsizing of OEMs and the dependency of smaller firms on these local clients. Since then, this central characteristic of the region has remained remarkably stable.

Many small and medium-sized suppliers still should expand their focus outside the region or develop into system suppliers. There are still too few firms capable of acting as high quality main-suppliers with internal development capabilities.

Nevertheless, the sudden shock of downsizing OEMs in the 1990s has alerted both businesses and policy-makers. Since then the region has shown a remarkable ability to co-operate and seize opportunities for improving the regional economic situation. Whether the region will fully succeed in its transition processes remains to be seen. But at this moment it seems that there are sufficient elements in the regional innovation system that can keep the dynamism alive.

Acknowledgement

This chapter is an update of the original chapter written by Patries Boekholt and Edwin van der Weele in 1994.

Notes

1   Therefore, the official name of this sub-region is South-East North Brabant, but because of this confusing name one usually refers to it as South-East Brabant.
2   The survey was part of a research project by the Technical University of Eindhoven, in which Edwin van der Weele, collaborating in the original chapter, was one of the participating researchers.
3   Boston Group study for the Regional Development Agency BOM (2002).

Chapter 3
The changing institutional structure and performance of the Catalan innovation system

Jordi Bacaria, Susana Borràs Alomar and Andrea Fernàndez-Ribas

Introduction

Despite being a region characterized by its dynamic industrial structure, Catalonia has long suffered from the lack of appropriate industrial technological innovation. Such difficulties have been a constant feature of the Catalan model of economic development. As in most of the European regions with an industrial tradition, the early industrial revolution was based on market expansion, agricultural productivity (giving rise to a massive labour migration to the towns and cities) and the introduction of sophisticated machinery in various production processes. Catalan industry did not itself produce technological innovations, but rather introduced them from abroad. The historical problems of technological innovation in Catalonia were mainly related to two phenomena: the traditionally closed nature of the Spanish market and the region's low investment in research. Spain has been the 'natural' market for Catalan products for many decades. The closed market affected the nature of product competition and the forms of innovation processes in the industrial realm. The lack of strong market incentives prevented investment in endogenous technology, and technological innovations were mostly imported. However, this trend does not mean an obstacle for technological development *per se*. The main problem in Spain and Catalonia was that such foreign novelties were almost always introduced late, reducing the possibilities for a process of 'learning by using' that would have helped reverse the situation.

Catalonia has shown great dynamism through the important changes made in its industrial and economic setting since the mid-1970s. Although from the regional innovation system point of view we should differentiate between the decades 1980–90 and 1990–2000. The profound and rapid changes of the Catalan economy and innovation processes should be understood, first, within the Spanish sociopolitical and economic context of the past thirty years. The democratic transition since 1976[1] and regional decentralization at the beginning of the 1980s (by the process of devolution developed by the 1978 Spanish Constitution) are two crucial phenomena that have fostered important renewal trends in public administration and in society. Similarly, the Spanish economy has sustained an accelerated path of internationalization and openness that, in spite of being perceived as necessary, has also created great uncertainties about the competitiveness of the Catalan structure. Second, the Catalan economy has also seen fundamental changes in the financial market and educational system, as well as the increasing relevance of the service sector, which have also helped the rapid transformation of the industrial landscape. Yet, one of the most direct factors in the Catalan system of innovation has been the Spanish government's attempt to develop the Spanish national innovation system more effectively.

Something else has been changing since the beginning of the 1990s. First, the gradual integration of Spain in the European economy has had a new impact on the Catalan relation to the Spanish market. Nowadays, Catalan trade is more oriented towards the European market and less dependent on the Spanish market. This outcome is giving the Catalan economy new incentives to be more competitive. Second, the decentralized political system in Spain has given way to the consolidation of a 'Catalan governance' with a strong political will to be 'differentiated' from the Spanish polity. This has also been the case for R&D and innovation policies.

The Catalan innovation system follows its own clear path of development, not only because of its industrial setting but also due to its specific institutional and sociopolitical characteristics. The initiatives taken by the newly and significantly empowered regional government have mainly focused on developing a renewed network of research institutions, supporting agencies related to technological development, and fostering an 'innovation market'. Parallel to the strengthening of institutions and to these policy initiatives, the aggregate performance of the RIS has improved slowly. The rationale for this weak performance is, in short, the persistent gap between research and innovation in Catalonia. On the other hand, the political will in Catalonia that explains why a regional innovation system exists, requires some kind of political action different from the Spanish government, even in innovation policy. Therefore, the Catalan innovation system is searching for its own pace, and to achieve it, an improvement in the institutional dialogue between the social actors and business representatives is necessary, in order to identify what the real social needs for fostering innovation are. This chapter examines these later issues, providing an overview of the rapidly changing trends that have characterized the Catalan RIS since the 1980s, both in terms of institutional set-up and overall performance. The conclusion will summarize the findings and will discuss the open research questions for future investigation.

Catalan economic and innovation performance during the 1980s and the 1990s

Catalonia is one of the industrial poles in Spain, together with Valencia and the Ebro Valley (Aragon, Navarre and the Basque Country), which have had the most significant growth rates of GDP in the past decades. During the period 1987–90, the growth rate in these regions was 5.3 per cent, which is higher than the Spanish average. However, during the period 1991–93, the growth rate in these regions was only 0.5 per cent. For different reasons (mainly the impact of the services sector) Madrid and the Balearic Islands also have a significant growth rates. This means that Catalonia has a dual position in terms of its industrial development: it is one of the most active regions in Spain, but its technological potential is still quite low compared to other European regions with a history of industrialization.

One of the first issues to understand concerning the nature and evolution of the Catalan RIS is to situate Catalonia in the Spanish and European Union regional context with regard to some general dimensions and with respect to the characterization of the science and technology system. The present section introduces a brief analysis of the economic, institutional and sociopolitical dimension of the Catalan RIS. Because most of the innovative and R&D activities are still found in industry, the analysis pays special attention to the relevant industrial activities in the regional economy and their evolution since the 1980s. The next section will present some basic input and output indicators on R&D and innovation.

General indicators

The economic and social relevance of Catalonia within the national context can be shown by several indicators. Last available figures show that, with a per-capita GDP of 19,123 Euros, Catalonia has 6.3 million people that represents around 15.47 per cent of the total Spanish population, has a GDP of 117,770 million Euros which accounts for 19.34 per cent of Spain's GDP, attracts, on average, around 20.5 per cent of the total Foreign Direct Investment flows in Spain (1999–2000), and produces around 27 per cent of Spain's exports (Idescat, 2002).

Its manufacturing base is also very relevant in the national context. In 1989, Catalonia's industry provided 25.4 per cent of Spain's industrial gross added value. In 1998, although the importance of the industrial sector had decreased both at the national and regional level in favour of the service sector, Catalonia still represented 25.5 per cent of Spanish industrial production (Callejón and Garcia, 2000). Currently, the distribution of Catalonia's economy follows a similar pattern to that of other EU economically advanced regions. In 2000, 62.36 per cent of GDP came from services, in contrast to 27.9 per cent from industrial activities, 7.93 per cent from construction and 1.79 per cent from agriculture and fishing.

The origins of industry in Catalonia date back to the nineteenth century when the woollen industries began to concentrate near Barcelona. Nowadays, Catalan industry is characterized by a high degree of diversity and complexity. It is diverse because it has a complete system of industrial sectors, where none of them accounts for more than 15 per cent in the main macro-economic measures such as occupation, gross domestic production and number of firms. Traditional industries such as textiles, metalworking and foods are still the most important activities in terms of employees, and altogether represent around 36.5 per cent of the total number of workers. Chemicals, transport equipment and machinery also contribute an important share of the total industrial gross added value. It is complex because its predominant business model is of medium and small firms which are often family-owned. The total number of industrial firms is around 40,000, more than half of them having less than five workers and less than 1 per cent having more than 200 employees. The geographical concentration of industrial activity and population around the Metropolitan Area of Barcelona, approximately 70 per cent, is another salient feature of the Catalan economy (see Table 3.1 and Table 3.2).

Table 3.1 Evolution of main socio-economic indicators in Catalonia

Indicator	1980s	1990s
Area (sq.Km)	31,980	
Population density (inhabitant/ sq. Km) 1981, 2000	187	199
Overall Population (1,000) 1981, 2000	5,956.4	6,361.0
Between 15 and 64 years old (%) 1981, 2000	64.1	68.7
More than 65 years old (%) 1981, 2000	11.0	17.0
Growth (%) 1981–1991, 1991–1996	1.7	0.5
Electricity consumption per inhabitant (Kw/h) 1980, 2000	2,905	6,468
Active population (1,000) 1980, 2000	2,249	2,704
Activity rate (%) 1981, 1998	51.3	53.1
Men	74.1	65.3
Women	30.7	41.9
Unemployment rate (%) 1981, 1998	15.3	10.6
Men	14.1	7.3
Women	17.7	15.2
Ocupation by sectors (%) 1981, 1998		
Agriculture	18.8	3.5
Industry	26.5	29.0
Services	46.0	58.2
Construction	8.6	9.3
Gross Domestic Product m.p. (Million Euros) 1980, 2000	17,309	117,770
Gross Domestic Product per capita (Euros) 1980, 2000	2,909	19,123
Foreign Trade Ratio (Exports+Imports/GDP) (%) 1980, 2000	34.8	68.5

Source: Idescat (2002)

Table 3.2 Structure of industry in Catalonia, 2000

Activity	Workers		Gross added value (1,000 euros)	
	No.	%	No	%
Chemical industry	61,200	8.4	4,320,880	14.5
Food products, beverages and tobacco	79,800	10.9	3,263,018	10.9
Metallurgy and metal products	87,200	11.9	3,137,625	10.5
Coke, refined petroleum and energy	72,000	9.8	3,006,323	10.1
Paper, publishing, printing and reproduction	62,900	8.6	2,666,698	8.9
Transport equipment	54,900	7.5	2,654,318	8.9
Textiles	98,200	13.4	2,523,798	8.4
Machinery and mechanic equipment	54,400	7.4	2,098,396	7.0
Electrical and electronic equipment	40,200	5.5	1,619,068	5.4
Rubber and plastics products	37,900	5.2	1,510,462	5.1
Other non-metallic mineral products	24,800	3.4	1,310,596	4.4
Other industry	32,100	4.4	862,727	2.9
Office equipment	10,200	1.4	526,950	1.8
Wood and furniture	15,600	2.1	384,640	1.3
Total	731,400	100.0	29,885,499	100.0

Source: Idescat (2002)

Since Spain's accession to the European Union in 1986, the Catalan economy has experienced an important internationalization. During the period 1996–2000, Catalonia's exports grew by an average annual rate of 13.1 per cent. As a result, the degree of openness of the economy (measured as the share of exports in the final demand) reached 38.8 per cent, most going to the EU (70 per cent) and the United States (9 per cent); the foreign trade ratio (measured as the share of exports and imports with respect to the GDP) reached 68.5 per cent. Foreign Direct Investment (FDI) has increased its importance as well. As Table 3.3 shows, for the period 1988–97, Catalonia's annual average growth was around 28 per cent, capital increase and corporate acquisition being the most usual means for FDI to enter the Catalan market, representing 65 per cent of total FDI in Catalonia and 26 per cent respectively in 1991–97. This investment is relevant because it has been mostly associated with technology transfer and the introduction of new forms of industrial organization in Spain. The reason why foreign investment has flowed so massively into Catalonia can be found in the industrial basis and entrepreneurship of this Spanish region, and also in its well-developed system of transport and communications, as well as the social and cultural components found in Barcelona. This FDI has mostly been concentrated in sectors characterized as dynamic and with a relatively high level of R&D

Table 3.3 Foreign direct investment by economic sector in Catalonia, 1988–97

	FDI (%)	
Activity	*Catalonia*	*Other CCAAs*
Financial intermediation	27.0	38.1
Chemical industry	20.1	7.6
Trade and tourism	12.9	16.5
Transport equipment	12.6	7.8
Paper, publishing, printing and reproduction	7.3	4.3
Food products, beverages and tobacco	6.3	10.9
Office and electrical machinery	4.6	6.9
Rubber and plastics	3.8	1.6
Textiles	2.3	0.7
Metallic products	1.9	3.1
Transport services	0.5	1.8
Precision instruments	0.5	0.6
Total	100.0	100.0

Source: Caixa de Catalunya (2000a)

Foreign direct investment in Catalonia is concentrated in the industrial sector, which during the period 1986–2000 captured 50 per cent (and even 80 per cent in some years) of total foreign investment in Catalonia. On the other hand, the strategy of multinational firms has changed. Until the 1970s they sought the Spanish market. Between the 1980s and the 1990s they have been primarily oriented towards the European market. Nowadays, another trend can be identified. Some multinational firms located in Catalonia undertake some spending on R&D, most typically in applied research, while basic research is undertaken in their home countries (Fontrodona and Hernández, 2001). However, since 2000, the balance in foreign investment has changed. In 2000 Catalonia had for the first time a positive balance in foreign direct investment. In 2001 Catalonia had 164 multinational firms with 368 plants in foreign countries (ibid.). On the other hand, it should be noted that the financial sector in Catalonia has a particular characteristic, the weight of the saving banks. This structure has two effects. The first impact is on the financial system of the SMEs. The second impact is on the transfer of savings outside Catalonia, through the utilities owned by the savings banks, to the big industrial firms in Spain (Endesa, Repsol, Gas Natural, Telefonica), that have their research activities in other Autonomous Communities (usually in Madrid).

Innovation indicators

Catalonia is in a paradoxical position in terms of science and technology. On the one hand, it is jointly with another two regions, the Basque Country and the Madrid Community, a leading innovative region of Spain. On the other, it has been lagging behind several leading European regions and countries with a quite similar dimension such as the Nordic countries, Baden-Württemberg in Germany, or Lombardy and Lazio in Italy. For instance, R&D expenditures performed by all institutional sectors is around 1,027 million Euros (annual average for 1997–99). As a proportion of GDP, it gives an indicator of national technology performance. As Table 3.4 indicates, this measure represents only 1.07 per cent, which is notably below the European average and European regions.[2] See also Table 3.5.

Table 3.4 R&D Indicators in Catalonia compared to Spanish and European averages

Indicator	Catalonia (1998)	Spain (1998)	EU (1998)
Expenses on R&D (million euros)	1,070	4,693	142,002
Expenses on R&D compared to GDP	1.07	0.9	1.87
Private expenditure on R&D/			
Total expenditure on R&D (%)	64.7	50.8	63.9
R&D personnel	20,023	97,099	1,636,370
R&D as a % of the labour force	1.22	1.02	1.31
Researchers / R&D Personnel (%)	34.0	21.9	49.2
Patent applications	292	828	48,775
Scientific production (articles) (1997)	3,910	18,503	255,038
Scientific production by researcher (1997)	0.41	0.34	0.30
Citations	9,113	35,701	504,963
Innovative firms /Total firms (%)	13.0	10.0	51.0
Technological effort (innovation			
expenditures/turnover)	1.85	1.64	4.8
Private expenditure on R&D/ GDP (%)	0.65	0.43	1.2
Quality of Scientific production*	2.42	2.34	2.83
Concentration of national GERD (1997)	21.7	–	–
Concentration national researchers (1997)	17.7	–	–

Notes:

GERD: Gross Domestic Expenditure on R&D.
* Number of citations obtained in 1998 in relation to the number of articles produced between 1996 and 1997.

Sources: Eurostat (2002); INE (2000)

Table 3.5 Catalan R&D statistics in relation to other Spanish Autonomous Communities

Region	1987			1999		
	Million euros	*Total (%)*	*GDP (%)*	*Million euros*	*Total (%)*	*GDP (%)*
Andalucia	106.23	7.7	0.4	474.73	9.5	0.7
Aragón	33.72	2.4	0.5	134.17	2.7	0.7
Asturias	23.40	1.7	0.4	74.44	1.5	0.6
Balears	6.73	0.5	0.1	32.89	0.7	0.3
Canarias	15.22	1.1	0.2	104.79	2.1	0.5
Cantabria	9.97	0.7	0.4	42.08	0.8	0.6
Castilla León	39.76	2.9	0.3	201.99	4.0	0.6
C.-la Mancha	8.11	0.6	0.1	65.10	1.3	0.3
Catalonia	16.76	18.6	0.6	1129.76	22.6	1.1
Valencia	53.72	3.9	0.3	332.19	6.6	0.6
Estremadura	9.79	0.7	0.2	38.68	0.8	0.4
Galicia	29.56	2.1	0.2	165.09	3.3	0.5
Madrid	617.57	44.6	1.8	1589.41	31.8	1.6
Murcia	18.04	1.3	0.3	84.51	1.7	0.7
Navarra	18.84	1.4	0.5	91.15	1.8	0.9
Pais Vasco	116.43	8.4	0.8	414.09	8.3	1.2
La Rioja	1.00	0.1	0.1	20.30	0.4	0.5
Spain	1385.39	100.0	0.6	4995.36	100.0	0.9

Source: INE (2000)

In terms of human capital, convergence is not achieved either. Catalonia has around 20,375 people devoted to R&D (average 1997–99), of whom 54.5 per cent are full-time researchers. More than 45 per cent of R&D personnel and 63 per cent of researchers work in the public sector (universities and public research centres). This implies the existence of 3.6 researchers per each 1,000 labour force worker. Consequently, the Catalan situation is still far from the European average. Another trend is that few enterprises carry on innovative and R&D activities in Catalonia. Only 13 per cent of the total number of industrial firms that exist in Catalonia introduce product or process innovations. This percentage is clearly below the European average, which, using similar surveys, represents around 50 per cent (Evangelista *et al.*, 1997).

The weight of the private sector in the innovation system marks another significant difference between Catalonia and the other Autonomous Communities. In respect to R&D expenditure, the private sector accounted in 1998 for 65 per cent of the regional effort (Table 3.4). In spite of this trend that puts Catalonia closer to the European distribution of resources by institutional sectors, there is little mobilization of private investor or venture funds towards innovation and R&D a factor that makes it difficult to converge with European standards. According to sectors and Figure 3.1, the majority of expenditure is produced in the chemical and pharmaceutical industries (22.9 per cent), by transport equipment (20.1 per cent), the food industry (11.0 per cent), electrical and electronic equipment (10.7 per cent), and machinery and mechanical equipment (6.2 per cent).

It is also worth noting the good performance of Catalan firms and research teams in capturing competitive and pre-competitive funds both at the national and European level as will be shown in the next section. Their productivity in terms of articles by researchers and economic resources invested by patent is also high. The data provided by the Institute for Scientific Investigation in Philadelphia (ISI) assign to Catalonia 3,910 articles for the year 1997. This figure indicates 0.41 articles per researcher, a measure that exceeds the figures of many European regions. This measure indicates the dominance of basic research in contrast to applied research that, in general, generates less publications (Tarrach, 2001). In terms of citations and the impact of publications, results are poorer. For instance, according to DURSI (2001), the impact of Catalan publications in 1998 as regards articles published in 1996–97, was 2.42 whereas in the United States it was 3.78, in Holland 3.44, in Denmark 3.37, in Sweden 3.34 and in Belgium 3.22. With regard to the number of applications for registering patents, in 2000, Catalonia recorded almost 35 per cent of Spain's total patent applications to the European

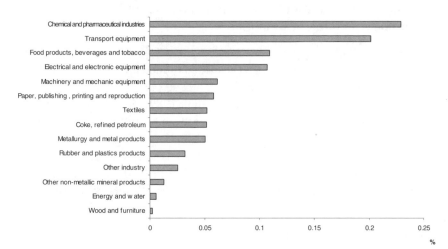

3.1 Innovation expenditures in Catalonia by industrial sectors, 1998
Source: INE (2000)

Patent Office (EPO). Nevertheless, the number of patent applications, 305 in 2000, is still far from leading regions such as Île de France (3,424) in France, Oberbayern (3,092) in Germany, Noord-Brabant (1,585) in Holland, Lombardia (1,371) in Italy, Denmark (903) or Uusimaa (806) in Finland. On the contrary, in terms of resources invested per each patent, Catalonia outperforms some leading regions. For example, in 1999 Catalonia registered one patent application per 3.7 million Euros invested on research and development, whereas Île de France invested 3.9 million Euros, East Anglia 6.7 million Euros, Vienna 5 million Euros and Attiki in Greece 7.24 million Euros (Eurostat, 2002).

Despite this evident gap, the data recorded in Figure 3.2 show that R&D expenditure grew in the public and private sectors during the period 1995–98. The number of personnel devoted to R&D activities and the number of researchers has also continuously increased since the 1980s. Nevertheless, and as can be seen in Table 3.4, Catalonia is failing to surpass its own ceiling in relation to the overall R&D expenditure as a percentage of GDP (1.07 per cent, as indicated in Table 3.4). That Catalan economic structure is controlled by small- and medium-sized enterprises (SMEs) is one possible explanation for this fact. Some studies have demonstrated that SMEs in Catalonia make a bigger innovation effort than large firms, both in terms of innovation expenditures in relation to their turnover and in terms of researchers with respect to employees (Fernàndez-Ribas, 2002), however, the amount of money they invest is smaller than the amount invested by large firms. As a result, it is very difficult to increase the amount devoted to R&D with respect to GDP, if there is not a substantial increase in private or public investment.

Policy shift: evolution of innovation, science and technology policies in Catalonia

The institutional dimension of the Catalan innovation system is a crucial aspect, since the policy initiatives intended to enhance innovation processes have produced a turning point in the available incentives. Three sets of policy activities devoted to R&D have coincided in Catalonia since the mid-1980s: first, those implemented by the Spanish government; second, those carried out by the Catalan government; and third, those set up by the European Union. Regarding the first, concrete measures were only developed in the late 1980s with the 'National Plan' for R&D, the transformation of the national public research centre (CSIC), and the industrial programmes for technological development from the Ministry of Industry.

The role of the state and the National Plan

Catalonia has been a net beneficiary of public allocations to scientific research under the different programmes of the Spanish National Plan.[3] During the period

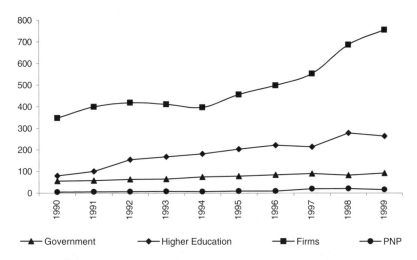

3.2 Evolution of R&D expenditure by institutional sectors in Catalonia, 1990–1999, million Euros
Note: PNP: Private non-profit sector
Source: INE (2000)

in which the First National Plan for R&D was in force, Catalonia received over 96.16 million Euros, 21.6 per cent of the total allocation. Most of the funds went to the areas of Quality of Life and Natural Resources (almost 50 per cent), to Production and Communication Technologies (40 per cent) and to the Fine Chemicals programme (8.5 per cent). During the period in which the 2nd National Plan of R&D was in force, from 1993 to 1995, Catalonia received a smaller amount of funds, around 60.10 million Euros, 23 per cent of the total sum (DURSI, 2002)[4]. However, Catalan participation in *industrial* programmes has been even higher. For instance, the amount allocated by the Spanish Centre for Technological and Industrial Development (CTID) to Catalan enterprises between 1988 and 1995, was approximately 246.41 million Euros, which means approximately 31 per cent of the total amount financed. For the most part, the financial incentives have been aimed at the sectors of advanced technologies for production, information and communication technologies, health and pharmacy, and materials.[5] Similarly, this region received 23.76 per cent of the amount in 1994–96 under the specific ATYCA programme.[6]

One of the latest political initiatives by the Spanish government in the area of knowledge production and innovation has been the re-organization of the university system, through the much disputed Organic Law of Universities approved by Congress at the end of 2001. This law covers the fields of education and vocational training, and is going to have a significant impact on university life and structure. This law has been a source of debate because it apparently significantly reduces university autonomy, and because it overlaps with some competences held by some regions, among them Catalonia. At the time of writing, the implementation of this Spanish law is well on its way, although the final financial allocations are still pending.

The impact of the Catalan government

The Catalan government has also developed a whole set of policy initiatives directed at R&D since the early 1980s. In 1979, under Article 9.7 of the Statute of Autonomy of Catalonia, the Catalan government established it would have exclusive competencies on R&D in co-ordination with the State. This means that national and regional policies have long co-existed in Catalonia. However, the limits of legal competencies between both levels of public action have not always been very clear. Political conflict on this subject emerged in 1987, when the Catalan government and Parliament filed a case of unconstitutionality against the Spanish 'Science Law' in the Constitutional Court. The two most important issues at stake were the transfer of economic resources to the regional government and the possible decentralization of CSIC. The Court passed judgment in July 1992, accepting the Spanish government's allegations and avoiding a model of clear separation of competencies.[7] Despite the important effects of this delay in the design of a single governmental strategy in Catalonia, the regional government developed a set of initiatives that are key factors for understanding the recent evolution of the RIS. These public initiatives have been twofold, aiming to improve the technological capacities of the region and to develop the regional innovation system more effectively.

In the early 1980s, the Catalan government created the Inter-ministerial Commission for Research and Technology Innovation (CIRIT) and the Centre of Entrepreneurial Information and Development (CIDEM). The CIRIT was founded as a body under the direct supervision of the Presidency Department to co-ordinate the scientific research activities carried out by the different departments of the Catalan government.[8] Among its most important activities were following up the state of scientific production in Catalonia and providing specific incentives (grants and subsidies) for scientific research. Although it was the agency most affected by the 'wait and see' situation before the Constitutional Court decision, after the decision its budget experienced an important boost. If in 1980, its funds were around 300,506 Euros, by the year 1983, they were 3.18 million Euros. Nevertheless, six years later, in 1989, CIRIT resources were slightly higher, around 3.8 million Euros. The policy effect was clear from 1990 to 1992, when resources increased faster than the first period (see Figure 3.3).

On the other hand, CIDEM is a regional agency for industrial development, aiming to foster technological development for Catalan industry, dependent on

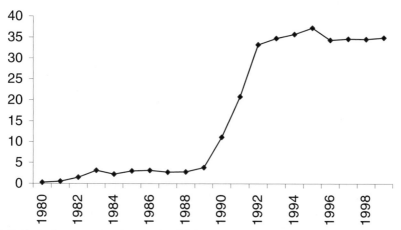

3.3 Budget of some regional supporting R&D organisations in Catalonia, 1980–1999, million Euros
Source: Cruz-Castro *et al.* (2002) based on DURSI (2000).

the Department of Industry, Commerce and Tourism.[9] It has so far been the more active of the two in terms of the impact of its initiatives. Its most salient activities have been the boost given to a network of laboratories[10] and technology transfer centres in the region. In this sense, it has been, jointly with the Department of Universities, Research and Information Society (DURSI), created in 2000, the main implementer of government strategy to articulate the RIS. Some of its key actions have been the renovation of the General Laboratory of Experiments and Investigation (LGAI),[11] the creation and/or support of a whole set of semi-public technological services for industries[12] and participation in the Vallés Technological Park.[13] Finally, it has been in charge of designing and implementing the First Innovation Plan of Catalonia.

Following the Constitutional Court decision, there have been new directions in the Catalan government's policy approach to innovation. At the beginning of the 1990s it became evident that the long-expected financial transfer from the Spanish government, achieved in the field of agriculture at the beginning of 1980s, was never going to be effective. As a result, the Catalan government adopted a 'catalyst position' based on preparing Catalan firms and individuals to find more funds from other sources outside the region. The objective has then been improving the performance of firms and individuals in order to put them in optimal conditions to effectively use other instruments of scientific policy such as the National Plans promoted by the state administration and the European Union Framework Programmes.[14] During the period 1990–92, the Catalan government injected an important amount of resources into R&D (see Figure 3.3). In 1990 the Inter-ministerial Commission for Research and Technological Innovation (CIRIT) and the General Directorate of Research had a budget of 11.08 million Euros, whereas in 1992 their budget was approximately 33.23 million Euros. In line with this economic push to regional R&D, in 1992 the Catalan government created the Commissioner for Universities and Research,[15] restructured the CIRIT,[16] and reached an agreement regarding the establishment of four-year Research Plans to co-ordinate all research actions.

The First Research Plan, which came about in 1993, was an important financial and organizational effort towards fostering scientific research in Catalonia as well. It was divided into two large sectors: a generic programme called 'General Promotion of Research' and a set of specific programmes. The implementation of the Plan was complex not only because of the large number of governmental departments that implement it, but also because of the procedures for its implementation in terms of the priority tasks periodically chosen.[17] CIRIT was the main co-ordinator, but the General Directorate of Research also carried out some direct functions in the management of the plan. Around 142.31 million Euros were spent on R&D during this period by the Government of Catalonia, implying an annual average of 35.53 million Euros, CIRIT managed around 60 per cent of the total amount whereas the General Directorate of Research administered the rest. Two bodies were also created to implement it, namely, an Assessment Commission and a Council of Scientific and Technical Evaluation, both formed by government representatives and experts. The implementation procedures were as intricate as the implementing bodies. The generic 'general promotion' programme had a set of 'global actions', such as training of research personnel, international scientific co-operation or infrastructure, which are the tasks carried out earlier by CIRIT. On the other hand, the programme of priority tasks, of a specific nature, identified relevant scientific areas. However, not all of them were supported simultaneously: a periodical evaluation selects some for financing. The result was a variable collection of programmes that made up the regional R&D plan.

The Second Research Plan (1997–2000) partly followed the previous structure, but it also aimed at focusing slightly more on technology transfer. The possibility of delegating some actions from CIRIT to other public or private organizations, related or not to the regional government, was another novelty of the Second Research Plan. During the first two years of the implementation of the Second Research Plan, the budget managed by CIRIT and the General Directorate of Research decreased. In total, 69.18 million Euros were invested in R&D, which means an annual average of 34.59 million Euros.

During 2000 the institutional bias towards the support of scientific research, continued. Yet, a perception that more emphasis had to be placed on technological development and innovation at large induced some institutional reforms. First, the creation of the Department of Universities, Research and Information Society

(DURSI) in 2000 represented an important step forward for the advance of the institutional dimension of the RIS (Bacaria *et al.*, 2001). For the first time, the RIS had an organ with sufficient administrative range to design, manage and co-ordinate scientific policies at the regional level. Its performance, though, is still controversial. The agency was created through the unification of existing bodies, namely the Commissioner for Universities and Research, an agency under the direct supervision of the Presidency Department, and some competencies previously in hands of other departments. As a result, DURSI is not functioning as a compact department yet.

Other significant reforms came with the approval of the Third Research Plan (2001–4), namely, new bodies like the Inter-University Council of Catalonia (CIC) co-ordinating the university system, the Catalan Institute for Research and Advanced Studies (ICREA), devoted to increasing the amount of research afrom broad, the Agency for Administration of University and Research Grants (AUR), specializing in managing R&D in Higher Education and the Assessment and Monitoring Council (CASA), which still is not operative. On the top of this, the political aim is to increase R&D expenditure up to 1.4 per cent by 2004. In a quite 'optimistic scenario' where the Catalan GDP increases annually around 5 per cent, the government of Catalonia has worked out that, in order to achieve 1.4 per cent of GDP, the Third Research Plan must increase its budget from 1,262.2 million Euros in 2000 to 1,905.29 million Euros in 2004. Two years into the period, this aim was far from being achieved.

One of the most relevant institutional novelties of the Catalan RIS in the early 2000s was the creation of the Innovation Plan (2001–4). Designed following the indications of the EU in the context of the RITTS initiative (Regional Innovation and Technology Transfer Strategies), this Plan signals a shift in the analytical framework adopted by regional policy-makers. As has happened in other parts of Europe, linear views of technological change have been replaced gradually with dynamic approaches based on the theoretical assumptions of the evolutionary economics of technical change (Biegelbauer and Borrás, 2002). Managed by CIDEM, the plan has been organized around five horizontal action programmes: innovation management, technology market, entrepreneurial spirit, digitalization of companies and manufacturing and logistics, the first three being the most developed so far.[18] The programme called 'technological market', which accounts for almost 50 per cent of the total budget of the plan (130.41 million Euros for the period 2001–4, meaning an annual average of 32.60 million Euros), is based on the assumption that SMEs should buy technology from universities and public research centres instead of undertaking it themselves. Creating an efficient and agile technological market to buy and sell technology is actually an essential task to improve Catalan firms' performance, but the 'policy discourse' forgets that firms which also do R&D have the strongest absorptive capacity (Cohen and

Levinthal, 1990). In order to guarantee the dynamism of the RIS, it is also necessary to increase the learning capacity of firms, fostering private intramural R&D and links among public and private agents. In fact, increasing the commitment of private firms in R&D has been one of the objectives of recent public–private partnerships established in the RIS (Bacaria and Fernàndez-Ribas, 2001).

Finally, it is worth pointing out that since the 1980s, the Catalan regional policy has shown a strong willingness to internationalize the Catalan economy and innovation. A set of strategies have been developed in this sense which directly or indirectly affect the RIS. First, through the creation/expansion of vast scientific/research institutions with external projection. A clear example of this is the General Laboratory of Assays and Research (LGAI) with large international contacts, and the Vallés Technology Park, that has attracted foreign companies. The semi-public 'Patronat Català Pro-Europa' is a business support service that channels detailed information about EU R&D programmes and represents specific Catalan interests in Brussels. Indeed, one of the most salient initiatives has been the establishment of several co-operation agreements with other neighbouring (or not) European regions (Borrás, 1995). Agreements such as Euroregio, 'Four Motors' and the 'Arc Méditerrannéen' contain important clauses to foster co-operation in R&D and/or technology transfer. Finally, the creation of an 'export office' called COPCA (with representative offices in the most important Catalan markets) can also be seen as an indirect measure to internationalize the innovation system.

The impact of the European Union

Several EU regional funds have contributed financially to such regional public efforts, mainly through FEDER (ERDF) and the Framework Programmes. In particular, during the period extending from 1989 to 1998 the contributions made by FEDER to the co-financing of infrastructures and research projects in Catalonia rose to 40.26 million Euros, which meant an annual average of nearly 3.6 million Euros (DURSI, 2002). Also during the period in which the 3rd European Union Framework Programme was in force (1990–94) Catalonia received 42.07 million Euros (implying an annual average of 8.41 million Euros, which meant 18 per cent of the funds returned to Spain by the EU, being mostly destined to the areas of information and communication technologies, human resources and mobility, industrial technologies and materials. During the period in which the 4th Framework Programme was in force (1994–98) Catalonia doubled the amount of resources received from competitive funds, nearly 84.14 million Euros, implying an annual average of 21.03 million Euros, which means nearly 20 per cent of the funds returned to the Spanish State (DURSI, 2002). Also, as mentioned previously, being part of the EU has had an important impact on the design of the regional innovation policy. Thanks to RIS (Regional Innovation Strategies) and RITTS (Regional Innovation and Technology Transfer Strategies) initiatives, promoted and partially funded by the European Union with ERDF funds (see Table 3.6), Catalonia has elaborated its own regional innovation plan. Perhaps it is too soon to say how this plan has succeeded in creating an integrated RTD infrastructure.

All in all, the Catalan innovation system is today a good example of how political and social willingness (despite the mentioned conflicts) can succeed in rapidly creating an institutional ensemble with the objective of fostering innovation. Yet, further mechanisms for establishing better horizontal co-ordination (within Catalonia) and vertical co-ordination (with the Spanish government) are still needed.

Innovative activities in Catalonia

In the 1980s profound and rapid changes occurred in the Catalan RIS. For an in-depth look at these transformations three crucial dimensions of the system are significant:

- technological monitoring;
- basic and applied research;
- technology transfer.

All of these dimensions have experienced rapid growth since the mid-1980s parallel to the larger political commitment. This means that in general most of the initiatives under each of them are of a semi-public nature, either as a result of the participation of public resources in already existing private initiatives, or as a direct public action engaging private actors; mixed ownership and product of an extended co-operation between private and public entities.

Table 3.6 Public funding in Catalonia by administrative levels

Organism or programmes	Period	Public finding (million Euros)	Total (%)
Generalitat de Catalunya*	1996–1999	123.2	55.12
State Administration (universities)	1996–1999	28.16	12.59
State Administration – CDTI (firms)	1998–1999	49.96	22.35
EU – IV Framework Program	1995–1998	21.04	9.4
Local administration (universities)	1996–1999	1.14	0.51
Total annual (average)		223.5	100.0

Note: * Including all departments

Sources: Author's own calculations, DURSI, CDTI and MCYT

Technological monitoring

Technological monitoring in Catalonia is mainly carried out through *semi-private institutions* of a multidisciplinary nature,[19] or through the specialized services provided by sectoral or professional associations. Although all these services know each other and co-operate occasionally, there is nothing like a systematically organized structure providing up-to-date scientific and technological information in the region. The creation of the 'Institute of Technology' in the Vallés Technology Park at the beginning of the 1980s was the most salient attempt to create a flexible, open and networked centre of technology monitoring in Catalonia, due to a lack of interest from industry.

Basic and applied research

Basic research is mainly carried out in public research centres, such as the CSIC centres in Catalonia, by the autonomous government and the universities. There are 16 CSIC centres in Catalonia of different sizes' in six scientific fields and types of activities, nine of which are within the category of basic research.[20] The Catalan centres have been among the most active centres of the CSIC, in terms of the internationalization of their activities, and of the relative number of contracts with enterprises.

The political tension between the Catalan and Spanish governments in the second half of the 1980s affected the relationship of the CSIC centres in Catalonia with the regional government. Today there are new lines of co-operation. Individual agreements between these centres and the Catalan government have been signed in order to integrate them more effectively into the RIS,[21] and they can participate on an equal basis in the new regional plan of R&D. Lately, the Catalan government has considered the idea of developing Catalan research centre. However, this has so far not seen the light.

Historically, Catalan (and Spanish) universities have given almost exclusive priority to teaching activities. Research was not encouraged and the relatively few activities in this respect arose out of the personal motivation of some individuals or departments. This trend is undergoing a profound transformation. The new resources provided by the Spanish and Catalan authorities have dramatically fostered scientific research in the university world, and the new regulatory measures have meant more contact with industry and therefore a move away from their traditional 'isolationism'. However, the main reason that R&D policy in Catalonia has developed a system with few links with the industrial sector (as the Catalan government initially planned) was because the Catalan universities strongly influenced it so that the institutional design and the policy were more in the universities' interest. The reason for this 'power' in the universities was because the Catalan government did not give any priority in the budget to R&D policy, waiting for the transfer of competences from the Spanish government. This temporal lag gave the power of policy-making in science and technology to the academic realm. Thus it explains why the CIRIT (the Catalan Council for Research and Technology), designed to integrate industry into R&D policy-making, has since 1988 been dependent directly on the Commissioner of Universities of the Catalan government (Castro *et al.*, 2002). Since 2000 this influence has been stronger than before, the role of the Ministry of Universities (DURSI) is to co-ordinate R&D policy in Catalonia.

Technology transfer

There has always been a negative technology 'balance of payments' in Catalonia, because of the massive imports of industrial technology. The model of industrial development was based on the acquisition of foreign machinery, and that created a high degree of technological dependence. From the mid-1980s the fees for technical assistance, patents, designs and trademarks increased greatly. In this period the Catalan economy experienced rapid internationalization and a massive influx of foreign capital investment.

Two important features of the Catalan RIS can be deduced here. From the aggregate point of view, the level of 'technology production' in this region was clearly insufficient for the demand. This is clearly seen in the negative technological balance of payments since the expansion period of the regional economy, at the beginning of the 1960s. Second, the patterns of external dependency on foreign technology show important disparities by industrial sectors. Obviously, traditional sectors such as fabrics, or leather and shoes, with low technology strategy, have low dependency rates as well. In contrast, sectors such as electric tools or cars and trucks are highly dependent on foreign technology. This might be explained by the process of internationalization and the presence of multinationals in the sector all throughout this period. The sub-sector of machinery and tools is an exceptional case. Of relative importance within the regional industrial economy, it also has a very dynamic pattern of technological innovation, with a very low dependency rate. It is also interesting to note the characteristics of the chemistry sub-sector and its growing process of technology dependence. Two aspects can explain such a trend. First, the increased internationalization of this sector with massive foreign direct investment since the mid-1980s and the subsequent importation of technology. And second, the relatively low dependency rates show that basic chemistry still predominates over fine chemistry.

On the other hand, Catalonia has a pre-eminent position within the national context related to the number of patents registered (Escorsa and Valls, 1992). This demonstrates yet again the duality of the Catalan technological capacity in the national and European scenarios. In Catalonia the highest percentage of patents in Spain are registered, with 37.7 per cent in 1992, followed by Madrid and the Valencia Community, with 22 per cent and 10 per cent respectively. In our view, the prominence of the Catalan percentage, especially related to other regions with important technological and scientific infrastructure, can be partially explained by the eminently applied nature of the research undertaken in Catalonia, a good indicator of elements of a regional innovation system. By contrast, a recent empirical analysis (Riba and Leydesdorff, 2002) based on patent and scientific publications' data, shows the lack of relational linkages between Catalan innovators in some pro-patenting sectors. We contest this thesis because these authors omitted any reference to institutional arrangements, and concluded too prematurely the lack of systemic features of the innovation performed in Catalonia.

Regional policy-makers have sponsored strategic actions to increase the 'systemness' of the Catalan RIS. For instance, it is well known that the Department of Industry has been very active in promoting clusters in the past ten years. Other initiatives include support for international trade fairs and regional actors have also typically undertaken sectoral conferences. Although it is true that these measures have been taken with the intention of overcoming the networking problems of the RIS, the Government of Catalonia has also used them as an expression of their industrial policies both at the national and the international level.

Industrial networks

The ability to create 'industrial networks' is an indicator of the degree of openness and adaptation to new types of industrial organization or the ability to absorb some foreign 'industrial culture' through direct investments. On the other hand, relations between employers' organizations in the market (in either competition or co-operation) can explain the differences in what is called 'entrepreneurial culture' and hence can determine different kinds of behaviour in creating 'industrial networks'.

Although industrial networks and employers' organizations deal with separate functions, they have close relations, especially when the regional industrial fabric is full of SMEs, as is the case in Catalonia. Industrial networks among SMEs can be promoted either through industrial organizations or by the government. There is a new political form of jurisdictional co-operation that serves inter-industrial links (Bacaria, 1994). In the 1980s there was fierce competition among the employers' organizations in Catalonia to gain members and power. This did not happen in other regions in Spain, because they had a weak industrial tradition or few SMEs. This competition in Catalonia had some advantages for implementing regional industrial policies, for example, when the Catalan government was monitoring or promoting programmes of technology and research

(Programme of Quality and Productivity, IDIADA). However, sometimes this competition prevented the co-ordination of actions, such as vocational training. Even some corruption was found, using the EC social funds to finance other activities than vocational training. Also this competition was characterized by the strategies of each organization, to capture the majority of the market's membership, in order to have more political influence, to get more public funds to promote their activities (such as vocational training, innovation and trade promotion networks, among others).

In any case, connecting firms and organizations has been very important in providing goods that have spillover effects. Conejos (1993) observes that an industrial structure, such as that of Catalonia, needs both strong leadership and links with employers' associations in order to supply everything firms need in the fields of vocational training, applied research, technical services and information to be more competitive.

In the second half of the 1990s, the 'market' for employers' organizations became more stable, similar to what happened in governing the innovation system. This means that some of these organizations have merged (the case of Pimec and Sefes), or finished their legal 'conflicts' (as the case of the Chamber of Commerce regarding the functions and the system of financing derived from the 1993 Act). In short, it seems that each organization has its own space in the 'market' and this prevents any non-productive battle with the others.

Employers' organizations in Catalonia could be clustered into three groups, according to the different sets of both private and public goods they provide, and their degree of competition: (1) owner's organizations; (2) clubs; and (3) Chambers of Commerce.

The characteristic of 'owners' organizations' (non-industrial branch representative) is that they provide private goods and public goods. Some organizations in this group specialize in the production of services (hence private) and compete between themselves and private firms. However, most of the employers' organizations specialize in providing public goods. For the former, the organization provides different services such as tax consultancy, application for subsidies, joint ventures and industrial co-operation, supply partners, and foreign customers, among others. Information and promotion of 'industrial networks' are also among the services provided by these kinds of organizations.

However, the provision of services can be considered a subsidiary aim because the main objective of the employers' organization is to provide some public goods, such as interest groups with a political influence. They are constituted as non-specific pressure groups (because they represent a myriad of interests) to lobby for general advantages from the government in favour of entrepreneurs.

Their programme is more ideological and politically conservative (Fomento del Trabajo)[22] or Sefes[23] closer to the Christian Democrat ideology, which with

Pimec concentrate more on SMEs as a pressure group, and finally merged as Pimec-Sefes.[24] Other territorial organizations are another example of employers' organization whose strategy is to provide services.

The aims of clubs are different. A characteristic of club associations is that they provide 'club goods', which are characterized by economies of scale. They have both cultural and economic goals, and sometimes work as a think-tank that serves as a pressure group or lobby. Although they mostly provide collective goods to members, rather than marketed goods to individuals, the structure of these associations has the distinguishing feature of an *exclusion mechanism*, entry is not free and membership entails benefits. Voluntary membership of the club serves as one distinguishing factor between pure public goods and club goods (Cornes and Sandler, 1986: 159). An example of these organizations in Catalonia is the Instituto de la Empresa Familiar,[25] whose main purpose is to lobby in order to reduce taxation on the legacy and patrimony of the owners of family firms, and to promote efficient systems of succession in the management of firms. This club has been successfully consolidated in this period, mainly for this lobby effort in the Spanish government. Another old club, Circulo de Economia,[26] is a forum on economic ideas willing to exert influence on economic policy decisions.

Finally, the Chamber of Commerce is a classical example whose aims are the representation, promotion and protection of trade, industry and shipping.[27] This compulsory collective action financed by compulsory taxes is important for preventing free-rider incentives. However, after the sentence of the Constitutional Court[28] on the 1911 Act, there was controversy regarding their functions and system of financing because they sometimes provided private services and competed with other associations or private firms. What is most important is that their production satisfied neither larger nor small enterprises. For this reason, some organizations (FTN, PIMEC) complained against the 1993 Act, organizing a campaign against the payment of compulsory taxes to the Chambers, and hoping for a favourable sentence from the Constitutional Court.

In fact, the 1993 Chambers of Commerce Act followed the European model of chambers, that sets out both the obligatory membership of economic agents in the Spanish territory (activities in trade, industry and shipment) and the compulsory payments to the chambers by these agents. In 1996 the Constitutional Court accepted the 1993 Act as Constitutional. However, the paradox is that in 1993 the Government promoted the Foundation for Continuous Training (FORCEM) that legitimated some kind of monopolistic provision of vocational training in favour of owners' organizations at the same time that the Parliament approved the governmental bill on Chambers of Commerce that gave the right to entrepreneurs to organize vocational training. Regarding finance, the Chambers are financed by the 'permanent cameral resources' that is a percentage of the firms' taxes, and the FORCEM is funded by a portion of Social Security payments (provided by the workers) and the European Social Funds allocated for this purpose.

As result of this conflict, the Chambers of Commerce have reduced their efforts in vocational training and dramatically reduced spending on it in recent years. However, despite this the situation they could be considered stable at the end of the 1990s. Some kind of cost should be expected in the monitoring of vocational training of a extended RIS.

Conclusion

Like Spain, Catalonia is engaged in a double process: economic development and the consolidation of both democratic and regional institutions. From the standpoint of economic development, Catalonia is one of the fastest growing regions in Spain, and its GDP per capita is close to the EU average. The Catalan economy is very dependent on the demand-pull of the Spanish and European economies, and the structure dominated by small and medium-sized enterprises is an element that explains some resilience in times of recession. The levels of R&D expenditure as a percentage of GDP (1.07 per cent) are still below the EU average (1.87 per cent). Nevertheless, it is indicative that 65 per cent of that expenditure is private, showing a clear private dynamism in this regard. The industrial sectors where such innovative activity is most prominent are the chemical industry, and transport and equipment. In terms of human capital, Catalonia performs lower than the EU average in terms of R&D personnel per 1000 labour force. Yet, it is worth pointing to the fact that 45 per cent of R&D personnel work is in the public sector, indicating again a clear dynamic pattern from the private sector. Regarding innovation outputs, Catalonia recorded 35 per cent of Spanish patent applications to the EPO (European Patent Office), although it is still far from the patenting ratios of leading European regions. In terms of scientific publications Catalonia has had good indicators compared to other European regions, namely 0.41 articles per researcher, but their impact seems to have been lower than other regions. All in all, this aggregated picture of innovation performance confirms the notion that Catalonia is in a dual position, namely, a leading region within the Spanish context, and in a below-average performance ratio when compared to other European regions. The dynamism of the private sector should not be under-estimated, even when public initiatives and institutions seem to be most politically visible.

However, the dominant feature of the Catalan innovation system in the past two decades has been the astonishingly rapid establishment of innovation-related institutions, mainly created by public initiative, and hence of a public nature. Several important political features have influenced the nature and evolution of the institutional structure for the support of innovation in Catalonia. First, the nature of the Spanish state and its public administration, which is partly decentralized. Second, the initiatives of the public authorities in Catalonia in launching programmes and restructuring institutions. And third, the accession of Spain to the European Union in 1986. This points to the fact that the construction and consolidation of the innovation-support institutions in this region are the result of a truly multi-level polity where public decisions are neither always complementary nor conflict-free, but where there have been a rich bundle of public initiatives in many innovation-related areas.

The accommodation of the Spanish and the Catalan spheres of public initiatives in the domain of innovation and R&D policy has been difficult. The Catalan government failed to obtain its demands to decentralize the research policy, particularly the Spanish public research centre CSIC. The 1992 Constitutional Court ruling against that demand was a turning point for the institutional structure of the promotion of innovation in the region. Whereas in the 1980s the Catalan government had created and reinforced some innovation-related institutions, it was only at the beginning of the 1990s that a proper policy strategy came about, with the First Regional Plan of Research (1993), and several other institutions established in the second half of the 1990s. Despite this, overall public expenditure on R&D by the regional government has increased very slowly in that decade, even decreasing in the period 1996–98. At the same time, few mechanisms have been established to shorten the existing gap between scientific research done at universities and public research units, on the one hand, and technological innovation in firms, on the other. On the contrary, the trend to separate the RIS between two different subsystems has increased significantly. This persistent separation of the RIS has recently been institutionalized with the creation of an Innovation Plan (2001–4) willing to encourage and foster innovation undertaken by firms. The most obvious positive aspect of the Innovation Plan is that it represents the first step towards redressing the relative scarcity of public initiatives in this matter. The other side of the story is that it consolidates the bipolar institutional structure of the Catalan RIS, where scientific research and innovation are still kept apart.

On the basis of these general conclusions three normative postulates deserve some attention. First, and following from what has been mentioned briefly above, there is a need to redress the existing bipolarity in the institutional structure of the RIS. The Research Plan and the Innovation Plan are useful instruments in Catalan governmental efforts to enhance innovation in the region. However, a further consideration to integrate them both into one single Plan might be useful, not just to reduce the duplication of implementation costs, but mainly to bridge the gap between both spheres of research and innovation, that is still so persistent in Catalonia. Second, the repeated political tension between the Spanish and Catalan administration has had negative impacts on the institutional structure for innovation in the region. These squabbles have consumed a considerable amount of political energy, generating uncertainty and delays in policy action. The hitherto dominating political will on the Catalan side has been to generate a research policy that is different and entirely autonomous from the Spanish government. Instead, greater effort should be devoted in the future to develop genuine innovation-support institutions (and not regional-size copies of Spanish institutions) that are specifically adapted to the needs of Catalan innovators, and to develop a strategy that integrates Catalan researchers and innovators with the leading Spanish ones. Both efforts will be a necessary precondition for a successful Catalan RIS in the coming enlarged EU, characterized as it will be by increased multi-level governance structures, and by much larger research-innovation networks EU-wide and world-wide. Third, enhancing the innovation performance of a region is far too large a challenge to be addressed in a top-down form by a pro-active government. This requires greater transparency, direct participation and engagement from civil society in general, and innovators in particular. A first step in this direction would be to reinforce the existing channels of dialogue with social actors and business representatives, in order to identify what the real societal and industrial needs for fostering innovation are. Some issues to develop the dialogue could be: organizational change, knowledge production, appropriation and usage, and skills/competences development at individual and collective level.

Notes

1   As a matter of fact, the transition to the market economy started in 1959 with the first measures of liberalization after the Civil War.

2   In fact, Catalonia also devotes a smaller proportion of its GDP to R&D expenditure than the Basque Country and Comunidad de Madrid. On the contrary, it is the Spanish region that spends more resources on innovation. Many factors explain this trend. Catalonia's R&D expenditure performed by the public sector is smaller than Comunidad de Madrid's public expenditure. Strategic policy decisions taken by the Spanish government explain why the Madrid Community has concentrated on an important amount of R&D public infrastructure since the post-war period. In the case of the Basque Country the situation observed for R&D expenditure is different. Apart from their higher political and taxing autonomy, R&D expenditure on private technology centres has been more important there than in Catalonia.

3   The Spanish administration is ruled by the State governing the Autonomous Communities. In terms of policy competencies, it means that the State has 'exclusive competencies' on aspects such as defence, justice, legislation, the monetary system, or foreign affairs, among others. There are also 'shared competencies' with the governments of the Autonomous Communities such as agriculture, fishing, health, railways and roads, territorial and urban

organization, the promotion of tourism and sports. Finally, there are 'concurrent competencies' which imply that each administrator has its own policy, finances it with its own resources and then co-ordinates them with the other administrator. In the innovation policy domain, both the Spanish Constitution, set up in 1978, and the Science Law, enacted in 1986, foresee that the State should have exclusive competencies on the promotion and formulation of the science and technology policy. Regarding regional R&D activities, the Science Law establishes the possibility of including in the National Plan the R&D programmes of the Autonomous Communities, which would be financed totally or in part from State funds. It also creates the General Council for Science and Technology as a body to assure the co-ordination between the activities of the National Plan and those of the sub-national governments. Although this is a legal framework, some Autonomous Communities have increasingly assumed legal competencies in the domain of science and technology through their regional statutes and other laws.

4   It is worth noting that the selection criteria of the projects is based only on their 'scientific excellence', and not upon territorial distribution. Therefore, this figure shows again that the industrial and technological capacity of this region stands out within the Spanish context.

5   CDTI is a Spanish agency reporting to the Ministry of Science, Technology and Information Society, for financing applied and industrial R&D. Apart from funding out of its own budget, technology and R&D projects developed by Spanish firms, it eases access to financing from third parties such as the Spanish Official Credit Institution (ICO) and the EU. Its role is similar to that held by ANVAR in France, FFF in Austria, Tekes in Finland or Vinnova (former Nutek) in Sweden.

6   ATYCA is a national programme for encouraging technology, security and industrial quality (see COTEC, 1998).

7   The court defended the idea that State and regional legal competencies in this field should co-exist. A separation of activities would have *de facto* implied the introduction of federal principles similar to some characteristics of the German National System of Innovation. On the other hand, the court ruled that the State cannot develop its co-ordination role in such a detailed way as to 'empty' the regional governments' capacity of action. Therefore, the solution of the Constitutional Court follows the peculiar lines of the 'State of Autonomies'.

8   This body has changed its structure several times since its creation. The first reform came after the transfer of public universities, competencies from the State to the Government of Catalonia in 1986 when some pressures emerged from the Department of Education and Universities to relate more effectively CIRIT with universities and scientific research. After this debate, in 1988,

CIRIT was incorporated as one office of the Education Department (Cruz *et al.*, 2002).

9 Nowadays this agency is known as Centre of Entrepreneurial Innovation and Development.

10 Such as the Institute of Automobile Research (IDIADA), The Association of Research, Management and Services for the Woollen Textile Industry, the Cotton Textile Research Association (Associación de investigación textil algodonera), the Textile Research and Testing Laboratory of Terrassa (Laboratorio de ensayos e investigaciones textiles del acondicionamiento tarrasense), CESCA, the supercomputation Centre of Catalonia (Centre de Supercomputació de Catalunya).

11 LGAI is the largest and best equipped standardization and certification laboratory in the region, functioning as one of the 'nodal' points of innovation networks within the region and therefore as a crucial institution of the RSI (also in terms of its external relations).

12 Apart from the mentioned laboratories, the Generalitat has supported multi-disciplinary centres like the Catalan Institute of Technology (ICT), created by the association of civil engineers) or the Catalan Research Foundation (FCR) whose objective is diffusion. For an exhaustive list and typology of these centres in Catalonia, see Escorsa *et al.* (1993).

13 The Vallés Technological Park was created in 1989 on the initiative of the Consorci de la Zona Franca (following the dismantlement of the Corporació Metropolitana de Barcelona), and with the participation of the Catalan government. It is located in a 'golden area' (popularly known as 'Silicon Vallés') between the Autonomous University of Barcelona, the new establishments of the LGAI, some new CSIC centres and the industrial belt around the capital of the region.

14 The Catalan government has also encouraged Catalan firms to use other initiatives put into practice at national level such as fiscal incentives.

15 This new body emerged from the division of the Education Department into two branches, higher education and schools. Thus, up to that moment, the new Commissioner had overall responsibility for higher education and research.

16 The CIRIT restructure implied that it would be headed by the Commissioner for Universities and Research.

17 See CIRIT (1993b).

18 The programme for implementing information and communication technologies in companies has started in 2002, whereas the manufacturing and logistics horizontal programmes are planned to begin at the end of 2002.

19 Like the ICT, the Catalan Technology Institute (Institut Català de Tecnologia), or the 'Fundació Catalana per a la Recerca' was created in the second half of the 1980s.

20 In humanities and social sciences: 'Milà i Fontanals' (IMF), the Institut d'Anàlisi Econòmica (IAE); in biology: 'Centro de Investigación y Desarrollo', 'Instituto de Biología Molecular de Barcelona', 'Instituto de Investigaciones Biomédicas de Barcelona' (IIBB); in natural resources: 'Centro de Estudios Avanzados de Blanes' (CEAB), 'Instituto Botánico de Barcelona (IBB)' shared by the municipality of Barcelona, 'Instituto de Ciencias del Mar' (ICM), 'Instituto de Ciencias de la Tierra Jaume Almera' (ICTJA); in science and technology; of physics: 'Centro Nacional de Microelectrónica (CNM), 'Instituto de Investigación en Inteligencia Artificial' (IIIA), 'Instituto de Robótica e Informática Industrial' (IRI) shared by the Universitat Politècnica, 'Observatorio de Física Cósmica del Ebro'; in science and technology of materials: 'Instituto de Ciencia de Materiales de Barcelona' (ICMAB); in science and technology of chemistry: 'Centro de Investigación y Desarrollo' and the 'Instituto de Investigaciones Químicas y Ambientales de Barcelona: Josep Pascual Vila'.

21 CESCA, the supercomputation centre, the FCR, eight public universities (UB, UAB, UPC, UPF, UdG, URV, UdL and UOC) and the CSIC. The Botanic Institute betwenn CSIC and the municipality of Barcelona, the Institute for Space Studies (Institut d'Estudis Espaial de Catalunya), created in 1996, between the FCR, three public universities (UB, UAB, UPC) and the CSIC.

22 The Fomento del Trabajo Nacional (FTN) was founded in 1771. It is the main employers' organization in Catalonia. Its most important goal is to defend the entrepreneurs' interests in the face of the administration and trade unions. The FTN is a confederation of entrepreneurial organizations and covers a wide range of organizations.

23 A group of dissidents in Fomento created Sefes in 1987.

24 These two merged in the late 1990s.

25 This was created in 1992, it has 80 members among the larger family firms, and does not want to have more than 100.

26 Created in the 1960s by young entrepreneurs and academicians, it is in favour of economic liberalism.

27 Act 3/1993, of 22 March, on chambers of commerce.

28 Sentence 179/1994, 16 June.

Chapter 4
Ontario's regional innovation system
The evolution of knowledge-based institutional assets

Meric S. Gertler and David A. Wolfe

Introduction

The idea that place plays a key role in determining the innovative capabilities and performance of individual firms has become widely accepted in recent years. There is now a large and well-developed international literature on the regionally organized nature of the innovation process and, in particular, the social character of learning dynamics underlying successful regional clusters (Scott, 1988; 1996; Porter, 1990; Putnam, 1993; Saxenian, 1994; Storper, 1997; Cooke and Morgan, 1998; Gertler and Wolfe, 2002).

The central argument running consistently through this work is that the geography of economic advantage and innovative capability is highly uneven, owing primarily to spatial variation in the social-institutional character of places. In the lucky places, firms become 'embedded' in close vertical and horizontal relationships with nearby firms, and within a rich, thick local-institutional matrix that supports and facilitates the production (private and socially organized), transmission and propagation of new technologies (product and process). The ability of firms in such regions to do so is based on shared language, culture, norms and conventions, attitudes, values and expectations that generate trust and facilitate the all-important flow of tacit and proprietary knowledge between firms (Grabher, 1993; Amin and Thrift, 1994). In other words, a set of characteristic practices emerges and rapidly spreads to many firms within the region, becoming in turn a part of the shared conventions characteristic of the local production cluster (Storper, 1997).

Closely related to this set of arguments is the idea that such regions can be characterized as learning regions – that is, places which foster social learning processes among firms, between firms and other local organizations, and reflexive learning by local and regional economic development agencies in the public and quasi-public sector (Florida, 1995; Morgan, 1997).

The region's unique institutional endowment, which can act to support and reinforce local advantage, has now come to be viewed as one of its chief competitive assets. Because such assets exhibit strong tendencies of path-dependent development, they may be difficult to emulate by would-be imitators in other regions, thereby preserving the initial advantage of 'first mover' regions. Maskell and Malmberg argue:

> It is *the region's distinct institutional endowment* that embeds knowledge and allows for knowledge creation which – through interaction with available physical and human resources – *constitutes its capabilities and enhances or abates the competitiveness of the firms in the region.* The path-dependent nature of such localised capabilities makes them difficult to imitate and they thereby establish the basis of sustainable competitive advantage.
>
> (1999: 181, emphasis in original)

Under such conditions, the region has emerged as the scale best suited to the management of economic development and innovation. Especially significant institutional assets include research centres and universities, other educational and training institutions, local producers' associations, chambers of commerce, and technology-transfer agencies. Taken together, these elements have been characterized as constituting a regional innovation system, analogous to the earlier idea of the national innovation system. However, even the most dynamic of these regions remains firmly enmeshed in the framework of policies and institutions elaborated at the national level (Lundvall, 1992; Nelson, 1993). These institutional assets are primarily responsible for producing and reproducing the characteristic firm practices (both internal and inter-firm) that are so important to the economic success of such regions. Furthermore, even large multinational firms are said to be attracted to those places that produce strong concentrations of distinctive capabilities, since these firms are anxious to exploit the innovative richness which arises from the social dynamics of learning regions.

In response to these developments, governments at the sub-national level have adopted a variety of policy instruments to foster the kind of inter-firm networking and regional innovation patterns found in the more innovative regions of the knowledge-based economy. The efforts of these governments to engage in institutional innovation serves as one important indicator of an intelligent or learning region. These regions model themselves on learning organizations, continuously and systematically concerned with enhancing their ability to 'function as repositories of knowledge and ideas, and provide an underlying environment or infrastructure which facilitates the flow of knowledge, ideas and learning' (Florida, 1995).

This chapter documents the evolution of the regional innovation system in Ontario, Canada's largest province and the centre of its greatest concentration of economic activity. Ontario enjoyed a privileged economic position during the post-war golden age but has experienced a lengthy period of economic volatility since the early 1980s. This restructuring can be linked to broader processes of globalization, but it was accentuated after 1989 by Ontario's deeper integration into the North American economy following the signing of the Free Trade Agreement (FTA) with the USA and its successor, the North American Free Trade Agreement (NAFTA). Facing major declines in the number of workers and firms in mature, labour-intensive economic activities, the province came under considerable pressure to reposition its economy and to foster more knowledge-intensive forms of development. These changes have forced a number of critical responses on the part of both firms and the government of the province, as they have worked to meet the challenge of becoming more innovative and adopting the characteristics of learning regions. This experience is therefore highly relevant to other regions attempting to shift their traditional industrial base to a more knowledge-intensive economy.

Thus, we are led to ask: what are the principal characteristics and elements of Ontario's regional innovation system, including its infrastructure of public and private institutions, and how have these evolved in the past ten to twenty years? How is the system organized for conducting basic and applied research? What are the mechanisms for promoting technology transfer within the system? To what extent has the innovation process become organized on a social rather than a private basis, and what role have institutional actors played in this transition? Finally, how reflexive is the system as a whole in terms of monitoring its successes or failures and adopting the features associated with learning regions elsewhere?

The region and its economic character

Ontario is Canada's most populous province and the industrial heartland of its economy. Its 2001 population of almost 12 million (Table 4.1) represented 38 per cent of the nation's total, while its Gross Domestic Product in the same year ($443.9 billion) accounted for nearly 41 per cent of the national economy. Moreover, the figures with respect to manufacturing are even more striking: Ontario produces more than half the manufacturing output of the national economy and accounts for a similar proportion of Canada's total merchandise trade.

The resource and manufacturing sectors of Canada's economy have long been dominated by foreign interests, and this has been especially true of Ontario. Historically, much of Ontario's resource economy emerged to supply the US need for industrial materials, particularly in the case of minerals and pulp and paper, and it retains its dominant export orientation. In the earliest phases of industrialization, British firms were the principal sources of investment capital in Central Canada, though their dominant position was usurped by American interests beginning late in the nineteenth century, and the trend continued through the 1980s. Most of Ontario's manufacturing industry grew up behind the sheltering

Table 4.1 Main indicators for the Province of Ontario, 1991–2001

Indicator	1991	1996	2001
Population	10,427,621	11,100,876	11,874,436
Employment (in 000s)	5,016	5,181	5,963
– primary industry	165 (3.3%)	151 (2.9%)	122 (2.0%)
– manufacturing industry	905 (18.0%)	904 (17.4%)	1,088 (18.2%)
– service industry	3,596 (71.7%)	3,815 (73.6%)	4,361 (73.1%)
Unemployment rate	9.5%	9.0%	6.3%
Gross domestic product (per capita)[a]	$29,201	$30,971	$36,192
Gross domestic product (per employee)[a]	$60,706	$66,358	$72,195
Export ratio	0.52	0.66	0.69
Import ratio	0.47	0.55	0.57
Gross expenditure on R&D (% GDP)	1.7	1.9	2.2[b]
Key Industrial Clusters	auto, electrical and electronic, finance		

Notes
a   Real GDP in chained $1997
b   Figure is for 2000
Sources: Ontario Ministry of Finance, 2002, *Ontario Economic Outlook and Fiscal Review,* December; Statistics Canada (2002) *Service Bulletin: Science Statistics,* "Total spending on research and development in Canada, 1990 to 2002, and provinces, 1990 to 2000", vol. 26, no. 7, November.

walls of the protective tariff. As the industrial heartland of the national economy, Ontario benefited disproportionately from federal tariffs and other policies that promoted import substitution industrialization. The result was a truncated manufacturing sector, relying excessively on the presence of foreign branch plants, with production geared to supplying the domestic economy.

Ontario's economy remains strongly oriented towards trade, although the geographical structure of this trade has shifted from a predominantly east–west flow (with the rest of Canada) to one that is increasingly north–south (Courchene and Telmer, 1998). Despite the political boundary that divides the North American continent in half, Ontario has become ever more integrated into the US economy. In 2001, fully 93 per cent of its international exports were destined for the United States, with Western Europe a distant second at only 3.2 per cent (Ontario Ministry of Finance, 2002b). Most of this trade centres around the key sectors of automobile assembly and automotive parts (Holmes 2000).

The dominant position of the automobile assembly and parts industries in Ontario's industrial structure is clearly reflected in the data on the province's balance of trade. Exports of motor vehicles and parts accounted for 41 per cent of the province's total exports in 1999 and generated a trade surplus of $32.2 billion (Table 4.2). In contrast, the next two largest export sectors, machinery and

Table 4.2 Top ten exporting sectors in Ontario, 1999

Ranking	Industries	Exports ($ millions)	Share of total Ontario exports (%)	Imports ($ millions)	Balance ($ millions)
1	Motor vehicles and parts	80,385	41.1	48,209	32,176
2	Machinery and mechanical appliances	23,752	12.1	44,408	– 20,656
3	Electrical machinery and equipment	9,685	5.0	27,089	– 17,404
4	Plastics and plastic articles	6,073	3.1	7,587	– 1,514
5	Non-ferrous metals and allied products	5,987	3.1	7,084	– 1,097
6	Pulp, paper and allied products	5,850	3.0	4,040	1,810
7	Furniture and fixtures	4,828	2.5	3,794	1,034
8	Prepared food, beverage, and tobacco	3,862	2.0	4,574	– 712
9	Articles of iron and steel	3,279	1.7	4,319	– 1,040
10	Precious metals, stones, and coins	3,247	1.7	1,598	1,649
	Total (all sectors, Ontario)	195,523		211,412	– 15,889
	Total (all sectors, Canada)	365,233		326,843	38,390
	Ontario as a share of Canada	53.5		64.7	

Source: Ontario Ministry of Finance, 1999, *Ontario Economic Outlook and Review*.

mechanical appliances, and electrical machinery and equipment, accounted for just over 17 per cent of total exports and generated a deficit on merchandise trade that more than offset the surplus in the auto sector. Although Ontario accounted for 53.5 per cent of all Canadian exports, it also absorbed nearly 65 per cent of total imports into the country, resulting in a provincial trade deficit of $15.9 billion in 1999. This constituted something of a drain on the national economy's international trade position.

The changing structure of the regional economy

The most profound structural change in Ontario's economy has been a persistent decline in the relative importance of manufacturing employment since the early 1980s (Wolfe and Gertler, 2001). As Table 4.1 shows, this trend continued through the first half of the 1990s. From 1991 to 1996, while total provincial employment rose by 165,000, manufacturing employment declined by 1,000. As a result, manufacturing activity's share of total employment dropped from 18.0 to 17.4 per cent. However, since 1996, manufacturing employment has staged something of a comeback in both absolute and relative terms, adding over 184,000 jobs and increasing its share to 18.2 per cent of total employment in Ontario. Nevertheless, the vast majority of employment growth has been accounted for by the service sector, which increased from 3.6 million in 1991 to 4.4 million in 2001 (increasing its share from 71.7 to 73.1 per cent of total provincial employment).

This shift in industrial structure – especially the relative decline of manufacturing – appears considerably more muted when measured in terms of output (gross domestic product at factor cost), rather than employment. Manufacturing output has remained reasonably steady at between 20 and 25 per cent of total output since the mid-1980s. On a comparative basis, Ontario's industrial structure is fairly similar to that of its competitors in the Great Lakes states (Table 4.3). The size of its manufacturing sector relative to GDP places it squarely in the middle of the pack. The notable differences are the relatively smaller size of the wholesale/retail trade and services sectors in Ontario, as well as the relatively large government sector. The latter can be explained in part by one of the fundamental differences between Canada and the USA, since the Ontario government figure includes health and social services, while the figures for the US states do not. If we were to reclassify these activities as non-government, Ontario's figure for government would drop to 11.1 per cent, while its services category would rise to 19.1 per cent. Apart from these differences, Ontario's economic structure stands out amongst its peer group of northern US states for its uncommon degree of sectoral balance. It boasts the third largest financial services industry (behind New York and Massachusetts, and tied with Pennsylvania), but it also has a very significant manufacturing base (in relative

Table 4.3 Gross state/provincial product by industry, as percentage of total, 1998

State/Province	Primary[a]	Construction	Manufacturing	Transportation, public utilities	Wholesale and retail trade	Finance, insurance and real estate	Services	Government[b]	TOTAL[c] ($US billions)
Indiana	2.1	4.8	32	7.5	16.1	12.6	15.4	9.5	170.9
Wisconsin	2.5	4.2	27.8	6.9	16.3	15.3	16.4	10.6	155.3
Ohio	1.5	3.8	26.1	7.5	17.9	15.2	17.5	10.5	333.6
Michigan	1.3	4.1	27.3	6.6	18.3	14.2	18.3	9.9	288.0
Ontario[d]	2.0	4.2	23.5	9.8	12.4	17.9	12.9	17.3	312.0
Minnesota	3.0	4.5	18.6	7.2	18.9	18.0	19.6	10.2	157.9
Pennsylvania	1.4	3.8	20.6	8.9	16.1	17.9	21.4	9.9	353.1
Illinois	1.6	4.0	17.8	9.3	17.0	20.0	20.8	9.5	416.1
Massachusetts	0.6	3.3	14.7	6.1	16.5	23.6	26.0	9.2	232.9
New York	0.5	2.8	10.8	8.0	13.9	32.0	21.9	10.1	687.7

Notes

a Includes farms and agricultural services, forestry, fisheries, and mining.
b Includes Federal civilian and military and State/Provincial and local government. Figure for Ontario also includes health and social services and educational services.
c Total GDP for each US state reported in constant (1996) dollars, GDP for Ontario reported in current (1998) US dollars.
d GDP (Ontario) at factor cost by industry in $Cdn in millions (1992 prices), gross state product in chained (1992) $US in millions, by industry.

Sources: United States Department of Commerce (2001), Statistics Canada (2000)

terms, more than twice as large as New York, and over 50 per cent larger than Massachusetts).

The statistics on Ontario's merchandise trade balance reviewed above indicate that the automotive sector ranks as the dominant manufacturing industry in the province. The sector's leading position is confirmed by the figures on GDP by industry (Table 4.4). Transportation equipment (of which automotive assembly and parts make up roughly 90 per cent) is the largest single sector, directly constituting nearly 27 per cent of all manufacturing output. Ontario currently ranks as the second largest auto producer in North America after the state of Michigan and exports more vehicles to the USA than Japan does. This performance is due in part to the labour cost advantage of production in Ontario, estimated to be in the order of US$10 per hour, that includes savings resulting from publicly provided medical care for employees. It is also due to the reputation that the industry has acquired for both a highly skilled, reliable and productive labour force. Within the auto assembly sector, real productivity grew by an impressive 80 per cent between 1991 and 1999, and now exceeds US levels. Moreover, the average time required to assemble a vehicle is now 10 per cent less in Canada than in the USA (Stanford, 1999). It is not surprising then, that since the end of the early 1990s recession in 1992, every major North American and Japanese assembler operating in the province has announced investments in new and upgraded plants which together total over $12 billion (Table 4.5).

Although the transportation equipment industry stands out as the leader in Ontario's manufacturing sector, a number of other industries are notable as well, either for their absolute size or their rate of growth over the 1990s. These include the electrical and electronic products industry (at 11 per cent of manufacturing GDP), the food industries (at slightly below 9 per cent of manufacturing GDP), fabricated metal products and chemical products (both just under 8 per cent of manufacturing GDP) (Table 4.4). The plastics, furniture, and rubber industries, although constituting relatively small proportions of the total manufacturing sector, grew at dramatic rates (62, 62 and 75 per cent respectively) over the course of the decade. One other industry is also remarkable for its overall rate of growth in this decade and its relative contribution to the total increase in manufacturing GDP. The electrical and electronics products industry (including telecommunications) clearly rivals automotive products as the dynamic engine powering the growth of the manufacturing sector in the 1990s. It is the only industry which both grew at a faster rate than the transportation equipment sector (81 versus 78 per cent) and accounted for the second-largest share of increase in total manufacturing GDP (22 per cent) behind the transportation equipment sector. This result is not completely surprising given the critical role of electrical products as the core enabling technology in the emerging information technology paradigm.

Table 4.4 Output by industry for Ontario manufacturing, 1989 and 1999, in millions of 1992 dollars

Industries	1989	1989 per cent share	1999	1999 per cent share	Growth rates between 1989 and 1999 (%)	Share of total manufacturing GDP improvement (%)
Printing and publishing	4,795	8.3	3,403	4.6	−29	−8
Non-metallic mineral	1,937	3.4	1,837	2.5	−5	−1
Leather	308	0.5	112	0.1	−63	−1
Clothing	1,034	1.8	794	1.1	−23	−1
Beverage	1,619	2.8	1,540	2.1	−4	0
Paper and allied products	2,406	4.2	2,360	3.2	−1	0
Refined petroleum and coal	389	0.7	465	0.6	19	0
Machinery	3,116	5.4	3,335	4.5	7	1
Primary textile	586	1.0	744	1.0	26	1
Wood	1,111	1.9	1,354	1.8	21	1
Primary metal	3,314	5.7	3,420	4.6	3	1
Rubber	803	1.4	1,408	1.9	75	3
Furniture and fixture	1,161	2.0	1,883	2.5	62	4
Food	5,752	10.0	6,450	8.6	12	4
Fabricated metal	4,928	8.5	5,840	7.8	18	5
Plastic	1,426	2.5	2,314	3.1	62	5
Chemical	4,606	8.0	5,724	7.7	24	7
Electrical and electronic	4,550	7.9	8,275	11.1	81	22
Transportation equipment	11,214	19.4	19,998	26.8	78	52
Other manufacturing	2,653	4.6	3,286	4.4		
All Manufacturing	57,676	100.0	74,672	100.0	29	100

Source: Statistics Canada, 2001, *Provincial Gross Domestic Product by Industry, 1992–1998*. Cat. No. 15-203.

Table **4.5** Major automotive investments in Ontario

Completion date	Project	Investment ($ millions)
1992	Ford – New Oakville Paint Plant	439
1992	Chrysler – retooling Bramalea Assembly Plant	600
1992	Freightliner – new St. Thomas Assembly Plant	30
1993	Ford – new Windsor Cosworth Aluminum Casting Plant	200
1993	Ford – retooling Oakville Assembly Plant	560
1994	GM – retooling Windsor Transmission Plant	300
1994	Ford – expanding Windsor Essex Aluminum Casting Plant	100
1995	Ford – reopening Windsor Ensite Engine Plant	1.000
1995	Toyota – new Cambridge Engine Assembly Plant	30
1995	Chrysler – expanding Windsor Assembly Plant	600
1996	Honda – expanding Alliston Assembly Plant	20
1996	Ford – expanding Oakville Truck Plant	400
1997	Toyota – expanding Cambridge Assembly Plant	600
1997	Ford – expanding Windsor Engine Component Plant	650
1998	Honda – expanding Alliston Assembly Plant	300
1999	Toyota – expanding Cambridge Assembly Plant	650
2000	Ford – expanding Windsor and Essex Engine Plants	1.600
	Ford – expanding Oakville Assembly Plant	1.000
	Ford – new paint facility at St. Thomas Assembly	150
2000	Daimler Chrysler – expanding Windsor Pillette Assembly Plant	1.500
	Damler Chrysler – expanding Joint R&D Centre at University of Windsor	500
2000	GM – expanding St. Catharine's Engine Plant	440
	GM – expanding Oshawa Assembly Plant	300
	GM – expanding Oshawa Metal Centre	100
2002	Toyota – expanding Cambridge Assembly Plant	TBA

Sources: Ontario Ministry of Finance, 1994, 'Ontario on the Job and Looking Ahead', p. 15, 1994; Press releases and company websites.

Aggregate indicators of innovative activity

The impact of Canada's legacy of foreign control in manufacturing remains the subject of intense debate in the literature on innovation and technological change (Safarian, 1966; Watkins, 1968; Britton and Gilmour, 1978; McFetridge and Corvari, 1985). Much of the debate revolves around the effect exerted by foreign ownership on the innovative capability – both product and process – of Canadian manufacturing. Historically, both the national and provincial economies have lagged as relative under-performers with respect to levels of investment in R&D. Critics hold that foreign-owned firms are under-performers of R&D in their Canadian operations, relative to Canadian-owned firms in the same industry. They also claim that such firms focus on the production of relatively mature products in their Canadian plants. Others take the position that foreign-owned firms have raised the technological standard of production processes in Ontario and Canada by acting as an important source of advanced manufacturing technologies, which they have implemented in their Canadian operations. Research conducted for the federal government in the early 1990s found that, while foreign-owned firms increased their R&D expenditures by a faster rate than their Canadian-owned counterparts in the same industry, this difference was largely attributable to a similar differential in firm size. The authors concluded that size and not ownership is the major determinant of R&D intensity (Holbrook and Squires, 1996). One additional factor suggested to account for Canada's lower R&D level is the predominance of resource-based and other sectors that typically spend a lower percentage of sales on R&D (Schulz, 1994: 46). More recently, Le and Tang (2001: 9) revisited these questions, and concluded that:

> Canada lags behind most of its major competitors in R&D performance partly because of the large extent of foreign ownership and the low share of high-tech industries. The prevalence of small firms in Canada is not responsible for the under-performance.

Despite the historically low levels of investment in R&D, there has been strong secular growth in the level of gross expenditure on R&D (GERD) at both the national and provincial levels since 1989 (Table 4.6). Ontario accounts for a disproportionate share of total Canadian GERD, fluctuating between 45 and 52 per cent throughout this period. Furthermore, both Ontario's and Canada's expenditures on R&D expressed as a percentage of GDP have increased; but on a relative basis, they still lag considerably behind the leading industrial countries. The core of Ontario's strength in R&D is concentrated in several key sectors: telecommunications equipment, computers and peripheral equipment, aerospace, pharmaceuticals and other electronic equipment. Ontario's relative position is particularly noteworthy in the sectors of telecommunications equipment and computers where it accounts for roughly 86 per cent and 80 per cent of total R&D spending by industry in Canada (Table 4.7). The figures in the fourth column of Table 4.7 provide an interesting perspective on the relative importance of intramural R&D spending across the industrial sectors. In terms of their R&D spending to sales ratio, only three sectors exceed 10 per cent: telecommunications equipment, other electronic equipment, and aerospace. Interestingly, electrical

Table 4.6 Ontario's and Canada's gross expenditures on R&D, 1989–99

Year	Ontario in $millions	Ontario R&D as (%) of PGDP	Canada[a] in $millions	Canadian R&D as (%) of GDP	Ontario R&D as (%) of Canadian total
1989	4,600	1.7	8,786	1.4	52.3
1990	4,444	1.6	9,549	1.5	46.5
1991	4,616	1.7	10,037	1.6	46.0
1992	4,861	1.7	10,659	1.6	45.6
1993	5,343	1.8	11,438	1.7	46.7
1994	5,958	1.9	12,586	1.7	47.3
1995	6,217	1.9	13,027	1.7	47.7
1996	6,271	1.9	13,157	1.7	47.7
1997	6,893	1.9	14,058	1.7	49.0
1998	7,508	2.0	15,332	1.8	49.0
1999	7,941	2.0	16,436	1.8	48.3

Note:

a Does not include R&D expenditures in the National Capital Region.

Source: Statistics Canada (2001b).

Table 4.7 Distribution of intramural R&D expenditures by industry, Ontario and Canada, 1999

Selected Industries	Ontario in $millions	Canada in $millions	Ontario as (%) Canada	Average R&D to sales ratio[a]
Agriculture, forestry, fishing	23	58	39.6	5.5
Mining, oil and gas extraction	28	120	23.3	0.6
Food, beverages and tobacco	61	113	54.0	0.3
Rubber and plastics products	21	41	51.2	1.3–1.7[b]
Textiles	48	68	70.6	1.6
Wood	2	33	6.1	0.8
Furniture and fixtures	2	7	28.6	1.7
Paper and allied products	5	103	4.8	0.6
Printing and publishing	7	11	63.6	3.2
Primary metals	55	135	40.7	0.2–0.7[c]
Fabricated metal products	71	116	61.2	1.4
Machinery	149	239	62.3	4.0
Aerospace products and parts	508	1,143	44.4	10.2
Motor vehicles and parts	179	196	91.3	0.2
Other transportation equipment	1	9	11.1	2.1
Telecommunications equipment	1,813	2,113	85.8	15.8
Electronic parts and components	58	146	39.7	4.7
Other electronic equipment	203	404	50.2	10.7
Computer and peripherals	376	471	79.8	2.2

(continued)

Table 4.7 continued

Selected Industries	Ontario in $millions	Canada in $millions	Ontario as (%) Canada	Average R&D to sales ratio[a]
Electrical equipment and appliances	51	110	46.3	2.7
Nonmetallic mineral products	5	12	41.6	2.4
Pharmaceutical and medicine	286	625	45.7	7.8
Other chemical products	151	228	62.2	0.8
Scientific equipment	50	126	39.7	7.3
Total manufacturing	4,161	6,558	63.4	2.3
Construction	5	26	19.2	3.4
Utilities	67	185	36.2	1.1
Services	1,160	2,872	40.4	2.2
Total all industries	5,444	9,820	55.4	2.2

Notes

a   2000 figures, except for other transportation equipment (1998). Current intramural R&D expenditures as percentage of performing company revenues.
b   1.3% for rubber; 1.7% for plastics.
c   0.2% for primary metals (ferrous); 0.7% for primary metals (non-ferrous).
Source: Statistics Canada, 2001, *Industrial Research and Development – 2001 Intentions; 2002 Intentions*. Cat. No. 88-202X1B

machinery, which includes two of these sectors, is one of the few sectors where Canadian business spending exceeds the OECD average.

The industrial sector that is most striking, in contrast, is motor vehicles and parts where the predominance of the 'Big Three' (General Motors, Ford and Daimler-Chrysler) and several Japanese assemblers has, until recently (see the following section), generated virtually no domestic R&D performed in Ontario, despite its relative weight in the provincial economy.

The migration of major Japanese assemblers, Toyota, Honda, and Suzuki, to Ontario beginning in the 1980s encouraged many of their suppliers to follow them from Japan. Indeed, because of the high importance that these assemblers and their suppliers accord to the quality of their final product, and because of the increasing reliance of the assemblers on their parts suppliers for the performance of product development functions, quality improvements – in both products and processes – and a building up of innovative capacity have been forced throughout the Ontario auto parts sector. These transplant firms are also recognized as a key source of knowledge concerning best practices in production, serving to speed up the diffusion of such practices in the areas of quality control, simultaneous engineering, inventory management, and worker participation in design and production. Hence, although this recent form of activity may not be reflected in the R&D expenditure performance of the industry, it suggests that Ontario's innovative capacity in the automotive sector has been significantly enhanced.

The policy environment for innovation in Ontario

The public role in promoting regional innovation in Ontario has been a distinctly secondary one until recently. In the expansionary atmosphere of the post-war 'golden age', provincial governments relied upon federal macro-economic management and a positive trade policy to create the appropriate environment for economic development. To the extent they pursued a consistent economic development policy, it focused on the supply side. Provincial governments saw their primary role as investing in the physical infrastructure for highways, generating electric power, building water and sewage systems, and a dramatic expansion of the post-secondary educational system. The cornerstone of provincial economic development policy in the 1960s and 1970s was its strong investment in post-secondary education. This created a dense network of seventeen universities and twenty-two colleges of applied arts and technology which contributed to a substantial upgrading of the educational qualifications of the labour force essential for a knowledge-based economy. The single most important industrial policy in this period was the Automotive Products Agreement (Auto Pact) negotiated by the federal government with the USA in 1965. This agreement, which assured that production in Canada by US-based firms equalled the level of their sales in

Canada, was critical for the dynamic growth of the sector over the next three decades (Rea, 1985: 22–23, 204–205).

The public policy response began to change in the late 1980s as Ontario's industrial heartland experienced the economic slowdown and reshaping that affected most other industrial economies in the wake of the oil price shock and the subsequent restructuring (Gertler, 1995). These changes accelerated in the 1990s as Ontario was effectively integrated into the broader North American economy with the adoption of the North American Free Trade Agreement (NAFTA). In response to the profound restructuring that ensued, both the provincial and federal governments adopted a number of policies to facilitate the process of economic transition and the shift towards more technologically-intensive activities. Despite a high degree of electoral volatility (Ontario voters have elected five different governments involving all three major parties in the past fifteen years), policy-makers have sought to address a number of key challenges. First, as noted earlier, Ontario's manufacturing economy has for decades been characterized by an unusually high degree of foreign ownership. In the post-NAFTA environment, this has rendered a large number of US-owned operations vulnerable to the processes of rationalization and continental restructuring. This development has heightened the importance for both levels of government of strengthening the research base in the post-secondary educational sector, as well as in private industry, and promoting closer ties between the two. This is closely linked to the second concern, a chronic tendency on the part of Ontario firms to under-invest in R&D. As noted above, this is especially evident in the automotive assembly sector where, until very recently, neither the 'Big Three' nor the Japanese automakers had located research facilities in Ontario. This deficiency has been partially overcome in the last few years with decisions by Daimler-Chrysler and General Motors to locate new research facilities in Windsor and Oshawa respectively.

Third, and largely as a result of the second issue, public policy has sought to promote the transition towards more knowledge-intensive sectors within the Ontario economy. This was stimulated, in part, by the standout performance of home-grown companies such as Nortel Networks, JDS Uniphase, Newbridge Networks and others in the telecommunications equipment sector during the telecom and IT boom of the late 1990s, as well as a host of smaller companies in the computer software and digital media industries. All of these firms are both leading performers of research and development and highly successful exporters. Finally, policy-makers came to realize that firms in more mature sectors such as automotive parts, plastic products, fabricated metal products, furniture, and food products required assistance to upgrade the quality and technological sophistication of their products in order for them to meet the ever-increasing quality standards of industrial and consumer markets.

The provincial policy response – towards a learning region

It is beyond the scope of this chapter to provide a comprehensive description of the full array of industrial policy approaches pursued in Ontario during the past two decades.[1] However, it is important to highlight a number of specific forms of intervention designed to establish a learning economy in Ontario. First, since the 1960s, Ontario governments have consistently pursued a strategy of investing in the province's post-secondary education system. The resulting system of seventeen universities and twenty-two colleges of applied arts and technology has been responsible for a substantial increase in the general level of educational attainment in the province, placing Ontario above, or on par with, almost every other Canadian province or US state.[2] In 2000 over 53 per cent of the employed labour force in Ontario had some post-secondary education, up from 28 per cent in 1975, while 43 per cent held a post-secondary certificate or diploma, or a university degree, compared to 19 per cent in 1975 (Figure 4.1). In the 1980s and 1990s, additional funding was targeted specifically at the research activities of the post-secondary sector, previously regarded as the exclusive responsibility of the federal government. One of the most important initiatives was the creation of the Premier's Council Technology Fund by the Liberal government in 1986. The Fund financed a number of innovative programmes, the most significant of which was the creation of seven university-based Centres of Excellence, designed to strengthen research capacity in areas of strategic importance to the provincial economy. An explicit requirement of the Centres' mandate is that they engage in research collaboratively with industry partners who help to shape their research priorities. In this way, a learning dynamic between the university sector and private firms has been strengthened.

A more ambitious initiative was the attempt undertaken by the social democratic government in the early 1990s to create systems of social learning within leading sectors of the Ontario economy. In the early 1990s, the growing literature on the potential value of regional networking and cooperation in enhancing competitiveness provided a useful model to emulate. The NDP government placed a strong emphasis on working with sectors through the Sector Partnership Fund. This programme was designed to encourage social dialogue and extended interaction between major industry partners (including employers, producer associations, unions, educational and research institutions, and governments) essential for a process of social learning. The Sector Partnership Fund was a multi-year initiative that provided funds on a matching basis to pay for both a strategic planning exercise and a set of policy proposals and programmes flowing from this analysis. The objective was to animate a social process of negotiation and mutual learning in individual sectors, with the goal of moving towards higher value-added production and more innovative firms.

By any criteria, the initial stage of sector consultation and strategy formation was a success. Both the number of sectors involved, and the extent of participation

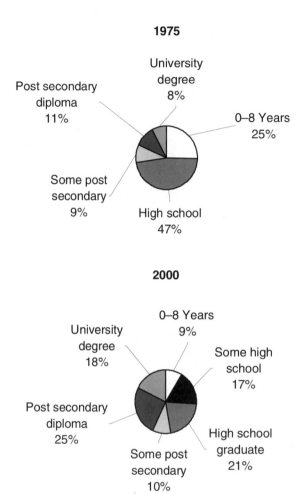

4.1 Educational attainment of Ontario's labour force
Source: Statistics Canada (2002) *Labour Force Historical Review*, CANSIM database.

by key sector players in the consultative process, exceeded the expectations of government officials. Between the summer of 1992 and the provincial election in June 1995, government ministries with sector responsibilities worked with a wide range of industry associations, trade unions and other stakeholders to develop sector strategies. Consultative efforts produced approved strategies in more than twenty sectors (Ontario, Ministry of Economic Development and Trade, 1995). Despite the number of sectors that participated in the strategy development process, the Sector Partnership Fund underspent its allocation in every year it existed and at the time it was terminated in July 1995, less than half the initial allocation had been committed. This was largely due to the government's insistence that private industry partly fund the initiatives; this 'quasi-market test' imposed a hurdle that many private sector participants found difficult to surmount. Although the Conservative government elected in 1995 formally terminated the Sector Partnership Fund, it subsequently refocused a number of its innovation policies around sectors, particularly in the area of information technology and biotechnology.[3]

Under both the Liberal and NDP governments, a growing number of sector-based institutions in the areas of industrial policy, labour market policy and financing mechanisms were created, with the explicit aim of creating inter-sectoral cooperation and establishing a stronger basis of trust around an agenda of increasing investments in firm-based training and innovation. In Neil Bradford's analysis of the reasons for the initial success of these efforts, and their ultimate collapse, he suggests that partisan factors, in the form of electoral results, were responsible for both their initiation and termination; that the capacity of state institutional structures exerted a strong influence over the success of certain initiatives, such as the Sector Partnership Fund, in achieving the limited degree of success it did; but ultimately societal constraints, in the form of the reluctance by a wide range of organized business interests to continue these cooperative endeavours after the defeat of the NDP government in 1995, dictated the end of this effort to build institutional relationships (1998: 541).

The Conservative government elected in 1995 campaigned on a platform, labelled the Common Sense Revolution, calling for an abrupt shift in the direction of government spending in general, and its economic development policies in particular. It evinced a preference for the use of broad framework policies, such as a reduction in the tax and regulatory burden on firms and individuals to stimulate growth, in contrast to the more targeted spending policies of its predecessors, such as the Premier's Council Technology Fund and the Sector Partnership Fund. Within the first six months of assuming office, nearly all of these inherited initiatives were wound down. All that remained were the Centres of Excellence, which were renewed in 1996 with a reduced budget and a consolidation of the seven centres down to four. The government indicated that the Centres would be tied even more closely to the private sector for the purpose of promoting economic growth and job creation. Their primary purpose was to encourage university–industry collaboration to give industry better access to university research expertise.

For the first two years of its mandate the issue of innovation policy seemed far from the concerns of the new government. However, in 1997 it re-emerged on the government's agenda. The budget introduced the $500 million R&D Challenge Fund designed to promote business–university partnerships and research excellence. The fund provides support for leading-edge research that benefits today's growing industries and helps create the industries of the future; financing investment in state-of-the-art equipment and facilities; and incentives for gifted researchers to work in Ontario, including endowed chairs. Funding is awarded on a competitive basis, according to the proposal's contribution to research excellence and economic growth. One criterion of economic benefit is the ability to attract private sector support (Eves, 1997: 177–183).

The reorientation of the government's policy focus continued in 1998. The budget identified strategic skills as the critical nexus between the emergence and rapid spread of new technologies and the resulting opportunities for growth in the local economy. Two new measures were designed to deal with critical skill shortages. The first was the creation of the $150 million Access to Opportunities Fund to generate 17,000 additional places at Ontario universities in the high demand computer science and engineering programmes in each of the next three years. This measure was adopted in response to intense lobbying from the province's dominant IT firms who were facing critical skill shortages as the telecom boom of the late 1990s gained momentum. In addition, the government provided $10 million to support four innovative training programmes at cooperative research institutes and community colleges in the areas of automotive parts design and manufacturing technology, new media skills, telecommunications and metal machining and engineering (Eves, 1998: 145–150).

This growing acknowledgment by the Conservative government of the importance of the innovation system and its contribution to the development of a knowledge-based economy gained further prominence in a vision document released shortly before the 1999 provincial election. The report by the Ontario Jobs and Investment Board, *A Road Map to Prosperity*, responded to a request from the Premier of the Province to develop an economic vision and action plan, with a strategy to ensure jobs, investment and economic prosperity for the province in the first two decades of the next century. The recommendations of this report were followed up in the 1999 Ontario Budget with the establishment of the Superbuild Growth Fund designed to consolidate all of the government's infrastructure spending under one programme and inject $20 billion into rebuilding the province's infrastructure over the next five years, half of which was to come from other public and private sector partners. In February 2000, the government announced one of its first investments by the Fund – $1.4 billion in new capital projects for the province's colleges and universities, the largest such investment in thirty years. Of the total, $742 million is funded by the province, with the remainder to come from other partners in the public sectors (such as municipalities) and the private sector. The new projects to be funded under this initiative are weighted heavily towards the information and communication technologies, as well as the health sciences.

The success of the government's innovation-oriented initiatives began to create internal funding pressures in all of the major new programmes in 2001–2, as the initial funding commitments were expended and the demand for new research funding, especially within the post-secondary educational system, continued. However, the provincial budget of June 2002 addressed many of these concerns as renewed funding was announced for each of the three centrepiece programmes – the Ontario Research and Development Challenge Fund with $250 million of new funding, the Ontario Innovation Trust with $300 million of additional funds, and the four provincial Centres of Excellence, which were given a new mandate and had their funding extended by $161 million. The government also used the occasion of the Bio2002 International Biotechnology Convention, held in Toronto in June 2002, to announce $51 million in funding for various biotechnology initiatives, widely recognized as one of the most potentially critical areas for future growth in the province. The funding included provincial support for the innovative MaRS[4] Discovery District to be developed adjacent to the University of Toronto's campus, situated among its dense network of teaching and research hospitals, to assist in incubating and commercializing new products generated by these research facilities (Research Money, 2002a).

The federal policy framework

Despite the growing prominence of the provincial role in innovation policy, the regional innovation system in Ontario remains strongly influenced by the federal policy environment. As the largest and most industrially concentrated province in the country, Ontario's economy is strongly impacted by federal policies to promote innovation. Federal science and technology policy has undergone two major shifts in the past decade and a half – the first in 1987 with the introduction of the 'InnovAction' programme by the Conservative government and the second in 1996 with the adoption of the results of the federal Science and Technology Review by the subsequent Liberal government. The most innovative element in this strategy was the NCE programme, which connects world-class researchers across the country from universities, hospitals and other centres in a series of joint research programmes. The programme was reviewed and extended in 1994, its funding was made permanent in 1997 (with $47 million annual funding) and further additions to its budget were announced in February 1999. The 1999 budget allocated $90 million of new funding over three years to the Networks of Centres of Excellence to create up to eight new networks. In 2000–1, 596 companies, 143 provincial and federal government departments and agencies, 44 hospitals, 149 universities, and more than 269 other organizations were involved in the NCE programme. In 2000–1, the networks stimulated outside investments of over $80 million, including more than $48 million by participating private-sector companies. The impact of the NCE programme is enhanced in Ontario where it built on the pre-existing base of the provincial Centres of Excellence programme. It is cited by the federal government as the prototypical example of the kind of partnership arrangement to generate and diffuse new technologies for the knowledge-based economy (Sulzenko, 1998: 292–293).

A key addition to the federal government's policy mix is the Canada Foundation for Innovation (CFI), introduced in the February 1997 budget, with an initial allocation of $800 million over a period of five years. The CFI provides funds on a matching basis to the provinces or industry and the universities for the modernization of research facilities in the natural sciences, engineering and health sciences at universities, colleges, research hospitals and non-profit research institutes. Contributions by the CFI cover up to 40% of the total cost of infrastructure projects, thereby leveraging a total of $2 billion in new infrastructure funding. CFI funding includes expenditures for the acquisition of state-of-the-art equipment, establishing computer networks and communication linkages and creating significant research data bases and information-processing capabilities (Sulzenko, 1998: 294). The 1999 budget allocated an additional $200 million to the CFI to help it meet the growing demand for research infrastructure in the areas of health, the environment, science and engineering. Ontario's Innovation Trust provides the matching provincial funding for this key federal initiative and, as was noted, the heavy uptake by provincial researchers necessitated a major new commitment of provincial funds in June 2002. The last budget before the 2000 general election introduced another new federal programme with major implications for the regional innovation system. The federal government set aside $900 million of federal funding over five years to create 2,000 new Canada Research Chairs at universities across the country, as well as a further $900 million to the Canada Foundation for Innovation, raising the federal government's total commitment to the CFI to $1.9 billion (Martin, 2000).

Another key contribution the federal government makes to the regional innovation system in Ontario is through its premier science and engineering organization, the National Research Council (NRC). The NRC has 3,000 staff located in ten centres across the country and accounts for 13 per cent of total spending on R&D by federal departments and agencies. Its primary objectives are: to undertake world-class research, to build partnerships with industry and other research organizations, and to concentrate on areas of research that raise Canada's competitiveness. A disproportionate share of federally funded and performed R&D in Ontario is accounted for by the large number of NRC laboratories located in the province. The role of the NRC was substantially enhanced with a set of measures introduced in 2000–1. At year-end 2000–1, the government granted NRC $110 million over the next five years to support cluster-based research centres in Atlantic Canada. The 2001 Budget provided an additional $110 million over three years to support similar initiatives in other parts of the country – including a National Institute for Nanotechnology in Alberta, the

Advanced Aluminum Technology Centre in Quebec, a new research programme at the Plant Biotechnology Institute in Saskatoon, fuel cell research in British Columbia and the Canadian Photonics Fabrication Facility in Ottawa deemed critical to the continued growth of that region's photonics cluster (Canada. Department of Finance, 2001: 115–125). These measures acknowledged the potential contribution that the NRC's research institutes, located across the country, can make to the emergence of technology-intensive clusters.

Complementary to its role in producing basic science and engineering research, the federal government's public infrastructure also supports the adoption and diffusion of technology. The principal federal programme in this area is the Industrial Research Assistance Program (IRAP), run by the NRC. IRAP was established in 1962 to provide assistance to Canadian firms to help solve technological problems in a timely and cost effective manner. It maintains a national network of 260 Industrial Technology Advisors (ITA) composed of staff from the NRC and some one hundred other organizations across the country, including universities, federal government organizations and provincial research organizations. The ITAs work with firms to identify possible sources to solve their technological problems, such as the NRC itself, other public research organizations, universities or private companies. IRAP also provides grants to client firms to acquire the necessary technology or hire staff to implement recommended solutions.

The regional innovation system

As the preceding discussion indicates, the regional innovation system in Ontario is marked by several paradoxes. On the one hand, the strongest industrial sector, transportation equipment, enjoys a significant competitive advantage, has taken steps to implement the latest process technologies and work practices in the industry, is a major international exporter, yet performs surprisingly little R&D. Other key sectors, such as electrical and electronic products, have enjoyed relatively strong growth, but remain major importers of goods into the Ontario economy. At the same time, a high and rising proportion of Ontario's labour force has completed post-secondary education. This factor is frequently cited by technology-intensive firms as critical to their decision to establish or expand operations in Ontario. The contradictory effects of these different factors represent the major challenges to, and opportunities for, the evolving regional innovation system in Ontario.

Systems of industrial governance: prospects for collaborative action

Our analysis thus far has described the most overt elements of innovation-inducing activity: direct R&D expenditures, technological infrastructure, education and training systems, and the government policy environment for innovation. And yet, the essence of regionally-based systems of innovation goes well beyond this. As noted at the outset of this chapter, it is also necessary to determine the extent to which socially organized, firm-based systems for learning, collaboration, co-operation and regulation have taken shape (Hollingsworth, *et al.* 1994; Cooke and Morgan, 1998): the non-government institutions (formal and informal), and regionally specific industrial cultures (defined as common, shared expectations, customs, norms and practices) through which firms in Ontario might enhance their innovative potential.

There are at least two significant obstacles to the development of strong, socially organized innovation systems in Ontario: a deeply entrenched individual-istic business culture, and the legacy of foreign ownership. First, Anglo-American business culture has long been recognized as being dominated by the ideal of rugged individualism, self-sufficiency and competitive rivalry, and Ontario's manufacturers have been strongly shaped by this ethic. The author of the most comprehensive study of business organizations within Ontario and the rest of the country has noted that 'business leaders in Canada possess what might be called an individualistic industry culture' (Coleman, 1988: 5). This culture is reflected in the attitudes and practices of individual firms, whose managers remain suspicious and sceptical of collective action and cooperation. The process of inter-firm cooperation in Ontario's manufacturing industries is therefore discouraged by the absence of the kind of strong sectoral coordinating mechanisms among firms provided by industry associations or Chambers of Commerce in some of the more regionally innovative industrial economies, such as Baden-Württemberg (Cooke and Morgan, 1994). Furthermore, until recently (see below) the majority of industry associations in Canada have been organized on a national, rather than a regional or provincial, basis (with the exception of Quebec), and sub-provincial organizations are even rarer (Coleman, 1988). The poorly developed regional basis for organization, the limited financial resources at their disposal, and their limited scope and mandate have all contributed to the inability of business organizations in Ontario to play a dynamic role in fostering more effective inter-firm cooperation. This weakness is compounded by the virtual absence of provincial-level sections of any of the major, sector-spanning associations that operate at the national level.

Many features of the institutional context surrounding the Ontario workplace – common to other jurisdictions which share the region's Anglo-American heritage – discourage and militate against meaningful inter-firm cooperation (Gertler, 2002). For example, cooperation between firms is difficult to achieve when, as a result of a highly decentralized training regime and a system of labour market regulation that encourages frequent turnover and instability, potential cooperators undermine a sense of mutual trust by poaching each other's skilled workers. Nor is the potential for cooperation advanced when firms in the same industry continue to compete with one another on the basis of wage rates (that is, when there is no mechanism to remove wages from the field of competition). Furthermore, the 'short-termism' engendered by the structure of Ontario's capital markets and system of industrial finance is not conducive to the establishment of long-term, close relations between cooperating firms. The continuing importance of these systemic framework variables underscores the difficulty of effecting change in the behaviour of firms within a given sector through exhortation alone, or through the modest policy initiatives described earlier. Sustainable and meaningful cooperation will be difficult to achieve unless greater attention is paid to these broader regulatory factors.

Second, there is strong evidence that the long history of dominance by foreign-owned manufacturing operations has suppressed opportunities for innovation based on inter-firm learning through interacting. Despite a growing recognition by global firms of the benefits arising from embedding themselves more deeply in close, learning-based relations with suppliers, customers, competitors, universities, research centres, and other innovation partners, the consensus view emerging from recent empirical work is that foreign-owned manufacturing establishments in Ontario – with a few exceptions noted below – have *not* overwhelmingly rushed to embrace these new possibilities (Gertler and DiGiovanna, 1997; Britton, 1999; Gertler *et* al., 2000). To the extent that they have formed collaborative relationships with other entities (whether these be firms or institutions), their partners tend to be found outside Ontario and Canada. For American-owned firms, these links are strongest with innovation partners in various regions of the United States, following paths that are well established through existing corporate relationships. On the other hand, Gertler *et al.*, (2000) find that Canadian-owned firms in their sample of Ontario firms *have* begun to develop closer, collaborative ties with local customers, suppliers, and innovation-supporting institutions (universities, research labs, technology transfer centres) in their home regions. They conclude that, despite the pervasive rhetoric about the global economy, nationality of ownership does still influence the behaviour and practices of private businesses (see also Britton, 1999).

The following sections outline the degree to which social interaction and coordination between private firms (and the institutions to promote them) have emerged in Ontario, focusing on two key sectors. Since socially organized systems for learning and innovation do not lend themselves to ready quantification, we adopt a more qualitative approach here, aiming to describe and analyze the mechanisms through which innovation-enhancing inter-firm behaviour is governed on a regional basis. Some of these mechanisms are directly mediated through institutions such as producer associations, co-operatively financed research consortia, and special-purpose organizations to promote industry-specific training, technology transfer, or marketing expertise. Others have arisen through important initiatives adopted at the local and community level, where effective action to coordinate and enhance the operation of the regional innovation system has proven more effective than at the provincial or sectoral level.

Automotive parts

Our earlier discussion of the sectoral composition of employment, output and trade highlighted the central role of the automotive sector in Ontario's industrial base. The industry consists of two pillars. The Big Three automobile manufacturers plus Toyota, Honda, and Suzuki (in a joint venture with General Motors) operate a total of thirteen assembly plants in Southern Ontario, from Windsor in the west to Oshawa in the east. Together, these plants produced nearly 2.9 million vehicles in 2000, over one million more than they produced in 1990 (DesRosiers, 2002). This assembly activity is supported by a large number of auto parts manufacturers, who supply assemblers throughout North America. As noted earlier, the 1965 Canada-US Auto Pact brought about a continental reorganization and rationalization of the industry, leading to a situation where Ontario-based parts producers could sell freely to assemblers in both Canada and the USA. One analysis of this sector (CIACC, 1994) estimated the number of plants in Canada at 750, with 90 per cent of these (or about 675) in Ontario.

The parts industry experienced a general upgrading of its quality, technical sophistication, skills base and innovativeness during the 1980s and 1990s. As noted earlier, much of this improvement has come about through the interaction between assemblers and suppliers within North America, as buyer–supplier relations were restructured to transfer more of the innovation function from assemblers to their suppliers. It should be noted, however, that the government of Ontario played a critical role in the early 1980s in laying the groundwork for this subsequent development. Through the creation of an industry-oriented technology transfer centre, and working closely with the Automotive Parts Manufacturers Association (APMA), the government assisted in the wider adoption of new manufacturing technologies, such as statistical process control, which helped producers increase the quality of their output and the reliability of their supply at precisely the time when assemblers began raising their standards for quality and timeliness of delivery. In so doing, they helped improve the competitive position of the automotive parts industry. As Table 4.8 indicates, the Canadian (largely Ontario) parts producers enjoyed steadily increasing output during the 1990s, and appear to have held their own in terms of market share in North America.

One further force underlying the resurgence of the automotive parts sector in Ontario in recent years has been the adoption of new process technologies, new ways of organizing work, and higher skill levels in the workforce. For example, the CIACC (1994) study estimates that, while unskilled workers constituted some 62 per cent of employment in the sector as recently as 1985, this proportion dropped to 33 per cent over the following decade. Furthermore, producers in the automotive sector have been among the quickest to adopt various forms of advanced manufacturing technologies in their production processes, including robotics, CNC machine tools, flexible manufacturing systems, and dedicated inter-company communications networks. The net result has been a dramatic increase in the industry's productivity, particularly since the early 1990s. Moreover, the once sizeable productivity gap between Canadian parts producers and their competitors in the USA has now been substantially closed.

Despite these impressive gains, the Ontario industry faces new challenges. Its member firms must continue to enhance their product development capabilities to satisfy assemblers' ever more stringent demands for improvements to product design, development and engineering. At the same time, parts producers are subject to ever-increasing downward pressure on prices, as assemblers move to source a higher proportion of their inputs on global markets. According to a recognized sector expert (DesRosiers, 2002), the core competencies of Ontario's auto parts

Table 4.8 Production in the Canadian automotive parts industry, 1991–2001

Year	Canadian OE* parts shipments ($Cdn millions)	Canadian share of North American OE[a] parts market (percent)
1991	11,495	8.5
1992	12,833	7.6
1993	14,741	7.3
1994	17,360	6.9
1995	19,750	7.7
1996	21,059	8.2
1997	24,121	9.0
1998	26,045	8.3
1999	30,420	8.3
2000	31,110	8.3
2001	29,420	8.6
2000/1991	170.6%	
2001/2000	– 5.4%	

Note: a OE refers to parts produced for 'original equipment' component of automotive market
Source: DesRosiers (2002).

industry can be found in their machinery, tool, die and mould capabilities which, when combined with plentiful supplies of high-quality raw material inputs (steel, aluminium, magnesium, plastic feedstock), yield further competencies in body stamping, structural components, interiors, wheels, tyres and exhaust systems. However, in many of the most knowledge-intensive areas of parts production – including such core component systems as electrical and electronic, drive train, steering, braking, engine, suspension, and fuel systems – the Ontario industry remains notably weak.

And yet, at precisely the time when knowledge-based inputs have become so crucial to firms' ability to improve their innovative capacity, the most recent comprehensive study of the industry has concluded that the sector faces a major impending shortage of skilled workers (APMA, 2003). The same study also concludes that the human resources problems are not confined to the shop floor, but also extend to the boardroom. With many original firm founders reaching retirement age, a high proportion of companies have no concrete succession plans in place, raising new uncertainties about future leadership in the industry. To compound the industry's difficulties still further, the implementation of the FTA in 1989 and subsequent rulings by the World Trade Organization first weakened and then eliminated the Auto Pact, removing provisions that had previously guaranteed a minimum level of vehicle production in Canada. Consequently, the 1990s saw a growing proportion of investments in new automotive assembly plants located in the southern USA and Mexico (Brieger, 2002; Mandel-Campbell, 2002). Given the long distances involved, it is becoming increasingly difficult for parts producers to serve these new markets from an Ontario base.

Not surprisingly, in the face of such pressing competitive challenges, all of the major players in the industry, including assemblers, parts producers (through the APMA) and the Canadian Auto Workers union, have called for significant new policy initiatives from both the provincial and federal governments. Proposals include a more aggressive approach to incentives for new assembly plant investments, as well as infrastructure improvements – particularly those that might facilitate trans-border shipments across the Windsor-Detroit and Niagara crossings in particular. Most recently, the APMA has issued a call to establish a new Centre of Excellence to support joint research and development in the automotive parts sector (APMA, 2003). The success of such a socially oriented approach may depend to some extent on the ability of individual firms to overcome their well-entrenched mindset of independence. A strategic analysis of the sector's prospects in Ontario, conducted in the early 1990s, highlighted the industry's strengths and weaknesses as it began to face new challenges. The study concluded that, while the 'fierce individualism and entrepreneurialism' so strongly evident in the sector has been the source of much of its strength (CIACC, 1994: 22), this same trait 'may serve as a barrier to timely collaboration among all the stakeholders to work effectively together' (ibid.: 23). There is little evidence that this prevailing mentality has changed in the interim.

Telecommunications, computing and software

The data presented earlier on the extent of research and development activity in Ontario highlighted the leading role played by firms in the information and communications sector, suggesting that it is one of the key generators of innovations in the Ontario economy. The telecommunications sector outpaced every other sector in the country, investing more than 20 per cent of sales in R&D activity. Firms in the sector have traditionally been among the leading R&D spenders in the country. Among the leaders was Northern Telecom (now Nortel), originally part of the Bell Canada Enterprises family of firms, but spun off in the late 1990s. It has traditionally been Ontario's (and Canada's) flagship producer of technology-intensive products, ranking among the top global manufacturers of telecommunications equipment. Much of the credit for Nortel's past success as an innovator can be attributed, either directly or indirectly, to the role of public policy. The firm's most important early market was provided through public (federal) regulation of telephone services, provided throughout large parts of Canada by its sister company, Bell Canada. Nortel took advantage of a virtual monopoly in the domestic telecommunications equipment market and a steady flow of revenues, which provided the financial resources and scale of operations necessary to underwrite its considerable R&D expenditures. Furthermore, the logistical challenges of building a network to supply high-quality telecommunications across a country as large as Canada spurred technological innovation. Its breakthrough into global markets came with the successful launching of its line of digital switching equipment in the late 1970s, a technology originally developed by Bell Labs. In the 1990s it was joined by a number of other major Ontario-based producers of telecom equipment, fibre optics and wireless communication devices, including Newbridge Networks (subsequently acquired by Alcatel), Mitel, JDS Fitel (later JDS Uniphase) and Research in Motion.

In addition to telecommunications, computer hardware, software and services constitute a dynamic and growing portion of the electronic industry sector. Major players in the hardware field include the Canadian subsidiaries of some of the largest US firms in the industry: IBM Canada and Hewlett-Packard (head-quartered in Toronto), and AT&T Global Systems and NCR (based in Waterloo). The operations of these firms have become more specialized in recent years with their plants often producing a single product with a world product mandate. A second group of firms produce and assemble PCs for the domestic market and some exports, while a third group specializes in the production of components, such as ATI, a Toronto-area firm that develops and produces high-performance video boards. Despite the strong basis of this segment of the industry, Ontario continues to import more than twice as much hardware equipment as it exports, signifying its continuing state of technological dependence.

In software, the Ontario industry is anchored by a small number of major firms, such as Cognos, Open Text, Hummingbird, Geac, and IBM Canada's Software Solutions Laboratory, as well as large numbers of small software houses. Of the top 100 software firms in Canada, thirty-eight are located in the Greater Toronto Area alone, accounting for $1.6B of the $3.4B in 1998 revenues generated by the top 100 firms (Deloitte and Touche *et al.*, 1999). Smaller innovative firms, such as Janna Systems (subsequently acquired by Seibel Systems), have demonstrated their capacity to bring world leading technology to market in a relatively short time frame and capture sufficient market share from their larger US competitors to become takeover targets. Ontario's leading software firms display strong capabilities in specific segments of the industry, such as text retrieval and document management, geographic information systems and computer-animated graphic systems for modelling and refining complex three-dimensional concepts. Once again, the supply of highly trained human resources has been key to the success of the computing industry, with world-renowned programmes at the Universities of Waterloo and Toronto leading the way.

The global downturn in telecoms since 2000 has not spared the computer and communications sector in Ontario. Despite the high profile layoffs that occurred in a number of leader computer and communications firms, principally Nortel, data from Statistics Canada suggest that both output and employment in the sector held up relatively well through the recession. Output in the sector peaked in the third quarter of 2000 and fell throughout the following year, although the overall decline masked a significant decrease in output in the manufacturing component while output in the service component of the ICT sector actually grew during 2001. When measured against the longer period since 1997, the ICT sector as a whole has experienced an annual growth rate of 14.1% compared to an annual growth rate of 3.5% for the economy as a whole (Industry Canada, 2002). The impact of the downturn was most marked in the area of R&D spending. Led by the telecommunications sector, predominantly based in Ontario, industrial R&D spending in Canada actually declined in 2001, the first year-over-year drop since the 1960s. Nortel's R&D spending alone fell by nearly $1 billion in 2001 with a further reduction forecast for 2002. Overall telecommunications R&D spending was forecast to decline by 23 per cent in 2002 (*Research Money*, 2002b).

Key players in the sector remain optimistic about its capacity to weather this major downturn and are positioning themselves to take advantage of new opportunities once the recovery is underway. They continue to draw upon the province's strong technological infrastructure for support in this regard. Of crucial significance for the sector's future prospects is the high-quality, publicly funded system of colleges and universities, which offer world-class degree programmes in electrical and computer engineering, computer science, and related fields. In addition to their strong linkages to the region's post-secondary institutions, members of the telecom and computing sector have developed a dense array of institutions to foster collaboration, interaction and exchange of information. Research consortia involving Ontario-based firms have been formed in the area of semiconductor design and telecommunications, at least in part as a response to federal and provincial policies aimed at promoting innovation in strategic technologies, and played a critical role in the growth of key firms in the sector. There are also a sizeable number of specialist industry associations with strong attachments to particular subregions of the province (e.g. Communitech in Waterloo, the York and Mississauga Technology Associations in the GTA and the Ottawa Centre for Research and Innovation).

Recent case studies of local, social learning exercises in two of Ontario's key ICT clusters (Ottawa and Waterloo) provide some evidence that the strength of the clusters in these communities draws not just upon their corporate and research foundations, but also from the highly networked forms of social capital that are being formed. A defining feature of the Ottawa cluster is the strength of the local 'institutions of collaboration'. The linchpin of these institutions is OCRI, the Ottawa Centre for Research and Innovation, a not-for-profit organization dedicated to helping the city's technology community shape its economic future. Founded in 1983 as a collaborative effort among partners from industry, the regional municipality, the local institutions of higher education and federal laboratories, OCRI currently has about 700 members and a budget of $4.5 million. OCRI sponsors a wide range of corporate programmes that involve up to 120 events annually and afford the members of the Ottawa ICT cluster frequent networking opportunities. OCRI is also involved in a dense network of partnerships with many of the federal and provincial organizations discussed above, aimed at strengthening the region's innovation capabilities. Partners in these relationships include the provincial Centres of Excellence, the Ottawa-Carleton Manufacturers Network, the Ottawa Photonics Cluster, and the NRC's Regional Innovation Centre (Wolfe, 2002c).

Although the ICT cluster in the Waterloo region is much smaller, it also benefits from the strong institutional linkages afforded by its industry association. Communitech is an industrial association founded in 1997 by a number of leading companies in Kitchener-Waterloo, including Open Text, Research in Motion, Descartes Systems, Mortis Kern Systems, and others. It currently has about 240 members, about half of whom are technology firms. Membership also includes a large number of service firms in the legal and accounting field with specialized knowledge related to technology-based development. Communitech's explicit purpose is to advance the needs of the technology-oriented firms in the region with respect to the different levels of government in the areas of training, marketing and export development, and the provision of infrastructure. Communitech runs an array of programmes similar to those sponsored by OCRI in Ottawa. It includes Peer to Peer groups, a mentoring programme, advocacy activities on behalf of the high tech cluster, seminars and events and the Business Accelerator Program which has assisted over 120 entrepreneurs since early 2000 and helped to raise $65 million in capital. Perhaps most importantly, the association has contributed to the creation of a 'buzz' about the technology potential of the region – greatly assisted by the dramatic emergence of high-profile success stories such as RIM, developer of the widely used Blackberry wireless e-mail device – and has attracted interest from as far away as Silicon Valley (Wolfe, 2002c).

These institutional features and developments suggest that a coherent system of innovation does indeed exist in this sector, with well-developed networks for inter-firm collaboration evolving in the past ten to fifteen years. In this sense, it forms something of an exception to the dominant industrial culture described above, and an encouraging alternative development path to the long-dominant branch plant-based mode of development in Ontario. Nevertheless, Ontario's clusters of activity in these industries are under almost continuous challenge from competitors in other regions and countries, as well as the vagaries of the global economy. A number of Ontario's leading 'success stories' in software and telecommunications have been the target of successful takeovers by larger US-based firms, including the takeover of Alias Research by Silicon Graphics of California, Newbridge Networks by Alcatel (France), and Janna by Seibel Systems (California).

While these developments underline the traditional precariousness of Ontario's manufacturing industries, it is worth noting that in most instances the new parent firms have recognized that the regionally-anchored human resource base constitutes an absolutely critical asset in their acquisition. This further underscores the need to preserve and enhance the public education infrastructure and other investments in quality of place that retain and attract highly educated and talented workers in Ontario's cities (Gertler et al., 2002). In the telecom equipment field, Nortel has also undergone a significant restructuring to cope with the global downturn in demand, as has JDS Uniphase in fibre optics. On the positive side, other firms have continued to invest in research through the downturn and to attract venture capital investment. A key challenge for the sector will be how strongly it emerges from the current recession to take advantage of new opportunities in the next upswing. In this light, there is encouraging evidence from within the Ottawa ICT cluster that a large proportion of the highly skilled workers laid off by Nortel and JDS Uniphase have been absorbed by other smaller technology-based firms in the region, including a substantial number of new start-ups established by these previously redundant workers (Dale, 2002; Stonehouse, 2003). Such developments strongly suggest that key components of Ontario's innovation system have achieved threshold levels of robustness and resilience, which bodes well in facing future challenges.

Conclusion

The preceding discussion paints the picture of a regional economy characterized by some strong contradictions. On the one hand, it stands out as the industrial leader in Canada: on most indicators, it ranks on a par with the Great Lakes states in the industrial heartland of the USA. Despite the dislocation caused by the economic restructuring of the late 1980s and early 1990s, it enjoys one of the highest living standards among the industrial countries. It benefits from an extensive post-secondary education system and has a highly skilled labour force. However, the traditional basis of the economy is in flux. The shift in terms of trade away from resources towards more knowledge-intensive industries means that the sources of Ontario's traditional economic strength will not make the same contribution to its future well-being as they have in the past. The virtual disappearance of tariff protection since the late 1980s led to the closing of many of the province's more labour-intensive manufacturing operations, but the emergence of newer more research-intensive firms in the knowledge-based sectors, along with a continued strong performance by the automotive sector, powered the province's strong growth in the late 1990s and into the new century. The key question is whether these underlying sources of strength in the regional innovation system are sufficiently well developed to weather the current downturn in knowledge-intensive sectors, such as information and communications tech-nologies, to play a similar role in the next upturn.

Over this period, provincial governments and some regionally based industry associations (at both the provincial and sub-provincial scale) have begun to create the new institutional infrastructure required to move Ontario towards a more socially organized and dynamic innovation system. The record to date, both from a public policy perspective and in terms of influencing private sector behaviour, is decidedly mixed. In a number of industrial sectors, the strong tradition of foreign ownership and reliance on imported technology has meant that Ontario's innovative capacity remains underdeveloped. At the provincial level, the manufacturing culture is marked by the legacy of individualism and non-cooperative behaviour. Yet, at the same time, a number of sectors, such as information and telecommunications technology and, to a more limited extent, automotive parts, have demonstrated a strong capacity for product innovation, as well as a capacity to develop strong sectoral and community-based institutions of collaboration. Ontario clearly has the institutional capacity needed to make the transition to a more innovative and knowledge-based regional economy. The question is whether it has absorbed the lessons necessary to overcome the weaknesses of its past and become an intelligent or learning region.

Acknowledgements

Research support for the original version of this chapter was provided by SSHRC Grant No. 809-95-0009. The authors are grateful to the Social Sciences and Humanities Research Council of Canada for its continuing support. Research assistance on the statistical material was originally provided by Ammon Salter, and Allison Bramwell ably assisted us in updating this. Thanks also to David Garkut for helpful comments and provision of key data.

Notes

1   For a more thorough review of recent innovation policy in Ontario, see Wolfe (1999).
2   In terms of levels of educational attainment in the labour force, only Massachusetts, California and British Columbia rank ahead of Ontario, and only by small margins.
3   A fuller discussion of Ontario's sector strategy can be found in Wolfe (2002a).
4   Medical and Related Sciences.

Part Two

Network-like Governances

Driving Forces, Modes of Cohesion and Means of Regional Polity

Chapter 5
Escaping path dependency
The case of Tampere, Finland

Gerd Schienstock, Mika Kautonen and Pasi Koski

From a resource-based to a knowledge-based economy

As in other small countries, regions have not played a major role in the Finnish national economy and its innovation system. There are at least three reasons for this. First, the Finnish political system was and still is characterized by a strong central state; all the important economic decisions are made in Helsinki, the country's capital. Second, from early industrialization onwards, the Finnish economy was dominated by an industrial cluster that had developed around the forest industry; indeed, sometimes Finland was called a forest-industrialized economy (Virkkala, 1994: 76). It follows that both the social institutions of the country and government policy were heavily influenced by, and adapted according to the needs and interests of, this single industry (Lilja *et al.*, 1992).

Third, it is often argued that Finland is very homogenous in terms of culture as well. Of course, this is partly due to the low population numbers, but it also has a more specific aspect. Technical development and economic progress are seen as forming an integral part of a strong sense of nationalism in the country, prompting some scholars to speak of a Finnish 'techno-economic nationalism' (Myllyntaus, 1992). Both technological development and economic progress can be interpreted as dimensions of the great project of building up an independent and prosperous Finland (Vuori and Vuorinen, 1994: 19).

The dependency upon a resource-based industry became a serious problem when Finland was hit by a severe economic crisis at the beginning of the 1990s, experiencing a large drop in productivity and exports and a dramatic increase in the unemployment rate. It became clear that in sticking to its traditional development path, Finland would not be able to get out of the economic crisis very rapidly. Creating a new development path based on knowledge-intensive industries was seen as the most promising option to cope with a sluggish economy and high unemployment. Although not triggered off by the deep recession, this major change nevertheless greatly supported the transition from a resource-based to a knowledge-based economy in Finland.

The regionalization of the Finnish production and innovation system progressed very slowly until the recession. There was also very little support from the political system. The development of a regional dimension of Finnish technology and innovation policy, as Lemola (1999) argues, was not based on rational decision-making but was mainly motivated by the regional policy of the EU, which Finland joined in 1995. The fundamental transformation of the Finnish economy, however, opened up new opportunities for economic restructuring also at the regional level. The Centres of Expertise Programme and the recent introduction in the Finnish education system of polytechnics with a strong regional orientation underline the new regional focus of Finnish innovation policy. Recently, the establishment of the new Employment and Economic Development Centres, whose main task is to develop their regional economies in a systemic way, has also strengthened the regional dimension of the innovation system (Schienstock and Hämäläinen, 2001).

Tampere and its environs have always played a particular role in the Finnish national economy. As early as 1840, Tampere, or 'Finland's Manchester' as it is known locally, was an industrialized city and home to some large-scale operations, and it was in Tampere that the industrialization of the whole country got under way. The main industrial forces of Tampere were the cotton mills and paper factories and later on its engineering workshops. Around the turn of the century the industrial base further expanded to the food-processing and chemical industries. The smoke-stack industries also formed the basis of economic development after the Second World War and later into the 1970s and 1980s. That is why the economy in the Tampere Region and in the city of Tampere was particularly hit by the recession in the 1990s and had to undergo fundamental changes. The Tampere region can be seen as a good example of how regions can get out of path dependency and create a new growth-oriented development path (see Schienstock and Hämäläinen, 2001), not only by modernizing traditional industries but also by developing new high-tech industries.

In the following, we first provide a general overview of the socio-economic development in the Tampere Region in recent years. The subsequent description of the regional innovation system starts with an analysis of the learning potential offered by the industrial structure and the organization of the production system. We then turn our attention to the set-up of support institutions, focusing particularly on the science and technology base, intermediaries and financial institutions. After that we discuss some aspects of the regional innovation policy carried out in the Tampere Region. Finally, we address problems challenging the regional innovation system and policy.

A socio-economic picture of the Tampere Region

With a population of 445,000 inhabitants, the Tampere Region is Finland's second largest region after the Helsinki Region (with approximately 1,300,000 inhabitants). About 9 per cent of the Finnish population live in the Tampere Region. Within the Central Tampere Region, the population is approximately 300,000. The number of employed people is 200,000, which is roughly in proportion to the region's share of the Finnish population. The central city of Tampere is clearly the second major economic centre in the country after Helsinki and its surroundings. During the past few years, increased migration in Finland has substantially favoured the four main industrial and university centres (Helsinki, Tampere, Turku and Oulu) and their environs, resulting in an approximately 1 per cent annual increase in their populations. The total Gross Regional Product per capita (GRP) for the Tampere Region was FIM 99,500 in 1997 and FIM 115,000 in 1999 (Finnish Ministry of Interior, 2001), which indicates the rapid economic growth that occurred during the last part of the 1990s.[1] However, within the region this growth has concentrated to a large extent in the central urban region of Tampere, while some parts of the region belong to the EU Structural Fund areas.

Analysis of the breakdown of the workforce by sector clearly highlights the industrial nature of the region. The pattern is of course largely the same as in all industrialized areas: a declining agrarian sector, a stagnating or declining industrial sector and a growing service sector (Table 5.1). However, the process of deindustrialization in the Tampere Region started on a large scale rather late in comparison with the rest of Finland. Nonetheless, in 2000 the industrial sector was still much bigger in the Tampere Region than in the rest of the country; on the other hand, the service sector in this region is smaller, in relative terms, than in Finland as a whole.

Table 5.1 Breakdown of labour force by sector in the Tampere Region and Finland, 1970–2000 (%)

	1970	1975	1980	1985	1990	1993	1995	1997	1999	2000*
Agriculture										
Tampere Region	15.3	11.7	9.9	8.3	6.6	6.6	5.1	4.4	3.9	3.4
Finland	20.5	15.2	13.0	10.7	8.7	8.7	7.2	6.3	5.5	4.9
Manufacturing										
Tampere Region	45.9	47.0	44.3	39.8	37.2	32.3	33.8	33.5	33.3	33.4
Finland	35.1	36.3	34.1	31.8	29.2	25.1	26.2	26.6	26.4	26.6
Services										
Tampere Region	38.8	41.3	45.8	51.9	56.2	58.9	58.6	60.2	61.1	61.3
Finland	44.4	48.5	52.9	57.5	61.6	63.7	64.2	65.1	66.2	66.6

Note: * forecast
Source: Statistics Finland

From 1950 until 1975, Finland enjoyed long periods of virtually full employment: the unemployment rate varied between 1.8 and 3.5 per cent. Towards the end of the 1970s, during the oil crisis, unemployment rose briefly to about 8 per cent, but then dropped back down again to around 4 per cent. The situation changed dramatically during the 1990s: at the beginning of the decade unemployment soared to unprecedented levels (about 20 per cent), but along with the economic recovery in the latter part of the decade, unemployment rates declined to about 10 per cent. Despite this positive trend, within the foreseeable future the Tampere Region will still have a high rate of long-term unemployment. Table 5.2 highlights the dramatic decline in employment in manufacturing and construction as well as in the private service sector since 1990. The situation has been more stable in the public sector.

The deep recession of the early 1990s – due to the collapse of trade with the Soviet Union, a bank crisis in Finland and the structural economic problems of the Finnish economy – gave impetus to substantial shifts in the strategies of the national and regional public authorities. A wide consensus emerged among firms and public authorities that the ICT sector offered the best possibilities for maintaining and renewing the industrial base. The policy response to the industrial crises of the 1990s, often referred to as a 'national project', brought about intensive public and joint private–public initiatives and activities intended to support the development of the ICT cluster, both at the national level and specifically within several regions, including the Tampere Region (Science and Technology Council of Finland, 2000).

The extent of this national project can be understood by considering the fact that approximately half of the research expenditure in Finland, including both private and public finance, has been spent until recently on maintaining and increasing the competitiveness of the ICT sector and related industries. Moreover,

Table 5.2 Changes in employment in different sectors in the Tampere Region and Finland, 1970–98 (%)

	1970–93		1990–93		1993–98	
	Tampere Region	*Finland*	*Tampere Region*	*Finland*	*Tampere Region*	*Finland*
agriculture	– 63.7	– 61.3	– 19.9	– 20.5	– 29.2	– 26.7
manufacturing	– 38.2	– 27.2	– 27.7	– 26.4	20.8	18.4
construction	– 50.3	– 40.6	– 50.4	– 50.8	41.2	35.6
private services			– 28.9	– 29.0	36.4	34.1
public services	25.8	30.6	– 12.5	– 8.6	4.8	– 1.2
total	– 18.3	– 10.4	– 20.1	– 19.5	17.9	13.6

Source: Statistics Finland, Council of the Tampere Region

approximately 35 per cent of the students at Finnish universities and polytechnics graduate in subjects related to ICT. Consequently, the industrial structure of Finland and the Tampere Region have changed exceptionally quickly and profoundly. For example, while in 1970 the electronics sector accounted for just 2 per cent of total Finnish exports, by 1990 this share was 11 per cent and by 1999 it had increased to 29 per cent. Tampere has been able to maintain and enhance its position as an important industrial region in this crucial industrial shift.

The innovation system of the Tampere Region

The industrial structure

The Tampere Region accounts for some 11 per cent of Finland's total output. In 2000 the region's manufacturing firms exported about 58 per cent of their total output, while the figure for the whole country was about 53 per cent. There are about 21,000 firms and plants in the Tampere Region, of which nearly 3,200 are industrial companies (Statistics Finland, 2001a). About 660 of them operate globally and a dozen of them are world market leaders. Nevertheless, the majority of firms in the Tampere Region are small.

The most important industrial agglomerations in the Tampere Region are the ICT sector, the pulp and paper industry and mechanical engineering, which together account for nearly 60 per cent of the total value of industrial production. Concerning employment, the pulp and paper industry and mechanical engineering have been fairly stable during recent years. The major growth has occurred within the ICT sector: it has shown annual growth rates of about 30 per cent in its employment (O'Gorman and Kautonen, 2001). The most important employer in the ICT sector, the Nokia Group, in 2001 employed approximately 3,600 white-collar workers in R&D-related functions in Tampere. The textile and clothing industry, which used to be the heart of the local industrial structure, has declined quite dramatically over the past two decades and now represents less than 5 per cent of total employment.

The process of industrialization in Finland has been closely interwoven with the country's natural resources, i.e. its extensive forests. Even today, the forest industry plays an important role in the Finnish economy – though its share of total industrial production has decreased. While in 1960 the forest industry accounted for almost 25 per cent of the country's total industrial production, in 2000 the figure was down to 21 per cent. However, the role of these resource-based branches in the formation of a significant industrial cluster should not be underestimated. Forest industries comprise a strategic bloc in the Finnish economy, including the mechanical forest industry (sawmill, plywood and chipboard, etc.), the chemical forest industry (pulp and paper), several related supplier industries (energy, chemicals, machines, maintenance, services, etc.) and customer industries (paper converters) (Lilja *et al.*, 1992: 137).

The importance of these industries to the Finnish economy is highlighted by the fact that they still account for the largest share of total Finnish exports, even though the share of the pulp, paper and wood industries declined dramatically from 70 per cent in the mid-1960s to around 30 per cent in 2000. About 65 per cent of the total production of the forest industries is exported. At the same time these industries have managed to maintain a very stable market share of around 15 per cent of total world exports in paper products. The production structure has nevertheless changed quite significantly in recent years, as the market share has dropped in the more standardized products (pulp) and increased in product categories of higher added value (Lilja *et al.*, 1992: 139). Paper production and processing is the biggest single forest industry branch in the Tampere Region, which generally specializes in products of higher value added. There are a number of relatively large firms manufacturing paper products in the region. The biggest production units are owned by UPM-Kymmene and M-REAL.

The metal industry in Finland has grown at a phenomenal rate during the past decade, with its share of total industrial production increasing by 49 per cent, including the production of electrical equipment. At the same time, rapid development towards a higher level of technological sophistication and internationalization has occurred. However, the metal industry has never formed the same sort of a coherent industrial cluster as the forest industries; instead it has specialized in producing capital goods for other sectors. A large part of the metal industry can be seen as belonging to the forest industries cluster and it is particularly in this area that it has its international strongholds. Finnish companies are among the world leaders in various types of paper machines, both in terms of market share and technical sophistication (Vuori and Vuorinen, 1994).

Until the rise of the electronics industries, the machine-building industry used to be the single most powerful branch in the region. The region's machine-building industry still plays a major role in the Finnish metal industry. There are a total of some 400 companies engaged in mechanical engineering and automation in the region, with a combined turnover in excess of FIM 10 billion (1.7 billion Euros). These companies employ nearly 20,000 people. Many companies are internationally oriented: Bronto Skylift, Sisu Terminal Systems, Metso Minerals, Sandvik-Tamrock, Timberjack and Neles Automation all have strong positions in global markets.

Electronics and telecommunications in particular have been growing very rapidly throughout Finland. In the past two decades the electrical industry and electronics have almost doubled their share within the metal industry and now account for approximately 50 per cent of the metal and engineering industries' total production. The growth of the electronics industry has been closely interwoven with the forestry sector: for instance, the growth and development of the automation industry are largely the result of close interaction between manufacturers in the electronics and paper industries. The diffusion and application of basic electronic technology to selected areas within the old production systems are often seen as a case *par excellence* of successful renewal in production processes. Today, telecommunications is leading the way for industrial renewal in Finland.

This renewal is evident in Tampere, where in less than five years the ICT sector has more than doubled in size. In 1996, there were a total of 170 ICT firms operating there, employing 5,200 people, with a total turnover of FIM 4590 million (€770 million). In 2000, the total turnover had doubled, totalling FIM 9180 million (€1.5 billion). Employment increased in private firms from 3,000 in 1994 to 6,800 in 1997, an increase of 125 per cent (Tampere Centre of Expertise, 1998). By 2000, the ICT sector in Tampere employed approximately 10,000 people and, if the media and new media sub-sector and the related services and commerce sub-sector are included, employment totalled 15,500 people (Statistics Finland, 2000).

Nokia, with its various business units, has accounted for over half of all the growth in the Tampere Region ICT sector, but during the last half of the 1990s, also nearly one hundred new business ventures were established. The growth in employment in the sector has been based, however, either on new business units established by firms having their headquarters elsewhere, or on the expansion of already existing firms, rather than on new firms *per se*. The ICT sector in the Tampere Region is characterized by a very diverse and versatile structure (O'Gorman and Kautonen, 2001; Kautonen *et al.*, 2002), which ranges from electronics and telecommunications production and R&D (Nokia), to telecommunication operation and services (Sonera, Soon Communication), to software and information system design and production (Fujitsu Invia, Tietoenator ja SecGo) and further to Internet and other new media content production (TV2, Alma Media).

The rubber, chemical and plastics industries are also quite significant branches in Pirkanmaa, but this is largely on account of one single operator, i.e. Nokian Tyres. Kemira Fibres and Pilkington Automotive Finland are other major firms with more than 500 employees. Figure 5.1 gives an overview of the contribution of the various sectors to industrial production in the Tampere Region.

It is clear from Figure 5.2 that, compared with Finland as a whole, the Tampere Region is still an important industrial centre. The Tampere Region has the largest textile industry in the country, but it also accounts for a large share of total production in the clothing industry, rubber and plastics industry, mechanical engineering, motor vehicles and transport equipment industries, as well as the electronics and telecommunications sector.

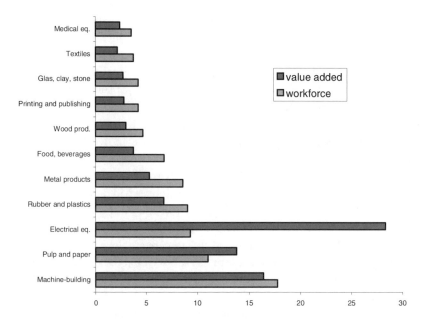

5.1 Industrial production in various sectors in the Tampere Region in 2000 (%)
Source: Statistics Finland (2002)

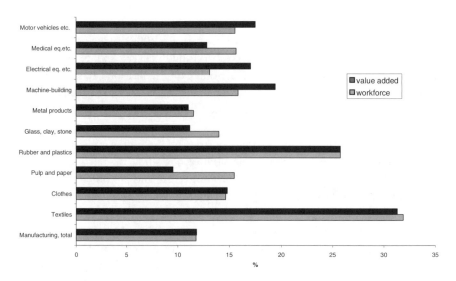

5.2 The Tampere Region's share as a proportion of total production in Finland (%)
Source: Statistics Finland (2002)

While the Tampere Region accounts for a significant share of industrial production in Finland, only two of the 100 largest companies in Finland have their headquarters there: GNT Finland (wholesale trade, IT products) and Nokian Tyres. This could become a problem for the region, as most corporate decisions are made at the headquarters. It is more difficult for regional management to participate in major decisions concerning new investments. The ten biggest employers in the Tampere Region in 2000 represented the following industries: metal industries (three companies), forest industries (two companies) and the rubber, chemical, graphic, food and electronics industries (one in each industry). However, some of Finland's biggest companies have major production units in the Tampere Region; this applies, for instance, to UPM-Kymmene (pulp and paper), M-REAL (pulp and paper), Metso (cranes, pulp and paper and automation technology) and Kemira Oy (fibres and synthetics).

In the past few years, some changes in ownership arrangements in large Finnish companies have occurred. The Finnish state has sold its companies to private sector investors. Another change has been the trend towards larger units due to take-overs by foreign companies and mergers of big firms. Here, the impact of these trends on the Tampere Region will be seen only in the future.

Restructuring of the production system

The autonomy of top management in making decisions on strategies concerning the organization of the production process and the use of labour has never been seriously questioned in Finland either by the state or by the trade union movement. Nowhere else in the Nordic countries has management been better placed to develop rationalization strategies with a view to preserving or improving the competitiveness of their companies without major restrictions. On the contrary, the state and the trade unions have both supported management strategies of restructuring production in the name of competitiveness. In fact, some scholars talk about a 'modernization pact' among unions, employers and the state (Alasoini, 1991: 55). Finnish trade union policy has been characterized as 'consensual adaptation' (Koistinen and Lilja, 1988), highlighting the point that strategic decision-making in the organization of production and the use of labour has been left to management.

During the 1960s and 1970s the organization model of Finnish companies was highly influenced by Fordist principles of the division of labour and management control. This can be explained partly by the traditionally very authoritarian nature of Finnish corporate culture. At this juncture it is important to bear in mind that the separation of ownership and control is a relatively recent phenomenon in Finland (see Kanniainen, 1994: 85). The fact that workers have not been sharply opposed to this practice may have to do with a distinctive work ethic and the dominance of traditional work values related to the recent agrarian past (Vuori and Vuorinen, 1994: 19). In addition, the educational level of the WWII generation in Finland was relatively poor.

Most Finnish firms, however, never developed a Fordist production model in the strict sense. We may therefore use the term flexi-Fordism to characterize the Finnish production model. The fact that industrial production in Finland is based mainly on small batches has prevented management from adopting too rigorous measures of work segmentation and de-qualification. And the comparatively small size of Finnish companies has impeded control over the production market and has forced them to be market-flexible, making it difficult to adopt Fordist rationalization strategies.

A major wave of restructuring production processes occurred during the 1970s and 1980s, which was to a great extent technology-driven. Modern ICTs were applied to make the rigid production structures more flexible, but strategies of organizational flexibilization and human resource management were not used in a systematic way during this first wave of modernizing the production system. This is not surprising, as most Finnish managers have an engineering background, which helps explain to some extent their technocratic approach towards issues of business renewal.

During the 1990s, however, the idea of needing a more profound change penetrated Finnish industry, focusing much more on the organizational dimension of restructuring and on human resource development. At the same time, Finnish companies became leading users of modern ICT among the OECD countries (Statistics Finland, 2001a). Particularly due to the fact that the Finnish economy was changing from being primarily resource-based to primarily knowledge-based, companies focused on learning and innovation, the logic of the most advanced form of economic competition. Recently the model of the network organization became the new production paradigm disseminated through a number of important restructuring programmes launched by public agents.[2]

Concepts such as the 'learning organization' and the 'network organization' of course have different meanings for different people. Although international comparative studies are missing, there seems to be some empirical evidence that nowadays Finland is one of the leading countries in the EU in terms of the spread of some key elements of network organizations, such as group work (Alasoini, 1999). Also partnership and co-operation became more common among Finnish companies during the 1990s (Prihti *et al.*, 2000). Furthermore, Community Innovation Survey (CIS) data reveal that the share of companies that engage in economic networks and co-operate with other firms as well as with support organizations in innovation processes is greater in Finland than in all other EU countries.

A significant number of companies in the Tampere Region have also been very active in transforming themselves into learning organizations. A recent comparative study[3] including eight European regions[4] revealed that companies in the Tampere Region were leading with respect to the introduction of group work, flat hierarchies, profit centres and supplier networks – the key dimensions of the network organization model. They were also very intensive users of network technology such as LAN and advanced communication technology, which are tools for accelerating information and knowledge flows. It is important to mention that user involvement in introducing and developing ICT was highest among companies in the Tampere Region, which indicates a trust-based organization culture. Particular emphasis was given to the high demand for management and organization competencies as well as communication skills. The interplay of these dimensions indicates that company restructuring strategies in the Tampere Region are increasingly influenced by the network logic of organizing business. Table 5.3 shows the extent to which different types of inter-firm networks are diffused in the economy of the Tampere Region.

The highly qualified workforce in the Tampere Region is a major strength of the region. Product quality, flexibility and innovativeness were also mentioned as major strengths by more than 50 per cent of the companies participating in a recent survey carried out in the region (Kautonen *et al.*, 2002). However, concerning the factor of price, companies in the Tampere Region do not consider themselves to be in a strong position (Figure 5.3). These findings indicate

Table 5.3 Types of company innovation networks in the Tampere Region (%)

Type of innovation network	Share of firms
No significant innovation networks	15.2
Inter-firm innovation networks along vertical production chains[a]	35.9
Both vertical and horizontal inter-firm innovation networks	19.7
Innovation networks consisting also of university units or research laboratories as members	17.5
Other types of innovation networks[b]	11.7
	100.0

Notes
N = 223
a A company's customer(s) and/or supplier(s) are involved in key stages of its new product or process development
b In addition to inter-firm relationships, this category of innovation networks consists also of co-operation with polytechnic(s) or other educational institution(s) (other than universities) or with public innovation support organisation(s)
Source: Kautonen *et al.* (2002)

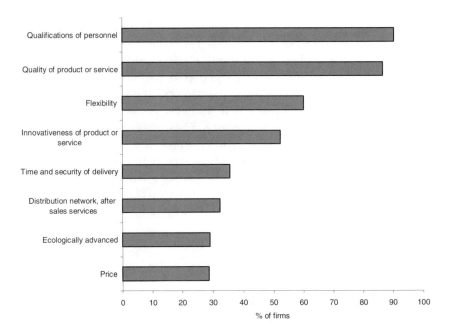

5.3 Tampere Region company views of own competitive strengths
Note: *N* = 245
Source: Kautonen, *et al.* (2002)

nonetheless that, overall, firms in the Tampere Region have adapted to the new competition criteria in the globalizing economy.

We can conclude that companies in the Tampere Region have improved their learning and innovation capacity significantly during the past ten years by introducing key elements of the network organization model. The use of network technology, organizational decentralization and functional integration, human resource development and participatory elements are nowadays much more common than they were a decade ago.

Nokia, the core company in Finland's highly competitive telecommunications industry, is also a key player in the economy of the Tampere Region, as one of its largest research centres is located there. The company has systematically improved its internal competences for promoting innovation by continuously increasing its R&D budget. It has also undergone several restructuring processes during the past fifteen years, becoming a global network firm. Nokia has adapted to the fact that flexibility and time have become the key competition criteria in global markets by turning itself into a flat and project-based organization; working in cross-functional design teams is common practice in the company. Internal co-operation is supported by a strong and distinctive corporate culture based on Nordic egalitarianism and reliability. Moreover, the company invests heavily in further training in order to keep the knowledge of its workers up to date, as knowledge in the telecommunications sector becomes outdated very rapidly. Nokia also tries to make use of the knowledge produced in the workplace through 'learning by doing' (Schienstock and Tulkki, 2001).

The company's researchers frequently co-operate in joint projects with their counterparts from technical universities and other research institutes. In addition, Nokia engages in strategic R&D partnerships not only with large leading companies in the telecommunications business, but also with small high-tech firms. Monitoring technological development very closely is another strategy for acquiring knowledge. For example, Nokia is a partner in most Finnish Centres of Expertise, which allows the company to monitor closely new technological developments in small Finnish high-tech firms.

Nokia has also changed significantly its mode of co-operation with suppliers and subcontractors (Ali-Yrkkö, 2001). In the beginning of the 1990s the company started to outsource its in-house manufacturing of accessories and to establish long-term partnerships with its subcontractors. In the mid-1990s the company restructured its entire production chain, reducing the number of co-operation partners by using assemblers and system suppliers. Nokia itself focused its efforts on such core competences as research, software production, final product design and brand management. There has also been a trend towards working with global suppliers; the company procures the components for its mobile phone system from suppliers in various parts of the world. In the past few years, Nokia has extended its range of co-operation partners, now using software and even R&D subcontractors. The next step in developing the network will be to introduce risk and profit sharing. The Tampere Region has benefited significantly from this development, as Nokia's activities in this region are focused on R&D.

Institutional set-up and innovation policies in the Tampere Region

The focus of technology policy in Finland has shifted from providing direct grants towards facilitating dialogue and co-operation and raising new initiatives. In the same manner, we may differentiate between a relatively stable innovation support infrastructure on the one hand and occasional new initiatives and programmes on the other. Stable services supply companies with support, lowering the threshold of risk-taking related to innovation activities. New initiatives bring actors together in a new way, highlight latent innovation support needs, increase innovation awareness and create positive pressures for renewal and learning.

Policy-makers in the Tampere Region focused on establishing an innovation support infrastructure by creating new organizations and services during the 1980s until the mid-1990s. Since then, the focus has shifted towards new, occasional initiatives and programmes. This is partly connected to the fact that policy-makers had to gain experience with the new programme-based policies and instruments. The new financial instruments (national and EU regional funding) were used in the beginning in such a way that dispersed the resources into small and often inefficient projects.

Science, technology and education

Tampere has a strong indigenous science and technology base, which matches the needs of industry due to a long tradition of university–industry co-operation and high-level research conducted in the two local universities (cf. also Jones-Evans, 2000). In addition, the region has many private and public research laboratories and a number of educational and training institutes, including polytechnics.

Key policy-makers in the Tampere Region consider the production of new scientific and technological knowledge to be the most important base of the innovation support system, followed by the education and training of a highly qualified workforce (Kautonen *et al.*, 2002). Therefore, there are good reasons for arguing that the universities and other higher education institutions form the backbone of the regional innovation system, together with large R&D-oriented companies.

Higher education has become very widespread in the Tampere Region, as in the rest of Finland. In 1999, the number of new students in higher education was about 50,000 and the share was as great as four-fifths of all 19–year-olds in Finland (Tulkki, 2001: 45). Some 23 per cent of adults in the country (as measured both on the national and regional levels) had a higher education degree (Statistics Finland, 2002).

In Finland as a whole, the total expenditure on research and development went up significantly after the recession. In 1993, FIM 11 billion were spent in R&D, while in 1995 the corresponding sum amounted to approximately FIM 13 billion and by 1999 the sum had grown to approximately FIM 23 billion. In the Tampere Region, the growth of R&D investments has been especially remarkable: the real annual change during 1995–99 was as high as 25 per cent compared to the national level of 14 per cent. In 1995, R&D expenditures in the Tampere Region still only accounted for about 10 per cent of Finland's entire R&D expenditures. Nowadays expenditures on R&D in the region, which have been growing particularly in the business sector, represent a share of about 14 per cent of national spending (Statistics Finland, 2001a). Nevertheless, the Helsinki Region strongly dominates R&D expenditures, with its share of 45 per cent. On the other hand, concerning the regional proportion of R&D personnel of the workforce, compared to the national average of 3.1 per cent, the Tampere Region accounts for 4.6 per cent.

Patent applications represent an important indicator with which to measure the outcome of R&D inputs. Helsinki has been the strongest of the Finnish regions in patent applications, with 39 per cent of the national total in 1999. The Tampere Region holds the second position not only in R&D expenditures but also in patents, with its 16 per cent share of the national total in the same year (Statistics Finland, 2001). The largest patent classes are electrical engineering (32.4%), processes and transport (18.8%) and physics (15.7%). The fairly even distribution of patenting activities among the various sectors reflects the widely diffused science and technology base of the region.

Of the two universities in the region, the Tampere University of Technology (TUT) has traditionally been a key actor. TUT was named a Centre of Excellence in Research in the fields of semiconductors, digital signal processing, hydraulics and automation. In all these fields of research, TUT has a long-standing tradition of co-operation with industry in the region. University–industry co-operation has been partly achieved through high labour mobility. Furthermore, students have written their master's theses in co-operation with firms and university staff has provided training courses for firms. University initiatives, such as part-time professorships for experts from industry, are also important as part of the close university–industry co-operation in the region. And a major part of the university's research activities – about 60 per cent – is financed externally, including financial support from industry. TUT, situated in the Hermia Science Park, where also the Nokia Group and approximately 150 smaller firms have located their R&D activities, has 1,100 employees and 7,600 students. The university played a central role for the Nokia Group in the 1990s, in fields such as digital signal processing, and it continues to be an important partner for Nokia (Ali-Yrkkö and Hermans, 2002).

In the 1990s, it was essential for the development of the regional innovation system that also the University of Tampere (UTA) and other research and educational institutions raised their regional profiles. The University of Tampere, with its 1,600 employees and 13,000 students, had traditionally been oriented toward the humanities and in educating a workforce for the public sector, whereas university–industry co-operation had developed only in the medical faculty. During the 1990s also computer science and information sciences, as well as hypermedia, became important fields of co-operation, which was one of the reasons for establishing a new Faculty of Information Science in the university in 2001. Concerning the ICT sector, the Tampere University of Technology and the University of Tampere together grant more than 200 Master's degrees annually in the fields of electronics, information and communication technologies and new media. The two universities in Tampere also played a crucial role in the emerging ICT sector, as senior researchers there established some of the first companies in the field.

VTT, the country's main technical research centre, is well represented in the Tampere Region. Its fields of strength overlap to a great extent with those of TUT: automation technology, as well as information and telecommunication technologies. VTT specializes in applied research, concentrating on the improvement of product and process technologies. Most of its research projects are commissioned by private companies or state-owned institutes, Tekes in particular, but the VTT institutes are also engaged in self-initiated research projects. Of VTT's nine research areas in Finland, five are present in Tampere, i.e. mechanical automation, construction, plastic and fibre technology, security technology and metallurgy and information technology. VTT has 250 employees in Tampere (Kautonen *et al.*, 2002).

There are also numerous educational and training institutions in the Tampere Region, including two recently established polytechnics, the Pirkanmaa Polytechnic, concentrating on social and health care sector education and the Tampere Polytechnic, the profile of which is to focus explicitly on activities significant to the needs of industry. There are also quite a few vocational training institutions in the Tampere Region. Figure 5.4 shows to what extent companies in the region engage in close co-operation with key knowledge producers. Altogether, approximately 80 per cent of the manufacturing and knowledge-intensive business service companies that employ ten or more people have at least some co-operation with these organizations.

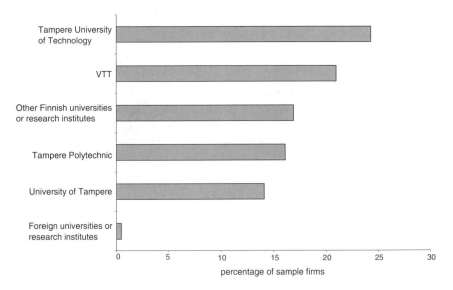

percentage of sample firms

5.4. Share of companies having frequent co-operation with some selected universities or research institutes
Notes: Likert-5, values 4–5, *N* = 195
Source: Kautonen *et al.*, 2002

Intermediaries and financiers of innovation activities

In the 1980s and 1990s, a number of intermediary and financial institutions were established in the innovation support infrastructure of the Tampere Region. These have served the actors in search of new growth paths. In particular, the municipal sector in Finland has remarkable autonomy guaranteed in legislation, which has opened up opportunities for an independent innovation policy at the regional level. Since the early 1970s, when municipalities established positions for industrial advisers, the municipal and sub-regional authorities have gained the power to support the setting up of new companies by founding science and technology parks, other intermediaries and regional venture capital funds. However, most of these are partly owned also by state-owned national organizations.

Most intermediaries and technology transfer companies in the Tampere Region are located in close proximity to TUT and VTT in the Hermia Science Park and in the newly established Finn-Medi Science Park. The latest high-technology agglomeration has developed in downtown Tampere, where the large, old industrial estates have been turned into a complex of software and new media companies. This sector is co-ordinated by Media Tampere Ltd. – a company that is mostly owned by private companies like Nokia and Fujitsu Invia. This commitment reflects the fact that these companies aim at using the city as their testing arena for new products and applications and as a seedbed for new business ventures, especially in the field of mobile and Internet technologies (Kautonen *et al.*, 2002).

In the ICT sector, several new institutions have been established to take up a bridging function between higher education institutions and industry. These include large research facilities such as the Digital Media Institute and the Optoelectronics Research Institute. Several bridging institutions are also located in the mechanical engineering and automation sector, including the Tampere Automation Centre, the Foundry Institute and the Rubber Institute. These institutes bring together firms, education and training institutions and other core actors representing certain fields of technology and expertise and they offer specialized services such as education and training, technology transfer and networking. Also many large-scale joint investments have been made that would otherwise have been too costly for any single company to finance (e.g. research facilities and pilot and prototype production equipment).

With respect to innovation support and financing, regional branches of state authorities have the most widely distributed clientele among companies in the Tampere Region. These include: the National Technology Agency (Tekes), the Regional Employment and Economic Development Centre of Tampere (EEDC) and Finnvera. Tekes provides funding in the form of R&D grants and loans for single companies. Tekes also initiates, co-ordinates and finances large national technology programmes, in which usually both the Tampere universities, regional research laboratories and industry participate. In 1999, Tekes financed company R&D in the Tampere Region totalling FIM 130 million (9 per cent of the national total) and in the same year its support for university and public research institute R&D totalled FIM 134 million (15 per cent of the national total).

Regional Employment and Economic Development Centres (EEDCs) were established in 1997 to bring together regional offices belonging to the administration of the Ministry of Trade and Industry, the Ministry of Labour and the Ministry of Forestry and Agriculture. One of the centres is located in Tampere. The regional offices provide companies with (1) advisory services; (2) training, consultancy and development services; (3) sector-specific information services; and (4) financial services. These include grants for development activities, investments, internationalization and to develop the operational environment of SMEs (incubators, technology transfer, etc.). EEDC had FIM 29 million for its operations in the Tampere Region in 1999.

Finnvera is a state-owned credit institution operating throughout Finland based on its fifteen regional offices. Finnvera's role as a financier of SMEs includes providing loans, guarantees and risk finance for growing and internationalizing companies. It concentrates on financing in manufacturing industries, tourism and various business services and providing short- and long-term loans for SMEs. In 1999, Finnvera spent altogether FIM 429 million (15 per cent of the national total) for various activities in the Tampere Region.

Altogether, state financing for the Tampere Region coming from the industrial policy budget accounted for FIM 1100 per capita (FIM 710 on the average in Finland) in 1999. The Tampere Region's share of national technology policy financing was even larger: in 1999, the financing was FIM 880 per capita, whereas the national average was only FIM 460 per capita. In particular, financial support coming from Tekes increased faster in the Tampere Region than in any other region of the country in the late 1990s. Compared to this financing based on competitive bidding, the Tampere Region's share of EU Structural Funds was only 3.4 per cent of the national total.

The availability of venture capital expanded rapidly during the 1990s, facilitating the setting up, growth and internationalization of knowledge-intensive small firms in Finland. For example, venture capital under management in Finland grew from a modest FIM 530 million in 1989 to FIM 13.6 billion in 2000 (Finnish Venture Capital Association, 2001). A major regional venture capital company, Sentio Invest Ltd., was established in 1996, partly owned by the City of Tampere and Finnvera Ltd. In 2000 Sentio Invest Ltd. disposed of a total capital of over FIM 90 million to invest in companies in the Tampere Region, most often in the form of a limited partial ownership contract during the first years of a company. In addition, a private–public consortium was established in 1998, backed up by the Finnish National Fund for Research and Development (Sitra), among others.

This consortium concentrates its support on pre-venture stages. Together with other financiers, the consortium invested some FIM 50 million in new business ventures in the Tampere Region in 2000.

The Council of the Tampere Region, established in 1990, is an inter-municipal joint authority, which bears statutory responsibility for regional development and planning. It is funded by its member municipalities, which receive state aid for this purpose. The Council's role is, broadly, to steer and monitor overall regional development, together with the key regional state authority, EEDC. The focus of public financing in the Tampere Region has been on industrial development in terms of innovation activities and enhanced qualification of the workforce, instead of physical infrastructure.

The City of Tampere itself either finances, owns or is a shareholder in a number of companies and establishments, such as the Tampere Technology Centre Ltd. and the Hermia Science Park, other regional funds, the Finn-Medi Medical Technology Centre, the Centre of Expertise Programme, the Tampere Polytechnic and so forth. In 2001 the City of Tampere also spent about FIM 23 million in order to finance business development programmes directly (Kautonen et al., 2002: 159).

The National Technology Agency (Tekes), the regional EEDC and Finnvera are the three most important public innovation support organizations for companies. Approximately 20–30 per cent of the companies in the region have fairly or very frequent co-operation with these three organizations (Figure 5.5). The local and regional agencies have smaller customer segments and in some cases their role is to serve in development at the cluster level. Of all the companies in the region, approximately 85 per cent have at least some co-operation with one or more public innovation support organizations (ibid.).

Regional and local innovation support organizations work with much smaller groups of customers. Intermediaries like science parks hosting technology transfer organizations, as well as regional venture capital funds in general co-operate with no more than 5 to 10 per cent of the regionally based companies (ibid.). In contrast to the regional offices of national organizations, the focus of these intermediaries' activities is on co-ordinating and networking instead of financing. Thus, there is a fairly clear division of responsibility between national and municipal organizations, in which the latter take care of 'innovation awareness', network formation and capability building, initiating new bsinesses and developing regional innovation and growth strategies.

Policy programmes and initiatives

Despite traditionally pursuing a relatively non-interventionist industrial policy, there have been intensive public initiatives and activities intended to support in

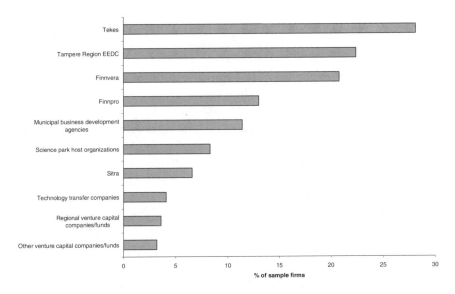

5.5 Share of companies located in the Tampere Region having frequent co-operation with some selected intermediary and financing organizations
Notes: Likert-5, values 4–5, N = 195
Source: Kautonen *et al.*, 2002

particular the development of the ICT cluster, both at the national level and in the Tampere Region. The Finnish government has initiated large research programmes focusing on technologies related to information and communication. National research and development expenditures grew from slightly more than 1 per cent of GNP in 1980 to 3 per cent of GNP by 1999. Since the ICT boom in the late 1990s, new knowledge-intensive sectors like biotechnology (Schienstock and Tulkki, 2001) have been increasingly looked upon as potential future growth areas.

So far, ICT has been a cornerstone of industrial renewal in the Tampere Region. According to an evaluation of the Centre of Expertise Programme (Finnish Ministry of Interior, 2002), the core expertise in firms and supporting organizations of the Tampere Region lies especially in the following areas:

- *Mechanical engineering and automation*, where the regional cluster revolves around production and the development of mobile machinery, process and production machines and process automation. Particularly strong fields of expertise lie in machine tool automation and mobile hydraulics, water hydraulics, control of dynamic phenomena, automated flexible production, integrated systems and regulating and measuring equipment for paper mills. This sector covers an industrial production base with a total gross turnover of FIM 17 billion in the region. This internationally important export industry is supported by a network of suppliers and by teaching and research services. The industrial base in this regional cluster has a total labour force of 24,000. One thousand people work in teaching and research activities, while an additional 1,500 people are engaged in design and service occupations that directly support the mechanical engineering and automation sector. The aims of the regional Centre of Expertise Programme are to preserve the current level of employment in major enterprises and to improve the regional supplier network so as to create 1,000 new jobs in firms by the year 2006.

- *Information and communication technology-based industries,* where the operations of the regional firms and business units focus on design, research and product development. The leading expertise of the Tampere Region ICT sector is in such areas as data communications, wireless networks, telecommunications networks, workstation software, team software, databases, mechatronics, process automation, sound, image and video processing, production control and logistics systems. The Tampere Region already has nearly 300 active ICT firms and business units employing some 8,500 people. The regional Centre of Expertise Programme aims to double the current number of jobs in the sector in the region by the year 2006. The Tampere Technology Centre Ltd. is responsible for the co-ordination of both the Mechanical Engineering and Automation and the ICT Centres of Expertise.
- *New media,* where the specific strengths in the communications sector are digitizing and mobile communications, digital content and distribution services, new media and the social impact of new communications technology. The media services operations of the Centre of Expertise – co-ordinated by Media Tampere Ltd. – cover a field employing a total of about 5,100 people. The aim of the programme is to increase the current turnover and employment impact of this sector. The projected turnover for the end of the period is FIM 5.5 billion and the target number of jobs in the sector is 7,600. Particular attention will be given to new media content production and services to be constructed on the basis of world-class technological expertise.
- *Health care technologies,* where particular specialization lies in implants, healthcare information systems and visualization, life management applications and certain vanguard projects in biotechnology. The number of jobs in this sector doubled during the 1990s and the turnover of its enterprises is currently growing by more than 15 per cent annually. The aim of the Centre of Expertise Programme is to diversify, globalize and expand this sector by 1,500 jobs and to develop the role of the Tampere Region as a centre for expertise in the industry. This programme is co-ordinated by Finn-Medi Research Ltd.

In addition to the nationally nominated Centres of Expertise, in 1998 the Tampere Region initiated a fifth sub-programme supporting the development of *knowledge-intensive business services* (KIBS). This sub-programme is seen as important not only because of the rapid growth of employment taking place in this field, but also because it has a significant impact on the innovation activities of other industrial sectors, as KIBS companies play an important role as creators, carriers and disseminators of new knowledge (Miles *et al.*, 1995). A new company, Professia Ltd., was established to co-ordinate the programme in this field.

The Tampere Centre of Expertise Programme functions as a catalyst in promoting new developments and bringing different actors together. It also acts as a mediator between national-level financiers, on the one hand, and service suppliers and local firms, on the other. The development projects co-ordinated by the programme aim to cover all the technological, market and social factors that are relevant to business success. In addition to development projects carried out with firms and networks of service organizations, the programme also intends to identify gaps and weak links in the regional system of innovation and to propose possible solutions (O'Gorman and Kautonen, 2002).

Figure 5.6 demonstrates the prosperous regional development that occurred during the late 1990s, showing the expansion of the key clusters and industrial sectors belonging to the Regional Centres of Expertise Programme. The ICT sector and the knowledge-intensive business services sector have been growing the most rapidly. Particularly in the ICT and KIBS sectors, the total turnover of the private companies more than doubled between 1995 and 2000. However, in 2001 the growth came to a halt due to the international stagnation of the global ICT boom. It remains to be seen whether the third generation of mobile telephony will create a new wave of growth. In mechanical engineering and automation, the most significant development occurring during the 1990s was that the companies and their environment were strongly transformed towards a more knowledge-intensive mode of production. This can be seen in the increase of R&D spending and productivity during the latter part of the 1990s, and it can also be seen in the technological level of the companies and their products (Kautonen *et al.*, 2002: 157).

In 2001, the eTampere Programme was launched to broaden and expand the ICT and the New Media Centres of Expertise. Because of its large budget of FIM 770 million (approx. 130 million Euros) for five years, the programme is considered to be very ambitious. Also because it consists of a great number of sub-programmes covering a wide range of activities from basic and applied research to business incubation and further to the development of information society citizenship, the programme can be seen as a major challenge for all actors involved. The programme covering technological, market and social aspects is seen as unique not only in Finland but also in Europe (Castells and Himanen, 2001). Within the

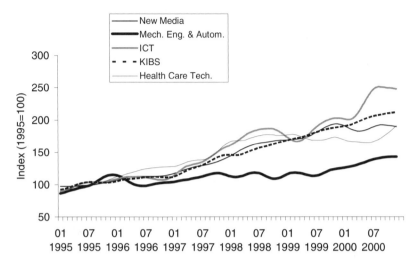

5.6 Development of total turnover in industries belonging to the Tampere Region Centre of Expertise Programme, 1995–2000, index
Source: Statistics Finland, Tampere Cityweb statistics (2002)

Programme, new virtual units have been set up, including the eBusiness Research Centre connecting TUT and UTA, the Information Society Research Institute at UTA and the ReLab of VTT (testing and applications, etc.).

As part of the eTampere Programme, a so-called eAccelerator was launched, which is based on the concept of a virtual, highly efficient business incubator oriented towards new technology-based companies. Its rather ambitious goal is to guide between twenty and twenty-five companies into international growth trajectories. This goal has not been formally re-examined because of the international stagnation of the ICT sector, although it is clear that in particular the weakening of the US venture capital market has made it much more difficult to attain such growth.

Innovation policy in the Tampere Region has two main goals, according to the key policy-makers (Kautonen *et al.*, 2002: 168, 173–175). The first is to maintain and strengthen the diversified and versatile industrial and technological base of the region, which can be seen as an important resource for continuous innovation activities in different sectoral and technological interfaces. A strong educational and research infrastructure is crucial in integrating large firms into the regional economy. The second aim is to develop the social and cultural amenities of the region in order to maintain its attractiveness to a highly qualified workforce. Recent nation-wide polls and surveys have shown that Tampere is currently the most attractive urban centre in Finland to which to migrate.

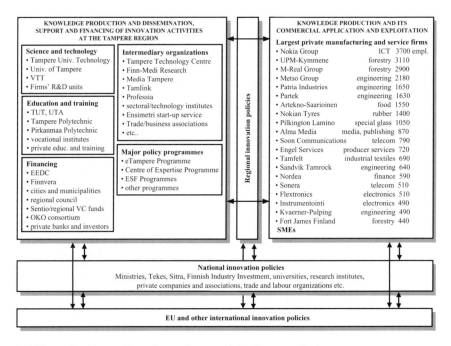

5.7 The regional innovation policy environment in the Tampere Region
Source: Kautonen *et al.* (2002: 159)

Conclusions

Escaping path dependency

The economic crisis in the beginning of the 1990s not only hit the Finnish economy severely, it also revealed major structural deficiencies. It became quite clear that to be able to cope with the problems caused by the economic crisis and in particular the extremely high unemployment rate, Finland would need brisk economic growth, which could not be expected from traditional resource-based industries. Therefore to avoid a long-term 'lock-in', causing the economy to deteriorate even further, Finland had to escape the traditional techno-economic development path and to create the basis for a new path which could stimulate rapid economic growth. There was widespread agreement that developing a knowledge-based economy would bring Finland back onto the high growth track.

During 1990s, the industrial structure of the Tampere Region changed profoundly. Industries which dominated the region ten years ago, such as pulp and paper, and mechanical engineering and automation, have maintained or even enhanced their competitive positions in global markets. However, the most significant development has been the rapid emergence of knowledge-intensive industries, especially the ICT sector and the knowledge-intensive business services sector. The total turnover of the private companies in these sectors more than doubled between 1995 and 2000. Approximately 10 to 12 per cent of the workforce in the region is employed in these two industrial sectors. The engine of growth has been the Nokia Group.

In addition to structural changes, the industries of the Tampere Region have been transformed towards a more knowledge-intensive mode of production. The companies have improved their learning and innovation capability significantly during the past ten years by introducing key elements of the network organization model. The use of network technology, inter-firm networks, organizational decentralization and functional integration, as well as human resource development and participatory elements are much more common now in the beginning of the new millennium than they were a decade ago. Here, the new knowledge-intensive industries have also contributed to the renewal of the traditional industries by local producer-user interaction and knowledge spillovers.

One of the key aspects enabling the growth of knowledge-intensive industries has been the ample provision of a workforce with tertiary education related to ICT. The Tampere University of Technology has traditionally participated in close co-operation with manufacturing companies. More recently, however, university–industry co-operation in the region has broadened to include the University of Tampere and new polytechnics as well as new knowledge-intensive industries. Overall, these relationships have produced a good match between the private and public knowledge bases in the region.

A number of intermediary and financial institutions were established in the innovation support infrastructure of the Tampere Region during the 1980s and 1990s. These have served in bridging the gap between industry and research institutions and in helping to bear the risks associated with long-term development projects. Various science, technology and innovation policy programmes have brought regional actors together with national and international sources of expertise. It was of utmost importance for the emergence of the knowledge-intensive industries that the interests of leading companies, the central government and the regional authorities intertwined from the recession onwards.

Challenges of regional innovation policy

The Tampere Region was quite successful in escaping the traditional resource-based path and forging ahead on a new knowledge-based development path indicated by rapid growth rates. However, the transformation process is still ongoing and is faced with some major problems.

The key challenges related to the expansion of knowledge-intensive industries in the Tampere Region lie in the exploitation of knowledge and the internationalization process. These consist of several aspects as follows. First, there has been a shortage of personnel having sufficient qualifications for and experience of international business. This has been due to a lack of provision for related education and training, as well as the fact that the activities of international trade have been largely concentrated in the capital city region. Second, companies seem to lack proper information related to their very often highly dynamic markets. Monitoring changes in foreign markets in particular can be seen as the most challenging task for SMEs and more support from the institutional environment is needed.

However, the threshold of internationalization for SMEs in the region has lowered quite considerably during the past five years. This is due to the fact that the high level of ICT expertise and related support infrastructure in the region has also been recognized internationally, indicated by growing foreign direct investment in the region and by the preparedness of venture capitalists to engage in higher investment in the region. The ICT industry and especially the Nokia Group have not only helped the regional economy to grow rapidly, but they have also opened up new markets in Europe, Asia and the USA for local companies.

A third challenge is that the number of newly established businesses in general and particularly within the growing industries has been rather low, if related to the overall company base of the region and the volume of research conducted in the local universities and research institutes. In the Tampere Region, the net growth in the number of companies has been smaller than in Finland on average. Between 1994 and 1997, the new company share of all companies in the region increased from 1 to 3 per cent, but recently dropped back to less than 1 per cent. The business services sector has been the most rapidly growing sector as measured by the number of new establishments.

The problem of low entrepreneurship has been recognized for a long time and it has been considered typical for a region that is mostly characterized by traditional large-scale industries. Since the 1980s various measures to tackle the problem have been introduced with little success. The problem still remains, since despite many efforts to facilitate and encourage university spin-offs, researchers in universities have either chosen to continue their scientific careers or to work with one of the large companies in the region. On the other hand, the availability of highly qualified research personnel has attracted many larger companies to locate their R&D activities in the region.

Along with the achievements and experiences of the past ten years, most of the policy-makers in the Tampere Region share the view that the future development of their region is highly dependent on its own active performance. National and international policies are seen to provide frames and resources for action, but successfully exploiting these opportunities, depends upon the autonomous development of the competences of the region's core companies and support institutions and on close co-operation among them. Continuous monitoring of internal and external developments and providing room for diversity within the Tampere Region are crucial in order to avoid future lock-ins.

Notes

1   1 Euro ≈ 6 FIM.
2   The Ministry of Labour, the National Technology Agency Tekes and the Academy of Finland are the most important organizations in Finnish network-facilitating policy (see Schienstock and Hämäläinen 2001).
3   Schienstock (2002b)
4   The following countries/regions were involved in the research project: Flanders, the Republic of Ireland, Lazio (Italy), Lower Austria, Portugal, the Stuttgart Region, the Tampere Region and West London. The sample of the company survey contains 800 companies, 100 companies per region. The regional/national samples were structured according to company size and industry.

Chapter 6
Learning in the village economy of Denmark
The role of institutions and policy in sustaining competitiveness

Peter Maskell

Introduction

Any process of territorial economic development will tend to be highly path-dependent. Localized capabilities are normally more durable than the assets upon which they were built. Yet, the rise and subsequent decline of what became known as 'the new economy' has been accompanied by a growing belief in 'big science' and formal R&D, and on the technology-intensive sectors.

Without any intention to add further to all this jazz one might, however, draw attention to the fact, that Denmark – one of the smallest of the OECD countries with a population of just over five million – has managed quite well, largely without becoming high-tech and in spite of an unfavourable location, few natural resources and with production costs in the top league of the world.

When trying to understand the reasons behind such a position there is something slightly unsatisfactory about the traditional explanatory factors like resource endowment, labour costs or capital ratio. The capital ratio, the use of new technologies, and level of formal education in Denmark are no higher than in many other countries. The small number of patentable innovations reflects the scarcity of large, globally oriented firms and the persistent low level of private sector research spending.[1] Even the labour productivity per hour has not been outstanding compared with major countries in the OECD (Table 8.1).

As Denmark nevertheless has a GDP per capita in the year 2000 exceeding 30,000 US$[2] and has been able to maintain and increase the standard of living (even in periods of rather high unemployment rates, see Table 6.2),[3] the explanation must be sought in a set of *qualitative* factors, which have led to the present rather favourable position occupied by the nation in the international division of labour.

Some of these qualitative factors are simply related to the national strategies that small countries have to adopt when confronted with international competition. But these strategies interact with the perceived outcome of the nation's and region's previous history and are embedded in a number of specific, though mostly informal, institutions. For want of a better term, the national and regional endowment of these informal institutions might here be called culture.

Table 6.1 Labour productivity (GDP per hour worked), 1950–98 (in 1990 US$ (PPP) per hour)

	1950	1973	1990	1998
Denmark	6.57	16.57	21.67	26.18
Germany	3.99	14.76	21.94	26.56
UK	7.93	15.97	21.42	27.45
France	5.82	18.02	29.47	33.72
USA	12.65	23.72	30.10	34.55
Japan	2.08	11.57	19.04	22.54

Note: The benchmark GDP estimates are in 1990 international dollars, based on purchasing power parity converters instead of exchange rates. The author relied on Geary-Khamis multilateral PPPs, available from the International Comparison Programme (ICP) of the United Nations, Eurostat and OECD.

Source: Maddison (2001:351).

Table 6.2 The unemployed as a percentage of the total Danish workforce

	1950	1960	1970	1980	1990	1997	1998	1999	2000
Total	3.0	1.7	1.2	6.8	9.4	7.8	6.5	5.6	5.3
Men	4.0	2.1	1.6	6.2	8.0	6.5	5.3	4.8	4.5
Women	0.9	0.7	0.5	7.5	11.1	9.3	7.8	6.5	6.2

Source: Statistics Denmark (2001) *Statistical Fifty-Year Review* (CD-ROM).

The main argument addressed in this chapter is that some national and regional cultures are more predisposed than others to support and advance the industry of today (Gertler, 1995). The national and regional cultures interact with natural and human resources, with formal institutions and with built structures in constituting a specific set of national and regional capabilities that contribute to the competitiveness of the firms localized in the country.

The underlying notion, however, is that the differences in national or regional capabilities to enhance the competitiveness of firms should be seen primarily as the result of territory-specific differences in the ability to create and use knowledge. The international economy favours firms that are able to learn, change and adapt a little faster than their competitors (OECD, 1994). The competitive edge has thus gradually shifted from static price competition towards dynamic improvements. The formation of regional or national institutions that actively support firms in coping with this process is now of crucial importance.

Formal (designed) and informal (self-grown) national or regional institutions both play a significant role in determining the success or failure of firms in the international competition, but it will be argued that informal institutions might often be fundamental for the long-term competitiveness of firms within such territorially defined economies (Krugman, 1994a).

The difficulties in creating economic progress through designed institutions have been made painfully clear through the meagre results of the past fifty years' development policies in many countries in the Third World. And the persistence of *intra*-national developmental problems in most industrial countries can hardly be seen only as a consequence of insufficient supply of well-designed institutions (Putnam, 1993; Hill, 1995). We might paraphrase Barney (1991) in submitting that the total informal *and* designed institutional endowment of a nation or a region can lead to sustainable advantages only if the resulting national or regional capabilities are valuable (they must allow the firms to create profit), rare (they cannot be in abundant supply), not subject to substitution and imperfectly replicable, meaning that policy-makers in other nations or regions cannot readily copy them.

While designed institutions or specific policies can more or less easily be imitated,[4] this is in no way the case with national or regional culture. Even when governments imitate each other's successful policies, the outcome always differs because the policies interact with firms, rooted in distinctive national and regional cultural settings (Zysman, 1994). If we want to understand the fundamentals behind the formation of sustainable international competitive positions, we need, then, to start with an understanding of the seemingly spontaneously established, economically important *informal* institutions.

In recent years, many have forwarded the idea that spatial agglomeration or clustering of related economic activities at a sub-national level – the industrial districts – promotes the competitiveness of firms, by condensing the effects of such informal institutions.[5] The clustering of the Danish furniture and clothing industry (Kristensen, 1992; Maskell, 1998) or the cluster of firms within radio communications in Northern Denmark (Dalum, 1995) might be used to illustrate this phenomenon, but compared with the population of many of the industrial districts elsewhere in Europe it might be more appropriate to take the whole of Denmark as a frame of reference. In doing this we must, however, keep in mind that regional cultural differences within the country's 43,000 square kilometres can be substantial, and that the number and the variety of instruments available to policy-makers and administrators are considerably greater than in most intra-national regions or districts.

By focusing on the whole of Denmark it is possible to demonstrate how a number of economically important informal institutions, which are sometimes associated with industrial districts in larger countries, have characterized the political and economic development of a small nation.

Informal institutions and small nations

Liberalization, specialization and path dependency

All small nations are faced with the same dilemma of openness. They need access to foreign resources and can only pay their way by exporting commodities or services at an internationally competitive price. This, in turn, forces the domestic producers to match or outstrip foreign firms in competitiveness and the only feasible way to ensure that the domestic firms keep pace with the best is by eliminating all barriers to trade. Protectionism is simply not a viable option for small nations. Small nations need to become *regions* in a broader economic entity with as little loss of political independence as possible. It is not surprising then, that many small developed nations of Europe – Denmark, Sweden, Norway, the Netherlands, Belgium, Austria and Switzerland – long ago opened their economies and actively advocated adopting a non-tariff, non-barrier world trade system (Balassa, 1969).

In the case of Denmark, liberalization has been an ongoing process beginning with commodities and later encompassing services, capital, knowledge and – to a degree – also labour.[6] In order to secure this process, and to balance the different sectoral interests along the road, a strong central government was needed – a government with detailed economic information on all major aspects of society, and with the power to co-ordinate the liberalization process. Close institutional and personal connections and extended informal networks between the central administration of government and the business associations, organized labour and the political parties, became a prerequisite for a successful outcome.

Once the domestic market for commodities had become sufficiently open, a process of industrial restructuring was set in motion whereby the small nations experienced a further specialization in certain groups of products in which they already had some market power. Even without any major initial advantage the growth in competence and the utilization of economies of scale enabled each of the nations to establish an internationally competitive manufacturing industry (Krugman, 1991). Over time, generations of rounds of investments – based on perceived international developments in demand and competition – together with embedded knowledge and other sunk costs have solidified the original distribution of investments and thus limited the range of possible avenues that might be taken in the time to come (Dosi, 1990).

Two size-related factors are here at play. First and foremost, the modest size of the national economy in small countries like Denmark places tight restrictions on the ability to function as a buffer for supernormal fluctuations in international demands. Second, the limited size of the national knowledge and capital base influences the range of industries in which small nations might successfully specialize.[7] If the technological spillovers are mainly domestic – as claimed by the 'new growth theory' (Grossman and Helpman, 1991, 1995) – large countries will profit more from any investment made in R&D than smaller countries, where some of the spill-over of any such investment is likely to benefit its trading partners.[8]

The restrictions of size have thus gradually channelled the process of specialization towards industries with rather stable demands and low price-elasticity.[9] These industries are often medium or low-tech, but can, nevertheless, yield high profits. Front edge, high-tech industries are to a high extent left to the bigger nations, either by choice or by necessity. Even a nation like Sweden has probably exhausted its economic ability to participate in the race for developing the next generation of advanced military aircraft in spite of an amazing track record of high performance and front-edge technologies in this field.

The Danish specialization pattern is typical in this respect with a long bias towards meat, fish, dairy products, beer (Carlsberg, Tuborg) and related machine industries. Only recently has Denmark also gained ground in non-natural resource, high-value sub-sectors ('niches') within traditional industries like consumer goods (LEGO), clothing, furniture and machinery (Dalum and Villadsen, 1994). It is furthermore striking, that the nation's few high-tech firms – in electronics, medical appliances and pharmaceuticals – are often historically rooted in the agro-industrial industry.

Domestic compensation

The specific profile of industrial specialization towards low-tech or medium-tech products with relatively stable demand and low price-elasticity raises little hope of creating high flyers with extraordinary growth rates[10] and vast net revenues. On the other hand, it does reduce the danger of damaging domestic economic consequences, if the international demand or competitive situation suddenly changes. However, the risk of such unexpected and unavoidable 'imported' dislocations can never be completely eliminated. This is especially the case when imports to Denmark (and other small nations such as the Netherlands) today cover more than 50% of the total national consumption and when almost 40% of the total national production is exported.

Larger nations might choose to reduce the domestic effects of sudden international economic eruptions by various protective measures. Small nations simply do not have the political power to do so, just as they fear immediate retaliation if they ever tried. Therefore, they are forced to react to sudden changes in the international economic environment with rapid adjustments of their *domestic production system*.

Being reactive sometimes implies jeopardizing the vested interest of firms, individuals or larger groups with the power to impede the process of national adjustment.[11] The ability to readjust to sudden changes in the international economy is thus closely connected with the ability to avoid such impediments[12] and specific institutions have been developed to accomplish precisely this. Although the small European nations have made use of profoundly different specific strategies, they have all developed systems to respond to dislocations by compensating those who are specially affected by sudden changes in the international economic environment. In his analysis of this phenomenon Peter Katzenstein notes that:

> elites in the small European states, while letting the international market force economic adjustments, choose a variety of economic and social policies that prevent the costs of change from causing political eruptions. They live with change by compensating for it.

> (1985: 24)

Once a functioning system of domestic compensation for damages endured by 'imported' disruptions is in place, the resistance to change is reduced to a point where the necessary rapid readjustment can take place when needed. The reactive, incremental and flexible pursuit of industrial adjustment might even take place *before* the question of domestic compensation has been settled, *if* these firms, groups or individuals, with the potential power to prevent or delay certain changes, trust that eventually they will be fully satisfied.[13]

Belief in government can therefore be crucial to the national response rate to external economic shocks. The investment in a reputation of reliability becomes a subtle, but essential element in the economic and industrial policy of small nations.

Negotiated economy

Small nations like Denmark have a tradition for working out broad compromises between stakeholders in business, politics and public life in *toto*. The consensus-seeking behaviour is rooted in a special sort of collective learning that takes place when all participants know that their chance of success in international business critically depends on the degree of domestic unity. Dissatisfied partners or neighbours mean continuous problems, which will have negative effects on all. The collective learning taking place when living together – yesterday, today, tomorrow and the day after[14] – seems to convey the message that yielding on some point in order to reach a compromise often gives better long-term results than taking full advantage of a temporarily strong bargaining position.

A common and distinct language, a shared cultural heritage, a sense of unity and participation all reinforce this tendency towards consensus-seeking (just as Belgium is a contemporary example of what might happen when some of these features are lacking). Within the consensus-seeking framework it can be implicitly or explicitly recognized, that criticism and conflict play a positive role in order to identify the arena of interests, where a compromise must be found. On the surface the political picture might look chaotic, but behind the screen the consensus-seeking process is at work. When, for instance, the number of political parties in Denmark rose steeply in the 1970s it was noted that 'Even in their fragmented political pattern there is a broader sense of unity than before' (Boyd, 1978: 30).

In Denmark the consensus-seeking process has interacted with century-old, deep-rooted egalitarian beliefs and an aversion towards conspicuous consumption (Veblen, 1899). Historically this egalitarianism affected not only the income distribution and the distributions of land holdings – both being more even than in the rest of Europe – but turned out to be a decisive factor in the local processing of growth impulses from the world market in ensuring that accumulated capital was directed into productive use[15] (Menzel, 1980). The difference in post-tax incomes between top and bottom in the work force is still very modest compared to other European nations, though a process of divergence has started and is likely to continue in the years to come. Nevertheless it is the extent of the egalitarian structure of the Danish society that continues to distinguish Denmark from most other small developed nations.

In the production and reproduction of the Danish political, cultural and economical identity, the egalitarian tradition and the consensus-seeking behaviour have amalgamated to form a common *informal* institution, which has shaped the means of *formal* decision-making. The result has sometimes been called the 'negotiated economy' (Hernes, 1979; Nielsen and Pederson, 1988), where interest groups from all walks of society are drawn into the decision-making process. A negotiated economy is a specific 'structuring of a society, where an essential part of the allocation of resources is conducted through institutional negotiations between independent decision-making centres in state, organizations and/or corporations' (Nielsen and Pedersen, 1991).

Few who have witnessed the functioning of the negotiated economy at close quarters are likely to feel tempted to praise its simplicity or effectiveness. However, its merit lies on another level: in the way whereby the process of reaching an agreement or decision simultaneously increases the insight in – and understanding of – the other participants' positions, interests and visions. Negotiation in this sense implies learning, which makes the next round of negotiation slightly easier and which enables not just the elites but sometimes even the society at large to reach a common perception of present and future challenges and of the way the society might proceed. When imported disruptions necessitate rapid adjustments in the domestic production system, an already existing platform for intervention is thus sometimes established.

Penalizing opportunism

It is difficult to act in a completely opportunistic manner in a village, without being severely penalized. Utilizing asymmetrical information,[16] or passing defective or sub-standard goods as first class, or creating hold-ups in order to benefit at the expense of others in the local community, will all be noticed. The information of such behaviour will be passed on to everyone, who in the future will tend to take their business elsewhere. Not so on the global market for standard goods, where customers as well as suppliers easily can be substituted. A dissatisfied customer has no way of warning all potential future buyers, hence opportunistic behaviour can continue and become an intrinsic part of the game.

The business community in a small nation like Denmark has very strong elements of the village mechanism. In most lines of business, and certainly within all sectors of the manufacturing industry, the domestic producers know each other either directly or indirectly. Most managers in larger enterprises will meet regularly and many will have known each other personally for years. Even in sectors dominated by a great number of small and medium-size enterprises like plastic production or furniture manufacturing, all producers will have a remarkable degree of knowledge of most other domestic producers in the sector, their main domestic and foreign suppliers and the most important customers (Kautonen, 1996). All firms in the sector will usually be organized in at least one association or guild with nation-wide coverage, with its own publications or newsletter and with annual or more frequent meetings. Many of the managers will share the same background and have received the same education, and most will have participated in some sort of joint activity on the local, the regional or the national level. Within the region the knowledge of each other is even higher and no major incident in a line of business passes unnoticed or uncommented.

The present trend towards sectoral clustering in Denmark and in the other Nordic countries (Maskell *et al.* 1998) reflects the advantage of proximity – not in supply cost or in low lead-time,[17] but in learning. Clusters or industrial districts are not designed. The most important internal institutions, which reinforce the process of clustering, are mainly informal: the quality of the financial services, the technological spill-over, the entrepreneurial rivalry between firms, etc. And most important: the proximity seems to create an even deeper village-like atmosphere where malfeasance is punished and trust relations can be built and utilized in knowledge creation (Maskell and Malmberg, 1999).[18]

Such a business climate does not necessarily lend itself to cooperation and interaction. In more cases than not, the opposite seems to be the case. Small firms in particular often envision the fellow producer down the street as their main competitor and often try hard to outsmart him without damaging the firm's own reputation. Local rivalry of this kind stimulates the entrepreneurial spirit and reinforces productivity in the cluster (Maskell, 2001a). At the same time, the shared history, values and culture nevertheless make certain types of exchange and co-operation easy (Aydalot, 1986). In regions and countries where the majority believe that opportunism is penalized, firms act as if they trust each other (Granovetter, 1985; Saxenian, 1994). And trust – as we know – is a remarkably efficient lubricant to economic exchange. Firms often compete while at the same time helping each other overcome technical problems, by lending materials and swapping surplus capacity or by exchanging information. Lawyers or written contracts are seldom used.[19]

The low barriers for interaction between firms – especially at the local and the regional level – have increasing importance as the use of knowledge gradually intensifies when developing new products and processes and when accessing new markets in new ways. As the developments in the international competition increase the demand for knowledge exchange, new network relations between firms seem to be built at a faster rate than ever before (Axelsson and Easton, 1992). In practice, the effects of a trust-enhancing environment and the active trust building through relation-specific sunk costs will be interconnected. In the pure market economy it is difficult to determine the price for information that will satisfy both buyer and seller (Nelson and Winter, 1982). The buyer wants to establish whether the information offered is worth the requested price, but given this information he or she is no longer on the market: 'its value for the purchaser is not known until he has the information, but then he has in effect acquired it without cost' (Arrow, 1970: 152) and further:

> The cost of transmitting a given body of information is frequently very low … In the absence of special legal protection, the owner cannot, however, simply sell information on the open market. Any one purchaser can destroy the monopoly, since he can reproduce the information at little or no cost.
>
> (Arrow, 1962: 614–615)

The knowledge of these mechanisms will discourage the seller from offering the information in the first place. Such *market failure* can be overcome by taking the transaction away from the market, by the development of long-term trust-based relations between two firms (Ford, 1990; Sabel, 1992) – secured by each firm's investment in relation-specific sunk costs (Eccles, 1981). The market failure can, however, also be overcome by placing the firms in situations where any violation of trust is so severely penalized that in effect, malfeasance becomes a non-option.

The village-like nature of business life in small nations like Denmark contributes to such a trust-creating environment, which does not force the firms to co-operate if they are not so inclined, but which makes co-operation possible for firms with a different frame of mind. Such informal institutions or conventions (Storper, 1994), which lower the barriers for interaction, co-operation or exchange and the creation of knowledge, increase rapidly in economic importance as we turn towards the knowledge-based economy (Maskell, 1999).

It has been shown (von Hippel, 1988) that on a local level, where firms share the same values, background and understanding of technical and commercial problems, such economically beneficial learning-by-interaction does, in fact, exist. In a relevant paper, Fagerberg (1995a)[20] takes this argument a little further by showing that it is not supply factors in each country, but domestic demand-induced innovation, which leads to international competitive advantage in modern Western economies (Porter, 1990). In his study of 16 countries, and 23 pairs[21] of user–producer relationships (Lundvall, 1985) in three years Fagerberg shows that advanced domestic users do have a positive impact on competitiveness, especially if the home market is exposed to foreign competition. He concludes that:

> interaction between users and producers of technology [is] a major impetus to technological change. Interaction, however, involves costs … these are a decreasing function of both the stability of the user-producer relationship and the degree of 'proximity', defined to include factors such as language, the legal system, the educational system etc. Hence, most stable user-producer relationships are of a *national* character.
>
> (Fagerberg, 1995a: 254)

The socially constructed framework, which enables firms to interchange otherwise purely internal information, constitutes an important part of the total set of capabilities which distinguish some nations or regions from others, and enhance the competitiveness of the firms located there.

Hence, Denmark is by and large following a medium or even a low road, rather than pursuing international competitiveness in high growth or high-tech sectors.[22] The relatively high wage level, and the higher value-added, are only to a point related to the supply of capital or labour but are closely related to the nation's total competence.

Competence in an economic system can reside in the individual employees as the result of acquired skills, education, qualification and training. Competence can also reside in the fixed capital of the firms through its investments in machines, etc. And competence can reside in the organizational structure of the firms, where insignificant incremental improvements from learning-by-doing and from repeating tasks all accumulate and gradually result in new and better ways of doing things (Maskell, 2001b). These improvements will in due course be embedded in the daily life of the firm as cost-reducing *routines*, representing 'the transmission in time of our accumulated stock of knowledge' (von Hayek, 1960: 27).

In the Danish case the combined effect of the three forms of competence can, perhaps, explain how the economy is able to sustain the relatively high level of income year after year. However, it seems likely that a major contribution must come from a fourth type of competence: *interorganizational competence*.

Interorganizational competence includes the routines and conventions that make the economic system function without undue fuss and with accordingly small transaction costs: the costs of identifying a possible business partner and of persuading, negotiating, co-ordinating, understanding and controlling each step in the transaction(s) with the partner. It is enhanced by the shared culture of the nation or region described in an earlier section of this chapter (Dei Ottati, 2002).

For instance, the collective learning in the handling and processing of fish, in agro-industry, in the processing of wood to furniture and so on, continuously eliminates technical and organizational problems and converts them to a matter of routine: this is the way we do things, and nobody needs to give it further thought for the time being. Such a procedure will often be fatal on the high road of development, with its sudden shifts in technological trajectory, demand pattern or fierceness of competition.[23] It is, however, rather safe when moving slowly on the quiet and less glorious road of low-tech learning, avoiding the disruptions of rapidly changing technology or of sudden demand shifts.

All progress in the refinement of inter-organizational routines increases efficiency by lowering the total transaction costs (Langlois, 1992). When long-term national or regional collective learning has taken place in a line of business, the costs of using the market – as opposed to relying only on intra-firm activities – diminish to a point at which a territorial industrial configuration of small firms only might become even more efficient than a configuration with larger firms, burdened with the cost of internal control and measures against shirking (Alchian and Demsetz, 1972).[24] Thus, a business environment that enhances trust will always make an economic difference, but when the traditional, static, cost-related international competition is superseded by competition based on dynamic improvements and learning (Lundvall and Maskell, 2000), the importance of such an environment increases dramatically.

Formal institutions

The discussion thus far might be thought to neglect the role played by designed or formal institutions. This imbalance will be partly rectified in the following sections, starting with a general introduction to some of the central elements in the Danish political system.

Governance structure and policy stances

There is something slightly surprising in the fact that though the Danish Social-Democratic Party has been in power for a large part of the twentieth century, no 'master plan' has been drafted, nor has any detailed working programme for the overall industrial development been put to work. On the contrary, the Danish industrial policy of the past thirty years can only be described as liberal (Sidenius, 1983), with dominant elements of 'hands off' policies. There is, furthermore, no tradition dictating the government to bail out corporate basket cases so when the country's only steelwork went bankrupt in the spring of 2002 bringing about the loss of more than 1,000 jobs in the small community it dominated, no political party, no union or organization, not even the local municipality argued that the government should step in.[25]

In general, the government is not perceived as having superior knowledge of the business world, which would enable it to intervene in the 'natural' course of events or in the trajectory of the technological development. Although the emphasis surely differs, the strong interest groups for both employers and employees all agree on the broader point, that the government should concentrate on establishing a stable and favourable macro-economic environment with low inflation rates, fixed exchange rates, gradual and controlled growth in domestic costs, including wage levels (Table 6.3) and taxes (Table 6.4),[26] and a rate of interest close to (or preferably below) the German one. The government is

Table 6.3 Real wage per employed (index 1965 = 100)

	1970	1980	1990	1998	1999	2000
Denmark	121	146	166	183	185	186
Sweden	120	147	159	176	179	184
Germany	133	183	206	186	188	187
UK	122	159	188	203	209	217
USA	110	120	127	138	142	145
Japan	150	217	252	259	258	261

Source: OECD (2001) and Statistics Denmark: *Statistical Fifty-Year Review 2001* (CD-ROM)

Table 6.4 The tax burden 1950–2000 (as a percentage of GNP)

Denmark	1950	1960	1970	1980	1990	1999	2000
Income tax etc.	9.2	12.3	21.0	25.0	28.3	30.1	28.9
VAT	0.0	0.0	7.4	9.8	9.8	9.7	9.4
Other indirect taxes	9.7	12.6	10.1	8.2	7.3	8.3	7.5
Other taxes	1.6	1.4	1.7	1.0	1.7	2.3	2.4
Total	20.5	26.4	40.2	44.1	47.1	50.4	48.2

Source: Statistics Denmark: *Statistical Fifty-Year Review* (2001) (CD-ROM)

habitually only called to step in if and when serious imported disruptions necessitate compensatory measures.

On all the major macro-economic issues, the difference between social democratic and conservative-led governments of the period has chiefly been marginal, thus reflecting the consensus-seeking nature of the negotiated economy. However, this has not prevented notions of 'leading sectors' and 'sundown'-industries from entering the public debate, supported by quarters in the Social Democratic party, the left wing, a few but politically important unions and parts of the governmental apparatus. Plans have been forwarded – with some initial success in the late 1980s and early 1990s – to develop an 'active' industrial policy, based on public economic support for the supposed 'winners' of tomorrow in order to increase their competitiveness and thereby put the nation on the fast track (Rasmussen, 1989). These ideas have now more or less petered out as many of the perceived winners went bust, while allegedly doomed industries thrived. New research results and understanding of the roots of sustained competitiveness – mainly through the works of Porter (1990) and the subsequent revival of Penrosian resource-based thinking – further fuelled this development.

An important device in this process has been the ongoing studies of the major Danish industrial strongholds (resource areas), consisting of value-chain analysis of interrelated industries – often with an above-average market share – including their upstream suppliers, their supporting industries as well as their main customers.[27] The studies were originated by the Council of Industrial Development *(Erhvervsudviklingsrådet,* now discontinued) with representatives from the largest firms, the federation of industrialists, the unions, the SMEs, the universities, and so on; in short, a typically Danish consensus-seeking body. The eight most important strongholds covering approximately 90% of all economic activity in Denmark (93% of value added, 87% of total export, 89% of employment) have been published, identifying the main strategic issues for each stronghold (Box 6.1). A further breakdown of the total Danish export and import on countries is shown in Table 6.5 for the whole period from 1945 to 1994. The development in the annual growth etc. of Danish exports and imports is shown in Table 6.6.

As a result of these studies and reflections a different paradigm is now emerging in Danish industrial policy. It is market-conformist in the sense that it explicitly avoids even Commission-permitted subsidies to individual firms or industries (the domestic implications of EU agricultural policy being the major exception) and mainly depends on the workings of the market mechanism. However, it is at the same time selective in its recognition of the necessity to build on the distinctive industrial pattern of specialization in Denmark.

Together, these two elements have redirected industrial policy towards improving the framework conditions of each industry: the technological and physical infrastructure, the skills and qualifications available on the labour market,

BOX 6.1: Identified industrial strongholds ('resource areas')

Food: 14% of value added,[28] 14% of employment, 21% of export

Strategic issues: Over-capacity. Regulation-based supply problems. Regulation and problems of market access: retailers increasing power.

Construction, housing: 13% of value added, 15% of employment, 7% of export
Strategic issues: Low productivity and low international competence. Low quality levels in management and bad logistic performance.

Medico/health: 3% of value added, 2% of employment, 4% of export
Strategic issues: High growth and high risk, leading to increasing capital demand. Growing importance of international R&D and collaboration with hospitals and doctors.

Transport/Communication: 11% of value added, 12% of employment, 20% of export
Strategic issues: Highly fragmented industry, low levels of competence and increasing competition, partly as a result of trends towards international deregulation.

Environment/Energy: 6% of value added, 4% of employment, 6% of export
Strategic issues: Increasing demands for financial competence, internationalization and accelerated innovations. Importance of customer demand for future product development.

Tourism/Leisure: 6% of value added, 6% of employment, 3% of export
Strategic issues: Many free riders and few producers of tourist products. Lack of relevant transfer mechanism from the beneficiaries (hotels, restaurants, transport services) to the producers of attractions. No one responsible for the product.

Consumer goods: 4% of value added, 6% of employment, 3% of export
Strategic issues: Lack of co-operation. Bad quality management. Increasing power at retailers.

Service (incl. retailing and wholesales): 33% of value added, 30% of employment, 23% of export

Table 6.5 Danish export and import of commodities (current prices in billion[4] DKK)

	1950	1960	1970	1980	1990	1995	2000
Total Export	5	10	25	96	216	264	403
Finland				2	6	7	14
Sweden			4	12	28	26	53
Belgium[1]				2	5	5	7
France[2]				5	13	15	20
Greece					2	2	3
Netherlands				4	10	12	20
Italy				5	11	10	13
Portugal					1	2	2
Spain					4	5	9
UK	2	3	5	14	23	21	40
Germany		2	3	19	43	61	76
E. Germany							
W. Germany		2	3	18			
Austria					2	3	4
USA			2	4	11	11	14
Japan				2	7	11	15
Total Import	6	12	33	109	196	232	361
Finland				4	6	7	10
Sweden		1	5	14	23	28	44
Belgium[1]				4	6	9	40
France[2]			1	5	10	13	18
Greece						0	1
Netherlands			1	8	11	17	27
Italy			1	3	8	10	16
Portugal					2	3	3
Spain					2	3	5
UK	2	2	5	13	15	16	31
Germany					45	52	76
E. Germany							
W. Germany		3	6	20			
Austria				1	2	2	4
USA		1	2	7	12	12	15
Japan				2	8	6	5
DKK/US$ exchange rate[3]	6.92	6.89	7.49	5.63	6.18	5.60	8.08

Notes:
1 Including Luxembourg.
2 Including Monaco.
3 Monthly average.
4 American billion, corresponding to one thousand million, or one British trillion.

Source: Statistics Denmark. *Statistical Yearbook* (1996:364, 366–367 and 200: 371). *Exchange rates:* OECD Main Economic Indicators Database and Statistics Denmark: *Statistical Fifty-Year Review* (2001) (CD-ROM).

Table 6.6 Development in prices for export and import

Denmark	1950	1960	1970	1980	1990	1999	2000
Export prices, goods (1948 = 100)	98	109	141	318	483	532	564
Export prices, goods (1948 = 100)	109	112	131	368	489	492	529
Balance of trade, goods (1948 = 100)	90	97	107	86	99	108	107

Source: Statistics Denmark, *Statistical Fifty-Year Review* (2001) (CD-ROM)

the functioning of the capital market, the quality of the supply system, and so on.[29] This turn in policy is reflected in govermental statements such as:

> The macro policy cannot produce a permanent increase in the national standard of living. The supply, quality and productivity of such factors of production as equipment, knowledge, labour and infrastructure are decisive for the national economic performance in the long run.
>
> (Ministry of Finance, 1992)

> The tendency until now has been to concentrate the industrial policy on grants and other such economic incentives to industry. However, detailed studies of firms' framework conditions show that initiatives in areas such as traffic and communication, publicly financed research, education, demand from the public sector, regulation and service all have greater impact on the development of the firms in any industry.
>
> (Ministry of Industry, 1993)

The appropriate instruments to enhance the competitiveness of firms in, for instance, pharmaceuticals (medico/health) might be public investments in R&D and public support for building contacts between industry and research to disseminate new knowledge. It might further be the creation of demanding customers through investments in public health programs and through specialization in hospitals.

However, the appropriate instruments in other industries would be very different. Infrastructure investments and programmes to improve market access (language training, network formation to strengthen market bargaining power, etc.) are of the highest priority for firms in the consumer goods industries. Educational programmes are more important in, for example, the leisure industry.

The conclusion drawn from this exercise is that a good industrial policy is also a *differentiated* industrial policy. The role of macro-economic policy is to ensure stability and incentives to work and produce. The role of industrial policy is to eliminate bottlenecks and barriers on the path that the industry (and not the government) has chosen to follow and to increase the competitiveness of firms by supplying a favourable environment of demanding and supporting entities.

As the economic resources available are limited, a number of short-lived advisory boards and committees are almost continuously set up to identify the best way of doing this in practice. They interact and, in a sense, compete with a large amount of sometimes even more influential organizations and interest groups outside the formal structure of government. The negotiated economy is in play.

Institutions for diffusion of technological innovations

A number of surveys have been conducted over the years on how Danish firms learn about global innovations. Not surprisingly, the results differ with firm size. The large, globally oriented firms usually have R&D departments of their own, monitoring international progress within the firms' field of interest. Sometimes these large firms plug into knowledge pools throughout the world by outsourcing parts of the current research portfolio and reaping the results, by obtaining access to foreign labs through co-operation or procurement, and by establishing their own facilities in international research growth points.

However, many SMEs obtain the bulk of their information on new products, new processes, new materials and other input, and on new production equipment through the market – by visits of sales representatives, service personnel and consultants from upstream suppliers. Sometimes these sources might be supplemented by information emerging downstream. This is, for instance, the case within the furniture industry, where Ikea, the global outlet for household furniture, on a regular basis informs their suppliers and subcontractors of innovations and improvements. Also, trade organizations, fairs, catalogues and other written material are important.

As a supplement – and only as a supplement (though the officers employed often tend to inflate its importance) – to these established channels of information, the Danish government has established an elaborate system to monitor and disseminate knowledge (mainly technological) of relevance for the SMEs. Within agriculture, this long-term effort has probably been decisive for the high productivity levels reached. The parallel system aimed at assisting the manufacturing industry, etc. was established more than eighty years ago, and comprises the Technological Institute (TI) – where the two departments[30] with a turnover in 2001 of US$ 81m (678m DKK) now employ approximately 900 people and have a connected network of sixteen local Technological Information Centres (TIC) spread throughout the

BOX 6.2: Medicon Valley in the Øresund Region

The establishment of several different industry centres within, for example, medico/life science, ICT, food processing, maritime industry and telecommunication, illustrates the ambition to develop the Øresund Region into one of Europe's most integrated and functional border regions.

'The Øresund region' is the chosen label for a cross-border area spanning the Metropolitan Copenhagen Region (governed by the co-ordinating cross-county body HUR) in Denmark and stretching into southern Sweden, including the province of Scania (governed by a regional council). In total the area has a population of 3.2 million inhabitants and a strong concentration of universities, research institutions and science parks. An 'Øresund Committee' was established in 1993 by the Greater Copenhagen county authorities, (the counties of Copenhagen, Frederiksborg and Roskilde, and the municipalities of Copenhagen and Frederiksberg) as well as regional and local authorities of Scania (Sweden). In 1999 the membership was extended to comprise neighbouring Danish counties outside the metropolitan area (Vestsjælland, Storstrøm and Bornholm.)

The idea of creating a centre for pharmaceutical and biotechnological companies was introduced in the early 1990s when governmental reports identified the potential of business development within life sciences, as 60 per cent of all Scandinavian pharmaceutical firms were located in the region. Both Denmark and Sweden have a strong pharmaceutical research tradition and an industry whose exports of pharmaceutical products are sufficiently high to put both countries in the group of five highest exporters per capita. By 1997, the Øresund Committee had initiated the creation of 'The Medicon Valley Academy' (MVA) to spur development and support interaction between private companies, universities, hospitals, science parks, research institutions and providers of knowledge-intensive services.

As of 2002, the research environment includes the main universities of Lund and Malmö (Sweden) and Copenhagen and Roskilde (Denmark), together with independent research institutions, such as the Wallenberg Neuroscience Centre, the Department of Biotech – Centre for Biological Sequence Analysis, the Institute of Medical Biochem and Genetics and the Swedish Institute of Food & Biotechnology, as well as public hospitals where clinical research is a main competence. The Science Parks (Ideon, Medeon, Symbion and the Danish Science Park in Hørsholm) in Medicon Valley, of which Ideon Science Park in Lund is the oldest and largest in Scandinavia, house a number of small and medium-sized companies specializing in biotechnology and IT and also have a strong profile within biotechnology.

Medicon Valley's research position has been ranked no. 3 in Europe for R&D spending in the pharmaceutical industry and biomedicine. In the European Top 10 list of health care regions, Medicon Valley has a strong position within the fields of biotechnology and applied microbiology, immunology, endocrinology, diabetes and metabolism, infectious diseases, neuroscience, oncology, biochemistry and molecular biology. The scientific research in these areas has generated a number of new companies and attracted foreign pharmaceutical and biotechnological companies while others are the result of local spin-offs. Many first-tier multinational pharmaceutical companies have chosen to set up offices in the region (such as Beaufort Ibsen, Biogen, Ferring Pharmaceuticals, Pfizer, Yamanouchi Pharmaceuticals, Eli Lily, GlaxoSmithKline, Bristol Myers Squibb and Amgen) in order to gain direct access to the knowledge created and exchanged within the region. The attractiveness of the region is enhanced by the constant inflow of government funding to basic research and by the formation of very targeted venture capital companies such as HealthCap, BankInvest, Medicon Valley Capital and Novo A/S – a new investment company created and fully owned by the Novo Nordisk Foundation. In recent years, several international venture companies, such as the UK based 3i, the Finnish BIO Fund and the Geneva-based Index Ventures hare also actively invested in funding new companies and expansion capital for existing companies in the region.

Other major regional activities include the building of a formal consortium between the twelve local universities to encourage the co-ordinating of courses and the creation of joint PhD programmes, though this activity is still at a very initial stage. The Øresund Science region was established with the purpose of promoting innovation, growth and the transfer of knowledge through co-operation between the various institutions (Medicon Valley Academy, IT Øresund, Øresund Food Network, Øresund Environment and the Øresund Science Region).

Even though the activity level has been high and the political backing substantial, it must be admitted that the cross-border co-operation has been somewhat restricted and the realized spill-overs much fewer than perhaps initially hoped for. The many unanticipated problems of integrating institutions developed separately in different national contexts have, together with differences in culture and business practices, contributed to dampen the previously high expectations. However, with the gradual emergence of a more sober and less sanguine approach, there is still reason to expect that the policy initiatives taken will eventually on balance merit the costs by providing benefits beyond what could be expected if a purely hands-off stand had been taken.

country[31] – and FORCE/DELTA, which specializes in supplying advanced technological information within selected areas.[32] On top of this established structure new government-led initiatives have come into existence in recent years.[33]

Finally, the universities, business schools and polytechnics all play a role in servicing industry. Most important in this respect is by far the knowledge conveyed through new generations of university candidates employed in industry, but some incidents of a closer day-to-day interaction have been recorded. The small cluster of highly specialized firms producing mobile phones and advanced radio communication equipment in Northern Jutland has thus benefited from their co-operation with the local Aalborg University (Dalum and Villumsen, 1994; Dalum, 1995) as has the emergence of a significant agglomeration of biotech firms ('Medicon Valley' – see Box 6.2) in the Copenhagen region on both the Swedish and Danish sides of the border (Maskell and Törnqvist, 1999).

Environmental institutions

A new actor in the technological game is the environmental authorities at the local, regional and national levels. Together with public opinion and customer demand they have had a growing influence on the investment pattern and internal restructuring in many industries. The Ministry of the Environment has set (and controlled) firm- or industry-specific pollution limits, and has introduced economic incentives, information programmes, and so on. The Parliament has further implemented a system of 'green' taxation on natural resources (water, energy) and waste. As a result, the manufacturing industry has moved – or is in the process of moving – from 'end-of-pipe' solutions to new technologies with some degree of recycling, resource savings and reduction in the use or production of environmentally damaging materials or waste.

The most important change in attitude – according to sample surveys – has not been brought about by environmental legislation or through the efforts of the environmental agencies to distribute smart pamphlets or establish on-line databases with green information on products or processes, but through market-conformist impulses: rapid (designed) increase in resource-prices and pressure from employees who see the connection between improved working conditions and the greening of industry. Perhaps even more important is the industry's recognition that customers actually might want environmentally sound products and production processes, and that their competitors are starting to meet this demand. The resulting innovative activity even in small firms is sometimes truly amazing, and sometimes the results can even be sold at a profit.

The often heated public discussion on the economic growth-inhibiting effects of all greening of industry has gradually diminished as practical experience has been gained, profits earned, and the inevitability of the process accepted.

Human capital and employment

The Danish educational level only slightly exceeds the OECD average – with the main difference being a stronger tradition for secondary schooling – but significantly below the levels found in the USA (Table 6.7). The former gap in the average length of education between men and woman is, however, rapidly closing, and the proportion of female university candidates in areas like medicine and law exceeds the male. The same has long been the case in for example, teacher training and social sector educations.

International comparative surveys point out that in spite of substantially higher annual costs per primary school pupil compared to most other countries, the testable skills (in reading and mathematics, etc.) are not at all impressive. Certain improvements in standards in the Danish primary school system seem to be slowly materializing as a result. The universities and business schools are experiencing the same tendencies towards bibliometric evaluation and a similar output-related interest from the government as in many other countries in Europe, and have felt a need to proceed with and expand on already established procedures for quality control in research and in educational activities (Maskell and Törnqvist, 1999).

The intermediate layer of education has experienced a gradual shift in the students' interest away from technical specialities and towards commercial and humanistic areas. Here, too, restructuring – with decentralization of responsibility and power – is in progress.

The vocational training system in Denmark consists of a great many different institutions that offer courses of very variable length and content. A summation of all these activities show that in 2000, vocational training corresponded to more than 95,400 'full-year courses'[34] with a total budget of US$ 543m (with 84 per cent covered by public subsidies to salaries, facilities and administration). A breakdown of the participants into age groups shows that the Danish vocational training programmes place a comparatively greater emphasis on the older members of the workforce (Table 6.8).

Since 1974 the number of industrial disputes – though already at a low level – has further decreased, just as the number of working days lost because of, for example, sickness is only a fraction of what it was in the 1960s. However, the risk of unemployment is closely associated with the level of education received: an unskilled person faces the risk of becoming completely unemployed two to three times higher than an individual who has received more than five years post-primary school education.

White-collar workers are guaranteed a minimum notice if laid off and the length of the notice is regulated in accordance with the number of years they have been employed in the firm, but many will have an individual contract specifying

Table 6.7 Education levels in selected OECD countries, 1999

	Highest education attained by the population (aged 25 to 64) (%)			
	Primary	*Secondary*	*Tertiary*	*Total*
Denmark	20	53	27	100
Sweden	23	48	29	100
Germany	19	58	23	100
UK	18	57	25	100
France	38	41	21	100
USA	13	52	35	100
OECD total	36	42	22	100

Source: Statistics Denmark, *Statistical Yearbook* (2001: 532)

Table 6.8 Participation in training outside formal education: expected hours of training outside formal education and net participation rates, 1994–98

		Participation rate, by age group				
	Years of participation[1]	*25–34*	*35–44*	*45–54*	*55–64*	*Total 25–64*
Austria	1.0	30	32	26	18	27
Belgium (Fl.)	0.8	23	20	21	12	20
Canada	N/A	32	37	28	12	30
Denmark	2.7	50	59	56	34	51
Finland	3.2	59	62	57	31	54
Italy	0.7	21	25	19	9	19
Netherlands	1.7	38	35	30	16	31
Norway	2.0	46	49	46	26	44
Poland	0.9	17	17	14	N/A	13
Portugal	N/A	25	12	10	5	12
Sweden	N/A	48	56	56	38	51
UK	1.4	43	45	38	22	38
USA	1.4	35	41	43	28	38

Note:
1   The estimate is based on all courses regardless of length or form being converted to full-time equivalents of 30 hours coursework per week and 40 weeks per year.

Source: International Adult Literacy Survey, 1995–1998. Here quoted from: OECD (2001, Table C1.5: 137).

an even longer period. The exceptionally large group of civil servants in Denmark (Table 6.9) has historically had a very high degree of job security, though cuts in the public sector have gradually diminished the security from its one-time high. The blue-collar workers, however, have no job guarantee and can be fired at very short notice – officially in order to increase the flexibility of the labour market and ensure that the employers will not be restrained in creating jobs because of fear of being stuck with an excess workforce tomorrow. A large proportion of blue-collar workers are thus hit by unemployment for longer or (often) shorter spells throughout the year. In order to make such a system function high levels of unemployment benefits must be available (Estevez-Abé *et al.*, 2001).[35]

Due to the high rate of unionization in the Danish workforce (Table 6.10), the unions or their federations have throughout the last quarter of a century been important and active players in the negotiated economy, not just on questions related to the labour market, but also on tax and financial policy, cultural and social policy, industrial and technological policy, and so on. In recent years, parts of the biannual negotiation of wage and working conditions between the unions and the employers have been decentralized to the individual firms, enabling the management and the employees to find local solutions. It is too early to comment on the results of this development but it signals a general move from a very collective system with uniform solutions and a high degree of predictability of future earnings and openings for the individual towards a much more diverse, individualistic and rights-based society. However, it is worth stressing that, though this emerging trend has increased the difference between regions, the redistribution of income and costs through the elaborate system of public taxes and transfers has until now kept the gaps within tighter limits than in any other country in the OECD. The egalitarian underpinning of all political processes has so far succeeded in reducing the gale of liberalization to a mild and almost agreeable breeze that evidently appeal to most walks of society.

The future

Supported by the somewhat favourable present development in Denmark's economic performance (OECD annual country reports, etc.) and a significant annual surplus on the balance of payment, it is generally felt that the country is on the right track.

The economic upswing in the latter part of the 1990s has completely changed the situation on the labour market in many of the former peripheral and unemployment-ridden regional development areas in Denmark – where some sectors report of full employment and others of a growing number of unfilled jobs available. In the most recent years, the larger cities and especially the Copenhagen Region have gained new momentum after several decades of

Table 6.9 Employment in Denmark 1948–2000

Denmark	1950	1960	1970	1980	1990	1999	2000
Primary sector	580	449	270	194	143	102	100
Secondary sector	683	767	858	690	647	613	615
Tertiary sector, private	780	859	946	999	1,081	1,175	1,194
Tertiary sector, public	143	203	389	651	734	775	778
Total employment	2,187	2,279	2,463	2,534	2,606	2,665	2,686
Total employment (excl. self-employed)	1,715	1,818	2,069	2,212	2,366	2,468	2,490
Percentage							
Primary sector	26	20	11	8	6	4	4
Secondary sector	31	34	35	27	25	23	23
Tertiary sector, private	36	38	38	39	42	44	44
Tertiary sector, public	6	9	16	26	28	29	29

Note: in 000s.
Source: Statistics Denmark, *Statistical Fifty-Year Review* (2001) (CD-ROM).

Table 6.10 Total workforce (including the unemployed), 1950–1999/2000 and union membership

Denmark	1950	1960	1970	1980	1990	1999	2000
Total workforce (persons in thousands)	2063	2094	2390	2746	2908	2880	2877
Total workforce (as percentage of the total population aged 15–69)	71%	67%	70%	77%	79%	76%	76%
– Men	96%	94%	87%	86%	84%	81%	81%
– Women	47%	41%	54%	68%	73%	71%	71%
Ratio of union membership (as percentage of the total workforce)	35%	46%	48%	64%	71%	75%	75%

Sources: Statistics Denmark, *Statistical Fifty-Year Review* (2001) (CD-ROM) and *Statistical Ten-Year Review* (2001: 47–48)

stagnation. The process is fuelled by the growth in the skills-based services that favour a location in the larger cities, and by the growing emphasis placed on building relations between the major companies and the universities. Furthermore, it is supported by the development on the real estate market where private property investments in the larger cities are expected to give a much better payback than buying a house in a rural setting or a small and remote town. However, the redistribution policies, widespread usage of ICT[36] and the improvements in the country's physical infrastructure (construction of major high capacity motorways and bridges and rail improvements) have together significantly lessened the burden of a remote location.

The main point of political disagreement concerns the way to handle immigration. A much tougher stand has gradually been taken by the social democrats and the liberal parties alike regarding acceptance of new immigrants from less developed countries, just as a broad consensus is emerging on the need for new policy measures to improve integration of accepted immigrants, some of which (especially from the Middle East and Africa) have had very low labour market participation rates while receiving various forms of social security on an almost permanent basis. In addition to questioning the wisdom of the special way the Danish welfare system functions, many legislators became worried by the prospect of continuously high unemployment rates also for the second and third generation of immigrants (Table 6.11) and the low *female* labour market participation rate for immigrants, etc. (48 per cent) compared to Danish citizens (74 per cent). Even though the present favourable economic conditions have occasioned a general scarcity of labour in many industries and regions, the unemployment rates among immigrants from less developed countries is still far above average and the best way to cope with this fact is bound to remain a heated issue in the years to come.

Conclusion

This chapter has argued that the influence of the national and the regional institutional endowment on economic development is fundamental and that crucial features and distinctions are not at all washed away by the formation of global markets. What appears to be a global, convergent development is in fact constituted by firms deeply rooted in specific territorial settings, and the influence of the firms' locational setting is, furthermore, often of paramount significance for their long-term competitiveness.

The evidence presented from Denmark indicates that although policy and formal institutions surely play a role, much of today's advances in economic life are in reality shaped by informal institutions and conventions, which are constantly reproduced and modified through the interaction and learning which has taken

Table **6.11** Unemployed immigrants (first and subsequent generation) as a percentage of immigrants (first and subsequent generation)in the workforce 1992–2000

	1992	1994	1996	1998	2000
From more developed countries[1]	17	19	15	12	9
– First generation[2]	18	20	15	12	9
– Subsequent generations[3]	15	15	12	9	6
From less developed countries[1]	37	43	32	23	18
– First generation[2]	37	44	33	24	18
– Subsequent generations[3]	12	16	13	9	8
Total	26	29	22	17	13
Total (number of persons)	27,955	34,713	28,586	24,047	19,250

Notes:
1   More developed countries include the USA, Canada, Japan, Australia, New Zealand and all European countries except Turkey, Cypress, Azerbaijan, Armenia, Uzbekistan, Turkmenistan, Georgia, Tadzhikistan, Kazakhstan, Kyrgizstan (but including Russia, Eastern Europe and the Baltic republics). Less developed countries include all other countries (based on UN: World Population Prospects 1994).
2   Persons born outside Denmark by parents both being non-Danish citizens.
3   Persons born in Denmark by parents, who were both born outside Denmark while being non-Danish citizens.
Source: Statistics Denmark (2001a).

place between and within groups at all levels of the society. The market economy is in this sense a conglomerate of territorially defined entities, each with a specific and embedded mixture of peculiarities resulting from the specific development path taken. Time and space interact in creating restrictions on the distribution of opportunities available to the firms of today where the influence of government can only be marginal, indirect and long term.

Acknowledgements

This is a slightly updated version of a chapter published in: H.-J. Braczyk, P. Cooke and M. Heidenreich (eds) *Regional Innovation Systems. The Role of Governance in a Globalized World* (1997), London: UCL-Press, pp. 190–213. The table updates were carried out by Maria-Theresa Larsen, while Louise Stefansen, provided the specific information included in this update on Medicon Valley. I acknowledge the support provided by FORA/Center for Business and Economic Research during the update.

Notes

1   The cost of research in private firms was 0.4% of GDP in Denmark in 1970, compared with 0.9 in Sweden and 1.5 in Germany and in the UK. In 1993 the Danish level had risen to 1.1% compared to 1.4 in the UK, 1.7 in Germany and 2.2 in Sweden. By 1999, business enterprise expenditure on R&D was 1.2% of GDP in Denmark, 2.8% in Sweden, 1.7% in Germany, 1.2% in the UK and 1.4% in the whole of the OECD (OECD, 2002, 1: 23).

2   This might be compared with (thousand US$ per capita (2000)) the UK's 24, Germany's 23, France's 22, Italy's 19, the USA's 36 or Japan's 38 (OECD Statistics, Online). Annual comparison of levels of GDP per capita (July 2002), available on http://www.oecd.org/M00018000/M00018518.pdf.

3   Immigration (see later sections) tends to increase the average unemployment rate. The proportion unemployed of all Danish citizens in the workforce in 2001 was 5.0 % compared to 6–7% from immigrants from North America or the other EU countries, 14% if from the rest of Europe including Turkey, 18% for African immigrants and above 25% for immigrants from Iraq or Lebanon (Statistics Denmark: *Statistical Yearbook 2001*).

4   This process of imitation sometimes also witnesses the existence of leaks in the national scientific and technological system, leading to a process of territorial dispersal or 'trickling-down' (Hirshmann, 1975: 187–190), which is an important part of less developed nations or regions 'catching up' with the most developed (Cornwall 1969, 1977; Olson, 1982).

5   Reviews and discussions of this swelling literature can be found in Malmberg and Maskell (1997, 2002).

6   It must be mentioned that the European movements of labour across borders are very insignificant and have until now only involved a little cross-border commuting, a few workers engaged in temporary jobs in the construction industry or some workers in the transport sector, and finally a group of bureaucrats. They are, however, nowhere near what was anticipated when this issue was originally discussed before the signing of the Treaty of Rome. The low mobility is significantly different from the situation in the USA. Even on a cross-regional scale, labour can hardly be considered a mobile factor of production in most European countries.

7   Drèze (1989) was the first to forward this 'standard goods hypothesis', and Melchior (1995) presents new empirical evidence on this, while Fagerberg (1995b) uses a different approach to address the same question. One should note that the specific specialization of small countries like Austria and Switzerland is very different from the specialization in the Benelux countries, which again is different from the Nordic countries. All have by and large a specialization in natural resource-based products. The specific products that

dominate the Nordic Countries include metal and ore, paper and pulp, fish and wood, etc. For a further discussion on specialization patterns and divergence/convergence, see Dalum, (1996).

8 See also Zander and Kogut (1995) on this. Furthermore, the 'new trade theory' (Krugman, 1994b) maintains that countries are likely to specialize in sectors and commodities for which the domestic market is of particular importance. The home market for high-tech commodities seldom plays such a role in small countries. Empirical investigations indicate, however, a limited effect of such spill-overs in manufacturing industries (Fagerberg, 1995b).

9 The empirical evidence of a low price-elasticity is, however, not very solid and might still be questioned.

10 The limited number of workers available often acts as a further barrier to rapid growth in one sector and a sustained demand might just fuel inflation.

11 For a discussion on the resulting national or regional lock-in, see David (1985), Arthur (1989) and Friedrichs (1993). In his analysis of changes in the rate of economic growth and development at the level of the nation state Mancur Olson (1982) presents further evidence to suggest that vested interest increasingly encumber economies during periods of stability, and therefore results in a deceleration of economic growth (cf. North, 1994).

12 Imai *et al.* (1986: 373) contribute an important part of Japan's economic success to the ability to unlearn former organizational or institutional rigidities through the acceptance of managerial declarations of a state of emergency or crisis, which makes radical changes easier to swallow.

13 Although such a mechanism sometimes increases the rate of response of small nations, this is neither universal nor unlimited. On the contrary, it is often possible to find specific situations where a group with a vested interest in maintaining the status quo may block necessary changes for a shorter or longer time.

14 The low mobility rate in European countries thus plays an economically important though often overlooked role.

15 If Adam Smith was right in claiming that 'The chief enjoyment of riches consists of the parade of riches', a society which bans conspicuous consumption and praises egalitarianism will tend to direct any surplus created into the available and socially acceptable outlet: new productive investments.

16 The problems of asymmetrical information are illustrated by Barzel:

> For example, determining the weight of an orange may be a low-cost, accurate operation. Yet what is weighed is seldom what is truly valued. The skin of the orange hides its pulp, making a direct measurement of the desired attributes costly. Thus the taste and the amount of juice it contains are always a bit surprising. The grower, more knowledgeable than the consumer, may gain by making the surprise an unpleasant one. The potential errors in

weighing the commodity and in assessing its attributes permit manipulations and therefore require safeguards.

(1982: 27)

17   That lead-time plays a minor role is confirmed by a number of interviews with business in such clusters in Denmark and reflects the efficiency of distribution systems in Northern Europe: goods can be ordered from warehouses located in Northern Germany or Sweden one day, and be at the factory gate the next.

18   It is interesting to note that the experimental literature indicates that income-maximizing individuals' ideas about fairness etc. – which is part of the egalitarian perception of the world – may have significant consequences for the off-the-equilibrium-path incentives and subsequent off-the-equilibrium-path behaviour in a way that influences the outcome (Prasnikar and Roth, 1992).

19   In his still very readable account of this phenomenon, Macaulay could have been addressing the situation in Denmark when he observes that

> even when the parties have a detailed and carefully planned agreement which indicates what is to happen if, say, the seller fails to deliver on time, often they will never refer to the agreement but will negotiate a solution when the problem arises as if there never had been any original contract.

(1963: 61)

20   Following Linder (1961).

21   A pair consists of an export product and a home market sector. 'Milking machines' and 'dairy products' will, for instance, constitute a pair as will 'sewing machinery' and 'clothing'.

22   Thus, direct foreign investments in Denmark have traditionally been on a rather modest level compared with most of the country's EU partners. The first foreign firms to be established in Denmark include ABB (1920), Colgate (1926), Phillips (1933) and Shell (1939). Today around 2,500 firms (out of 280,000 = 9%), with approximately 150,000 employees are owned by legal entities outside Denmark. The larger foreign-owned firms include ABB (with 2,300 employees in 2001 and a turnover of US$400m); Hydro Texaco (222 employees, US$350m in turnover) Shell (1475 employees and US$1100m) and MAN B&W Diesel A/S (2280 employees and US$200m in turnover in 2000).

23   The concept of a 'high road' of constructive competition was introduced in Sengenberger and Pyke (1992: 12), in the somewhat different context of assessing the developmental effects of labour standards.

24   The existence of such general relative benefits for smaller firms are not the same as saying that no larger firms can exist. Denmark does, in fact, have a number of larger enterprises, though their proportion of the total industry is

smaller than in most other countries. Only 19% of Danish firms had more than 500 employees, compared with 36% in Germany, 32% in the UK, 33% in France and 42% in Sweden. Only Italy shared Denmark's size structure. The average turnover for the 100 largest enterprises in Denmark was US$697,000 million in 1992 compared with US$8,921,000 million in Germany, US$9,469,000 million in the UK, US$8,887,000 million in France and US$2,963,000 million in Sweden (Strandskov *et al.*, 1994: 39). The largest Danish firms include ISS with 115,000 employees, mainly employed outside Denmark.

25 Only agriculture and the shipyards have received economic support of a considerable size over a number of years, mainly as a consequence of decisions taken on a European level, though indirect support has been given to the wind power industry and other presumably environmental friendly technologies by rigging the market prices on energy, etc.

26 After growing through decades the total tax burden has now been stabilized and is showing signs of a slight drop in later years, the liberal-conservative government that took over in December 2001 have declared a total hold on new taxes. Though popular if believed (a great deal of well-founded scepticism can be found in all layers of the society), the policy has been very strict in the first half of 2002, decreasing the room for manoeuvre when changes are made in many other policy areas.

27 Each report contains an identification of the stronghold, an outline of the economic development of the industry and the industry's present situation, and a description of the external conditions (the international framework conditions and the market development), as well as the internal conditions (the competition between Danish firms, their resource base, their strong and weak sides). Each report also analyses the relevant infrastructure, regulation, educational situation, R&D, technological service, industrial policy, etc. and identifies the most important strategic issues for the industry (see Box 6.1). Finally, it discusses the tendencies, scenarios and possible policy recommendations. The reports were written by a group of one or more professional management consulting firms with one or more university researchers in close dialogue with selected industry representatives (10–20) and assisted by five 'monitors'. The whole project was financed by the Ministry of Industry, Department of Industrial Development (*Erhvervsfremme Styrelsen*), and is carried on by the Ministry of Economic and Business Affairs after the change of government in late 2001.

28 All percentages shown are of the total value added in Danish industry, the total Danish employment and total Danish exports.

29 More than fifty task forces working under the Ministry of Industry forwarded suggestions on how to implement such a policy within every sector of industry.

Each task force consisted of representatives from business, unions, universities and the relevant parts of the public sector.

30   One of the departments is situated in Taastrup in the vicinity of Copenhagen and the other in the country's second largest town of Aarhus. Smaller units are placed in a few provincial towns (such as Herning). TI was formerly known as DTI (Danish Technological Institute).

31   Each TIC is a legally independent, non-profit organization that employs four to six consultants and has a secretarial staff of one or two. Founded in 1971 and becoming independent in 1996, TICs offer expertise and consultancy services free of charge to SMEs primarily within manufacturing industries, technology-based trade and knowledge-based services. Each TIC also functions as a point of contact to relevant experts and knowledge centres. All the sixteen regional TICs are jointly served by 'TIC Denmark', which provides common staff functions, HRM, marketing and financial services. The running costs of 104m DKK (2002) are split evenly between the government and the county councils with a trickle arriving from municipals, various EU grants and other sources.

32   FORCE Technology is an authorized knowledge centre with representatives in all parts of the country employing a total of 825 persons (2001) and a total turnover of US$70m. It owns a subsidiary in Sweden and is now generating an increasing turnover from activities abroad.

DELTA, Danish Electronics, Light and Acoustics, is a government-recognized private, independent organization supplying businesses with knowledge about new technology in products, processes and environment. DELTA is a leading test, design, service, consulting and education organization within the field of electronics, software technology, optics and acoustics. In 2000, DELTA had 253 employees and a turnover of approximately US$47m.

33   These initiatives attempt (1) to increase the co-ordination at the local level between the various public and semi-public friends of the private enterprise (*Erhvervsknudepunkter*); (2) to support local initiatives to strengthen a comparative advantages in a particular field (*Vækstmiljøer*) e.g. horticulture (Fyn), wind energy (Ringkoebing), IT (Ringkoebing), Furniture (Viborg), biotech (Aarhus), offshore technologies (Ribe), plastic (Ribe), tourism (South Jutland); and (3) to augment regional ICT-capabilities (Det Digitale Danmark) by targeted efforts with strong local public and private participation in Northern Jutland (IT-fyrtårn) and Copenhagen.

34   For instance, ten persons each following two courses with an average length of 2½ weeks makes one full-year course.

35   This particular combination of low barriers for firms to hire and fire in combination with high levels of compensations is sometimes internationally referred to as the Danish labour market 'model'.

36   The share of Danish households having access to the Internet is 46% (2001), while 87% of the Danish firms with more than 10 employees are on-line. These rates of coverage are among the highest in the world only surpassed by Sweden (for households: 48%) and by Finland (for firms: 91%) (Statistics Denmark, 2002b).

Chapter 7
The Baden-Württemberg production and innovation regime
Past successes and new challenges

Martin Heidenreich and Gerhard Krauss

Introduction

By the 1980s at the latest, the crisis of Tayloristic, bureaucratically organized mass production was obvious. In the highly industrialized societies of the Western world, the production of standardized industrial products at competitive prices was no longer viable. The comparative advantages these countries had enjoyed, primarily the competence and capital required for organizing mass production, had declined or lost their significance. This raises the question as to the remaining locational advantages: what products or services can still be profitably manufactured or rendered, given the labour costs in Western Europe?

Baden-Württemberg also faces this question. Initially, this may seem somewhat surprising when one considers that the region's success was based less on Tayloristic mass production concepts and far more on the flexible manufacturing of high-quality industrial products (Piore and Sabel, 1984; Streeck, 1991). Over many decades, flexible high-quality production enabled manufacturing companies in this regional state in south-west Germany to avoid price-based competition against which they could hardly have won. This manufacturing concept was successful as long as it was pursued as a complementary approach to mass production (and not as a radical alternative). The demand for investment goods, as well as for quality-orientated sophisticated market segments that could not be served by standardized products, was satisfied by companies whose special strengths lay in the flexible supply of high-quality products. With the advent of the much debated knowledge-based economy – this situation changed completely. In contrast to the post-war period of prosperity, companies are no longer faced with the decision of either turning out low-cost mass products or diversified quality products. What is now demanded are innovative high-quality, flexibly supplied and low-cost products and services. Lean production, development and marketing concepts are undermining the former complementary position between flexible specialization and mass production. This also undermines the former comparative strengths of industrial districts and other types of regional economies. One can no longer assume that there is a naturally evolved superiority of regional production and institutional networks characterized by a multitude of small and large industrial and service companies, regional co-operation and supply relations between companies, as well as a supporting network of regional institutions (banks, training systems, research and development institutions, regional labour relations, etc.) (Pyke and Sengenberger, 1992).

This brings us to discussion on the strengths and the limitations inherent in regional production systems. Baden-Württemberg (or the greater Stuttgart area to be more precise; cf. Sabel, 1989), as well as the central Italian and French industrial districts, was frequently quoted as a prominent example of such regional systems. The success of these regions was attributed to the concept of flexible specialization, based on close co-operative relations between companies and general institutional conditions that barred companies from the option of hire-and-fire policies and drastic labour cost reductions, and thereby reinforced the imperative of permanent innovation (cf. also the concept of co-ordinated market economies generalizing similar observations; Hall and Soskice, 2001). Only adherence to collectively binding regulations and agreements was able to prevent companies from 'free-riding' (in the form of refraining from training or research investments, or wage-dumping practices, etc.), approaches that may appear efficient and rational in the short term, yet prove detrimental in the long term. Qualified employees in long-term working relationships, co-operation-based employer–employee relations and an intensive regional information exchange between different companies will facilitate the orientation to demanding high-quality market segments, and this orientation is also needed in order to secure safe jobs for the core workforce of unionized employees. Apart from general institutional conditions, co-operative supplier–buyer relations and regional company clusters (Porter, 1990; OECD 1999) are of considerable importance for the success of regional production and innovation concepts, as such company networks facilitate the smooth exchange of information and enhance technical and business competence (Powell, 1990).

Streeck (1991) takes the credit for freeing the concept of flexible special-ization from a certain *Mittelstand* or neo-artisan romanticism. In the model of diversified quality production that he proposed, large-scale companies also find their place, whereas the close regional context is abandoned, and national, govern-mental regulation structures (labour law, training systems, etc.) are integrated into the model. The balance between competition and co-operation, which is central to flexible co-operation strategies, is not so much ensured by personal agreements and trust-based relations, but more by national institutions and legal and collective agreements. Streeck emphasizes in particular the significance of industry-wide wage agreements, uniform and national training regulations, and collectively bargained wages and working-hours agreements. Thus, regional and national training systems and industrial policies, industrial relations, professional and business associations, and regional and national financial systems, are the central pillars of such intercompany regulation structures and production regimes.[1]

Within the context of increasing worldwide competition, networked and regionally concentrated manufacturing structures and a 'rich' institutional environment are no longer regarded as adequate preconditions for success. Whether we look to government-supported scientific regions such as the Midi-Pyrénées, high-tech regions such as Silicon Valley, traditional industrial districts such as Tuscany, or metropolitan financial and service centres (global cities) – all of these different production and innovation concepts rely on a rich institutional environment and on close intercompany co-operation-based relations. With the rising significance of regionally anchored economic structures, the differences between the respective variants are of central interest. Although the concepts of flexible specialization and diversified quality production are primarily based on the strengths of regional production and institutional networks, the relative stability and consistency of regional production structures may also be associated with considerable innovation obstacles. The institutional stabilization of interorganizational networks is a prerequisite for the success of industrial districts, yet on the other hand this very stabilization may prove disadvantageous as it hampers the active search for new product and production concepts (Saxenian, 1989; Grabher, 1993). Regional or national lock-in effects tend to cement yesterday's success formulas as permanent institutions. In view of increased demands made on flexibility, quality and innovation, the stabilization of communication and co-operation relations (and the associated barriers between different employee groups, companies, branches and sectors of the economy) may begin to prove dysfunctional.

This possibility can no longer be excluded for Baden-Württemberg (Braczyk *et al.*, 1996), even though this highly industrialized German state with its 10.4 million inhabitants, and its 5 million employees is one of the most prosperous and most innovative European regions: this is reflected by a GDP of 295 billion Euros (2000; more than the Swiss, Danish, Finnish or Austrian gross domestic product), its per-capita average income of nearly 27,000 Euros (1999; well above the German (23,400 Euros) and European (20,000 Euros) average), and its research intensity of 3.9 per cent of its GDP (Germany: 2.3 per cent; European Union: 1.8 per cent). Its employment rate (percentage of population aged 15–64) is well above the German and European level (1999: 69.5 per cent in comparison with 65.4 per cent and 62.8 per cent), its unemployment rate well below these levels (1999: 5.1 per cent in comparison with 8.9 per cent and 9.4 per cent), the rate of European patent applications per million people (average 1997–99) is the highest of all European NUTS2–regions (416.4 in comparison with 227.3 in Germany and 119.4 in Europe) (European Commission, 2001).

Despite these impressive performances, the first symptoms of the limitations of the regional production system became increasingly apparent in the first half of the 1990s. During the crisis between 1992 and 1994, the economy of Baden-Württemberg suffered more than the other states of the former West Germany. GDP declined by 4.7 per cent (1993), the unemployment rate of the dependent labour force rose from 3.7 per cent (1991) to 8.7 per cent (1997). The crisis affected mostly the economic core region of Baden-Württemberg, the region of Stuttgart (cf. Krauss, 1999: 359). However, it was quickly overcome because the region could over-proportionally benefit from the unexpected boom of the automotive industry in the second half of the 1990s: In 2000, the GDP grew by 4.5 per cent, the highest growth since 1992. Employment numbers increased significantly during the last years of the 1990s. In October 2000, Baden-Württemberg's unemployment rate reached an eight-year-low of 5.5 per cent; the number of employees now is even higher than at the beginning of the crisis at the beginning of the 1990s (1991: 4,831,000 employees; 2001: 4,976,800 employees). Nevertheless, the fundamental situation of the region, especially its strong and also increasing dependence on two complex, but increasingly mature products (cars and machines) still persists. The share of service employment (1999: 57 per cent) is much lower than in Germany (63 per cent) and in the European Union (66 per cent) reflecting the classical industrial strengths of the region especially in the investment goods sector (car production, machinery, electrical equipment). Also, the economic recovery at the turn of the century cannot hide the fact that newly created jobs in the industrial core branches compensate only for a portion of the jobs lost during the crisis and that in fact, those branches in the long run are likely to further lose workers (the number of employees in manufacturing industry declined from 1.5 (1990) to 1.2 million in 1999).

These indicators outline the limits, but also the potentials of the production and innovation regime to date. In the following discussion we will analyse this regime in order to shed light on this new situation and the ongoing transformation of the regional innovation regime.

In the following discussion we will initially describe the extraordinarily successful economic development that Baden-Württemberg underwent in the post-war years. These successes resulted in an economic structure that is presently proving problematic in view of the altered general conditions of the global economy. This will be followed by an account of the institutional environment in Baden-Württemberg (i.e. the research and development facilities, the vocational training system, industrial relations and financial services). These institutions represent a major precondition for special strengths in the area of advanced, predominantly mature technologies. However, the inertia of these institutions explains several weaknesses in the sector of new knowledge-intensive high technologies. In conclusion, we will summarize the strengths and weaknesses of the present production and innovation regime and point out some attempts at a new positioning of the Baden-Württemberg production and innovation regime.

Industrial modernization of Baden-Württemberg after the Second World War

In the prosperous early post-war decades, Baden-Württemberg's economy succeeded in charting an extraordinarily successful course of development. This federal state, or *Land*, in the southwest of Germany – which has existed in its present form only since the fusion of the three *Länder* of Baden, Württemberg-Hohenzollern and Württemberg in 1952 – recorded higher growth rates than the entire Federal Republic. During the 1950s especially, the Baden-Württemberg economy expanded a great deal faster than the West German economy as a whole. However, from the 1970s onwards it also become apparent that Baden-Württemberg's economy was more strongly affected by recessionary phases than was the rest of Germany, thus reflecting the drawbacks of a strong export orientation (Figure 7.1).

This extraordinary growth was associated with the dynamic (catching-up) industrialization of the federal state. The agricultural sector, which had accounted for a quarter of the workforce at the beginning of the 1950s, dwindled very quickly, whereas the number of employees in manufacturing industry rose from 1.4 million (1950) to 2.3 million (1970), reaching an absolute peak value (with a 55.9 per cent share of the labour force in Baden-Württemberg – compared with a 48.9 per cent average on a national level). In 2001, the 40.3 per cent share of employees active in production industry was still considerably above the German average (1999: 34.5 per cent). Compared with other OECD countries (with the exception of Portugal and some Central European Countries), Baden-Württemberg (and Germany) still exhibits an above-average share of industrial employment (see Figure 7.4).

The successful industrialization strategy was based primarily on the investment goods industry or, more precisely, on the mechanical engineering industry, the automotive industry and the electrical engineering industry (see Figure 7.2). These three branches (and especially the automotive industry) form the economic backbone of the industrialization model of Baden-Württemberg. From 1950 to 2000 the number of employees in these three branches more than tripled (1950: 225,000 employees; 1991: 800,000; 2000: 700,000 employees), whereas the number of employees in the textile industry – the most important industrial sector in 1950 and a major factor driving the development of the mechanical engineering industry in the nineteenth century (Sabel, 1989) – declined to less than one-third of its original volume.

These three branches are at the centre of two relatively autonomous industrial clusters located mainly in the region of Stuttgart – the automotive industry and its suppliers (approximately 335,000 employees in 1998) and the mechanical engineering industry producing a wide spectrum of production technologies in mostly small and medium-sized companies. As well as these traditional clusters,

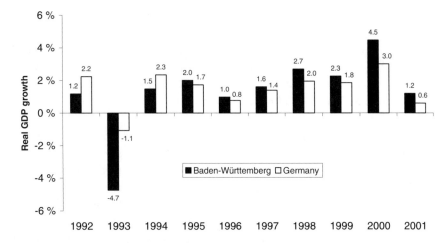

7.1 GDP growth in Baden-Württemberg and Germany (1992–2001)

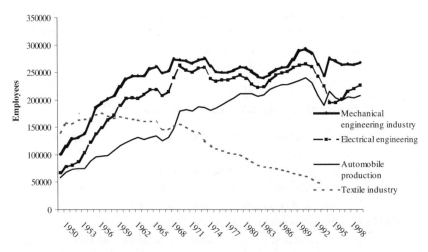

7.2 Employment in the core branches of the economy of Baden-Württemberg (1950–2000)
Source: Statistisches Landesamt Baden-Württemberg (2000)

in the past decades have emerged a new cluster of business-related software and service companies (such as SAP, IBM, Hewlett-Packard, or the once successful Brokat[2]) with 55,000 employees. Besides these three established clusters, different studies have identified some smaller, mostly local clusters (for example, biotechnology, multimedia, photonics, health).

The growth of the regional labour force is another indicator of the successful industrialization of the state (1950: 3.1 million; 2000: 5 million). During the same period the total population rose from 6.4 million to 10.5 million. The influx of exiles from the former German regions in eastern Europe accounted for the first rise and was followed by the inflow of people from other federal states and abroad (the proportion of foreigners rose considerably in the period between 1959 and 1973, and foreigners accounted for 12.2 per cent of the population in 2000). The regional unemployment rate was always lower than the German average (Figure 7.3).

The export rates that exceeded the German average over decades are an additional indicator of the success of Baden-Württemberg's economy. In 1999, 29 per cent of regional production was exported – a considerable increase since 1993 (23 per cent). This success can be attributed to the concentration of three branches of the investment goods industry (namely mechanical engineering, electrical engineering and the automotive industry). In 1999 the three core sectors of Baden-Württemberg's economy recorded 49.0 per cent (mechanical engineering), 55.4 per cent (automotive industry) and 46.8 per cent (electrical engineering) of their sales outside Germany. There can be no doubt as to the outstanding success of economic development in Baden-Württemberg in the post-war years. These outstanding successes were reflected in a considerable rise in the number of employees (and the total population), high export rates, above-average growth and an unemployment rate below the national average.

Economic structures – an obstacle to innovation?

Baden-Württemberg's post-war prosperity was enabled by a co-ordinated ensemble of regional economic structures and general institutional conditions. In the following we will analyse regional economic structures in terms of accumulated capabilities and potential inertia and thus will show how the necessary transformation of the regional economy is difficult. In doing so, we will concentrate on possible lock-in effects resulting from the formation of regional clusters. We feel this approach is valid and justified, as the strengths of Baden-Württemberg's economic structure – consisting of many globally active corporations (DaimlerChrysler, Robert Bosch, IBM Deutschland, Heidelberger Zement, ZF, SAP, Porsche, etc.), a multitude of successful *Mittelstand* companies and institutions of world renown – have been adequately portrayed in other places (Sabel *et al.*, 1989; Herrigel, 1996).

As Table 7.1 shows, the growth rates of Baden-Württemberg's economy in the 1990s were below the national average – mainly due to the deep structural crisis at the beginning of the decade. At the same time, the branches with the highest growth rates – financial and business services – expanded slower than at the national level. The regional shares of these highly productive and dynamically expanding services are close to the relatively low German average.

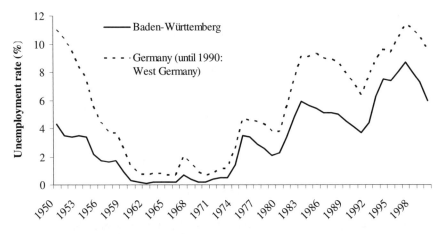

7.3 Unemployment in Baden-Württemberg and West Germany 1950–2000.
Source: Statistisches Landesamt Baden-Württemberg (2000)

Table 7.1 Economic and employment structure of the Baden-Württemberg economy (1991–2000)

	Gross value added (at constant 1995 prices)				Employment			
	% share of economy (1999)		Development 1991–1999		% share of economy (1999)		Development 1991–1999	
	B-W	Ger	B-W	Ger	B-W	Ger	B-W	Ger
Agriculture and forestry	1.2	1.0	41.9	19.1	2.2	2.6	–31.2	–37.3
Industry	32.3	24.0	–0.1	–4.5	30.6	22.5	–14.9	–24.5
Construction	4.4	6.0	–17.9	0	6.0	7.4	–7.7	1.1
Wholesale and retail trade, restaurants, hotels and transport	14.7	18.0	10.7	13.7	22.5	25.2	2.9	2.4
Finance, insurance, real estate and business services	27.0	30.0	29.3	38.0	13.9	13.9	45.4	42.1
Public administration, education, health, social work and other services	16.1	21.0	12.7	12.7	24.8	28.4	15.0	10.6
All branches	100.0	100.0	7.7	13.6	100.0	100.0	1.3	–1.3

Source: Statisches Landesamt Baden-Württemberg, 2000: Lange Reihen 1950–1999 and Statistisches Bundesamt, STATIS

The question arises why, in spite of Baden-Württemberg's exceptional success in the investment goods industry, its economy did not succeed in staging a stronger reorientation to sectors promising greater growth potential. Why did Baden-Württemberg's economy fail to stake out a greater share in new areas such as information and communications technology, new materials, biotechnology, environmental and power technology, microsystem technology, and production services (Faust *et al.*, 1995), although the industrial, structural and institutional preconditions in each of the cited areas were certainly not unfavourable? This question also leads us to consider the inertia of established production structures.

In the following we will discuss three aspects of this inertia or resistance to change. First, we will document that the share of in-house production (value added divided by sales) of Baden-Württemberg's industrial companies is still above the West German average and is extraordinarily high by international comparison. As a high share of in-house production is frequently associated with disadvantages in terms of costs and flexibility, the high degree of integration of regional manufacturing may prove a considerable handicap in facing international competition. Second, we will demonstrate that the share of internally rendered services is exceptionally high and that Baden-Württemberg's industrial companies use external service providers to a very limited extent. This factor may also prove to be a handicap in coping with worldwide innovation, flexibility and cost competition. Third, we will illustrate that close regional integration and interlinking are primarily vertical, while regional co-operation activities mainly consist of supplier and service relations within an industrial cluster. Co-operation between competitors – a factor regarded as crucial for innovative product and production concepts (Piore and Sabel, 1984) – plays a relatively insignificant role in Baden-Württemberg.

On the way to lean production?

Considering the years of discussions on lean production concepts, make-or-buy or JIT ('just-in-time') issues, one could expect a considerable reduction of in-house production. Surprisingly, however, the average extent of in-house production of all companies in Baden-Württemberg has remained constant (1978: 49 per cent; 1990: 48.7 per cent; West Germany 1990: 48.2). This stability is the result of opposite developments: as the share of more strongly integrated service areas increased, the extent of in-house production in the manufacturing industry declined slightly (1978: 42 per cent; 1990: 40 per cent). As the average extent of in-house production in West Germany was recorded at 38.1 per cent (1990), Baden-Württemberg's industry can hardly be regarded as being in the vanguard of developments. Particularly in the automotive and the electrical engineering industry, the extent of in-house manufacturing has reduced considerably over recent years. Nevertheless, the share of in-house production in the electrical engineering industry (1990: 50.2 per cent; West Germany: 48.1 per cent) and in the mechanical engineering industry (1990: 43.6 per cent; West Germany: 42.4 per cent) is still comparatively high. Only in the automotive sector (1990: 33.6 per cent; West Germany: 33.3 per cent) and in the food, beverages and tobacco industry was the share of in-house manufacturing considerably lower than the average in the manufacturing industry. The number of employees in Baden-Württemberg procuring supplies for the automotive industry increased from 84,000 (1993) to 142,000 employees (1998; cf. *Baden-Württemberg in Wort und Zahl*, July 2001). As a high degree of integration in manufacturing is associated with a lack of openness towards competent, specialized suppliers and service providers, a high degree of in-house manufacturing may well hamper a reorientation to innovative products and flexible sales market segments (Münzenmaier, 1995).

On the way to an industrial service society?

In connection with the high, although decreasing, extent of in-house manufacturing in Baden-Württemberg's industry, a high 'internal tertiary rate' of Baden-Württemberg and West German companies is notable. The differentiation and organizational segregation of manufacturing and service activities are far less pronounced than in most other Western industrial nations (Figure 7.4); in other words, companies perform a great many production-related services themselves. This is reflected by the high share of employees in manufacturing industry who are active in the service professions (1993: 39.6%) or who are primarily assigned service tasks (1991: 41.9 per cent). These figures barely deviate from the West German average (38.8 per cent and 41.5 per cent, respectively).

The above was associated with the delayed development of the service sector. In comparison with other advanced industrial societies, Baden-Württemberg's share of service sector employment is relatively low (57 per cent in 1999; cf. Figure 7.4). The technology and export-orientated investment goods industries in particular, but also the consumer goods branches, use external service providers relatively little. Only a quarter of the input factors requested by manufacturing industry are services (1990: 25.1%). Since 1978, however, this share has risen considerably. This is especially true for the automotive industry. In 1998, 53 per cent of external supplies consisted of services (consulting, engineering, marketing, development, etc.). Baden-Württemberg's companies have also sourced an increasing volume from external suppliers (especially the electrical engineering industry, with 29.2%). After deduction of their own 'exports', Baden-Württemberg procures 4.6% of services required from other German states or from abroad (1978: 3.4%). Therefore, Baden-Württemberg's service balance is negative. Financial, transport and other services account for two-thirds of this negative balance.

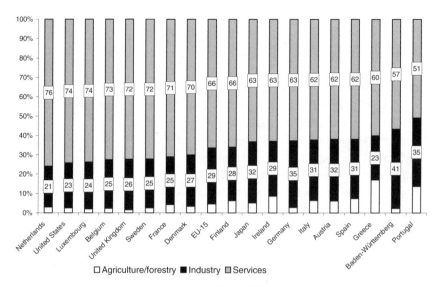

7.4 The employment structure of the economy of Baden-Württemberg in international perspective, civilian employment by economic sector, 1999
Source: OECD (2001a)

This points to a potential *vicious circle*. Especially in terms of sophisticated, manufacturing-related services, Baden-Württemberg's companies are unable to draw on regional external providers. As the use of remote or foreign external providers is associated with higher risks and transaction costs, companies refrain from procuring these services. This may pose an obstacle to globalization, innovation, flexibilization and diversification strategies, as companies are often not able to access or develop specific in-house competence and know-how (e.g. concerning Japanese customer wishes and tax legislation, efficient suppliers for biotechnological production techniques, or hardware/software solutions to specific problems, etc.). In many instances external services can be more efficiently developed, rationalized and systemized, whereas some customers may also benefit from the experiences of others. It cannot be generally assumed that leaner companies are actually more innovative and more efficient. But the extraordinary inertia of vertically organized companies will inhibit reorientation to new products and product models more strongly than the targeted access of innovative service providers and suppliers.

Innovation by co-operation between companies?

Intensive co-operation and communication networks within a region give rise to synergies that, according to the concept of flexible specialization, represent an important precondition for the success of industrial districts. In the case of Baden-

Württemberg, however, one must clearly differentiate between vertical and horizontal co-operation patterns. In Baden-Württemberg, the significance of vertical relations between suppliers and buyers is very high. In the age of internationalized production structures, Baden-Württemberg's manufacturing industry has retained a surprisingly high degree of regional sourcing. Of the required input factors, some 53 per cent of supplies were regionally procured in 1990, 26.7 per cent from other German states and 20.4 per cent from abroad (Münzenmaier, 1995). In mechanical engineering and the automotive industry, the share of regional sourcing has even increased in recent years. This reflects the extent to which the companies of the three core branches of automotive, electronic and mechanical engineering are tied in regional clusters.[3]

Relations between potential competitors are horizontal forms of co-operation. In Baden-Württemberg they are far less significant than the concepts of flexible specialization would suggest (Schmitz, 1992: 95, 101; Cooke *et al.*, 1993). Based on a representative survey of West German mechanical engineering companies, Kerst and Steffensen (1995) were able to demonstrate that the number of co-operating companies in Baden-Württemberg is by no means above average (excluding research and development – in which in 1993 55 per cent of Baden-Württemberg's and 48 per cent of West Germany's mechanical engineering companies co-operated). The share of co-operating mechanical engineering companies in Baden-Württemberg (1993: 37 per cent) is on par with the West German average (36 per cent). Therefore, it is doubtful that there is a higher incidence of co-operation activities between competing companies in Baden-Württemberg than in other West German states.

The assumption that the structure of Baden-Württemberg's economy is more strongly determined by *Mittelstand* companies than the rest of the West German economy is also a misconception. Based on the average size of the regional companies, there is no difference between Germany and Baden-Württemberg (cf. Statistisches Bundesamt: Fachserie 4, Reihe 4.1.2, Wiesbaden). On the contrary, the prosperity of the regional economy is based on the success of a large number of big companies: in 2000 25 companies in Baden-Württemberg employed more than 10,000 people, 46 companies had a revenue of more than a billion Euro – among them DaimlerChrysler (416.500; 163 bn €), Bosch (198,000; 32 bn €), Röchling (41,650; 6.1 bn €), Bilfinger+Berger (40,700; 4.4 bn €) and ZF (36,400; 6.5 bn €).

It can be concluded that Baden-Württemberg's metal industry is interlinked by vertical supply and service patterns. The regional economy is organized in closely knit industrial clusters, thus facilitating the exchange of information and vertical co-operation with customers and suppliers. Horizontal co-operation activities (at least in the mechanical engineering industry) are no more prominent than in other West German states.

The extent to which Baden-Württemberg's manufacturing industry procures industrial input and services from external providers is as low as in other West German regions. The share of in-house manufacturing is around 40 per cent in both cases. Services account for only one-quarter of input, whereas two-fifths of the employees in manufacturing companies are assigned service tasks. This implies that Baden-Württemberg and German industrial companies opt primarily for internally organized – and not market-mediated – forms of co-ordinating production and service activities. This contrasts with other market-driven high-tech regions in the world such as California where many services are offered by numerous highly specialized co-operating firms. In view of increasingly short innovation cycles and global production, investment, distribution and sourcing strategies, this course of action may incur higher transaction costs in connection with lower innovation rates.

The primarily vertical co-operation patterns, as well as the high share of in-house manufacturing and the low share of external services requested by industrial firms, indicate that the marked concentration of Baden-Württemberg's economy on the investment goods industry (automobiles, machines, electrical engineering) can hardly be broken up by intercompany co-operation activities. As Baden-Württemberg's industrial core is characterized by advanced technologies (reflected by the gross value added per wage and salary earner and by the growth rate of gross value added), the region's productive specialization is associated with considerable risks: communication and co-operation opportunities outside of historically evolved and institutionally and organizationally reinforced trajectories ('paths of development') can hardly be utilized. It is these 'barriers to learning' – and not the 'maturity' of Baden-Württemberg's product range itself – that can evolve into a major obstacle on the road to innovation-promoting company strategies.

The institutional regulation structures of Baden-Württemberg's economy

The region has enjoyed decades of economic prosperity because of its skilled labour, co-operative industrial relations, well-developed research structures, state and national industrial policies, and close and long-term relations between banks and companies. Many analyses (e.g. Schmitz, 1992; Herrigel, 1993) have reconstructed in detail the specific elements of this success story. Here we will therefore confine ourselves to providing a brief overview of Baden-Württemberg's production regime and point out the potential limitations of these regulatory structures – limitations that only come into effect in the face of increased demands in terms of flexibility, innovation, quality and efficiency.

Research, development and transfer institutions in Baden-Württemberg

Baden-Württemberg has a highly-developed research infrastructure with a total of 97,000 R&D personnel (full-time equivalent).[4] The regional R&D intensity is with 3.9 per cent of the GDP (1999) one of the highest regional rates in Europe; it is higher than the research intensity of all other industrialized nations (with Sweden investing 3.8 per cent in 1998). This accounts for a significant proportion of past success. Research and transfer institutions have helped to consolidate and extend the chosen path of development. Here, the concentration of regional research efforts on the dominant industrial clusters has led to Baden-Württemberg becoming especially strong in the areas of medium-high technologies,[5] where significant technological leaps are associated with high expenditure. However, in high-tech and other promising fields, Baden-Württemberg has certain weaknesses. The existence of a well-established research and transfer structure and a high regional concentration of R&D personnel is clearly not sufficient for the development of new products that will be successful on the market. Nonetheless, strengths in medium technology are an important requirement for the development of new, future-orientated fields of technology. As far as technology transfer to smaller and medium-size companies is concerned, Baden-Württemberg has a widespread network of specialized institutions, all of which belong to a state-wide umbrella organization, the Steinbeis-Stiftung für Wirtschaftsförderung (see Beise *et al.*, 1995).[6] In 1998, technology transfer became a private business activity and therefore was outsourced to a private firm called Steinbeis GmbH and Co. für Technologietransfer. This firm maintains a network of about 300 centres[7] for technology transfer, in most cases close to a *Fachhochschule* (university of applied sciences). These centres enable small and medium-size companies to develop their technological expertise, products and product quality in close collaboration with professors at the Fachhochschulen. Nonetheless, only 15% of Baden-Württemberg companies rate technology transfer centres as important information sources for innovative activities; 32% say that universities are an important information source (Heinemann *et al.* 1995: 21).

For several reasons, this transfer concept – which has been exceptionally successful to date – is now being examined critically. First, the commercial aspects of innovation are having to be considered alongside the purely technological aspects. Second, now that globalization is even affecting *Mittelstand* companies, a greater degree of internationalization is required in technology transfer. Third, the traditional transfer concept requires very precise demands on the part of the companies. The ability to find innovative questions for the transfer centres is not something that can necessarily be taken for granted, especially among smaller *Mittelstand* companies. So, transfer centres can generally respond only to problem-solving tasks, which can be dealt with within the framework of the highly limited contractual work at the Fachhochschulen (and to some extent at universities): From the companies' point of view, R&D co-operation in particular – i.e. jointly conducted R&D projects in which both partners are involved financially and extend their technological know-how – are under-represented in the transfer centres' spectrum of work (Beise *et al.*, 1995: 66).

Fourth, the restructuring of the regional economy is going hand in hand with a change in demand. What was once the central function of the transfer centres, that of 'systematically facilitating companies' access to new technologies – especially small companies' (Maier, 1989: 290), was going to become considerably less important. The number of transfer and consultation projects relating to the use of modern technologies declined by over 75 per cent between 1990 and 1994 (Steinbeis-Stiftung für Wirtschaftsförderung, 1994: 39), while the volume of individual projects increased considerably (by about 60% on average). Greater involvement in the area of research-intensive high-tech will also be in much demand in the future.

Fifth, the regionalization concept of the Fachhochschulen is also coming under increasing pressure. Many external centres of the Fachhochschulen and associated Steinbeis transfer centres have difficulties fulfilling the demands of a blanket-coverage technology-transfer network. Only a quarter of the companies surveyed had taken up offers of technology transfer in the previous five years. Technology transfer was thus only being used by a limited group of companies. What is more, given their limited resources, it is doubtful whether the small external centres at the Fachhochschulen are in a position to provide companies with sophisticated and comprehensive consultation.

R&D intensity of the Baden-Württemberg economy

In terms of the research intensity of its economy, Baden-Württemberg occupies the leading position among the federal states. Nevertheless, due to its regional specialization profile, the competitiveness of Baden-Württemberg's high-tech products is limited in international trade. The reasons for the relatively limited success in high-tech exports are mainly to be found in the traditional specialization profile of Baden-Württemberg's R&D system. Despite a rise in young developing high-tech districts in the region, such as biotechnology or multimedia clusters, with newly emerging innovation networks and specific transfer structures, the major R&D capacity and technology-transfer institutions are still concentrated in the industrial core sectors.

Baden-Württemberg's research system differs considerably from that of the rest of West Germany. For example, the proportion of R&D personnel working in the Baden-Württemberg economy is unusually high: in 1997, 71.4 per cent of R&D personnel were working in industry, whereas in West Germany as a whole this figure was only 62.2 per cent. Figure 7.5 shows that Baden-Württemberg employs considerably more R&D personnel per capita than the rest of the Federal Republic. The high R&D intensity of the Baden-Württemberg economy is also reflected in the rate of R&D expenditure per employee. In this respect, Baden-Württemberg occupies the leading position in Germany.

However, R&D personnel in Baden-Württemberg's economy are distributed unequally among the different sectors of industry. As far as company research capacity is concerned, 94 per cent are in manufacturing industry, and around 80 per cent in the three core industrial sectors (Table 7.2). Compared to Germany as a whole, R&D intensity is above average, especially in Baden-Württemberg's vehicle manufacture (Figure 7.5 and Table 7.2).

It therefore comes as no surprise that patent registrations were well above the German average. In 1999 1,120 domestic patent applications per million inhabitants were registered at the German and 416 at the European patent office (Germany: 650 and 227; cf. Statistisches Landesamt, 2001 and European Commission, 2001). This is the highest ratio among all sixteen German *Länder*. In 1998, the most important technological fields (with more than 5 per cent of all patent applications) were: Vehicles and transport; Electricity; Engines or turbines; Engineering in general; Measuring, testing, optics; Building (Greif, 2000). Electronics, communication technologies, biotechnology, computing and information storage are characterized by lower patent figures. This concentration on more traditional technological fields can also be demonstrated in comparison

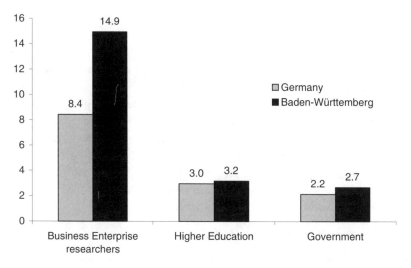

7.5 R&D personnel per thousand labour force (1997; full time equivalent)
Source: Bundesministerium für Bildung und Forschung (2000); Bundesbericht Forschung (2000: 547–552)

Table 7.2 Business Enterprise R&D personnel (FTE) in different branches of the Baden-Württemberg and German economy, 1997(%)

	Baden-Württemberg		Germany	
	No.	%	No.	%
Manufacturing Industry	63,935	94	262,916	93
among these:				
Chemical industry	4,434	6	49,012	17
Production and transformation of metal	1,282	2	6,933	2
Mechanical engineering	9,338	14	38,821	14
Data processing, electrical engineering	16,533	24	82,119	29
Automotive production	30,314	44	70,762	25
Other branches	6,369	9	34,792	12
Companies (total)	68,270	100	282,439	100

Source: Bundesministerium für Bildung und Forschung (2000): Bundesbericht Forschung (2000: 548–549)

with national patent patterns (Figure 7.6): Even in comparison with Germany, the regional R&D system is characterized by a specialization in technologies relevant for the construction of machines and cars. This strong concentration on specific technological fields in the second half of the 1990s was a major reason for the above average performance of Baden-Württemberg. But in the case of a downswing of these industries, it can have a profound negative impact on regional performance.

R&D-intensive economic sectors are of great importance in Baden-Württemberg, and the number of employees working in high- and medium-high-technology industries is also above the German average (1999: 92 per 1000 inhabitants in comparison with 55 in Germany; Statistisches Landesamt, 2001: 27). However, the weakness of Germany's and Baden-Württemberg's high- and medium-high-technology industries becomes clear when we consider the export structure of R&D-intensive products. In comparison to other highly developed countries, it is conspicuous that Germany has specialized in the field of medium-high-technology (cf. Figure 7.7). In Germany, only 19 per cent of all manufacturing exports are high-tech products (1999) – and the corresponding figure for Baden-Württemberg used to be even lower (*Baden-Württemberg in Wort und Zahl*, 12/92).

Vocational and further training in Baden-Württemberg

Baden-Württemberg has a well-established and widespread system of vocational and further training for skilled employees (Maier, 1989: 295–6). The strength of Baden-Württemberg's system of training is the high significance of practice-

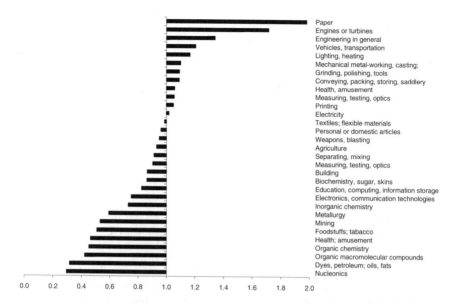

7.6 Patent specialization of Baden-Württemberg in comparison with Germany, 1998 Source: Own calculations on basis of Greif (2000)

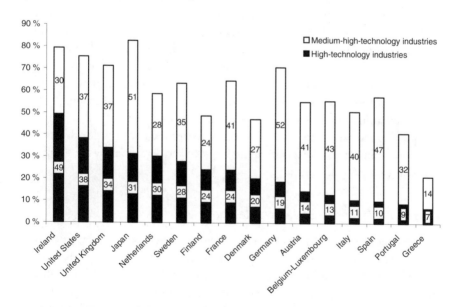

7.7 Share of high- and medium-high technology industries in manufacturing exports, 1999 Source: OECD (2001b)

orientated training courses in Berufsschulen, Fachschulen, Berufsakademien and Fachhochschulen. According to Herrigel, the close ties between training and practice at local and regional level are characteristic of Baden-Württemberg. 'Formal ties are extensive and informal exchanges occur systematically in the region' (Herrigel, 1993: 230). This is not reflected in the qualification levels of the labour force: the share of employees who have finished a vocational training is nearly the same as in West Germany (1999: 61.7 per cent and 61.4%). Also the share of employees with an academic degree (8.4 per cent) and the share of employees without vocational qualifications (22.6 per cent) is nearly the same as in West Germany. This points to the fact that the vocational education system is not a regional particularity, but a nationwide regulation. In an international perspective, this means that the percentage of the workforce who have completed tertiary education is much below the levels of Canada (1999: 43 per cent), the USA (39 per cent), Finland, Japan, Sweden and other advanced nations (OECD, 2001c).

In conclusion: the vocational training system in Baden-Württemberg has contributed significantly to the success of the regional economic model; the manufacturing-orientated production model and the vocational skills training model have had a mutually stabilizing effect. This is reflected, on the one hand, in a high proportion of vocationally skilled employees and, on the other, in an extremely well-developed training system. However, the outstanding importance of vocational training also means that its limitations and weak points present considerable problems, especially the rigid vertical and horizontal demarcations between defined vocational fields (Kern and Sabel, 1994: 606). The functional boundaries between different training courses and between different occupational groups impede the processes of collaboration and innovation that run across different vocational fields. This has led to a crisis in the vocational training system, especially during the 1990s, and to a shift of vocational and further training into companies, indicating an increasing distance between conventional forms of vocational training and the qualifications required and demanded by the companies (Heidenreich, 1998).

Industrial relations in Baden-Württemberg

The co-operative relations between unions and employers' associations are another central pillar of Baden-Württemberg's production regime. On the one hand, they prevent individual companies from resorting excessively to wage-cutting strategies, thus increasing the pressure for permanent innovation; on the other, they also allow a flexible, trust-based utilization of qualified employees by clearly separating industry-wide labour conflicts from within-company co-operative relations (Sabel, 1989: 25). If German labour relations can be described as a co-operative model of conflict regulation, then this applies in particular to Baden-Württemberg. For one thing, Baden-Württemberg boasts the largest regional membership of the union IG-Metall after North Rhine-Westphalia: at the end of 2000, 18.5 per cent of the 2.7 million members of IG-Metall were resident in Baden-Württemberg. Also, Baden-Württemberg has come to be regarded as the mainstay of the unions, having been the battleground of many national wage conflicts. Second, the regional unions (especially IG-Metall, which still has 500,000 employees, i.e. 52 per cent of all Baden-Württemberg's DGB union members) have always played a leading role in Germany. This trade union formulated proposals for the industrial renewal of the regional economy, for example, proposals for reorganizing the mechanical engineering industry. The unions were involved in the selective corporatism between regional business, science and politics – even if only in a subordinate position (Heinze and Schmid, 1994).

The current globalization of the regional economy and the individualization of employment relations suggest that this regional system of industrial relations is building up to a radical change, which is set to sweep away the institutional basis for the former corporatist regulation strategies. On the one hand, important regional companies are increasingly acting on a global level, on the other, the present crisis of industry-wide wage agreements and the trend towards company-level labour relations (with regard to wages and working hours) could shake the German system of employee–employer relations to its very foundations.[8] The tendency to devolve negotiations to company level, the threat of transferring production elsewhere, and the increasing chances of direct interest representation drastically reduce the influence of interest representation bodies.

The crisis of a successful production and innovation model?

In the previous sections we have described the productive and the institutional dimension of Baden-Württemberg's production and innovation regime. First, we analysed the structure of regional production in Baden-Württemberg and stressed the dominant position of the so-called capital-goods producing industry. The prominence of automotive, mechanical and electrical engineering explains the higher than average growth of production, export and employment; these branches were the source of Baden-Württemberg's post-war prosperity. However, this production structure may now prove to be an obstacle in adapting to new demands in terms of flexibility and innovation. First, established production structures and close-knit regional supply and service networks make it harder to tap into new market opportunities. These highly institutionalized structures and networks show remarkable stability and continuity, the major innovations being performed mainly by incumbent firms. New companies play a relatively insignificant role and start-ups are encouraged to adapt their innovation strategies and behaviour as far as possible to the established technology paths, in order to increase their chances of success or, inversely, to reduce their risk of failure (cf. Krauss, 1999). Second, industrial companies perform the greater part of production-related services themselves; the question that needs to be addressed here is whether this high proportion of in-house services inhibits not only the development of the service sector, but also the specialization and optimization of company-related services (e.g. management consulting, development, marketing, software development, logistics and financial services). Third, horizontal co-operation between companies in the same industrial sector is of minor importance in Baden-Württemberg, so that synergy effects (e.g. through joint market observation and research and development activities) are not utilized. These possible disadvantages are balanced against the strengths of a technically advanced, diversified and internationally competitive industrial structure; competence in production technology is an important basis for incremental, path-dependent innovations.

This production structure has been supported in the past by the establishment of a dense network of regional institutions (which are largely embedded and shaped by national regulations). Research and development activities, vocational and advanced training facilities, industrial relations and financial services have contributed substantially to the success of Baden-Württemberg's production model. However, this institutional environment has become so firmly rooted that a problem of lock-in is to be expected in the face of new demands.

First, despite the exceptionally well-established research and development system in Baden-Württemberg, successful exports are mainly achieved with advanced technologies; high-tech goods account for a relatively small proportion of the region's exports. This weakness in the high-tech sector is the downside of the region's extremely successful specialization in traditional technologies. Although this concentration on established technological trajectories is a sign of inertia, we should not overlook the fact that strengths in the field of 'mature' technologies are a good basis for success in the high-tech sector; however, this requires an intelligent recombination of existing potential, a diversification into new technological fields and the exploitation of new possibilities of utilization.

Second, in the field of education and further education, Baden-Württemberg's economy can draw on an efficient vocational training system and a higher-than-average proportion of youngsters leaving school with a certificate of secondary education. However, the regional vocational training system does share one of the weaknesses of the national education system: its orientation towards clearly defined fields of activity and occupational domains (instead of interdisciplinary, process-related qualifications). Such functional distinctions are proving an obstacle to interdisciplinary strategies aiming at greater innovation, economy and flexibility.

Third, Baden-Württemberg plays a leading role in the German system of industrial relations which has been described as one of the central pillars of a co-ordinated market economy (Hall and Soskice, 2001). It is to be feared that the current crisis in Germany's labour relations will not be able to be compensated for at the regional or even national level. The challenges posed by the current process of deregulation, globalization and individualization of labour relations threaten the foundations of industry-wide interest representation, and this in turn undermines the basis of regional patterns of regulation. Apart from negotiations between management and works councils (and the focusing and channelling of potential conflicts that such negotiations allow), we are increasingly seeing direct forms of interest representation (in project groups, semi-autonomous working groups, quality circles, etc.). This phenomenon is undermining the possibilities for co-ordination at intercompany (and hence also regional) level.

In conclusion, we can observe a reinforcement of those industrial and institutional patterns that have proved successful in the past. This hinders attempts to adapt to new industries and services or to reorientate innovative efforts, training services, patterns of interest representation and financial services. Indications that the limits of the regional production and innovation regime have been reached were registered mainly in the first half of the 1990s. The second half of the 1990s with its extraordinary successes especially for the German car industry meant an additional incentive to concentrate on traditional technological fields. The region faces the challenge of using its current strengths to find a new place in the changing world of international competition, and this can effectively be achieved only by the path-dependent reorganizing of its traditional industrial structure and institutional framework in order to create the conditions for an innovative environment.

First steps on the way to a new production and innovation regime

In Baden-Württemberg the basic preconditions for a new production and innovation regime are exceptionally favourable, as the state is able to draw on a unique network of successful industrial companies and supporting institutions. Many globally operating, major corporations are active in the state, and this is associated with a concentration of many strategically crucial corporate functions (research and development, administration, controlling, marketing, IT integration, logistics, etc.). Such corporate functions, with high value added, are a key prerequisite for a strong position within global innovation and locational competition. Although the employment volume will continue to decline in the traditional industrial core areas, the automobile, mechanical engineering and the electrical engineering industry – and above all the services that will be developed on the basis of this product range – will continue to take centre stage. The strengths in these areas will form the basis and the starting point for the diversification and systematic development of a new range of products and services.

Thus, the reorientation of this regional production and innovation regime must consist of transforming the mature industrial cluster, on the one hand, and promoting new technology fields, on the other – a dual strategy that was proposed by the influential Future Commission Economy 2000 (*Zukunftskommission Wirtschaft*, 2000) in a report issued in 1993. This recommendation does justice to the fact that an exclusive promotion of new, high technologies alone is not enough to open up new growth opportunities and employment areas. Fundamental technical innovations usually come about on the basis of evolved strengths. The transformation of the industrial core of the *Land* will primarily arise through the basic restructuring and globalization of manufacturing and development activities. In the medium term, they are an important precondition for shortening the development cycles of new products and their 'time to market'. Various government policies are also driving the restructuring of industrial core sectors and a multitude of new institutions such as four software centres, five biotechnology parks, centres for fuel cell technology, for new traffic control systems, etc. have been put into place to support these efforts (Wirtschaftsministerium Baden-Württemberg, 2000).

Beyond the state's established core industries, some forward-looking approaches have also been emerging. Excellent opportunities are perceived for Baden-Württemberg in the biotechnology sector (Schell and Mohr, 1995: 2). With almost 400 biotech companies, which are mainly situated in four 'BioRegions' (Freiburg/BioValley Upper Rhine, the Rhine-Neckar Triangle, Stuttgart/Neckar-Alb, and Ulm), Baden-Württemberg is a rather successful site for this technology (Dohse, 2000). Of the seven biotechnology clusters that Dohse (2000) identified nationwide in Germany, two were (partially) located in Baden-Württemberg.

In the area of multimedia services, Baden-Württemberg is also well positioned, as it can draw on an efficient electronics industry, as well as many publishing companies and research and educational facilities (in spite of the lack of a sizeable film industry). The *Land* government has started several programmes in order to support the development of the multimedia industry. In 1996, it founded the 'Medien- und Filmgesellschaft' (MFG) which is to co-ordinate various media projects and to function as a hub for media-related activities. The Land also started a state initiative called 'Baden-Württemberg medi@', a collection of various media-related projects. Some of these projects have been designed explicitly to build upon existing sectoral strengths in Baden-Württemberg and to develop multimedia in these sectors. For instance, the use of multimedia for service tasks in the mechanical engineering industry and an online market for small and medium-sized enterprises are being promoted. Finally, the *Land* government presented, in 1999, a new strategic vision for the media economy of Baden-Württemberg ('Leitbild für den Medienstandort Baden-Württemberg'). This is an attempt to improve the visibility of Baden-Württemberg's media sector and to better co-ordinate the industrial policy aiming to support multimedia.

However, Baden-Württemberg seems to have difficulties in competing with outstanding media locations such as Munich, Hamburg, Berlin, Frankfurt or Cologne and to build a reputation as an important multimedia site in Germany. One of the reasons for this is the dominance of manufacturing and research functions in Baden-Württemberg's electronics industry, while the development of new applications and the content side are underrepresented in Baden-Württemberg's economy. Furthermore, it seems there is little interaction going on between the major multinational corporations such as Bosch or Alcatel SEL and the small, specialized multimedia companies. Moreover, the region is often criticized for lacking a stimulating cultural atmosphere, which is an important factor in attracting companies and personnel in the multimedia business (Braczyk *et al.*, 1999; Fuchs and Wolf, 1998).

The search for new product and production concepts is being supported by many new institutions (such as a regional innovation council or the above mentioned Medien- und Filmgesellschaft) as well as by expert commissions, a dense network of regional technology transfer institutions and industry policy initiatives. The Future Commission Economy 2000 (*Zukunftskommission Wirtschaft 2000*), appointed in 1992, gave the starting signal for the search for 'ways out of the crisis'. This was followed by the Innovationsoffensive with a funding of DM1 billion committed to new technical faculties, data highways, biotechnology parks, software centres. In 1994 an Innovationsbeirat was set up and this council developed, among others, proposals for creating a biotechnology agency, a microsystem forum and better computer facilities in schools. Within the context of a 'Future Campaign' (*Zukunftsoffensive*) the state government has realized these proposals since 1996. An additional DM1 billion has been invested in upgrading technical colleges, colleges of advanced vocational studies, universities, clinics, schools and libraries. Since 1997, the state government has supported the establishment and expansion of five biotech parks at Freiburg, Heidelberg, Esslingen, Ulm and Reutlingen/Tübingen with a total of 12.5 million Euro. Support has also been given to business start-ups, networked research projects and regional trade fairs. Start-up companies, for example, have been supported by subsidy programmes, investment shares, and a venture capital fund which was set up in 1998. Within the framework of the programmes 'Young Innovators' and 'Start-up Founders on Campus' the government has supported founders from universities and research institutes.

Experiments with new political approaches have been launched with the intention of initiating and supporting regional innovation networks. One of the most successful examples of these network strategies is the 'Technology region Karlsruhe' and its technology park 'Technology factory Karlsruhe' which since 1984 has been the origin for 150 companies, thus creating nearly 3,000 jobs. Other examples of these network strategies are the 'Innovative region Ulm' (formerly Wissenschaftsstadt Ulm) and especially the already mentioned four biotechnology regions in Baden-Württemberg. Encouraged by a federal 'BioRegio' programme, several networking initiatives in four sub-regions of Baden-Württemberg with research potential in biotechnology research were set up by local actors in order to promote the development of a regionally anchored biotechnology industry. What was special about the BioRegio programme was an approach which offered to assist the development of regional biotechnology clusters, making regions compete with one another and then, in the final phase, concentrating on three selected, promising regions. The Baden-Württemberg Ministry of Science and Research also supported the development of biotechnology with a networked research programme. The sponsoring of regionally anchored biotechnology was part of a new policy geared to advancing new industries beyond the mature core branches. In 1996, one of the biotechnology regions of Baden-Württemberg, the so-called 'Rhine-Neckar Triangle' (partially located in two other German *Länder*), was awarded the coveted status of a 'model region'. Internationally renowned institutions such as the German Cancer Research Centre, the European Molecular Biology Laboratory, the Max Planck Institute for Medical Research, and the Centre for Molecular Biology at Heidelberg served as points of crystallization of this regional cluster. The winners of this Bioregio contest were assigned public subsidies of DM 50 million over a period of five years (from January 1997) that should provide the starting point for additional private investments. Much more important was that they received priority in the appropriation of funds from the Federal Research Ministry. These resources have been committed with the aim of improving the regional organization involved in the transfer of biotechnological knowledge in economic products and services. To this end, targeted assistance has been granted to advance co-operation between science, business, public administration and important societal groups.

The above mentioned 'BioRegio contest' also sparked initiatives in other regions of Baden-Württemberg as in the Greater Ulm region, the Stuttgart-Neckar-Alb area or in and around Freiburg. Here, increased efforts have been made to bring the relevant actors together and create greater networking and co-operation. However, the relatively important number of different sub-regions in biotechnology confronts Baden-Württemberg with particular problems, namely the impossibility of concentrating public resources on the most promising region. In Baden-Württemberg, the *Land* government therefore follows a particular approach to support the development of the biotechnology industry by subsidising biotechnology projects not primarily in the already prized model region of the Rhine-Neckar Triangle, but ensuring that the other emerging biotechnology regions of the *Land* also receive public funding (Krauss and Stahlecker, 2000; Dohse, 2000). An important element of this policy of the Land was the creation of a biotechnology agency (*Biotechnologie-Agentur*) which has the task of co-ordinating Baden-Württemberg's support for the biotechnology industry in the different sub-regions of the Land. This reflects the attempt of the regional government to distribute public money evenly to all bioregions in Baden-Württemberg and not to accord special favour to the Rhine-Neckar Triangle. Similar to the case of multimedia, such a 'decentralized' approach is not completely undisputed, since the development of the biotechnology sector may need a concentration of resources on a relatively small number of fields and geographic areas. This points to the fact that a cluster policy which requires the regional concentration of public means is difficult to implement in such a heterogeneous, polycentric *Land* as Baden-Württemberg. The 'joint decision trap' analysed by Fritz W. Scharpf (1988) taking the example of the relationship between the federal and the *Bundesland* level, is not limited to this relationship but is also reflected in the relationships between the *Land* of Baden-Württemberg and its four 'government districts' (*Regierungsbezirke*) Freiburg, Karlsruhe, Stuttgart and Tübingen and its twelve subordinate regions.

The development of strategies for institutional learning remains a challenge to be mastered. While many 'institutionally poor' economic regions seek to adopt the seemingly exemplary institutions of other countries, Baden-Württemberg is faced with the challenge of restructuring and transforming an exceedingly rich institutional landscape. We have provided a relatively detailed account of this endeavour in the sectors of research and development, technology transfer, training and industrial relations. All of these challenges put the well-considered (and concerted) modernization of regional institutions at the top of our agenda. The expedient further development of communication and co-operation promoting institutions is therefore a central precondition for the design and rejuvenation of innovation-friendly environments. But it has also been demonstrated that institutional reforms and a transformation of existing productive structures are a difficult and extremely risky endeavour – especially when the global success of the dominant regional industries (especially the car and mechanical engineering industry) apparently make it unnecessary (at least temporally) to develop new institutional and organizational capabilities. These are the two facets of path-dependency: on one hand, it implies a singular accumulation of experiences, of technological and organizational know-how, of facilitating institutions; on the other, it also implies the difficulties in changing the existing industrial and institutional order in order to incorporate new technologies, new organizational competencies, and new qualifications.

Notes

1   The terms 'production' or 'plant regime' denote the institutionalized patterns of interpretation and behaviour within, between, over and beyond companies

that shape company product and production concepts and the conflict and co-operation relations between various employee groups and management. Production regimes can be institutionalized at the level of companies, corporations, branches, organizational fields (Scott, 1995), regions, nations and groups of nations. Industrial relations (including labour law and the organization of employer and employee interests in associations), as well as the general educational and vocational training institutions, can be regarded as the traditional institutional forms of national production regimes. Government industrial policies, the financial system, the distribution and sales market structures, and the respective branch and industry structures (including networks and integration between companies) can also be interpreted as institutionalized co-operation patterns between various protagonists in the economic system. The term 'production regime' is similar to the term industrial order proposed by Herrigel (1993) and Lane (1994).

2   Brokat, founded in 1994 in the Stuttgart Region, and specializing in software and support for electronic services, quickly became a strongly expanding company before finally running into insolvency in November 2001, then being forced to undertake a radical reorganization.

3   The state's mechanical engineering and automotive companies procured a considerable share of their total supplies (1990: 21.2 per cent of DM 91 billion) from Baden-Württemberg companies in the following branches: iron, non-ferrous metals, foundries, other mechanical engineering and automotive companies, the electrical engineering industry and the iron, sheets, metal goods branch. Given tight regional interlocking it can be assumed that, in addition to the 207,500 employees in the automotive industry (1987), 63,000 gainfully employed persons are active in other industrial branches as suppliers to the automotive industry. In 1987, 15.7 per cent of all wage and salary earners in the manufacturing industry were directly or indirectly active in connection with the automotive industry (Münzenmaier, 1988: 521). In 1993, 84,000 and, in 1998, 142,000 regional employees procured supplies for the automotive industry. Together with the 193,000 employees in the automotive industry, 6.6 per cent of the total regional employment and 21.3 per cent of the industrial employment directly or indirectly provided by the car industry. The result of the automotive boom of the second half of the 1990s therefore is an increasing specialization in this product.

4   The 2000 federal report on research (Bundesministerium für Bildung und Forschung, 2000: 221) states that Baden-Württemberg was one of the regions of Europe with the highest concentration of research. The state research report of Baden-Württemberg in 1995 (Ministerium für Wissenschaft und Forschung, 1995) highlights that Baden-Württemberg is the state with the most universities and colleges in the Federal Republic of Germany. It has a well-established research infrastructure in the field of basic research and in applied research. This

infrastructure includes nine universities, two recently founded private universities, six Pädagogische Hochschulen (colleges of education), eight colleges of art, twenty-two state-owned Fachhochschulen (including sixteen with a technical orientation), ten private Fachhochschulen, seven colleges for administration and eight Berufsakademien (Bundesbericht Forschung 2000: 221).

5   Classification into low technology, medium technology and high tech is based on the R&D intensity resulting from the ratio of R&D efforts to the production value of the product or its product range. Products with an R&D intensity below 3.5 per cent are regarded as low, between 3.5 per cent and 8.5 per cent as medium, and above 8.5 per cent as high technology. This method can be applied in industrial sectors as well. The list of R&D-intensive industries need not necessarily be the same as the list of R&D product ranges (Gehrke and Grupp, 1994: 45). The OECD proposes in its 'Science, Technology and Industry Scoreboard 2001' a similar distinction between high-technology industries (Aircraft and spacecraft, Pharmaceuticals, Office, accounting and computing machinery, Radio, television and communications equipment, Medical, precision and optical instruments) and medium-high-technology industries (Electrical machinery and apparatus, Motor vehicles, trailers and semi-trailers, Chemicals excluding pharmaceuticals, Railroad equipment and transport equipment, Machinery and equipment).

6   Similar services are also offered by other institutions, although on a smaller scale. An example in this case would be the chambers of industry and commerce (Schmitz, 1992: 110).

7   By the end of 2000 (31 December), Baden-Württemberg was hosting 301 Steinbeis transfer centres. While Steinbeis increasingly creates new centres also in other German and foreign regions, Baden-Württemberg still remains the main location of this organization (there are 127 Steinbeis centers in other parts of Germany and 8 centres abroad).

8   For example, the following statements by the chairman of the Baden-Württemberg metal and electrical industry association:

A much bigger problem than the withdrawals [from the employer's associations] is the steadily increasing number of companies which negotiate individual contracts with their labour force and their works council without regard for the collective wage agreement. Such contracts include working hour models and wage settlements outside the wage agreement, e.g. longer working hours for no extra pay. Such contracts within individual companies … undermine the collective wage agreement. Unions and employers' associations should therefore have a strong interest in opening the existing wage agreements and establishing general conditions under which these company-internal contracts can be reintegrated.

(*Stuttgarter Zeitung* 1995: 13)

Chapter 8
The regional innovation system in Wales
Evolution or eclipse?

Philip Cooke

Introduction

In the first edition of this book an initial attempt was made to reveal some evidently path-breaking trends whereby Wales as a pioneer of the first industrial revolution was, in the 1990s, leading an unusual pathway out of 'lock-in' and path dependence on a legacy of declining coal and steel industries that had begun production as far back as the 1780s. Unlike, say, the Ruhr region in Germany, where endogenous or, in evolutionary terms 'generative growth' of environmental technologies from steel and coal was apparent (Heinze *et al.*, 1998), Wales was being lifted by the arrival of global transplant firms, mainly from Japan and later the Asian 'Tigers' specialising in electronics and automotive industries. These were familiar with operating in clusters and the chapter showed how, in concert with the Welsh Development Agency (WDA), vertical, supply chain clusters were being built, especially in south Wales. Where indigenous suppliers were competitive and innovative, firms received contracts, although these were a minority but regionally significant. Sony, for instance, developed twenty-five regional suppliers in south Wales, from a total of 300 in the European Union. If the locals were unable to meet requirements, the WDA recruited suppliers, or firms like Sony and Matsushita brought them in from their own *keiretsu*.

Importantly, for the core issues of this book, these Asian firms injected a propulsive innovation element into the economy by demanding globally competitive quality at costs that typically declined by at least 3 per cent per contract period, normally two to three years. This made suppliers innovate in ways they had never been used to before. Firms were generally pressed to take innovation seriously even where they were not supplying the transplants as the Welsh Development Agency became an ambassador for, among other things, 'lean production', 'global sourcing and supplying' and 'technology marketing'. So much so, that Wales became, for a brief period in the mid-1990s, a darling of the Regional Policy Directorate of the European Union, recognised as such by being given the first pilot Regional Technology Plan contract in 1994. These later became Regional Innovation Strategies, which with the EU Regional Innovation and Technology Transfer Strategies resulted in over one hundred EU regions having such plans by the turn of the century (Landabaso, 1997).

This chapter reviews that hopeful period, taking the account up to late 2002 when published employment data showed Wales had lost 44,000 manufacturing jobs in the period between November 1998 and November 2002 (UK Office of National Statistics, 2003a). The previous set of statistics showed 23,287 manufacturing jobs had disappeared from the March dates for those years, hence statistics show a catastrophic acceleration in a nine-month period. This is particularly significant since, as will be shown below and in line with statistics appearing in the first edition of this book, Wales was growing as a manufacturing economy within UK. Indeed, as may also be seen from Table 8.1, Wales was the only part of the UK in which manufacturing employment was not in decline but actually showing an increase from 1991 to 1998. Thus, views of critics dismissive of a prevalent perspective of the early and mid-1990s that Wales was experiencing something of an 'industrial renaissance' by comparison with elsewhere in the UK, and even large parts of the EU (Cooke *et al.*, 1994) are clearly to be discounted. What is of far more importance is trying to understand what happened from 1998 to 2002, what its implications for innovation and competitiveness capabilities have been, and what, if any, new forms of innovation and enterprise support have been forthcoming. The chapter is thus organised to tackle these three crucial issues. It does this by, in some places, summarising key events leading to a waxing of innovativeness in Wales as a context for what subsequently can only be characterised as its waning. Elsewhere wholly new data are mobilised to seek to show how, as evolutionary theorist Thorstein Veblen (1899) noted, economies are not determinate in their trajectory, history can be absurd, and downward trajectories are as likely as those pointing upwards.

The waxing and waning of innovation in Wales: what happened to the regional innovation system?

In the post-war years government policy had encouraged engineering and other manufacturing firms to relocate to the industrial belts of south and north Wales. Thus, companies such as Ford, Hoover, Ferodo, GEC, Ferranti, Hotpoint, Borg-Warner and 3M became established, many demonstrating the importance of American investment in a UK economy dependent for a time on Marshall Aid and seeking to recover traditional markets throughout the world. At this time (1945–75) there was no obvious pattern to the incoming foreign investments other than that they were classical branch plants, mainly in consumption goods industries, seeking and finding large numbers of semi-skilled shopfloor workers, both male and female. Few of these arrivals ever sourced much of their supplies locally with the exception of peripheral items such as packaging and transportation.

The establishment of the Welsh Development Agency in 1976 meant that, for the first time, Wales had a body capable of promoting strategic economic development. Though the WDA never produced an economic plan for Wales, not even producing a corporate plan until 1992, nevertheless there developed a tacit sector strategy to intensify the level of investment, both domestic and overseas, in automotive and electronic engineering. This strategy took off spectacularly in the 1980s, mainly because this was the period of most intense job loss in coal, steel and the first round of manufacturing industries. For a period of approximately ten years from 1983 to 1993 Wales, with 5 per cent of the UK's population and GDP, consistently attracted between 15 per cent and 20 per cent of inward investment in the UK (Cooke, 1995).

Much of this was Japanese, American and European (especially German) investment in engineering. Sony arrived in 1974, followed by Hitachi, Panasonic (Matsushita), Aiwa, Brother, Sharp and Orion, all in some way involved in consumer or office electronics. Later, LG from Korea, wafer fabrication firms International Rectifier (US) and Trikon (UK), and components firms from Hong Kong and Singapore joined the cluster. Since 1998, Sony has reduced employment by around 700, as has Panasonic, while Hitachi, Aiwa and, in effect, LG have closed their operations in Wales. In automotive industries, Ford opened an engine plant at Bridgend in south Wales in 1978 and this was followed by acquisitions or new, greenfield investments by Calsonic, Valeo, Lucas-SEI, Robert Bosch, Trico, ITT-Alfred Teves, Ina Bearings, Sekisui, Yuasa, Gillet, Grundy and Hoesch-Camford. Since 1998, Valeo and Lucas-SEI have retreated, the latter to Slovakia and Poland. By 1992 production of 200,000 engines a year by Toyota began as supply to their assembly plant in Derby and for export back to Japan. From 1999, the Ford Bridgend engine plant became the sole Zetec engine source, annually producing 700,000 of these and 55,000 Jaguar AJ26 V8 engines. In 2001 a new range of Jaguar engines was announced, to be produced at a rate of 325,000 per year. Toyota engine production had expanded to 500,000 engines by 2003. Wales had evolved into a key centre of high-quality, high-skill automotive engine production in Europe, with 2,400 employed at Bridgend and 600 at Deeside in north Wales.

According to Rhys (2002) the component base consists of some 150 companies, 40 of which are first-tier suppliers, 70 second-tier and the rest lower in the supply chain. Joining global leaders like Bosch and Calsonic since 1995 are TRW, Visteon, Meritor and Magna. These and indigenously developed supplier companies have built a customer base which includes all the UK and major European manufacturers in the automotive industry sector. These firms retain some forty direct and indirect supply relationships to assemblers such as Volvo, Saab, Fiat, Opel and Renault. Of much greater importance are the supply-chain links from Welsh automotive components firms to UK-based, domestically and foreign-owned assemblers such as Rover, Ford, Jaguar, Nissan, Toyota, Honda, GM and Peugeot. Welsh suppliers have over sixty direct supply contracts with these firms and some 130 in which they supply the final customer indirectly through another member of the supply chain. However, Rhys (2002) also notes that gross value per head is below the UK average by some 7 per cent and net capital expenditure by 20 per cent. Thus, although increasingly capital-intensive, the automotive industry in Wales lags in productivity, something to which we shall return.

A cluster story can be told for electronics and information and communication technology (ICT). By 1990, the main industries in this sector were office automation and consumer electronics. Other important industries were telecommunications equipment, instrumentation, components and software. Between 1980 and 1990 these industries grew in employment terms by an average of 110 per cent. However, whereas in the automotive industry all of the Welsh and Welsh-based firms are components, systems or engine suppliers, in IT and electronics, components only account for 13 per cent of the industry. The vast majority of production firms are final assemblers, many of them Japanese such as Panasonic, Orion, Sony, Sharp and Brother. Such firms sought to source their supply requirements within Wales. An example was the Japanese-German television and VDU screen joint venture NEC-Schott, now wholly NEC-owned, located in Cardiff, joining other overseas supply companies located in Wales such as Matsushita Components, Diaplastics, Ninkaplast, and Meiki. This largely explains how Wales became both more of a manufacturing economy than it was and, proportionately, more of a manufacturing economy than the UK.

What now demands investigation is what happened and why to reverse the burgeoning trajectory of the Welsh manufacturing sector, much of it supporting the electronics cluster and the automotive supply chain, especially Corus, the Anglo-Dutch joint venture that absorbed British Steel and has cut employment most. In Table 8.1 comparative statistics of manufacturing job change 1991–2001 show the point at which the reverse occurred. Table 8.2 then explores what happened until November 2002, the last date for which Labour Force Survey statistics are available at the time of writing. Briefly, Table 8.1 shows three relevant things. First, the marginally and uniquely positive growth statistic for Welsh manufacturing 1991–98. Second, the higher than average rate of job loss in manufacturing 1998–2001 should be noted (which nevertheless translates into a relatively modest 9,287 jobs, Cooke *et al.*, 2003) shared with North-east England behind the West Midlands. Accordingly, third, slippage from third to fourth in regional manufacturing employment share in Britain. The crucial question to be answered next is whether large or small and medium enterprises mainly account for that manufacturing employment decline. The answer is, overwhelmingly, large firms. Official statistics at UK level show large firms (> 250 employees) accounted for 228,000 of the UK's 348,000 manufacturing job loss 1998–2001, approximately two-thirds, and there is no reason to think Wales was any different (Office

Table 8.1 Manufacturing employment change in Great Britain, 1991–2001 (March)

Region	2001 (%)	1998 (%)	1991 (%)	%Change 1991–2001	%Change 1991–98	%Change 1998–2001
E. Midlands	20.5	21.5	26.7	–6.2	–1.2	–1.0
Eastern	14.5	17.1	19.7	–5.2	–2.6	–2.6
London	6.4	7.8	10.0	–3.6	–2.2	–1.4
North East	16.5	21.1	21.6	–5.1	–0.5	–4.6
North West	16.4	20.2	22.1	–5.7	–1.9	–3.8
South East	11.2	13.9	15.5	–4.3	–1.6	–2.7
South West	14.2	13.9	15.5	–3.2	–0.7	–2.5
W. Midlands	19.9	25.7	28.0	–8.1	–2.3	–5.8
Yorks. & H.	17.8	21.3	23.0	–5.2	–1.7	–3.5
Scotland	12.8	15.4	17.6	–4.8	–2.2	–2.6
Wales	17.1	21.7	21.6	–4.5	+0.1	–4.6
GB	14.1	17.4	19.3	–5.2	–1.9	–3.3

Source: Office of National Statistics

Table 8.2 Regional manufacturing employment change, 1994–2002 (November)

Region (000s)	2002 (%)	2001 (%)	2000 (%)	1998 (%)	1994 (%)
E. Midlands	434 (21.0)	453 (21.9)	455 (22.6)	481 (24.1)	494 (26.4)
Eastern	430 (15.5)	460 (16.6)	444 (16.2)	465 (17.6)	475 (19.0)
London	287 (8.0)	284 (8.0)	282 (8.1)	319 (9.4)	310 (10.1)
North East	194 (17.6)	210 (19.1)	220 (19.9)	233 (21.7)	205 (19.6)
North West	557 (17.4)	569 (18.2)	594 (19.1)	622 (20.4)	665 (22.6)
Scotland	336 (13.9)	337 (14.1)	368 (15.3)	375 (16.1)	380 (16.7)
South East	569 (13.6)	582 (14.0)	567 (13.8)	656 (16.3)	600 (16.2)
South West	366 (14.7)	364 (14.8)	385 (15.8)	378 (16.2)	377 (17.1)
Wales	206 (15.8)	220 (17.4)	223 (17.7)	250 (20.4)	237 (19.9)
W. Midlands	563 (22.5)	572 (22.8)	567 (23.2)	639 (25.8)	629 (26.7)
Yorks. & H.	444 (18.7)	440 (18.7)	479 (20.3)	477 (20.8)	471 (21.3)
GB	4,386 (15.7)	4,491 (16.2)	4,584 (16.7)	4,893 (18.2)	4,843 (19.1)

Source: Office of National Statistics

of National Statistics, 2003b). Now the analysis moves to absolute statistics as well as percentages and the period covered takes us up to November 2002, as shown in Table 8.2. Table 8.2 reveals a number of important features, especially for the 1998–2002 period. First, although not the largest magnitude in absolute numbers, the Welsh percentage decline in manufacturing was, at 4.6 per cent, the steepest. Second, the two-to-one ratio of large firm to SME job loss suggests that large firms accounted for approximately 30,000 of the 44,000 jobs lost in 1998–2002. Wales slipped from fourth to sixth in regional manufacturing employment share in approximately one year. Wales is now closer to the profile of 'post-industrial' regions like the South-East and South-West in its modest share of manufacturing employment than to manufacturing regions like the Midlands towards which its trajectory pointed up to 1998.

This point is being laboured because of the swiftness with which change has happened, the manner in which inward investment firms and the linked remnants of the Welsh steel heritage have contracted, and their importance to the emergent regional innovation system that had been evolving around engineering sectors or clusters and which now is beginning to unravel. The unravelling occurs when, for instance, a firm like Hitachi, or Aiwa with its local suppliers association shared partly with its parent Sony, disappears. It impacts when a firm such as LG (later LG-Philips) that set up with fanfares and research grants for university academics retrenches and, in crisis, is forced by the South Korean government to sell its undeveloped, last generation semiconductor production and R&D facility to its rival Hyundai, whose subsidiary Hynix wishes to sell it back to the WDA who built it in the first place. It occurs when Corus shuts down its 200-person materials research laboratory, as happened in 2001. Embryonic 'Triple Helix' relations among universities, businesses and government agencies atrophy and die with the loss of regional personnel to act as interlocutors and commissioners of research. This, in brief, is what happened to the, always hierarchical, ultimately WDA-animated, but FDI-facilitated regional innovation system in Wales after 1998.

Of course, this kind of economic evolution is part and parcel of global competitiveness as inward investors activate new locational selection mechanisms in light of changed market conditions. But such experiences betray an important feature about innovation systems for policy-makers and academe alike. Systems, by definition, represent and thrive upon stability and reasonable institutional and organisational continuity. Innovation creates uncertainty and is destabilising. The relationship is somewhat like that Latour (1998) specified between 'science' and 'research' as discussed in the Introduction to this book. Regional innovation systems in particular must develop highly refined sensitivities to change. That this happens in settings like Massachusetts where mini-computing disappeared but biosciences rose to global prominence is testimony to the flexibility to market opportunities inherent in what were referred to in the introduction as Entrepreneurial Regional Innovation Systems (ERIS). This is more difficult in the interventionist Institutional Regional Innovation Systems (IRIS) typical of Europe and paradigmatic in Wales.

So what has been the innovation system's policy response in Wales, and what, crucially, has been the effectiveness of the response? These questions are explored in the section that follows, but as a prelude three major input shifts, one of which also reveals a significant output shift may be mentioned. First, as devolution was meeting demand for a democratic Assembly in Wales, power to determine financial allocations was wrested away from administrators. A re-mapping of Welsh GDP performance led to the discovery that more than half the area of Wales warranted EU Structural Funds Objective 1 designation. Dividing Wales into zones containing wealthy and poor localities had obscured this hitherto. A sum of £1.2 billion over six years was thus earmarked for economic restructuring, including regional innovation expenditure, starting in 2000. Second, the planning process necessary to achieve this objective led to two further economic development strategies. These marked an end to the WDA's love affair with inward investment, now seen to have dried up, something also recognised in the thinking of other regional systems, notably Scotland as discussed in the Introduction to this book. These documents shifted the strategic economic development spotlight on to *entrepreneurship*, with a key instrument modelled on the old Regional Technology Plan but transformed into the Entrepreneurship Action Plan. A new investment vehicle, Finance Wales, was set up to channel EU and private funds into loans and equity investments for SMEs and start-up businesses. A 'Knowledge Exploitation Fund' was set up to facilitate exploitation of university research.

As we shall see, apart from the achievement of Objective 1 status, itself automatic once the boundary conditions were complied with, actions involved paper strategies, establishment of delivery mechanisms, renewal of tasks for existing personnel, and recruitment of new public administrators. Coincidentally, the Vocational Training set-up (known by the acronym ELWA) was completely overhauled, at least organisationally, and its size and budget doubled to twice that of the WDA. Finally, the National Health Service in Wales was twice reorganised following the setting up of the Assembly in 1999 and, as in the rest of the UK, large injections of public finance have been provided to bring standards up to the average for the EU, which entails a UK health budget rise to £105 billion from its current £65 billion. The 2003 health budget in Wales was £3.8 billion. Thus, the Welsh Assembly Government had swiftly turned its attention to administrative reforms, absorbing large amounts of new money, and centralising control of expenditure and management of these budgets.

The effect of this is revealed starkly in Table 8.3, which gives a comparative analysis of changes in public administration (education, government, and health) employment in British regions since 1994. Wales now has the highest percentage share of public administration in the land. Reflecting back on the 1998–2002 period that saw a major downturn in the manufacturing labour market, the 67,000

Table 8.3 Regional public administration employment change, 1994–2002 (November)

Region (000s)	2002 (%)	2001 (%)	2000 (%)	1998 (%)	1994 (%)
E. Midlands	502 (24.3)	488 (23.6)	467 (23.2)	438 (21.9)	400 (21.4)
Eastern	640 (23.1)	633 (22.9)	637 (23.2)	570 (21.6)	475 (19.0)
London	850 (23.8)	851 (24.0)	771 (22.1)	769 (22.7)	731 (23.7)
North East	326 (29.6)	327 (29.7)	301 (27.3)	283 (26.4)	263 (25.2)
North West	874 (27.4)	856 (27.4)	853 (27.4)	756 (24.8)	720 (24.5)
Scotland	690 (28.6)	671 (28.1)	649 (27.0)	635 (27.2)	583 (25.6)
South East	1,004 (24.0)	974 (23.4)	987 (24.0)	960 (23.8)	864 (23.3)
South West	653 (26.1)	626 (25.4)	642 (26.4)	588 (25.2)	564 (25.6)
Wales	415 (31.8)	368 (29.1)	368 (29.2)	348 (28.4)	311 (26.1)
W. Midlands	606 (24.2)	621 (24.8)	568 (23.2)	559 (22.5)	516 (21.9)
Yorks. & H.	634 (26.7)	592 (25.2)	604 (25.6)	552 (24.1)	513 (23.1)
GB	7,193 (25.7)	7,008 (25.3)	6,846 (24.9)	6,459 (24.1)	5,964 (23.5)

Source: Office of National Statistics

rise in public administration employment more than made up for the 44,000 manufacturing jobs lost in that period.

Indeed, employment overall in Wales has risen, with the ubiquitous 'other business services' growing somewhat, but not the more knowledge-intensive financial services. Hence, two questions arise: one concerns the effectiveness of the implementation of innovation targeted measures, now aimed at SMEs rather than FDI, the other concerns an even more interesting issue as to whether a public sector-led strategy of employment generation is simply a drag on the 'real economy' (Pritchard, 2003) or whether within it, there might be the seeds of a novel innovation strategy for a more socially nuanced and sustainable regional economy. These and related matters are discussed in the following section.

Innovation performance: Wales compared

While it was true to say in the previous edition that there was a bewildering array of enterprise support instruments available in Wales in the mid-1990s, by 2003 there was, at some 250 listed on the WDA website, a positive cornucopia of aids. Strictly regarding innovation, the most valuable of these in the past were a prototype RITTS and the pilot RTP, since updated under the RIS 2 programme funded by the EU. The latter was evaluated by EU assessors as being good regarding provision of organisational inputs to the programme, organising numerous meetings bringing 'Triple Helix' type actors to meetings to discuss required actions, and, accordingly, building consensus about future development imperatives. However, it was marked down on the outputs and outcomes aspects, the evaluators seeing little by way of new initiatives and much re-packaging of existing instruments drawn from the above-mentioned 250 (Technopolis, 1998). Rather than go into detail on a miasma of policy instruments, the following maximises use of the limited space available to first examine, in this section, some comparative innovation indicators involving Wales, and in the following one, discuss a few key initiatives before drawing conclusions about prospects for the Welsh innovation system as it faces an uncertain future.

Three innovation studies involving Wales were published between 1998 and 2002. The first was the EU-funded Targeted Socio-Economic Research (TSER) project called *Regional Innovation Systems: Designing for the Future* co-ordinated by the present author (Cooke *et al.*, 2000). The second is the UK Innovation Survey conducted by the UK government in 2001 (DTI, 2001), while the third is a study by the Harvard Business School conducted, using secondary data, by Michael Porter (Porter, 2002).

Beginning with the TSER study, this compared Wales and ten other European regions (two in Central Europe) in respect of whether and to what extent regional innovation operated interactively as is proposed in the innovation systems literature. Of the eleven regions, many of which, like the Basque Country in Spain, Styria in Austria, Tampere in Finland and Wallonia in Belgium were old industrial regions reconverting to newer, more innovative sectors Wales was agreed to be one of only four that warranted being denoted a regional innovation system. Like the three others, this was because of conscious practice and policies established at regional level to promote interactive innovation among firms and between them and universities and economic development agencies or ministries. Baden-Württemberg was one, not a reconversion but rather a high performance engineering economy, the Basque Country and Styria the others. Because whole economies could not be surveyed with the resources and timescale available, participant research teams identified their regionally important, propulsive sectors for in-depth study. In Wales this meant the aforementioned automotive and electronics engineering industries plus, perhaps presciently, healthcare. Most other regions had varieties of engineering as their propulsive sectors also, but only a few like Tampere selected healthcare. The reason why healthcare is important for innovation is that it belongs to a technological innovation system that includes Life Sciences, pharmaceuticals and biotechnology as well as care of patients. In some countries this grouping accounts for up to 25 per cent of GDP and even (in the UK) 25 per cent of the total R&D budget. We saw in Table 8.3 that the broad employment sector in which UK official statistics place healthcare (excluding Life Sciences, pharmaceuticals and biotechnology) is substantially larger than manufacturing and more than double the size of manufacturing in Wales. The research, technological and production activities associated with healthcare contain the highest levels of private R&D expenditure given the world pharmaceuticals average of 17.5 per cent of sales in 2002 (worth at least $28 billion in 2002) and some of the most innovative, advanced technologies known in history. The annual US public R&D budget for the National Institutes of Health in 2003 is $27.3 billion, most of which is spent in Medical and Life Sciences research centres in US universities (Cooke, 2004). Public health research expenditure in the European Union was estimated at some $10 billion (Senker and Van Zwanenberg, 2001).

The following consists of key innovation indicators arising from the TSER study of Wales and its ten comparator regions. Firms were surveyed regionally by postal questionnaire and asked a range of innovation-related questions. A key one, frequently used in surveys of this kind was how much product, process and organisational innovation had been conducted by the firm during the preceding three years. This referred both to innovations new to the market and those new to the firm. In Baden-Württemberg 64 per cent of firms had innovated products new to the market but only 12 per cent had done so for processes. In Wales 45 per cent had innovated products new to the market and 19 per cent processes new to the market. Regarding organisational innovation, the most commonly introduced measure among the regions studied was the ISO 9000 business process quality standard. In Baden-Württemberg 68 per cent had introduced this between 1993 and 1996 whereas in Wales the figure was 70 per cent. On total quality management (TQM) the two were equal, both with 50 per cent of firms having introduced TQM during the three years preceding the survey. Recall that this was during the period when the Welsh innovation system was being constructed as 'scaffolding' for the burgeoning automotive and electronics industries. The German region used in the above comparisons was particularly relevant since it was probably Europe's leading region in these industries.

However, to get at the systemic aspects of innovation within and then beyond the region required investigating collaboration among firms and 'Triple Helix' partners among others. This was done by postal survey questionnaire also, and true to most such surveys done subsequently, the leading partner *within the region* on average is the customer, the second is the supplier and the third, in this survey but not all, was universities. Of all firms surveyed, the mean was 44 per cent of firms having innovation partnership with regional customers, 35 per cent suppliers and 24 per cent universities. In Baden-Württemberg the figures were 89 per cent, 80 per cent and 25 per cent respectively, while in Wales they were 28 per cent, 22 per cent and 25 per cent. Interestingly, in light of what has already been said about the public governance leadership of the Welsh innovation system even in the early 1990s, the highest-ranking innovation partner, with 29 per cent of firms recording it, was 'government'. Thus in those days the panoply of enterprise support schemes meant that at least that percentage of firms was using them, receiving government advice on innovation, but interacting with customers and suppliers far less than the average.

But this reflects also the greater strength of the globally leading German region's innovation system compared with the more open relations already described between firms located in Wales but owned or trading elsewhere. Thus when the question of innovation partners at national level was posed, although Baden-Württemberg firms' innovation interactions with national customers rose to an astounding 93 per cent and with suppliers a still healthy 75 per cent, the equivalents in Wales rose to 56 per cent and 51 per cent respectively. Thereafter, when the question was posed regarding European innovation partners, Wales slipped back to a poor 22 per cent customer and 26 per cent supplier innovation interaction while the German region scored 73 per cent and 36 per cent respectively. Universities at European level were insignificant partners for both in contrast to nationally where the German region had 19 per cent of firms engaged and Wales 25 per cent.

These data and many more published in Cooke *et al.*, (2000) paint a picture of firms in Wales being innovative, though not placing Wales as a European region in the top tier of innovators. They show Wales being modestly interactive for innovation with firms in the region and as much users of university innovation support in the region as the leading performer. Network relationships were high nationally for Welsh firms but nowhere near as high as those of the European regional leader. Notable also is the mid-1990s 'grant-dependence' in Wales suggested by the higher government innovation partnership than for any other of the eleven regions.

The two other studies compare Wales' economic performance with other regions of the UK, and of the two, the government study (DTI, 2001) is the more comprehensive. It shows Wales vying with Northern Ireland for bottom position in Business R&D Expenditure (BERD) over the 1998–2000 period and a declining employment in private R&D by 2000. These statistics reflected the 200 R&D jobs lost at Corus in late 2000. The DTI survey measured innovation performance regionally for SMEs and large firms over the 1998–2000 period. Wales was shown to have 45 per cent of its SMEs active in innovation compared to the UK mean of 46 per cent. Contrariwise, 82 per cent of large firms were active by comparison with the UK mean of 67 per cent, only the North-East scoring higher at 89 per cent. Both are branch-plant economies and the statistics confirm the argument of this chapter, which is that it is the FDI sector that is innovative, and weakening of its presence weakens regional innovation in Wales. The DTI study also confirms the TSER findings on Wales' prominence as a process innovating region with 18 per cent of enterprises active compared to 15 per cent UK-wide. This is underlined by reference to what is called 'novel innovation' (new to the market) where Welsh SMEs are in first position, 50 per cent above the UK mean. Here large enterprises score below the UK mean. For novel product innovations Welsh SMEs again score higher than average and large firms in Wales score third highest (24 per cent of enterprises producing novel product innovations against an 18 per cent UK mean). Moreover, the mean percentage of turnover from novel products places Welsh SMEs second only to London although for large firms this variable scores well below average. This is where Wales' productivity problem re-appears. Finally, regarding networking and interactive innovation Wales scored above the UK mean of 28 per cent of firms reporting institutional inform-ation exchange as being of value to innovation, but at 29 per cent only marginally and less than four other regions.

This rather rosier picture of innovation performance in Wales suggests three things of importance. The first is the propulsive effect on the supply chain of exacting customers such as those in the FDI sector, the presence of which looks to be waning. Second, and somewhat unusually, two separate surveys have shown Welsh firms to be pronounced process innovators compared to other regional firms in the UK and selected European regions. SMEs are prominent in this, which may again reflect the impact of demanding exogenous customers. Finally, we see that the ten-year and more history of institutional regional innovation system (IRIS) building receives an echo in the marginally higher than average networking propensity of Welsh enterprises, but in truth at 1 percentage point above the mean and on a fairly weak indicator, this tells us relatively little about all the system building effort that has gone on, save that it has hardly constituted a systemic 'quantum leap'.

Finally, we can take a brief look at the results of Michael Porter's reflections upon the Welsh innovation condition (Porter, 2002). Porter shows, first, that Welsh economic performance is below the regression line that associates per capita income and annual growth in employment 1996–2000. He also shows Welsh productivity levels to be in the weak quadrant (along with all but London and the South-East) on gross value added related to productivity change over the same period. However, it is closer to the national averages on both than most UK regions. This can be interpreted as another effect of the FDI sector that raises productivity somewhat more than the domestic sector though not massively, but enough to have given a boost to the Welsh statistic. In the past, EU data have shown GDP per worker high in Wales but all statistical sources show GDP per person low, a reflection of low male and female economic activity rates deriving from past generations of deindustrialisation. Porter places overall (not just BERD) R&D activity below average but higher than three other UK regions. He also shows manufacturing 1990–2000 to have been, along with healthcare, Wales' higher than average large employment location quotient sectors. Finally, and interestingly he shows Cardiff University (with 7) to be Wales' third highest US patent holder, behind Dow Corning and local biomedical devices firm Gyrus Medical Ltd. Cardiff University is also shown to be thirteenth among UK universities on the same indicator. But the leader, Imperial College, London has only 36 compared to the US leader, the University of California with 1,585. Porter's action agenda for Wales is to improve the Welsh business environment, develop clusters, develop subregional strategies, and create an integrated vision and organisational structure to deliver it. Porter's view on the aforementioned Welsh Assembly Government economic development strategies (Porter, 2002) was that they were a 'wish list' with no obvious mechanisms for delivering success. It was once said of a Welsh shepherd that he guessed the profession 'management consultant' accurately when one of them asked, if he guessed the number of sheep in the flock correctly could he have one? Agreeing to the challenge, the shepherd asked in return if he could have it back if he guessed the challenger's profession. Using global satellite positioning connected to his laptop, the man got the number right, chose his animal then waited. 'How did you guess I was a management consultant?' the astonished consultant asked. 'Because you cost a fortune, you tell me what I already know, and you know nothing about my business. Now give me my dog back'.

Devolved Wales and its key innovation instruments

We have observed many of the key and evolving difficulties faced by the Welsh economy and its faltering regional innovation system. In the following, four of the key policy mechanisms for re-tracking the Welsh innovation system are examined to give a flavour of the often noble aspirations embodied as inputs to their supporting policies and the unyielding nature of brute reality when it comes to making judgements on effectiveness measured in terms of outputs. The first example is the large, £1.2 billion EU Objective 1 funding for 2000–6 in the older industrial and western seaboard belts known officially as West Wales and the Valleys. Not all of this funding is available for innovation; under EU rules measures to promote community enterprise and regeneration, training and general assistance to SMEs are covered as well. Nevertheless, some funding is earmarked for innovation support. One sphere in which such funding is used is meeting the Welsh Development Agency's strategy of constructing twenty business incubators or Techniums, many in the Objective 1 area.

From the outset, as in many earlier recipients of Objective 1 aid in southern Europe, there was a problem of absorptive capacity by the institutional set-up in Wales. Initially an office in the Assembly was created for an Objective 1 'tsar' and the body responsible for managing the previous Objective 2 programme, the Welsh European Funding Organisation (WEFO) was given responsibility for disbursing project funding. The process of drawing up the priorities on which the money was to be spent was complex and not entirely successful. Participation by representatives of local government, business and the voluntary sector had led to deadlock with the voluntary sector complaining of being out-manoeuvred by the other parties. Accordingly, the new First Minister dismantled the administrative machinery set up by his predecessor and handed the task to the civil service. Time was short as the final submission deadline to Brussels was looming, so they simply allocated the funding in the same proportions as it had been divided in the old Objective 2 programmes. Some of the resulting imbalances were raised in the UK Parliament's Select Committee on Welsh Affairs investigation into The Structural Funds in Wales, and from the evidence given by the First Minister, the above account of administrative expedience emerged (Welsh Affairs Committee, 2000).

An extremely complex system of interlocking committees was set up as responsible for each programme area, involving Assembly and other government, business, voluntary and academic representatives and experts who were recruited to fill these committees, whose main task was to judge whether grant applications for funding should be approved. At the end of the first year of this process an unofficial estimate of 1,700 was made, by a former European Union senior official who had returned to advise the Assembly on this financial absorption and allocation nightmare of the number of people that had been recruited to manage the approval system and support it administratively. Such were the complaints from, particularly, the business community at the glacial progress of implementation of the Objective 1 programme that reforms were instituted, consisting of the insertion of a new layer of committees given a 'troubleshooting' function to break the administrative log-jams that kept recurring.

Thereafter, it was assumed that project funding was being allocated, projects were being implemented, monitored and evaluated with job targets being achieved. Announcements to the effect that, for example, £82 million had been allocated for Techniums and other, community and training measures in Swansea or £60 million had been allocated to hard-hit former manufacturing communities in West Wales appeared regularly on the Assembly website (www.wales.gov.uk). However, in 2003 the Economic Development Minister was asked by the all-party Economic Development Committee for a progress report on the Objective 1 programme and the Director of WEFO obliged, the resulting report being lodged in the public domain in the Assembly Library (WEFO, 2003). Astonishingly, this official report revealed that only £74 million in EU grants and match funding had been paid out and, even more surprisingly, only 44 of a projected 26,000 jobs had been created, with a further 14 being safeguarded. Opposition politicians quickly took the Labour Minister to task on value for money grounds, pointing out that each job appeared to have cost £1.74 million to create. Later, the Minister blamed a computer for the misinformation and claimed the actual number was 'over 6,000' but offered no supporting evidence (Shipton, 2003).

Thus it was evident that the absorptive capacity problem had not been satisfactorily dealt with and there were fears that Brussels would have to be repaid a substantial tranche of the funding allocated. In late 2003, the Labour administration announced that WEFO was to be absorbed into the Assembly as from January 2004. Briefly, we can see how three innovation support policies have been affected by governance problems of a different kind arising from an increasingly centralised mode of animating the regional innovation system. *A Winning Wales*, the WAG economic strategy document condemned by Michael Porter as a 'wish list', refers to the importance of innovation on its first page. Even its widely criticised predecessor, the *National Economic Development Strategy* was associated with setting up 'Finance Wales' the public–private venture fund for innovation, and the 'Knowledge Exploitation Fund' for academic knowledge exploitation, although the Technium idea is more recent. In 2003 a *Wales for Innovation* plan was launched and was quickly shown to be largely another 're-packaging'.

Beginning with a preliminary 'sense-making' account of Techniums, it is worth recalling that twenty of these are planned, some already in operation by 2003. In line with UK government policy on building a knowledge-based economy, which supports building incubators as 'seed crystals' for clusters, Techniums aim to offer hosting facilities for university start-ups and other high technology businesses, including those from abroad. Thus far, the first, on the Swansea waterfront, has found tenants and a second one was completed in late 2003. But Agilent, a small American software business that was one of the first, widely trumpeted, arrivals closed at the end of 2002 and other tenant firms were moved to the Technium from a 1980s' Innovation Centre on the campus of Swansea University required for academic expansion. Other Techniums in planning or construction stages were to have sectoral focus, like the Bio-Technium at Wales' National Botanic Gardens, and media Techniums in Cardiff and west Wales. all of these faced major obstacles due to financial stringency in 2003. A possible set of design flaws in the policy include, first, an inclination to replicate old incubation approaches that failed to prioritise management assistance, including allocating part-time space to such services as venture capital, legal advice and management accountancy. Second, true to WDA traditions, they are properties leasing space, now for SMEs – previously for FDI businesses, thus they are not in themselves innovative. Finally, they assume 400 or more incubator spaces can be filled. A study of this question calculated that, from academia in Wales, where there are less than 1,000 tenured scientists and engineers, some 20 to 30 spinouts could be anticipated during the lifetimes of those academics if international rates of academic entrepreneurship prevailed (Jones-Evans, 2002). Clearly, a major 'recruitment' effort is underway to aspirations to have any chance of being fulfilled.

The Knowledge Exploitation Fund (KEF) has aspirations that fit the Technium idea in principle, but in practice will make very little impact upon filling the Technium incubators. This is because, like many policies, it was designed by and for the public sector. So, to exploit academic knowledge, KEF funds Further Education (Community) colleges and Higher Education Institutions to offer training to firms on the advantages of such activities as business networking. This networking approach also applies to higher education itself, as a £1.1 million grant to partners Cardiff University, the University of Wales Medical School and Techniquest, a science museum, to establish a Gene Park testifies. This admirable initiative involves, as a first stage, setting up a virtual Gene Park between the Life Sciences departments of the main universities. Hence much of the funding is earmarked for high speed data transmission cabling and technology. This is one of the more significant research infrastructure investments KEF will have made. However, firms approaching KEF for support are informed that the KEF remit is to support public knowledge exploitation as a priority, leaving SMEs frustrated and wondering how this Training Agency-funded initiative, supposedly spending between £24 million and £28 million per year, can actually help them in other than trivial ways. In 2003 KEF was taken from the Training Agency (ELWa) and placed in the WDA.

Finally, Finance Wales was set up in 2000 to fill the perceived funding gap for innovative businesses seeking investment of a scale beyond that normally met by seed corn funding or business angel networks (in Wales the angel fund Xenox is also managed by Finance Wales). In addition, upon establishment, small firms loan funds were created to assist non-high technology businesses and community enterprises. Although targets were set for the number of firms officially to be assisted with venture capital from the Wales Innovation Fund (resourced by the EU Objective 1 funding, the WDA and NatWest Bank), interview results from a research project on innovative financing of economic development reveal that an average of only three investments per year have been forthcoming (Cooke and Clifton, 2003). On the other hand, the Small Firms Loan Fund has been over-subscribed. A restructuring of the many initial funds into fewer, larger funds has worsened the position in three ways. First, because of some failed investments an internal rate of return double that required by the venture capital industry has been set, thus further discouraging approaches due to more stringent conditions being applied to applicants. Second, administrative expediency by WAG has diverted non-venture capital financial problems Assembly civil servants are incapable of managing into Finance Wales. Key staff are thus diverted from building up a customer base by firefighting on activities the institution was not designed to fulfil.

Thus, third, because core demand for both equity investment and economic development grants has been slow, especially during the post dot.com stock market 'meltdown', administrators fearful of questions being asked of low performance and concerned not to make future risky investments, have set up rules that require a venture capital-seeking firm to first win a Regional Selective Assistance grant for half the sum being sought. The rationale is that the regional aids division does the due diligence on the equity request and the linkage results in 'two hits for the price of one' for the administrators. This flies in the face of modern public investment theory, which is to wean SMEs away from grant-dependence towards a mixed equity and loan package, thus encouraging better entepreneurship. In Northern Ireland and Scotland steps have been taken to reduce grant dependence among SMEs but in Wales the opposite is the case. Thus, to conclude this section on 'sense making' regarding the Welsh Assembly Government's attempts to grapple with retracking the Welsh regional innovation system, it is clear that the 'public enterprise' approach, popular elsewhere in the 1970s, that is being taken has good intentions but is failing dismally to foster entrepreneurship and innovation. This is because of risk aversity and an unwillingness to loosen an over-centralised grip on control of budgets and the design of enterprise and innovation support instruments for public more than private benefit.

Conclusion

This chapter has sought to achieve three objectives, the first of which is to reprise after a decade the evolution of a particular type of state-animated and multinational capital facilitated regional innovation system that could clearly be seen emerging when foreign investment was flooding into Wales, supply chain integration was being effected, and innovative cluster interactions were being formed as global firms embedded themselves in a receptive regional economy, equipped with appropriate skills and public subsidies. The second has been to investigate recent economic change, which, as was shown, has been dramatic, heralding the ending of the inward investment boom, the establishment of a devolved, democratic regional administration, its new focus on innovation and entrepreneurship and power to generate jobs in public administration. As we have seen, only the last-named power to invest in employment in public services can currently be called a success. This raises problems for innovation theory and practice, since it is unclear but an open question as to whether the public sector can be a 'pacer' in this particular vein, as suggested by Gregersen (1992). The third aim was to examine some key innovation-driving initiatives that have been designed and implemented in Wales since devolution as a 'sense-making' exercise (Weick, 1995; Nooteboom, 2001) into why initiatives taken to foster innovation and entrepreneurship, given the turning away from inward investment, should have proven so recalcitrant and intractable to policy leverage.

Regarding the first aim, the research showed that much had changed since the early 1990s when the previous edition was being researched. In Wales, which was the UK's only growing manufacturing region in employment terms, manufacturing job loss rose sharply after 1998. The reasons for this are complex but affected larger firms mostly, many of which were FDI businesses. Some were relocating to Central and Eastern Europe or North Africa where, in the former case, accession to the EU at substantially lower labour costs was the incentive. In the latter case even lower wage costs attracted, for example, clothing suppliers to UK retailer Marks & Spencer, itself squeezed by intense competition in its home market, leading it also to vacate export markets. Process innovation had been pronounced in M&S supplier firms like Dewhirst, contributor of over 1,000 job losses, as the wholesale transhipment of advanced technology and workforce trainers to Morocco testified. The UK's overvalued currency *vis-à-vis* Euroland also gave reason to manufacturers, notably those from East Asia, that had been located in Wales for, in some cases, more than a quarter of a century to re-invest in plant and equipment in new locations. Thus, supply chains have become more extended and innovation interactions through the value chain weakened as the WDA, responsible for animating countless support initiatives in the past, turned away from FDI to concentrate on the stimulation of endogenous growth.

This has proven to be a hard nut to crack. Assessments of performance regarding initiatives such as the Entrepreneurship Action Plan, the Knowledge Exploitation Fund and Finance Wales are seldom published but research currently being conducted (Cooke and Clifton, 2003) indicates that the Entrepreneurship Action Plan has only impacted a third of its target businesses since establishment (1,800 SMES out of a target of 4,600), a report on KEF shows that despite budgets of well over £20 million per year being spent, only 5 per cent more entrepreneurship modules were being taught in universities and other higher education institutes, although 25 per cent more were taught in further education colleges. But 75 per cent of the latter had no or few mechanisms for technology transfer, while the statistic for universities was 25 per cent. It can be concluded that there was a significant disconnect in this particular part of the entrepreneurship-driven renewal of the regional innovation system in Wales (Steele and Levie, 2001). The earlier analysis of Finance Wales, a vehicle designed to supply venture capital to innovative SMEs and start-up businesses because of a perceived market failure in private provision, showed that such disconnects register in the far lower than targeted number of businesses coming forward in quest of equity investment. Accordingly, public venture capitalists are redeployed on firefighting problems with co-funding grant packages for, *inter alia*, a holiday village development in the Objective 1 area. Further administrative expediency and risk aversion have the effect of slowing down and making more difficult acquiring equity investment while encouraging SMEs to become more grant-dependent than many wish to be.

Thus, we come to a success story in terms of job generation which is the 67,000 new jobs created from the Welsh Assembly Government's own block grant financial resources transferred from London. The breakdown between health, education and public administration between June 1999 and June 2002 was 22,000, 18,000 and 3,000 (Cooke *et al.*, 2003). Both health and education contribute to innovation, the first in patient treatment, and the second in producing talent. But, as services, they are frequently seen as parasitic on the real economy. Universities perform a valuable export function for the Welsh economy because, of the roughly 15,000 graduates produced each year by the thirteen higher education institutions, half are from outside Wales. Each is worth, notionally, £15,000 per year to the economy or, together, £112.5 million, which over a typical three-year degree course is an 'export' value of £337.5 million. If to that are added the Welsh students, the figure doubles to £675 million, and adding in the salaries of employees, the sum is over £1 billion, though the 'export' value remains at a third of that (Coombes *et al.*, 2002).

As we have seen, the Welsh healthcare budget is £3.8 billion and healthcare has even greater innovation systems potential because of the central role of Life Sciences, pharmaceuticals and biotechnology in scientific and technical support of it. Mention was made above of the winning by a Cardiff-based academic consortium of £4 million from the UK government and Welsh Assembly Government (through KEF) to build a Gene Park. This is virtual to begin with, then after two to three years a real Gene Park will be built in Cardiff's waterfront district. This connects to ambitious plans being realised in 2003 to merge the hitherto separate Cardiff University and University of Wales Medical School, creating two colleges within the new institution, one for Life and Medical Sciences, the other for Science, Engineering, Arts and Humanities. In support of the Biosciences capability that underpins the merger, Cardiff University invested substantially in attracting the 'star' scientist in stem cell research, Lasker Prize-winning Welshman Martin Evans and his research team from Cambridge University. A new Biosciences Centre has been built to house the expanded Molecular and Medical Biology department, now renamed School of Biosciences. An existing Medipark in the medical school houses some thirty biotechnology start-up businesses and these will move as they grow on to the Gene Park. In other words, there is the seed crystal of a possible biosciences cluster for which the healthcare demand and the education and research supply are crucial components. Government support in and beyond Wales assisted all features in this development, but mainly through research and infrastructure funding. Augmentation of the pharmaceuticals sector is needed, given that Amersham-Pharmacia and Bayer are the principal global representatives of the sector currently in Wales since Parke-Davis and Warner Lambert joined the manufacturing exodus. This is a task in which the WDA ought to be the key source of expertise. But in the absence of a 'knowledge economy' strategy comparable to that operating in Scotland, as described in the introduction, such a possibility remains unrealised.

Thus, in conclusion, the title of this chapter inquires of the regional innovation system in Wales whether the economic shifts of the past decade have resulted in its evolution or its eclipse. The account given leans eventually to the judgement that the old FDI-dependent systems interaction among the engineering Triple Helix (Etkowitz and Leydesdorff, 1997) has effectively been eclipsed, that the efforts of the WAG to develop a new one focused upon generic entre-preneurship and innovation has so far failed to achieve its objectives, but that a new type of public sector interaction involving healthcare and higher education offers a possibility of evolution into an innovative, university-led type of innovation system designed to fit the demands of the new 'knowledge economy'.

Acknowledgements

I am grateful for assistance in writing this chapter to my colleagues at the Centre for Advanced Studies, Nick Clifton, Carla De Laurentis and Rob Wilson. Dylan Jones-Evans from the University of Wales, Bangor, gave unstinting advice and information based on his report on R&D to the Economic Development Committee of the National Assembly for Wales. John De La Mothe, University of Ottawa, was interesting to talk to about the prospects for 'public' innovation systems. I want to thank our editor, Helen Ibbotson and my co-editor Martin Heidenreich for their patience. None bears any responsibility for what was written.

Chapter 9
Industrial clusters and the governance of change
Lessons from North Rhine-Westphalia

Josef Hilbert, Jürgen Nordhause-Janz, Dieter Rehfeld and Rolf G. Heinze

Economic performance and industrial policy

North Rhine-Westphalia (NRW) is one of Germany's sixteen federal states, and is situated in the heart of Europe, bordering on Belgium and the Netherlands. With a population of 18 million in 2001, NRW is the most densely populated federal state in Germany. It accounts for 22 per cent of Germany's total population.

NRW is not only one of Europe's largest conurbations, but it also represents Germany's most significant industrial area. Approximately 23 per cent of German GNP, 22 per cent of industrial output and 26 per cent of exports originate from here. North Rhine-Westphalia's gross domestic product in 2000 was about 455 billion Euro.

NRW's leading industrial sectors are chemicals (e.g. Bayer), plastics, mechanical engineering and steel construction, electrical engineering and electronics, and the food industry. A third of Germany's top 500 international companies have their headquarters in NRW. However, there are also more than 500,000 small and medium-sized enterprises.

By and large, the economic profile of NRW and its different subregions is characterized by diversity and change. North Rhine-Westphalian business activities cover almost all existing sectors and branches, ranging from coal mining and energy (in the Ruhr Area) via such traditional industries as furniture (in the Lower Rhine area, as well as in the eastern part of Westphalia) and food processing (e.g. meat processing in the Münsterland) to modern service industries such as telecommunications and mass media (particularly in Cologne and its environs).

In such a broad and differentiated economy, it is difficult to identify one (or at least the main) factor driving the dynamics of change, but the dominant trend is the shift from production to services (see Figure 9. 1). Clearly, it is the above-average decline in such traditional sectors as mining, steel and investment goods that is the most powerful reason for the 'wind of change' being experienced in the regional economy (Nordhause-Janz, 2002).

The North Rhine-Westphalian decline in traditional industries has its particular focus in the Ruhr Area, the former industrial heart of both NRW and Germany. This area has about 30 per cent of the *Land*'s population and 28 per cent of industrial output and was dominated for a long time by its traditional

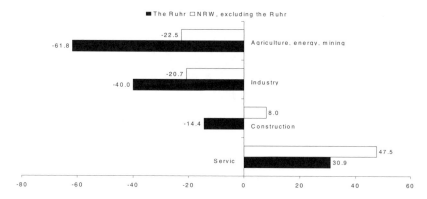

9.1 Sectoral employment in the Ruhr Area and NRW: percentage changes 1982–2000
Source: Own calculations on basis of LAA statistics

sectors: coal mining and steel. Although these sectors employed fewer than 80,000 people in the year 2001, the production networks, concepts and regimes in this area have been characterized by traditional linkage patterns for a longer time.

The problems of structural change and renewal in the Ruhr Area have a rather negative impact on the economic performance indicators of NRW in general. Figure 9.2 shows that NRW employment has developed at less than the (West) German average. The impact of employment decline in the Ruhr explains this. Correspondingly, unemployment in NRW is above the German average and peaks (up to 14 per cent) in some cities of the Ruhr Area.

The disappointing performance of the NRW labour market has raised political awareness and made industrial policy a top priority for the NRW government. In this context, probably the most pressing challenge in the Ruhr Area is to motivate and enable existing firms to diversify and to stimulate new start-ups.

NRW industries are very advanced technologically; however, in the Ruhr Area many are still operating in traditional and shrinking markets. Therefore, a key challenge for industrial policy in NRW is to help industry change from its traditional roots and adjust to more promising markets. However, for firms operating in declining business sectors, there are risks in seeking new products and markets. Established ties to customers and suppliers protect the orientation of enterprises and promise market predictability. New markets are at best unknown and incalculable, or even hostile towards new competitors, and this increases the probability of failure. Encouraging existing firms to shift to new businesses means enabling them to develop helpful links within the business cluster they are entering. This is a key reason why networking has become an issue for modern industrial policy. At the same time during the last few years the foundation of new start-up firms has been the focus of regional policies.

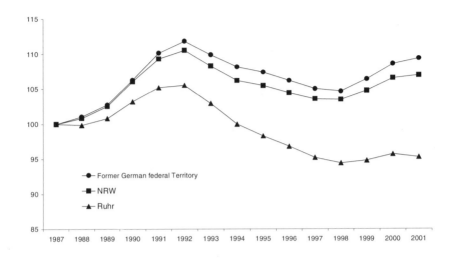

9.2 Employees covered by social security: 1987 = 100
Source: Own calculations on basis of LAA statistics

In contrast to countries such as France, Sweden, the UK or Italy, Germany's policy is decentralized and is characterized by strong participation and self-regulation procedures (particularly for the *Länder*). However, this does not mean that NRW can pursue an independent industrial or structural policy. Particularly in terms of financial resources, for example, the NRW government has to act in co-operation with the federal government in Berlin and with the European Commission in Brussels. Sometimes, co-operation with Berlin is difficult, because it is complicated by party politics. Since 1966 NRW has been governed by the Social Democrats (either in coalitions or in majority governments) and the federal government (between 1983 and 1998) has been controlled by a coalition of Christian Democrats and Liberals.

Industrial clusters and political intervention

About ten years ago, when Piore and Sabel (1984) published the *Second Industrial Divide*, they initiated a discussion about the new meaning of flexible specialization for the future of industrial development. Referring to the industrial districts in the Third Italy or in Baden-Württemberg, they also highlighted the new meaning of a flexible and innovative regional base of global competitiveness. Industrial districts and synergies, agglomeration advantages and regional networks – these are the salient topics in the new discussion about regional development, which holds out the possibility of a sustainable development for all types of region, high-tech and traditional.

However, we should be careful with simple concepts and high expectations. On the one hand, the most promising models of flexible specialization, the Third Italy and Baden-Württemberg, are today experiencing a fundamental structural shift. On the other, we should remember the fate of older industrial regions. These older regions were organized as agglomerations or networks for a long time, but only very few have handled the challenges of structural change successfully.

The increasing significance of regional networks therefore also involves risks of failure, the problems of organizing a sustainable regional restructuring, and not least, the limits of regional strategies in the context of global economies and national and European politics.

Looking at the North Rhine-Westphalian case, we can discuss the problems of traditional regional networks (production clusters) and the possible development of new regional networks. We will focus on four production clusters, each at a very different stage of development:

- the production cluster around the coal and steel industry in the Ruhr Area is an example of an old cluster that is disintegrating;
- the environmental industry is an example of a new production cluster that has its roots in the old industrial structures of the Ruhr Area and is one of the fastest-growing industrial sectors;
- the media/telecommunications cluster is young and very promising, focused on Cologne;
- the healthcare businesses as a service-orientated cluster with potential for economic and occupational growth.

The downward spiral of the Ruhr iron and steel industry

The evolution of the coal and steel cluster in the Ruhr Area and the region's rise to being the main location of Germany's economically leading production chains have been described many times before, so there is no need to outline them in detail here (Schlieper, 1986; Kiesewetter, 1986: 187ff.; Radkau, 1989: 115ff.; Hamm and Wienert, 1990: 144ff.; Weber, 1990).

Looking back to the roots of industrialization in the middle of the nineteenth century, it was not local technological competence that explains the rise of the Ruhr Area. The most important innovations in steel production came from England and the most important technical universities for the mining sector had been founded outside the Ruhr Area in Aachen and Clausthal-Zellerfeld. It was the use of technologies developed elsewhere that brought out the materially related connection of coal and steel. Consecutively, the materially related connections expanded: first, by the expansion into product processing segments either via a direct material relation such as the one between foundries and blast furnaces or via the ensuing progress in thermal economics. Second, two more industries were integrated into the coal, iron and steel-based production cluster:

- In 1902, power generation and steel production became connected by steel producers Stinnes & Thyssen taking over 86 per cent of RWEs (the regional power generating and distribution company) shares; power stations and steel plants exchanged raw materials and energy over the following years. This started the boom in large lignite power stations, which introduced low energy prices – which, in turn, attracted high energy-consuming heavy industries.
- Around this time, by-products of both mining and steel industries, such as alum or sulphur, were increasingly used as raw materials for the chemical industry (which was to become rather important during the Second World War policy of autarky and its autonomous coal-based industry, the Kohle-chemie).

The organization of the production cluster in the Ruhr Area is to be seen in the context of the possibilities of these materially determined interlinkages. Whereas steel production and the steel-working industry had been spatially separated up to the middle of the nineteenth century, the corporate policy of the Ruhr Area's steel companies aimed at concentrating production and distributive functions of this production chain – mining, as well as processing, and even scrap collecting for recycling purposes – into integrated groups.

Thus, the evolution of groups and consortia became a structural element of the Ruhr Area as early as in its initial expansion phase. The product groups of small and medium-sized enterprises, especially those in mechanical engineering, stayed close to the large-scale enterprises of the coal, iron and steel industry. Contrary to production clusters in other regions, the Ruhr Area's large companies succeeded in retaining the services of the most important engineers so that outsourcing and subsequent foundation of new rivals were correspondingly rare (cf. Weber, 1990: 222, 228).

The growth of this production cluster is both the success story of the Ruhr Area and the main reason for its problems, when coal mining in the Ruhr Area came under pressure from global competition in the late 1950s and steel production likewise since the early 1970s. The process of deindustrialization in the Ruhr Area is well known as being the original crisis that produced the downturn of the industrial core in this region (cf. Petzina, 1987; Montankommission, 1989). Therefore, we will focus on another aspect of this development: the disintegration of the production cluster.

There are two main reasons for this trend towards vertical disintegration (Rehfeld, 1993, 1995). First, there is a trend of dissolving the materially related production interlinkages. In this context, for instance, we can consider:

- new technologies in steel-generating or downstream production, such as the foundries; these new technologies facilitated the organizational and spatial separation of what had been closely connected production steps;
- the change from coal-based chemistry in the Ruhr Area to petrochemicals, and the declining importance of coal for steel-generating;
- the increasing use of microelectronic and sensor-technical components in mining; these components cannot be delivered by the local mining suppliers and have to be imported from outside; that is one reason that traditional supplier–user relations are weakening;
- very low transportation costs; therefore very heavy and bulky components can also be transported worldwide.

Second, of further importance for the Ruhr Area's production interlinkages was how the dominant groups reacted to changed global conditions. Their strategies led to a change in organizational integration, which became possible through the vertical disintegration mentioned above. The dominant groups in the coal, iron and steel production cluster followed three strategies of organizational restructuring:

1   The dominant Ruhr Area enterprises – especially those of the steel industry – have grown into multinational, globally acting groups. In the 1950s they took part in establishing steelworks in Third World countries and then founded branch enterprises, mainly for further processing activities.
2   In the face of increasing difficulties in the final market, the steel groups started diversifying in the 1960s. They bought both plants and companies in the mechanical engineering industry, as well as those engaged in plant construction, supply to the motor industry, and ship-building. These activities are mainly located outside the Ruhr Area, so there was a large exodus of capital (cf. Petzina *et al.*, 1990).
3   Some steel and energy groups have diversified in information and communication technology. At the end of the 1990s most of these activities had been sold to other companies like Vodafone. Nevertheless, the information and communication activities are still located in the Ruhr Area or in the neighborhood. They are one of the key elements for the restructuring of the Ruhr Area.

Despite these trends of deindustrialization and disintegration, a cluster of coal, iron and steel and related industries still remains, which, although much smaller than it was, still dominates the region with its economic and organizational power and its importance in terms of employment: even today more than two-thirds of the West German coal output and iron and steel production is concentrated in the Ruhr Area.

In the early 1990s, nearly half of the industrial employment in the Ruhr Area still depended on this cluster. Another 12 per cent of industrial employment depended on further energy-consuming heavy industries. Only a quarter of industrial workers were employed by the dominant industries of past decades, such as mechanical and electrical engineering, the motor and plastic industries, and those parts of the chemical industry that are not part of primary industry. Finally, about one-tenth of industrial employment depended on consumer-related industries.

The task of restructuring in the Ruhr Area is not simply an economic challenge. The growth of these leading sectors also shaped all of the regional structures, which is still apparent today. The connection between industrialization, population growth and urbanization is well known. Originally, mining existed as a sector alongside agriculture. However, the development of sparsely populated areas attracted an enormous influx of workers, coming increasingly from eastern Germany and foreign countries. The large housing estates built for miners, and those for the employees of other large companies, dominated not only the settlement structure but also the lifestyle and consumer standards of the whole region. Furthermore, the transport infrastructure was geared to the demands of the growing industry, especially in terms of the supply of raw materials such as ore and scrap, and the distribution of products. This is reflected in the region's highly developed railway system and other modes of transport.

Finally, long-standing employment of unskilled or semi-skilled workers in mass production plants of heavy industry led to certain skills profiles and highly organized industrial relations. The latter have contributed to delaying structural change while helping the sociopolitical reduction of its impact. The Ruhr Area's adjustment to changed global conditions cannot be explained only in terms of economics. The dominating influence of the coal, iron and steel industries must be seen in relation to the social, cultural and political structures, to the settlement structures and the infrastructure.

Phoenix from the ashes: the environmental protection industry

Environmental problems in the Ruhr Area have existed for many decades. Waste water and air pollution, contaminated soil and hazardous waste have been closely related to the process of economic growth in this region. In the early 1970s, for the first time there were broad discussions about environmental problems and the beginning of innovative political measures aimed at reducing pollution and contamination. This is the crucial point concerning the rise of the environmental protection industry in the Ruhr Area, because these new measures were organized in a way that can be termed 'the transformation of problems into markets' (Nordhause-Janz and Rehfeld, 1995).

The creation of new markets is only one important aspect of the rise of environmental technology in the Ruhr Area. Another decisive aspect concerns a strong spatial interrelation between problem-causing and problem-solving industrial activities. Nearly half of German industrial investment in environmental technologies occurred in NRW, most of it in the Ruhr Area. Therefore, the great steel, energy, mining and chemical companies can be regarded as lead users, who forced their suppliers, first of all in mechanical engineering, to develop new technologies for the reduction of pollution, contamination and waste. In this context, the development of internal solutions to environmental problems in the research departments of the steel industry, the founding of new specialized companies by engineers from these departments, different modes of outsourcing – have been important origins of the rise of an environmental technology industry in NRW (Figure 9.3).

The environmental protection industry started to develop in the Ruhr Area as early as the 1960s. In the 1990s a wide range of enterprises were engaged in this new market. The most important groups of enterprises are:

- builders of machinery and facilities (mainly engineering companies from the regional steel producers, constructors of power plants and power plant components), engaged in environmental technology and the construction of systems and facilities such as purification plants and detoxification systems;

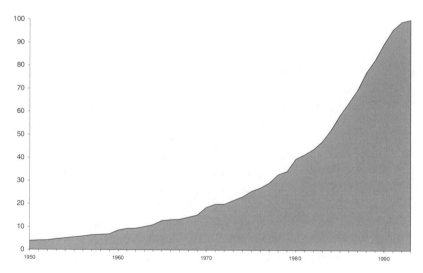

9.3 New entries of enterprises in the environmental market
Source: Nordhause-Janz and Rehfeld (1995)

- regionally based mining and energy companies, that have diversified in recent years and in many cases have externalized their activities in waste management by founding new companies;
- regionally based plants and companies, especially automobile assembling plants and the chemical industry, that have announced new policies for recycling;
- specialized regionally based enterprises with a long tradition in waste management and soil recycling, especially construction and service firms;
- diversifying suppliers of the mining industry, especially mechanical engineers; they started to construct systems for dust removal and air pollution prevention in the 1960s;
- a wide range of new small and medium-sized firms, engaged in planning and advertising, software development, producing systems and apparatus for measuring and controlling, producing special components and basic chemical materials;
- enterprises engaged in related activities such as transport, biotechnology, processing, and so on.

Annual market entries by firms rose incrementally and expanded from the early 1960s (Figure 9.3). In 1996 about 90,000 people worked in private environmental companies in NRW, more than in the remaining mining sector.

But it is not only the rise in absolute numbers of new entries that is remarkable, it is the broad range of diversification too. Since the late 1980s, an increasing number of consultancy, planning and other service companies have been founded (Figure 9.4). As a result, today in NRW a broad range of different activities and functions are concerned with environmental problems. Our studies have shown many different inter-firm relations between these companies. These inter-relationships have given rise to new production clusters which are becoming ever more international.

Co-operation between agents in the NRW environmental protection industry is not uncommon. Among the more significant of these are the following:

- between regionally based mining, steel and energy companies, specialized enterprises engaged in waste management and affected car producers aiming at developing new concepts in automobile recycling;
- between steel, energy companies and the local authorities in Duisburg, organizing the 'Entsorgungszentrum Duisburg' in order to develop new concepts in hazardous waste removal;
- between three regionally based enterprises of the energy and environmental protection sector in the cleaning of contaminated soil ;
- between energy and waste management firms in a waste utilization company;

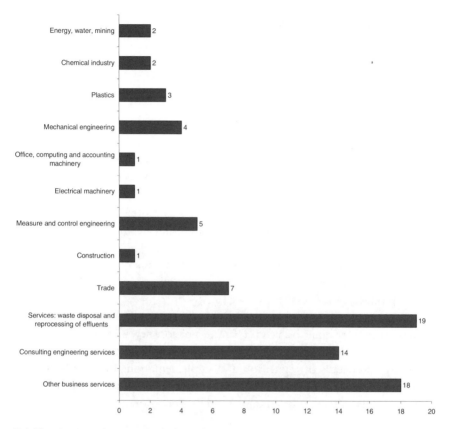

9.4 The structure of new entries in the environmental market since 1990
Source: Nordhause-Janz and Rehfeld (1995)

- between chemical industry companies, a steel producer and a public research institute in implementing a facility to transfer used plastics to oil products;
- between regionally based enterprises in the context of the Institute for Environmental Technology in Duisburg;
- between the Duisburg Institute, local authorities in Essen and others in electronic waste removal;
- between the local authorities in Gladbeck, Bottrop and Gelsenkirchen and a waste management company planning a facility to sort packaging waste;
- between local authorities from Gladbeck, Bottrop, Gelsenkirchen and Essen and a regionally based construction company to manage rubble.

To understand the development of environmental technology in NRW, we must remember that regional suppliers to the traditional production clusters (mining, steel) were able to master new tasks in environmental protection. In this context the development of the North Rhine-Westphalian environmental protection industry is of general interest in the discussion of regionally based diversification strategies. It can be explained not only by one dominating technical competence, but by many different avenues that helped to link the new markets in a successful way. Among the important factors here are:

- a long tradition in waste management, especially in scrap collecting for recycling purposes;
- experience in the construction of ventilation systems for mining companies;
- a tradition of co-operation with local authorities, especially in energy supply and water purification;
- experience in the transportation of hazardous waste;
- the availability of waste dumps and sites for incineration facilities.

In addition, innovation has been important for entrants to new markets. More than half of all market entries have been based on internal spin-off developments in new products or services (Figure 9.5).

The impression is that, in the late 1990s, the dynamic of the environmental protection industry came to an end. There are no more new incentives for environmental law. In some fields such as automobile recycling there is no security regarding the details of regulation and implementation. In other fields like contaminated soil or waste water systems there is a lack of public finances. The rate of new market entries has slumped and the concentration has been rising on

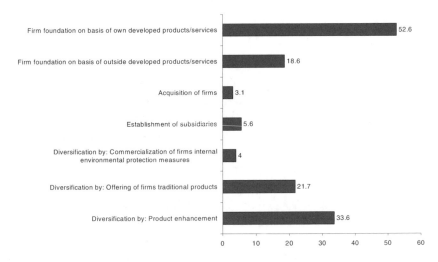

9.5 Strategies of entry into the environmental market
Source: Nordhause-Janz and Rehfeld (1995)

a global level. Over-capacity and a stiff competition dominate the market. Nevertheless, the situation has to do with consolidation, with business as usual, there is no crisis. The level of employment is still high and innovation occurs step by step which has to do with both company strategies and political regulation.

Increasingly isolated solutions are a matter of political regulation; most of them can be called 'end of pipe-solutions'. That means that the solutions take place after the problems have arisen. But there is a new trend of focusing more on waste avoidance than on waste management, and we can no longer be sure that the German way of separating and collecting waste is the best way – in economic as well as in ecological terms. The main reason for this trend is the growing understanding that the traditional process of waste management will produce more problems or will be very expensive in the future. For instance, the new measures in waste management in Germany have raised new questions concerning the rising transportation services needed to organize the recycling process and the emissions from waste incineration.

In the long run, therefore, we can assume that a shift from isolated solutions in environmental protection to integrated approaches of ecologically guided planning and producing will take place. No doubt, this alternative solution will also create new markets. But these markets will differ from recent markets for environmental technologies. The integration of advertising, planning, and the construction of new materials and new products will become more important and organizational solutions will be more effective than technological solutions.

The expertise that is needed to develop such new solutions is available in North Rhine-Westphalia. The problem is to recombine and reintegrate the existing competences. The key problem is that the EPI in North Rhine-Westphalia, and this argument seems to be crucial for the German EPI in general, remains embedded in the overall German innovation system. A strong focus on techno-logical solutions is one aspect. This focus an essential characteristic of German mechanical engineering companies, and most companies that provide environ-ment technology have long-standing roots in mechanical engineering. Even today they remain rooted in this tradition and they feel themselves more like mechanical engineering companies than 'green companies'.

The dominance of fragmented markets is a second aspect. There are ambitious innovations in details, but these innovations ignore the interlinkages between the different environmental media. This is also partly attributable to a strong price regime. As long as the price for depositing or burning waste remains low because of over-capacities, nobody really cares about saving material.

Nevertheless, there are examples of a new way of managing the environment. So, on regional level projects to reduce waste, traffic and energy become more and more important. In this respect, environmental protection does not primarily refer to compensating or reducing waste but to avoiding the production of waste. Therefore, the local task of the years to come will not only be the organization of waste management, but to find new activities in order to reduce waste, traffic and energy use in the interest of increasing the level of quality of life.

At the level of the production chain, regulations of waste management – especially the obligation to take back old products no longer in use – are concerned with saving material. Recently, we find reflections on new materials, of collective traffic-organization – for instance, in supplying components – or the durability and renewability of products.

And, not least, we find new ways in handling the problem of environment and the dissipation of energy and materials at the plant level. The rising costs of increasing single solutions to reduce waste bring out concepts of integrated material planning. Ecological control, environmental management or integrated material circuits are such concepts which are attracting interest.

New media and telecommunications: the dim star cluster

In the past years new media and the information and communication sector (ICT) has been top of the agenda of business firms and politicians. Politicians hope for new jobs from a new industry, and business people either look for new instruments to increase the competitiveness of their firms or want to exploit new media for the development and design of new products or services. According to many market observers the ICT market was regarded as a fast and steadily growing job machine (Seufert, 1994).

Although recent developments on new market stock exchanges have caused a more realistic view of the sector, there is no doubt that ICT has been an important factor in the last years in the context of regional development and structural change. This especially is correct in the case of North Rhine-Westphalia. In spite of many economic problems which are still rooted in the decline of traditional economic sectors like steel and coal mining, there are also remarkable patterns of structural change. One prominent example of the latter is certainly ICT, which in recent years has undergone fundamental changes. One of the most cited buzz-words, which describes an important part of these changes appears to be 'multimedia'. In the beginning, almost not more than a technical concept, the discussion on multimedia more and more centred around the emergence of a new economic sector or new business cluster.

Although many different prognoses on predictable market volumes and jobs exist, there is no official definition of what multimedia means from a sectoral point of view. In a technical sense, multimedia applications are characterized by three important features:

1   interactive usage;
2   integration of different media types;
3   treatment and storage on the basis of digital technologies.

This short description of the basic features shows that multimedia applications not only have a typical cross-sectional character in a technological sense but obviously from a sectoral point of view, as well. The production of multimedia applications requires the combination of goods, services and competences of different actors and sectors. In particular, this demand for combination and co-operation can be regarded as the main reason why some analyses speak of production chain multimedia or new media, involving the audiovisual and print media sector, advertising companies, software and hardware producers and telecommunication providers. As a consequence, sectoral borders between traditional parts of ICT and media-orientated sectors became fluent. The term convergence describes this development, which is still open-ended.

NRW has good reason to look at this process optimistically (Nordhause-Janz and Rehfeld, 1999). The region can be regarded as one of the ICT centres in Germany. In 2000 the ICT sector in NRW accounted for more than 31,000 companies. In comparison to 1996 the number of firms has grown about 33 per cent. In the same time turnover grew from 67 billion Euro to more than 89 billion Euro. With more than 256,000 people in 2001, NRW covers more than 23 per cent of the West German sectoral employment.

Without doubt, the most promising and expanding ICT cluster in NRW is located in Cologne. The roots of this cluster originate in a specific set of conditions. First of all, Cologne represents the location of the Westdeutscher Rundfunk (WDR), the second largest broadcasting company in Europe. In addition, Cologne is well known for its very broad and attractive cultural milieu, in which development was closely linked to the expansion of the WDR. In the 1960s, the recording studios of the WDR attracted artists like John Cage, Nam June Park or Karlheinz Stockhausen, followed by ambitious gallery managers, who organized the first world-wide art fair in Cologne. As a result of this engagement, Cologne grew into one of the most dynamic art locations in the world. Finally, proximity to Bonn as the former German capital and Brussels as the location of the EC Commission made Cologne attractive as a base for headquarters for a broad range of media associations.

In particular, the foundation of the German RTL headquarters in Cologne functioned as a catalyst for the Cologne cultural and media seedbed. More and more broadcasting stations followed RTL, and some of them relocated their head-quarters from Munich or Berlin to Cologne. Regional suppliers have specialized in media-related services and today the most prominent world-wide media companies like Sony, Warner Brothers, EMI, Pioneer, Bertelsmann and so on are found in Cologne.

A second promising example is located in the Ruhr Area. Dortmund has become an important centre for software and IT-service in NRW. On the basis of 900 enterprises with 13,000 employees, the software branch with its great growth potential is an integral part of the structural change in Dortmund, in a city marked historically by the coal, steel and beer industries.

The majority of the firms dominating the software market in Dortmund were founded in the 1970s and 1980s. The roots of these companies lie in the milieu of the University of Dortmund with the largest informatics department in Germany and with the technical university. At present, approximately 4,500 students are enrolled in eight different IT-related degree programmes offered by these institutions.

In addition to the project and practical experience gained through several university activities and co-operation with industry, outsourcing in the traditional sectors such as the mining industry and its suppliers has been regarded as a further factor leading to the start-ups in the software sector.

Proximity to the university was regarded as good for research potential in the past. Nowadays, however, companies settling in Dortmund view the university as a valuable souce of potential employees. The spatial core constitutes the university and the technological park in Dortmund, although settlements are becoming dispersed everywhere in Dortmund especially by new foundations. The Settlement of Technology Park Dortmund aims at the transfer of know-how and technologies on a high level of research and innovation and has also contributed to the further development of software and IT-branches in Dortmund.

In summary, NRW has become an important regional player in the ICT sector. At the same time, because of strong regional concentrations and specializations, not all subregions of NRW have benefited from the positive economic effects of ICT. Nor will they be able to catch up to the existing location advantages of the ICT core regions in the future.

Another important aspect for future development in ICT can be found in recent telecommunication-based developments. Telecommunication providers have made vast investments in UMTS licences, although many observers doubt if economic success can be achieved. Hardware companies, especially those which are engaged in network equipment, certainly will profit from the necessary infrastructure investments. But this sector traditionally is located more in the southern part of Germany than in NRW. Whether other parts of the ICT sector, such as software developers and telecommunication providers, can profit in the same way will depend heavily on whether they can offer attractive services, and last but not least, a competitive price. All in all, the post-2000 world-wide observable decline in demand in ICT can be regarded as a hint that the growth rates of the past can no longer be extrapolated to the future.

Cluster in transition: Healthcare businesses not a burden but an asset to economic and occupational growth

Almost all advanced societies and economies are characterized by the increasing relevance of healthcare expenditure and healthcare industry employment (Figure 9.6). The main driving forces of this process are:

- socio-demographic changes such as the ageing of population and the decreasing relevance of family and neighbourhood support and care;
- promising progress of both medical science and technology as well as medical and care delivery systems (e.g. remote health monitoring);
- a bureaucratization of health regulations resulting in inefficient and fat health and care delivery systems;
- increasing willingness of consumers to pay for healthcare and promotion products and services (like wellness, emergency alarm systems or diet food).

In 1998 – at the end of the last decade – healthcare was by far the biggest business cluster of the North Rhine-westphalian economy. By and large, one million people worked here: 40 per cent of them with in-patient institutions like hospitals or nursing homes for the elderly; another 40 per cent with out-patient services; and the rest supply and administration businesses, or with neighbouring sectors (like health tourism).

In Germany (as in many other countries) the vast majority of economists and economic policy-makers have many problems concerning the growth of healthcare. In the long run, they fear, the increasing costs of health will become a severe burden on the economy, because more health expenditure means more taxes or more contributions to social insurances which could reduce the room for manoeuvre and the international competitiveness of other business sectors such as the automotive industry or tourism. As a solution to this problem, traditional economists and politicians argue either for cost cutting (if they are liberal) or for a new offensive to increase productivity in health service delivery (if they are social-democratic or conservative). Since mid-1995 this traditional pattern of debate has been changing, and a growing number of researchers, as well as (regional) policy-makers, argue for fostering the economic relevance and growth of healthcare, instead of limiting it. If healthcare businesses manage both to increase productivity and to mobilize additional private purchasing, this sector could continue to be one of the biggest business clusters and become an engine of growth to enhance economic dynamics in supply and neighbouring sectors.

In 2001 the NRW Ministry of Health published an expert investigation report (FFG/IAT/MHH, 2001) outlining quantitative scenarios on the future prospects of the NRW healthcare cluster. If growth conditions are bad, i.e. if there are big productivity gains, severe cutbacks in public health expenditure and

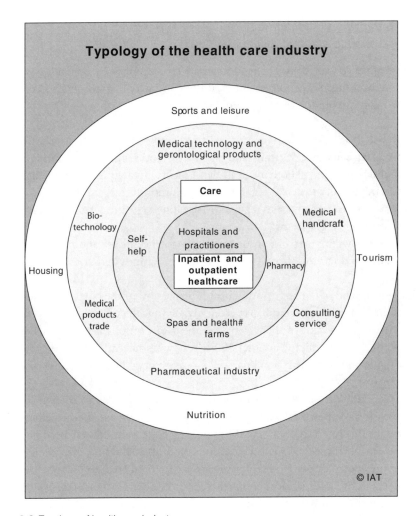

9.6 Typology of healthcare industry

no growth in private health consumption, the healthcare industry will only grow about 70,000 additional employees, caused by the increasing need of an ageing population for health support. If conditions improve – no severe cutbacks and an increasing willingness of private consumers to spend money on health products and services – occupational growth could result in about 200,000 new jobs.

For a couple of years, this paradigm shift – perceiving healthcare as an asset to economic growth, and not a burden or master plan – has infected regional innovation activities in NRW. Although, up to now, a great design (a master plan) to develop healthcare industries in NRW has been missing, there is a wide (sometimes even wild) variety of different initiatives all designed to encourage hospitals, nursing homes, supply and neighbouring businesses place emphasis on for productivity, innovation and new products and services. In the following we will describe the three most relevant and most promising activities of this kind:

1   *Health Care NRW e. V.:* Health Care NRW e. V. is both a business interest association and a kind of dialogue forum bringing together different firms, business people, researchers and consultants. Although Health Care NRW e. V. is open to members from all different subsectors of the healthcare industry, both the list of members as well as the list of main activities prove, that the main focus is on life sciences (i.e. on biotechnology). As well as interests representation and organizing dialogues and expertise exchange among members, Health Care NRW publishes a news letter and is co-organizer of a well-known yearly congress ('MCC Health World') which takes place in NRW and gives interesting new perspectives with respect to innovation trends and policy regulation. Health Care NRW members come from all over the state of NRW, however, more than 50 per cent of them are located in the Rhine Area of NRW. Both the founding phase as well as the first years of operation of the Health Care NRW e. V. were significantly supported by public money from the NRW Ministry of Economic Affairs.

2   *Zentrum für Innovation in der Gesundheitswirtschaft Ostwestfalen* (East-westphalian Centre for Innovation in Healthcare Businesses; ZIG): ZIG is a healthcare industry business interest association located in the eastern part of NRW. In this region above-average relevance is placed on healthcare because of the following reasons:

    (a) It houses around ten so-called Kurbäder, i.e. villages or small towns which are profiled by healing spas, rehabilitation hospitals and a wide variety of wellness-providing service firms (e.g. 'fitness factories', beauty farms, health tourism).

    (b) It is home to two of the leading German healthcare providing enter-prises: the 'Anstalt Bethel' and the 'Evangelisches Johanneswerk'.

    (c) It is the location of the biggest and world-famous Heart Surgery Centre in Bad Oeynhausen.

    (d) In this region there are the headquarters and the main development and manufacturing sites of some large medical equipment providers (e.g. Stiegelmeyer, Europe's no. 1 in beds for hospitals and nursing homes).

    In 1998, encouraged by a local business development agency, around twelve to fifteen business people and some healthcare researchers founded the ZIG, with the aim of promoting the healthcare business cluster in this region. One of the advantages the ZIG members expect from their initiative is to develop cross-border collaboration and innovation, in order to strengthen both firm and regional competitiveness. Another reason for founding the

ZIG was that healthcare business people from the eastern part of NRW did not feel adequately represented in the Health Care NRW e.V., which, from their point of view, seemed to be too biased towards the Rhine Area and too dominated by life science firms

3   *Landesinitiative Seniorenwirtschaft* (State Initiative for Elderly People Support Business): in 1998 two well-known economic and gerontological research institutes in NRW published a memorandum called: *Economic Opportunities of an Ageing Society* (FFG/IAT, 1999, see also Hilbert/Naegele, 2001). In NRW, as well as in most other European countries and regions, a significant part of the aged population enjoys a relatively high income, and this may result in an acceleration of the demand for products and services that make life easier for the elderly and the handicapped. To encourage firms to seize this opportunity and to develop an ambitious elderly people support expertise, the NRW state government established the Landesinitiative Seniorenwirtschaft. This initiative consists of three working groups – on housing, on new technologies, and on leisure and tourism – which try to develop and conduct both collaborative products and service innovation, as well as collaborative marketing. This work is organized by the 'Geschäftsstelle Seniorenwirtschaft' (office to promote support business for elderly people) in Gelsenkirchen at the Institute for Work and Technology (IAT). This office has very strong working ties with regional actors in three NRW subregions: East-Westphalia, lower Rhine and the southern Ruhr Area. Furthermore, there is significant support from small firm business interest associations to encourage their members to target the support equipment for the elderly business in local markets (e.g. bathroom modernization or barrier-free flats).

To summarize and to conclude, compared to new media and telecommunication, the healthcare cluster is rather different. Although it is very well established as a gigantic business sector, it has problems identifying and developing its future growth potential. Therefore, it needs industrial policy to push this sector to adopt a growth strategy. However, public policy-makers hesitate to take the initiative because they are still debating whether or not healthcare growth is an engine or a hindrance to economic and occupational growth in the rest of the economy. These doubts and hesitation are the background for both NRW's lack of a grand design, a master plan to develop healthcare industry and the polycentric profile of the exciting landscape of regional development initiatives and associations.

Up to now, industrial policy is only beginning to become aware of the potential and challenges of this business sector and it is still looking for adequate strategies to foster the further emergence of this cluster. The coming years will tell whether and how policies can contribute to both an improvement of the quality of healthcare delivery in NRW and the development and promotion of a promising growth business.

Cluster policies in North Rhine-Westphalia: First steps towards a reorientation in structural policies

Particularly in regions like the Ruhr Area, cluster policies have had a very negative bias because this region suffers from the decline of the long dominant steel and mining cluster. Cluster policies focus on sectoral specialization, and specialization is very risky because the prognoses about industrial development are often very vague and short-term. Nevertheless, the situation changed in the late 1990s, and today cluster policies are very prominent in all parts of NRW. There are several reasons why the industrial development institutions and actors changed their mind.

First, some regions happened to be successful in industrial restructuring. The most prominent example is the take-off of the media cluster in Cologne in the late 1980s (cf. Rehfeld and Wompel, 1997), and the most ambitious one is the Dortmund project that aims for the renewal of the local industrial structure, guided by the innovative sectors software/e-commerce, micro technologies and logistics (cf. Rehfeld and Wompel, 1997; Stadt Dortmund, 2001).

Second, industrial policy programmes have changed the strategic focus. European industrial policies, German technology policy and North Rhine-Westphalian industrial policy have focused more and more on cluster building. Local and regional industrial policies are strongly dependent on these programmes and were forced to accept the new instruments.

Third, cluster policy in Germany has a specific focus that has its roots in the German tradition of non-interventionist industrial policy. If you look at concepts to promote industrial policies in Germany, the label 'cluster' is found vere rarely. Concepts and strategies are labelled 'fields of competence', 'innovation cores' or 'innovation poles'. The reason is that cluster policies in Germany are strongly related to technology policy (innovation) and labour market policy (competence). Cluster policy with a conceptually strong meaning is still suspected of being interventionist and has to be stopped, especially by the Chambers of Commerce, one of the most important players in local and regional policy.

Discussing cluster policies in NRW, one has to bear in mind that this is still a very young concept that is still in an experimental stage and that is taking place in a specific conceptual context. No wonder, therefore, that there is neither an example of a cluster that can be regarded as a result of cluster policies, nor there are established routines in cluster policies. Nevertheless, policies did influence or shape the way and speed of restructuring and in this sense a lot of different policies are relevant also for cluster development. In our context five levels of policy-making are of interest.

First, at national level, tax policies, policies of regulation and privatization, labour market and environmental policies, as well as infrastructure and spatial development policies provide general frameworks that guide and change markets and sectors. Research and development policies are more sectorally guided and since the mid-1990s there has been a supplementary focus on regional networking.

Second, Germany is a federal state and this means that the implementation is strongly shaped by the federal states, in this case by the state government of North Rhine-Westphalia. This is relevant, for instance, for the location of nationally funded research and development institutions, and for the details of implementing environmental regulation. Additionally, the NRW state government has been engaged in its own funding programmes to promote new technologies.

Third, the local level is the lowest level of implementation, as well as the level of urban planning. The local level has to co-ordinate the different programmes and use them for a specific industrial development strategy.

Fourth, the regional level has been institutionalized in NRW since the late 1980s, and it focuses on optimizing and the co-ordination of local policies. The reason is that industrial networks and clusters cross administrative borders. Furthermore, at the regional level, industrial policy is dominated by different modes of public–private partnership: the Chambers of Commerce, trade unions, labour market agencies, training agencies and other associations are partners in this policy-making context. Despite institutionalization, the regional level in NRW is hard to follow. One finds a lot of sub-regions that try to co-ordinate regional policy, and one finds about one dozen regional agencies that are in charge of labour market policy: in the Ruhr Area the Project Ruhr GmbH has additional integrative functions. Finally one can find a lot of co-operation throughout these sub-regions.

Fifth, European policy is present at all levels. In particular, regional policy and the rise of the related regional level are not comprehensible without European structural policy. In NRW most parts of the Ruhr Area benefit from EU Structural Funds, and the programmes give orientation to all the other regions in North Rhine-Westphalia.

The most important level for cluster policy is the North Rhine-Westphalian state government. All in all, there are about fifty initiatives (*Landesinitiativen*) in North Rhine-Westphalia. These initiatives co-ordinate the following activities:

- Sector analyses, including an overview of NRW's strengths and weaknesses as well as handbooks and related information presenting the most important companies, research institutes and public agencies.
- The co-ordination of public programmes aimed at lead-user projects, especially co-operation projects.

- Support for advanced infrastructure such as specialized research agencies, the regulation of training policy, specialized technology agencies or the traditional infrastructure such as data networks.
- Not least, these initiatives provide a framework for regional and local activities in cluster building.

The regional level is more confusing because it differs from sector to sector and from region to region. Nevertheless, the regional level is the most important one, because there is no general innovation system in NRW, but there are specific regional innovation systems. The most ambitious regional project is an initiative to develop twelve fields of competence as leading sectors for the future development of the Ruhr Area. The project was initiated by the Ministry of Economics and Small Businesses, Technology and Transport for North Rhine-Westphalia. In the framework of a study carried out by the consultancy firm Roland Berger & Partners, six competency fields – energy, transport/logistics, information and communications, new materials, microsystem technologies and medical technologies – have been identified in the Ruhr Area (Roland Berger & Partners, 2001). Any support for these and a further six fields would help the region to keep and strengthen its leading technological position in Europe. Together with the regional Structural Funds from the European Union and other resources, a total of 3.6 billion euros could be allocated to the development of the Ruhr Area by 2006.

These fields of competence are to be developed by different instruments, in particular:

- co-ordinating agencies and institutes;
- research institutes;
- inter-industrial networking;
- an initiative to found new companies;
- acquisition in order to close the production chain;
- export – promoting policy;
- training policy.

Summing up, we have to bear in mind that in NRW there a lot of initiatives that are important for sector development and cluster building, but policies explicitly aimed at cluster building are very new and not really established yet. Therefore, cluster policy is in an experimental stage today and a lot of things remain to do to make it work in a solid and professional way.

The problems of cluster policy can be illustrated by the results of an evaluation of thirty-five regional projects aimed at cluster building in NRW (Rehfeld *et* al., 2000). On the one hand, the projects provide a good illustration of the potentials of cluster policy. Location management, acquisition policy, training programmes, the improvement of public implementation strategy, urban planning, activating co-operation, as well as formal contacts, are results that can be seen as very important toward cluster development.

On the other hand, a lot of problems are found. The competence in cluster management is very different from region to region. Little experience of project management, deficits in co-ordination (horizontal as well as vertical), and problems in priority-setting are key problems in the public sector regarding cluster policy.

Furthermore, we have to bear in mind that there is no common evidence on the possibilities and the limits of cluster policy. We know a lot about the way successful clusters work, but this knowledge has nothing to do with the kind of knowledge needed for cluster building. Three arguments may illustrate this problem.

First, according to Porter (1991, 1999), clusters work by combining co-operative and competitive elements. Without any doubt, public policy can initiate co-operation but it is difficult to organize competition in a co-operative way.

Second, there is no evidence about the right time for a policy of cluster-building. So far as cluster policy can be regarded as successful in NRW, it concerns clusters that are already expanding. Therefore, good practice in cluster policy concerns instruments to keep a cluster working, and to speed it up. The case is much more difficult when a cluster is more a potential than a reality, because then you need to initiate a self-enforcing dynamic.

Third, successful clusters are based on informal communication, face-to-face contacts and trust. Processes like this only work aqway from the public eye. Politics, in contrast, needs to be done in public: it has to be presented in the media, it needs discussion in parliament and it needs public legitimation.

The three aspects only illustrate basic problems in successful policies regarding clusters. As long as these problems are not solved and policy focusing on cluster management is more indirect, it is impossible to analyse the intentional impact of politics on cluster building in a solid way. To improve competence in cluster management, referring to our own experience and evaluation, five aspects are important in the short and middle term in North Rhine-Westphalia in order to improve cluster management.

First, there is a need for a shared understanding about cluster-related policies. In North Rhine-Westphalia the conceptual and strategic situation is quite confusing. Most actors avoid talking about clusters or cluster policy because of ideological terms. From a liberal point of view the cluster approach is suspected of being an interventionist one. Therefore, cluster-related policy is called regional innovation policy, innovation systems, regional joint projects, regional networking or strengthening regional competencies. The problem is that there is great hope in this new approach, but nobody really knows if this approach is a promising one, what the preconditions for successful cluster management in structural as well as in strategic terms are, and what more results can be realistically expected.

Second, to implement a professional cluster-related policy a lot of competencies that are not usually found in economic development agencies are needed. Until the 1990s local development agencies had been concentrated on acquisition and on organizing incentives. But as competition for investment became very strong at a global level, the focus of the activities of economic development agencies has shifted to strengthen the local base of innovation and economical strength. For the new tasks of cluster-related policy or cluster management, a lot of new competencies are needed, especially (Bratl and Trippl, 2001):

- strategic development;
- location marketing;
- human resource management;
- innovation and technology management;
- internal and external networking;
- knowledge management;
- conflict management;
- control.

Third, cluster-related policy only makes sense when the companies participate. Sometimes the initiatives for cluster management come from the companies. But in most cases, it is initiated by local development agencies, by trade unions or by European or national programmes. In the latter case, cluster management often has to face the situation that most companies are not really interested in cluster policy because the region is not really part of their plan. Therefore, cluster management depends on motivating and activating, and this means first of all demonstrating that companies benefit from cluster management in the short term too. The differences between the strategic orientation of the companies, on the one hand, and the local development agencies, on the other, have been the most critical aspect in most cluster projects. There is a strong need in common learning strategies to overcome this bottleneck.

Fourth, cluster-related policy needs to be integrated into an overall strategy of local or regional economic development. Concentrating local economic development on cluster management runs the risk of ignoring other tasks and potentials of local development policies. This is the case because cluster management covers only one part of local development policy. On the one hand, not all regions have the preconditions for successful cluster management because they have a very dispersed and weak industrial base. On the other, there are other parts of the local economy, sectors related to local demand, like the public sector, cultural and social activities, quality of life, shopping, leisure and so on that are very important for the economic future of a location, but that are not the focus of cluster management. Furthermore, a lot of new industries are clustered in specific regions, but they depend on continuing proximity to their customers. This is the case for the services for the elderly or parts of ICT and, despite clustering, they are supposed to become important for all regions. This means locations have to strengthen these sectors, even if they cannot hope to build clusters based on them.

Fifth, and not least, professional cluster management needs methods of evaluation. As Diez (2001) points out, cluster management is not based on a linear causal relationships between resources, activities, results, effects and regional impact. There are no well-defined objectives and many difficulties in quantifying effects because of very complex systemic interactions. So ex-post evaluation is not really valid, and we need to change to a flexible and dynamic evaluation design.

Part Three
The Leviathan Approach
Steering Innovation and Growth in Interregional Contexts
by the State

Chapter 10
Regional innovation systems in the less-favoured region of Japan
The case of Tohoku

Shiro Abe

Introduction

In the past decade, strong interest has been expressed by academics and practitioners in regional innovation systems (RISs), their similarities and differences in comparative perspective, and the extent and manner that these differences explain variation in regional advantage. This is a response to a paradoxical situation of local and regional self-help in the context of growing globalization of the economy. As the boundaries between the global, national and local-regional blur, there is doubt about how much local-regional initiatives can enable regions to make their own history. There is also strong motivation for firms and governments to be innovative to enhance the region's ability to meet the uncertainties of structural change and to realign itself into a new competitive position.

The concept of RISs which could be said to be an analytical framework linking techno-economic dynamics to territorial development and competitiveness, and describing the complex mixture of institutions and policies that influence innovation processes at the regional level, is interpreted in many different ways. There are different points of view between different regions and within the respective region about what constitutes those systems and how their effectiveness should be measured. A clearly stated set of operational goals is needed to evaluate their effectiveness, but the goals are multiple and complex, because they are emerging or built up territorially. The theme of RISs is a practical and political question as well as a theoretical one, in that it poses some harsh challenges to people living and working in the region concerned. Regions have limited instruments for stimulating innovation by themselves and are uncertain how effective they are in achieving high performance. Also, advances in forging systems of innovation on a regional scale are in constant evolution as a trial-and-error process defined by place and time. New insights into the dynamics of the innovation process might be added, and new ways of conceptualizing regional innovation potential would be elaborated (Cooke *et al.*, 1988; Archibugi *et al.*, 1999; Morgan and Nauwelaers, 1999).

Although the region is a territorial unit, the definition of the region itself is in contention, and its innovation system is not a single systematic mechanism but rather a cluster of various internal and external policies and institutions operating in that space. Among the strategic variables for strengthening the working of RISs are a variety of measures ranging from instruments fostering endogenous business initiatives to national government industrial policy and regional development policy. But the creative and dynamic aspects of RISs lie in their organizing and co-ordinating capabilities. This implies the capacity to mobilize creativity and hidden resources from a range of fields and to favour synergetic collective learning, but also to make national and even supranational policies function as a catalyst to promote a decentralized process of regional self-organization.

Reviewing the case of Tohoku as an example of the less-favoured region in the country with a unitary political tradition might mean focusing on the complexities of central/local-regional dynamics or, put another way, the interaction of regionalization and regionalism as dual sequential processes. As definitions of regionalization and regionalism themselves take different forms in different places (Hilpert, 1991; Keating, 1997; Acs et al., 2000; Cooke, 2002), regionalization in the Japanese context is not always synonymous with the devolution of powers, but rather refers to a process whereby a number of central government departments define regional policies and impose their guidelines on regions, and, on some occasion, this breeds veiled or overt discord with regionalism from the bottom up.

On the other hand, if the local region such as Tohoku is to find its position and survive in the increasingly globalized world, it seems to need to increase its capabilities for social innovation more than to develop its technological competence. But this task is not easy owing to unavoidable circumstances as not only the position but also the mind-set of the local region have been extremely confined in the trinity the of dynamics of the changing spatial division of labour in the globalizing economy, the central-local relationship in the political and administrative structure, and the changing patterns of urbanization. As a result, regionalism used to take the form of a vicious circle of depending on the central government and playing the blame game about its policies.

This means that the form and nature of the interaction between regionalization and regionalism in a unitary state tends to be two sides of the same coin. Therefore, the task of forging systems of innovation on a regional scale has to involve tackling dual challenges so that regionalization might provide regions with the ability to respond to negative external shocks and proactively to take advantage of opportunities, and regionalism might induce regions to take the initiative and responsibility for their own future.

The regional system in Japan

Tohoku region is a 'non-metropolitan' area in the administrative framework of Japan. As the Japanese archipelago has been divided into two parts designated 'metropolitan' and 'non-metropolitan' or 'rural' in terms of the NCD (National Comprehensive Development) Plan, much attention has been focused strictly on the metropolitan area, whose land areas account for only 10 per cent of all Japan. Metropolitan areas were designated 'relocation-out' areas under the Industry Relocation Law of 1972. Tsukuba Science City, Kanagawa High-Tech Park, and Kansai High-Tech Cities – all of which are located in those areas – have often been referred to as typical examples of Japanese technopolis, although they were excluded from application of the Technopolis Law of 1983, which was, in effect, a revised version of the Industry Relocation Law in an era of high technology.

From the point of view of socio-economic cleavage, referred to sometimes as 'dual Japan' (Ozawa, 1997; Porter *et al.*, 2000), Tohoku region is a 'backward' (in Japanese usage) or 'less-favoured' (in European usage) area where a number of structural problems are inforce their comparative disadvantages with respect to innovative capacities. The national economy is not only a global unit but also a mix of regional economies with differing industrial and social structures and various propensities for economic innovation and change. There have been some complicated dynamics in region-to-region relations on a national scale and relations among regions on a global scale. Historically speaking, Japan, as a latecomer in the process of industrialization, had experienced both advanced and backward conditions in different regions. The advanced industrialized regions could gain their development dynamics at the expense of disadvantaged regions, which tended to be forced to stay at a 'backward' or monoculture stage within the division of labour. But this impetus, drawn from uneven and disproportionate development, did not always continue to generate or to diffuse regional development dynamics. In order to reduce and readjust regional disparities, another working system consisting of price, financial and fiscal mechanisms had to be formed. Furthermore, although these adjustment devices could generate domestic regional development dynamics, they could not always succeed on the global scale, because they often intensified international friction (Okamoto, 1986; Aoki, 1997). As a result, the national economy has been confronted with difficult economic management problems and with conflicts between domestic and international requirements. And, in turn, the backward regions have been faced with an awkward dilemma. They have suffered profoundly from their vulnerability in adapting to rapid modernization in the past and the globalization of the economy today. Such was the position of the Tohoku region.

The use of the term 'region' is often ambiguous, depending on the context in which the concept and term are employed. If it denotes a territorial unit that is smaller than the national territory, but larger than prefectures and municipalities, there seems to be, as Samuels (1983) observes of Japan, rather less than usual substance to the idea of 'region'. Japan has three tiers of government – central, prefectural and municipal – but not regional. 'Region' at the meso-level has been exclusively the policy language of the central government, which was more concerned with identifying those areas most appropriate for administrative convenience and political integration. Although various kinds of 'regional schemes' to create regional government organs were often debated before and after the Second World War, they have never been implemented. But that does not mean that there have been no geographical groupings which shared certain historical and cultural identities with a territorial unit beyond the prefectural boundaries and regional consciousness. The reason that regional identities have not been a critical force in Japanese politics since the early Meiji era, when the building of the modern centralized nation–state started, must be attributable to the incontrovertible fact that their claims as regions have been voluntarily or involuntarily latent under the more dominant ideology of modernization, with its main premises of the nationalization of politics, economy and culture.

Until 1947, prefectural governments were semi-self-governing organizations, in that governors were not autonomous and they acted as centrally appointed officials. After the post-war reform, the prefecture and municipality governments were classified as 'ordinary local public entities' which means *de jure* autonomy, and both the chief executive and assembly members of all entities are elected by direct vote by the residents. However, the hierarchical system of administrative functions between national and local governments has not changed so radically. Some 80 per cent of functions at the prefectural level and 50 per cent at the municipal level have been acquired by delegation from the national government. Ministers direct and supervise governors, who are similarly responsible for directing and supervising mayors, to whom they delegate tasks within their responsibility. By the Decentralization Reform of 1999, this agency delegation system was abolished and a significant increase in the formal autonomy of local governments was expected. But no major change in the tax system has yet been introduced, so the financial authority and sources of revenue of the local public bodies are still heavily controlled by the administrative and legislative participation of the national government. Thus, there is substantially a three-tier hierarchy of executives under central control, parallel to the three-tier government system (Neary, 2002).

At the regional level, there are regional organizations of six national associations of local bodies (governors, prefectural assembly chairmen, mayors, city assembly chiefs, towns and villages, town and village assembly chiefs), each of which functions mainly as a sort of budgetary acquisition group and whose founding dates back to various pre-war periods. On the other hand, the regional framework of planning was institutionalized by a series of region-specific development acts after the NCD Act of 1950. The national government, in parallel with the institutionalization of the implementation process in the way that the national plan is broken down into the subnational and regional plans, has set up different kinds of regional bureaux of ministries to supplement the national programme and measures on a regional basis. But the size and shape of the regional area defined by them vary with issues and ministries. Relating to the Tohoku region, each Tohoku bureau of ministries, MAFF (agriculture, forestry and fisheries), MITI (international trade and industry), MT (transport), MPT (posts and telecommunications) and MC (construction) had jurisdiction over six prefectures, but the Tohoku District Development Office of NLA (National Land Agency) has competence over seven prefectures.[1] Also, six Tohoku associations of local bodies cover six prefectures, but the Council of Tohoku Local Public Bodies consists of members representing prefecture governments and economic organizations of seven prefectures. Thus, prefectural political and administrative institutions are still seen as intermediary organs in the Japanese governmental system, but, simultaneously, 'region' has increased in importance as the territorial framework for public policy to redress regional unevenness.

Two opposing trends occurred 'because of needs arising from the globalization of Japanese flexible production' (Fujita, 1991) since the end of the 1970s, and they were accompanied by a series of waves of offshore investment, which had a decisive domestic spatial impact. Japan's regional structure had been a complex spatial system determined largely by location of industries and administrative systems of both public bodies and private corporations, but since the mid-1980s became increasingly clear that the growing internationalization of Japan's economy and the coming of the information society had promoted regional restructuring, resulting in the growth of the Tokyo metropolitan area and consequent regional inequality. Simultaneously, this inspired the emergence of a new regionalism against Tokyo's unipolar regional structure (Fujita and Hill, 1993; Abe and NIRA, 1994; Abe and Study Group of the Province Centre Cities, 1995; Yada, 1996).

The greater the distinction between global, national, regional and local blurs, the more it becomes difficult to grasp and elucidate the dynamics of regional structural changes. Viewing the region as a more significant terrain of strategic actions, the RISs operate within a variety of global, national, and local-regional regulatory milieu. Adjustment and innovation policies that come down from above as part of centralized macroeconomic management are interrelated with innovative attempts from below, mobilizing endogenous resources, initiating developments and co-operating with various actors to identify and create the specific set of conditions under which their strategies might be successful in securing a place in the global political economy. At the same time, there are certain fundamental disjunctures between economy, culture and politics, and between the representational or symbolic realms and material activities of the local region. To explain this in full is beyond the scope of this chapter, its purpose being limited to take up only certain aspects of the RISs in Japan, and especially to focus attention on the local–regional development and innovation initiatives by referring to the case of the Tohoku region, which comprises seven prefectures – Aomori, Iwate, Akita, Miyagi, Yamagata, Fukushima and Niigata.

Profile of the Tohoku region

Major economic indices

Although the Tohoku region covers 21.0 per cent of Japan, its share of population is only around 10 per cent. Tohoku's share of population in both 1920 and 1955 was about 13 per cent. Meanwhile, the Tokyo metropolitan area's share of population increased from 13.7 per cent to 17.3 per cent. During the consequent period of high economic growth, the population of Tohoku declined rapidly, although, at all times since the war, interprefectural net migration has remained net emigration on balance.

Even some time after the end of the high-growth period, the Tohoku region still experienced the long-term shift in the balance of the industrial structure generally referred to as 'industrialization'. Furthermore, a change in the size of manufacturing establishments was discernible from 1980 (the share of medium-sized establishments was increasing) attributable to a rapid increase in the number of factories in the Tohoku region. But the share of small and medium-sized industry in Tohoku is still overwhelming, with only 5.3 per cent of employment in firms of 100 people or more in 1999.

GDP statistical data indicate some features of the Tohoku region. As mentioned earlier, the region still experiences the double structural changes of industrialization and de-industrialization, and Tohoku's share of GDP had been declining through the process of de-industrialization as well as in the process of industrialization. In both the secondary or tertiary industries, the shared percentage of output is continuously less than the shared percentage of working persons engaged in each industry in the Tohoku region (Table 10.1). As for agriculture, the reason that Tohoku's share of output is relatively high is that the agriculture of this region has its monocultural structure concentrated in rice production. And, for the same reason, many high-tech factories moved to locate in Tohoku. In rice-farming regions where new factories rise like castles above rice paddies, eldest sons and their wives who live together with their farming parents are employed in high-tech industries. Such households are also part-time farms, which, because of the modernization of rice farming, do not require constant work in the rice fields. On the other hand, the Tohoku region lags far behind metropolitan areas in new industries such as information technology (Tohoku's share of people engaged in information service industry was 4.1 per cent in 1997). The indices of foreign trade in the Tohoku region are also very low (Tohoku's share of value of exports was only 0.97 per cent in 1999), although official statistics are based on

Table 10.1 Gross domestic product by industry, Tohoku and Japan

		1965	1970	1975	1980	1985	1990	1995	1997
Japan	Primary	9.9	6.5	5.3	3.5	2.9	2.1	1.5	1.4
	Secondary	37.4	42.4	38.7	37.9	37.1	37.1	32.8	31.5
	Tertiary	52.8	54.8	59.9	61.9	63.7	65.9	65.6	67.0
Tohoku Region	Primary	23.9	17.1	13.9	8.1	7.5	5.4	3.6	3.2
	Secondary	24.0	29.6	31.2	31.9	30.9	34.0	32.5	31.0
	Tertiary	52.1	56.7	58.1	63.0	64.7	63.9	63.9	65.7

Note: All = 100.
Source: Economic Planning Agency.

Custom House location, so there may be some under-assessment. This means that many high-tech firms located in Tohoku are export industries, much influenced by the exchange rate of the yen.

The enduring structure whereby the region's share of income is less than its share of population, and the region's share of local government expenditure and administrative investment in public works is more than the share of population is unchanging. Table 10.2 shows that much of the administrative investment was concentrated on the metropolitan areas during the high growth era. During the Third NCD Plan period (1977–87) since the oil shock, the emphasis in public works has been shifting to non-metropolitan areas, but since the beginning of the Fourth NCD Plan, the previous trend has been reversed slightly.

Change in the character of the Tohoku region

Table 10.3 shows changes in the number of applications for construction of new factories since the late 1970s, and how high-tech industries have concentrated. This shows, apparently, that the Tohoku region assumed a special status as a very important high-tech related area in present Japan.

From the macro-economic point of view, one explanation is that, in order to overcome the so-called 'Nixon Shock' and the 'Oil Shock' in the early 1970s, an increase in consumption and higher-yielding capital investment was needed domestically. Surplus capital poured into the Tohoku region (invested first in land speculation), because Tohoku's backwardness meant that it was the last remaining region in Japan that could potentially receive new industries. Induced by public investment, which increased along with the general rise of prices and income as a result of the oil shock, housing and factory construction boomed in the Tohoku region for the first time (Okamoto, 1985).

Table 10.2 Prefectural income, local government expenditure and administrative investment, per capita

	1965	1970	1975	1980	1985	1990	1995
Prefectural income							
Tohoku	64.0	71.0	89.0	87.0	84.0	80.0	86.5
Tokyo	149.0	152.0	166.0	160.0	162.0	152.0	136.7
Local government expenditure							
Tohoku	112.0	116.0	122.0	128.0	122.0	118.0	120.0
Tokyo	91.0	92.0	85.0	81.0	84.0	90.0	88.0
Local taxes for all revenue(%)							
Tohoku	13.6	17.6	15.4	12.0	19.6	20.9	18.7
Tokyo	53.7	60.2	51.9	57.8	63.7	64.9	56.6
Administrative investment							
Tohoku	92.0	95.0	112.0	129.0	118.0	111.0	117.8
Tokyo	118.0	107.0	89.0	82.0	82.0	100.0	105.1

Note: National average = 100
Sources: Economic Planning Agency and Ministry of Home Affairs.

Table 10.3 Tohoku share of industrial location by type of factory

	1976–80	1980	1980–5	1985	1985–90	1990	1990–5	1995	1997
Factory[1]	15.8	16.6	19.6	21.1	22.5	21.6	20.6	19.8	21.6
Selected factory[2]		14.6	16.7	20.3	18.8	20.9	19.1	15.3	16.6
Fabricated metal		10.7	12.2	13.8	19.3	26.3	20.1	2.6	16.2
General machinery		14.3	18.6	21.1	23.0	28.0	21.5	12.5	19.3
Electrical machinery		21.7	30.3	31.5	30.4	28.5	29.3	36.4	22.1
High-tech[3]	30.4	32.3	32.8	34.1	37.7	33.0	30.6	29.2	20.1

Notes
Japan = 100.
1 Site > 1000m².
2 Site > 1000m² or premises > 3000m².
3 Drugs, medicines, communications and electronic equipment, medical instruments and optical instruments apparatus, and lenses.

From the Tohoku region's point of view, its advantages in terms of resources and space have resulted in a 'high-tech land'. There were many reasons that direct investment in the Tohoku region has been made subsequently. First, the Tohoku Shinkansen (high-speed train) and the Tohoku Expressway (opened during the late 1970s and the early 1980s) have facilitated the movement of people from all parts of Tohoku to the Tokyo metropolitan area. Second, there was an abundant supply of energy and water for industrial use. Third, rich farmland, virgin forests and the surrounding sea all made the kind of attractive environment then sought by new high-tech industries. However, more than anything else, more specific reasons that business people should seriously consider direct regional investment there were land prices and the nature of the labour force available in the Tohoku region. The average price of land for manufacturing sites in coastal industrial parks in the metropolitan areas was ten or more times that of industrial parks in the Tohoku region. Wage rates were on average approximately 20–30 per cent lower in the Tohoku region than in metropolitan areas, and the people of Tohoku were known for being industrious, patient and kind.

How much has the agro-industrial complex structure – formed as a result of the location of high-tech firms in recent decades – changed the indices that had been referred to as evidence of the 'backwardness' of the Tohoku region? Until 1970, the decline in the population of the Tohoku region was largely attributable to young workers moving from Tohoku to the Kanto industrial region (including Tokyo). Even now, the percentage of students who go on to university is relatively low (44.1 per cent for Japan and 33.0 per cent in Tohoku in 1999), and for university graduates seeking employment opportunities the environment is still less favourable there.

The value added of manufactured goods shipments has certainly increased every five years and Tohoku's share of Japan's total has also steadily increased (from 4.6 per cent in 1965 to 7.3 per cent in 1997). But it is regrettable that regional differences in productivity between the Tohoku region and metropolitan areas have hardly been reduced (Tokyo Metropolitan = 114 and Tohoku = 70, with a productivity base 100 for all of Japan, in 1997). The more regional economies are buffeted not only by international competition and fluctuating currency rates but also by regional competition within the national economy, the more the incentive factors attracting R&D functions and foreign investment become essential to respond to the global competitive challenge and secure the basis for self-sustaining growth. But statistical data concerning the location of private R&D by region (Tohoku's share 8.15 per cent, 1985–97) and patent applications by region (1.8 per cent in Tohoku and 86.1 per cent in the three metropolitan areas of Tokyo, Nagoya, Osaka in 1998) show how poorly the Tohoku region fares in its share of regional strategic resources.

Looking in more detail at differential growth between industries to glimpse the prospects for 'high-tech Tohoku', which was the expression fashionable in the 1980s when 'high-tech fantasy' prevailed, it is most striking that, in recent years, the leading industry in the Tohoku region is now electronics, which accounts for a third of all manufacturing in the 1990s, from only 5 per cent at the beginning of the 1960s. However, excessive concentration in that particular industry and its relatively low productivity are to be interpreted rather as weaknesses in terms of the regional economy, because it is increasingly at the mercy of external economic changes. Since the late 1980s, the rush for a Tohoku location by high-tech firms has reversed, resulting in the 'hollowing out' of the regional economy. In particular, the electrical industry has begun to shift mass production and labour-intensive production to NIEs (newly industrializing economies) in response to the high exchange rate of the yen since 1985, and to shift value-added and capital-intensive production and parts production to China and ASEAN in addition to NIEs in the early 1990s. The majority of high-tech industries located in the Tohoku region are branch plants, carrying out routine production functions with relatively low-status jobs, whose top management and most R&D activities are located outside the region, usually in Tokyo. Branch plants purchase much input from outside the regions and have close technical links with others in the Tokyo metropolitan area.

The main cause of relatively low value-added productivity in the Tohoku region is largely attributable to the labour-intensive firms and the low rates of technological innovation. In seeking to link itself to the continuing global processes of techno-industrial innovation, the Tohoku region faces strong disadvantages because of its initial conditions of relative backwardness, although opportunities to attract more advanced production are by no means ignored.

Regionalization of innovation

Before the Technopolis Plan

Under the governmental system of Japan, local governments had limited instruments available to encourage innovation and diversify their area's economic base. Major institutions sought to strengthen technological capability throughout the country under the modernization project; in SMEs the Public Experimental Stations owned by prefecture government were of key importance. Some of the oldest *Kohsetsushi* (Public Experiment Stations) were initially established in the Meiji period, and trends in establishment have reflected the social and economic conditions of the times: agriculture-, forestry-, and fishery-related stations were established first, followed by industrial stations, then post-war sanitation laboratories and other healthcare-related stations, and finally in the late 1960s pollution research centres and other environment-related institutions. Incidentally, half of all public research institutions owned by prefectural governments were established before 1950. As the policy implication of the establishment of those institutions was to modernize local technologies and to stimulate technological innovation activities in SMEs, the major functions of those institutions were focused on technical guidance, testing and analysis. Prefectural governments were not familiar with research management or knowledge to utilize results of research for local regional economic development and enhancement of quality of life, except in very limited fields such as the improvement of rice plants. They had mainly been modernizing local industries, which were principally SMEs, and attempting to develop new industrial zones by luring manufacturing enterprises. It was 1983 when the technopolis project was initiated by MITI, and since then there has been a growing recognition that the level of research and technological innovation in a local area or region is a major long-term influence on its economic growth and development.

In the days of the traditional 'exogenous' regional policies of the national government, such as the creation of employment by financial and fiscal incentives to large industrial corporations to establish branch plants, or to all sizes of industrial and other organizations to relocate, the main policy objective of local government was to succeed in becoming part of a national government programme. The race to gain such a designation took hold of almost all prefectural governments under the NICP (New Industrial Cities Promotion) Act of 1962. Although bureaucrats in the central government and the national big business community initially wanted only two or three growth poles, located within the Inland Sea close to the Pacific Belt, fifteen sites were designated ultimately, as a result of the 'distributive' pressure from the political representatives of local regions, among which five sites in the Tohoku region were included.

In NICP, the main policy instruments were public investment in industrial infrastructure, including coastal industrial sites, port facilities and roads, and local tax concessions, which were intended to make the districts attractive to manufacturing locations. Government financial institutions such as the Hokkaido-Tohoku Development Corporation (established in 1956), and the Public Corporation for Promotion of Small and Medium Enterprises (established by prefectural government), provided loans for manufacturing investment in the district. The Japan Regional Development Corporation (established in 1962) and local development corporations (established by prefectural government or municipal government for the temporary purpose of acquiring land for industrial development and for housing, securing developmental funds and bonding) were the main institutions taking charge of developing sites. But what beneficial effects these measures had on the reduction in regional economic differentials and laying the basis for self-generated growth remain an open question, since almost every prefectural government sought later to gain another designation overlapping the same district designated as NIC (Sasao, 1991; Sazanami, 1991).

In retrospect, it seemed to be explained by an increasing divergence between the logic of industry and the expectation of local regions that the results of the diversionary policies of the 1960s and 1970s (especially the NICP) programmes and their implementation proved disappointing. The main components of those programmes were the development of industrial and trading sites and traffic infrastructure in order to enhance the attractiveness of distinctive locations for large firms, which were dominant at the initial stages of the phenomenal Japanese post-war boom. However, according to structural analysis of the patterns and complexities of regional restructuring (Massey, 1979; Yada, 1990), regional industrial structure could be seen as a complex result of different layers of investment within the series of wider national and international-spatial divisions of labour. As for the heavy and chemical industries that were encouraged to disperse, their spatial pattern of production within Japan might be that of 'sectoral spatial specialization'. These industries, concentrated along the Pacific Belt, had little need to seek cheap labour supplies by locating in rural regions such as Tohoku, depending on either massive rural outmigration until the end of the 1960s or offshore investment since the beginning of the 1970s. On the other hand, for emerging industries such as electrical goods and manufacturing assembly, their vocational requirements were different from the premise of the NICP policy, because of the different form of spatial differentiation that those industries used, which might be 'an intra-sectoral division of labour' within the overall process of production. Thus, for want of true insight into the underlying mechanisms linking industrial change and regional restructuring, a discrepancy between the policy goal and its performance has resulted.

Technopolis fever

The idea of 'technopolis' (technology-intensive cities) fleshed out in MITI's Vision for the 1980s (1980) differed in its basic approach from the conventional ideas of regional development centring on land utilization and infrastructural improvements. It was a hybrid of two concepts: that of a centre for the promotion of R&D and innovative technology, such as Silicon Valley, and that of even much older Garden City notions that were imported from England early in the twentieth century and were revived as one of the chief planks of the Ohhira government platform. In the initial phase of discussions concerning technopolis, the main theme was to be the building of another Tsukuba (a huge conglomeration of technological and production facilities, as well as universities), or miniature conglomerations modelled on Tokyo, as the model in a few selected regions. But when this idea was made public by MITI, it provoked the unwanted attention of local government planners. Of Japan's forty-seven prefectures, forty immediately volunteered to host such high-technology cities. At this time, as in the case of NICP, under pressure from politicians intent on generating distributive benefits for constituents, in 1982 MITI altered its initial efficiency-orientated plan. In the Technopolis Law (a law for accelerating regional development based on high-technology industrial complexes) passed by the National Diet in 1983, its rationale became not merely the creation of high-technology production centres but also development of local innovative R&D capacity to help stimulate development of existing industries locally. Ultimately, twenty-six districts were designated, among which all seven prefectures in the Tohoku region were included.

Particularly in less-favoured regions such as Tohoku, the idea of the technopolis has struck a responsive chord. It held forth the prospect of building an enduring infrastructure, ideally suited to the emerging era of high technology; such an infrastructure would produce revenue, employment, prosperity and demographic balance. Thus, at first, local governments welcomed this policy as a new way of obtaining subsidies for building local factories, without any particular concern for R&D. In this process, however, strong competition occurred among candidate prefectures, and MITI decreed that without explicit R&D planning a district could not be accepted as a technopolis district. This strongly encouraged independent effort by local governments to design new organizations for R&D that aimed at the transfer of high technology to local industries (such as the Technopolis Foundation), and to stimulate local industries to organize their action clubs.

The goals of the technopolis policy were to promote manufacturing-orientated R&D that aimed at incremental improvements in existing production systems by transferring R&D capacity, and to establish knowledge-orientated R&D with the goal of designing a new frontier or making a breakthrough in existing systems, which might eventually create new industries. To realize these goals, a new organizational structure was considered that would link industries, universities and government. However, how synergies among governmental institutions, local industries and universities could be created was quite unknown, and neither local governments nor MITI knew precisely how to do this. In addition, although the policy instruments of central government to promote synergies were incentive measures such as the tax system (special depreciation and loss allowances, the reduction of local taxes), finance (a special lending system), and a subsidy system for R&D, the background of policy implementation had largely changed, because reduction in the budget deficit (so-called fiscal reconstruction) had become one of the most important objectives of economic policy since 1980. So, the policy instrument of the Technopolis project rejected public works in favour of a 'soft' infrastructure of trained people, new technologies, information services, venture capital and telecommunications services. In turn, and ironically, prefectural governments had to concentrate on 'hard' infrastructure – roads, airports, laboratory facilities, technology centres and industrial and research parks – and too little on the 'soft' infrastructure of R&D consortia, venture capital funds and co-operating research funds (Ito *et al.*, 1995).

Immediately after the first step of the technopolis programme (1984–90) started, enormous changes were seen far beyond ones observed during the preceding three decades; on the external side, following the Plaza Accord of 1985, the increasing volatility of foreign exchange rates and the rapid and huge appreciation of the Japanese yen, further liberalization of trade in goods and services, and a remarkable expansion of foreign direct investment; on the domestic scence, the bubble of shares and real estates prices in far greater size, a large outflow of Japanese manufacturing investment, and the ageing of the population with its impact on the social security system. All these changes have affected Japanese economic growth, and the national government announced a set of fiscal and monetary policies designed to counteract the recessionary effects of rapid yen appreciation and to boost domestic demand (the Maekawa Report by the Research Council on Economic Structural Adjustment for International Co-operation, which emphasized the need to steer the nation's course away from a 'production-oriented' economy towards a 'living-oriented' one, and its industrial policy version, the Basic Vision of Industrial Society in the twenty-first Century by the Industrial Structure Council, MITI, in 1986).

These measures strongly influenced industrial development in the technopolis. The technopolis programme at the starting point was primarily aimed at relocating high-tech manufacturing firms from congested metropolitan areas to the districts designated. But the percentage of firms located in the technopolis was not necessarily as high as expected. This was because manufacturing companies had been shifting their production facilities overseas instead of to the technopolis. To counter this offshore movement, MITI spurred regional economic organizations to establish the Industrial Vitalization Centres for regions to implement policy measures, one of which was established in the Tohoku region in 1988. And MITI developed the Regional Research Core Concept (passed by the National Diet in 1986 as the 'Private Participation Promotion Law' and in 1988 as the 'Brain Location Law') to promote the regionalization of high-tech research and to strengthen local R&D facilities. As a result, the same districts designated by the Technopolis Act were designated doubly or trebly by these Acts too. On the other hand, recognizing the uneven regional effects of the first round, prefectural governments in the Tohoku region began to establish, or to prepare for the establishment of, science and research parks instead of conventional industrial parks.

At the same time, the Ministry of Education started to promote joint research or entrusted research programmes with the private sector by enacting the Law for Facilitating Governmental Research Exchange in 1986. In order to develop creativity, it was essential not only for industry, university and government to do their best in their respective capacities, but also for them to co-ordinate and share the work. Technological changes now required a higher level of co-operative R&D activities and close interaction between basic science and product and process technology. Thus, the university-industry connection was essential for enhancing basic research and innovation development linkage. Particularly in local regions, the university is a key centre for basic research, but has difficulties pushing R&D

itself without sufficient funds. Industry wants to acquire new innovative technology by utilizing human resources and facilities in universities. Co-operative research is one measure and joint research another. Although university–industry co-operative research was generally not active in provincial regions before 1983, the technopolis project changed the situation because of the initiative of science and technology promotion policies of prefectural governments. And ME started to establish the Co-operative Research Centre attached to the university in 1987. However, such a development was a late arrival in the Tohoku region.

The second stage of the technopolis programme (1991–95) started after the MITI Vision for the 1990s (1990) was issued. It is interesting that technopolis had little news value as a political symbol in that Vision which emphasized less strategic sectors, but quality-of-life priorities, such as resorts, interior decorating and fashion. And the Skellton Planning of the second period laid stress on endogenous modes of development such as the improvement of the quality of regional industries and manufacturing establishments, the promotion of the foundation of industrial enterprises and technology transfer.

Concerning the location of R&D institutions too, there has been an acute regional imbalance. The two prefectures of Greater Tokyo and Ibaragi, where Tsukuba Science City is located, had two-thirds of national R&D owned by the central government (5.9 per cent in Tohoku), and the three prefectures of Greater Tokyo, Kanagawa and Osaka had about half of total private R&D (2.6 per cent in Tohoku). During the 1980s, many high-tech firms relocated to the Tohoku region, but they have been mainly limited either to the making of parts for shipment to metropolitan regions or overseas, or routine assembly. Although local governments expected the technopolis to be a method of technology transfer, very little techno-logy transfer has occurred between incoming factories and local industries. Since the expansion of basic research activities and promotion of technology fusion between different fields is expected to lead to increasing market opportunities for technologically innovative areas in the future (especially for small businesses to convert their activities and develop their new fields under conditions of economic structural change), prefectural governments have been forced to build (or plan to build) their own new R&D projects, or to strengthen functions of prefectural research institutions through organizational restructuring in order to introduce state-of-the-art technology into the local region.

Historically, the establishment of universities or colleges and the expansion of existing ones were at a peak during the high-growth era of the 1960s. The aim of establishing a university in those days gave more priority to practical aspects of promoting industrialization in science and technology, which has helped Japan to catch up in the development of industrial technology and the modernization of society. As it became essential for Japan to develop technologies of its own instead of improving and applying imported technologies in the catch-up process, the expected role of universities has changed towards creation of new technology as a seed for future production. With this background, there are two movements: much emphasis is laid on establishment or expansion of graduate schools rather than undergraduate courses, and establishment of research-type (rather than teaching) universities by prefectural government. In Tohoku, every prefectural government established new universities or planned to build them (eleven universities were established or partly funded by local governments in 1988–95 in Tohoku).

It was in 1997, two years behind schedule, that the basic strategy of the third stage (1995–2000) was decided. In 1994, the last year of the second stage, the Industrial Structure Council issued the policy document, *Industrial Structure in the 21st Century*, which forcibly appealed to a greater need for Japan to make a kind of paradigm shift in industrial policy. And, in 1998, the next year after the third stage started, the Technopolis Law was abolished and its programmes were absorbed into the Law for Promotion of New Enterprises.

There are many ways of evaluating the technopolis programme (Glasmeier, 1988; Stöhr and Pönighaus, 1992; Castells and Hall, 1994; Sternberg, 1995; Park, 1997; Yamazaki, 1992; Ito, 1998; JILC, 1999), and the assessment based on comparison of the degree of goal achievement with respect to employment, turnover and population since their implementation has proved largely disappointing. However, evaluation of their success or failure in terms of the development of innovation systems should be flexible because that is a long-term project.

The Technopolis Plan was seen as a regional industrial policy to initiate development based on high-tech industrial complexes, but it had two objectives that did not seem necessarily compatible from the point of view of provincial regions outside the 3M areas: industrial policy and regional policy, or national development and regional development. Historically, regional policies could be seen in many cases as adjuncts to industrial policy, because of their aim to improve infrastructure to contribute to national economic growth, rather than to ameliorate the problem of regional differentials. In some cases, they could even be considered a form of social policy in disguise, through implementing measures (via some sort of public investment) to compensate those regions where private business investment was scarce or existing industries were declining. As mentioned earlier, the Technopolis Plan was originally designed as the industrial policy to upgrade the entire industrial structure to the level of the knowledge-intensive industries. This would enhance Japan's international competitiveness and establish the basis for an inward-orientated development trajectory which would ease international trade friction. But, in the law-making process, it turned into a regional policy because of political pressures from local regions, other government ministries and by the anti-high-growth climate of the age. Thus, designation and implementation happened through consultation between central and local government, but neither necessarily had the know-how needed for technopolis construction and operation.

In terms of regional policy, the national government sought to redistribute growth spatially by establishing dispersed high-technology industrial complexes through stimulating and harnessing the innovative potential of SMEs and new enterprises. However, in local regions such as Tohoku, local government, which had to take the initiative in acquiring the designation of the plan and its implementation, tended to see it as a device to attract high-tech firms into hitherto empty state-led industrial sites.

Originally, the Technopolis Plan was a learned response, based upon the difficult experiences of western countries with which Japan was to catch up, and was run with little understanding of the geography of the high technology age. Most shortcomings in performance of the technopolis programme in the implementation process – such as low growth of output value and employment, low capabilities to generate new frontier R&Ds and little emergence of new venture business – were brought about by both external and internal factors. The first was that the technopolis strategy had been undermined by the regional impact of the surge in Japanese foreign investment during the 1980s, when, because of the strong yen and the global localization strategy of Japanese corporations, the 'hollowing out' of not only production facilities but also R&D facilities had begun. The second concerned a failure to generate synergy through innovative cross-fertilization. Local linkages within the technopolis area still appear weak, and most branch subsidiaries retain strong vertical links with their headquarters, rather than opening up new production spaces for local firms (Table 10.4).

The last point is worth noting in the sense that, as a regional development policy aimed at setting up high-tech industry complexes, the Technopolis Plan can be seen to be a case of international 'institutional borrowing'. The strategies on which that plan was based were naïvely copied from the Silicon Valley model. Furthermore, programmes for particular technopolises were copies of copies, emulating each other as well as conforming to the state-led model. And, paradoxically, that model was applied not to the metropolitan areas but to provincial regions which were severely handicapped by the lack of policy and institutional resources. Basic essentials of the Silicon Valley model were seen to be a regional network-based industrial system, where, depending on both geographical and cultural proximity, relationships of shared identities and mutual trust exist. These are repeatedly reinvested through shifting patterns of competition and collaboration among specialized producers, scientific institutes and various supporting institutions (Smilor et al., 1988; Saxenian, 1994; Markusen, 1997). However, as some institutional economists and industrial sociologists have argued, another kind of network system to sustain flexible specialization developed during the

Table 10.4 Technopoles in Tohoku

Prefecture	Aomori	Iwate	Miyagi	Akita	Yamagata	Fukushima	Niigata
Name of Technopolis	Aomori	Kitakami	Sendai North	Akita	Yamagata	Koriyama	Shinanogawa
Mother city	Aomori	Morioka	Sendai	Akita	Yamagata	Koriyama	Nanogawa
Start of the plan	1984	1987	1986	1984	1987	1986	1987
Developed Parks(ha)	230	412	732	144	186	399	307
Established Research Institute	2 (1988, 1994)	3 (1993, 1995, 1999)	2 (1992, 1999)	2 (1992, 1995)	3 (1988, 1993, 1994)		4 (1988, 1989, 1992, 1995)
Established Public Universities	2 (1993[1], 1999)	1 (1998)	1 (1997)	1 (1999)	2 (1992, 2000)	1 (1993)	4 [1] (1988, 1994, 1994, 1995)
Center for Cooperative Research	Hirosaki U. 1997	Iwate U. 1993	Tohoku U. 1998	Akita U. 1993	Yamagata U. 1992	Fukushima U. 2001	Nagaoka U. 1981
Center for Industrial Promotion	2 (1992, 1996)	4 (1994, 1997, 1997, 1999)	4 (1988, 1993, 1998, 1999)	1 (2000)	3 (1989, 1994, 1999)	2 (1992, 1998)	3 (1988, 1991, 1999)
Designated National Project[2]	a 1964, b 1987, 1992, c 1986, g 1994	b 1984, c 1987, 1991, 1999, d 1987, f 1994 g 1993, h 1997	a 1964, c 1985, d 1989, e 1988	a 1965, c 1986	c 1985, f 1992, e 1989, g 1994	a 1964, b 1987, c 1993, f 1991	c 1992, e 1987, 1989, g 1993, h 1997
Rate of an increase (1995/1985)[3]							
in population	.99	1.04	1.14	1.04	1.03	1.07	1.00
in labour force	1.24	1.16	1.01	1.15	1.00	.96	1.00
in industry labourer	1.18	1.22	1.22	1.16	1.04	1.11	1.03
in shipment of manufacture	1.54	2.01	1.30	1.38	1.54	1.36	1.35
Location 1985–1997 number & share (JAPAN=100)							
All firms	219 (0.67)	198 (0.61)	204 (0.63)	99 (0.30)	290 (0.89)	159 (0.49)	658 (2.03)
High-tech firms	18	38	28	15	58	30	40
Research Institutes	0	1	17	0	3	1	2

Notes

1　Private Universities supported by prefecture governments

2　a: New Industrial Cities (1964), b: New Media Community (MITI-1983), c: Teletopia (MPT-1983), d: Intelligent City (MC-1986), e: Private Sector Resources Utilization Law (1986), f: Key Facilities Siting Law (1988), g: Office Arcadia Law (1992), h: Regional Industrial Concentration Reinvigoration Law (1996)

3　Rate of an increase (1995/1985) in All JAPAN, population, 1.03; labour force, 0.94; industry labourer, 1.04; shipment manufacture, 1.15.

1980s in Japan, which was characterized as the 'Japanese system of innovation' (Freeman 1987), 'relational contracting' (Dore, 1987) or 'horizontal integration between research, design, development, production and marketing' (Aoki, 1988; Lash and Urry, 1994). Thus, the technopolis project implied a most burdensome dual challenge for the local region. Not only had it to conquer established vertical linkages, it also had to build up locally a new kind of horizontal network system linked into this emergent 'Japanese form of production system'.

Structural reforms and post-technopolis

The bursting of the bubble economy in the early 1990s and the consequent financial and economic woes have dramatically shaken Japanese confidence in their economic institutions, unleashing demand for reform and change, such as the deregulation and decentralization of public administration. In addition, the previously stable party system had been completely reconfigured by the split in the ruling Liberal Democratic Party, and the public confidence in the once vaunted Japanese bureaucracy caused to decline by a series of well-documented cases of corruption (Stockwin, 1997).

The Basic Law for Science and Technology of 1995 seemed to be the saving grace to the nation which was in the situation of soul searching, because it laid down the basic framework for future S&T policy and aimed to be an advanced science-and technology-oriented nation in the twenty-first century. The Law and its Basic Plan of 1996 called for the promotion of S&T overall and of university–industry linkages in particular. Furthermore, the Law incorporated the adoption and implementation of policies calling on local governments to engage in the promotion of S&T in order to serve as a basic framework for the future of S&T policy in Japan. The First S&T Plan stressed the importance of promoting research activities in regional areas, and called for the promotion of co-ordination and exchanges among local industries, academic and governments in accordance with the Basic Guideline for Vitalization of S&T Activities in Local Areas, which was approved by the Prime Minister in 1995. Thus, the prefectural governments were stimulated to make efforts to promote S&T by establishing councils to deliberate their own policies and adopting outlines and guidelines for their policies, and taking actions to reorganize or improve their public research institutions and working to strengthen R&D capabilities.

Based on the S&T Basic Plan, national measures for S&T promotion in regional areas also started; Basic Research for Life and Society of 1995 and Regional Science Promotion Program of 1996, STA; Venture Business Laboratories Program of 1996, ME; Regional Advanced Technology Joint Research and Development Promotion Program of 1996, MAFF; Regional Consortium R&D System of 1997, MITI; Multimedia Pilot Town of 1997, MPT, etc. And new laws were enacted and administered: Regional Industrial Concentration Reinvigoration Law of 1997, as a measure to meet the situation of severe hollowing out of local industries; Law for Promotion of New Enterprises of 1998, to promote the creation of new enterprises that make use of local industrial resources; Law to Promote Technology Transfer from Universities of 1998, to establish technology licensing organization such as Tohoku Technoarch Co. Ltd established by Tohoku University and others.

But in 1997 due to the Asian crisis, the worst records were yet to be made of GDP growth rate, unemployment rate, government fiscal deficits and Japan's competitive place in the white paper of International Institute for Management Development. Then, recommendations and reports of Councils were rushed out; the recommendations on the 'preparation of industrial technology strategies', the Industrial Structure Council of MITI, 1998; the Report of Economic Council of EPA, which argued that, defining present Japan as being at a turning point, Japanese socio-economy should be one with an economic structure and disposition that pursues prosperity and joy through self-help and competition; the Report *Strategy for the Recovery of Japanese Economy* by the newly established Economic Strategy Council of the Office of the Prime Minister, which argued the need to change Japan from an 'equity and equality' to 'efficiency and fairness' society, focusing on strengthening Japan's competitiveness, in 1999; the final Report of the Industrial Competitiveness Council of PMO, which demanded newer policies and legislation to strengthen competitiveness, such as realization of true co-operation among industry, academics and government, promotion of reforms of universities and restructuring of government systems, in 2000. And these recommendations have resulted in the enactment of the Industrial Revitalization Law (Japanese version of the US Bayh-Dole Act) of 1999 and the Industrial Technology Enhancement Law of 2000.

Two long-term policy documents issued at that time have registered a significant shift on the part of national government. *The Grand Design of National Land in the 21st Century* (1998), in replacing the fourth NCDP, moves away from an earlier master plan-type conception of regional planning, and the focus has moved from diversionary policies to the need to exploit the region's endogenous potential and regional networks. *Challenges and Prospects for Economic and Industrial Policy in the 21st Century* (2000), equivalent to MITI's Vision 2000, avowed the aim to strengthen 'the competitiveness through technological innovation and create institutionally wide-ranging opportunities for jobs and social participation throughout a life-time of dreams and incentive'. Based on similar ideas, the second S&T Basic Plan launched in 2001 argues for Japan to be a nation with international competitiveness and the ability to sustain development. In this connection, the need to reform the university system, with a mind to enhancing research productivity and competitiveness, is widely acknowledged, and the ninety-nine state universities and colleges are to be reclassified as independent administrative agencies in 2003.

Viewed from the regionalization of innovation policy, there are three new programmes which are characterized in terms of the introduction of new concepts such as geographic specialization and cluster formation, by favouring most dynamic sectors and locations in order to maximize national competitiveness.

One is the Research Results Utilization Plazas Programme implemented by JST (Japan Science and Technology Corporation), whose plazas have been constructed in seven cities including Sendai (Tohoku) up to 2002. The second is MEST's 'Intellectual Cluster' Program, stimulating the building of a technology innovation system around public research institutes that possess R&D seeds characteristic to the region. Ten clusters are starting from April 2002, among which Sendai Cyber-Forest Plan is included as the only one plan designated in the Tohoku region.

The third is METI's 'Industrial Cluster' Programme, which was decided as a measure to cope with industrial restructuring and employment problems by the Cabinet in September 2001. It is aimed principally at developing specialization at the regional level to fuel productivity improvement and foster innovation. In the Tohoku region, two projects promoting the development of industries dealing with the ageing society and the recycling society are set underway by the initiative of the Tohoku bureau of METI (formerly MITI).

However, in Tohoku region, being at a disadvantage with respect to science and technology activities indices (Table 10.5), whether these measures designed with both local input and national co-ordination will eventually result in stimulating and widening the endogenous technological capabilities of each regional economy, or whether the heavy emphasis on competitiveness of regions and local areas in terms of the values and rhetoric of the market will intensively develop local and regional culture, is still an open question.

From the observation of the initial stage in the Tohoku case, the impact of these cluster programmes on the revitalization of the local-regional economy or the forging of regional systems of innovation seems to be rather low in comparison with that of Technopolis policy. In startling contrast to the good times of the early 1980s when the Technopolis policy stimulated a whirlwind of 'high-tech fantasy' as futurological conjecture, in these days of severe depression, broader and enlightened challenges are needed which will help the local-region break out of a cycle of pessimism, keep people thinking about change and push their horizon toward a vision of a hopeful future. However, these cluster programmes do not seem to possess such vigour but are technocratic in nature. In order to achieve the objectives which these programmes set forth, to build 'clusters', they require working across various sectors of the local-region and dealing with multiple constituencies, calling for critical self-understanding of the parties involved, and

Table 10.5a Some indicators of science and technology activities in Tohoku

Prefecture	Universities: numbers and share (2002)			Number of university students share (1998)		Number of national research institutes & researchers (1998)		Number of public experiment and research institutes and researchers (1997)		
	national	local	private	undergraduate	graduate	institutes	researchers	institutes	all researchers	researchers with doctorate
Aomori	1(1.0)	2(2.6)	6(1.1)	(0.7)	(0.3)	0	(0)	26(2.8)	(2.3)	(1.2)
Akita	1(1.0)	1(1.3)	1(0.2)	(0.3)	(0.3)	0	(0)	19(2.0)	(1.7)	(2.2)
Iwate	1(1.0)	2(2.6)	3(0.6)	(0.4)	(0.5)	1	(1.5)	15(1.6)	(1.8)	(0.7)
Miyagi	2(2.0)	1(1.3)	10(1.9)	(1.8)	(3.3)	2	(0.5)	17(1.8)	(1.8)	(1.0)
Yamagata	1(1.0)	1(1.3)	2(0.4)	(0.4)	(0.6)	0	(0)	18(1.9)	(1.9)	(0.9)
Fukushima	1(1.0)	2(2.6)	4(0.8)	(0.7)	(0.4)	0	(0)	25(2.7)	(1.8)	(1.3)
Niigata	3(3.0)	1(1.3)	11(2.1)	(0.9)	(2.0)	2	(0.9)	25(2.7)	(2.1)	(0.9)
Tokyo	12(12.1)	3(4.0)	101(19.7)	(24.3)	(26.4)	29	(24.2)	28(3.0)	(5.6)	(3.8)

Table 10.5b Some indicators of science and technology activities in Tohoku

	Number of research institutes in private companies		Expenditure on science and technology per capita (yen)		Number of patent applications (share)		Number of venture companies		
	1991	1998	1992	1997	1992	1996	1992	1998	1998
Aomori	2 (0.05)	2 (0.05)	7.031	11.287	(0.01)	(0.04)	8 (0.4)	5 (0.2)	3(0.3)
Akita	3 (0.08)	7 (0.08)	11.460	11.793	(0.01)	(0.08)	6 (0.3)	10 (0.4)	4(0.4)
Iwate	5 (0.13)	5 (0.13)	8.263	42.131	(0.07)	(0.03)	7 (0.3)	13 (0.5)	2(0.2)
Miyagi	24 (0.63)	19 (0.51)	4.638	5.878	(0.28)	(0.40)	10 (0.5)	22 (0.9)	1(0.1)
Yamagata	9 (0.23)	11 (0.29)	10.476	11.566	(0.18)	(0.19)	10 (0.5)	23 (0.9)	9(1.0)
Fukushima	21 (0.55)	31 (0.83)	15.616	16.673	(0.10)	(0.15)	8 (0.4)	17 (0.7)	3(0.3)
Niigata	34 (0.89)	46 (1.23)	3.219	4.245	(0.22)	(0.47)	22 (1.1)	31 (1.2)	7(0.8)
Tokyo	814 (21.4)	686 (18.4)	2.982	4.465	(49.9)	(49.24)	529 (27.7)	689 (28.6)	345(40.0)

Note: Japan = 100

Sources: Compiled from Science and Technology Indications: 1994, 1997, 2000; National Institute of Science and Technology Policy, Science and Technology Agency.

overcoming the inertia of old habits and removing existing institutional framework constraints, that is social innovation while developing a shared vision of future prospects. In the actual state, in the case of the Intellectual Cluster Programme, the university's involvement is based on a rather small number of dedicated professors but has not yet become institutionalized, and in the case of Industrial Cluster Programmes, they are developed at the initiation of well-meaning bureaucrats but with less real input from local-regional industry. What makes the Tohoku people sceptical of new initiatives might be the legacy of the past poor process of the same sort of policies and the rather moderate level of public funding for these programmes. But, more than anything else, it might be due to the fact that the policy languages of these programmes are somehow new but the modes of policy, that is perception and manner of implementation of programmes, are largely conventional. Then whether these programmes prove successful seems to be highly dependent on their innovation processes in themselves.

New regionalism

During the plan-making process of the fourth NCDP, a new regionalism emerged, which, resisting the conventional 'top-down' strategies, explored alternative new trajectories of regional development. It was to resemble the claim for 'regional states' (Ohmae, 1995) in the sense that development programmes based on 'bottom-up' strategies must be a creative response to the serious impact of the global economy at the regional level. By resizing the reduced capability of the national government to provide satisfactory solutions to growing regional unevenness, a claim for the transfer of central competences and functions to regional and local levels was justified. However, for regions to design mechanisms and institutional arrangements to cope with the growing complexity and uncertainty of the globalization of the economy, their own institutional innovation and productivity are preconditions. Yet, as things stand, their powers are not sufficient. Because of the limited scope of their actions, they cannot avoid requesting resources from the national government to develop skills and infrastructure. Therefore, the new regionalism is characterized by an ambivalent combination of resistance and dependence. What is distinctive about it is that the boundaries of the regional framework are defined autonomously in terms of the strategic calculations of the local region concerned. It might be paradoxical that the definition of the region can be highly variable because of the absence of a regional government system, although that absence has often been seen as the precondition for public policy to counterbalance regional problems.

The new regionalism took shape in different ways in different regions, since it was tailored to specific problems, conditions and strategies of particular regions (Sakamoto *et al.*, 1989; Fujita and Hill, 1993). The TICP (Tohoku Intelligent

Cosmos Plan) was a regional development project jointly initiated in 1987 by the leading industrial, academic and administrative bodies of the entire region, which promoted the creation of bases for advancement of industrial technology and the enhancement of the information function, technological capacity and academic expertise in the region, including seven prefectures in the global and longer-term perspective. But aiming at far more than regional development, it addressed the structural problems of Japan as a whole, and it will provide more credible solutions for them: the ageing population, the problem of investment, the nature of the future industrial structure, and the nation's need to find an ethically acceptable role suited to its capacities and ambitions. It intends to build a new philosophy and to shrug off the past conceptual framework which served the country well in the 'catch-up era' but which is quickly becoming obsolete.

In the Tohoku region, the originators of TIC project have resolved to make their own contribution to the world by developing new technology and future-orientated industries in which humanity and creativity are integral constituents. 'Cosmos', first of all, implies an ordered universe, one that neither grows haphazardly nor degenerates into entropy, but in which the hand of design and of deliberate creation is visible. This universe would be 'intelligent' in that it will make, to changes in its environment, responses that are both rational and appropriate to its overriding concern with the quality of life and humanity. It intends to be driven neither by a crass concern with mere profit nor by a headlong impulse to exploit all or any of the capacities of scientific discovery, come what may (Abe, 1997).

Looking back upon its plan-making process, there were three unprecedented characteristics differing from other regional plans. First, this was a plan not from 'top down' but from ' bottom up' , since, in the past, the regional development plan had been formulated by the central government, based on drafts written by central departments. In 1987, just before the Japanese government issued the fourth NCDP, some members of the TIC promotion committee (especially academic members) proposed their plan enthusiastically as the alternative to promote the future development of the Tohoku region. The conceptions of their plan and that of the national plan were not the same, but they worked with the national government in order to acquire resources to carry it into effect and they succeeded in the attempt to incorporate the aims of their plan into the national plan. Second, this was not merely the sum of prefectural plans in the conventional mode of budgetary acquisition groups, but the regional plan in which seven prefectures are linked laterally with each other under the 'holon' philosophy, meaning dynamic equilibrium between whole and individual or competition and collaboration (Koestler, 1978). In the Japanese government system, where there are some regional bureaux of central government but no regional government, each prefectural government is usually independent of the others and rather competitive in seeking subsidies and benefits from the central government, so mutual co-operation is difficult. In this case, it took ten months for them to agree to sit round the same table and to consent to make the regional plan from the bottom up, and another year and a half to draw up the plan. However, in the end, they overcame historical difficulties. Third, this was a project not initiated by local governments but originally proposed by academics, who played decisive roles as go-betweens, bringing together seven prefectural governments and also acting as persuasive agents to the central government (Abe, 1990; Nishizawa, 1995; Ishida, 1996).

The plan, encompassing a vision for the coming thirty-year period and for goals and strategies appropriate to it, can also be interpreted as the region's bid for an enhanced status on both the national and global stage. For this to become a reality, the plan envisaged a twofold strategy: first, it sought to achieve a qualitative enhancement and an absolute increase in the supply of information, technological capacity and academic expertise; second, by establishing certain pivotal centres linked at various levels (personnel, information and research) to a wider network, seven prefectures would be able to function globally as a single unit.

More specifically, innovative research and development were to be promoted. Results of this concentrated drive towards greater scientific and technological creativity would then be funnelled through to industry and the economy by an applications system built for the purpose. It was considered of prime importance for strong and mutually supportive links to be forged between industry, pure science, and technology. An inherent part of this is an increased emphasis upon provision and availability of information, an expanded three-way flow of knowledge between Tohoku and the rest of Japan, and then to the rest of the world. This in turn necessitates attracting many scientists and other professionals in various fields from both Japan and overseas and creating conditions specifically to facilitate such mobility.

The TIC Plan has been steadily making progress since its proposal in 1987. In the implementation of its first objective to promote innovative scientific and technological R&D, a systematic institutional structure has been developed for this purpose, as well as the design of a research-friendly environment. In addition, the foundation of actual R&D companies and organizations was already promoted, and an integrated network for their most efficient and co-ordinated management was formed.

One is ICR (Intelligent Cosmos Research KK, capital 8.456 billion yen), an organization specifically designed to support strategic R&D efforts and to facilitate industrial applications of R&D. As of 2001, fourteen R&D corporations had been established through joint investments (total amount of investment, 22.7 billion yen) by national and local governments and private companies. The targets of these corporations are both generic and specific technologies making a special contribution towards solving problems peculiar to Tohoku (as one of the results, numbers of patent applications, are over 400). ICR has worked to initiate twelve research projects under the Regional Consortium R&D System of MITI, from 1997 to 2001, and plays the role of the managing bureau in both the Intellectual Cluster Programme of MEST and the METI's Industrial Cluster Program from 2002. And, one year before, the Plaza of Research Results Utilization Programme of JST was located in the site of ICR.

Second is the Academic Society inaugurated in 1990, intending to establish and synthesize creative academic activities with a view to the future as well as to contribute to purposeful regional development, which transformed into the Intelligent Cosmos Academic Foundation in 1996 (number of academic members affiliated, 2620, and funds, 450 million yen). Third, the Tohoku Region Entrepreneur Expansion Network (about 800 industrialists affiliated) was founded in 1995 to enhance the internal dynamism for entrepreneurship. However, while the establishment of such institutions has been developing, the industrial commercialization of the results of R&D is slow to emerge.

In parallel with implementation efforts inside the region, the TIC group worked on the national government to regionalize regional policy, eventually leading to support and encouragement for regional initiatives, since carrying their plan into effect would require both radical policy changes at the national level and regional institutional innovation. They won government approval to make a comprehensive survey of measures for promoting the TIC plan (Co-ordination Budget for NCDP 1987–9, 1994–6), and survey committees made up of members of the academic, industrial and governmental communities from Tohoku as well as Tokyo were formed by eight ministries (NLA, ME, STA, MAFF, MITI, MC, MPT, and MT) respectively. It was unusual for ME and STA to organize their own survey committee concerning regional development. But at that time, neither ministry had the concept of 'region' in their policy thinking. The TICP group made a proposal to both ministries to position the concept of a 'RIS' in their national policy promotion. Whether this proposal had great material effect or not is unclear, but it was the first time that a regional framework was adopted to scrutinize national S&T promotion policies in the White Paper of STA of 1991. And, in 1995, the Council for Science and Technology issued Recommendation 22, entitled 'Regional Science and Technology Promotion',[2] which was sanctioned as 'the master principle for promoting science and technology activities in the local region' by the national government in December 1995. Then, in White Paper of Science and Technology 2002, the term 'RISs' became one of the official policies.

TICP is a sort of experiment of the subnational region at the meso-level, intending a shift from exogenous, satellite-type platforms of the Technopolis Policy to endogenous development, by enhancing capabilities to formulate and implement its own development policies on its own initiative as well as to urge the structural reform projects from within. At the first half stage, it opened a new sort of overall regional policy forum to discuss possible futures in terms of raising innovation in the region. Now, at the midway stage, it is faced with self-monitoring its practices to fit a new situation.

Viewed from the problems to be overcome in future policies, it must be recognized that local-regional systems of innovation are still very fragile. One problem is the discrepancy between institution building and attitudinal changes. The existing local institutions such as governments, industrial associations and even universities are implicated in clientistic networks and leaders of those institutions tend to step forward only out of narrow self-interest with less strategic and systemic thinking or reflexivity. Another is the great dependency on the crucial role of human factors, especially the personal dynamism of promoters. A long-term project such as TICP, whose approach is to be first of all about building social capital for collective innovation activities, requires catalysts or social entrepreneurs to foster new co-operation between local actors as well as to tie the region to relevant external partners. Thus the destinies of the project are swayed greatly by the exit of important promoters, due to ageing or regrettable events.

For TICP to sustain itself as an ongoing experiment and continuous movement forward requires constant process innovation, that is a process to identify and address new issues by thinking out of the box and getting fuelled up with lnew energy. The challenge of TICP at the midway stage seems to be to make an extra effort to involve new ideas and new leaders, and to rebuild platforms for continuing collaboration.

Conclusion

RISs are shaped largely by the national political-economic structure in which they are embedded like a jigsaw puzzle, and are not unaffected by cyclical swings in the macro-economic climate. And under the recessional or depressional trends after the bursting of the bubble, and the unstable party system after the end of the previously enduring conservative rule, government policies drift between the uneasy combination of conflicting elements of piecemeal solutions or quick fixes and a consistent line to address the nation's extensive structural problems, among priorities placed on anti-recessional policies in the short term and structural changes essential for the long term, and among competing and often contradictory visions for the future (Porter, *et al.*, 2000; Dore, 2000). Consequently these are reflected in the fact that lines of innovation policy action in the regions too become more haphazard and piecemeal.

Long-term strategic thinking and action in the less-favoured regions are in an awkward dilemma. The idea of 'local-regional initiative' has gained increasing importance since the 1980s to cope with the problems and challenges offered by globalization and subsequent global restructuring for specific regions. However, the national government's programme of structural reform (one recent example is the Local Independence and Revitalization Program, in 'Basic Policies' of the Koizumi Cabinet, June 2001) declares a shift of priority to 'unique regional development' and 'revitalization of wisdoms and development efforts through competition' on the one hand, but in reality, local public finance has been in a state of crisis because local governments had to expand their debt to cover their public works spending and permanent local tax cuts accompanying the central government's economic stimulus packages.

In addition, through processes of administrative reform at both the national and local level, which linked often to the neo-liberal agenda 'minimizing the cost and maximizing the benefit', it is not easy for local governments to set up their independent and long-term ventures when it is unclear what tangible results will follow. Furthermore, the recent regional and technology policies of the central government, intending to integrate the competitive advantages of the regions into its strategies in favour of national competitiveness, are liable to foster competition among regions for investment and market shares, but not necessarily accelerate their release from the tyranny of zero-sum games among parochial local units, and strengthen a culture of co-operation and a social cohesion which are highly valued in a context where innovation is conceived as collective learning process.

There is still a great discrepancy among inevitable dual strategies of the local region: to devote its endogenous efforts to induce self-sustaining development on the regional level and to participate actively in the national innovation process from the perspective of globalization. To turn the discrepancy into the mutually complementary resonance, the need to achieve the right balance between regionalization and regionalism is keenly felt. The Japanese style of regionalization has tended to mobilize local leaders to build new quasi-government organizations or new councils almost from programme to programme of the central department, so that the bulk of organizations piled up, overlapping each time. This has been liable to sap the energies of regionalism essential to make national government investment in a programme effective to encourage competition rather than collaboration in the local-region, and to deprive it of centripetal force to design its own strategy. As long as the national government (even now just like 'the developmental state') defines and drives entirely local-regional economic strategy, there will be no simple solutions to the problem. However, it might be a platitude, but a step out of the dilemma for the local-region seems to lie nowhere other than continuing its challenges to build strongly on its own initiative, and keep up with patience, the co-ordinating formula and platforms to address significant issues that strike at the heart of its future, so that it might help people residing there to break out of a cycle of pessimism which has been caused by the straying of national government policies of proactive and reactive effects, to develop their delicate art and skills of mixing the top-down programme with the bottom-up demand, and to take responsibility for and make positive choices about their future.

Notes

1   By reorganization of the Central Government Offices (in January 2001), the numbers of ministries was reduced from 22 to 13; four ministries of MT, MC, NLA and HDA to MLIT, three ministries of MPT, MHA and MCA to MPM, two ministries of ME and STA to MEST, and MITI to METI (Ministry of Economy, Trade and Industry), etc.

2   The present author was a chairman of subcommittee drafting Recommendation 22, in 'Basic Guidelines for Boosting Regional Scientific and Technological Activities' Committee, CST.

Chapter 11
Innovative milieu and co-operation networks
State initiatives and partnership for restructuring in Singapore

Hing Ai Yun

Introduction

Relevant theorization of economic space centring on the concept of innovative milieu/environment (Aydalot, 1985; Lakshmanan, 1995) has opened up opportunities for exploring economic dynamics in terms of territorial relationships. Economic space, according to Camagni (1991), became 'relational space, the field of social interactions, interpersonal synergies and social collective actions that determine the innovative capability and the economic success of specific local areas'. The process of creation and innovation for economic development, according to Camagni, should be viewed as the result of

> a collective learning process, fed by such social phenomena as intergenerational transfer of know-how, imitation of successful managerial practices and technological innovations, interpersonal face-to-face contacts, formal or informal co-operation between firms, tacit circulation of commercial, financial or technological information.
>
> (ibid.: 1)

This chapter is an attempt to explore one particular dimension of the relational aspect of the innovative milieu, that is, the state's role and its potential for constituting the environment for continuous innovation. To achieve this objective, we will use the case of Singapore, one of the economically successful NIEs (newly industrializing economies), to study how the state has set about building the capacity for renewal to combat tendencies of entropy inherent in capitalism.

The chapter is organized into three broad sections. The first part portrays details of the economic and political profile of Singapore society. The second part covers various features of the innovation system, and the final section deals with the nature of the 'extended' innovation system, which includes the areas of education, industrial relations and the financial underpinning supporting innovation.

Background context to Singapore's development

Under British rule, which began in 1819, Singapore, an island of about 600 km^2 in the heart of Southeast Asia, was turned into a major regional communication and business centre at the end of the nineteenth century. It also managed to attain a standard of living far superior to that enjoyed by countries in the surrounding region, even until today. Mainly through a conjuncture of historical trends and suitable policies that differed quite substantially from neoclassical orthodoxy and implemented by a strong regulatory state, Singapore has managed not only to stay ahead but to thrive as a viable economic entity since attaining independence in 1965, despite a gross lack in the material basis of production.

Economic development and transformation of the industrial structure

The early composition of Singapore's industrial structure reflects its urban mercantile character, with manufacturing weakly developed, contributing to only 17.6 per cent of the GDP (Table 11.1). Just prior to the attainment of independence, trade and services alone contributed to 63 per cent of the GDP in 1960 (at current market prices), showing its pre-eminent role as entrepot, trading, transport and processing centre for the vast resource-rich Southeast Asian hinterland. Singapore's initial foray into industrialization was based on import substitution which at that time was the commonly accepted model for industrialization. Despite political upheavals associated with this phase of industrialization (1961–67), manufacturing registered a respectable growth rate of 15 per cent per

Table 11.1 Gross domestic product by industry in Singapore

Sectors	Average for the decade			
	1960	1970	1980	1993
Manufacturing (%)	17.6	24.9	28.6	26.1
Construction (%)	5.6	9.5	6.9	6.3
Commerce (%)	26.0	22.1	18.4	16.9
Transport and communications (%)	9.3	7.3	11.6	13.8
Finance and business services (%)	14.8	17.0	19.9	25.4
Others (%)	26.7	19.2	14.6	11.5
Total gross domestic production S$	5,058.5	12,172.4	28,832.5	71,211.9
Annual change (%)	9.9	15.1	10.7	10.1

Note: S$ million at 1985 market prices

Source: Economic Development Board (EDB), *Annual Report 1993/94*; Ministry of Trade and Industry, various years.

annum, led mainly by the capital-intensive petroleum refinery sector and a small labour-intensive textile and garments sector. But when Singapore left the Malaysian Federation, it had to abandon ISI and make the switch to export-orientated industrialization (EOI).

Industrialization really took off vigorously during this first phase of EOI, with growth averaging almost 20 per cent between 1967 and 1973. This time around, apart from the labour-intensive export-orientated textile and garment industry, the electric sector (primarily electronic products and components) and oil-rig building combined to propel the surge in manufacturing.

Growth during this period was spurred by external demand, and industries that grew fastest were export-orientated. This in turn was encouraged by the externalization of the American economy and US policy to develop Japan and the frontline states as instruments in the containment of the Soviet Union (Hersh, 1993). By 1970, manufacturing had increased to 24.9 per cent of the GDP, whereas the share of commerce, transport and business and financial services had dropped to its historic low of 46.4 per cent (Table 11.1). In the meantime, with the tremendous expansion of the GDP, the labour market began experiencing uncomfortable shortages. This has proved an abiding problem ever since. Now that the situation had reversed, a new phase (1973–79) of industrialization was begun, with the state becoming more focused in the selection and promotion of foreign investments which by 1980 made up 67.1 per cent of manufacturing investments (Table 11.2 and see Table 11.6).

Unfortunately, because of the recessionary spell of 1974–75, the constraining impact of initial measures taken to transform the economy to a high-tech one contributed to a sharp drop in manufacturing growth to 8.8 per cent over the period. Even this reduced rate of expansion was achieved only through horizontal means, by the addition of new labour such as women and immigrant workers (see Table 11.3 on labour force expansion).

By the end of the 1970s, pressure from the emerging economies of ASEAN and China, and problems posed by a growing force of immigrant labour, combined to prompt the drafting of a more serious and systematic policy of industrial upgrading, called the 'Second Industrial Revolution' .

The key strategy used was a three-year (1979–81) corrective high-wage policy, which it hoped would discourage the use of a scarce resource. Unfortunately, this measure alone was inadequate without a ready supply of skilled/ educated labour to support the switch. Tables 11.4 and 11.5 reveal that a substantial majority of Singapore's workforce had primary school education or less, and this was reinforced by a small sprinkling of professional workers. With the help of pump-priming through state-sponsored construction activities, which averaged 21.5 per cent per annum between 1979 and 1984, and the re-emergence of financial/business service dynamism (growing at 15 per cent per annum), GDP

Table 11.2 Gross fixed assets (S$ million)

Capital structure	1980	1985	1990	1992
Foreign	67.1	65.0	72.8	72.9
Local	32.9	35.0	27.2	27.1
Total (100%) S$	10,561	20,260	32,815	39,168
Japan %	11.2	14.5	23.0	23.2

Source: Compiled from EDB *Annual Report* 1990/91 various years

Table 11.3 Labour force participation in Singapore

Year	1980	1984	1990	2001
Male	81.5	81.2	79.1	77.8
Female	44.3	45.8	50.6	54.3
Total	63.2	63.4	66.0	65.4
Labour force	1,068,932	1,207,369	1,562,800	2,119,700

Source: Department of Statistics (various years); Singapore Census of Population (1990, 2000)

Table 11.4 Labour force by education in Singapore

Education level[a]	1980	1990	1992	2001
Primary and below	58.5	53.3	45.8	19.8
Secondary	28.9	28.5	29.8	42.1
Post-secondary/diploma	9.3	12.2	16.2	21.0
Tertiary	3.2	6.0	8.2	16.9

Note [a] Change in categories over the years
Source: Department of Statistics (various years)

Table 11.5 Occupational distribution, various years

Occupation	1970	1980	1990	2001
Professional and technical	8.6	11.7	15.7	28.4
Administrators/managers	2.4	6.3	8.6	13.5
Clerical	12.7	13.8	13.1	13.4
Sales and service	29.4	14.6	13.8	11.3
Agriculture and fishing	4.1	1.6	0.3	*
Production workers	39.2	46.2	44.5	29.6
Unclassified	3.6	5.8	4.0	3.7

Note: * For 2001, Fishing and Agriculture is combined in 'unclassified'
Source: Department of Statistics (various years), Singapore Census of Population (2000)

growth during this period could continue at a respectable rate of 8.5 per cent. By 1980, the manufacturing share of GDP reached its peak of 28.6 per cent.

Over the years, the effects of domestic rigidities had been accumulating without causing undue problems until hit by the impact of recession from the advanced industrialized economies. The high level of forced savings (47 per cent of GDP, the highest gross domestic saving rate in the world, according to the Monetary Authority of Singapore, MAS), a swathe of assorted levies imposed on labour combined with high statutory board charges and public sector surplus, exacerbated the contractionary effects of the 1985 recession to produce the sharpest economic reversal experienced in peacetime Singapore.

It must be noted that figures indicating the broad expansion of manufacturing hide behind them a complex process of birth/rebirth and demise of various subsectors over the whole timespan of the development trajectory. The bifurcation characterizing the early phase of industrialization (1961–67) bears witness to the significant contribution of labour-intensive (usually locally owned and domestically orientated) food, printing and publishing sub-sectors towards employment creation, whereas the petroleum refinery sector, on the other hand, registered an annual value added per worker reaching \$970581[1] in the 1960s compared to \$6791 for the food sector. By way of contrast, the food sector provided 5,918 jobs during this period (1961–9), whereas only 593 were employed in the petroleum sector, which was established in Singapore because of its location in the heart of Southeast Asia.

By the 1970s, electronics had gained enough prominence to overtake petroleum in terms of annual value added. In 1970–79, the electronics sector was already employing the largest number of workers and it continues to do so till today. The share of electronics export peaked at 58 per cent in 1998. Also, by 1990s, Singapore had reduced its dependence on ASEAN and Japan for its growth. In their place, the USA became a dominant influence with 1 per cent of US growth reflected at slightly more than 1 per cent in Singapore's growth rate (Ministry of Trade and Industry, 2001, 2002). The current recession in Singapore reflects the coincidence of the sluggish US economy and global overcapacity in the electronics sector. Nonetheless, the EPE cluster (comprising electronics and precision engineering) continues to remain Singapore's key engine of manufacturing growth, contributing \$5 billion or 61 per cent of fixed asset investments secured for 2001 (*EDB Annual Report* 2001: 32). Additionally, this cluster provided 58 per cent of the total jobs created. The industrial sector is nurtured based on the strategy of cluster development. There are currently five clusters in manufacturing. They are Electronics and Precision engineering, Chemicals, Infocomms and Media, Logistics and Transport, Biomedical Sciences. More focused attention is now paid to developing the Services cluster to comprise the second engine of growth.

Governance

In the overall context of a generally low level of education and discouragement of local industry under British rule, the legacy of an overwhelmingly developed state apparatus (especially one built up over the years to combat communist insurgency) had placed a great deal of power in the hands of those favoured/trusted to rule after independence. The vast distance separating rulers and the ruled has persisted up until today, expressed by the staggering wage imbalance found between different classes. The PHP Institute (1995) reported that top managers in Singapore are paid more than those in Paris (11 per cent more) and London (50 per cent more), whereas the gross median monthly wage for Singapore was only $1234 in 1994.

Local political leaders favoured by the British to take over the reins of power were largely Western-trained professionals imbued with the singular belief that human agency is the dominant force in the shaping of destiny. Strong centralized state rule is proudly touted publicly to give a sense of government in control: 'All ministries speak with one voice ... Strong government has worked for Singapore. It enables us to move swiftly' (H.L. Lee, 1995: 7).

In view of the persistent strength of foreign multinationals (MNCS) – currently, they produce 77.8 per cent of manufacturing output and 90.5 per cent of operating surplus apart from contributing to 55.8 per cent of wages (Table 11.6) – the state cannot wield unmitigated power, rhetoric aside. A commissioned study by the Economic Development Board (EDB), the prima donna of the state's economic apparatus, asserts that:

> In the initial years, the EDB started as a pseudo 'Ministry of Foreign Affairs' to foster external investment and business links. Over time, it has evolved into a super hospitality agency for foreign MNCS, a paternal promotional agency for local enterprises ... as well as an agency devoted to economic development. While the economic strategies are set by political leadership at the cabinet level and its parent Ministry of Trade and Industry (MTI), the EDB is at the ground and implementational level.
>
> (Low, 1993: 62)

Obviously, since the MNCs have been linked to Singapore's survival, their well-being figures prominently in any policy decision.

The thrust of state intervention is projected as decidedly pro-market, generally speaking. Yet, when implementing the whole range of economics-related policy matters, tensions are evident between the state and the business community over divergences of competing interests. As the chief landlord, with control over more than three-quarters of Singapore's landmass, the state has been denigrated for fuelling real estate prices to the detriment of manufacturing interests.[2] Equally, some corporate sources are forever disparaging the high levy they have to pay for

Table 11.6 Principal statistics of manufacturing by nationality of capital source 1999 (%)

Nationality of capital source	Establish-ments	Workers	Output	Remun-eration	Net value added	Net operating surplus	Net assets	Direct exports
Singapore	79.1	50.4	22.2	44.2	24.3	9.5	30.9	12.9
Foreign	20.9	49.6	77.8	55.8	75.7	90.5	87.1	87.1

Note: 50% equity as cut-off
Source: Department of Statistics (1999) *Report on the Census of Industrial Production*

using foreign labour. During the current recession (1998–2002), top of business wish-list is a repeat of past requests to cut utility costs (77 per cent), land and rental costs (67 per cent), government fees/rates, and GST (51 per cent) (Remuneration Data Specialist, in *Straits Times* Interactive, 14 August 2002). In fact, cut in CPF (workers' pension fund) was only mentioned by 12 per cent of those polled. Employers have also complained that the emphasis on meritocracy (the ideological linchpin underlying an elitist bent in state–people relations) is proving a formidable barrier at the shop-floor level, where teamwork has to be encouraged to help firms compete in the increasingly competitive global market. Moves towards privatization has led to an aggressive build up of state-linked companies (GLC) as major regional players. This has made the state a serious challenge to private interests.

Certainly, there are also times when state and private sector's interests coincide, as when the state acts strictly to regulate the labour force, it is at one and the same time providing employers with a disciplined and conforming workforce. More recently, state success in negotiating free trade agreements (FTA) with several countries will save the business classes about $1 billion in tariffs over the next five years (*Goh CT Business Times*, 5 November 2002). A more significant move is the FTA with China (landmark framework agreement recently signed with Chinese Premier Zhu during the ASEAN summit (*Today* 2000, 5 November, 3)) which is expected to cover a market of 1.7 billion with aggregate gross domestic product of almost US$2 trillion and two-way trade worth US$1.2 trillion. FTAs work to enhance Singapore's economic space and the preferential market access from FTAs in themselves tend to attract more investments.

In other cases, the state has been known to work around corporate interests to minimize the outcome of its own disadvantaged position. When corporate management has been forced to relocate because of costs, land and labour constraints ever since the 1970s, and despite voices expressing fears about de-industrialization and a hollowing out of the economy, the state had perforce to realign to offer new incentives (e.g. for operational headquarters, international purchasing offices (IPOS), an approved international traders scheme, and an approved oil trading scheme) to entice MNCs to retain their core functions and use Singapore as the beachhead for penetrating the region (Singapore International Chamber of Commerce, 1994). The purpose is to 'create an economic space beyond Singapore when local companies and Singapore-based multinationals invest overseas in operations which are linked to and which enhance their entities in Singapore' (Economic Development Board, 1993/4: 3). However, the very act of establishing MNCs as the chief engine of growth has served to constrain the state's role, because ultimately MNCs respond only to the market and their own imperatives. This was clearly brought out since the first short oil-induced recessionary spell of 1974, further reinforced by the serious downturn of 1984 and repeated during the Asian financial crisis. Chastened by the bitter experiences of 1984, when it was 'abandoned' by MNCS, the state had initiated a regular and systematic process of incorporating corporate views to build the long-term viability of Singapore enterprises to make them 'industry leaders of tomorrow' (ibid.: 50).

At first glance, Singapore's infamously tough stand on law and order issues would have projected the state as an assertive agent in Singapore's economic development. Instead, evaluations of the reasons behind the dreadful recession of 1984 have placed the state as 'rather reactive in promoting investment and charting the industrial strategies for Singapore' (Low, 1993: 105). Its decisions now do not appear so far-sighted. A difficult international economic environment and fierce competition worldwide (and especially in the region) have combined with greater differentiation of the Singapore economy to make it more difficult for the EDB to enforce its will.

To overcome these new challenges, the state had to establish mechanisms to generate regular feedback from the corporate world – new ideas and criticism that would then help in goal-setting and in devising appropriate strategies and in discarding measures deemed obsolete. This approach is in line with a new orientation, first announced as a major objective of the Strategic Economic Plan (SEP), which 'sets the strategies and programmes for Singapore to realise a vision – to attain the status and characteristics of a first-league developed country within the next 30–40 years' (Economic Planning Committee, 1991: 2) and to 'initiate a national planning process which is consultative and evolutionary in character' (ibid.: 3). As a follow-up, a tripartite panel – the Economic Panel – was established as 'a forum for consultation and discussion of major economic issues among the three key sectors of the economy viz labour, business and government' (ibid.: 99). Regular economic forums would be organized 'to discuss the economic environment, performance and strategies' (ibid.: 101).

As an example, the Singapore Economic Forum (organized by the Economic Promotion Club, an informal grouping of chiefs of state agencies involved in economic and business development), held in July 1995, was attended by about

600 business people and relevant senior bureaucrats. In his speech, the Deputy Prime Minister (H.L. Lee, 1995) reiterated the mode of governance that would underline Singapore's response to the changing economic environment. According to him, the government

> must set the direction for the country, mobilize the population and create the stable social and political framework within which the free market economy can work smoothly ... there are certain things which are beyond the scope of the private sector, for example, planning for the manpower needs ... investing in infrastructure requirements like industrial estates, and taking stakes in exceptionally large projects to spread some of their risks ['nurturing winners'] ... the government must still co-operate closely with the private sector to promote economic development, and make judgement on the most promising areas to push for ... EDB has identified several industry clusters [chemical industries, water fabrication parks for the electronic industry cluster and information infrastructure for the IT industry]. Provision of skills training and specialized infrastructure will add to Singapore's competitive advantage in these areas.

The Economic Review Committee (comprising seven subcommittees), established in 2001, is the most recent example of the establishment of such groups, in this case, to 'fundamentally review our development strategy and formulate a blue print to restructure the economy' (EDB online) This targeting of feedback from the private sector is not new. The EDB has a long tradition of seeking out expertise from CEOs from the private sector. (Appendices I and II list the advisory members on the Board of EDB, A*Star, and the panel set up to revamp the Technology Plan.) One result of such close interaction is that state investment policies will be dynamic and always attuned to the needs of foreign investors and global trends.

In addition, as these business–state forums are given a high public profile, they also serve to refocus the country's collective consciousness to meet these new challenges. They are a visible representation of public relations efforts, aimed regularly at exaggerating anxiety, that serve to spur workers to ever greater efforts, apart from artfully using patriotic feelings both to energize the implementation of development initiatives and to enhance acceptance of costs and deprivations.

Internally, regular strategic planning meetings (SPMs) have been held since 1987, aimed at setting targets and devising suitable strategies to further enhance Singapore's economic capability. So began the series of annual corporate meetings, incorporating senior personnel and set up to examine past performance and to chart directions for the next year's development.

The manifold new functions, emerging within the EDB and then spun off to be developed or sustained by other agencies, are a reflection of both the increasing differentiation of the economy and the growing sophistication of agencies trusted with the responsibility of leading Singapore's economic future. Although some have expressed apprehension that the highly rated EDB (with exaggerated powers) could become 'conceited and complacent' (Low, 1993: 117), more worrying is the greater need for co-ordination of multi-agency responsibilities in gearing Singapore for high-tech development. For, accompanying the need to develop non-manufacturing sectors and increasing internationalization of Singapore's economy, the parallel processes have arisen of diversification and decentralization of agencies dealing with economic development. As these agencies develop their own speciality and autonomous character, problems may develop as a result of competing interests and contention for turf, despite the fact that mechanisms have been put in place precisely to ensure co-operation and teamwork. Interlocking management posts are in good measure a crucial tool that help enhance interagency co-operation and collaboration. The chairman of A*Star (previously the National Science and Technology Board) is also the Co-Chairman of EDB.

In brief, the major thrust of development policy is still to remain sharply competitive and globally orientated (based on exports and MNC investments), and firmly under the helm of the bureaucratic elite. Although repeated calls from corporate sources for greater deregulation and a reduction of bureaucratic controls have been resisted by officialdom, the policy has also at the same time led to the state becoming more socially inclusive in the crafting of policies. The increasing intrusion of external forces has indeed made it more difficult for the state to enforce its will on all levels of society. More importantly, with the passing of time, credible assessments of state performance have built up to expose some weaknesses in an overrated bureaucracy, for instance, especially with regard to comparison with free-wheeling Hong Kong, whose success was achieved without having to support an expensive bureaucracy (World Bank, 1993).

On the labour front, disdainful of confrontational politics, a system of tripartism initially established to determine wages is now commonly held responsible for the prevalence of harmonious relations. But this does not deny the lead role played by the state in advising/rationalizing the trade unions movement. The current process of restructuring has led to declining and unstable union membership, and this worries the state. For while disdaining a closed-shop policy, without a minimal mass of trade union members it would be difficult to mobilize workers to support state-directed policies. Because of this need to maintain a continuously close watch over unions and their tendency towards autonomously reinforcing their own strength, tripartism is needed to keep them in close embrace. Alarmed at the persistent recalcitrance of airline workers, Senior Minister Lee warned that it was necessary to think of 'new ways to twine the political and trade union leadership' (May 1995). The Prime Minister, commenting on Lee's suggestion, had remarked that government scholars and administrators sent to the NTUC (National Trade Union Congress) to 'help' workers could be asked to serve short stints in the government as part of the 'criss-crossing' of top people from both sides (*Straits Times*, 8 May 1995).

In the current prolonged recession (after the Asian financial crisis and September 11), it became clear that while a strong state had benefited Singapore in the early days of industrialization, its monopolistic hold on power is proving to be the Achilles' heel especially when fundamental transformation necessitates redistribution of state power. The Asian Development Bank in its most recent report on Singapore had this to say: 'Although the government's past interventions in industrial development have been beneficial, there is some concern that continued interventions on this scale could impede necessary corporate restructuring' (*Straits Times*, 26 April 2000, 37). The Chairman of the Singapore Exchange in a frank interview had revealed 'we lost a number of years, ... decades ... behind our main competitor Hong Kong [to become Asia's pre-eminent financial centre] ... but they didn't listen to stray voices in the wilderness' (*Straits Times*, 19 July 2001, S14). Most recently, in a keynote address at a local conference on the new economy, M. Porter urged the contraction of the influence of government-linked companies (*Straits Times* Interactive, 24 November 2001). Returning to Singapore in 2002, he repeated his advice thus, 'we have to get the government out of the way, it is moving but the pace is too slow' (*Straits Times* Interactive, 31 July 2002).

Other performance indicators

Socio-economic performance

When Singapore first ventured along the path of industrialization, unemployment was rife at nearly 15 per cent. Today, with a labour force of 2,119,700 (Ministry of Manpower, 2001), total participation rate is high at 64.5 per cent (up from 42.3 per cent in 1966); 79.6 per cent for male and 50.9 per cent for female. Immigrant labour makes up 20 per cent of the workforce (Asian Development Bank, 1994: 71). Industrial development has unequivocally promoted the interests of the masses. Development benefits such as housing, healthcare and work have reached a substantial majority. In 1990, 87.5 per cent owned their homes. The infant mortality rate is 5 per thousand, putting Singapore on a par with countries such as Japan (Germany's figure is 6).

Labour Force Surveys have found a consistent upward trend in the median monthly income received from $613 in 1984 to $1234 in 1994 and $2000 in 2001. Income distribution as indicated by the Gini coefficient has improved too, from 0.477 in 1980 to 0.432 in 1990. However, despite such improvements, relative to that of other NIES, Singapore's performance in this respect is still dismal. The Gini coefficients for Taiwan and South Korea are 0.311 (1990) and 0.400 (1988) respectively. Likewise, the UN's Human Development Report (1993) has ranked Singapore 43 (on the Human Development Index), a position well behind its GNP ranking of 26. Note that such oil-rich fiefdoms as Brunei, Qatar, Kuwait and Bahrain have a similar disparity. Not surprisingly, former socialist economies have outpaced Singapore on the Human Development Index, achieving a converse pattern of human development far in advance of their GNP attainment (Czechoslovakia 26/49; Hungary 28/52; Estonia 34/42). Singapore's NIE competitors also boast more balanced ratios between HDI and GNP. Hong Kong's was 24/24 and South Korea registered 33/37.

More serious is the fact that, despite years of a flourishing economy, Singapore's expenditure on education as a percentage of public expenditure, at 11.5 per cent, is well behind that of Korea (22.4 per cent) and Hong Kong (15.9 per cent) for the period 1988–90. And even then, Singapore spends the largest proportion on higher education (31 per cent) when compared to Hong Kong (25 per cent) and Korea (7 per cent). Additionally, Singapore's expenditure is lower for primary plus secondary education (65 per cent), in contrast to Hong Kong (70 per cent) and Korea (78 per cent). The accumulated consequence is reflected in Singapore's low ratings for education (placed in position 39 and 37 for illiteracy rate as a percentage of population and public expenditure on education as percentage of GDP respectively) in *The World Competitiveness Yearbook* (2002). Its ranking for tertiary enrolment is equally low, at position 28 in the Global Competitiveness Report 2001–2002 (World Economic Forum). Unable to reach the skill profile desired by ranking agencies such as the World Competitiveness Report (WCR), Singapore has taken to importing more tertiary educated foreign talents (see Table 11.7) to supplement those that could not be created domestically. In 2000, 32.7 per cent of permanent residents had tertiary education whereas the comparable figure was 9.5 per cent for citizens. This strategy allows Singapore to spend less on the education of slow learners. With strategies such as these, Singapore managed to retain its position as the fourth most competitive economy in the world despite last year's (2001) sharp recession (WCR, 2002–3).

Singapore's elitism now appears dated in the face of the ascendance of flexible production. The model company in the fast-paced markets of the 1990s, we are informed, 'is irreverent about hierarchy and it even tolerates some organizational unruliness' (*Business Week*, 12 December 1994: 47). Even though elitism is deeply resented and has been vigorously opposed (e.g. loss of electoral seats as a result of imposing a graduate mother scheme which encourages educated women to have children), it continues to underpin the general mode of decision-making in Singapore society, despite evidence that it has counter-productive outcomes. For instance, Odaka's (1989) study of skills in Asia had concluded that workers in

Table 11.7 Highest qualification attained by nationality

	Citizens		Permanent residents	
	1990	2000	1990	2000
No qualifications	31.5	20.9	27.2	7.5
Primary	26.8	23.6	30.9	17.6
Secondary	27.0	25.3	16.7	18.5
Upper Secondary	7.3	14.5	7.1	18.4
Polytechnic	3.4	6.3	3.8	5.2
University	4.0	9.5	14.2	32.7
Total	100	100	100	100

Source: Census of Population (2000)

equivalent skill levels are less productive outside Japan because of low levels of motivation. Japan's Gini coefficient is only 0.35.

> As long as people worry about speaking their mind, Singapore's climb up the economic ladder could be much slower than the government wants … While Singapore is having a good deal of success in wooing fund managers, it trails Hong Kong in equities trading. Politics has 'everything' to do with that, says a Western banker. He argues that Singapore will be hobbled as a regional financial centre unless it has a strong equities focus, as opposed to fund management or bond operations. The trouble is that equity analysts tend to be more acerbic in their comments than their fixed income counterparts. 'We can't get our good people to go to Singapore,' says the banker. 'That gets to freedom of the press'.
>
> (Businessweek online April 5 1999)

These observations are reinforced by the International Survey Research Corporation (ISR) study from 1999–2001 of 60,000 Singaporean employees working in top companies (including government bodies) which tells us 'that a lot of companies here are well managed but not well-led' (senior consultant P Record). 'Employees see the leaders as lacking both the intellectual capital to craft aspirational goals and the emotional intelligence necessary to achieve them' (*Business Times*, 6 September 2002). Management, according to ISR, is about keeping the current system functioning. It works through hierarchy and through systems and is 'hard … and cold'. Leadership, on the other hand is about producing non-incremental changes, 'it works through people and through culture', and is 'soft … and hot'. The firm measured commitment levels of employees in forty major global clients. 'I wasn't expecting the scores to be that bad' says P Record

'... Bizarrely, [the Singapore numbers] are even worse than Hong Kong' (*Business Times*, 6 September 2002). Tracking the financial performance of firms, ISR also found that organizations with high levels of employee commitment achieved significant gains in financial performance, consistently outperforming those with low scores. Interviews with integrated circuit design engineers have solicited the view that 'being in R&D (here) ... , we don't get the kind of recognition that we would get if we were in the US. Here, managers get more recognition than people in R&D' (*Straits Times* Interactive, 21 January 2002).

Despite many previous studies linking performance with alienation, the state is hesitant to move politically. For instance, a 1992–93 survey conducted by Chicago-based International Survey Research Corporation found that, of the 330,000 workers studied from six countries (the USA, the UK, Hong Kong, Singapore, Malaysia and Australia), Singapore had the lowest proportion (31 per cent) of workers reporting that their pay was at least as good, if not better than, their counterparts in other companies, compared to 48 per cent from the USA and 43 per cent from Malaysia, a low-wage country. Additionally, Singaporean workers were the least satisfied with management (*Straits Times*, 26 April 1993).

For some time now, what Singapore has done is to continue with its old strategy of adding more material inputs to up productivity. According to the World Bank (1993), Hong Kong's total factor productivity (TFP) has increased consistently, whereas Singapore's TFP is in consistent decline. Recent pronouncements by the state to restructure the National Productivity Board (NPB) and other related organizations are aimed at giving Singapore's productivity drive a fresh impetus (Trade and Industry Minister Yeo, *Straits Times*, 1 July 1995), a move that reflects the twin problems of declining productivity and increasing nominal wage.

Steep management hierarchies result in undue stress and this has fundamentally affected the quality of life of its people. V. Goh's study presented at the 7th Asian Congress of Sexology alleged that Singaporean men and women experience miserable sex lives. Those aged below 40 have sex only six times a month compared to three times a week reported for most countries, and, 'it goes downhill from there ... they are disinterested or they cannot perform' (*Straits Times* Interactive, 18 November 2002).

Recent moves to privatize public services and restructure the economy would most certainly affect weaker groups adversely. For instance, with privatization and restructuring of hospitals, there are worries that the poor may not get adequate care. Says MP Dr M. Lim, 'medical and nursing staff felt restructured hospitals cared more for bottom lines than staff or listening to feedback' when reiterating his belief that 'push' rather than 'pull' factors are responsible for many doctors leaving. His concerns are echoed by the President of the Singapore Medical Council, Professor Balachandran (1995) when addressing the Sixth Annual Scientific Meeting:

putting greater emphasis on money has affected training ... consultants and department heads lacked time to listen or to teach ... this hospital does not need entrepreneurs. Departments have become too big ... too many meetings to allow time ... for adequate supervision and teaching and maintenance of proper standards of medical care.

In fact, health as a proportion of total government operating expenditure had declined from 8.3 per cent in 1982 to 6.1 per cent in 1992. When total health expenditure is measured as a percentage of GDP, Singapore's position is 43 as measured by the WCY (2002). Health economist Phua KH alleges that 'Singapore appears to have one of the lowest shares of government subsidy in the world, at about a third of total expenditure (*Straits Times* Interactive, 2 October 2002).

Environment

The establishment of the first Anti-Pollution Unit under the Prime Minister's Department in April 1970 and then the setting up of the Ministry of Environment (MOE) in September 1972 (Singapore Anti-Pollution Department 1970–72) both indicate the significance of environment quality in Singapore's attitude towards development. Today, the Pollution Control Department (PCD) under the MOE is specifically charged with the prevention and control of environmental pollution (Ministry of Environment, 1993). The department ensures that its aims are fulfilled through four processes:

- environment management measures are incorporated into the design of new developments;
- the department is consulted by planning and development agencies on new development proposals;
- regulation of industrial and residential development;
- monitoring of industrial processes and acceptable levels of environment management.

The department also carries out regular monitoring of both air and water quality. It is supposed to have now instituted fifteen automated remote monitoring stations, which can instantaneously track air pollution levels via a telemetric system. The Pollutant Standards Index (PSI), an indication of air quality developed by the USEPA (US Environmental Protection Agency), is now employed as the basis for ensuring ambient air quality in Singapore. USEPA acceptable benchmarks and Singapore measurement recordings for 1993 are juxtaposed in Table 11.8.

Table 11.8 Pollutants in Singapore against international benchmarks, 1993.

Pollutants	Singapore (per Nm³)	International standard (USEPA per Nm³)
1. Sulphur dioxide (9 monitoring stations)	18	80
2. Nitrogen dioxide (10 monitoring stations)	15	100
3. Suspended particles (8 monitoring stations)	55	75
4. Ozone	concentration pphm 7–10	USEPA I-hour ozone concentration: not to exceed 12 pphm
5. Lead	0.1 per Nm³	USEPA ambient air quality std 1.5 per Nm³
6. Smoke (6 monitoring stations)	26 per Nm³	WHO long-term goal 40 per Nm³ WHO long-term goal and USEPA
7. Carbon monoxide	1–3 ppm	9 ppm (parts per million)

Source: Compiled from Ministry of Environment (1993)

Chapter 45 of the Clean Air Act and its regulations provide for the control and monitoring of industrial pollution. 'Scheduled premises' – industries that have the potential to cause serious air pollution (e.g. chemical, cement plants and factories with large boilers) – require permission to operate and these are given only after pollution control requirements have been met. Additionally, plants are also subjected to tests of gaseous emission, fuel analyses and smoke observation of chimneys. At the same time, industrial boilers with a generating capacity of 2300 kg per hour are required to install smoke density meters to monitor compliance with the appropriate (Ringelmann 2) standard.

Another role of the PCD concerns the regular monitoring of various inland bodies of water and coastal areas. The parameters analysed for inland non-catchment areas include pH, dissolved oxygen, biochemical oxygen demand, total suspended solids, ammonia and sulphide. The PCD monitors 129 USEPA priority pollutants at least once a year, including chloroform, benzene, toluene, trichloro-methane, pyrone and chlordane. For 1993, water quality for both inland bodies (catchment and non-catchment) and coastal water remains good and within WHO guidelines.

More importantly, Singapore has continued to press for more stringent standards in pollution control. For instance, the permissible level of sulphur in automotive diesel fuel has been reduced from 0.5 per cent to 0.3 per cent by weight.

Because of its location at the crossroads of Asia's most busy sea lanes, cross-boundary pollution poses a constant source of potential large-scale disaster for Singapore. Singapore became part of the ASEAN Working Group on Transboundary Pollution and the ASEAN Workshop on Pollution Standards Index to further the long-term goal of ambient air quality. Nearer to home, Singapore also works with Malaysia on the Malaysian-Singapore Joint Committee on Environment to work on environment issues of mutual concern. Singapore is also part of the Oil Spill Prepares and Responses for Asia, a co-operative conference group established to harness regional co-operation towards ensuring prompt and concerted regional response to tackling unpredictable oil spills. Concerned to stay at par with what is possible, Singapore is keeping in close touch with international standards and best practices through the use of consultants (e.g. a WHO consultant was invited in February 1970 to assist and advise on the framework for air pollution control); sending staff to international conferences (e.g. in 1993 the Ministry of Environment's officials attended a total of thirty-one overseas meetings and conferences) and the use of up-to-date equipment for testing and monitoring.

Apart from the benefits of enjoying a cleaner environment (e.g. more than two-thirds of the days in Singapore were classified as 'good' in terms of the Pollutant Standards Index, Ministry of Environment 1993), Singapore is now reaping an unforeseen advantage of possessing the knowledge and skills to become a 'consultant' to the less developed countries in ASEAN. Its more advanced position on environment controls has also made Singapore a model candidate for organizing and hosting environmental training in the region.

Crisis awareness

The state in Singapore has exerted every possible means to more than secure a crisis mentality among its people. Singapore's position on a whole range of benchmarks is regularly put on public display to show how competitive or uncompetitive the nation has become and how much more it has to endeavour to succeed internationally.

After the 1985 recession, MTI closely monitors the competitiveness of Singapore by 'constantly developing improved indicators of short-term competitiveness, and creating other indicators of medium to long-term competitiveness' (The Economic Planning Committee, 1991: 82). For instance, the relative unit labour cost (RULC) and the return on investment (ROI) have been developed as aids for signalling both the start of a recession and threats from overheating. Both indices represent indicators of short-term competitiveness. The SEP'S medium to long-term indicators include rate of investment outflow and overall share weighted by export gross value added (GVA). A working group comprising representatives from MTI, MAS and EDB were supposed to be set up 'to regularly review information on trends in competitiveness and make appropriate recommendations' (The Economic Planning Committee, 1991: 86). At the same time, databases on which decisions can be based have expanded tremendously with the institution of regular national surveys on a whole variety of topics of economic relevance. In November 1997, the Committee on Singapore's Competitiveness was formed to make a thorough review of Singapore's competitiveness over the next ten years. The Asian financial crisis hit Singapore in 1998.

If one theme can be said to underscore state–people relations in Singapore, it is that, in creating anxiety among the people, political elites have often succeeded in cashing in on mass vulnerability to capture and successfully mobilize mass support for their policies. The ideology of survival has become a regular catchphrase in ministerial speeches, which almost invariably link patriotism with sacrifice, hard work and discipline.

Foreign employers, astounded by never-ending exhortations to better the workforce, have on their part pleaded for some degree of moderation to avoid the unintended consequences of a backlash. The German Business Group, in response to government request for feedback, said 'we would caution against driving the workforce too hard as this may result in non-co-operation. Contrary to "Keep Singapore Clean" and "Courtesy Campaigns", a hard driving productivity campaign may have adverse results' (31 August 1982). More remarkable is the press statement of the American Business Council (20 August 1992) in responding to the same request for feedback.

> Most employers view the Singapore workers as being generally hard-working, positive in attitude and highly motivated … Therefore we would like to see campaigns aimed at improvement taking a positive tone. Rather than continuously telling the Singapore worker how bad he is.

More specifically, to facilitate monitoring of responses to state policies, the Feedback Unit was set up to dialogue with designated groups and to gather the views of people on various topics. The discussions would then be submitted to the Prime Minister. However, feedback groups cannot replace the democratic process. This could be one reason why despite having seventeen feedback groups, constituents are still clamouring for democracy and liberalization of politics

In reality, Singapore's ability to create the niche role for itself is based on a combination of factors. First, years of tending to every need of MNCS have provided EDB with deep intelligence about the direction of corporate strategies in its endless search for profits. Second, the success of Singapore's positivistic rational bureaucracy has gained it the confidence of the region's less developed economies to the extent that it is often consulted and put up as a model for emulation. Third, the transformation of the more advanced economies, such as the EC and Japan, has spurred the outward migration of SMEs in search of lower-cost profit centres. Lacking in resources, these SMEs require the expertise of a intermediary to facilitate their relocation.

The innovation system

Singapore, in the throes of a radical restructuring process, is now undergoing a drastic transformation, a process initiated by the government in the early 1970s but not taken up vigorously by the private sector until the mid-1980s. For society, restructuring was a great challenge, carried out in the belief in the common aim of raising Singapore to a standard of living on a par with the Swiss. However, these aims could not be imposed on foreign companies, which overwhelmingly dominate economic output. Except for the very few well-managed companies, restructuring was often carried out rather late in the day and only when they saw no other way out. For many, crippled and battered by paper-thin margins, arguments for restructuring are mainly presented as a defensive move, rather than as part of a continuous long-term strategy of monitoring one's competitive position *vis-à-vis* a fast-churning market. Besides, state revision of investment incentives has favoured a particular strategy of restructuring (moving up the technology ladder) over a host of other available restructuring modes.

Corporate strategies and industrial restructuring: general

This section presents a rough typology of actual strategies adopted by firms in their adjustment to current problems of low margins: the appreciation of the Singapore dollar, the shortage of labour, increasing wages (unit labour costs have increased by 33 per cent between 1988 and 1994) and rising retail rentals (23 per cent over the same period. Our examination of fifty companies reveals that the route maps taken by individual enterprises are a wild mixture of adjustment strategies, with the technological mode making up only one of a larger number of strategies open to companies, depending on the product market, company strength and weakness, length of operation and a whole gamut of empirical peculiarities in which companies are embedded.

Despite the across-the-board cost increases, some companies have opted to stay on in Singapore and even to take the step of expanding production. Petroleum refineries that have stayed with Singapore, since its initial hesitant first step on the road to industrialization, are among the stayers. Having sunk many hundreds of millions of dollars into Singapore, relocation would be doubly expensive. Despite stabilization of the domestic market, companies see themselves located in the centre of the booming Asian market. In their view, it would be more economical to upgrade and catch the market on its upward surge (demand for high-quality lubricants in the Asia-Pacific region is expected to grow at 4–6 per cent per annum) rather than start a new plant in a lower-cost neighbouring country.

Because of a different market, cost and price structures, Singapore-based Japanese companies are dealing with the tight margins in a slightly different manner. The appreciation of the yen has caused manufacturers of electronic products to shift production to Southeast Asia, according to Chairman Kazuhiro of Matsushita Technology (Mastec), Singapore. For Japanese companies with existing plants in Singapore, it has now became more economical to produce some lines here. Mastec Managing Director Shuichi said that it would cost 20 per cent less to manufacture the Panasert MK2F in Mastec now, despite the $4.5 million cost of transferring the surface-mount technology from Japan to Singapore, an amount spent largely on upgrading both the present facility and training.

While expanding and upgrading existing production facilities, firms such as Hitachi Cable (S) Pte Ltd have also moved older labour-intensive lines to Singapore' s low-cost production neighbours. Hitachi has invested $15 million to expand its production of integrated-circuit lead frames in Singapore, even as it shifts its enamelled copper wire production from Singapore to its Johor plant. Of the sixty employees affected by the move, production operators were redeployed to other plants in Singapore, whereas engineers had the option to stay in Singapore or relocate to Johor.

For Sanyo Electric, high wage costs have caused a shift to a less labour-intensive manufacturing strategy, according to Human Resource Manager Choo. The Singapore company will now focus on manufacturing high value-added products such as the 20-inch colour television for export to Japan, whereas its audio equipment line will be shifted to the cheaper production base of Johor. Additionally, it will enhance its production design capabilities and expand its parts procurement function for the group's factories in Singapore, Malaysia, Indonesia and even Mexico. The company's function as inventory and service base in Singapore will be enhanced, because of the expected increase in sales of electronic parts to other audio equipment and computer manufacturers.

Local companies, technologically weak and having to break into new markets overseas, have been pushed to devise their own peculiar strategies for combating lowering profits. To help it move to the production of higher-end products, a local company such as Asiamatric has acquired a related business from an American engineering firm (Wilmont Engineering) for $2.4 million. Technological upgrading aside, this move also provides access to the huge US market. Fears that its position as a contract manufacturer to MNCS could easily be jeopardized by its overdependence on crucial customers have caused the company to try to attract new shareholders, who are major electronic firms. Like so many other manufacturing companies, Asiamatrix has tried lowering its risk profile by going beyond its traditional concerns with electronic components and semi-conductors. It is looking into property, hotel and residential development.

Other local companies whose fates are closely intertwined with that of their major customers (e.g. JIT Electronics, that specializes in printed circuit board assembly, contract manufacturing of finished electronic products and wire harnessing) have to move with them. Says Managing Director Goh of JIT, 'Sanyo and Mitsubishi are our customers. When they relocated their factories to Johor, we followed them in as well so as to be able to service them at their doorsteps.' Of course, the fact that Malaysia is a lower-cost producer helps. The company has moved its labour-intensive low-priced products to a $5 million factory in Tampoi and a joint-venture factory in Penang.

Companies that relocate to low-cost neighbouring countries, according to Managing Director Tan of Apple Computer Singapore, are making consumer products such as television and telephones. 'Innovation is limited for such products ... everything is cost driven.' In contrast, the personal computer industry has a different logic.

> We're continuing to add new features to our computers like multimedia communication capabilities, many of which did not exist just two years ago ... our products are going to become more and more complex, so that our main challenge would not be to find cheaper countries to make them in, but a country that is able to make them at all.

What worries Managing Director Tan more than just cost is how local supporting industries can improve their quality and supporting efficiency. 'Costs *per se* are a secondary concern compared to the quality and breadth of the cluster of supporting industries.' Of concern too is the presence here of new technologies such as flat panel displays.

As more than 80 per cent of Apple's costs are for materials purchased in US dollars and sales of products are in yen and other non-American currencies, the changes in the currency situation have resulted in net benefit to Apple, whose sales in Asia have grown 55 per cent alone for 1994. To combat pay hikes (exacerbated by 10 per cent because of the appreciation of the Singapore dollar), Apple moved to a seven-day week to enhance return on investment, which includes the new $55 million logistics building that frees space for more lines while leading to capacity expansion of 20 per cent. The company admitted that because of increased R&D costs (nearly equivalent to that of the USA), it would not have set up its R&D facilities here if it had not received state grants to support them: $9.3 million for a design centre and part funding for its $16 million .joint research centre with the Institute of Systems Science.

State incentives do indeed have an important role in restraining firms from relocating all of their functions abroad. For Siemens Components (integrated circuit chip maker), which was awarded the business headquarters status (sales of its chips in the region had brought in a sum of $1 billion in 1994 and this was expected to expand by 30 per cent in 1995), the company now enjoys tax incentives such as ten-year tax holidays and 90 per cent tax exemption of chargeable income for export of services. In exchange, having already invested over $300 million to date, the company will invest in an application laboratory to help original equipment manufacturers (OEM) from the region to design electronic products based on its chips which are made there.

Details from the adjustment strategies of companies presented above very clearly show the status of technological innovation in the web of reform strategies, which includes relocation, technological innovation (process and product), labour shedding, training and reassignment of staff, market realignment, acquisitions, and more commonly a combination/mix of these strategies depending on their own individual peculiarities and direction of state support.

New corporate players in emerging industries have entered the fray, encouraged by generous state incentives (see 'funding schemes' on the website of A*Star). As a result of urgent state action in pushing intensively for the growth of this sector, biomedical's share of manufacturing output shot up to 5 per cent while its value added comprised 12 per cent of manufacturing sector's overall value-added.

Since the thrust of development is to encourage MNCs and state-linked companies, local/indigenous SMEs are left in benign neglect. According to Ng *et al.* (1986: 31):

> among the ASEAN Countries, Singapore has had the most experience in the use of fiscal incentives to support its science and technology plans. It also has the most elaborate set of incentive schemes ... to encourage skills and manpower development, R&D, and other forms of technology transfer.

Yet, the same study concluded that, among the ASEAN countries, economic linkages to MNCs 'is particularly low' (ibid.: 40) and indicates 'the low technical capabilities of the local subcontractors and input suppliers'. Weakness in this aspect of technological infrastructure has still to be addressed today. A report by JETRO (1992) pointed to the continued inflow of subcontractors into Singapore, despite the government's stated support for local industries, and had attributed this trend to the underdevelopment of indigenous supporting industries. The Global Competitiveness Report (2001–2002) has rated Singapore relatively low on local availability of components, process machinery, research and training services (in positions 38, 41, and 32 respectively). Singapore's weak position *vis-à-vis* MNCs has forced it to be less ambitious. 'An indigenous technology generating capacity is not an immediate or even a medium-term objective ... instead, it seeks to become an important regional centre for the production of high technology, science-based products' (Ng *et al.* 1986: 30).

R&D in Singapore

Singapore began systematically monitoring its R&D track record in 1978, when it recognized that 'to maintain our competitive edge, Singapore needs to move to an innovation phase of our development and promote activities with more innovation and design contents'. To this end, the NSTB (National Science and Technology Board), renamed the Agency for Science, Technology and Research (A*Star) since January 2002, was formed with the mission to 'develop Singapore into a centre of excellence in selected fields of science and technology so as to enhance our national competitiveness in the industrial and services sectors' (H.L. Lee). Deputy Prime Minister H.L. Lee had observed that, compared to some NIEs and industrialized economies, 'Singapore still has some way to go ... a concerted effort by government is needed to uplift our strength in science and technology ... This is a crucial task in the next phase of Singapore's economic growth' (H.L. Lee) The most recent National Survey of R&D (2000) revealed that R&D expenditure had reached $3.01 billion, very much higher than 1992's $50 million. The annual growth rate between 1991 and 1993 had registered 15 per cent

The commitment to R&D had succeeded in pushing an ascending trend from 1978 to 2000 when the GERD rose from 0.2 in 1978 to 1.89 in 2000. Relative to NIEs for which figures are available, Singapore's ratio is lower than that for Taiwan (2.05 for 1999), and Korea (2.46 in 1999), but above that of the international norm of 2 per cent. The Economic Development Board's international advisory board had recommended that GERD to GDP should expand to at least 2 per cent to maintain Singapore's competitiveness.

Since the establishment of the NSTB, local R&D has become more focused. R&D in Singapore has always thrived on private sector initiative. The contribution of this sector had expanded consistently from 50 per cent in 1984–85 to 60 per cent in 1992 to 62 per cent in 2000. Electronics (53 per cent), engineering (20 per cent), and ITC (11 per cent) represent areas of dominant R&D interest. Of the gross R&D expenditure of $3009.52 million for 2000, 51.3 per cent was expended on engineering while 20.8 per cent went to computer and related sciences.

The NTP had targeted for a ratio of 90 research scientists and engineers (RSEs) per 10,000 people in the labour force by 2005. The 2000 National Survey of R&D found the ratio reached 83.5 in 2000 (Japan's RSE is 97 in 1999 compared to Taiwan's 71 and Finland's 99 during the same period).

Until now, two five-year technology plans have been implemented (National Technology Plan from 1991–95 with a $2 billion budget; and the National Science and Technology Plan with a $4 billion budget). A*Star is the leading agency for implementation of the Science and Technology 2001–5 Plan with a budget of $7 billion over the next five years. Much more is now being done in the field of intellectual property. Singapore has acceded to the Paris Convention, the Patent Co-operation Treaty and the Budapest Treaty (*Straits Times*, 28 January 1995).

Singapore has described its approach to R&D (and for that matter to any issue) as realistic and pragmatic. The Economic Committee was set up in 1985 to develop measures to turn the economy around and has recommended that Singapore's R&D efforts be directed towards improving product design and development capability and developing competence in technologies relevant to the nation's economic activities. The practical approach to R&D is again underlined in the National Science and Technology Board (1991); that is, with its limited resources, Singapore should concern itself with applied research and experimental development where knowledge gained can be put to commercial use, citing the wisdom of this policy as practised by the Japanese in the 1960s and 1970s.

Although the private sector has become the leading force in Singapore's R&D effort, contributing 62 per cent of the total national GERD, the state sector can be credited for accelerating this trend. Apart from the provision of tax incentives and funding schemes to encourage the building of R&D capability in the private sector (see also Singapore International Chamber of Commerce, 1994), vigorous efforts have been made to expand the local supply of R&D personnel (increasing both local production of R&D manpower and liberalizing immigration policies to enhance the inflow of foreign R&D personnel), to further the development of the necessary R&D infrastructure (science parks and industry – public research institution collaboration), and improvements in the protection of intellectual property rights.

Apart from the EDB, the Singapore Institute of Standards and Industrial Research (renamed Spring Singapore) and the A*STAR are the leading agencies concerned with the development of technology in Singapore. Because the approach to R&D is mainly for its commercial benefits, its development has come under the purview of the Ministry of Trade and Industry. The MTI Minister was the first to announce the upgrading of the 1991 NTP, and the NSTB itself was formed under the MTI with the mission 'to promote industry driven R&D' (National Science and Technology Board, 1991: 23). Nonetheless, the National Science and Technology Board (1991) had also envisaged a broader goal for R&D: to serve educational (Ministry of Education) and service goals (Ministry of Health and non-commercial statutory boards).

Technological monitoring

A*Star, as one of the lead institutions concerned with the shaping of R&D development in Singapore, has a broad list of international sources from which it culls its information on R&D activities, standards and benchmarks worldwide. It then sets its own standards after taking into consideration the constraints and strengths of Singapore. Because of the small size of its population, Singapore has to be discerning and discriminating in increasing expenditure in this area.

For instance, with the help of 200 experts and practitioners in R&D from both the public and private sectors, the NSTB crafted the National Technology Plan (1991), which then identified nine key technology areas most relevant for future economic growth and thus most deserving of state support. They include:

- information technology
- microelectronics
- electronic systems
- manufacturing technology
- materials technology
- energy, water and environmental resources
- biotechnology
- food and agrotechnology
- medical science.

Apart from developing a broad-based R&D capability, clusters of technology competencies have been identified for developing niche areas where a high standard of competitiveness will be maintained (The Economic Planning Committee, 1991: 7). On the broader front, the Committee for Singapore's Competitiveness was established in May 1997 (announcement was made for a thorough review of Singapore's economic competitiveness by the Prime Minister in November 1996) to keep track of Singapore's position. An important method of maintaining Singapore's competitive position is by constant innovation The twin engines of growth lies with manufacturing and services (high value added) but innovation, in terms of attitude and infrastructure, undergirds the development of these sectors. EDB's own study of 4,000 manufacturing companies show that 'companies that have undertaken innovation and R&D have consistently outperformed national manufacturing average' in terms of new products, sales revenue generated and royalties derived from patents developed in Singapore (EDB, online, 'Innovation').

Among the problems limiting R&D in Singapore, the largest proportion (almost three-quarters) of private sector firms cited a shortage of research personnel (note that 40 per cent of RSE for 1992 (total N = 6454) were not Singaporeans). More than 60 per cent cited high risks compared to expected returns and high costs of R&D start-ups. Although large MNCs such as SGS Thomson Micro-electronics would agree that the level of support given to R&D by the government via bodies such as the NSTB is impressive (Senior Manager of Technology Programmes, K. Das), there are also others who bemoan the narrow focus on application. According to general manager of Azfin Semi-conductors (which was awarded a Research Incentive for Singapore Companies grant), 'The impression is that everything has to be done on an accelerated short-term basis. Research has more of an application flavour, but abstract concepts which might not have any immediate application are important too.' Azfin is a non-fabricating semi-conductor design house which does no manufacturing but concentrates solely on design work. K. Das of SGS Thomson also raises another difficulty faced by Singapore: 'Singapore faces a problem of attracting people to the R&D profession because the bias is towards manufacturing and production ... they [Singapore engineers] need to go abroad for a few years, get fully immersed in an R&D environment and bring this kind of culture back home.'

Extended innovation system

Education

Some competitive reports worldwide have ranked Singapore's workforce as being among the world's most competitive. Since 1980, Beri, an international business risk and consultancy firm, has rated Singapore workers very highly. But again, there are others that show up considerable deficiencies in various aspects of Singapore's human resource development. The National Productivity Board's CEO Lee noted that the 1995 World Competitiveness Report ranked Singapore 35th in terms of skilled labour (*Straits Times*, 5 November 1995). The problem probably stems from the elitist cast of policies premised on the belief (similarly professed by late eighteenth- and early nineteenth-century European ideologues of progress such as Condorcet, Saint-Simon and Comte) that elites are the national managers/vanguard of the new industrial society (and their ideological position, referred to by von Hayek as the 'religion of engineers'). Only these elites should receive education, whereas the masses are trained to be obedient and apolitical.

On the other hand, fostering individual responsibility to the extreme (as opposed to the welfare state) has resulted in selfishness and in some cases even subversion of total organizational goals. In the same press statement, it was noted

> There are still indications that much of the motivation is directed towards personal success, without recognition that individual economic success is tied to the corporate success which, in turn, is achieved through a group effort and teamwork ... in addition, we believe that it is essential for the basic educational process to emphasise teamwork and group achievement.

There is still a large gap between communitarian ideology and practice. Until now, teaching of this aspect of work organization had yet to proceed to the school level.

As early as 1985, when the Economic Committee was set up to chart new directions for the economy, innovation, and more specifically R&D, education was targeted as a solution to sustaining Singapore's development for the next lap. We are reminded that a cornerstone of the SEP 1991 is to build 'a social and institutional structure which supports innovation' (The Economic Planning Committee, 1991: 8). However, the translation of this goal into the education system was not realized until the announcement by the Minister of Education Lee Y. S. (*Straits Times*, June 1995) that 'Singapore's education system will move away from the current emphasis on mastery of content to one that will give students more opportunities to acquire thinking and learning skills.' But the Minister also added that 'it has to be a gradual process'.

The sub-committee of the Economic Review Committee on human resources, when submitting its recommendations for the remaking of Singapore had to reiterate suggestions 'many of which have been made over the years by critics' (*Straits Times* Interactive, 12 November 2002). Singapore Human Resource Institute executive director D. Ang said, 'They are not totally new but there is an urgency to realise these recommendations now that Singapore is in a transition phase of economic development.' Apparently, the sub-committee had found the education reforms lagging behind, 'its pace is apparently not fast enough'.

Skills training

As early as 1961, upon the recommendation of the CCK Commission of Inquiry into Vocational and Technical Education, a technical bias was introduced into the school curriculum. This bias was underscored by the establishment in 1968 of the Technical Education Department within the Ministry of Education. A more focused and speedy programme of skills training was set up at the same time with the establishment of training centres for specialist trades such as the metal industries, electromechanical and precision engineering. In 1979, the Skills Development Fund levy was established on workers earning less than $750 per month. In that year, the formal educational system was also restructured to allow for streaming of pupils, such that the less able could then be diverted to vocational schools. Thus emerged the association between school dropouts and technical education, an association that has proved quite difficult to remove.

It was only in 1992 that the Institute of Technical Education (ITE) was established as a post-secondary institution (taking over the responsibilities of the former Vocational and Industrial Training Board), so that skills training could begin to be accorded its proper respect. ITE is the national authority on certification of technical skills and it also conducts skills tests and examinations for public candidates.

Apart from providing full-time technical and business courses for secondary school leavers, the ITE also runs the New Apprenticeship System (modelled on

Germany's Dual Training System) which allows school leavers to earn as they learn. The Modular Skills Training Scheme provides opportunities for the acquisition of new skills or for upgrading. In view of the current tide of restructuring and serious efforts to attract high-tech industries using skilled labour, the ITE had a $360 million revamp announced in April 1995. In part, the exercise represents another major effort to transform the education system, which in 1994 started the ten-year schooling system. Students who would previously have dropped out after primary school now join the normal (technical) course in secondary school. They will then go on to the ITE (about 70 per cent), thereby reducing the dropout rate in the transition to post-secondary schooling. A parallel move was also made to encourage workers to join on-the-job training schemes to complete their secondary education (Worker Improvement through Secondary Education, WISE). As the Basic Education for Skills Training (BEST) has achieved close to 90 per cent of its targeted pool of 225,000 workers since its inception in 1983, it is time now to shift the focus to a higher level of training, said Chairman Sinnakaruppan of the Advisory Council for continuing education and training (4 June 1995).

The specialist training centres run by EDB play a very special role of producing artisans and trainers. Feedback from the promotional activities of EDB is channelled towards the centre's planning and production of artisans required by incoming new investments. The small size of these centres, producing 100–200 technologists, allows rapid revision of courses, recruits and approaches used, so that they can move speedily in tandem with the requirements of industry. The centres are run jointly with MNCS, for instance, with Philips (Singapore) Pte Ltd in 1975; bilaterally, for instance the German-Singapore Institute GSI with the German government in 1982, based on the German Handwerks- and Industriemeister-System, and more recently also with MNCS, for instance, the GSI was able to embrace MNCs such as Hewlett-Packard, Asea Brown Boveri (ABB) and Siemens-Nixdorf.

Singapore ranks high for staff training and development, outshining even the 'elite global high-performing companies, according to ISR' (*Business Times*, 23 September 2002). However, what must be addressed is the appropriateness of training which could have resulted due to the current system of tying training grants to employers rather than leaving the choice to workers. A Manpower Ministry survey on Adult Training in 2000 found that only one in five workers found training relevant for their future jobs.

Industrial relations

The minimum terms and conditions of employment and labour relations are set out in the Industrial Relations Act (IRA) and Employment Act, and additional terms of service are negotiated between unions and management and are then embodied in collective agreements certified by the Industrial Arbitration Court. Certain management functions (such as matters relating to promotion, transfer, recruitment, etc.) are excluded from negotiation. Clearly, the policy stand is for conciliation and arbitration. Industrial disputes are eschewed and severely curbed.

Over the years, both Acts have been amended to suit new economic development, mainly to improve Singapore's competitive position. For instance, in the 1980s, employers were given greater flexibility to schedule working hours and to link pay to company performance and productivity. In addition, the rationalization of the bureaucracy has also moved large areas, previously open to negotiation, into the hands of state bureaucrats.

The National Wage Council, set up in 1972, remains the tripartite body responsible for orderly wage adjustment and for setting guidelines for wages. In 1993–94 NWC was composed of five employers, five union representatives and four representatives from the government. In 1986, it made an in-depth study into how 'flexi wages' can be implemented, so companies can be allowed to respond more quickly to changing business conditions. Companies were encouraged to pay as much of the wage increases as possible in the variable component to maintain flexibility. In 1995, 76 per cent of employers adopted flexible wage systems, with the flexible component making up 16 per cent of workers' total wages. In citing these figures, Minister of Labour Lee added: 'This means that employers are better prepared to survive sudden business downturns and can make adjustments to wage costs with minimal disruption to workers.' He was addressing 2,500 workers at the Jurong Shipyard's National Day ceremony (12 August 1995).

According to Senior Minister Lee (K.Y. Lee, 1995), unemployment resulting from restructuring, new technology and workers not upgrading are three issues that should be the major concerns of the trade union movement. The trade union movement has a dual role. It should check on backward-looking companies so they do not go under, bringing undesirable consequences to workers. Also, they should pool their resources to provide workers with facilities (e.g. golf course) so they can have a taste of the life-style of their bosses.

Trade unions have been roped in to participate and support a variety of issues such as industrial safety, training, and change in retirement age. Assistant Secretary General of the NTUC Yu-Foo (who is also an MP) had called upon unions to help small companies set up safety committees to deal with occupational and health issues. For while the Factories (Safety) Regulation provides for larger companies employing more than fifty workers to set up these committees, there is no such provision for the smaller companies. These exhortations were sparked by a couple of fatal accidents preceding the speech. In fact, according to the Political Secretary without Portfolio Lim, B.H. the NTUC Shipyard Safety

Consultative Committee was set up in February, prompted by the spate of serious accidents over the past two years in which several people died. And most of these accidents were preventable.

As for training, defined as another pressing issue facing the economy, the NTUC is actively involved in various training programmes, either on its own (e.g. computer classes) or jointly (e.g. with the ITE in organizing courses for office skills and business studies). It also helped train 17 per cent of workers undergoing the Workers, Improvement through Secondary Education (WISE – mathematics and English at secondary level) launched in 1987. According to the head of the NTUC Skill Development Department, workers are hesitant to go for training because of family commitments, shift work, overtime work, and the need to hold down more than one job. In fact, the National Productivity Board, which manages the SDF, has reported a surplus of $204 million. According to nominated Labour MP DePayva, this could have come about only because of the scant attention given by employers to the training of workers. Currently, a 1 per cent levy is charged to the payroll of workers earning less than $1000 (*NTUC News Weekly*, March 1995) for the Skills Development Fund.

However, as disclosed by Labour Minister Lee (May 1995), it is encouraging that training clauses have increasingly been included in collective agreements (CAS). Whereas in 1993 only 7 per cent of CAs had training clauses, the situation was much improved by 1994 when training clauses were included in 27 per cent of CAs signed that year.

Singapore's policy since the late 1970s has always been aimed towards labour saving and to advance the cause of training in order to upgrade the skills of the workforce continuously. In fact, the percentage of workers undergoing training and number of training places are included as key performance indicators (*PSB Annual Report*, 2000/2001). Any shortfall is then to be made up by the importation of foreign labour, which is, to say the least, tightly regulated. A system of levies and quotas has been put in place to wean companies off the need for cheaper labour. The levy is aimed not only at discouraging employers from an over-reliance on cheap labour but at the same time serves to break the fall in local wages that could have resulted by an uncontrolled influx of foreign labour.

Trade unions have also pushed for the rationalization of production organization. In his 1995 May Day message, NTUC President Oliveiro reiterated the government's call for companies to automate so they can operate with a smaller but more skilful workforce:

> the trouble is that many companies baulk at investing in new machinery ... they pay little attention to the training need of the workers ... when they need new employees they merely offer to pay higher wages. This could lead to a wage spiral and hurt our competitiveness.

Financial supports

The National Survey of R&D in Singapore (2000) reveals that out of the total of $1866.05 million expended on R&D by the private sector, 83 per cent was internally sourced. In fact, despite much fanfare, government funding constitutes only about 8 per cent of private sector R&D expenditure. From the comments of companies regarding strategies for restructuring, we can get a very rough idea of the direction in the flow of R&D funds. According to the Singapore International Chamber of Commerce, 'a dynamic venture capital industry has developed in Singapore over the past seven years' (1994: 32). Total funds under management now exceed $2.5 billion.

To spur the development of small technology-based companies, the EDB has set up two venture capital funds, EDB Ventures Pte Ltd (EDBV) and Singapore Bio-Innovation Pte Ltd (SBI). These are aimed at investing in venture capital funds and projects. It will also co-invest in projects with local companies and to encourage local entrepreneurship. Apart from outright grants that help lower the cost of R&D (e.g. the Research Incentive Scheme for Companies), the state has used the consortium model to reduce the costs of R&D further by teaming up companies in the same or related industry. The NSTB funds the consortia, but allows research institutes such as GINTIC (see Appendix I) to work with groups of companies to develop new technology that will help them stay competitive. For instance, the first consortium was formed to develop ball grid array in April 1994. The Institute of Microelectronics worked with twelve companies in developing the technology, and GINTIC collaborated with seven in teaching them how to use the technology in their products and processes. The most recent consortium was organized in 1995 for ceramic/tape/micro ball grid array assembly and printer circuit board assembly.

Conclusions

As newly emerging economies look set to dwarf the achievements of the rich industrial world, their market-friendly reforms and governance have increasingly come under close scrutiny. Worries about competition have probably brought about exaggerated accounts of the success of emerging economies and how their prowess would pose a danger to First World prosperity. A more realistic assessment of the strong growth of NIES, at least for the Singapore case, would most probably lead one to agree with the conclusion of Krugman (May 1995) that, with the exception of Japan, Asian growth is largely 'input driven'.

The Singapore state has finally agreed that, despite a per capita income of US$20470 'our economy does not yet have the depth, breadth and maturity of theirs [European countries], whether in terms of educated manpower, technological know-how, or well established MNCs' (Deputy Prime Minister H.L.

Lee, 1995). In the two decades after 1970, the manufacturing sector had grown only because more capital and labour were used. The level of total factor productivity (TFP) actually saw a 6 per cent drop compared to Hong Kong, where TFP increases accounted for more than 56 per cent of manufacturing growth during that period. In its 1994 Annual Report, MAS noted that between 1991 and 1993, the increase in TFP accounted for only 2 percentage points of the 7.5 per cent growth that the economy experienced. The rest were contributed by a higher employment level (3.8 per cent), greater capital intensity (1.2 per cent) and cyclical factors (0.5 per cent). Of the 7–8 per cent growth projected by MAS till the end of the century, TFP is expected to contribute only 2 percentage points. The bulk (3.5–4 per cent) is expected to come from an expanded workforce, and the remaining 1.5–2 per cent will come from increased capital intensity. If additional labour continues to be the chief source of growth, diminishing returns of such input growth as forewarned by Krugman, not to mention the small size of Singapore and the social problems already encountered with an increasing immigrant workforce, will face Singapore in the not too distant future; hence, the sudden and frenetic emphasis given to moving students and workers towards the thinking mode and the seriousness in raising state funding for R&D. With a huge surplus of $70 billion in 1994, Singapore's problem has less to do with capital but much more significantly is related to its ability to maximize the potential of everyone in its workforce. A senior principal consultant of Hay Management Consultants observed that companies are experiencing 12.5 per cent turnover and the cost is 'definitely a productivity killer … there is a push factor associated with the perception of the climate in the organization'. One personnel manager had advised that any firm facing a turnover of more than 5 per cent should review its management practices.

Since the mid-1960s, the rationalization of production and service organizations and fortuitous external circumstances have coupled to spark Singapore's industrial development. But it would seem that the turn to rationalization has assumed an overly positivistic slant, such that too much weight is placed on quantitative measures, hence emphasizing only Weberian technical rationality. Too little value has been given to reflexive thinking and substantive rationality. Thus, the race was only to raise per capita income, without attending too much to the means of achieving that figure. Goals attained (e.g. growth) therefore are not supported by a base that can sustain it in the long term.

If we recall the two extreme ways of defining rationality in the Enlightenment Project, we can now understand the anti-Western and unique Eastern values debate currently in vogue in Asia as reflecting the classic debate between positivists and rationalism/metaphysics, rather than as a question of opposing liberal Western values with Eastern authoritarianism. We can then also comprehend Singapore's inclination towards elite control and disregard for politics. However, the force of intense competition has now encouraged a more participatory style of management and politics, which can replace the spiralling price of monetary rewards. In addition, the social foundations underpinning productivity for a past era, premised upon technical rationality, coercion and hegemony, have perhaps lost their efficacy in today's world of turbulence and heated competition.

But Singapore would have to work very hard to reverse the authoritarian legacy of the past. Authoritarianism and elitism have imposed heavy costs. Neglecting small companies (which now constitute less than 80 per cent of manufacturing companies but which achieve only 9.5 per cent of the operating surplus generated in that sector) and inadequate attention paid to the education of the masses (as opposed to focusing on large foreign MNCs and nurturing of tertiary students and gifted children) could have partially accounted for the underdevelopment of its human infrastructure. Today, competition leading to a massive relocation of foreign companies and the need for a thinking workforce has forced a turnaround of policies to focus on developing local MNCs and empowerment of every worker.

Nonetheless, state initiatives to foster innovation through the forging of co-operative networks, especially in the current process of restructuring, must be given due recognition, if only for their psychological impact. For many years, working with MNCs has gained the state a wealth of knowledge on the workings and development trajectories of the world's major MNCs. The state has made good use of this fund of intelligence information to carve a niche role for itself as middleman serving the relocation needs of local SMEs and of SMEs from abroad (e.g. from Germany). With its long experience of scouring the world for investors, the EDB has learned to judge the swirl of undercurrents shaping global capital movements, and its relative autonomy from political jostling has permitted rapid retailoring of its broad range of incentives to capture new inward investment. However, the state's role cannot be viewed as an unqualified success, with perhaps the greatest threat coming from the iron rule of oligarchy.

Appendix I

A*Star (Agency for Science, Technology and Research) currently funds and oversees thirteen national research institutes:

- Bioinformatics Institute
- Bioprocessing Technology Centre
- Data Storage Institute
- Genome Institute of Singapore
- Institute of Communications research
- Institute of Bioengineering

- Institute of Chemical and Engineering Sciences
- Institute of High Performance Computing
- Institute of Materials Research and Engineering
- Institute of Microelectronics
- Institute of Molecular and Cell Biology
- Laboratories for IT
- Singapore Institute of Manufacturing Technology.

Out of the nineteen Board Members of A*Star, nine are foreigners from MNCs and foreign research institutes:

- Sydney Brenner (Salk Institute for Biological Studies)
- Goran Ando (Pharmacia and Upjohn Inc)
- Paul Guehler (3M Co.)
- Alice Shih–hou (California Institute of Technology)
- Jonathan Knowles (F Hoffmann-La Roche Ltd)
- Richard Lampman (Hewlett Packard Co)
- Ronald Oxburgh (House of Lords Select Committee on Science and Technology)
- Masatoshi Takahashi (Sumitomo Chemical Co Ltd)
- Seiichi Watanabe (Sony Corporation).

Appendix II

The EDB International Advisory Council is made up of the following:

- CEOs from US, European, Japanese Corporations
- Asahi Glass Co. Ltd
- BASF Aktiengesellschaft
- Daimler Chrysler AG
- Quintiles Transnational Corp.
- Philips Electronics
- Seagate Technology
- Sony Corporation
- ST Microelectronics
- Sumitomo Chemical Company.

(EDB *Annual ReportI, 2001/2002*)

These companies represent industries important to Singapore's economic future.

Composition of the National Technology Plan is as follows:

- ten chief technology officers from companies represented on the Advisory Council;
- five chief technology officers from other companies with significant R&D experience/expenditure, e.g. Hewlett-Packard.

These officers each manage a budget exceeding US$3 billion (S$4.3 billion), total US$45 billion.

Appendix III

Examples of state–private sector initiatives

Research Incentive Scheme for companies

- *Aztech Systems* (local SME) Start of digital signal processing-based audio boards with fax/modem features, electro-optical devices and microelectronics. Provided with grant of $8.5 million.
- *Sony Systems Design International* R&D centre costing $10 million focusing on developing multimedia and microchip software. Now working on multi-media retrieving and archiving system and improved microchip designs for CD-ROM data storage devices and video cassette recorders. Provided with grant worth $250,000.

State-private sector joint venture is the Singlab Joint venture by IBM Singapore, EDB, Institute of Systems Science, CSA Holdings, Singapore Computer Systems. Singlab was appointed as IBM'S Asia-Pacific regional R&D centre. Singlab focus on:

- multimodel human interface research leveraging combination of multimedia, pen-based voice input/output and speech recognition technologies;
- multimedia solutions R&D centre;
- application development centre;
- development consultancy centre for software products.

Polytechnic–private sector collaboration/alliance ($5 million) is the Ngee Ann Polytechnic/AT&T/NCR Centre for Advanced Technology. This collaboration aims to do the following:

- spearhead joint training and R&D in open systems technology and newly emerging technologies such as parallel computing;
- to provide technical and professional consulting services to A T&T/NCR companies in Hong Kong, China, Indonesia, Malaysia, the Philippines, Singapore, India, Sri Lanka, Taiwan, Korea and Thailand.

State–foreign university collaboration is the Singapore Institute of Standards and Industrial Research collaborating with the Chinese University of Zhejiang on projects related to coating materials (thin film technology) to generate commercial applications.

The main aims of state-private sector initiatives are:

- to develop IT systems to serve sectoral needs and to enhance the sector's contribution to the economy, for instance, an integrated network for the construction and real estate industry called CORENET, a joint initiative by the Ministry of National Development and the NCB;
- To network major state offices and their clients to improve overall productivity.

Notes

1 All denominations are in Singapore dollars unless otherwise stated (S$2.35 = £1.00, May 1997).

2 The German Business Group, in response to state request for feedback on productivity, stressed instead the problem of real estate inflation (19 July 1982):

> Industrial development and real estate speculation are actually contradictory because industrial development depends on constancy in land prices. The huge influx of capital here has led to speculation in real estate that has become an unfavourable influence on investment. When even a state-owned body like the Jurong Town Corporation is asking up to S$400 to S$500 for a square metre of land it becomes impossible for industry to cope with such prices. Rent increases by government bodies of 20–30% and even more are being imposed – even during tax relief incentive periods which seem to cast doubt on the government's stated policy of fighting inflation.

Chapter 12
Regional innovation support systems in South Korea
The case of Gyeonggi

Robert Hassink

Introduction

Systems of innovation are formed by firms interacting with other actors in an innovation context for interactive learning. These systems have become popular as a conceptual framework to explain differences in competitiveness both between firms and sectors, at the local, regional, national and supranational level since the beginning of the 1990s (Edquist, 1997). Starting with national innovation systems, this approach has been recently extended by sectoral innovation systems and regional (subnational) or local innovation systems (Edquist, 1997; Braczyk *et al.*, 1998; de la Mothe and Paquet, 1998; Mytelka, 2000). In general, these kind of systems are divided into two subsystems: the production system and the institutional system. As this chapter's core theme is innovation support systems, it will focus on the institutional part of regional innovation systems. In this chapter institutions are considered as 'formal structures with an explicit purpose', also called organisations, rather than 'things that pattern behavior' such as norms, rules and laws (Edquist, 1997: 26). The focus will be on those organisations that support the innovativeness of small and medium-sized enterprises (SMEs) and that can be defined, if they actively co-operate as a group, as innovation support systems. An innovation support system consists of all agencies found in three support stages, namely the provision of general information, technological advice and joint R&D projects, between firms (of which technology-following SMEs are the main group) and higher education institutes (HEIs) and public research establishments (PREs). Agencies found in these stages try to help to solve the innovation problems of technology-following SMEs either by giving them advice themselves or by referring them to other agencies in a further stage of support. If it concerns a highly complicated technological problem, the SMEs might finally be referred to a university or PRE. The agencies can be mainly supranationally, nationally or regionally initiated.

This chapter will shed light on how far the process of regional innovation support systems has evolved in South Korea, a politically highly centralised country with nearly 47 million inhabitants where recently some political power has been transferred from central government to regional authorities. The chapter aims to find answers to two main questions. First, based on a case study of innovation support agencies in Gyeonggi (Figure 12.1), to what extent can we find *regionally embedded* innovation support systems in South Korea's regions and can we talk about support *systems* (actively co-operating agencies) or is it more appropriate to speak about *infrastructures* (lack of co-operation)? Second, is the establishment of regionally embedded innovation support systems necessary to change South Korea's stage of economic development from an investment-driven one to an innovation-driven one? This chapter does not consider embeddedness as commonly seen from a firm's point of view, which stresses social interaction between the firm and its environment (Granovetter, 1985; Oinas, 1997). As innovation support agencies in regions are the topic, we will work with the notions of institutional embeddedness (Barnes, 1999) and spatial (regional or national?) embeddedness (Oinas, 1997). Institutional embeddedness is seen as co-operative action of individual agencies as well as several sorts of local coalitions in securing interests in processes of regional development, whereas spatial embeddedness is defined as actors 'being embedded in social relations on different spatial scales' (ibid.: 29). Institutional embeddedness thus stresses co-operative action, whereas spatial embeddedness stresses the spatial level of embeddedness. The question will be whether support agencies are deeply and firmly fixed in social relations with other institutions in the region (which is a combination of institutional embeddedness and spatial embeddedness confined to the region), so that we can speak about regional innovation support systems.

The chapter will focus on the Gyeonggi Province (8.9 million inhabitants) around Seoul for two reasons. First, Gyeonggi can be regarded as the economic and innovative powerhouse in South Korea (Park, 2000). Second, it has a strong manufacturing and institutional density, diversified production structure and a strong tradition of SME-based manufacturing.

In order to be able to tackle the questions concerning regional innovation support systems in Gyeonggi, two frameworks need to be created. A theoretical framework on regional innovation support systems will first be presented and then South Korea's national policy and economic framework will be described.

Theoretical framework on regional innovation support systems

The recent popularity of the concept of regional innovation systems is closely related to the surge in regional innovation policies in many industrialised countries of the world. The importance of the regional level is namely increasing with regard to diffusion-oriented innovation support policies (Ergas, 1987; Jessop, 1994; Dodgson and Bessant, 1996: 5; Cooke and Morgan, 1998; Amin, 1999; Lorenzen, 2001). Partly supported by national and supranational support programmes and

12.1 The location of Gyeonggi in South Korea

encouraged by thick institutional set-ups found in successful regional economies such as Baden-Württemberg in Germany and Emilia-Romagna in Italy, many regions in industrialised countries have been setting up science parks, technopoles, technological financial aid schemes and innovation support agencies since the second half of the 1980s. The central aim of these policies is to support regional endogenous potential by encouraging the diffusion of new technologies both from universities and PREs to SMEs, between SMEs and large enterprises (vertical co-operation) and between SMEs themselves (horizontal co-operation).

This increasing importance of regions for innovation policy can be considered the outcome of a converging of regional and technology policy since the early 1980s (Rothwell and Dodgson, 1992). These two policy fields converged into regional innovation policies since their aim became partly the same, namely to support the innovative capabilities and thus the competitiveness of SMEs. It also fits into what Amin (1999) recently observed as a shift from a firm-centred, incentive-based, state-driven and standardised regional economic development policies to bottom-up, region-specific, longer-term and plural-actor policies. These policy trends cannot only be seen in European countries, but also in North America and some countries in Asia (Markusen *et al.*, 1999). Although we can therefore speak about a general phenomenon, there are of course large differences between individual regions and countries concerning the extent to which these trends take place. Generally, contributory factors to regional innovation policies are a federal political system, decentralisation, strong regional institutions and governance, a strong industrial specialisation in the region, socio-cultural homogeneity and thus trust relationships, large economic restructuring problems and the strong commit-ment of regional political leaders (Atkinson, 1991).

One of the main strengths of the regional level for innovation support has been called the 'garden argument' (Paquet, 1994): if the economy is regarded as a garden with all kinds of trees and plants, for the gardener (government) there is no simple rule likely to apply to all plants. Growth is therefore best orchestrated from its sources at the level of cities and regions. At this level, rather than at the national level, policy-makers can better tailor policy to demand. Regionalisation, therefore, allows for differentiation in policies, which is necessary because of differing regional economic conditions and thus the different support needs of industries and firms (Park, 1998: 198). Regionalisation also raises the enthusiasm and motivation of regional policy-makers, as they are now able to devise 'their own' policies. Moreover, because of the large variety of institutional set-ups and initiatives in Europe and North America, these laboratories of experimentation offer both national and regional policy-makers plenty of institutional learning opportunities (Hassink and Lagendijk, 2001).

In many regions in Europe, however, an increasing functional overlap between agencies, that is at least more than one agency in the different stages of innovation support delivering the same kind of services, and a lack of policy co-ordination at the regional level have been observed (Hassink, 1996). The target group of most of the agencies, that is technology-following SMEs (SMEs for which it is not important to develop or apply the newest technologies), have increasing difficulty in finding their way in the jungle of support agencies. As a policy reaction to this problem, which is partly caused by multilevel (regional, national, European) funding, the European Commission launched several support programmes for regions from 1994 onwards. These Regional Technology Plans (RTP), Regional Innovation Strategy (RIS) and Regional Innovation and Techno-logy Transfer Strategies (RITTS) Programmes aim at supporting regions in Europe to (re)organise their innovation policies in order to meet the demands of firms more than they did before.

After regional innovation policies started emerging in the mid-1980s, several academics have developed theoretical and conceptual ideas on regional innovation strategies in the mid-1990s. These concepts, that is regional innovation systems (Cooke, 1998; De la Mothe and Paquet, 1998), the learning region (Morgan, 1997) and the idea of institutional thickness (Amin and Thrift, 1994), have been partly developed for policy reasons, namely as a response to the organisational and strategic weaknesses of regions. Scholars also wanted to derive conceptual policy lessons from successful regional economies and to make clear why the regional level is an important level as a source for learning and innovation. The institutional thickness concept, for instance, which takes the thickness of institutions as its starting-point of analysis, was launched after scholars found out that successful industrial districts in Europe are characterised by a 'thick' tissue of support institutions. Institutional thickness, which nourishes relations of trust, is characterised by inter-institutional interaction and synergy, collective representation by many bodies, a common industrial purpose and shared cultural norms and values (Amin and Thrift, 1994: 15).

To derive policy lessons from successful regional economies, however, is not new in economic geography, as older theory-led development models, such as industrial districts and innovative milieu, are also based on experiences in growth regions such as Silicon Valley, Baden-Württemberg and the Third Italy (Schamp, 2000). What distinguishes the concept of regional innovation systems from these somewhat older concepts is that it is not derived from experiences in any particular kind of region. It can therefore be applied to a broader range of regions than the other models, which turned out to be difficult to transfer to structurally weak regions. In addition, due to the evolutionary character of the concept and its typology (see below), it can be used to examine the development path of regions over time and to recommend to regional policy-makers what direction to follow (Cooke *et al.*, 1998).

Of the recently developed concepts, that is the learning region and institutional thickness, the regional innovation systems concept is most widely dealt with in the literature both in a conceptual way (Cooke, 1998; Cooke *et al.*, 1998; De la Mothe and Paquet, 1998) and concerning empirical case studies, including North American and Asian ones (Braczyk *et al.*, 1998; De la Mothe and Paquet, 1998; Chung, 1999b). Cooke *et al.*, (1998: 1581) define regional innovation systems as systems 'in which firms and other organisations [such as research institutes, universities, innovation support agencies, chambers of commerce, banks, government departments] are systematically engaged in interactive learning through an institutional milieu characterised by embeddedness'. The aim of regional innovation systems is to integrate traditional, context-linked, regional knowledge and codified, world-wide available knowledge in order to stimulate regional endogenous potentials.

A typology of regional innovation support systems as presented in the Introduction of this book helps to apply the concept to a broad range of regions and to clarify the 'scale' of public policy involvement, that is from mainly national to mainly local. It also clarifies the relationship between national and regional innovation support systems. Such a typology consists of grassroots systems, network systems and *dirigiste* systems (for other typologies in relation to regional innovation policies, see Tsipouri, 1999, and Nauwelaers and Wintjes, 2000). Grassroots and network systems deserve to be called systems, as extensive and well co-ordinated interaction between institutionally embedded agencies makes them more than just a sum of their parts (which could be called an infrastructure). These two systems show similarities with what Amin (1999) has labelled bottom-up, region-specific, longer-term and plural-actor kind of regional economic development policies. In nationally initiated *dirigiste* systems, on the other hand, intra-regional institutional embeddedness and 'systemness' tend to be weaker. They come close to the firm-centred, incentive-based, state-driven and standardised kind of regional economic development policies (Amin, 1999).

Two factors can have a great impact on what type of systems tend to predominate under what circumstances. First, there might be a relationship between the development stage of a country and the required type of system. A *dirigiste* kind of system might work better if a country is in an investment-driven stage of development, whereas network and grassroots, that is more decentralised, kinds of systems work better if a country has entered an innovation-driven stage of development (Porter, 1990). Second, there is a clear relationship between the political-administrative system and the predominating kind of support system. In countries with a federal or similar political system such as Germany, Austria, Spain and Belgium, one tends to find more often grassroots or network kinds of systems than in countries with a more centralised political system, such as the Netherlands, Denmark and Great Britain.

Regional Innovation Support Systems in South Korea

Thus, recent theoretical discussions suggest an increasing importance of the regional level for innovation support. On the basis of the case study of Gyeonggi, this section will give practical evidence on this trend in South Korea. It will start, though, by presenting South Korea's policy framework for regional innovation support systems and subsequently the case region's economic profile.

South Korea's policy context for regional innovation support systems

In recent years one can observe a fundamental change in South Korea's institutional framework and the content of its industrial, technology and regional policies. This has been necessary to achieve the restructuring of its economy from a low-technology, labour-intensive, 'mass production' type of industry to a high-technology, capital- and skill-intensive, 'flexible specialisation' type of industry (Porter, 1990). This involves a shift in emphasis from hierarchical control to decentralised governance, both at the level of the state and at the level of the firm. According to many, however, these institutional changes are taking place at a too slow pace, particularly where the central government is involved (Kim, 2000). This slow pace of reforms partly resulted in the economic crisis of 1997, the worst one since the Korean War in the early 1950s. During the recent economic crisis voices in favour of more market and less state and more decentralisation and less centralisation have therefore become even louder.

In the 1980s, the government gradually shifted emphasis from industrial policy to technology policy (Kim, 2000). This shift in government policy led to a sharp increase in R&D expenditure levels: R&D expenditures as a percentage of GNP grew from 0.38 per cent in 1970 to 2.46 per cent in 1999 (Kim, 1997). It now has the highest R&D intensity of all East Asian economies and recently even surpassed the United Kingdom (ibid.). Particularly striking is the relatively low share of government expenditures and hence the relatively high proportion of private sector involvement in R&D investments. Not only R&D expenditures increased, also the high-tech industries' employment share of total manufacturing employment grew from 9.1 per cent in 1983 to 16.6 per cent in 1994 (Wessel, 1997). The strong increase in patent registrations is another important indicator of South Korea's rapid development in industrial R&D (Kim, 1997). Both private R&D expenditures, high-tech employment and patent registrations are strongly concentrated in large enterprises.

Considering the fact that Korea was one of the poorest countries in the world in the 1950s with an extremely low R&D input, strong technology policy has led to these relatively high scores on R&D-related indicators. The main ministry involved in technology policy is the Ministry of Science and Technology (MOST). The ministry has two related institutes, the Science and Technology Policy Institute (STEPI), MOST's think tank, and the Korea Institute of Science and Technology Evaluation and Planning (KISTEP), MOST's policy management and evaluation institute. Another player in the field of innovation support for SMEs is the Ministry of Commerce, Industry and Energy (MOCIE). Despite the increasing government involvement in technology policy, Kim (2000) observes several weaknesses in South Korea's innovation system: research at universities is relatively weak, there is a fundamental lack of interplay between universities and the private sector, there are relatively few technological spin-offs and there is a dearth of diffusion mechanisms to transfer research results from PREs to industry and particularly to SMEs. There are signs that the character of South Korea's technology policy is moving from a mission-oriented one, which is focusing on public research institutes and big science projects, to a diffusion-oriented one, which stresses the environment, the transfer of knowledge and technical education (Ergas, 1987; Hassink, 2001). Recently, for instance, the central government has increasingly been supporting the innovativeness of SMEs and inter-firm networks. These SME-oriented innovation support policies are much better developed than one would expect after reading the literature and press articles on South Korea's general economic policy. In those publications the South Korean government is often blamed for just supporting the *chaebol* (large, family-based conglomerates) and neglecting SMEs, of which many lack boundary-spanning functions, such as R&D. The strength of the Korean SME-oriented innovation support, however, is contradictory judged by the literature (see Hassink, 2001), which might partly be caused by the lack of a systematic evaluation (Chung, 1999a). There is more agreement on what could be improved in the support policies, namely a stronger involvement of local and regional authorities (OECD, 1996: 174; Park, 1998; Suh, 2000; OECD, 2001) and a stronger voice from the SMEs themselves in the agencies, which are mostly set up by the central government (Park, 1998: 195).

One factor that led to the recent economic crisis is the weakness of the system of research institutes and universities. The latter are too focused on teaching and devote too little on research. The imbalance between teaching and research at universities is illustrated by the fact that in 1994 universities employed 33 per cent of South Korea's total R&D personnel, whereas they received no more than about 7.7 per cent of the national R&D expenditure (Kim, 1997). In addition, given the teaching orientation at universities, there is a fundamental lack of interaction between universities and the private sector and there are relatively few technological spin-offs (ibid.). Although the government extensively financed the establishment of a whole range of PREs (80 per cent of public R&D spending goes to PREs, compared with 41 per cent in Germany and 24 per cent in the USA), these institutes lack diffusion mechanisms to transfer research results to industry and particularly to SMEs (Kim, 1997).

South Korea's regional policy, another bordering policy field of regional innovation support systems, has been 'heavily reliant on programmes involving construction of industrial sites and infrastructure development, as well as regulation of metropolitan growth' (Hong, 1997: 421), whereas soft goals such as net-working, institutional frameworks, public–private partnerships and the provision of information and consulting services have been neglected. Many ministries and agencies are directly or indirectly involved in regional economic policy (no less than five ministries at the central level). In general, regional policy has had a limited effect on spatial development in general and on reducing regional economic inequalities in particular (Kang, 1997). It has been weakly implemented, 'often succumbing to national short run economic pressures' (Hong, 1997: 419). Many scholars have been arguing that regional policy should be changed away from 'top-down' decentralisation policies, mainly implemented in the 1970s (large-scale heavy industrial complexes in the central and particularly south-eastern parts of South Korea) and 1980s (mainly PREs to Daedeok Science Town in Daejeon) to 'bottom-up' decentralisation policies of developing endogenous potentials (mainly SMEs) in the regions (Hong, 1997; Kang, 1997; Park, 1998). The emergence of these latter policies have been facilitated by political decentralisation reforms in 1995 (Hassink, 2001).

Case study of Gyeonggi

South Korea's rapid industrialisation in the 1960s and 1970s and the rise of high-tech industries from the mid-1980s onwards have caused a strong concentration of economic activities in the north-western and south-eastern parts of the country and thus considerable regional disparities (OECD, 2001). The heavy industrialisation in the central and south-eastern provinces also generated monostructural industrial complexes dominated by branch plants of *chaebol* which are mainly steered from Seoul. The national government and *chaebol* dominated the formation of most of these districts. Local and regional actors, such as regional development agencies and universities, did not play an important role. The strong growth of these districts is thus almost entirely exogenously, rather than endogenously, generated.

In contrast to the spatial production structure in the south-eastern part of Korea, which has a production structure that is characterised by the strong geographical concentration of some large industrial complexes in some localities (externally steered local innovation systems), Gyeonggi has a more diversified production structure. The biggest manufacturing industries are electronics (mainly because of Samsung electronics' production complex in Gyeonggi's capital Suwon), rubber and plastics products, electrical machinery, assembling metal products and textile (Table 12.1).

According to Lee (2001), Gyeonggi has three strong clusters in the following industries: automobile components (see also Lee, 2002), semi-conductors and pharmaceutics, which are all concentrated in the southern part of the region (Lee, 2001). It can be regarded, together with Seoul and Incheon, as the innovation centre of South Korea. In fact, due to the decentralisation of high-tech manufacturing industries from Seoul, its position as an innovation centre has even been strengthened (Park, 2000; Lee, 2001). At the same time, however, these industries are still dependent on Seoul for the supply of producer services (Park and Markusen, 1999). The strong position of Gyeonggi as an innovation centre is illustrated by several statistical data, such as its relatively high R&D intensity (number of R&D workers per 1,000 inhabitants), its high share of patents of the South Korean total, its over-representation of employment in high-tech industries and its leading position in South Korea when it comes to business start-ups (see Table 12.1, Hassink, 2001; Lee, 2001). Although Gyeonggi is characterised by a high industrial diversity and many independent, highly innovative SMEs, it has been hit relatively hard by the crisis in 1998. This might be explained by the predominance of SMEs in this region (Table 12.1), which have suffered more from the economic crisis than the large externally controlled branch plants of the *chaebol* in the south-eastern part of the country. Meanwhile, however, the Gyeonggi economy has quickly recovered as below-average unemployment rates and above-average growth rates show (Table 12.1).

Table 12.1 Some comparative statistics on Gyeonggi and South Korea

	Gyeonggi	South Korea
Growth rates[1]		
1998	5.0%	– 1.8%
1999	12.6%	9.7%
2000	11.0%	6.6%
Unemployment rates[1]		
1998	8.2%	6.8%
1999	6.9%	6.3%
2000	3.7%	4.1%
SME-share of total employment in 2000[1]	82.6%	79.2%
Employment share of largest manufacturing industries in Gyeonggi in 2000[1] (location quotient)		
– electronic components, radio, TV and communication equipment	16.0% (152)	10.5%
– rubber and plastic products	7.5% (125)	6.0%
– electrical-machinery and converter	7.4% (140)	5.3%
– assembling metal products and outfits	7.3% (106)	6.9%
– textile	7.1% (82)	8.7%
R&D personnel per 1,000 inhabitants in 1997[2]		
• total	6.2	4.5
• in universities and PREs	1.4	2.3
• in companies	4.8	2.2
R&D expenditures in million won per 1,000 inhabitants in 1997[2]		
• total	420.8	232.0
• in universities and PREs	40.5	62.2
• in companies	380.4	169.9
Patents (share of total)[3]		
• 1985	10.0%	100%
• 1995	33.2%	100%
Share of technology intensive industry of total manufacturing employment in 1994[4]	40.5%	100%
Share of manufacturing employment in 1994	25.8%	100%

Sources:
1 National Statistical Office Republic of Korea and own calculations.
2 Ministry of Science and Technology and own calculations.
3 Park (1998).
4 Wessel (1997).

Local linkages between companies and suppliers, customers and competitors seem to be more important in Gyeonggi than in the monostructural industrial complexes in the South East of the country, such as in Gumi (Park, 2000; Lee, 2001). At the same time, however, firms in Gyeonggi are increasingly internationally active, foreign direct investment has been strongly increasing after the economic crisis at the end of the 1990s and even if their customers relocate to other regions, they tend to stay in Gyeonggi due to agglomeration advantages. A telling example is the car supplier industry in Gyeonggi, which used to be focused on some main car plants, such Daewoo and Kia. After the major car producers, such as Hyundai, established car manufacturing plants in other parts of the country, only limited number of bulky parts producers moved to these locations, but a large part of the suppliers stayed in the Capital Region.

> Regardless of the location of the assembly plants, suppliers who work with several assemblers and produce either high-tech parts or standardized parts choose their location by searching for benefits from the accessibility to a skilled labor force, banks, R&D functions, and government institutions, and remain in the Seoul metropolitan area.
>
> (Lee, 2002: 1017)

All in all, Gyeonggi's regional economy can be regarded as one of the most innovative and robust in South Korea. In the following, the region's system that is supposed to support the innovativeness of the regional economy will be portrayed. The most important elements of the innovation support system in Gyeonggi stem from nationally devised initiatives, that is intermediary agencies, a consortium programme and a programme to support so-called technoparks. A smaller part consists of locally and regionally devised initiatives. In the following a selection of recently established key innovation support agencies and initiatives in Gyeonggi will briefly be described, starting with the nationally devised ones (see also Hassink, 2001; Lee, 2001).

One of the main innovation support agencies in Gyeonggi is the Small and Medium Business Administration (SMBA), an organisation which was established by the central government in 1996 and which has eleven regional offices in South Korea. The office in Gyeonggi (located in Suwon) has about fifty employees. These regional offices' main functions are to inform SMEs on the spot about national aid schemes, management and sales and purchase issues, to assess applications for aid schemes, to provide regional SMEs with technological advice and test and analysis equipment and to refer SMEs to other agencies. Very similar to the SMBA is the Small and Medium Industry Promotion Corporation (SMIPC), which also has eleven regional offices and is also fully supported by the central government. The Gyeonggi office is located in Suwon and has about twenty employees, including about five technology consultants, who are, in contrast to SMBA's consultants, professional engineers with a long company experience. Kim and Nugent (1994: 13) consider the SMIPC as the 'most important public agency providing technical support exclusively for SMEs'. Despite some small differences between the SMBA and SMIPC, these agencies, as well as the more densely spread offices of the Chambers of Commerce, are very similar to each other. Even according to some managers of the agencies, SMEs mix up these very similar agencies.

The central government also recently established a network of thirty-seven so-called Regional Research Centers (RRCs), which are located at universities across the whole country. They are specialised in those technologies that dominate in the region's industry: in Gyeonggi, there are three RRCs: the RRC for Electronic Materials and Components in Ansan, the Center for Environmental and Clean Technologies in Suwon and the RRC on Ceramic Engineering in Yongin. The centres aim at fostering co-operation between universities and SMEs in the regions and are meant to upgrade research facilities at universities so that they become interesting partners for SMEs to co-operate with. They offer SMEs in the region the following services: technological advice, joint R&D projects, seminars, training courses and the use of scientific equipment for tests and experiments. A recent survey among SMEs in South Korea seems to confirm the success of the RRCs, as it shows that the share of SMEs co-operating with universities on innovation projects increased from 12.8 per cent in 1995 to 28.0 per cent in 1997 (Chung, 1999a). Concerning the particular case of Gyeonggi, the institutional embeddedness of these centres in the region is relatively weak, as the interviewed RRCs in Gyeonggi mainly co-operate with agencies that are located outside the region. This weak intra-regional co-operation is probably due to a relatively weak industrial specialisation and clustering in Gyeonggi.

Furthermore, the central government has recently selected six so-called technoparks for long-term financial support, of which one is located in Gyeonggi, namely Gyeonggi Technopark in Ansan. In contrast to most science parks in Great Britain and Gründer- und Technologiezentren in Germany, which mainly focus on technology-oriented start-ups and SMEs, South Korea's technoparks are also supposed to contain R&D centres and production plants of *chaebol*, pilot plants or learning factories which are both used by university students and SMEs and small business support centres. Technoparks are developed and financed by a wide range of participants including central government, local and regional authorities and universities.

In addition to the presented nationally initiated measures, locally and regionally initiated policy measures have recently been increasing. Gyeonggi Province (2.67 per cent) spends about the same share of its budget on science and technology policy (S&T) as the average of all provinces (2.58 per cent) (Chung, 1999b).

Looking at the provincial budgets for this policy, however, the lion's share is devoted to co-financing the above-described recently developed nationally devised policy initiatives (Hassink, 2001). Because Gyeonggi Province has the largest absolute S&T budget of all the provinces in South Korea (Chung, 1999b), it has more room to set up and finance some innovation policy measures. It is the only province in South Korea that has set up a regional version of RRCs. Three centres that were not selected by MOST to become an RRC received support from the province and are now called Gyeonggi Regional Research Centers (GRRCs). Furthermore, the province has established its own intermediary agency for SMEs in 1996, called the Gyeonggi Small Business Foundation (GSBF). The GSBF, which has forty-one employees and has been recently renamed into Gyeonggi Small Business Center, has two aims. First, it promotes business start-ups and existing SMEs that develop new products. It has an 'on-spot innovation team', consisting of engineers with extensive company experience who technologically advise Gyeonggi SMEs. Second, the GSBF is going to set up a science park in Suwon, the capital of Gyeonggi, within the coming two years. In contrast to the above-mentioned technoparks, this science park will only provide high-tech, R&D-oriented business start-ups (so no production) with office space. In addition to the office space for about 100 high-tech business start-ups, the science park will also become a new home for twenty-five innovation support agencies of the Gyeonggi Province in a so-called 'under-one-roof one-stop shopping center'.

All in all, the strong increase in initiatives of the central government in which regions participate as co-financiers has clearly boosted the role of regions in innovation policies. However, innovation policy still has a strong national character, as in nearly all the cases, provinces can only co-finance initiatives that are devised and implemented by the central government. South Korea's provinces clearly lack the capabilities to co-ordinate innovation support measures and to strategically and reflectively think about innovation support (see also Hassink, 2001; Lee, 2001). These lacking capabilities to co-ordinate innovation policies at the regional level show that South Korea does not yet have ideal regional innovation support systems, let alone reflective learning regions.

Conclusion

This chapter made clear that in South Korea the central government's innovation policy focused on SMEs has recently been strongly developed. The network of RRCs and consortium initiative, in particular, are important steps to sharing the universities' equipment and knowledge with SMEs in the regions. However, to what extent does the regional level play a role in these innovation support policies and can we speak about support systems or is it more appropriate to speak about infrastructures?

The decentralisation of SME-oriented innovation policy, which has been requested by many, has been facilitated by the political reforms of 1995. The strong increase in initiatives of the central government in which regions participate as co-financiers, such as the technoparks, the consortium programme and the RRCs, have clearly boosted the role of regions in innovation policies. Nevertheless, innovation policy still has a strong national character, as in most of the cases, provinces can only co-finance initiatives that are devised and implemented by the central government. South Korea's regional innovation support systems, therefore, can be classified as *dirigiste* in the typology of innovation support systems (Table 12.2), showing clear similarities with France's *dirigiste* innovation support system (Cooke, 1992). However, Gyeonggi, which is the most populous province, has recently set up some initiatives parallel to the central government initiatives. Gyeonggi, therefore, seems to be moving from a *dirigiste* to a network kind of regional innovation support system. Moreover, other recently developed regionally initiated projects, such as the Milano Project in Daegu, the Gyeongnam Mechanical Engineering Industry Technobelt Project (Park and Lee, 2000) and the initiative to strengthen the opto-electronic cluster in Gwangju (Chung, 2001), all point in a general trend towards network systems in South Korea. Since these initiatives are all set up and partly financed by coalitions of regional institutions, they are much more strongly institutionally embedded in the regions than top-down initiatives set up by central government agencies.

The existence of *dirigiste* innovation support systems and therefore the limited role of regions in them can first and foremost be explained by their inability to levy taxes and hence their lacking financial resources to finance initiatives. Furthermore, in contrast to the situation in Europe, South Korea's regions lack a supranational sponsor and promoter of regional innovation policies which has an interest in 'hollowing out' the nation-state.

One can rightly ask, however, whether the establishment of regionally embedded innovation support systems is necessary at all to change South Korea's economic development from an investment-driven stage to an innovation-driven one. In other words, does it matter whether SME-oriented innovation support is organised at a regional or national level?

There are two clear disadvantages of the current *dirigiste* kind of system in South Korea in which the central government dominates SME-oriented innovation policies. First, this *dirigiste* kind of system generates too homogenous innovation support agencies which are not focused enough on specific regional economic demand. The regional offices of the main agencies, SMBA and SMIPC, offer about the same standard services in all regions of the country, regardless of the specific regional economic needs and problems. In addition, they are too dependent on financial support from the central government. In a society which changes at an increasingly rapid pace, central governments are less able to adapt their

Table 12.2 Characteristics of Gyeonggi's regional innovation support system

Type of system	Definition
Initiation	mainly central government, but increasing role of provincial government
Funding	mainly national agencies, but increasing role of provincial government
Research and support	mixed
Specialisation	low
Intra-regional co-operation	low
Co-ordination	low
Type of system	*dirigiste*, but moving towards network system

innovation support policies to the fast changing demand of companies. Therefore, the closer the proximity, both geographically, socio-culturally and organisationally, between the agencies and SMEs, the more flexible and efficient they are. Too much dependence on central government support leads both to inflexibility and to rent-seeking instead of innovation-seeking behaviour of the agencies.

Second, this kind of system often generates horizontal policy co-ordination problems. Agencies in the regions, such as the SMBA, SMIPC and RRCs, are highly vertically dependent on national ministries, that is the Ministry of Trade and Industry and the Ministry of Science and Technology respectively, for financial support. Horizontal co-ordination problems are caused by the lack of co-ordination and co-operation between these national ministries, on the one hand, and the weakness of regional governments to strategically guide and co-ordinate the initiatives that are implemented by national ministries into their region as well as local and regional initiatives, on the other hand. Despite the establishment of the SMBA, which is supposed to co-ordinate innovation support for SMEs, the support infrastructure can be characterised as fragmented with overlapping activities and agencies, particularly in the first stage of innovation support (the SMBA and SMIPC, in particular). Since the division of labour between the agencies is not clear and interaction between them is at a low level, they form an innovation support infrastructure rather than a system.

However, it would be short-sighted to consider a causal link between the decentralisation versus centralisation phenomenon and co-ordinated versus unco-ordinated innovation support. This might be just one relationship. There are many other factors that affect the level of co-ordination in an innovation support infra-structure, such as the existence of personal networks between the directors of the agencies and, interrelated to this factor, the duration and stability of the institutional set-up. It will be difficult to come to some form of 'systemness', if the innovation support infrastructure changes every four years because a newly elected central government decides to replace agencies. Since South Korea only recently set up many of its initiatives, also time will be needed to develop to a system.

Nevertheless, despite this restriction, regionally embedded innovation support systems are clearly preferable to *dirigiste* ones for South Korea in its current development stage (between investment-driven and innovation-driven). The *dirigiste* system might have been successful in the investment-driven stage, when it achieved economic catch-up with industrialised countries mainly on the basis of central government's supply-oriented support of large enterprises and satellite industrial districts. The system, however, clearly reaches its limits in the innovation-driven stage which South Korea has now entered. To meet the support requirements of that stage of development, regionally embedded, demand- and diffusion-oriented support systems need to replace the outdated support structure. However, given the specific South Korean economic, industrial, financial, institutional and political context with the strong position of government-backed *chaebol*, too much focus on an SME-based endogenous, grassroots type of regional innovation system would be inappropriate. It will be more realistic to concentrate on an network approach which is also to some extent bottom-up, but more planned and co-ordinated by regional government and based on partnerships between a broader set of actors, namely regionally and nationally initiated support agencies, large enterprises, SMEs, universities and PREs. Such a system will help to promote the formation of innovation networks between these actors in South Korea's many satellite and hub and spoke industrial districts, which lack intra-regional networking.

However, to change a *dirigiste* kind of innovation support system into a network kind of system is not an easy process. Central government officials are often not willing to give up decision-making authority to lower levels of government and are reluctant to devolve power to the regions, as they fear the inability of regional policy-makers to devise and implement sound policies. Although the political reforms of 1995 changed the political system, it will take a long time to change the centrally oriented and dependent attitude of politicians and policy-makers in provincial administrations. However, this is in a way a chicken-and-egg problem, since regional policy-makers can only build experience and ability if they are enabled to devise and implement their own policies. Central government, therefore, should put the principle of subsidiarity more into practice: it should give regional governments greater access to sources of revenue and help them more to develop skills and knowledge, so that they can become responsible for those initiatives and agencies that can be perfectly operated by regional authorities, such as the SMBA and SMIPC.

Decentralisation, however, does not mean that the central government no longer has a role to play. Apart from being responsible for basic, pre-competitive technology development, it also needs to co-ordinate, evaluate and publish on regionally initiated innovation policies, so that regions can learn from each other. It also has to make sure that monies are channelled to structurally weak regions so that decentralisation does not lead to the strengthening of existing regional economic inequalities. Furthermore, it should carefully monitor whether certain regions defend their traditional end-of-the-product life-cycle industries and hinder restructuring or the promotion of new industries. In such a case it needs to intervene in order to avoid the emergence of policy and cognitive lock-ins. Thus, a partnership between central and provincial governments is necessary which is characterised by a clear division of labour. This partnership should be characterised by consultation and negotiation rather than hierarchical top-down relationships and should allow for local initiatives and diversity. A decentralisation of innovation policies to the regional level embedded in such a partnership will contribute to an efficiently operating and co-ordinated innovation support infrastructure, which will help South Korea to generate innovation-driven growth.

Acknowledgements

The chapter reports on a research project on regional innovation support systems in South Korea and Japan which was carried out by the author from February 1998 until October 1999. Large parts of this chapter have previously been published (see Hassink, 2000, 2001). The project was sponsored by the European Union Science and Technology Fellowship Programme Korea.

Chapter 13
Slovenia
A fragmented innovation system?

Knut Koschatzky

System transformation and system building

At the beginning of the 1990s, the central and eastern European countries (CEEC) were suddenly forced to thoroughly transform their political and economic order and to open their economy to the world market. This drastic situation is unique in history. With the transformation process, high expectations arose regarding policy, economy and science. The initial conditions during the 1990s were far from promising. Industrial structures and levels of technological development being ill-adopted to market requirements were the legacy of decades of central planning. Production was inefficiently resource-intensive and quality standards were often low. As a matter of fact, CEECs suffered from a technological gap since the socialist system had hampered flexibility of industries and economic growth.

In this respect, innovation plays an important role in long-term economic success. Process innovation harnesses technological restructuring through introducing new resource-saving techniques into production. Product innovation responding to market needs represents the opportunity for industries to compete in international markets and to survive domestically. The nature of the innovation process and the preconditions differ greatly according to industry sector and company size (e.g. Pavitt, 1984).

Internal resources and co-operation with other actors represent complementary sources of innovation. The ability to innovate and to utilize external, innovation-relevant knowledge depends on the absorptive capacity of a firm (Cohen and Levinthal, 1990: 128). The higher the absorptive capacity, the better firms are able to organize innovation processes. Learning within enterprises can be implemented at different levels (Reid and Garnsey, 1998), whereas learning by interacting between customers and producers, competitors, and other enterprises as well as research establishments substantially affects innovation ability (Lundvall, 1988). Networking is an essential means of knowledge exchange and learning. Networks bring actors, resources and activities together and are thus a specific institutional arrangement. Part of this arrangement are innovation networks. They are understood as all organizational forms between market and hierarchy which serve the purpose of information, knowledge and resource exchange and which help to implement innovation by mutual learning between the network partners (Fritsch *et al.*, 1998).

The importance of spatial and social proximity in learning, the exchange of non-codified knowledge, and in innovation activities and networking is emphazized by the concept of regional innovation systems (RIS). This analyses the regional generation of innovation by incorporating elements from innovation, network, knowledge and transaction costs economics. According to the concept (cf. Braczyk *et al.*, 1998; Cooke *et al.*, 1997; Cooke, 2002), RIS are characterized by the following:

- close networking between firms, universities, research institutes, inter-mediaries, financial organisations and other agencies;
- the existence of a local capital market;
- a certain degree of autonomous public spending competence;
- the responsibility for the extension of classical infrastructural facilities;
- an innovative atmosphere and a learning orientation of firms and the whole population.

Usually, RIS are parts of a national innovation system (Nelson, 1993; Edquist, 1997), although they are not mere copies of the national institutional fabric, but have specific characteristics and functions. According to the given criteria it becomes clear that not all regional entities of a country fulfil the specific conditions of an innovation system. Since new, and in its early stage, implicit knowledge is bound to locations (localized knowledge), those locations which offer a broad range of knowledge producers are considered to be the most advantageous ones by knowledge users (Asheim and Isaksen, 2002). This is particularly true for agglomerations and regions with a diversity of companies and manifold research institutions (Storper, 1995, 1997).

Innovation is also expected to depend strongly on transformation-related and organizational characteristics of firms such as corporate governance structures. Investments in R&D and human capital are crucial determinants of firms' innovation capabilities. Since a linear innovation model according to the Soviet-Leninist science push predominated in CEECs during the socialist period, interactive learning processes and the feedback of users' requirements were either under-developed or non-existent. This was also shown by the high degree of fragmentation which existed between the individual innovation institutions (Dyker and Perrin, 1997; Meske, 1998). These structural characteristics are linked to behaviours and routines which might have outlasted system transformation both in companies and in research institutes, and which now possibly hinder the co-operative organization of innovation processes.

Although external co-operation and networks are praised as sources of innovation also in transition economies, evidence from different CEECs (Grabher and Stark, 1997; Harter, 1997; Radosevic, 2001) shows that many regions (and countries) are still characterized by fragmented innovation systems (cf. Landabaso et al., 2001: 249). This is due to the fact that during the socialist period, horizontal co-operation only had a complementary character. It was mainly used for the acquisition of material resources, but not for the acquisition of knowledge. Since most of the research institutes were and still are thoroughly basic research-oriented, they are not very well qualified to act as co-operation partners for innovation support and market-oriented knowledge exchange with an industrial sector producing at an average technological level.

More than a decade after the start of the reform processes in CEECs, an analysis of their development and innovation potentials has therefore to adopt a new perspective: On the one hand, it can be expected that the legacy of the former economic system still prevails and influences today's innovative performance. On the other, the outcome of the industrial restructuring programmes and their impact on innovation and firms' competitiveness have to be carefully assessed, even if these effects will be fully evident only in the long run. The question is whether pre-conditions do exist for innovative activities in firms, the development of innovation networks and thus for the emergence of regional innovation systems in transition countries, or if socialist history and the succeeding institutional system still hinder the full exploitation of economic, technological and innovative potentials. As one of the CEECs which will be integrated in the European Union, the Republic of Slovenia serves as case study to answer the question whether an innovation systems has already been developed in this country or whether the different innovation actors are still fragmented. Although Slovenia has to be regarded as a national (innovation) system, its small size qualifies it as a good example of a regional system with well-developed and autonomous institutions. Distance within Slovenia plays a minor role compared to larger countries and thus spatial proximity between the different agents in the innovation process might be more pronounced than in other national innovation systems.

Slovenia – institutional background of an accession country

Slovenia is a relatively small economy with 2 million inhabitants covering a surface of 20,256 km^2. The gross national income per capita in 2001 amounted to US$ 9,780, the annual GDP growth rates reached 3.7 per cent during the period 1991–2001, 4.6 per cent in 2000 and 3.0 per cent in 2001 (World Bank, 2002); in 1997, the unemployment rate was 14.4 per cent (IMAD, 1998; Raiser and Sanfey, 1998). The largest towns are Ljubljana and Maribor with 276,000 and 108,000 inhabitants respectively. The country was the strongest developed region in the former Yugoslavia: while it accounted for only 8 per cent of Yugoslavia's surface, 29 per cent of the federal republic's exports originated in Slovenia (European Commission, 1993: 5). Even after its independence in 1991, the small country has remained primarily export-oriented. The collapse of the former Yugoslavia, however, led to a drastic decline in trade. Given the small internal market, integration into international trade relations, especially with western Europe, is very important. Its favourable geographic situation bordering Italy, Austria, Hungary and Croatia as a gateway to other central European and south eastern European countries and the traditional openness of the country facilitate such a strategy. Today, the EU market contributes more than 70 per cent of the Slovenian export volume. Due to the process of economic adaptation, a drop in production was noted in all branches. Economic collapse especially threatened traditional industrial sectors such as steel and heavy machine construction, the automobile industry, and the textile and furniture sector. Although the transition of the industrial sector is not yet complete, the number of business enterprises has obviously grown in the past years, especially in the areas of small enterprises and the service sector.

Slovenia possesses a noticeable research potential. About 52,000 students are enrolled at the universities of Ljubljana and Maribor. As well as these important organizations, the Academy of Science and Arts and approximately fifty other independent research institutes, among which the Jozef Stefan Institute and the National Chemistry Institute are the largest, contribute to research and scientific development in Slovenia. According to figures from the Slovenian statistical office, 7,000 researchers work in Slovenia, of which 43 per cent are teachers at the two universities, 15 per cent are researchers at the government research institutes, 22 per cent are employed by other organizations and 20 per cent work in business research labs (Government of Slovenia, 2000). More than 200 research organizations are active in the business sector and about 180 R&D units can be found in industrial enterprises. As well as these organizations, there are about twenty private foundations promoting education and research, of which the Slovenian Science Foundation is the largest. The share of R&D investments in GDP amounted to 1.5 per cent in 1998 and was planned to reach 1.6 per cent in 2000. Slovenia implements a science and technology policy with a stronger focus on science than on technology. Responsible for most public programmes in this field is the Ministry of Education, Science and Sports, a successor to the former Ministry of Science and Technology. With regard to the different organizations involved in science and technology policy, the institutional fabric looks rather fragmented. Since the Slovenian Innovation Agency, developed by a PHARE project in 1998, has not yet been founded, no clear entry point into the Slovenian innovation support system exists (Stanič et al., 2002).

Despite the different political activities in promoting science and technology, the readiness to co-operate both in the research sector and between science and industry was lacking for a long time. Consequently, the Slovenian research and innovation potential could not be fully utilized (Stanovnik, 1998). Traditional behaviour and an incentive scheme not oriented towards industrial research needs made co-operative ties with industrial clients not very attractive for many of the institutes (Walter and Bross, 1997).

The data used in this analysis come from a postal innovation survey carried out by the Fraunhofer Institute for Systems and Innovation Research (ISI), Karlsruhe, in co-operation with the Institute of Economic Research (IER), Ljubljana, among industrial companies and research institutes, between October 1997 and March 1998.[1] The main aim of the survey was to analyse those linkages among firms and between firms and research institutes which contribute to the realization of innovation. Conventional production chain-based producer–supplier linkages without any reference to innovation were not considered. The sample consists of 416 manufacturing firms from NACE categories 15–37 and 60 research and transfer organizations (cf. Table 13.1). Regarding branch structure and size, the manufacturing sample may be considered a relatively representative image of the Slovenian manufacturing industry; in the research sample, university institutes

Table 13.1 Composition of the industrial and the research sample

NACE	Industrial branch	Total population		Sample	
		Number	(%)	Number	(%)
15, 16	Food, Beverages, Tobacco	118	8.8	33	7.9
17–19	Textiles, Clothing	160	12.0	46	11.1
20–22, 36	Wood, Paper, Printing	293	21.9	79	19.0
23–26	Chemical products, Plastics	194	14.5	54	13.0
27, 28	Metal processing	200	15.0	77	18.5
29, 34, 35, 37	Mechanical engineering, Vehicles	203	15.2	63	15.1
30–33	Electrical and optical equipment	168	12.6	64	15.4
Total		1,336	100.0	416	100.0
Type of research institute					
University institutes		38	30.2	13	21.7
Public research institutes and transfer offices		53	42.1	30	50.0
Other research institutes		35	27.8	17	28.3
Total		126	100.0	60	100.0

Source: ERIS Slovenia

are slightly under-represented compared to the basic population, while public research institutes and transfer offices are slightly over-represented.[2]

Innovation activity in the manufacturing sector

More than three-quarters (76.4 per cent) of Slovenian manufacturing companies in the sample reported product and/or process innovation in the three-year-period from 1994 to 1996.[3] The majority of the Slovenian companies (53.4 per cent) carried out both product and process innovation. This reflects the situation that product innovation often could not be realized without improving firms' outdated technologies. In addition, cost efficiency could not be realized without reducing the high levels of overstaffing prevailing in the former system by introducing new forms of work organization. From the data, the investment in new technologies or new capital goods cannot be traced. A share of 17 per cent of firms carried out product innovation only, 6 per cent process innovation only.

R&D personnel constitutes an important part of the human capital of firms and their innovation potential. A high average share of R&D personnel can be found in the electrical and optical equipment industry (9.9 per cent) and in mechanical engineering and vehicle production (6.9 per cent; cf. Table 13.2). The first two are also among the sectors with highest export share. R&D departments of industrial firms were in many cases absorbed in the everyday operation of running and maintaining technological equipment and have, with very few exceptions, suffered serious financial and personnel cuts (Stanovnik, 1998). Measured as share of R&D expenses of turnover, the R&D intensity is relatively high in the electrical and optical equipment industry with 6.5 per cent on average. R&D intensity is also above average in metal processing (5.2 per cent) and mechanical engineering (4.1 per cent). Surprisingly, companies in the chemical and plastics sector invest only relatively little in R&D with an average share of 2.6 per cent of sales.

In the sample, two-thirds of manufacturing companies reached an R&D intensity up to 3.5 per cent and 20.4 per cent up to 8.5 per cent. The remaining 12.5 per cent can be classified as high-tech companies with an R&D intensity of above 8.5 per cent. A share of 67 per cent of innovating firms carried out development activities permanently, 29 per cent occasionally and only 4 per cent never. Among firms which have not innovated during 1994 until 1996, 17 per cent carried out development work but without attaining results, 43 per cent of non-innovators perform development occasionally and 40 per cent never. On the other hand, research is mainly carried out on an occasional basis (49 per cent of the innovating firms). While innovation consists to a large extent of improvements of existing products and processes, those with a higher degree of novelty and technological advance relying on new technological knowledge amount to the

Table 13.2 Share of R&D personnel and R&D intensity by sector (%)

Sector		R&D intensity (R&D expenses as share of sales)	Share of R&D personnel
Food, Beverages,	Mean	3.8	3.8
Tobacco	Median	2.0	1.7
Textiles,	Mean	2.4	3.7
Clothing	Median	1.0	1.2
Wood, Paper,	Mean	2.0	2.8
Printing	Median	1.0	2.8
Chemical products,	Mean	2.6	4.9
Plastics	Median	2.0	3.8
Metal processing	Mean	5.2	3.9
	Median	2.0	2.1
Mechanical	Mean	4.1	6.9
engineering, vehicles	Median	3.0	4.2
Electrical and	Mean	6.5	9.9
optical equipment	Median	5.0	5.7
Total	Mean	3.8	5.2
	Median	2.0	2.6

Source: ERIS Slovenia

smaller share of all innovations. This underlines the importance of development work for innovative activity.

An indicator of the realization of product innovation is the share of new products in total sales volume.[4] Almost one-third (31 per cent) of companies which have performed product innovation during 1994–96 earned more than 50 per cent of their total sales from the new products. This can be interpreted as a high commercialization success. Another third (33 per cent) earned between 10 per cent and 25 per cent of their turnover from new products. The degree of novelty and the technological content of innovations are indicated by the share of completely new product developments compared to improvements of existing products as a share of all reported product innovations; 42 per cent of firms with product innovation reported that half or more than half of their product innovation were completely new developments. Almost the same share of companies (38 per cent) had completely newly developed less than a quarter of their products, but mainly relied on improvements of existing products.

Table 13.3 Structural characteristics of innovating firms and non-innovators

	Innovating firms (Mean)	Non-innovators (Mean)	T-Test	Non-parametric Test: Kolmogorov-Smirnov-Z
Age	33.3	27.8	1.278	1.073
			(0.203)	(0.200)
Employees 1996	279.0	106.0	*2.538	**2.521
			(0.012)	(0.000)
Sales 1996	24.4	8.4	*2.200	**2.513
(Mio DM)			(0.028)	(0.000)
Sales per employee	92.7	90.4	0.164	1.308
(thousand DM)			(0.870)	(0.065)
R&D personnel	9.7	1.0	**2.785	**4.814
			(0.006)	(0.000)
Share of R&D personnel of	6.3	1.6	**8.319	**4.794
total staff in percent			(0.000)	(0.000)
Share of employees with	7.9	4.0	**2.946	**1.745
university degree in per cent			(0.003)	(0.005)

Notes:
According to the Levene Test the T-Test has been performed assuming unequal variances for age, sales per employee and share of R&D personnel of total staff.
Significance in brackets, with significance on the 1% level ** and significance at the 5% level *.
Source: ERIS Slovenia

Regarding innovating and non-innovating Slovenian manufacturing firms, their main differences are summarized in Table 13.3. As both the T-Test and the non-parametric test confirm, there is a significant difference in the structural variables between innovating firms and non-innovators. Significant differences can be found in number of employees 1996, sales 1996, absolute number of staff employed in R&D, share of R&D personnel and share of employees holding an academic degree.

Innovation linkages of manufacturing firms

According to modern innovation theory, the relation between innovation input and innovation output is rather complex. As well as input factors, the management of the innovation process is of prominent importance. Innovation can be understood as an interactive process between various individuals and departments within the firm but also extending interaction to external co-operation partners. The interactive nature of the innovation process requires the incorporation of market needs right at the beginning of the process and foresees continuous feedback between different stages of the development process (Kline and Rosenberg, 1986). Networks are assumed to facilitate the open exchange of information leading to interactive learning capabilities, the reduction of uncertainty and increase in flexibility to adopt to market changes (Messner, 1995; Fritsch, 2001). Close interactions between suppliers and users are especially effective for product innovations in manufacturing (Andersen and Lundvall, 1988; Koschatzky, 1998; Lundvall, 1992).

Innovation co-operation is a very important information and knowledge resource for Slovenian companies. Of the 416 firms included in the industrial survey, 385 confirmed that their co-operation with at least one partner surpassed normal business relationships in the case of innovation-relevant activities. This is a remarkably high number considering that 318 companies (76.4 per cent of the sample) accomplished product or process innovation between 1994 and 1996. It can therefore be concluded that not all of the cited co-operative relationships are innovation-related contacts, but that 'normal' business relationships were also mentioned especially concerning co-operation with service companies. Therefore, business-related service companies represented the most important co-operation partner; their role was emphasized by 80 per cent of the interviewed companies. Contacts with customers (72 per cent) and suppliers (56 per cent) reflect the importance of networks within the vertical value added chain. Co-operations which are characterized by a high degree of freedom in partner search are distinctly less significant for information and knowledge exchange: 37 per cent of the companies co-operated with research institutes, 27 per cent with other companies. There is hardly any difference between the co-operation behaviour of Slovenian companies and the co-operation patterns identified in other regions by the ERIS survey. In the case of Saxony, for example, co-operation partners were called on in a comparable sequence and with similar frequency (Fritsch *et al.*, 1996: 21).

The significance of vertical co-operation is also shown by the changes which have taken place in external collaboration since 1991; 64 per cent of the companies have increased their contacts with customers and 58 per cent of them have increased their number of suppliers, whereas only 6 per cent and 5 per cent respectively of the firms have reduced their co-operation relationships. This increase shows the changes which have taken place in industrial co-operation since the decline of the socialist economic system. Contacts with business-related service companies have also been intensified, however less strongly, since only 38 per cent of the firms indicated such an increase in co-operation. An interesting fact is that former relationships with universities and industrial research institutes have been broken off since 1991. Whereas 11 per cent of the companies entered new co-operations, 14 per cent of them gave up their contacts. Changes in the originally linear innovation model could have caused the decrease in co-operative behaviour. Industrial research requirements were apparently not always satisfied by the formerly mandatory co-operation relationships, so that discontent has led to a breaking off of former contacts. On the other hand, viewed by the research institutes, co-operation with companies has improved since independence in 1991: this was confirmed by 36.2 per cent of all research institutions. For more than half of them, co-operation has remained the same, and only 12.1 per cent considered it as worse than before. This contradiction might be explained by the fact that the institutes are more optimistic about the impacts of their co-operative relationships with firms than the firms themselves and that the institutes do not have developed sufficient competences to assess the success or failure of their networking with external partners. In addition, the economic transition process also brought with it significant reductions in the companies' R&D budgets, so that research institutes were called upon less often.

A difference in co-operation behaviour is also found between the various branches of the manufacturing industry. It can also be seen in the case of Slovenia that innovating companies show more tendency for co-operation than all companies on average. Whereas, in comparison with the average co-operation frequency, fewer companies in the food processing industry exchanged information and knowledge with their customers (probably due to the high number of final consumers), contacts with suppliers and information exchange with research institutions played an above-average role in this branch. The most intense co-operation with all three of the groups of partners was found in the chemical and plastics industry and the electrical and optical equipment industry (cf. Table 13.4).

Table **13.4** Co-operation partners according to branches

Co-operation partners	Customers		Suppliers		Research institutes	
Branches	all firms	innov. firms	all firms	innov. firms	all firms	innov. firms
Food, Beverages, Tobacco	57.6	66.7	63.4	74.1	42.4	48.1
Textiles, Clothing	71.7	91.2	56.5	67.6	30.4	38.2
Wood, Paper, Printing	63.3	80.4	49.4	62.5	25.3	33.9
Chemical products, Plastics	75.9	88.1	61.1	73.8	50.0	57.1
Metal processing	76.6	92.7	49.4	60.0	31.2	41.8
Mechanical eng., Vehicles	74.6	87.5	55.6	68.8	27.0	33.3
Electrical and optical equipm.	78.1	85.7	62.6	66.1	53.1	57.1
Total	71.9	85.5	55.8	66.7	36.1	44.0

Note: Share of firms in %.
Source: ERIS Slovenia

Both branches also excel with the highest intensity of scientific contacts. In the light of the generally decreasing number of co-operation activities with research organizations, this could point to a demand-oriented research offer for these companies, as well as to a high absorptive capacity due to the high technological standard in these sectors.

Regarding transition-specific aspects in innovation co-operation, the most intensive network connections with partners (in particular with customers) were maintained by Slovenian public enterprises, which is certainly also due to the larger size of these companies. Only gradual differences existed between the remaining types of ownership (social ownership, foreign ownership, private companies with Slovene owners) especially regarding co-operation activities with research institutes. Consequently, the type of ownership did not significantly influence the choice of partners for innovation networking. The most important co-operation shares were shown by companies which were privatized by 1992, whereas a lower degree of co-operation intensity was shown by firms which had only recently been privatized, or which had not yet been privatized at the moment of the survey. This pattern is due to several reasons: competitive companies with intense external co-operation relationships were the first to be privatized; in comparison with companies which were privatized later, they have had more time to establish new contacts and gain experience of innovation networks.

Co-operation pattern of Slovenian research institutes

For the Slovenian research and transfer institutes in the sample, companies from the production and service sector represented the most important co-operation partners (cf. Figure 13.1). 82.5 per cent of the sample institutes co-operated with firms, 80.7 per cent co-operated with other research institutes. These are fairly high shares compared with other regions of the ERIS sample: in the German federal state of Saxony, also a region under transition, 78 per cent of all research institutes covered by the survey co-operated for innovation purposes with firms; in Barcelona it was 71 per cent, in Stockholm 64 per cent and in Vienna 55 per cent (Fritsch and Schwirten, 1998; Revilla Diez, 2000). The successive positions in Slovenia were held by public administration (59.6 per cent), trade associations (49.1 per cent), transfer institutions (43.9 per cent), research organizations which participated in common research programmes promoted by the EC (42.1 per cent), as well as banks and financial institutes (15.8 per cent). As well as contacts with other research organizations, this distribution shows a strong orientation towards the business sector by the Slovenian research institutes, mostly, however, targeting larger companies. While over 70 per cent of the firms with more than 500 employees co-operated with research institutes, less than 20 per cent of those with up to 100 employees had similar contacts. Regarding both knowledge

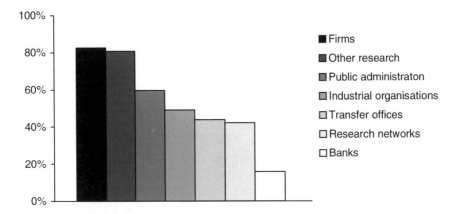

13.1 Co-operation partners of Slovenian research institutes (share of institutes with respective co-operation in %)
Source: ERIS Slovenia

exchange and the financing of universities and national research institutes, the government (public administration) also played an important role.

Distinguishing between university institutes, public R&D organizations or transfer agencies and other, mainly private research institutes, differences become obvious concerning the intensity of co-operation shared with companies and other research organisations (cf. Table 13.5). Although these are not statistically significant due to the small number of cases, they point to the fact that university institutes co-operated less intensely with companies than the other two groups of research institutes. This is partly due to the predominance of the educational role played by universities in the socialist system, so that research capacities had to be improved following the country's independence. The closest co-operation existed between Slovenian university institutes and the public administration (66.7 per cent indicated intense or very intense co-operation), which reveals a close relationship between university research activities and the public sector. In contrast to this, other, mainly private institutes were clearly more oriented towards industry. As far as the mixed group of public R&D and transfer institutes is concerned, they also showed an above-average orientation towards both companies and other research institutions; therefore, they were more intensely embedded in innovation networks with these partners than the other organizations.

The establishment of contact between research institutes and companies can have different aspects. The more relationships are oriented towards the common realization of R&D projects, or the market introduction of new products, the more they must be formal (and reliable). Learning processes can be realized above all in R&D-oriented co-operation due to the fact that not only information is exchanged, but also knowledge and competences. The most important element

Table 13.5 Intensity of research institutes' co-operation with firms and other partners

Type of institute	Co-operation with...					
	Firms		Institutes		Public administration	
	Low	Intensive	Low	Intensive	Low	Intensive
University institute (n=12)	58.3	41.7	50.0	50.0	33.3	66.7
Public research institutes/ transfer office (n=30)	36.7	63.3	40.0	60.0	50.0	50.0
other research institute (n=17)	41.2	58.8	70.6	29.4	76.5	23.5

Note: Shares in %.
Source: ERIS Slovenia

of co-operation is the development of prototypes, on which thirty-eight of the fifty-three institutes (71.7 per cent) worked intensely to very intensely with companies from the industry and service sector. This is reflected by the production-oriented competence by the institutes, attained during the socialist period; many of the institutes had even created their own small production units in order to earn money. Other important aspects of co-operation are conceptual work and the generation of new ideas.

One of the roles of research institutes is to serve as a bridgehead for small and medium-sized companies, whose co-operative behaviour is mostly limited to their regional environment (Feldman, 1994), by providing internationally available information and scientific know-how. In order to accomplish this function, they must have access to international knowledge networks. This points to the spatial reach of co-operation with research institutes in one respect, and with firms in another. Figure 13. 2 shows the numbers of research organisations intensely co-operating with other institutes from Slovenia, from the neighbouring countries of Italy, Croatia, Hungary and Austria, as well as from other European and non-European countries. It is shown that especially the other, non-governmental R&D institutes of the sample are not able to fulfil a science-oriented bridgehead function. Their scientific co-operation is almost exclusively oriented towards Slovenia. Noteworthy international links are non-existent. University and public R&D institutes are subject to different conditions.[5] About 40 per cent of them are integrated into European and world-wide knowledge networks, a share which is fairly similar to those recorded for other ERIS regions: in Barcelona, 46 per cent of scientific co-operations are of international character, in Stockholm 38 per cent and in Vienna 52 per cent (Revilla Diez, 2000). Consequently, these two

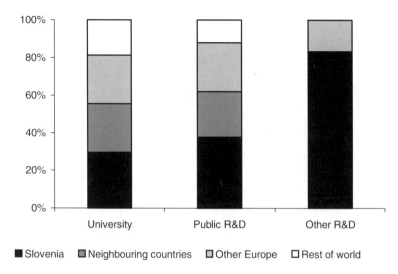

13.2 Spatial pattern of co-operation with other research institutes (share of co-operating institutes in %)
Source: ERIS Slovenia

groups should be able to make international knowledge accessible to companies. On the one hand, university institutes have the potential for these kind of positive network effects; on the other, due to the fact that they co-operate less with firms than the other two groups, this potential is not yet sufficiently known about and made use of by companies.

Regarding co-operation with companies, both university and public research institutes focus on Slovenian co-operation partners (cf. Figure 13.3). This share is approximately 55 per cent for the university institutes and more than 70 per cent for public organizations. Slovenian research institutes are thus closely linked with the national enterprise sector. Similar degrees of domestic innovation-relevant linkages with firms were recorded for the other ERIS regions Barcelona (70 per cent) and Stockholm (67 per cent), while in Saxony only 6 per cent of the university institutes co-operated with industrial firms from outside Germany (Fritsch and Schwirten, 1998; Revilla Diez, 2000). Consequently, not only public institutes but also university institutes fulfil the function of a national bridgehead by providing Slovenian companies with their own knowledge and with knowledge acquired at an international level. On the other hand, it is also possible to conclude that Slovenian university institutes and public research institutes do not represent interesting co-operation partners for many foreign companies, since their services are only called upon in a limited way. Private institutes show different co-operation behaviour; their innovation co-operation with industrial partners has a distinctly more international character. Since they are less integrated in scientific networks,

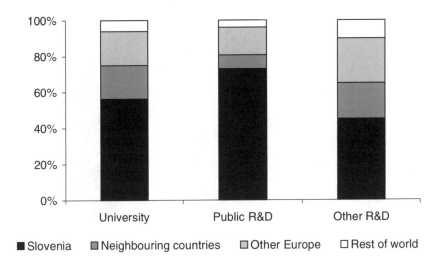

13.3 Spatial pattern of co-operation with companies (share of co-operating institutes in %)
Source: ERIS Slovenia

companies are their most important co-operation partners and their most important sources of knowledge. Innovation-relevant knowledge, which qualifies them as interesting co-operation partners, can be accumulated not only through scientific networking but also through learning processes which are induced by industrial co-operation.

From fragmentation to system integration – a long way to go

According to their self-assessment, an unexpected high share of Slovene manufacturing firms introduced product or process innovation between 1994 and 1996. This high share of innovation reflects the need for reorientation after the loss of traditional markets and for modernization of outdated capital stock and over-staffed organizations. As revealed by the share of sales from product innovation and the share of completely new developments versus incremental improvements, innovation seems to be a success factor for Slovene firms. Specific sectors could be identified according to their above-average performance. Nevertheless, the analyses of the empirical data point to the fact that the Slovenian system transformation has not yet finished, and that not all opportunities for mutual co-operation have been exploited. The most important characteristics of an efficiently functioning regional or national innovation system are the mutual interactions of its constitutional elements (e.g. universities, non-university research institutes, technology transfer agencies, consultants, advanced training institutions, public and private financing institutions, small, medium-sized and large companies and other organizations integrated in innovation processes), as well as their involvement with other innovation systems (Cooke, 1998). If essential elements in the system, such as companies and research organizations, are not involved in mutual interaction, then not only is the system fragmented, but the system denomination itself must be questioned.

According to the data from the manufacturing survey, the chances of common interactive learning processes and of implicit knowledge transfer were not fully utilized, despite a relatively high share of co-operating companies at first glance. Co-operation took place first of all on the level of information exchange and less so on the level of joint research and development. Compared with vertical co-operation, Slovenian industry showed a lack of horizontal linkages with research institutes, which is a typical pattern for all central and eastern European transition countries. Co-operation with foreign research institutes, in particular, was, at least during the time covered by the survey, almost non-existent.

Due to the fact that they co-operate mainly with companies from their own country, the survey among research institutes revealed that the Slovenian institutes are fairly well integrated into the national innovation system. An interesting fact is that even for the generally basic research-oriented university institutes, one of the focal contents of co-operation with companies is the support of market introduction. As already pointed out, integration into global research networks and international industrial networks is indispensable for gaining new knowledge. In this area, at least a partial docking function is assumed by Slovenian research institutes. Since many of them are integrated into international knowledge networks, they fulfil the important function of bridgeheads for scientific and technological knowledge which is available at an international level. These results were not necessarily to be expected in a formerly socialist country. It must be noted, however, that university institutes hold the smallest share of co-operation with companies among the three groups of organizations. When co-operating with companies, they are able to deliver market-related research and transfer services. Nevertheless, the share of these contacts remained below that of the other organizations. It is also clear that particularly larger institutes co-operate with bigger companies; small institutes hardly enter into contact with small companies. In spite of existing co-operation, this points to a fragmentation of the Slovenian innovation system, since all of the innovation agents are not equally integrated in information and knowledge exchange; this is true both of companies and of the research sector.

This fragmentation is supported by several developments within the institutional framework. The Ministry for Science and Technology which was founded in 1991 was in charge of policy-setting, design and implementation of programmes for R&D. Partly because of an influential scientific community, the dominant concept is the financing of academic research. Basic research traditionally absorbs the majority of all budgeted funds for science and technology (Stanovnik, 1998: 101). Although a technological development programme was formulated in 1994, according to which funds for supporting technological developments were expected to grow by 10 per cent per year, severe budget constraints led to a decline of resources for science and technology in recent years. Additionally, the availability of loans or equity to finance innovation is very limited. Banks are rather hesitant and high interest rates often cannot be paid from the profits of research and development projects. There is only an underdeveloped venture capital market in Slovenia (Bross and Walter, 1998).

According to a study by Coopers & Lybrand, commissioned by the European Commission, the major drawbacks of the Slovenian innovation system are (see European Commission, 1999; Špilek, 2000):

- R&D investment is still focused on academic and research and less on the needs of manufacturing enterprises.
- The research system is characterized by rigid institutional structures.
- The contribution of the research system to the Slovenian industry is weak and thus industrial innovation is less pronounced compared to the industrial sector in western countries.
- Priorities of the government for research and innovation are not evident or only vaguely defined.

Many ministries and other funds and agencies have launch programmes to support innovation in industrial enterprises. Due to the fact that the Slovenian innovation agency has not been founded yet, there is no clear entry point into the Slovenian support system. Nevertheless, in 1999 two programmes were implemented which aim at the efficient co-operation between different ministries, development corporations and agencies for supporting innovation in firms. Whether this activity also reduces bureaucratic hurdles in the practical execution of the promotion programmes still remains an open question.

Recently, two projects financed by the European Union should contribute to a better exploitation of the Slovenian innovation potential. The innovation relay centre Slovenia started its activities in July 2002 and tries to enhance the innovative level of the Slovenian industrial sector and its international competitive position (Stanič *et al.*, 2002). The centre is not only integrated in the European IRC network with fifty-eight centres in thirty different countries, but has a national network itself with the Josef Stefan Institute as co-ordinator, the University of Maribor, the Slovenian Chamber of Commerce and Industry, and the Institute of Economic Research as partners. The second activity is the SLORITTS project which started in November 2001. This should increase the innovative activity in

Slovenia through the promotion of co-operation between SMEs, research institutes, public bodies and development agencies. Five objectives are pursued: consensus building around the project's objectives, development of guidelines for one-stop-shop services for SMEs, better exploitation of research and university potentials in the business sector, development of know-how transfer mechanisms in co-operation with the regions of Umbria and Shannon, and provision of a framework for the future use of national and EU funds (ibid.).

These activities are important steps in fostering interregional and international co-operation and networking. Whether these will be successful steps in overcoming the still existing system fragmentation and the legacy of the former socialist system will be shown by the development during the next years. Compared to other successful regions of a similar size to Slovenia, the country still lacks a co-ordinating organization such as the Slovenian innovation agency and an innovation and funding systems which meets the requirements of both research and industry. This demands not only an intensification of networking between research and transfer institutes and the business sector, but also a closer networking between the different ministries and agencies that are involved in the promotion of science, technology and innovation. As long as the internal hurdles are higher than the synergetic effects resulting from co-operation, the Slovenian innovation system remains fragmented and the way to go towards system integration remains long.

Notes

1   This survey was part of the European Regional Innovation Survey (ERIS) carried out in eleven European regions by the department of economic geography at Hanover University, the Chair of Economic Policy at Technical University Bergakademie Freiberg, the Department of Economic and Social Geography at the University of Cologne, and the Fraunhofer Institute for systems and innovation research, Karlsruhe. ERIS was financially supported by the German research council (cf. Koschatzky and Sternberg, 2000, and Sternberg 2000 for a summary of results).

2   For more information about the sample structure, see Koschatzky *et al.* (2001) and Koschatzky (2002).

3   According to this definition a firm is classified as being innovative if it realized innovations within a three-year period. Compared to other surveys asking for innovations within a shorter range of time this might lead to an over-estimation of innovative *activity*, but reflects better the innovative *potential* of the firms under investigation.

4   According to the definition used in the questionnaire, products were classified as new when introduced into the market between 1994 and 1996. It should be

noted that new products might not only be the result of own innovation activity, but can also be purchased by other firms (re-selling).

5   Due to their status, the so-called 'national institutes' benefit from higher basic funding and have good chances of being granted state assistance for projects. In central and eastern European countries these financing sources represent an important pre-condition for the establishment of international co-operation relationships.

Chapter 14
Conclusion
The dilemmas of regional innovation systems

Martin Heidenreich

Regional innovation systems were initially defined as 'interacting knowledge generation and exploitation sub-systems linked to global, national and other regional systems for commercialising new knowledge'. In the preceding chapters, authors from all over the world have analysed thirteen European, Asian and American regions in order to put flesh on the notion of knowledge-generating and exploiting sub-systems. Our central thesis in this concluding chapter is that knowledge-generation in regional innovation systems is always faced with various different types of dilemmas and that the strength of regional innovation systems does not depend on a specific set of institutions, technologies, and firms, but on the ability to face the numerous dilemmas connected to territorially bounded production and innovation processes. These problems reflect the fundamental dilemma of innovation: satisficing (even if not optimal) results can be obtained with previous routines, products, technologies, and institutions, while new routines, products, technologies, and institutions require extraordinary investments and the outcomes remain uncertain.

To summarize some of the lessons we can extract from our case studies, we will first condense the basic features of the thirteen regions previously described. We will then reconstruct four dilemmas territorially bounded innovations are confronted with. Then, on the basis of the initially introduced three concepts of regional governance (grassroots, networks and *dirigiste* RIS), we will distinguish different ways of dealing with these dilemmas.

Basic characteristics of institutional regional innovation systems

In the introduction two different types of regional innovation systems were distinguished: entrepreneurial and institutional regional innovation systems. These concepts reflect the distinction between entrepreneurial and institutionalised technological regimes proposed by Winter (1984) and Audretsch (1994). Most of the regions previously analysed can be classified as institutional regional innovation systems (IRIS) – with the partial exception of Tuscany, Denmark and Singapore. Industrialized regions like Ontario, Wales, Baden-

Württemberg, North Rhine-Westphalia, Tohoku, Brabant, Catalonia, Tampere/ Pirkanmaa, Gyeonggi and Slovenia are characterised by the following features (see also the Appendix):

- an industrial structure with a strong position of low and medium technology, in general, quite developed production-related services, but only a small share of high-tech production;
- a governance structure which is dominated by formal, in general public institutions (especially in the fields of research, technology transfer, education and training, and marketing in foreign markets). These institutions are in general integrated in the political and administrative context of the national innovation system – even if they are in a legal and operational sense autonomous from the national level.
- a business structure characterised by the important role of multinational companies which are in different ways and to a varying extent integrated into regional production networks.

These regions are often the industrial core regions of their respective countries; this is especially true for Ontario, Gyeonggi, North Brabant, Baden-Württemberg, North Rhine-Westphalia, Catalonia and Tampere.

This type of national or European industrial core region differs from the industrial or service-oriented business districts dominated by small and medium-sized enterprises (SME) in Denmark or Tuscany. Other types of economic regions not represented in our sample are the destroyed industrial regions (for example, in Eastern Germany) and the metropolitan design, research, communication and culture-based service regions which have been described as global or regional cities (Sassen, 2000; Simmie *et al.*, 2002). Most of the regions previously analysed cannot hope to develop a value chain which is predominantly based on services (public relations, finance, advertising, controlling, consulting, mass media). Production is an essential feature of their economic model, which provides an explanation for the relative stability and even inertia of these regions. Huge investments in production facilities and the mastery of specific technologies hamper radical innovations as these innovations would destroy most of the former investments and qualifications. Perhaps Stuttgart, Cardiff, Eindhoven and Barcelona may have the possibility to specialise mainly in advanced services – but Baden-Württemberg, Wales, Southeast North Brabant or Catalonia will not become a new Silicon Valley, a financial district like the City of London or a global media city such as Paris or Munich. Most of the regions we have analysed are bound to their industrial heritage – and they have to face the challenges of a globalised, innovation-centred knowledge economy on this basis, with their specific limitations and opportunities:

- A crucial problem of all the IRIS regions is the systematic discrepancy between research and innovation. This has explicitly been reported in the chapters on the RIS in Ontario, Catalonia, Baden-Württemberg. Only in Baden-Württemberg, where R&D expenditures are extremely high (1999: 3.9 per cent of the GDP, more than double the European level), was it possible to employ 17.8 per cent of the employees in the production of high and medium-high technologies. In the other European regions this percentage is below 10 per cent (see Appendix).

- Only a minority of regions (especially Singapore, Denmark and Wales) has a strong position in knowledge-intensive services (telecommunication, financial services, education, health, culture). This also points to the legacy of a successful industrial past.

- The potential vulnerability of the regions is a direct consequence of the dependency of large firms which are the entrepreneurial backbone in many of the regional innovation systems analysed in the preceding chapters (Philips, NedCar, DAF, ASML, Océ and Rank Xerox in Southeast Brabant, DaimlerChrysler and Bosch in Baden-Württemberg, Bayer, RWE, Bertelsmann or Thyssen-Krupp in North Rhine-Westphalia, the US, Japanese and European automotive companies in Ontario and Wales, Nokia in the Tampere region). These multinational companies have in principle the opportunity to choose their production sites world-wide with the best mix of production costs, subsidies, and qualifications – possibly leading to delocalisation decisions (see the examples of Tohoku and Wales). And even if the central firms in general do not decide to relocate their production (Dunning, 2000), the regional employment level is directly influenced both by the negative or positive development of these firms and by changing supply strategies (see, for example, the case studies on Brabant and Baden-Württemberg).

- The high mobility of firms, plants, and supplier relations is not matched by a similar flexibility in regional capabilities. The capabilities of a region are anchored in its organisational capabilities (in its firms, its industrial structure, and its patterns of specialisation) and in its governance structure (Crouch *et al.*, 2001). These governance structures are the institutional 'memory' of a region, the result of path-dependent experiences of co-operation and conflict (North, 1990; Crouch and Farrell, 2002). They have been described as *conventions* (Storper, 1997). The relative stability of these conventions and their path-dependent development was comprehensively described in the first edition of this book (Braczyk and Heidenreich, 1998).

The regions described in the preceding chapters are, therefore, trapped in a dilemma which reflects their specific position in a globalised, innovation-centred knowledge economy: on the one hand, they are often the most innovative regions of their respective nations. They are characterised by good or excellent research and development facilities and a qualified labour force. On the other hand, even a high, in general public engagement in the production of regional 'collective competition goods' (Le Galès and Voelzkow, 2001) is no guarantee for an uncontested position in the global economy. Investments in education and training, research and development, technology transfer and marketing will not automatically 'produce' innovations. They are not entrepreneurial regions as they are lacking a sufficient number of SMEs and creative entrepreneurs in new technological fields. The uncertainties and fragility of the chosen paths of specialisation appear in the form of relocation decisions of firms, mergers, plant closures, external sourcing, and corresponding reductions at the employment level. These risks have become much clearer since the first edition of this book. The promises of a new economy where IT, multimedia, biotechnology, and advanced services could guarantee a similarly uncontested competitive position similar to the post-war period of predominantly national capitalisms have largely been disappointed.

Therefore, the preceding chapters focus much stronger than in the first edition on the risks of the chosen specialisation: Gertler and Wolfe conclude that 'the strong tradition of foreign ownership and reliance on imported technology has meant that Ontario's innovative capacity remains underdeveloped'. Boekholt and de Jager mention 'overlaps and fragmentations of efforts' in the case of Southeast Brabant; Koschatzky 'points to a fragmentation of the Slovenian innovation system, since all of the innovation agents are not equally integrated in information and knowledge exchange'; Cooke demonstrates that the innovation capability of Wales could not upgrade because the links between the mainly public innovation infrastructure and the new, foreign industrial basis has proved to be too weak; Heidenreich and Krauss refer to the fragile bases of the automotive boom of the 1990s which in a short-term perspective helped to overcome the crisis at the beginning of the 1990s, but which once again intensifies the specialisation on the car industry; Bacaria, Borràs and Fernàndez-Ribas point to a 'gap between scientific research done at universities and public research units, on the one hand, and technological innovation at firms, on the other'; Hilbert *et al.* point to the necessity of encouraging existing firms in North Rhine-Westphalia to shift to new businesses.

These diagnoses illustrate major challenges institutional regional innovation systems are facing: the bridging of the gap between R&D and innovation, between global and local knowledge, between established industrial strengths and new technological trajectories, between successful global companies and a diversified industrial structure of innovative SMEs. In the following, these challenges will be analysed on a slightly more general basis.

Regional innovation processes between opening and closure

Regional innovation systems are 'places where close inter-firm communication, socio-cultural structures and institutional environment may stimulate socially and territorially embedded collective learning and continuous innovation (Asheim and Isaksen, 2002: 83). Similar to the notion of a conservative innovator or a learning organisation, this concept is an oxymoron expressing two antithetical processes (Weick and Westley, 1996). While the system concept stresses the role of stable regional orders, the concept of innovation emphasises the process of creative destruction (Schumpeter 1935). The corresponding dilemma is not specificity of regional innovation systems but reflects the uncertainty, the openness, and the risks of innovation processes.

The concept of innovation refers to 'the transformation of an idea into a marketable product or service, a new or improved manufacturing or distribution process, or a new method of social service' (European Commission, 1995: 4). Innovations in this sense always have to be pushed through against resistance, for example, the inertia or the opposition of the successful businesses. This was emphasised by Schumpeter, who defined the enforcement of innovation to be the central function of a charismatic entrepreneur. The achievement of an entrepreneur does not consist in the invention or the development of a new technology but in the enforcement of a new production function. The entrepreneur succeeds in overcoming insecurity and resistances. He/she is not necessarily a successful researcher or an inventor but 'the revolutionary of the economy – and the involuntary pioneer of social and political revolution' (Schumpeter, 1935: 130).

This positive appraisal of innovation ignores the dilemmas each innovator is confronted with. On the one hand, innovations are risky, with mostly high costs, results remain uncertain. On the other, previous investments, competences, habits, and qualifications are devalued by innovation. The benefits of innovations and the risks of omitted innovations, therefore, always have to be balanced against the costs of successful innovation and the benefits of omitted innovations. Hence, from an individualistic and short-term perspective, resistance against innovation may often be quite rational. This dilemma can also be formulated as a dilemma between redundancy ('slack') and specialisation/efficiency (Crouch and Farrell, 2002: 20–21).

Additionally, successful innovations are often a barrier to further innovation: not only is the better the enemy of the good. This also holds true vice versa. Stabilisation of successful innovation is a necessary prerequisite for each innovation process. In evolutionary theories of innovation (Nelson and Winter, 1982; David, 1985; Dosi 1988), the contradictory unity of innovation and institutionalisation is taken into account by the distinction of variation and stabilisation phases. Tushman and Rosenberg (1992), for example, distinguish four different phases of technological innovation: technological discontinuities, eras of ferment, dominant designs, and eras of incremental change. In opposition to this temporal differentiation, innovation system approaches distinguish between learning and knowledge, on the one hand, and institutions on the other without being able to precisely specify the connection between institutions and innovations:[1] How can relatively stable regional orders contribute to innovation? What are the crucial features of the relationship between variety and redundancy in the case of regional innovation systems?

The described dilemmas are familiar to innovation theories (cf. for example for the organisational level, Zaltman *et al.*, 1973; Rammert, 1988; Hage and Hollingsworth, 2000: 978). Also, in the debate on national and regional innovation systems several of these dilemmas have been mentioned: On the one hand, it has been emphasised that networks can be a central prerequisite for innovations. On the other, it has been observed that corporations have the power to block innovations due to lock-in-effects (cf. Grabher, 1993; Fritsch, 2001). Also, emphasis has been put on the importance of regional processes of closure; but contrariwise, it has been stressed that the performance of regional innovation systems essentially depends on a global exploitation of new opportunities (Amin and Thrift, 1994). On the one hand, industrial districts have been defined by their local communities; on the other, Piore and Sabel (1984) have stressed that they are based on competition between co-operating businesses. Very often, however, these dilemmas of innovation and innovation systems have also been ignored. There were attempts to identify a suitable bundle of factors representing the necessary and sufficient conditions for the success of regional innovation systems. Strong regional identities, collective goods, network moderators, transaction-cost saving network, and an adequate design of the innovation-supporting infrastructure should do the trick.

Controversially, in the following we will develop an opposing idea. *We suppose that the capability of regional innovation systems is to be sought in the ability to deal with the contradictory challenges and dilemmas of regionally concentrated innovation processes.* There is no universally applicable set of innovation-conducive institutions or a magic formula for regional competitiveness but only the ability to handle the contradictions and conflicting goals of regional innovation processes. In order to develop this thesis, we will now discuss four dilemmas of regionally concentrated innovation processes. These dilemmas refer to the spatial, social, material, and temporal dimension of these processes; they specify the initially mentioned tension between innovation and institutionalisation, or, put in more broadly terms, the dilemma between opening and closure. In this respect, the concept of 'opening' refers to spatial, cognitive, and institutional boundary-spanning processes in science, economy, technology, and organisations; processes of social closure, on the other hand, describe new spatial, cognitive, and institutional forms of regulation and limitation.

Regional economic structures between regionalisation and globalisation

In the spatial dimension, the dilemma of opening and closure is represented by the tension between globalisation and regionalisation. On the one hand, the knowledge society is characterised by the disembedding of social relationships from their local context of interaction (Giddens, 1990). For the regionally embedded company this can result into the need to look for suppliers outside its home region. Concerning the regional market, this development can lead to a loss of its role as pilot market as well as to increased competition with companies from all over the world. The exodus of important suppliers, customers, and competitors can result in the destruction of regional networks:

> Globalisation can thus be defined as the intensification of worldwide social relations which link distant localities in such a way that local happenings are shaped by events occurring many miles away and vice versa ... Local transformation is as much a part of globalisation as the lateral extension of social connections across time and space ... what happens in a local neighbourhood is likely to be influenced by factors – such as world money and commodity markets – operating at an indefinite distance away from that neighbourhood itself.
>
> (Giddens, 1990: 64)

Consequently, the success of regional networks increasingly depends on their ability to become a nodal point in national and supranational information, communication, investment, and production flows. The relatively closed industrial districts described by Marshall belong to the past (Amin and Thrift, 1992).

Simultaneously, the globalisation of economic exchanges does not imply that geographic proximity loses its importance. On the contrary: regional, location-specific factors become even more important in the context of world-wide competition based on costs and innovativeness. This is proved by an increasingly regional differentiation of production and technological capabilities (Archibugi *et al.*, 1999). While technological and scientific knowledge is produced on a world-wide basis, increasingly implicit, applied knowledge and experience in particular play a role in the most innovative regions of the world. While by means of world-wide information, communication, and transportation facilities spatial distances are increasingly losing their importance, nevertheless, the economic success of industrial and metropolitan business districts points to the key role of spatial proximity and personal communication. While even SMEs more frequently use world-wide development, production, and distribution structures, the core competences of businesses as well as the strategic suppliers and customers are nevertheless still concentrated in a region (Archibugi and Michie, 1995; Patel and Pavitt, 1998). Regional capabilities build precisely on the regional use of world-wide information, innovation, and market chances. '[I]ndustrial districts or innovative milieus are compelled to integrate extra-regional contributions as an essential component of the regional innovation process itself' (Gordon, 1995: 195).

The dilemma of regionalisation and globalisation determines the relationship between dominant, globally oriented groups and smaller companies oriented towards regional and national markets. The insertion of regional economies into world-wide information, trade, and investment flows is effected by multinational, in general, bigger companies. Despite decreasing communication, co-ordination and transportation costs, the degree of internationalisation is still linked to the size of an organisation. This becomes problematic if the entire technological knowledge of a region is concentrated in these focal companies while the innovativeness of other regional companies remains extremely limited. Also vertical co-operation networks, i.e. predominantly supplier relationships, can become an obstacle to learning and innovation as the economic fate of a region is closely linked to a specific technology, a specific product or even to a specific company, such as the case in Wales and Tohoku. Also in Brabant, Baden-Württemberg and Ontario the economic structure of the region is dominated by a few focal companies and their plants and suppliers. A more diversified business structure with horizontal networks, such as in Tuscany, Denmark and Catalonia, is also favourable for focal firms. This especially holds true if these are engaged in the development and production of complex products bringing about a dependency on close development and production networks with smaller firms.

Regional networks between fragility, regional learning and lock-in-effects

In the social dimension, the dilemma of opening and closure shapes regional co-operation networks. Due to interorganisational mobility of employees, different forms of 'network moderators', and intensive social and professional contacts regional co-operation relationships can facilitate the exchange of information between potential competitors (Powell *et al.*, 1996). The learning and innovation opportunities connected to spatial proximity represent a crucial condition for the advancement of the basis of regional competence.

However, the contribution of co-operation networks to regional innovativeness is put at risk by lock-in-effects of established networks, on the one hand, and, on the other, by individualistic business strategies. In this respect, for instance Chesbrough and Teece (1996: 68) stress that the stability of interorganisational forms of co-operation is always endangered by changing and potentially diverging interests of companies:

Each company wants the other to do more, while each is also looking for ways to realize the most gain from the innovation. Information sharing can be reduced or biased, as each seeks to get the most at the other's expense. In most cases, the open exchange of information that fuels systemic innovation will be easier and safer within a company than across company boundaries. The inevitable conflicts and choices that arise as a systemic innovation develops can best be resolved by an integrated company's internal management processes.

Interorganisational networks, therefore, always have to be stabilised by *regional orders*. These orders can be defined as ensembles of institutionalised expectations, routines, and methods which shape the organisational, economic, technical, scientific, and political relationships in a region (cf. for a similar concept, the concept of 'worlds of production' Salais and Storper, 1993). These patterns encompass both formalised expectations (rules, laws) and informal habits, methods, and cultural frames and perceptions (Scott, 1998: 107–114; Crouch and Trigilia, 2001: 224–229). These informal patterns have additionally been defined by Storper (1997: 38) as conventions, as 'taken-for-granted mutually coherent expectations, routines, and practices'.

Regional orders can contribute to the capability of regional innovation systems in two different ways: they can reduce the uncertainties, risks, and ambiguities always linked to innovations. Regional unions and associations, regional schools and training facilities, informal contacts and networks each contribute to the production of certainties. This cognitive function of regional networks has already been stressed by the so-called Californian school of new regional economics (cf. Storper, 1997: 9–14) – even if here the reduction of uncertainties was analysed exclusively under the perspective of reducing transaction costs:

> Culture formation depends on (though is certainly not fully explained by) a structure of transactions ... the greater the substantive complexity, irregularity, uncertainty, unpredictability and uncodifiability of transactions, the greater their sensitivity to geographical distance. In all these circumstances, the cost of covering distance will rise dramatically.
>
> (Storper and Scott, 1995: 506)

However, the availability of information on new technologies and markets, qualifications as well as subventions is not only a problem of costs. Innovative companies are facing considerable uncertainties concerning their future strategies – these uncertainties may be reduced by close and intensive contacts with other regional companies as well as by the production for regional pilot clients. This cognitive function of regional orders – the creation of subjective certainties in order to facilitate action – is equivalent to *trust* (Lane and Bachman, 1998). The (perceived) risks of innovation are reduced by the use of regional experiences, information, methods, and certainties. Simultaneously, however, such cognitive lock-in-processes are always risky: they not only facilitate collective rules of interpretation and appropriateness of innovation, they also enable the continuation of previous paths and blindness to new challenges.

On the other hand, by means of providing 'local collective competition goods' (Crouch *et al.*, 2001), regional orders can also help to overcome the problems of collective action and interorganisational co-operation as regional institutions provide necessary resources required for innovation (public research and development facilities, technology transfer, education and training). By establishing collective rules of interpretation and behaviour and by providing collective resources, regional orders make an essential contribution to the innovative potential of regional companies.

Such processes of cognitive and political closure can facilitate co-operation between regional actors, links between different cognitive arenas (Hage and Hollingsworth, 2000) and the discovery of new paths of action. However, regional networks can also contribute to blindness to new challenges and opportunities. In addition, collective resources (for example, subsidies) can delay adaptation. In order to prevent a devaluation of previous competences and investments, accumulated experiences and knowledge can impede the search for new strategies (see Grabher, 1993). The dilemma of social opening and closure is, therefore, translated into the tension between fragility of interorganisational patterns of co-operation, regional learning, and regional lock-in-effects.

Regional research, development and technology transfer institutions between learning and institutionalisation

In the substantive dimension, the tension between closure and opening is materialised in the tension between normatively stylised, and knowledge-based innovation systems. These two types of innovation systems are characterised by different forms of structural coupling among social subsystems. In the first case – which has initially been termed Institutional Regional Innovation System (IRIS) – knowledge-based subsystems are closely coupled with social systems favouring stable, predictable paths of innovation. In the second case – introduced as Entrepreneurial Regional Innovation System (ERIS) – closely coupled knowledge-based subsystems favour science- or technology-driven innovations.

In both cases, systematic, permanent inconsistencies between science, technology, economy, politics, and the public has been institutionalised. The different social systems (science, technology, economy, politics) do not follow only their own logic as assumed in an ideal-typical model of a modern, functionally differentiated society: Science is not only engaged in the falsification of propositions, economy not only in the reproduction of liquidity, technology not only in the construction of working artefacts, politics not only in the production of collectively binding rules because these systems also take into account their different perspectives and logics. Innovation systems require the closer coupling of economic, technological, scientific, and political perspectives; innovations are facilitated by relatively stable interactions between scientific, economic, technical, and political perspectives. Based on the work of the systems theoretician Niklas Luhmann, two forms of such a structural coupling can be distinguished, namely, knowledge-based and normatively based forms. Luhmann (1994) defines knowledge as cognitive expectations which are ready to be disappointed and revised if disproved by contradicting evidence. Knowledge is, therefore, characterised by a cognitive style; the social systems represented by these expectations are prepared to learn. Normatively based expectations, however, are not revised even if they are disappointed. While the economy and science are characterised primarily through knowledge-based forms of expectation, politics, administration, and jurisdiction are dominated by normatively stylised expectations (Luhmann, 1975).

Both in knowledge-based and normatively stylised innovation systems, innovative individuals, organisations and networks are coupled with social institutions. In normatively coupled innovation systems, calculability and stability are much more important than the revision of disappointed expectations. This refers to a dominance of normatively stylised subsystems. Scientific discoveries and technical inventions can be converted into economically relevant innovations only when political, legal, social, and cultural points of view are taken into consideration, for example, in the context of a 'co-ordinated market economy' (Hall and Soskice, 2001). Innovative companies are closely coupled with other social spheres, especially with research, technology transfer, unions, business associations, schools, banks, the labour law, and politics. This facilitates the design and incremental improvement of complex technical systems, for example, cars, machinery, chemistry, and other investment goods. The requests of the environment are interpreted as requests for reliable, calculable, long-term oriented decisions; the long-term accumulation of organisational and technical knowledge is more important than the short-term maximisation of shareholder-value. Such innovation systems are characterised by path dependency and inertia.

Instead, in knowledge-based innovation systems, established interests and regulation structures have to be less considered (Cooke, 2002). The readiness to learn is more important than calculability. The innovation strategies of firms are restricted less by legal, political, ethical, and social considerations; they are more closely coupled with economic, scientific, and technical perspectives.

This *dilemma between fragmented, knowledge-based and normatively regulated innovation systems* also shapes the tension between publicly financed research, development, and technology transfer infrastructure, and technological innovation. While explicit knowledge is in general crucial for the advancement of sciences, technological knowledge is to a great extent implicit; it is applied knowledge (see Faulkner, 1994): 'A significant amount of innovations and improvements are originated through "learning-by-doing" and "learning-by-using"' (Dosi, 1988: 223). The knowledge required for the development, construction, and implementation of new technologies cannot be reduced to scientific discoveries: 'Technological knowledge is much less well articulated than is scientific knowledge; much of it is not written down and is implicit in "experience", skills, etc.' (Dosi, 1982: 153). Without rules of thumb, practical experiences, proved design, and construction principles technologies can hardly be developed. Additionally, the development of new technologies and procedures requires the recombination of specific knowledge from different sources, consumers and clients, technology and science, and law and politics. In this respect, technological innovations are considerably facilitated by the structural coupling of technical, economic, scientific, political, and cultural subsystems.

Regional research, development, and technology transfer institutions can, therefore, be distinguished according to the different forms of structural coupling. In knowledge-based orders this coupling increases the learning capacities of the involved subsystems; in normatively stylised orders the coherence and calculability of regional innovation processes are more important.

Regional economic policy between previous strengths and new technological fields

In the temporal dimension, regional innovation systems are characterised by the tension between previous strengths and new technological fields. The success of an RIS depends both on the development of previous strengths and technological trajectories and on openings for new developments and chances. In this respect, regions face the dilemma of being especially successful in a short-term perspective if the innovation supporting institutional infrastructure (education and research, investment systems, technology transfer, industrial policy) is optimally adjusted to dominant industrial clusters (cf. the example of Baden-Württemberg). This, however, may impede positioning in new technological fields (information and communication technologies, biotechnology, new materials) and the recombination of previous knowledge (micro system technology, nanotechnology, optoelectronics, mechatronics). While the existing technological and organisational patterns of specialisation must be supported by regional institutions, new technological fields can only be reached if the region and its firms and institutions open up to new perspectives, co-operation partners, and technologies. This, however, is equivalent to a suboptimal adaptation to existing core sectors.

This dilemma of redundancy and variety arises from the cumulative character and the path-dependency of regional and technological development (Dosi, 1982; Edquist, 1997; Braczyk and Heidenreich, 1998). Regional and technological learning are cumulative processes. Experiences and practical knowledge accumulated in the course of the development and utilisation of a technology also outline the further development of a region. Such technological path-dependencies cannot be easily broken up by industrial policies. Singapore, for example, was only able to gain its top position as South-east Asia's service and logistics centre after the development of industrial competences in the petro-chemical, electrical engineering and electronics industries. Regional trajectories, therefore, refer to the competences, methods, problem definitions, and technologies found in a region. These regional knowledge assets, deeply rooted in the rules and routines of regional employees and firms, are transmitted and further developed in regional networks. It is therefore difficult to establish a new Silicon Valley if there is already a successful and innovative one.

The dilemma between previous strengths and new technological paths also shapes regional economic policy. On the one hand, regional policies can focus on previous and present strengths. The competences and networks developed in the course of decades of industrial experience are the strengths of a region. Additionally, new economic strengths like production-related services can be developed on the basis of already existing competences. This can be done by cluster policies which stimulate and support the emergence of 'networks of production of strongly interdependent firms (including specialised suppliers), knowledge producing agents (universities, research institutes, engineering companies), bridging institutions (brokers, consultants), and customers linked to each other in a value-adding production chain' (Boekholt and Thuriaux, 1999: 381). Simultaneously, however, the development of regional competences requires their diversification by supporting newly founded firms and SMEs outside established networks as well as lines of technological specialisation.

In conclusion: innovation processes are always accompanied by dilemmas due to the liability of newness and the advantages of omitted innovations. They are shaped by the tension between the advantageous exploitation of previous technologies and products and the preservation of sunk investments as well as the uncertainties of new technologies, product specialisations, institutions, markets, and procedures. In the case of regional innovation systems, this dilemma brings about a tension between spatial, social, substantial and temporal dimensions of processes of opening and closure. In the spatial dimension, it refers to the tension between globalisation and regionalisation. The social dimension is characterised by the tension between the openness of global developments and relations and the stabilising lock-in-effects of regional networks. Concerning the substantive dimension, this is illustrated by the tension between knowledge-based and normative forms of structural coupling. Finally, referring to the temporal dimension, this dilemma emerges in the tension between the continuation of previous technological development paths and the assertion in new technological fields. These four dilemmas shape regional economic structures, regional patterns of co-operation, the innovation-supporting infrastructure (research, development, and technology transfer) as well as economic policies.

Facing the dilemmas of regional innovation systems

In this section, we will discuss how the former-mentioned spatial, social, substantive, and temporal dimensions of the innovation dilemma shape the innovation systems in the 13 regions previously analysed. We concentrate on the question how these four dilemmas shape regional economic structure, patterns of co-operation, regional research, development, and technology transfer infrastructure, as well as regional economic policy. Referring to the three types of structure of regional governance Cooke has initially distinguished (grassroots, network and *dirigiste* RIS), we will reconstruct the different forms these dilemmas assume in the following. The results of this analysis are summarised in Table 14.1. The supporting statistical indicators to the analysis are put together in the Appendix tables.

The dilemmas of informal and market-driven forms of co-ordination

Grassroots RISs are characterised by flexible interorganisational networks between mostly SMEs, which are connected to the global market by a number of major global companies. An example of this pattern is provided by California, where the economic structure is marked by a multiplicity of local economic districts – for example in the area of jewellery, furniture, automobile design, entertainment, computers, biotechnology, and multimedia – and some world-wide successful companies.

On the contrary, the industrial districts in the Tuscany region have chosen a different, very particular way of dealing with the dilemma of regionalisation and globalisation. Unlike California and most other regions of the world these districts are not dominated by large focal companies connecting the regional economic structure with the world market. Additionally, the generally very small companies in Tuscany region are not bought by external bigger competitors. The 'more conscious and planned form of integration' usually associated with bigger businesses is replaced by more or less strongly formalised co-operation networks ('enterprise groups'). The integration into global markets, therefore, does not require the abolition of essential features of Italian industrial districts.

Table 14.1 Dilemmas of regional innovation systems

Regional governance	Regions	Regional economic structures between regionalisation and globalisation	Regional networks between fragmentation, regional learning and lock-in effects	Regional research, development and technology transfer institutions between learning and institutionalisation	Regional economic policy between previous strengths and new technological fields
Grassroots	Tuscany, Ontario, Brabant, Catalonia	Between focal companies (global player) and regional diversity	Between flexibility ('fierce individualism') and institutionally stabilised co-operation	Between applied development and systematic research activities	Between previous strengths and new technological fields
Network	Tampere, Denmark Baden-Württemberg, North Rhine-Westphalia, Wales	Successful global companies and innovative SMEs. Two partially contradicting conditions for regional competitiveness	Danger of institutional lock-in-effects	Marginal returns of high R&D expenditures in established technological fields	Between the general public support of a knowledge infrastructure and differentiated (cluster) policies
Dirigiste	Slovenia, Tohoku, Gyeonggi, Singapore	Between publicly subsidised new plants and the internal development of regional competences	Fragmentation; low impact of inter-organisational networks	Decoupling of national R&D agencies and private companies	Between an unified national industrial policy and first steps to decentralisation

The Canadian way of dealing with the dilemma of globalisation and regionalisation is much more widely spread than the Tuscan way. According to Gertler and Wolfe, the economic structure of Ontario is heavily shaped by US and Japanese automobile companies. The most important conditions for the location of these plants were proximity to an attractive market, relatively low labour costs, as well as different forms of political support. Concisely, it was possible to integrate foreign plants into the network of regional suppliers. Nevertheless, the development of an autonomous regional basis for innovation only succeeded partially as research and development capacities are still mainly concentrated in the home country of the foreign groups.

In this respect, in this region the dilemma of globalisation and regionalisation emerges in a latent threat to the regional economic structure: Either the focal companies are no longer able to face the pressures of the international competition or – due to an increasing attractiveness of other regions – they decide to relocate their production, their supplier contracts or their research facilities to other locations. This risk is reduced by the strong position of the smaller companies which seems to be a characteristic feature of grassroots regions.

The second dilemma refers to the question of which collective goods are produced by regional co-operation networks and how these networks can be stabilised. The 'enterprise groups' described by Dei Ottati in Tuscany are an impressive example of such co-operation structures. Design, marketing, product innovation, and production are distributed among different firms of the groups which are mainly integrated by personal ties, supplier relationships or capital links. However, this model of a decentralised, self-organised co-operation also reaches limits. More strongly institutionalised forms of co-operation are required. Dei Ottati emphasises (p. 39):

> Effective collective action is required for the accelerated renewal and upgrading of localized knowledge ... the increased speed and variety of innovations call for the injection and wide diffusion of new, partially heterogeneous, skills; but such a need, especially in a system of small and medium-sized firms, can be met only by some form of collective provision.

In Ontario, multipurpose centres exist in two subregions, namely in Ottawa and in Waterloo (cf. the descriptions of the Ottawa Centre for Research and Innovation (OCRI) and Communitech in Chapter 4). But even in Ontario the existence of institutionally stabilised patterns of co-operation is rather an exception than the rule. In general, interorganisational patterns of co-operation are shaped by 'fierce individualism and entrepreneurialism'.

In grassroots regions, therefore, dynamic SMEs operate in a field of tension between individual initiatives and institutionally stabilised forms of co-operation.

Their success is based on their initiative and their entrepreneurial commitment. In an innovation-centred economy, however, the exploitation of new possibilities increasingly depends on the co-operation and exchange of information with other firms in order to develop new products and to open up new, especially foreign markets. Such arenas of interorganisational learning can be stabilised only to a certain extent by personal relationships and hierarchies of reputation. Often public institutions are required in order to put intercompany relationships on a permanent basis (see, for example, the detailed analysis of owners' organisations, clubs und Chambers of Commerce in the Catalonian example). The co-operation dilemma of grassroots regions can, hence, be characterised as tension between individualised entrepreneurialism and institutionalised learning.

The tension between applied, highly specific development activities and more broadly oriented and systematic research refers to a third dilemma of grassroots regions. In this respect, Bacaria *et al.* illustrate the important role of applied research in the Catalonian innovation system. At the same time, this orientation is accompanied by a 'lack of relational linkages between Catalan innovators in some pro-patenting sectors'. In particular, the flexible SMEs of this region can hardly profit from public research activities. Considerable innovation activities such as their 'learning capacity' in new technological fields prove to be too weak. As a result, the strong role of applied research reveals itself to be a barrier to the link with more systematic research and development activities.

A fourth dilemma is the consequence of the path-dependency of regional trajectories (Braczyk and Heidenreich, 1998). The regions previously described bear considerable strengths in their traditional technological fields: Catalonia in the field of textiles, metal working, and food, Ontario and Brabant in the automotive industry, in electrical, and electronic products, Tuscany in textiles, clothing, and furniture. However, it is precisely the previous successes with these mature industries which impede the development of strengths in new technological fields as the available resources and manpower are already invested in the established technological trajectories. This dilemma between previous strengths and new fields can partially be reduced by funds for risk capital. In general, however, the required radical innovations cannot be financed internally. This is true even for California (Castells and Hall, 1994; Leslie, 2000): a considerable extent of the success of this region has been enabled by military research. Without an adequate industrial policy, the rise of new industries is in general not possible. In this respect, Gertler and Wolfe emphasise the role of the state for the central business of the Canadian telecommunications industry. The state can promote new technological trajectories both by direct public subsidies and orders and by funding research facilities and academic education.

In conclusion: on the one hand, grassroots RIS are distinguished by 'fierce individualism' and rather weak public governance structures. This endangers the stability of the institutional order in the region. However, the regional economic structure is also shaped by dynamic SMEs which provide the innovative performance considerably to increase interorganisational networks. The capability of the grassroots regions is, therefore, shaped by the tension between fragile governance structures and innovation-centred economic structures.

The dilemmas of network-like governances

In networked innovation systems (Tampere, Denmark, Baden-Württemberg, North Rhine-Westphalia, Wales), the established technological paths are stabilised both by innovation-supporting institutions, especially by research, technology transfer and education facilities, and by interorganisational networks.

A first dilemma of these regions results from the dependence on a relatively small number of global players: Nokia in the Tampere Region, Daimler-Chrysler and Bosch in Baden-Württemberg, Philips and DAF in North Brabant, Thyssen-Krupp, Bayer, RWE and the WestLB in North Rhine-Westphalia dominate the regional economic structure. With the exception of Wales, these companies are only partially embedded into the regional networks of innovative regional suppliers. In Baden-Württemberg and in Denmark, however, the competencies of the smaller, regionally anchored firms seem to be much more extended and diversified. A diversified structure of innovative SMEs, however, is a crucial asset for the regional embedding of the focal companies into a region. This is demonstrated, for example, by the relocation and downsizing decisions of a limited number of foreign companies in Wales. Even if the foreign plants could be embedded into regional networks of competence, an upgrading to more research and development intensive activities might fail. The regional capability of a region, therefore, depends on the global competitive position of focal companies as well as on a diversified population of innovative, internationally oriented businesses. These two pillars of regional competitiveness do not automatically stabilise each other. Larger companies will rather contribute to focus regional capabilities on their specific technological fields than to a regional variety. This tension between variety and short-term economic efficiency can be called a 'global player dilemma' of regional innovation systems.

Second, the regional patterns of co-operation in network regions are institutionalised in a much more stable way than in the grassroots regions. While the institutional basis for co-operative arrangements are very fragile in Ontario and Tuscany, interorganisational patterns of co-operation are effectively stabilised by institutions such as the Steinbeis Foundation in Baden-Württemberg, the North Rhine-Westphalian SME policies, the German Chambers of Commerce, the Danish Technology Institute, the Welsh Development Agency or the national Technology Agency in Finland. These are institutionalised 'knowledge bridges' bringing together different partners from economy, science, politics, and the public and represent a crucial asset for each economic region.

Both the strengths and the limits of these institutions can be illustrated referring to the example of Wales: After the decline of the regional steel and mining industry, in the 1970s and 1980s Wales became a preferred location for Japanese, American and German automobile and electronics plants. In the first edition of this book Cooke wrote: 'Wales had become one of the key centres of high-quality, high-skill automotive engine and components production in Europe.' The Welsh Development Agency tried to integrate the newly created industrial plants into the institutional and industrial infrastructure of the region, by means of technology transfer centres, science and technology parks, supplier groups, common research projects, as well as by means of education and training facilities. As a result, the foreign production plants were meant to be used as industrial kernels for the construction of new production clusters. With the revaluation of the British pound and the availability of Central European production locations, however, this FDI-driven reindustrialisation model reached its limits (cf. the analysis by Cooke in Chapter 8). Albeit network activities in Wales are still stronger than the national average, the regional embedding of the newly established plants did not prove to be sufficient for the durable upgrading of the region's innovative capabilities.

In comparison to Wales, co-operation relationships are considerably more intensive in Baden-Württemberg. Cooke reported: 'Of all firms surveyed, the mean was 44 per cent of firms having innovation partnership with regional customers, 35 per cent suppliers and 24 per cent universities. In Baden-Württemberg the figures were 89 per cent, 80 per cent and 25 per cent respectively, while in Wales they were 28 per cent, 22 per cent and 25 per cent.' However, most of the co-operation relationships in Baden-Württemberg are of a vertical nature. Horizontal forms of co-operation, meaning relations between potential competitors, play a relatively subordinate role. This points to the limits of regional institutions: the internationalisation of production, distribution and development, common research and development activities, as well as consultancy on business management cannot be provided adequately by the established institutions. Heidenreich and Krauss conclude (p. 205):

> Established production structures and close-knit regional supply and service networks make it harder to tap into new market opportunities. These highly institutionalized structures and networks show a remarkable stability and continuity … New companies play a relatively insignificant role and start-ups are encouraged to adapt their innovation strategies and behaviour as far as possible to the established technology paths, in order to increase their chances of success or, inversely, to reduce their risk of failure.

Additionally, the North Rhine-Westphalian economy is profiled by the path-dependent nature of established co-operation networks. This is illustrated by Hilbert *et al*. in in Chapter 9 in the example of the regional environmental industry in NRW. While the region has succeeded in specialising in this new field after the decline of the coal and steel industry, the accumulated technological competences favour environment protection concepts which are primarily less innovative 'end-of-pipe solutions'. New concepts of environmental protection aimed at the reorganisation of the production and consumption processes, however, are not supported by the 'long-standing roots in mechanical engineering' of the region.

Third, in comparison to grassroots regions, network regions increasingly invest in research and development. Research expenditures, however, are no guarantee of innovation – especially if they are mainly concentrated on the established technologies. In particular, patent specialisation illustrates that the regions are mainly continuing their successful specialisation of the past: Baden-Württemberg exhibits distinctive strengths in the field of transportation technologies and mechanical engineering; North Rhine-Westphalia in the field of the engineering, chemistry and metallurgy; the Tampere Region (that belongs to the Etelä-Suomi region) in the field of electricity and physics, and Denmark in the area of human necessities (food).

Apart from these limitations, in comparison to other regions, the regions assigned by Cooke to the type of networked innovation systems have nevertheless succeeded best in leaving the previous trajectories and in placing themselves in new technological and economic domains (see Appendix Table A.3).

*   Denmark and Wales have chosen a service-oriented path of development: Denmark traditionally has a higher share of employment in the service sector. Also in the knowledge-intensive services, Denmark – closely following the European service metropoles (London, Stockholm, Paris, Brussels, Helsinki) – shows one of the highest regional employment shares in Europe. Wales joined this path *volens nolens* after the end of its 'industrial renaissance', i.e. after the partial retreat of foreign production plants. The high share of knowledge-based services (1999: 37.5 per cent in comparison to the European average of 32 per cent) points to the role of the public service (cf. Chapter 8 by Cooke).
*   The Tampere Region successfully specialised on advanced technologies beyond the established paths. While the Finnish economy was traditionally focused on resource-based industries and their spring-offs (pulp and paper, mechanical engineering and automation), in the 1990s it started a new technological trajectory in the ICT sector and knowledge-intensive services. One-third of the labour force is already employed in knowledge-intensive services (1999). This success is not only based on isolated companies such

as Nokia, but is backed by a high share of academically trained people (2001: 32 per cent of the working-age population), high research and development expenditures (2.4 per cent of the GDP), and a high patent quota (248 per million residents) in the Etelä-Suomi Region, to which Tampere belongs. Additionally, systematically interorganisational networks have been developed (see Chapter 5 by Schienstock *et al.*).

- Also Baden-Württemberg and North Rhine-Westphalia hold a strong position in advanced technologies. The number of patents (595 and 260 per million inhabitants) is far above the European average (140). To a large extent, these regions are continuing their paths of specialisation. This is demonstrated by the patent specialisation of these regions and the share of advanced technologies (chemistry, mechanical engineering, transportation and ICT technologies), which is far above the European average (see Appendix Table A.2). An indicator of the limits of this 'path-preserving' model, however, is represented by the share of R&D expenditures and the share of academically trained employees in North Rhine-Westphalia, which is below the European average.

Network regions, therefore, are characterised by efficient research and development structures focusing on their particular profile of regional specialisation. The Tampere Region has been the most successful in establishing new technological trajectories, but this is less so for Wales and North Rhine-Westphalia.

Fourth, the mostly successful development of networked innovation systems can additionally be attributed to a successful balance between both a general and a differentiated economic policy. The case studies illustrate the difficulties of a balance. In the two German federal states analysed in this volume, which are bigger than most European states with 10 and 18 million inhabitants, only basic attempts are made in supporting innovative clusters. A reason for this restraint is that cluster policies imply the selective support of single subregions and, hence, counteract the politically desired homogeneity of living conditions. As well as this political risk, the economic risks of cluster policy are also a considerable factor. An alleged future technology can prove to be a stalemate. As a result, most regions and countries – especially the German ones – support mainly the general 'knowledge infrastructure' of a region (research and development, education). Additionally, Denmark and Tampere have developed a 'differentiated industrial policy' (see, for example, the Regional Centres of Expertise Programme in Finland, the network of local technological information centres in Denmark or the publicly financed 'real services' – marketing, technological advice, quality assurance, organisation consulting, information on markets and standards – in other regions). Hence, a regionalised economic policy has to face the tension between a differentiated and a general support of the economic development.

In conclusion, the networked RIS have developed effective and sound innovation-supporting institutions. Their economic structure is shaped by global players as well as by networked SMEs. The risks of these regions arise above all from their success: the established technological, organisational, and institutional structures can become a barrier for further innovations.

The dilemmas of dirigiste, state-dominated innovation systems

Finally, there is a *dirigiste* type of regional innovation systems to which in the Introduction Slovenia, Tohoku, Gyeonggi and Singapore were ascribed. In these regions, in opposition to regional protagonists the state holds a relatively dominant position. Accordingly, these regions are shaped by the tension between an active, largely centralised state and regional actors translating (in a more or less sufficient way) public incentives and new results drawn from research and development into innovations. Against the background of these linear patterns of innovation, networked patterns are only slowly becoming more important.

The first dilemma referring to this regional economic structure can be illustrated by the example of Singapore. The institutional prerequisite for its industrial development was a strong government consistently subordinating the interests of domestic entrepreneurs to the interests of foreign businesses. Initially in the 1960s, refineries and labour-intensive textile and clothing plants were built. In the 1970s, with the help of foreign direct investment (FDI) a capital-intensive electronics industry was generated. Since the 1980s, Singapore has developed into a highly qualified finance and logistics centre for the South-East Asian region. As a result, the dependency of the region on investment decisions from foreign companies remains high. According to Hing Ai Yun in Chapter 11, the strong state may even become the Achilles' heel of the further development in Singapore. Correspondingly, there is a dilemma referring to the tension between a state-induced and FDI-based industrialisation and the development of its own, independent research, and competence basis.

Tohoku is an extreme example of the vulnerability of a region favouring external, state-induced investments. According to Shiro Abe in Chapter 10, who describes the 'hollowing out' of Tohoku, the labour cost-intensive mass production of electronic products which was the basis of the regional economic success in the 1980s has progressively been transferred to other Asian countries since the end of the 1980s.

The example of the South Korean region of Gyeonggi additionally demonstrates the strengths of regional variety in the context of a *dirigiste* innovation system. Also this region was strongly hit by the Asian crisis in 1998. However, according to Robert Hassink in Chapter 12, 'the Gyeonggi economy has quickly recovered ... firms in Gyeonggi are increasingly internationally active, foreign direct investment has been strongly increasing after the economic crisis at the end of the 1990s and even if their customers relocate to other regions, they tend to stay in Gyeonggi due to agglomeration advantages' (p. 337).

In conclusion, a strong state can contribute to the industrialisation of a region especially by means of public subsidies or other types of support for globally active companies. If the development of an endogenous qualification, research, and competence basis fails and if the newly established factories cannot be embedded in regional networks, these factories remain 'cathedrals in the desert'. In this case, the region can easily be hit by relocation decisions and economic crises.

Regional co-operation networks can hardly be promoted by a strong state; at least, in our case studies we found only little supportive indications to this argument. The *dirigiste* counterpart to the support of networks seems to be the state-sponsored foundation of technology parks and science cities. The 'techno-polis', technology-intensive cities described by Shiro Abe, are an example of this public role. Like the Welsh Development Agency, the powerful Japanese Ministry of International Trade and Industry (MITI) has succeeded in transferring production plants into the rural region of Tohoku. However, not even the technopolis-initiative was able to strengthen regional networks: 'Local linkages within the technopolis area still appear weak, and most branch subsidiaries retain strong vertical links with their headquarters, rather than opening up new production spaces for local firms' (p. 277).

Korea also shows a similar point of departure. According to Robert Hassink, the level of regional networking is very low in Gyeonggi. The regional companies are part of a national production system (especially in automobile production). The main task of the public innovation support infrastructure is to improve contacts with public research facilities and to inform them about public funding programmes. The support of regional networks is not part of its remit. Such a centralist innovation support structure increasingly reaches its limits: with the transition from an investment- to an innovation-driven stage of industrial development, the requests for stronger regional networks intensify. Nationally homogeneous agencies increasingly cannot tackle the more diversified regional requests: 'Gyeonggi, therefore, seems to move from a *dirigiste* to a network kind of regional innovation support system' (p. 340).

For such a transition, Slovenia provides excellent conditions. Even if its innovation system has to be characterised as *dirigiste* and fragmented (due to the socialist legacies), Knut Koschatzky in Chapter 13 describes extraordinarily intensive interorganisational patterns of co-operation: 93 per cent of the questioned companies 'confirmed that their co-operation with at least one partner surpassed normal business relationships in the case of innovation relevant activities' (p. 352). However, these are mainly vertical relationships, namely relations to business-related service companies, to customers, and suppliers. Contacts with competitors or with the public research and development infrastructure are considerably more fragile.

In conclusion, the *dirigiste* innovation systems are mainly characterised by a national supportive infrastructure. Up to now, regional co-operation networks have had a minor role in the current development concepts. Slovenia, Gyeonggi, Singapore, and Tohoku are, therefore, not characterised by fully developed regional innovation systems. However, with the increasing importance of more complex, non-linear innovation processes, regional networks are increasingly growing in importance in order to face the uncertainties of systemic, recursive innovation strategies. First indicators for such a shift towards network-based innovation concepts can be observed in all five regions – in Tohoku, in particular, they are already supported by regional institutions.

This transition from linear to systemic innovation concepts also shapes the third of the four dimensions examined here, namely the relationship between companies and research, development, and technology transfer infrastructures. Up to now, companies and institutions have been largely decoupled. In Slovenia, for example, 'The closest co-operation existed between Slovenian university institutes and the public administration ... other, mainly private institutes were clearly more oriented towards industry.' This is correspondingly documented by the structure of R&D expenditures: even if expenditures are quite high (1.5 per cent of GDP), only 54 per cent of these originate from private businesses.

In Japan and Korea, national actors try to overcome the institutional decoupling between research and businesses by founding technology parks and regional research centres. In the extraordinarily research-intensive region Gyeonggi, the regional research centres succeeded in prompting numerous SMEs, however, mostly outside the region. In the Japanese region of Tohoku it was not possible to strengthen the regional research and development capacities in a persistent way. It can, therefore, be concluded that *dirigiste* RIS did not succeed in the regionalisation of national research and development activities and a closer coupling with the enterprise sector.

Fourth: in the past, the strong states dominating the *dirigiste* innovation systems originally did not favour a regionalisation of industrial politics. Gradually this changed in Japan and Korea. In such unitary states like Japan, however, it is a very difficult task to pursue diversified industrial policies. The development of the technopolis initiatives clearly demonstrates this argument. Not only did this initiative pursue the objective to promote knowledge-intensive industries: 'In some cases, they could even be considered as a form of social policy in disguise, through implementing measures (via some sort of public investment) to compensate those regions where private business investment was scarce or existing industries were declining' (p. 276). Without stronger political regions and a different, more networked development model, diversified industrial politics can hardly be implemented. Simultaneously, disadvantaged regions like Tohoku hardly have the opportunity to profit from such regionalisation.

In Table 14.1 key aspects of the previous argumentation are summarised. As a major result of the discussion it can be concluded that a regional innovation infrastructure is only partially institutionalised in grassroots and *dirigiste* regions. In the case of the first, regional governance structures are the result of a provisional regulation of individual business strategies; in the second case, the regional level is rather weak in comparison to the national level. This points to the fragility of regional governance structures, which are dependent on two conditions: first, regional companies must be able to benefit from the implicit, regionally distributed competences of other businesses. This requires an innovation strategy supported by close co-operation with suppliers and competitors as well as by close contacts with universities and research institutes. This, however, is not the case in regions still dominated by standardised mass production of less complex products where companies are primarily interested in low capital and labour costs or in subsidies, not in the development of regional competences. Partially this seems to be the case in Gyeonggi, Ontario, Wales and Tohoku. Second, the state must be ready to decentralise competences and responsibilities and to accept a diversified regional development. This problem is not only relevant in countries with *dirigiste* innovation systems (France, Slovenia, Japan, Korea, Singapore), but also in Finland (Tampere), Spain (Catalonia) und Germany. Bacaria *et al.*, for example, not only described considerable frictions between the national and the regional level, but also the tendency to split the Catalonian innovation system into two separate support structures, into a national and a regional one. Similar problems apply to the two German regions as these are too large for a diversified economic policy.

If both conditions (decentralisation of political competences and innovation-centred business strategies) are met, the essential prerequisites for a fully-fledged regional innovation system – which are basically characterised by a regional order and regional co-operation and innovation networks – are found. Even successful innovation systems of this type, however, are still threatened by the reverse of their success, namely from institutional lock-in-effects and from the specialisation in specific technologies and industries. As a result of their past successes, regional economies erode if new firms, products and technologies are not simultaneously promoted.

Conclusion

In this concluding chapter, central dilemmas of the thirteen regional innovation systems previously analysed have been summarised. The starting point was the dilemma between innovation and institutionalisation: given the enormous risks of innovation it is partially rational for individual entrepreneurs, organisations, and networks to preserve the previous competences and specialisation profiles and to gradually develop them towards new directions. The risks of omitted innovations, however, are opposed by the risks of failed innovations: successful innovations in one field can devaluate previously accumulated competences, technologies, investments, and plants in other fields. On the one hand, regional actors have to open up to new demands, challenges, and technologies; on the other, a relative regional closure is a precondition for the continuation of previous recipes of success and for the incremental accumulation of competences.

In the case of spatially concentrated innovation processes, this innovation dilemma is translated in four different dilemmas: first, businesses must assert themselves in an increasingly world-wide competition. In the most innovative regions of the world, this is accompanied by the increasing importance of local, experience-based, context-bound knowledge. Second, innovative firms are dependent on distributed knowledge of innovation networks, i.e. on trust-based patterns of co-operation between firms, schools, research institutes, political authorities, and users as these networks facilitate the recombination of technical knowledge and the embeddedness of new technologies. However, these networks may also be accompanied by lock-in-effects. Regional competitiveness, therefore, also depends on a diversification of the regional economic structure and the opening up to new competences, technologies, and businesses. Third, a close coupling of scientific, economic, political, technical, and cultural actors facilitates the reciprocal adjustment of perspectives and actions. This, however, may also hamper radical scientific, economic or technical innovations. Fourth, regional competitiveness is based on the accumulation and path-dependent development of competences. This, however, may also impede new technological trajectories. These four dilemmas shape regional economic structure ('between regionalisation and globalisation'), regional co-operation networks ('between fragility, regional learning and lock-in-effects'), regional development and technology transfer institutions ('between learning and normative regulations'), and regional economic policies ('between previous strengths and new technological fields').

In the third section of this chapter, it was described how the thirteen regions face these four dilemmas. It was found that the three types of governance structures initially proposed by Philip Cooke are characterised by different patterns. In the case of the grassroots regions, the institutional orders of these regions are highly fragile. They are continuously threatened by 'fierce individualism' among mostly small enterprises and a relatively weak position of the local authorities. *Dirigiste* structures, on the other hand, reflect a linear innovation concept, in which basic research, applied research, development, and production can still be decoupled, demonstrated by minimal regional co-operation; regional companies are mainly connected by vertical supplier-customer relationships. The state guarantees the stability of the institutional order; the organisational interests in a decentralised regional order are still relatively weak. In networked RIS, entrepreneurial interests in the regional support of distributed innovation processes are matched by a regionalisation of research, development, technology transfer, and economic policy. In this case, regional innovation networks and innovation-supporting institutions can develop. However, even these networked innovation systems are always threatened by their previous successes, namely by the inertia of previous technological specialisations and institutions. This indicates the challenges, regional innovation systems have to face in a knowledge-based economy.

Acknowledgement

I am grateful to Philip Cooke for comments on a previous version of this chapter.

Notes

1   Cf. Lundvall (1992), Nelson (1993), Edquist (1997) and Archibugi *et al.* (1999). Metcalfe (1995), for example, defines national systems of innovation as

> that set of distinct institutions which jointly and individually contribute to the development and diffusion of new technologies and which provides the framework within which governments form and implement policies to influence the innovation process. As such it is a system of interconnected institutions to create, store and transfer the knowledge, skills and artefacts which define new technologies.

It remains open in which way the creation, storage and transfer of knowledge is effectuated. There have been attempts to fill this gap with the concept of co-operation or networks which should be able to facilitate innovations (Hage and Hollingsworth, 2000). But Fritsch (2001) has shown that the assumed connection 'between the co-operative behaviour of firms and the performance of the regional innovation system' cannot be proved.

Appendix: statistical indicators

Table A.1 Economic performance, industrial structure and unemployment in nine European regions

	EU15	Baden-Württemberg	Catalonia	Denmark	Etelä-Suomi	North-Brabant	North Rhine-Westphalia	Slovenia	Tuscany	Wales
GDP/head (PPS) EU15=100										
1995	100.0	123.2	95.5	118.1	90.6	106.4	114.2	62.8	112.6	80.8
2000	100.0	122.0	99.5	118.6	96.0	110.0	108.6	67.2	113.5	80.6
average 1998–1999	100.0	120.8	98.2	118.6	94.4	112.0	108.5	67.3	113.4	81.5
GDP/head (PPS) EU25=100										
2000	110.2	134.5	109.7	130.7	105.8	121.3	119.8	74.0	125.1	88.8
Employment by sector (% of total) 2001										
Agriculture	4.1	2.4	2.5	3.5	6.1	3.2	1.6	10.0	4.2	2.2
Industry	28.5	40.8	39.2	25.4	32.7	26.0	32.9	38.6	34.1	26.9
Services	66.7	56.8	58.3	70.9	61.0	65.1	65.5	51.4	61.7	70.8
Unemployment rate (% total)										
1991	7.9	2.3	11.8	8.5	7.6	5.4	5.4	:	6.4	9.1
2001	7.6	4.1	8.8	4.4	9.8	2.0	7.5	5.7	5.0	5.9
Unemployment rate (%) 2001										
Female	8.9	4.4	11.9	5.1	11.2	2.7	7.5	6.0	7.9	5.0
Young	15.1	4.3	16.6	8.7	22.5	4.8	8.9	15.7	17.3	14.6
Long-term unemployed, 2001 (% of total unemployed)	42.6	42.9	42.4	22.0	23.8	36.6	48.1	63.3	41.0	26.8

Source: European Commission (2003) Second progress report on economic and social cohesion. Brussels, COM (2003) 34/4. (hhtp://www.europa.eu.int/comm/regional_policy/sources/docoffic/offical/reports/pdf/interim2/tables_01_12_en.pdf: February 25th, 2003); European Commission (2002).

Table A.2 Employment, population, education and R&D in nine European regions

	EU15	Baden-Württemberg	Catalonia	Denmark	Eteläe-Suomi	North-Brabant	North Rhine-Westphalia	Slovenia	Tuscany	Wales
Employment rate (ages 15–64 as % of population aged 15–64), 2001										
Total	64.3	69.9	71.6	75.9	69.1	73.8	63.5	63.6	60.7	65.2
Female	55.1	62.4	57.4	71.4	66.0	63.9	54.7	58.6	49.6	59.1
Male	73.5	77.5	85.9	80.2	72.1	83.3	72.2	68.5	71.9	71.1
Population (2000)										
Total (000s)	378,914	10,499	6,170	5,338	1,818	2,365	17,998	1,990	3,543	2,958
Density (inhabitants/km²)	118.7	293.7	193.2	123.9	34.5	479.5	528.1	98.2	154.1	142.4
aged < 15 (%)	16.8	16.8	13.9	18.4	17.3	18.6	16.3	16.1	11.5	19.0
aged 15–64 (%)	66.9	67.7	68.6	66.8	66.3	68.6	67.1	70.0	66.6	63.8
aged 65+ (%)	16.3	15.5	17.5	14.8	16.4	12.8	16.6	13.9	21.9	17.3
Educational attainment: population aged 25–59 (as % of total) 2001										
Low	34.2	20.0	55.1	18.5	24.4	32.6	19.2	22.8	55.0	23.4
Medium	43.5	54.3	18.7	54.2	43.4	44.7	59.9	62.6	35.3	50.4
High	22.3	25.7	26.3	27.3	32.2	22.7	20.8	14.6	9.7	26.2
R&D expenditure (1997)										
in % of the GDP	1.8	3.8	0.9	1.9	2.4		1.7	1.5	0.7*	0.8
Business sector (% of total)		77.1	64.6	62.0	64.3		63.2	53.8	55.9	44.1
Public sector (% of total)		11.8	10.5	15.6	19.1		15.2	28.6	44.1	12.5
Higher education (% of total)		11.1	24.9	22.4	16.6		21.6	17.6	0.0	43.4
Employment 1999										
High-tech manufacturing	7.8	17.8	9.3	6.4	8.3	6.8	9.9		5.8	9.0
Knowledge-intensive services	32.3	28.4	25.1	41.6	33.9	32.6	29.5		24.2	37.5

Source: European Commission (2003) Second progress report on economic and social cohesion. Brussels, COM (2003) 34/4. (hhtp://www.europa.eu.int/comm/regional_policy/sources/docoffic/offical/reports/pdf/interim2/tables_01_12_en.pdf: February 25th, 2003); European Commission (2002).
Note: * Figures for 1993

Table A.3 Technical specialisation of nine European regions (patents applications by IPC section, 2000)

	Baden-Württemberg	Catalonia	Denmark	Etelä-Suomi	North-Brabant	North Rhine-Westphalia	Slovenia	Tuscany	Wales
EPO patent applications per million									
inhabitants, average 1998–1999–2000	495.9	51.2	159.2	247.8	577.8	260.8	21.2	59.2	64.4
Human necessities	515	76	224	41	106	674		56	35
Performing operations, transporting	1.349	69	119	68	113	1.162		59	37
Chemistry, metallurgy	482	43	163	37	74	1.146		28	22
Textiles, paper	151	12	17	51	8	127		21	2
Fixed construction	234	23	50	17	16	350		10	10
Mechanical engineering, lighting, heating, weapons, blasting	1.157	19	70	22	53	600		20	8
Physics	797	25	127	82	486	528		24	32
Electricity	841	38	133	186	730	681		28	11
EPO patent applications; 2000; total	**5.525**	**305**	**903**	**503**	**1.585**	**5.267**		**247**	**156**

Source: European Commission (2002).

Note: The table shows the patent intensity and the technological sector of the patent applications to the European Patent Office for each region, according to the international patent classification (IPC). The data for Wales refer to 1998.

Table A.4 Statistical indicators for Singapore

Indicator	1980	2000
Inhabitants (in 1000)	2,413.9	4,017.7
Civilian labour force (in 1000)	1,064.8	2,094.8
Civilian labour force by sector	(in 1000)	(in 1000)
agriculture	21.4	–
industry	424.9	434.9
services	556.9	1176.9
not classifiable	61.8	12.8
Unemployment rate	3.0	3.1
Gross domestic product (GDP)		
per capita (in current prices, in Singapore $)	not available	39,585
per employee (in current prices, in Singapore $)	9,940	not available
Direct investment (in Singapore $, mill.)		
from abroad in the region	11,201.7	18,900.0
from the region abroad	1,615.9	22,000.0
GERD (gross expenditure on R&D, in per cent of the GDP)	0.3 (in 1981/2)	1.89
Qualification structure of the workforce :		(year 2001)
Pre-primary:	72.4	20.0
Secondary:	16.3	42.1
Post Secondary/ Diploma:	7.7	21.0
Tertiary:	3.6	16.9
	100.0	100.0
Most important industrial/economic clusters	petroleum/products, electronics/ electrical	electronics/ petroleum/ electrical products

Table A.5 Statistical indicators for Tohoku

Indicator	1980	1997
Inhabitants (000s)	12,103	12,365
Civilian labour force (000s)	6,006	6,487
Civilian labour force by sector	000 (%)	000 (%)
• Agriculture	1,288 (21.4)	660 (10.2)
• Industry	1,755 (29.2)	2,116 (32.6)
• Services	2,961 (49.3)	3,696 (57.0)
Unemployment rate (%)	1.8	3.5
GDP per capita (thousand yen)	1,724	3,527
Per employee (thousand yen)	3,474	6,723
Export rate (%)˙	0.25 (1989)	0.79
Import rate (%)	2.25 (1989)	2.39
Direct investment	Not available	Not available
GERD (% of GDP)	0.18 (1990)	0.38
Qualification structure of the workforce (%)		
Blue-collar	29.7	33.5
Green-collar	21.2	10.0
White-collar	25.0	31.7
Grey-collar	24.0	24.8
Most important industrial/economic clusters	Food, Electronics	

Note: ˙These ratios are according to the Ministry of Finance's statistics in which value of exports and imports by region are calculated by location of each custom house (port of clearance).

Bibliography

Introduction: regional innovation systems – an evolutionary approach

Antonelli, C. and Momigliano, S. (1981) 'Problems and experiences of regional innovation policy in Italy', *Micros*, 2: 45–58.

Asheim, B. (2002) 'Temporary organisations and spatial embeddedness of learning and knowledge creation', *Geografiska Annaler*, 84: 111–124.

Asheim, B. and Isaksen, A. (2002) 'Regional innovation systems: the integration of local "sticky" and global "ubiquitous" knowledge', *The Journal of Technology Transfer*, 27: 77–86.

Audretsch, D. (2002) 'The innovative advantage of US cities', *European Planning Studies*, 10: 165–176

Aydalot, P. (ed.) (1986) *Milieux Innovateurs en Europe*, Paris, GREMI.

Becattini, G. (1989) 'Sectors or districts: some remarks on the conceptual foundations of industrial economics', in E. Goodman *et al.* (eds) *Small Firms and Industrial Districts in Italy*, London: Routledge.

Bergman, E. and Feser, E. (2001) 'Innovation system effects on technological adoption in a regional value chain', *European Planning Studies*, 9: 631–650.

Bergman, E., Maier, G. and Tödtling, F. (eds) (1991) *Regions Reconsidered*, London, Mansell.

Braczyk, H., Cooke, P. and Heidenreich, M. (eds) (1998) *Regional Innovation Systems*, London: UCL Press.

Brail, S. and Gertler, M. (1999) 'The digital regional economy: emergence and evolution of Toronto's multimedia cluster', in H. Braczyk, G. Fuchs and H. Wolf (eds) *Multimedia and Regional Economic Restructuring*, London: Routledge.

Bruun, H. (2001) 'Regional development and biotechnology: a network analysis of the local Bio-grouping in Turku, Finland', *Technology, Society, Environment*, 3: 97–128 (Espoo: Helsinki University of Technology, Laboratory of Environmental Protection).

Bruun, H. (2002) 'Mobilising a regional lighthouse: a study of the Digital North Denmark programme', paper presented to the Digital North Denmark Research Seminar, Aalborg, 21–22 November.

Brusco, S. (1990) 'The idea of the industrial district: its genesis', in F. Pyke, G. Becattini and W. Sengenberger (eds) *Industrial Districts and Inter-Firm Co-operation in Italy*, Geneva: IILS.

Camagni, R. (ed.) (1991) *Innovation Networks*, London: Belhaven.

Carlsson, B. (2004) 'Innovation systems: a survey of the literature from a Schumpeterian perspective', in A. Pyka (ed.) *The Companion to Neo-Schumpeterian Economics,* Cheltenham: Edward Elgar.

Castilla, E., Hwang, H., Granovetter, E. and Granovetter, M. (2000) 'Social networks in Silicon Valley', in C. Lee *et al.* (eds) *The Silicon Valley Edge,* Stanford, CA: Stanford University Press.

Cooke, P. (1985) 'Regional innovation policy: problems and strategies in Britain and France', *Environment and Planning C: Government and Policy,* 3: 253–267.

Cooke, P. (1992) 'Regional innovation systems: competitive regulation in the new Europe', *Geoforum,* 23: 365–382.

Cooke, P. (2001) 'Regional innovation systems, clusters, and the knowledge economy', *Industrial and Corporate Change,* 10: 945–973.

Cooke, P. (2002) *Knowledge Economies: Clusters, Learning and Cooperative Advantage,* London: Routledge.

Cooke, P., Boekholt, P. and Tödtling, F. (2000) *The Governance of Innovation in Europe,* London: Pinter.

Cooke, P., De Laurentis, C. and Wilson, R. (2003) *The Future of Manufacturing Jobs in Europe: Wales as a Case Study,* Brussels: The European Parliament.

Cooke, P. and Hughes, G. (1999) 'Creating a multimedia cluster in Cardiff Bay', in H. Braczyk *et al.* (eds) *Multimedia and Regional Economic Restructuring,* London: Routledge.

Cooke, P. and Morgan, K. (1994) 'The creative milieu: a regional perspective on innovation', in M. Dodgson and R. Rothwell (eds) *The Handbook of Industrial Innovation,* Aldershot: Edward Elgar.

Dalum, B. (1995) 'Local and global linkages: the telecommunications cluster in northern Denmark', *Journal of Industry Studies,* 2: 89–109.

De la Mothe, J. (2003) 'Constructing advantage through distributed innovation', paper presented at OECD Expert Mission on 'International Knowledge Flows', Glasgow, 25–29 November 2002.

Dicken, P. (2001) 'Chains and networks, territories and scales: towards a relational framework for analysing the global economy', *Global Networks,* 1: 89–112.

Edquist, C. (ed.) (1997) *Systems of Innovation,* London: Pinter.

Florida, R. (2002) *The Rise of the Creative Class,* New York: Basic Books.

Foray, D. and Freeman, C. (1993) *Technology and the Wealth of Nations: The Dynamics of Constructed Advantage,* London: Pinter

Gereffi, G. (1999) 'International trade and industrial upgrading in the apparel commodity chain', *Journal of International Economics,* 48: 37–70.

Gibbons, J. (2000) 'The role of Stanford University: a Dean's reflections', in C. Lee *et al.* (eds) *The Silicon Valley Edge,* Stanford, CA: Stanford University Press.

Hassink, R. (2000) 'Regional innovation support systems in South Korea and Japan compared', *Zeitschrift für Wirtschaftsgeographie,* 44: 228–245.

Hing, A. (1998) 'Innovative milieu and cooperation networks: state initiatives and partnership for restructuring Singapore', in H. Braczyk, P. Cooke and M. Heidenreich (eds) *Regional Innovation Systems,* London: UCL Press.

Hood, N., Peat, J., Peters, E. and Young, S. (eds) (2002) *Scotland in a Global Economy: The 2020 Vision,* London: Palgrave.

Isaacs, A. (2002) 'Silicon Valley as a Case of Regional Innovation', presentation to UNIDO international conference on 'The Process of Innovation and Learning in Dynamic City-Regions', Shenzen, China, 7–9 December.

Latouche, D. (1998) 'Do regions make a difference? The case of science and technology policies in Quebec', in, H. Braczyk, P. Cooke and M. Heindenreich (eds) *Regional Innovation Systems*, London: UCL Press.

Latour, B. (1998) 'From the world of science to the world of research?' *Science*, 280: 208–209.

Lundequist, C. and Power, D. (2002) 'Practices of regional cluster building: evidence from Sweden', *European Planning Studies*, 10: 685–704.

Lundvall, B. (ed.) (1992) *National Systems of Innovation: Towards a Theory of Innovation and Interactive Learning*, London: Pinter.

Lundvall, B. (1994) 'The global unemployment problem and national systems of innovation, in D. O'Doherty (ed.) *Globalisation, Networking and Small Firm Innovation*, London: Graham & Trotman.

Maillat, D. (1991) 'Local dynamism, milieu and innovative enterprises' in J. Brotchie *et al.* (eds) *Cities of the 21st Century*, London: Longman.

Maillat, D. and Vasserot, P. (1986) 'Les milieux innovateurs', in P. Aydalot (ed.) *Milieux Innovateurs en Europe*, Paris: GREMI.

Malecki, E. (1991) *Technology and Economic Development*, London: Longman.

Marshall, A. ((1890)1961) *Principles of Economics*, London: Macmillan.

Marshall, A. (1919) *Industry and Trade*, London: Macmillan.

Meyer-Krahmer, F. (1985) 'Innovation behaviour and regional indigenous potential', *Regional Studies*, 19: 523–534.

Nelson, R. (ed.) *National Innovation Systems: A Comparative Study*, Oxford: Oxford University Press.

Noisi, J. (2002) 'Clusters in high technology: aerospace, biotechnology and software compared'. Presentation a conference at Dept of Management and Technology, University of Quebec, Montreal, 1 November.

Norton, R. (2000) *Creating the New Economy: The Entrepreneur and the US Resurgence*, Cheltenham: Edward Elgar.

Nowotny, H., Scott, P. and Gibbons, M. (2001) *Re-Thinking Science*, Cambridge: Polity Press.

Piore, M. and Sabel, C. (1984) *The Second Industrial Divide*, New York: Basic Books.

Revilla Diez, J. (2000) 'The importance of public research institutes in innovative networks – empirical results from the metropolitan innovation systems of Barcelona, Stockholm and Vienna', *European Planning Studies*, 8: 451–464.

Rothwell, R. and Dodgson, M. (1991) 'Regional technology policies', in J. Botchie, *et al.* (eds) *Cities of the 21st Century*, London: Longman.

Sabel, C. (1992) 'Studied trust: building new forms of co-operation in a volatile economy', in F. Pyke and W. Sengenberger (eds) *Industrial Districts and Local Economic Regeneration*, Geneva: IILS.

Sabel, C., Herrigel, G. and Kern, H. (1989) *Collaborative Manufacturing: New Supplier Relations in the Automobile Industry and the Redefinition of the Industrial Corporation*, MIT, Sloan School of Management Report, published as 'Kooperative Produktion: Neue Formen der Zusammenarbeit zwischen Endfertigern und Zulieferern in der Automobilindustrie und die Neuordnung der Firma', in H. Mendius and U. Wendeling-Schröder (eds), *Zulieferer im Netz: Zwischen Abhängigkeit und Partnerschaft*, Cologne: Bund Verlag, 1991, pp. 203–227.

Sako, M. (1989) 'Neither markets nor hierarchies', paper presented at conference at Bellagio, May 29–June 2.

Schmitz, H. (1999) 'Global competition and local cooperation: success and failure in the Sinos Valley, Brazil', *World Development*, 27: 1627–1650.

Schumpeter, J. (1975) *Capitalism, Socialism and Democracy,* New York: Harper.

Scott, A. (1988) *New Industrial Spaces*, London: Pion.

Scott, A. (1994) *Technopolis*, Los Angeles: University of California Press.

Simmie, J. and Wood, P. (eds) (2002) 'Innovation and competitive cities in the global economy; introduction to the special issue', *European Planning Studies*, 10: 149–152.

Stewart, T. (2001) *The Wealth of Knowledge*, London: Nicholas Brealey.

Strambach, S. (2002) 'Change in the innovation process; new knowledge production and competitive cities – the case of Stuttgart', *European Planning Studies*, 10: 215–232.

Towill, D. (1993) 'Systems dynamics – background, methodology and applications', *Computing and Control Engineering Journal*, December: 261–268.

Tulkki, P, Järvensivu and Lyytinen, A. (2002) *The Emergence of Finnish Life Sciences Industries*, Sitra Reports Series 12, Helsinki: Sitra.

UNIDO (2002) *Industrial Development Report 2002/2003: Competing Through Innovation and Learning*, Vienna: United Nations Industrial Development Organisation.

Winter S. (1984) 'Schumpeterian competition in alternative technological regimes', *Journal of Economic Behaviour and Organization* 5, 287–320.

1   The remarkable resilience of the industrial districts of Tuscany

Amin, A. (1994) 'Santa Croce in context or how industrial districts respond to the restructuring of world market', in R. Leonardi and R. Nanetti (eds) *Regional Development in a Modern European Economy*, London: Pinter.

Arpes (1982) *Studio conoscitivo sul settore della concia, pelletteria e calzature*, Florence: Regione Toscana.

Bacci, L. (2002) *Sistemi locali in Toscana: Modelli e percorsi territoriali dello sviluppo regionale*, Irpet, Milan: Franco Angeli.

Bartolini, S. (1994) 'Dinamiche di concentrazione della proprietà a Santa Croce sull'Arno', in M. Bellandi and M. Russo (eds) *Distretti industriali e cambiamento economico locale*, Turin: Rosenberg & Sellier.

Becattini, G. (1978) 'The economic development of Tuscany: an interpretation', *Economic Notes*, 2–3: 106–123; republished in G. Becattini *et al.* (2003).

Becattini, G. (1989) 'Sectors and/or districts: some remarks on the conceptual foundations of industrial economics', in E. Goodman and J. Bamford (eds) *Small Firms and Industrial Districts in Italy*, London: Routledge.

Becattini, G. (1990) 'The Marshallian industrial district as a socio-economic notion', in F. Pyke, G. Becattini and W. Sengenberger (eds) *Industrial Districts and Interfirm Co-operation in Italy*, Geneva: International Institute for Labour Studies.

Becattini, G. (1991) 'The industrial district as a creative milieu', in G. Benko and M. Dunford (eds) *Industrial Change and Regional Development*, London: Belhaven Press.

Becattini, G. (1999) *L'Industrializzazione leggera della Toscana: Ricerca sul campo e confronto delle idee*, Irpet, Milan: Franco Angeli.

Becattini, G. (2001) *The Caterpillar and the Butterfly: An Exemplary Case of Development in the Italy of Industrial Districts*, Florence: Le Monnier.

Becattini, G., Bellandi, M., Dei Ottati, G. and Sforzi, F. (2003) *From Industrial District to Local Development: An Itinerary of Research*, Cheltenham: Edward Elgar.

Becattini, G. and Rullani, E. (1996) 'Local systems and global connections: the role of knowledge', in F. Cossentino, F. Pyke and W. Sengenberger (eds) *Local and Regional Response to Global Pressure*, Geneva: International Institute for Labour Studies.

Bell, C. (1988) 'Credit markets and interlinked transactions', in H. Chenery and T. Srinivasan (eds) *Handbook of Development Economics*, Amsterdam: North Holland.

Bellandi, M. (1992) 'The incentives to decentralized industrial creativity in local systems of small firms', *Revue d'économie industrielle*, 59: 99–110; republished in G. Becattini *et al.* (2003).

Bellandi, M. (1996), 'Innovation and change in the Marshallian industrial district', *European Planning Studies*, 4, 3: 357–368.

Bellandi, M. and Russo, M. (eds) (1994) *Distretti industriali e cambiamento economico locale*, Turin: Rosenberg & Sellier.

Benko, G. and Lipietz, A. (eds) (1992) *Les régions qui gagnent. Districts et réseaux: les nouveaux paradigmes de la géographie économique*, Paris: Puf.

Best, M. (1990) *The New Competition: Institutions of Industrial Restructuring*, Cambridge: Polity Press.

Bianchi, P. and Gualtieri, G. (1990) 'Emilia-Romagna and its industrial districts: the evolution of a model', in R. Leonardi and R. Nanetti (eds) *The Regions and European Integration: The Case of Emilia-Romagna*, London: Pinter Publishers.

Blim, M. (1992) 'Flexibly specialized industrial districts at middle age: a preliminary exploration of their present and future prospects', manuscript, Northeastern University, Boston.

Bortolotti, F. (1994) 'L'Alta Valdelsa. La crescita dell'industria meccanica', in F. Bortolotti (ed.) *Il mosaico e il progetto*, Ires Toscana, Milan: Franco Angeli.

Bortolotti, F. and Casai, L. (1994) 'Il Valdarno inferiore. Un distretto esemplare', in F. Bortolotti (ed.) *Il mosaico e il progetto*, Ires Toscana, Milan: Franco Angeli.

Brusco, S. (1995) 'Local productive systems and new industrial policy in Italy', in A. Bagnasco and C. Sabel (eds) *Small and Medium-size Enterprises*, London: Pinter Publishers.

Caporale, A. (1995) 'Internazionalizzazione e decentramento produttivo nel distretto conciario di Santa Croce sull'Arno', in A. Cavalieri (ed.) *L'Internazionalizzazione del processo produttivo nei sistemi locali de piccola impresa in Toscana*, Irpet, Milan: Franco Angeli.

Cappiello, M.A. (1992) 'I distretti industriali calzaturieri della Toscana e delle Marche', in F. Nuti (ed.) *I distretti dell'industria manifatturiera in Italia*, vol. II, Milan: Franco Angeli.

Cavalieri, A. (ed.) (1995) *L'Internazionalizzazione del processo produttivo nei sistemi locali di piccola impresa in Toscana*, Irpet, Milan: Franco Angeli.

Cee-Force (1993) 'Fabbisogni di competenze professionali dei lavoratori e degli imprenditori e dei servizi alle imprese nel settore calzaturiero nell'area di Pistoia', Pistoia.

Cossentino, F., Pyke, F. and Sengenberger, W. (eds) (1996) *Local and Regional Response to Global Pressure: The Case of Italy and its Industrial Districts*, Geneva: International Institute for Labour Studies.

Costi, D. (1993) 'Un'indagine sui gruppi di imprese nel distretto industriale di Prato', unpublished thesis, Faculty of Economics, University of Florence.

Dei Ottati, G. (1991) 'The economic bases of diffuse industrialization', *International Studies of Management & Organization*, 21, 1: 53–74; republished in G. Becattini *et al.* (2003).

Dei Ottati, G. (1993), 'Il sistema tessile pratese nel secondo dopoguerra: nascita, sviluppo e trasformazione di un distretto industriale', in *Atti del convegno Ambienti e tipologie dell'industrializzazione*, Regione Piemonte, Turin: Fondazione Luigi Einaudi.

Dei Ottati, G. (1994a) 'Trust, interlinking transactions and credit in the industrial district', *Cambridge Journal of Economics*, 18, 6: 529–546; republished in G. Becattini *et al.* (2003).

Dei Ottati, G. (1994b) 'Prato and its evolution in a European context', in R. Leonardi and R. Nanetti (eds) *Regional Development in a Modern European Economy*, London: Pinter.

Dei Ottati, G. (1994c) 'Cooperation and competition in the industrial district as an organization model', *European Planning Studies*, 4: 463–483.

Dei Ottati, G. (1996) 'Economic changes in the district of Prato during the '80s: towards a more conscious and organized industrial district', *European Planning Studies*, 2: 35–52.

Dei Ottati, G. (2002) 'Social concertation and local development: the case of industrial districts', *European Planning Studies*, 10, 4: 449–466.

Forlai, L. (1993) 'Prato tra crisi e nuove strategie', *Quaderni dell'Osservatorio*, 1, Prato: Associazione intercomunale pratese.

Freschi, A. (1992) *I centri di servizio alle imprese in Toscana*, Florence: Regione Toscana.

Goodman, E. and Bamford, J. (eds) (1989) *Small Firms and Industrial Districts in Italy*, London: Routledge.

Graziani, A. (1994) 'L'esperienza italiana nel Sistema Monetario Europeo', in F.R. Pizzuti (ed.) *L'Economia italiana dagli anni Settanta agli anni Novanta*, Milan: McGraw-Hill.

Harrison, B. (1994a) 'The Italian industrial districts and the crisis of the cooperative form: Part I and Part II', *European Planning Studies*, 2, 1–2: 159–174.

Harrison, B. (1994b) *Lean and Mean. The Changing Landscape of Corporate Power in the Age of Flexibility*, New York: Basic Books.

Iris (1994) *Società, economia e territorio a Prato: Indagine per il nuovo piano regolatore*, Prato: Comune di Prato.

Irpet (1975) *Lo sviluppo economico della Toscana con particolare riguardo all'industrializzazione leggera*, ed. G. Becattini, Florence: Guaraldi.

Istat (1981a) *12° Censimento generale della popolazione*, Rome: Istituto Nazionale di Statistica.

Istat (1981b) *6° Censimento generale dell'industria e dei servizi*, Rome: Istituto Nazionale di Statistica.

Istat (1991a) *13° Censimento generale della popolazione*, Rome: Istituto Nazionale di Statistica.

Istat (1991b) *7° Censimento generale dell'industria e dei servizi*, Rome: Istituto Nazionale di Statistica.

Istat (1996) *Censimento intermedio*, Rome: Istituto Nazionale di Statistica.

Istat (2001a) *14° Censimento generale della popolazione*, Rome: Istituto Nazionale di Statistica.

Istat (2001b) *8° Censimento generale dell'industria e dei servizi*, Rome: Istituto Nazionale di Statistica.

Leonardi, R. and Nanetti, R. (eds) (1994) *Regional Development in a Modern European Economy: The Case of Tuscany*, London: Pinter Publishers.

Loasby, B.J. (1998) 'Industrial districts as knowledge communities', in M. Bellet and C. L'Harmet (eds) *Industry, Space and Competition: The Contribution of Economists of the Past*, Cheltenham: Edward Elgar.

Mariani, G. (1992) 'Il distretto conciario del Valdarno Inferiore', in F. Nuti (ed.) *I distretti dell'industria manifatturiera in Italia*, vol. II, Milan: Franco Angeli.

Marshall, A. (1919) *Industry and Trade*, 5th edn, London: Macmillan.

Pdup (Partito di unità proletaria per il comunismo) (1975) 'Decentramento produttivo, crisi tessile, alternativa di classe', mimeo, Prato.

Piore, M. and Sabel, C. (1984) *The Second Industrial Divide*, New York: Basic Books.

Porter, M. (1990) *The Competitive Advantage of Nations*, London: Macmillan.

Promomoda (1993) 'Il distretto industriale di Empoli: analisi del settore abbigliamento', mimeo, Empoli.

Pyke, F., Becattini, G. and Sengenberger, W. (eds) (1990) *Industrial Districts and Inter-firm Co-operation in Italy*, Geneva: International Institute for Labour Studies.

Pyke, F. and Sengenberger, W. (eds) (1992) *Industrial Districts and Local Economic Regeneration*, Geneva: International Institute for Labour Studies.

Romagnoli, S. (1995) 'L'area empolese fra crisi e decentramento internazionale', in A. Cavalieri (ed.) *L'Internazionalizzazione del processo produttivo nei sistemi locali di piccola impresa in Toscana*, Irpet, Milan: Franco Angeli.

Scott, A. (1995) 'The geographic foundations of industrial performance', paper presented at the International Conference on Competitividad territorial y recomposición socio-política, El Colegio de México, Mexico City, 25–27 April.

Sengenberger, W. (1994) 'Labour standards: an institutional framework for restructuring and development', in W. Sengenberger and D. Campbell (eds) *Creating Economic Opportunities: The Role of Labour Standards in Industrial Restructuring*, Geneva: International Institute for Labour Studies.

Sengenberger, W. and Pyke, F. (1992) 'Industrial districts and local economic regeneration: research and policy issues', in F. Pyke and W. Sengenberger (eds) *Industrial Districts and Local Economic Regeneration*, Geneva: International Institute for Labour Studies.

Sforzi, F. (1994) 'The Tuscan model: an interpretation in light of recent trends', un Leornardi, R. and Nanetti, R. (eds) *Regional Development in a Modern European Economy: The Case of Tuscany*, London: Pinter Publishers; reprinted in G. Becattini *et al.* (2003).

Signorini, F. (1994) 'The price of Prato, or measuring the industrial district effect', *Journal of the Regional Science Association International*, 73, 4: 369–392.

Storper, M. and Scott, A. (eds) (1992) *Pathways to Industrialization and Regional Development*, London: Routledge.

Tessieri, N. (2000) 'Multinazionali e distretti industriali in Italia', *Sviluppo locale*, 13: 71–99.

Uip (Unione Industriale Pratese) (1990) *Relazione del consiglio direttivo*, Prato.

Wilkinson, F. and You, J. (1994) 'Competition and cooperation: toward understanding industrial districts', *Review of Political Economy*, July: 259–278.

Zagnoli, P. (1993) *Percorsi di diversificazione dei distretti industriali: il caso di Prato*, Turin: Giappichelli.

2 South-East Brabant: A regional innovation system in transition

Amin, A. and Thrift, N. (eds) (1994) *Globalization, Institutions, and Regional Development in Europe*, Oxford, Oxford University Press.

Beek, W.J., Keus, E. and Rijntjes, G.J.P. (1994) *Technologie-initiatieven in Nederland: De regionale agenda*, The Hague: SMO.

Bianchi, P. and Miller, L. (1992) 'Systems of Innovation and the EC policy-making approach', paper presented at workshop Systems of Innovation (SPRINT/FAST), Bologne.

Boekholt, P. (1994) 'The European Community and Innovation Policy: Reorienting towards diffusion', PhD thesis: Aston University.

Boekholt, P. (1995) 'Clusters in de metaalelektro', in D. Jacobs, A.-P. de Man and A. aan den Rijn (eds) *Clusters en Concurrentiekracht*, Samson, pp. 61–78

Boekholt, P. (1997) 'Innovative clusters in the regions, possibilities for University-Enterprise partnerships', in J. Mitra and P. Formica (eds) *Innovation and Economic Development: University-Enterprise Partnerships in Action*, London: Oak Tree Press.

Bosman, A., Burgers, J., Martens, H., Van Ootmarsum, C., Vermeulen, V., Van der Weele, E., Van Deer Weil, M. and Van Woerden, J. (1993) *Innovaties in Regionaal Economische Netwerken: Een studie naar regionale KMO's in Zuid-oost Brabant* [Innovations in regional economic networks, a study of industrial SMEs in South-East Brabant], Eindhoven: Technische Universiteit Eindhoven.

Boston Consulting Group (2002) *De toekomst van de maakindustrie in Zuid-Nederland* [The future of the manufacturing industries in the Southern part of the Netherlands], Venlo: Knoops B.V..

Cadmos, S.A., Netherlands Economic Institute (NEI) and Berger, Roland (1991) *European Scenarios on Technological Change and Social and Economic Cohesion*, Brussels: Commission of the European Communities, MONITOR-FAST Programme, Prospective Dossier No.1, vol. 16, FOP 240.

Camagni, R. (1991) *Innovation Networks: Spatial Perspectives*, London: Belhaven Press.

Cooke, P. (1994) *The New Wave of Regional Innovation Networks: Analysis, Characteristics and Strategy*, Cardiff: University of Wales, CASS.

Cooke, P., Boekholt, P. and Tödtling, F. (2000) *The Governance of Innovation in Europe: Regional Perspectives on Global Competitiveness*, London: Pinter.

Dosi, G., Freeman, C., Nelson, R.R., Silverberg, G. and Soete, L. (1988) *Technical Change and Economic Theory*, London: Pinter Publishers.

ETIN (2002) *Economic Profile Eindhoven Region*, Tilburg: ETIN Adviseurs.

Fahrenkrog, G. and Boekholt, P. (1993) *Report for the SPRINT/EIMS, Policy Workshop 'Public Measures to Support the Clustering and Networks of Innovative SMEs', Luxembourg, 6–7 December, Commission of the European Communities*, Apeldoorn: TNO-Centre for Technology and Policy Studies.

Freeman, C. (1987) *Technology Policy and Economic Performance: Lessons from Japan*, London: SPRU, Pinter Publishers.

Freeman, C. (1992) 'Formal scientific and technical institutions in the National System of Innovation', in B.-A. Lundvall (ed.) *National Systems of Innovation: Towards a Theory of Innovation and Interactive Learning*, London: Pinter.

Grabher, G. (1993) 'The weakness of strong ties: the lock-in of regional development in the Ruhr area', in G. Grabher (ed.) *The Embedded Firm: On the Socioeconomics of Industrial Networks*, London: Routledge pp. 255–277.

Håkansson, H. (ed.) (1989) *Corporate Technological Behaviour: Cooperation and Networks*, London: Routledge.
Holland, C. (1994) *Technologiebeleid in de regio, een inventarisatie*, The Hague: Consultium.
Horizon Programme (2002) *Opportunities for the 'Eindhoven' Technology Region*, The Committee for Regional Opportunities, Eindhoven, June 2002.
Jacobs, D., Braendgaard, A. and Boekholt, O. (1991) *Globalization of Science and Technology and Small Advanced Countries (Benelux, Denmark)*, Brussels: European Commission, Monitor/FAST, Vol. 18, FOP 290.
Jacobs, D., Boekholt, P. and Zegveld, W. (1990) *De economische kracht van Nederland*, The Hague: SMO.
Jacobs, D., de Man, A.-P. and aan den Rijn. A. (eds) (1995) *Clusters en Concurrentie-kracht*, Samson.
Lundvall, B.-Å. (ed.) (1992) *National Systems of Innovation: Towards a Theory of Innovation and Interactive Learning*, London: Pinter Publishers.
Metcalfe, S. (1995) 'The economic foundations of technology policy: equilibrium and evolutionary perspectives', in P. Stoneman (ed.) *Handbook of the Economics of Innovation and Technological Change*, Oxford: Blackwell Publishers, pp. 409–512.
Morgan, K. (1996) 'The learning region: institutions, innovation and regional renewal', *Regional Studies*, 31(5): 491–503.
Nelson, R.R. (ed.) (1993) *National Innovation Systems: A Comparative Analysis*, Oxford: Oxford University Press.
Nelson, R.R. and Rosenberg, N. (1993) 'Technical innovations and national systems', in R.R. Nelson (ed.) *National Systems of Innovation: A Comparative Analysis*, Oxford: Oxford University Press.
North-Brabant Development Agency (1999) *Innovatie Profiel Brabant* [InnovationProfile Brabant], Tilburg: North-Brabant Development Agency.
North-Brabant Development Agency (2000) *Eindrapport RITTS* [RITTS final report], Tilburg: North-Brabant Development Agency.
North-Brabant Development Agency (2002) *Innovative Actions Brabant*, Tilburg: North-Brabant Development Agency.
OECD (1999) *Boosting Innovation: The Cluster Approach*, Paris: OECD.
Porter, M. (1990) *The Competitive Advantage of Nations*, New York: Free Press.
Praat, H. (1992) *Mainsuppliers en hun netwerken: Naar een effectieve structuur van de Nederlandse toeleveringsindustrie* [Main suppliers and their networks: Towards an effective structure in the Dutch supply industry], Nijmegen: Katholieke Universiteit Nijmegen, Nederlandse Vereniging Algemene Toelevering.
Praat, H., van der Weele, E. and Gosselink, P. (1995) *De kracht van het specialisme: succesvol toeleveren door kleur bekennen* [The power of specialising: success in supplying by showing one's colours], Apeldoorn: Nederlandse Vereniging Algemene Toelevering / TVO-STB
Praat, H., van Dishoeck, N. and van Weele, A. (1994) *De winst van uitbesteden, samenwerking vanuit ketenperspectief* [The benefit of sub-contracting, collaboration from the supply chain perspective], TNO Beleidsstudies, Holland Consulting Group, Nederlandse Vereniging Algemene Toelevering.
Provincie Noord-Brabant (2002) *Uitvoeringsprogramma Regionaal Economisch Beleid* [Implementation Programme Regional Economic Policy]', 's-Hertogenbosch.

Regional Economic Development Corporation REDE (2002) *Facts and Figures Eindhoven Region*, Tilburg: Etin Adviseurs.

Royen, E.J.G., Raaymakers, A., Schippers, A. and Verbong, G. (1991) *Philips en zijn toeleveranciers: uitbesteden en toeleveren in de regio Brabant, 1945–1991* [Philips and its suppliers: sub-contracting and supplying in the Brabant region, 1945–1991], Eindhoven: Kamers van Koophandel en Fabrieken voor Zuid-oost-Brabant.

SEO (1994) *De regionale dimensie van innovatie in de Nederlandse industrie en dienstverlening* [The regional dimension of innovation in the Dutch industry and services], Amsterdam: University of Amsterdam.

Stoop, S. (1992) 'De sociale fabriek: sociale politiek bij Philips Eindhoven, Bayer Leverkusen en Hoogovens IJmuiden', [The social factory: Social politics at Philips Eindhoven, Bayer Leverkusen and Hoogovens IJmuiden], PhD thesis, University of Utrecht: Stenfert Kroese.

3 The changing institutional structure and performance of the Catalan innovation system

Bacaria, J. (1994) 'Competition and co-operation among jurisdictions: the case of regional co-operation in science and technology in Europe', *European Planning Studies*, 2(3): 287–302.

Bacaria, J., Borràs, S. and Fernàndez-Ribas, A. (2000) 'Public action and innovation-support institutions in new technological agglomerations: the case of the Vallès Occidental County', *European Urban and Regional Studies*, 9(4): 283–296.

Bacaria, J., Borràs, S. and Fernàndez-Ribas, A. (2001) 'El sistema de innovación regional en Cataluña', in M. Olazaran and M. Gómez Uranga (eds) *Sistemas de innovación regional*, Aideia: Servicio de publicaciones de la Universidad del País Vasco.

Bacaria, J. and Fernàndez-Ribas, A. (2002): 'Public-private partnerships in research and technology development in Spain' in *Covoseco: From Co-operation between to Co-evolution of Science and Technology*, IHP-STRATA program DG Research, Bremen: University of Bremen.

Biegelbauer, P. and Borrás, S. (eds) (2002) *Innovation Policies in Europe and the US: The New Agenda*, Ashgate: Aldershot.

Borràs, S. (1995) 'Interregional co-operation in Europe during the eighties and early nineties', in N.A. Sørensen (ed.) *European Identities: Cultural Diversity and Integration in Europe since 1700*, Odense: Odense University Press.

Caixa de Catalunya (2000a)*Anuari Econòmic Comarcal*, Caixa de Catalunya: Barcelona.

Caixa de Catalunya (2000b) *Informe sobre la situació i les perspectives de l'economia catalana, primavera 2000*, Caixa de Catalunya: Barcelona.

Callejón, M. and García Quevedo, J. (2000) 'Economía y política del cambio tecnológico en la industria de Cataluña', *Economía Industrial*, 335–336.

Castro, L., Fernández, M. and Sanz, L (2002) 'La importancia de los intereses académicos en la política científica y tecnológica catalana', unpublished paper. Madrid: Unidad de Políticas Comparadas. CSIC.

CDTI (1999) *Memoria de investigación: Año 1999*, Madrid: MCYT.

CIRIT (1993a) 'R&D a Catalunya: Despeses i activitats dels sectors públic i privat (1990)', in *Collecció informes No.8*, Barcelona: CIRIT.

CIRIT (1993b) *Pla de Recerca de Catalunya 1993–1996*, Barcelona: Generalitat de Catalunya.

Cohen, W.M. and Levinthal, D.A. (1990) 'Absorptive capacity: a new perspective on learning and innovation', *Administrative Science Quarterly*, 35: 128–152.

Conejos, Jordi (1993) 'Models Industrials de Futur per a Catalunya', *Banca Catalana Revista Econòmica*, pp. 11–20.

Cornes, R. and Sandler, T. (1986) *The Theory of Externalities: Public Goods, and Club Goods*, Cambridge: Cambridge University Press.

COTEC (1998) *El sistema español de innovación. Diagnósticos y recomendaciones. Libro Blanco*, Fundación Cotec para la Innovación Tecnológica. Available http://www.cotec.es.

Departament de Indústria, Comerç i Turisme (2001) *Pla d'Innovació de Catalunya*, Barcelona: Generalitat de Catalunya. Online. Available http://www.gencat.es/cidem/innocat.

DURSI (2001) *III Pla de Recerca de Catalunya 2001–2004*, Barcelona: Generalitat de Catalunya. Online. Available http://www.gencat.es/dursi.

DURSI (2002) *Memoria d'activitats 2001*, Barcelona: DURSI. Available http://www.gencat.es/dursi.

Escorsa, P. and Valls, J. (1992) *La recerca i la tecnologia*, Quaderns de Competitivitat 12, Barcelona: Direcció General d'Indústria, Generalitat de Catalunya.

Escorsa, P. *et al.* (1993) *R&D a Catalunya: despeses i activitats dels sectors públic i privat: 1990*, Barcelona: Generalitat de Catalunya, Commissió Interdepartmental de Recerca i Innovació Tecnológica.

Eurostat (2002) 'Research and development expenditure and personnel in European regions', Online. Available http://europa.eu.int/comm/Eurostat.

Evangelista, R., Perani, G., Rapiti, F. and Archibugui, D. (1997) 'Nature and impact of innovation in manufacturing industry: some evidence from the Italian innovation survey', *Research Policy*, 26, (4–5): 521–536.

Fernàndez-Ribas, A. (2002) 'El model d´innovació català', unpublished paper for the Government of Catalonia, Pla Governamental Cat21, June.

Fontrodona, J. and Hernández, J.M. (2001) *Les multinacionals industrials catalanes 2001*, Barcelona: Generalitat de Catalunya Departament de Comerç i Turisme.

Giráldez Pidal, E. (1994) 'Relacions financeres i tecnològiques amb l'estranger' in Banco Bilbao Vizcaya (ed) *L'economia catalana davant del canvi de segle*, Barcelona: BBV.

Institut de Estadística de Catalunya (2002) *Figures for Catalonia 2002*, Barcelona: Generalitat de Catalunya IDESCAT. Online: http://www.idescat.es

Instituto Nacional de Estadística (2000a) 'Encuesta de innovación tecnológica en las empresas 1998', Madrid:INE. Online: http://www.ine.es/inebase/cgi/um

Instituto Nacional de Estadística (2000b) 'Estadistica sobre las actividades en Investigación Científica y Desarrollo Tecnológico (I+D)', Madrid: INE. Online: http://www.ine.es/inebase/cgi/um

Ministerio de Ciencia y Tecnología (MCYT) (1999) 'Indicadores del sistema español de ciencia y tecnología', Madrid: MCYT. Online: http://www.mcyt.es/Estudios_Publica/PDF/Indicadores%20CyT%202000.pdf.

Presidencia del Gobierno, Oficina de Ciencia y Tecnología (2000) *National Plan for Scientific Research, Technological Development and Innovation (2000–2003)*, vol. I 'Objectives and Structure', Madrid: Ministerio de la Presidencia. Online: http://www.mcyt.es/sepct/pdf/pnidi-1i.pdf

Riba, M. and Leydesdorff, L. (2002) 'Why Catalonia cannot be considered as a Regional Innovation System', *Scientometrics*, 50(2): 215–240.

Servei de Programació i Anàlisi Industrial (1989) 'Política de desenvolupament tecnològic: el cas de Catalunya', unpublished paper. Barcelona: Generalitat de Catalunya, Direcció General de Industria.

Tarrach, A. (2001) *La situació de l'R&D a Catalunya i el III Pla de recerca 2001–2004*, Nota d'economia 69–70, 2nd quarter, Barcelona.

4 Ontario's regional innovation system

Amin, A. and Thrift, N.J. (1994) 'Living in the global', in A. Amin and N.J. Thrift (eds) *Globalization, Institutions and Regional Development in Europe*, Oxford: Oxford University Press.

APMA (2003) *Autoshift 2002: Action Strategies for the Automotive Components Industry in the 21st Century*, Toronto: Automotive Parts Manufacturers' Association, January.

Bradford, N. (1998) 'Prospects for associative governance: lessons from Ontario, Canada', *Politics and Society* 26: 539–573.

Brieger, P. (2002) 'A "riches to rags" story', *National Post*, 24 April.

Britton, J.N.H. (1999) 'Does nationality still matter? The new competition and the foreign ownership question revisited', in T.J. Barnes and M.S. Gertler (eds) *The New Industrial Geograph*, London: Routledge, pp. 238–264.

Britton, J.N.H. and Gilmour, J.M. (1978) *The Weakest Link: A Technological Perspective on Canadian Industrial Underdevelopment*, Background Study No. 43, Ottawa: Science Council of Canada.

Canada, Department of Finance (1998) *The Canadian Opportunities Strategy, Budget 1998*, Ottawa: Department of Finance.

Canada, Department of Finance (2001) *The Budget Plan 2001*, Ottawa: Department of Finance.

Canadian Independent Automotive Components Committee (1994) *Strategic Action Plan*, Toronto: CIACC.

Coleman, W.D. (1988) *Business and Politics: A Study in Collective Action*, Montreal and Kingston: McGill-Queen's University Press.

Cooke, P. and Morgan, K. (1994) 'The Regional Innovation System in Baden-Württemberg', *International Journal of Technology Management*, 9(3/4): 394–429.

Cooke, P. and Morgan, K. (1998) *The Associational Economy*, Oxford: Oxford University Press.

Courchene, T. and Telmer, C. (1998) *From Heartland to North American Region State: The Social, Fiscal and Federal Evolution of Ontario*, Toronto: Centre for Public Management, Faculty of Management, University of Toronto.

Dale, J. (2002) 'Innovation in Ottawa's technology clusters', paper presented at the Ontario Innovation Summit, Ontario Ministry of Enterprise, Opportunity and Innovation, Toronto, 5 November.

Deloitte & Touche, Greater Toronto Marketing Alliance, SMART Toronto and Human Resources Development Canada (1999) *Canada's SMART Community: The Greater Toronto Area's Information Technology and Telecommunications Industry*, Toronto.

DesRosiers, D. (2002) 'Is our auto sector in trouble? If so, where? What do we do about it?', paper presented to the Canadian Urban Institute, 7 March.

Eves, E. (1997) 'The R&D opportunity: cutting taxes and creating jobs', Budget Paper E, in *1997 Ontario Budget*, Toronto: Queen's Printer for Ontario.

Eves, E. (1998) 'Strategic skills: investing in jobs for the future today', Budget Paper E, in *1998 Ontario Budget*, Toronto: Queen's Printer for Ontario.

Florida, R. (1995) 'Toward the learning region', *Futures*, 27: 527–536.

Gertler, M.S. (1995) 'Groping towards reflexivity: responding to industrial change in Ontario' in P. Cooke (ed.) *The Rise of the Rustbelt*, London: University College London Press, pp. 103–124.

Gertler, M.S. (2002) 'Technology, culture and social learning: regional and national institutions of governance', in M.S. Gertler and D.A. Wolfe (eds) *Innovation and Social Learning: Institutional Adaptation in an Era of Technological Change*, Basingstoke: Palgrave Macmillan, pp. 111–134.

Gertler, M.S. and DiGiovanna, S. (1997) 'In search of the new social economy: collaborative relations between producers and users of advanced manufacturing technologies', *Environment and Planning A*, 29: 1585–1602.

Gertler, M.S., Florida, R., Gates, G. and Vinodrai, T. (2002) *Competing on Creativity: Placing Ontario's Cities in North American Context*, Toronto: Institute for Competitiveness and Prosperity and the Ontario Ministry of Enterprise, Opportunity and Innovation. Available online at: www.competeprosper.ca.

Gertler, M.S. and Wolfe, D.A. (eds) (2002) *Innovation and Social Learning*, Basingstoke: Palgrave Macmillan.

Gertler, M.S., Wolfe, D.A. and Garkut, D. (2000) 'No place like home? The embeddedness of innovation in a regional economy', *Review of International Political Economy*, 7: 1–31.

Grabher, G. (ed.) (1993) *The Embedded Firm*, London: Routledge.

Holbrook, J.A.D. and Squires, R.J. (1996) 'Firm level analysis of determinants of Canadian industrial R&D performance', *Science and Public Policy*, 23(6): 369–74.

Hollingsworth, J.R., Schmitter, P. and Streeck, W. (eds) (1994) *Governing Capitalist Economies: Performance and Control of Economic Sectors*, Oxford: Oxford University Press.

Holmes, J. (2000) 'Regional economic integration in North America', in G.L. Clark, M.P. Feldman, and M.S. Gertler (eds) *The Oxford Handbook of Economic Geography*, Oxford: Oxford University Press, pp. 649–670.

Industry Canada (2002) *Canadian ICT Sector Profile: Information and Communications Technologies Branch*, Ottawa, April.

Le, C.D. and Tang, J. (2001) 'Why does Canada spend less on R&D than its key trade competitors?', paper presented at the 2001 Economic Conference, Statistics Canada, May, Ottawa.

Lundvall, B.-Å. (ed.) (1992) *National Systems of Innovation: Towards a Theory of Innovation and Interactive Learning*, London: Pinter.

Mandel-Campbell, A. (2002) 'Driving production down Mexico way', *National Post*, 23 April.

Martin, P. (2000) *Budget Speech 2000*, Ottawa: Department of Finance.

Maskell, P. and Malmberg, A. (1999) 'Localised learning and industrial competitiveness', *Cambridge Journal of Economics*, 23: 167–186.

McFetridge, D.G. and Corvari, R.J. (1985) 'Technology diffusion: a survey of Canadian evidence and public policy issues', in D.G. McFetridge (ed.) *Technological Change in Canadian Industry*, Background Study, vol. 3, Royal Commission on the Economic Union and Development Prospects for Canada, Toronto: University of Toronto Press, pp. 177–231.

Morgan, K. (1997) 'The learning region: institutions, innovation and regional renewal', *Regional Studies*, 31: 491–504.

Nelson, R.R. (ed.) (1993) *National Innovation Systems: A Comparative Analysis*, Oxford: Oxford University Press.

Ontario Jobs and Investment Board (1999) *A Road Map to Prosperity: An Economic Plan for Jobs in the 21st Century*, Toronto: Ontario Jobs and Investment Board.

Ontario Ministry of Economic Development and Trade (1995) *Ontario Sector Snapshots: A Progress Report on the Sector Development Approach*, Toronto: Ontario Ministry of Economic Development and Trade.

Ontario Ministry of Enterprise, Opportunity and Innovation (2002) *Ontario Innovation 2002 Index*, Toronto: Ontario Science and Innovation Council.

Ontario Ministry of Finance (2002a) 'Ontario's dynamic workforce', March, www.2ontario.com/welcome/oolf_303.asp.

Ontario Ministry of Finance (2002b) 'Ontario fact sheet', 4 December, www.gov.on.ca/FIN/english/economy/factedec02.htm.

Porter, M.E. (1990) *The Competitive Advantage of Nations*, New York: The Free Press.

Putnam, R. (1993) *Making Democracy Work*, Princeton, NJ: Princeton University Press.

Rea, K.J. (1985) *The Prosperous Years: The Economic History of Ontario, 1939–1975*, Toronto: University of Toronto Press.

Research Money (2002a) 'Innovation remains front and centre as Ontario renews central R&D programs', 16: 10, 21 June.

Research Money (2002b) 'Slumping telecommunications sector drags down industrial R&D spending', 16: 2, 29 July.

Safarian, A.E. (1966) *Foreign Ownership of Canadian Industry*, Toronto: McGraw-Hill.

Saxenian, A. (1994) *Regional Advantage: Culture and Competition in Silicon Valley and Route 128*, Cambridge, MA: Harvard University Press.

Schulz, T. (1994) 'How much should Canada spend on R&D?', in Industry Canada, Secretariat for Science and Technology Review, *Resource Book for Science and Technology Consultations*, vol. II, Ottawa: Minister of Supply and Services Canada, pp. 43–46.

Scott, A.J. (1988) *New Industrial Spaces*, London: Pion.

Scott, A.J. (1996) 'Regional motors of the global economy', *Futures*, 28: 391–411.

Stanford, J. (1999) 'Auto workers and productivity', *National Post*, 27 September, p. C5.

Statistics Canada (2000) *Provincial Gross Domestic Product by Industry, 1984–1999*, CANSIM II Database, Ottawa: Statistics Canada.

Statistics Canada (2001a) *Provincial Gross Domestic Product by Industry, 1992–1998*, Ottawa: Statistics Canada.

Statistics Canada (2001b) *Service Bulletin: Science Statistics*, 25(8), November.

Statistics Canada (2001c) *Industrial Research and Development: 2002 Intentions*, Ottawa: Statistics Canada.

Stonehouse, D. (2003) 'How we rank: study shows Ottawa "well positioned to compete", but not all is smooth sailing', *Ottawa Citizen*, 6 February.

Storper, M. (1997) *The Regional World*, New York: Guilford Press.

Sulzenko, A. (1998) 'Technology and innovation policy for the knowledge-based economy: the changing view in Canada', *OECD STI Review*, 22: 285–305.

US Department of Commerce (2001) *Statistical Abstract of the United States 2001*, Washington, DC: US Department of Commerce.

Watkins, M.H. *et al.* (1968) *Foreign Ownership and the Structure of Canadian Industry*, Ottawa: Privy Council Office, Government of Canada.

Wolfe, D.A. (1999) 'Harnessing the region: changing perspectives on innovation policy in Ontario', in T.J. Barnes and M.S. Gertler (eds) *The New Industrial Geography: Regions, Regulation and Institutions*, London: Routledge, pp. 127–154.

Wolfe, D.A. (2002a) 'Negotiating order: sectoral policies and social learning in Ontario', in M.S. Gertler and D.A. Wolfe (eds) *Innovation and Social Learning: Institutional Adaptation in an Era of Technological Change*, Basingstoke: Palgrave Macmillan, pp. 227–250.

Wolfe, D.A. (2002b) 'Innovation policy for the knowledge-based economy: from the red book to the White Paper', in G.B. Doern (ed.) *How Ottawa Spends 2002–2003: The Security Aftermath and National Priorities*, Toronto: Oxford University Press, pp. 137–156.

Wolfe, D.A. (2002c) 'Knowledge, learning and social capital in Ontario's ICT clusters', paper prepared for the Annual Meeting of the Canadian Political Science Association, University of Toronto, Toronto, Ontario, 29–31 May.

Wolfe, D.A. and Gertler, M.S. (2001) 'Globalization and economic restructuring in Ontario: from industrial heartland to learning region?', *European Planning Studies*, 9(5): 575–592.

5 Escaping path dependency: the case of Tampere, Finland

Alasoini, T. (1991) 'Modernization strategies in Finnish manufacture: past experiences, prospects for the 1990s', in A. Kasvio, C. Makó and M. McDaid (eds) *Work and Social Innovations in Europe*, Tampere: University of Tampere, Research Institute for Social Sciences, Work Research Centre. Working Papers 25/1991, pp. 39–68.

Alasoini, T. (1999) 'Organisational innovations as a source of competitive advantage: new challenges for Finnish companies and the national workplace development infrastructure', in G. Schienstock and O. Kuusi (eds) *Transformation Towards a Learning Economy: The Challenge for the Finnish Innovation System*, SITRA 213, Helsinki: SITRA.

Ali-Yrkkö, J. (2001) *Nokia's Network – Gaining Competitiveness from Co-operation*, Vantaa: Taloustieto Oy.

Ali-Yrkkö, J. and Hermans, R. (2002) *Nokia Suomen innovaatiojärjestelmässä*, Keskustelunaihe nr. 799. Helsinki: ETLA.

Castells, M. and Himanen, P. (2001) *The Finnish Model of the Information Society*, Helsinki: SITRA and WSOY.

Finnish Ministry of Interior (2002) Osaamiskeskusohjelman kotisivut (web pages of the Centre of Expertise Programme. Available online at: http://www.intermin.fi/intermin/home.nsf/pages

Finnish Venture Capital Association (2001) *Tilastotietoja toimialasta* (Sectoral Statistics), Helsinki: Statistics Finland.

Jones-Evans, D. (2000) 'Entrepreneurial universities: policies, strategies, and practice', in P. Conceicao, D.V. Gibson, M.V. Heitor and S. Shariq (eds) *Science, Technology, and Innovation Policy: Opportunities and Challenges for the Knowledge Economy*, London: Quorum Books.

Kanniainen, V. (1994) 'Growth and technical change in Finland: the role of collective sharing of economic risks', in S. Vuori and P. Vuorinen (eds) *Explaining Technical Change in a Small Country: The Finnish National Innovation System*, Heidelberg: Physica-Verlag in Association with ETLA, Helsinki.

Kautonen, M., Kolehmainen, J. and Koski, P. (2002) *Yritysten innovaatioympäristöt. Tutkimus yritysten innovaatiotoiminnasta ja alueellisesta innovaatiopolitiikasta Pirkanmaalla ja Keski-Suomessa*, Teknologiakatsaus 120/2002. Helsinki: TEKES.

Koistinen, P. and Lilja, K. (1988) 'Consensual adaptation to new technology: The Finnish case', in R. Hyman and W. Streeck (eds) *New Technology and Industrial Relations*, Oxford: Basil Blackwell, pp. 263–271.

Lemola, T. (1999) 'Economic development and phases of technology policy in Finland', unpublished paper prepared for the International Symposium Towards an R&D Strategy for Israel, 16–17 June 1999, Jerusalem.

Lilja, K., Räsänen, K. and Tainio, R. (1992) 'A dominant business recipe: the forest sector in Finland', in R. Whitley (ed.) *European Business Systems: Firms and Markets in their National Contexts*, London: Sage, pp. 137–154.

Miles, I. and Kastrinos, N. with Flanagan, K., Bilderbeek, R. and Den Hertog, P., Huntik, W. and Bouman, M. (1995) *Knowledge-Intensive Business Services: Users, Carriers and Sources of Innovation*, European Innovation Monitoring System (EIMS).

Myllyntaus, T. (1992) 'Technology transfer and the contextual filter in the Finnish setting: transfer channels and mechanisms in a historical perspective', in Vuori, S., Ylä-Anttila, P. (eds) Helsinki: *Mastering Technology Diffusion – The Finnish Experience*, Helsinki: ETLA (The Research Institute of the Finnish Economy), pp. 195–252.

O'Gorman, C. and Kautonen, M. (2001) 'Policies for new prosperity: promoting agglomerations of knowledge intensive industries', conference proceedings of Technological Entrepreneurship in Emerging Regions, 28–30 June 2001, Singapore, National University of Singapore.

Prihti, A., Geoghiou, L., Helander, E., Juusela, J., Meyer-Kramer, F., Roslin, B., Santamäki-Vuori, T. and Gröhn, M. (2000) *Assessment of the Additional Appropriation of Research*, Helsinki: Sitra.

Science and Technology Council of Finland (2000) *Review 2000: Challenges of Knowledge and Know-How* (in Finnish).

Schienstock, G. (2002a) *Information Society, Work, and the Generation of New Forms of Social Exclusion*, Final Report. TSER Programme.

Schienstock, G. (2002b) Final report of the project 'Information Society, Work and the Generation of New Forms of Social Exclusion', funded by the European Commission/DG XII under the TSER Programme, Tampere (Finland).

Schienstock, G. and Hämäläinen, T. (2001) *Transformation of the Finnish Innovation System: A Network Approach*, Sitra Report series 7, Helsinki: Sitra.

Schienstock, G., Räsänen, H. and Kautonen, M. (1999) 'From smoke-stack industries to information society: multimedia industry in the Tampere region', in H.-J.

Braczyk, G. Fuchs and H.G. Wolf (eds) *Multimedia and Regional Economic Restructuring*, London: Routledge, pp. 320–345.

Schienstock, G. and Tulkki, P. (2001) 'The fourth pillar? An assessment of the situation of the Finnish biotechnology, *Small Business Economics*, 17: 105–122.

Schienstock, G. and Tulkki, P. (2001) 'From foreign domination to global strength: transformation of the Finnish telecommunications industry', unpublished report for the project National Systems of Innovation and Networks in the Idea-Innovation Chain in Science-based Industries, funded by the European Commission/DG XII under the TSER Programme, Tampere (Finland).

Statistics Finland (2000) *Industrial Statistics for CityWeb Statistics Service*, accessed 18 October, City of Tampere.

Statistics Finland, *StatFin* (2001a) Available online at: http://statfin.stat.fi/StatWeb/start.asp.?LA=fr8,1p=home.

Statistics Finland (2001b) *Tiede ja teknologia 2000* (Science and Technology 2000). Helsinki: Statistics Finland.

Statistics Finland, *StatFin* (2002).

Tampereen seudun osaamiskeskusohjelma 1999–2006 (1998) Tampere: Pirkanmaan liitto.

Tulkki, P. (2001) 'Finnish way to information society: expanding engineer education', *European Journal of Engineering Education*, 26(1): 39–52.

Virkkala, S. (1994) 'Economic restructuring and regional development in Finland', in J. Doling, B. Koskiaho and S. Virkkala (eds) *Restructuring in Old Industrial Towns in Finland*, Tampere: University of Tampere. Department of Social Policy and Social Work, pp. 69–104.

Vuori, S. and Vuorinen, P. (1994) 'Outlines of the Finnish innovation system: the institutional setup and performance', in S. Vuori and P. Vuorinen (eds) *Explaining Technical Change in a Small Country: The Finnish National Innovation System*, Heidelberg: Physica-Verlag in Association with ETLA, Helsinki, pp. 1–42.

6 Learning in the village economy of Denmark

Alchian, A. and Demsetz, H. (1972) 'Production, information costs, and economic organization', *American Economic Review*, 62: 777–795.

Arrow, Kenneth J. (1962) 'Economic welfare and the allocation of resources for invention', in R. Nelson (ed.) *The Rate and Direction of Inventive Activity: Economic and Social Factors*, Princeton, NJ: Princeton University Press, pp. 609–30.

Arrow, Kenneth J. (1970) *Essays on the Theory of Risk Bearing*, Chicago: Markham.

Arthur, W.B. (1989) 'Competing technologies, increasing returns, and lock-ins by historical events', *Economic Journal*, 99: 116–131.

Axelsson, Björn and Easton, Geoffery (eds) (1992) *Industrial Networks: A New View of Reality*, London.

Aydalot, P. (1986) *Milieux Innovateurs en Europe*, Paris: GREMI.

Balassa, Bela (1969) 'Industrial development in an open economy: the case of Norway', *Oxford Economic Papers*, new series, 21: 344–359.

Barney, J. (1991) 'Firm resources and sustained competitive advantage', *Journal of Management*, 17: 99–120.

Barzel, Y. (1982) 'Measurement cost and the organization of markets', *Journal of Law and Economics*, 25(1): 27–48.

Boyd, Andrew (1978) 'How the storm changed the signs', *The Economist* (Survey), 28 January.

Christensen, Jens Frøslev (1993) *Innovation i dansk erhvervsliv* (Innovation in Danish industry) Copenhagen: Erhvervsfremme Styrelsen.

Collis, David J. (1991) 'A resource-based analysis of global competition: the case of the bearings industry', *Strategic Management Journal*, 12: 49–68

Cornwall, John (1969) 'Postwar growth in Western Europe: a reevaluation', *The Review of Economics and Statistics*, L (3): 361–368.

Cornwall, John (1977) *Modern Capitalism: Its Growth and Transformation*, Oxford: Oxford University Press.

Dalum, Bent (1995) 'Local and global linkages: the radiocommunications cluster', Northern Denmark, paper presented at the Journal of Industry Studies and Industrial Relations Research Centre, University of New South Wales, Sydney, 30–31 August.

Dalum, Bent and Villumsen, Gert (1994) *National erhvervsudvikling og konkurrenceevne* (National industrial development and the competitiveness), Copenhagen: Erhvervsfremme Styrelsen.

Dalum, B., Laursen, K. and Villumsen, G. (1998) Structural change in OECD export specialisation and stickiness. *International Journal of Applied Economics*, 13(3): 423–443.

David, Paul (1985) 'Clio and the economics of QWERTY', *American Economic Review*, 75: 332–337.

Dei Ottati, Gabi (2002) 'Social concertation and local development: The case of industrial districts', *European Planning Studies*, 10(4): 449–466.

Dosi, G. (1990) 'Finance, innovation and industrial change', *Journal of Economic Behaviour and Organization*, 13: 299–319.

Drèze, Jacques H. (1960) 'Quelques réflexions sereines sur l'adaption de l'industrie belge au Marché Commun', *Comptes Rendus des travaux de la Société d'Economie Politique de Belgique* du 20 décembre 1960 (17.45–19.15) 275: 4–37. (A translated and revised version with the title 'The standard goods hypothesis' is included in Alexis Jaquemin and André Sapir (eds) *The European Internal Market: Trade and Competition*', Oxford: Oxford University Press, 1989: 13–32.

Eccles, Robert (1981) 'The quasifirm in the construction industry', *Journal of Economic Behaviour and organization*, 2: 335–357.

Erhvervsministeriet (1995a) *Regionalpolitisk redegørelse* (Ministry of Industry: Report on regional policy), Copenhagen: Erhvervsministeriet.

Erhvervsministeriet (1995b) *Erhvervsredegørelse 1995* (Ministry of Industry: Annual report on industrial policy), Copenhagen: Erhvervsministeriet.

Estevez-Abé, Margarita, Iversen, Torben and Soskice, David (2001) 'Social protection and the formation of skills: a reinterpretation of the welfare state', in Peter A. Hall and David Soskice (eds) *Varieties of Capitalism: The Institutional Foundations of Comparative Advantage*, Oxford: Oxford University Press.

European Commission (1993) *White Paper on Growth, Competitiveness and Employment*. December, Brussels: European Commission.

Fagerberg, Jan (1995a) 'User-producer interaction, learning and comparative advantage', *Cambridge Journal of Economics*, 19(1): 243–256.

Fagerberg, Jan (1995b) 'Competitiveness, Scale and R&D', paper presented at the NUIP/FIEF conference on Technology and International Trade at Leangkollen, Oslo, 6–9 October.

Federal Reserve Bank of Kansas City (1995) *Reducing Unemployment: Current Issues and Policy Options*, Jackson Hole, 25–27 August, 1994.

Ford, David (ed.) (1990) *Understanding Business Markets: Interaction, Relationships, Networks*, London: Thomson Learning.

Freeman, Chris (1995) 'The "National System of Innovation" in historic perspective', *Cambridge Journal of Economics*, 19(1): 5–24.

Friedrichs, Jürgen (1993) 'A theory of urban decline: economy, democracy and political elites', *Urban Studies*, 30(6): 907–917.

Gertler, Meric S. (1995) 'Manufacturing culture: the spatial construction of capital', paper presented at the annual conference of the Institute of British Geographers, Newcastle Upon Tyne, 3–6 January.

Granovetter, M. (1985) 'Economic action and social structure: the problem of embeddedness', *American Journal of Sociology*, 91: ???–364

Grossman, Gene M. and Helpman, Elhanan (1991) *Innovation and Growth in the Global Economy,* Cambridge, MA: Harvard University Press.

Grossman, Gene M. and Helpman, Elhanan (1995) *Technology and Trade*, CEPR discussion paper no. 1134, February, London: CEPR.

Hernes, Gudmund (1979) *Forhandlingsøkonomi og blandingsadministration*, Oslo: Universitetsforlaget.

Hill, Charles W.L. (1995) 'National institutional structures, transaction cost economizing and competitive advantage: the case of Japan', *Organization Science*, 6(1): 119–131.

Hirschman, Albert O. (1958) *The Strategy of Economic Development*, 17th printing 1975, Yale: Yale University Press.

Imai, Ken-ichi, Nonaka, Ikujiro and Takeuchi, Hirotaka (1986) 'Managing the new product development process: companies learn and unlearn' in Kim B. Clark, Robert H.Hayes and Christopher Lorenz (eds) *The Uneasy Alliance: Managing the Productivity-Technology Dilemma*, Boston: Harvard Business School, pp. 337–86.

Katzenstein, Peter J. (1985) *Small State in World Markets: Industrial Policy in Europe*, Ithaca, NY: Cornell University Press.

Kautonen, Mika (1996) 'Emerging innovative networks and milieux: the case of the furniture industry in the Lahti Region of Finland', *European Planning Studies*, 4(4): 439–456.

Kongstad, J. and Larsen, L. (1990) 'The sectorial impact of the internal market in Denmark', *European Economy*, special edition on Social Europe, Directorate-General for Economic and Financial Affairs, Brussels: Commission of the European Communities, pp. 140–153.

Kristensen, Peer Hull (1992) 'Industrial districts in West Jutland, Denmark', in F. Pyke and W. Sengenberger (eds) *Industrial Districts and Local Economic Regeneration*, Geneva, pp. 122–174.

Krugman, Paul (1991) 'Increasing returns and economic geography', *Journal of Political Economy*, 99: 483–499.

Krugman, Paul (1994a) 'Competitiveness – a dangerous obsession', *Foreign Affairs*, 73(2): 28–44.

Krugman, Paul (1994b) 'Empirical evidence on the new trade theories: the current state of play', in *New Trade Theories: A Look at the Empirical Evidence*, London: Centre for Economic Policy Research (CEPR), pp. 11–31.

Krugman, Paul and Venables, Anthony J. (1993) *Integration, Specialization and Adjustment*, NBER Working paper no. 4559, Cambridge: NBER.

Langlois, Richard N. (1992) 'Transaction-cost economics in real time', *Industrial and Corporate Change*, 1(1): 99–127.

Linder, S.B. (1961) *An Essay on Trade and Transformation*, Uppsala: Almqvist and Wiksell.

List, F. (1841) *The National System of Political Economy*, London: Longmans, Green and Co.

Lorenzen, Mark (2001) 'Localized learning and policy: academic advice on enhancing regional competitiveness through learning', *European Planning Studies*, 9(2): 163–185.

Lundvall, Bengt-Åke (1985) *Product innovation and User-Producer Interaction*, Industrial development research series no. 31, Aalborg: AUC.

Lundvall, Bengt-Åke and Maskell, Peter (2000) 'Nation states and economic development: from national systems of production to national systems of knowledge creation and learning', in G.L. Clark, M.P. Feldmann and M.S. Gertler (eds) *The Oxford Handbook of Economic Geography*, Oxford: Oxford University Press, pp. 333–372.

Macaulay, Stewart (1963) 'Non-contractual relations. business: a preliminary study', *American Sociological Review*, 28(1): 55–67.

Maddison, Angus (2001) *The World Economy: A Millenial Perspective*, Paris: OECD.

Malmberg, Anders and Maskell, Peter (1997) 'Towards an explanation of industry agglomeration and regional specialization', *European Planning Studies*, 5(1): 25–41.

Malmberg, Anders and Maskell, Peter (2002) 'The elusive concept of localization economies – towards a knowledge-based theory of spatial clustering, *Environment and Planning A*, 34(3): 429–449.

Maskell, Peter (1998) Successful low-tech industries in high-cost environments: the case of the Danish furniture industry', *European Urban and Regional Studies*, 5(2): 99–118.

Maskell, Peter (1999) 'Globalization and industrial competitiveness: the process and consequences of ubiquitification', in E.J. Malecki and P. Oinas (eds) *Making Connections: Technological Learning and Regional Economic Change*, Aldershot: Ashgate, pp. 35–60.

Maskell, Peter (2001a) 'Towards a knowledge-based theory of the geographical cluster', *Industrial and Corporate Change*, 10(4): 919–941.

Maskell, Peter (2001b) 'Knowledge creation and diffusion in geographic clusters', *International Journal of Innovation Management*, 5(2): 213–237.

Maskell, Peter, Eskelinen, Heikki, Hannibalsson, Ingjaldur, Malmberg, Anders and Vatne, Eirik (1998) *Competitiveness, Localised Learning and Regional Development: Specialization and Prosperity in Small Open Economies*, London: Routledge.

Maskell, Peter and Malmberg, Anders (1999) 'Localised learning and industrial competitiveness', *Cambridge Journal of Economics*, 23(2): 167–186.

Maskell, Peter and Törnqvist, Gunnar (1999) *Building a Cross-Border Learning Regio: The Emergence of the Northern European Øresund Region*, Copenhagen: Copenhagen Business School Press.

Melchior, Arne (1995) 'Technology and international trade: new theory and evidence on the standard goods hypothesis', paper presented at the NUIP/FIEF conference on Technology and International Trade at Leangkollen, Oslo, 6–9 October.

Menzel, Ulrich (1980) *Der Entwicklungsweg Dänemarks (1880–1940), Ein Beitrag zum Konzept autozentrierter Entwicklung*, Projekt Untersuchung zur

Grundlegung einer praxisorientierten Theorie autozentrierter Entwicklung, Bremen: Bremen University.

Nelson, Richard R. and Winter, Sidney G. (1982) *An Evolutionary Theory of Economic Change*, Cambridge, MA: Harvard Univserity Press.

Nielsen, Klaus and Pedersen, Ove Kaj (1988) 'The negotiated economy: ideal and history', *Scandinavian Political Studies*, 11(2): 79–101.

Nielsen, Klaus and Pedersen, Ove Kaj (1991) 'From the mixed economy to the negotiated economy: the Scandinavian countries', in R.M. Coughlin (ed.) *Morality, Rationality and Efficiency: New perspectives on Socio-Economics*, New York: M.E. Sharpe, pp. 145–168.

North, Douglass C. (1994) 'Economic performance through time', *The American Economic Review*, 84(3): 359–368.

OECD (1994) *Globalization of Industrial Activities*, I-II, Working paper 48, Paris: OECD.

OECD (1995) *Education at a Glance*, Paris: OECD.

OECD (2001) *The STAN database*, available online: www.oecd.org/document/15/0,2340.

OECD (2002) *Main Science and Technological Indicators*, Paris: OECD.

Olson, Mancur (1982) *The Rise and Decline of Nations. Economic Growth, Stagflation and Social Rigidities*, New Haven, CT: Yale University Press.

Porter, Michael E. (1990) *The Competitive Advantages of Nations*, London: Macmillan.

Prasnikar, Vesna and Roth, Alvin E. (1992) 'Considerations of fairness and strategy: experimental data from sequential games', *The Quarterly Journal of Economics*, August: pp. 865–888.

Putnam, Robert D. (with Robert Leonardi and Raffaella Y. Nanetti) (1993) *Making Democracy Work: Civic Traditions in Modern Italy*, Princeton, NJ: Princeton University Press.

Rasmussen, Poul Nyrop (1989) 'Industrilokomotiver og samfundsøkonomisk organisering', *Økonomi og politik*, 62: 7–10.

Sabel, Charles (1992) 'Studied trust: Building new forms of co-operation in a volatile economy', in F. Pyke and W. Sengenberger (eds) *Industrial districts and local economic regeneration*, Geneva: ILO, pp. 215–250.

Saxenian, Annalee (1994) *Regional Advantage*, Cambridge, MA: Harvard University Press.

Sengenberger, W. and Pyke, F. (1992) 'Industrial districts and local economic regeneration: Research and policy issues', in F. Pyke and W. Sengenberger (eds) *Industrial Districts and Local Economic Regeneration*, Genever: ILO, pp. 3–29.

Sidenius, Niels C. (1983) 'The policy role of legislatures, some preliminary reflections and observations on the decision-making process in Danish industrial policies', paper presented at the workshop on 'Parliament and Policy' in the ECPR joint sessions, Freiburg, 20–25 March.

Statistics Denmark (1995 and 2000) *Statistical Fifty year review*, available online at www.dst.dk/dst/dstframeset_800_en.asp.

Statistics Denmark (2001) *Statistical Yearbook*, available online at www.dst.dk/dst/dstframeset_800_en.asp.

Statistics Denmark (2002a) *Statistical Ten Year Review*, available online at www.dst.dk/dst/dstframeset_800_enasp.

Statistics Denmark (2002b) *Information Society Denmark – 2001. Focus: Use of Internet*, Copenhagen: Statistics Denmark.

Storper, Michael (1994) 'Institutions in a learning economy', paper presented at the OECD conference on 'Employment and Growth in a Knowledge-Based Economy', Copenhagen, 7–8 November.

Strandskov, Jesper *et al.* (1994) *Ejerforhold og konkurenceevne i dansk erhvervsliv*, Copenhagen: Erhvervsfremme Styrelsen.

Veblen, Thorstein (1899) *The Theory of the Leisure Class*, London.

von Hayek, Friederich A. (1960) *The Constitution of Liberty*, Chicago: University of Chicago Press.

von Hippel, Eric (1988) *The Sources of Innovation*, Oxford: Oxford University Press.

Zander, Udo and Kogut, Bruce (1995) 'Knowledge and the speed of the transfer and imitation of organizational capabilities: an empirical test', *Organizational Science*, 6(1): 76–92.

Zysman, John (1994) *National Roots of a 'Global' Economy*, Berkeley, CA: University of California Press.

7 The Baden-Württemberg production and innovation regime

Beise, M., Licht, G. and Spielkamp, A. (1995) *Technologietransfer an kleine und mittlere Unternehmen: Analysen und Perspektiven für Baden-Württemberg*, Baden-Baden: Nomos.

Braczyk, H.-J., Fuchs, G. and Wolf, H.-G. (eds) (1999) *Multimedia and Regional Economic Restructuring*, London and New York: Routledge.

Braczyk, H.-J., Schienstock, G. and Steffensen, B. (1996) 'Die Regionalökonomie Baden-Württembergs – Ursachen und Grenzen des Erfolgs', in H.-J. Braczyk and G. Schienstock (eds) *Kurswechsel in der Industrie*, Stuttgart/Berlin/Köln: Kohlhammer, pp. 24–51.

Bundesministerium für Bildung und Forschung (2000) *Bundesbericht Forschung 2000*, Bonn/Berlin: BMBF.

Cooke, P., Morgan, K. and Price, A. (1993) *The Future of the Mittelstand. Collaboration versus Competition*, Regional Industrial Research Report No. 13. Cardiff: University of Wales.

Dohse, D. (2000) 'Technology policy and the regions: the case of the BioRegio contest', *Research Policy* 29: 1111–1133.

Faust, K., Grupp, H., Hummel, M., Klee, G., Laube, T., Münzenmaier, W., Saul, C., Schmoch, U. and Waldkircher-Heyne, C. (1995) *Der Wirtschafts- und Forschungsstandort Baden-Württemberg: Potentiale und Perspektiven*, Ifo Studien zur Strukturforschung 19, Munich: Ifo Institut für Wirtschaftsforschung.

Fuchs, G. and Wolf, H.-G. (1998) 'The emergence of industrial clusters for multimedia: a comparison of California, Ireland, and Baden-Württemberg', *Current Politics and Economics of Europe*, 8, 225–255.

Gehrke, B. an Grupp, H. (1994) *Innovationspotential und Hochtechnologie: Technologische Position Deutschlands im internationalen Wettbewerb*, Heidelberg: Physica-Verlag.

Grabher, G. (1993) 'The weakness of strong ties: the lock-in of regional development in the Ruhr area', in G. Grabher (ed.) *The Embedded Firm*, London: Routledge, pp. 255–77.

Greif, S. (2000) *Regionale Verteilung von Innovations- und Technologiepotentialen in Deutschland im Spiegel von Patenten*, Munich: Deutsches Patent- und Markenamt.

Hall, P.A and Soskice, D. (2001) 'An introduction to varieties of capitalism', in P.A. Hall, and D. Soskice (eds) *Varieties of Capitalism: The Institutional Foundations of Comparative Advantage*, Oxford: Oxford University Press, pp. 1–68.

Heidenreich, M. (1998) Die duale Berufsausbildung zwischen industrieller Prägung und wissensgesellschaftlichen Herausforderungen', *Zeitschrift für Soziologie*, 27: 321–40.

Heinemann, F., Kukuk, M. and Westerheide, P. (1995) 'Das Innovationsverhalten der Baden-Württembergischen Unternehmen,' *Eine Auswertung der ZEW/infas-Innovationserhebung 1993*, Mannheim: ZEW-Dokumentation No. 95–05.

Heinze, R.G. and Schmid, J. (1994) *Industrieller Strukturwandel und die Kontingenz politischer Steuerung: Mesokorporatistische Strategien im Vergleich*, Arbeitspapier No. SIT-wp-2-94. Bochum: Ruhr-Universität Bochum.

Herrigel, G.B. (1993) 'Power and the redefinition of industrial districts: the case of Baden-Württemberg', in G. Grabher (ed.) *The Embedded Firm*, London: Routledge, pp. 227–251.

Kern, H. and Sabel, C. (1994) 'Verblaßte Tugenden: Zur Krise des deutschen Produktionsmodells', in N. Beckenbach and W. von Treeck (eds) *Umbrüche gesellschaftlicher Arbeit*, Göttingen, Schwartz and Co., pp. 605–624.

Kerst, C. and Steffensen, B. (1995) *Die Krise des Baden-Württembergischen Maschinenbaus im Spiegel des NIFA-Panels*, Stuttgart: Akademie für Technikfolgenabschätzung. Arbeitsbericht No. 49.

Krauss, G. (1999) 'Les problèmes d'adaptation d'une économie régionale forte: changement et inerties en Baden-Württemberg', *Revue d'Economie Régionale et Urbaine*, 2: 353–376.

Krauss, G. and Stahlecker, T. (2000) *Die BioRegion Rhein-Neckar-Dreieck: Von der Grundlagenforschung zur wirtschaftlichen Verwertung?* Stuttgart: Arbeitsbericht der Akademie für Technikfolgenabschätzung in Baden-Württemberg No. 158.

Lane, C. (1994) 'Industrial order and the transformation of industrial relations: Britain, Germany and France compared', in R. Hyman and A. Ferner (eds) *New Frontiers in European Industrial Relations*, Oxford: Blackwell, pp.167–95.

Maier, H.E. (1989) 'Industrieentwicklung und Industriepolitik in Baden-Württemberg: Überlegungen zu den institutionellen Voraussetzungen differenzierter Qualitätsproduktion', in J. Hucke and H. Wollmann (eds) *Dezentrale Technologiepolitik*, Berlin: Birkhäuser, pp. 261–303.

Ministerium für Wissenschaft und Forschung (1995) *Landesforschungsbericht Baden-Württemberg 1995*, Stuttgart.

Münzenmaier, W. (1988) 'Zur Abhängigkeit Baden-Württembergischer Arbeitsplätze vom Automobilbau', in Statistisches Landesamt (ed.) *Baden-Württemberg in Wort und Zahl 12/1988*, Stuttgart: Statistisches Landesamt, pp. 514–521.

Münzenmaier, W. (1993) 'Input-Output-Tabellen für Baden-Württemberg 1989 bis 1988', in Statistisches Landesamt (ed.) *Jahrbücher für Statistik und Landeskunde in Baden-Württemberg 1992*, Stuttgart: Statistisches Landesamt, pp. 181–192.

Münzenmaier, W. (1995) 'Input-Output-Tabellen 1990', in Statistisches Landesamt (ed.) *Baden-Württemberg in Wort und Zahl 12/1988*, Stuttgart: Statistisches Landesamt, pp. 235–241.

OECD (1999) *Boosting Innovation: The Cluster Approach*, Paris: OECD.

OECD (2001a) *OECD in Figures*, Paris: OECD.

OECD (2001b) *OECD Science, Technology and Industry Scoreboard 2001: Towards a Knowledge-Based Economy*, Paris. Paris: OECD.

OECD (2001c) *Education at a Glance*, Paris: OECD.

Piore, M.J. and Sabel, C. (1984) *The Second Industrial Divide: Possibilities for Prosperity*, New York: Basic Books.

Piore, M.J. and Sabel, C. (1985) *Das Ende der Massenproduktion: Studie über die Requalifizierung der Arbeit und die Rückkehr der Ökonomie in die Gesellschaft*, Berlin: Wagenbach.

Porter, M.E. (1990) *The Competitive Advantage of Nations*, New York: Free Press.

Powell, W.W. (1990) 'Neither market nor hierarchy: network forms of organization', *Research in Organizational Behavior*, 12: 295–336.

Pyke, F. and Sengenberger, W. (eds) (1992) *Industrial Districts and Local Economic Regeneration*, Geneva: International Institute for Labour Studies.

Sabel, C. (1989) 'Flexible specialisation and the re-emergence of regional economies', in P. Hirst and J. Zeitlin (eds) *Reversing Industrial Decline? Industrial Structure and Policy in Britain and her Competitors*, Oxford/New York: Berg und St. Martins, pp. 17–70.

Sabel, C., Herrigel, G.B., Deeg, R. and Kazis, R. (1989) 'Regional Prosperities Compared: Massachusetts and Baden-Württemberg in the 1980s', *Economy and Society*, 18(4): 374–404.

Saxenian, A. (1989) 'The Cheshire cat's grin: innovation, regional development and the Cambridge case', *Economy and Society*, 18: 448–477.

Scharpf, F.W. (1988) 'The joint decision trap: lessons from German federalism and European integration', *Public Administration*, 66: 239–278.

Schmitz, H. (1992) 'Industrial districts: model and reality in Baden-Württemberg, Germany', in F. Pyke and W. Sengenberger (eds) *Industrial Districts and Local Economic Regeneration*, Geneva: International Institute for Labour Studies, pp. 87–121.

Scott, W.R. (1995) *Institutions and Organizations*, London: Sage.

Statistisches Landesamt (ed.) (1992) *Baden Wüttemberg in Wort und Zahl*, Stuttgart: Statistisches Landesamt.

Statistisches Landesamt Baden-Württemberg (2001) *Monitor Baden-Württemberg: Materialien und Berichte No. 29*. Stuttgart: Statistisches Landesamt.

Steinbeis-Stiftung für Wirstschaftsförderung (ed.) (1994) *Bericht 1994*, Stuttgart.

Streeck, W. (1991) 'On the social and political conditions of diversified quality production', in E. Matzner and W. Streeck (eds) *Beyond Keynesianism: The Socio-Economics of Production and Full Employment*, Aldershot: Edward Elgar, pp. 21–61.

von Schell, T. and Mohr, H. (eds) (1995) *Biotechnologic-Gentechnik. Eine Chance für neue Industrien?* Heidenberg: Springer.

Wirtschaftsministerium Baden-Württemberg (2000) *Innovationssystem Baden-Württemberg. Innovations- und Technologieförderung als wirtschaftspolitische Aufgabe*, Stuttgart: Wirtschaftsministerium.

8 The regional innovation system in Wales

Cooke, P. (ed.) (1995) *The Rise of the Rustbelt*, London: UCL Press.

Cooke, P. (2004) 'Managing knowledge spillovers: the role of "megacentres" in biosciences', in C. Carlsson *et al.* (eds) *Knowledge Spillovers and Knowledge Management in Industrial Clusters and Industrial Networks*, Cheltenham: Edward Elgar.

Cooke, P., Boekholt, P. and Tödtling, F. (2000) *The Governance of Innovation in Europe: Regional Perspectives on Global Competitiveness*, London: Pinter.

Cooke, P. and Clifton, N. (2003) *Funding Economic Development in Wales*, ESRC Devolution and Constitutional Change Programme Report, Cardiff: Centre for Advanced Studies.

Cooke, P., De Laurentis, C. and Wilson, R. (2003) *The Future of Manufacturing Jobs in Europe: Wales as a Case Study*, Brussels and Strasbourg: report for the Green Alliance MEP Group, European Parliament.

Cooke, P., Morgan, K. and Price, A. (1994) 'The Welsh renaissance: inward investment and industrial innovation', *Regional Industrial Research Report No. 19*, Cardiff: Centre for Advanced Studies.

Coombes, L., Davies, C., Page, H. and Wilson, R. (2002) *An Analysis of First Destinations of Graduates from Welsh Higher Education Institutions*, Cardiff: ELWa-Higher Education Funding Council for Wales.

Department of Trade and Industry (2001) *Regional Innovation Performance in the UK*, London: DTI.

Etkowitz, H. and Leydesdorff, L. (eds) (1997) *Universities and the Global Knowledge Economy*, London: Pinter.

Gregersen, B. (1992) 'The public sector as a pacer in national systems of innovation', in B. Lundvall (ed.) *National Systems of Innovation*, London: Pinter.

Heinze, R., Hilbert, J., Nordhaus-Janz, J. and Rehfeld, D. (1998) 'Industrial clusters and the governance of change: lessons from North Rhine-Westphalia', in H.-J. Braczyk, P. Cooke and M. Heidenreich (eds) *Regional Innovation Systems*, London: UCL Press.

Jones-Evans, D. (2002) 'Research and development in Wales', paper to Economic Development Committee, National Assembly for Wales.

Landabaso, M. (1997) 'The promotion of innovation in regional policy: proposals for a Regional Innovation Strategy', *Entrepreneurship and Regional Development*, 9: 1–24.

Latour, B. (1998) 'From the world of science to the world of research?' *Science*, 280: 208–209.

Nooteboom, B. (2001) *Learning and Innovation in Organisations and Economies*, Oxford: Oxford University Press.

Office of National Statistics (2003a) *Labour Force Survey*, London: ONS.

Office of National Statistics (2003b) *Small Business Statistics*, London: ONS.

Porter, M. (2002) *Regional Foundations of Competitiveness: Issues for Wales*, Cambridge, MA: Harvard Business School.

Pritchard, J. (2003) 'Warning as jobs move away from industry', *Western Mail*, 13 February.

Rhys, G. (2002) 'The automotive sector in Wales: still alive and well', report to Third Autoconference, London, November (http://www.autoconference.co.uk).

Senker, J. and Van Zwanenberg, P. (2001) *European Biotechnology Innovation Systems*, Final Report to EU-TSER Programme, University of Sussex, SPRU.

Shipton, M. (2003) 'Just 44 jobs created by Euro cash so far', *Western Mail*, 18 January.

Steele, L. and Levie, J. (2001) *Entrepreneurship Education in Higher and Further Education in Wales: An Analysis of Returns from an Entrepreneurship Audit*, Report to Education and Learning Wales (ELWa), Glasgow: Hunter Centre for Entrepreneurship: University of Strathclyde.

Technopolis (1998) *An Evaluation of the Wales Regional Technology Plan*, Amsterdam: Technopolis.

Veblen, T. (1899) *The Theory of the Leisure Class: An Economic Study of Institutions*, New York: Macmillan.

Weick, K. (1995) *Sensemaking in Organisations*, London: Sage.

Welsh Affairs Committee (2000) *European Structural Funds*, London: The Stationery Office.

Welsh European Funding Organisation (2003) *European Structural Funds Programme: Partnership Data Report*, Cardiff: WEFO.

9 Industrial clusters and the governance of change

Bratl, H. and Trippl, M. (2001) *Innovation System Management Austria*, Vienna: Invent.

Diez, M.A. (2001) 'The evaluation of regional innovation and cluster policies: towards a participatory approach', *European Planning Studies*, 9: 907–923.

Forschungsgesellschaft für Gerontologie (FfG) / Institut Arbeit und Technik (IAT) (1999) *Memorandum, Wirtschaftskraft Alter*, Dortmund und Gelsenkirchen, available on: http://iat-info.iatge.de/aktuell/veroeff/buch/index.html.

Forschungsgesellschaft für Gerontologie (FfG) / Institut Arbeit und Technik (IAT) / Medizinische Hochschule Hannover (MHH) (2001) *Gesundheitswesen und Arbeitsmarkt in NRW: Dokumentation*, Düsseldorf: Ministerium für Frauen, Jugend, Familie und Gesundheit des Landes Nordrhein-Westfalen, available on: http://www.mfjfg.nrw.de/service/publikationen/regal/index.htm.

Hamm, R. and Wienert, H. (1990) *Strukturelle Anpassung altindustrieller Regionen im internationalen Vergleich*, Berlin: Duncker & Humboldt.

Hilbert, J. and Naegele, G. (2001) 'The economic power of ageing', in S. Pohlmann (ed.) *The Ageing of Society as a Global Challenge. German Impulses: Integrated Report on German Expert Contributions*, Berlin: Bundesministerium für Familie, Senioren, Frauen und Jugend, pp. 63–86.

Kiesewetter, H. (1986) 'Das wirtschaftliche Gefälle zwischen Nord- und Süddeutschland in historischer Perspektive', *Neues Archiv für Niedersachsen*, 35: 327–347.

Montankommission (1989) *Bericht der Kommission Montanregionen des Landes Nordrhein-Westfalen*, Düsseldorf: Ministerium für Wirtschaft, Mittelstand und Technologie.

Nordhause-Janz, J. (2002) *Das industrielle Herz schlägt nicht mehr im Ruhrgebiet: Veränderungen der Beschäftigungsstruktur in Nordrhein-Westfalen*, Internet Document. Gelsenkirchen: IAT, IAT-Report No. 2002–03.

Nordhause-Janz, J. and Rehfeld, D. (1995) *Umweltschutz 'made in NRW': Eine empirische Untersuchung der Umweltschutzwirtschaft in NRW*, Munich and Mering: Hampp.

Nordhause-Janz, J. and Rehfeld, D. (1999) *Informations- und Kommunikationswirtschaft Nordrhein-Westfalen*, Gelsenkirchen: IAT Graue Reihe.

Petzina, D. (1987) 'Wirtschaftliche Ungleichgewichte in Deutschland', in H.G. Wehling and Hans Georg Wehling (eds) *Nord-Süd in Deutschland? Vorurteile und Tatsachen*, Stuttgart: Kohlhammer, pp. 59–81.

Petzina, D., Plumpe, W. and Unger, S. (1990) *Diversifizierungsprozesse im Ruhrgebiet in wirtschaftstheoretischer Perspektive*, Bochum: Zentrums für interdisziplinäre Ruhrgebietsforschung der Ruhr Universität Bochum.

Piore, M. and Sabel, C. (1984) *The Second Industrial Divide*, New York: Basic Books.
Porter, M.E. (1991) *Nationale Wettbewerbsvorteile: Erfolgreich Konkurrieren auf dem Weltmarkt*, Munich: Droemer Knaur.
Porter, M.E. (1999) *Wettbewerbsstrategie: Methoden zur Analyse von Branchen und Konkurrenten*, Frankfurt: Campus.
Radkau, J. (1989) *Technik in Deutschland: Vom 18. Jahrhundert bis zur Gegenwart*, Frankfurt/M: Suhrkamp.
Rehfeld, D. (1993) *The Ruhrgebiet: Patterns of Economic Restructuring in an Area of Industrial Decline*, Brussels: European Commission.
Rehfeld, D. (1995) 'Disintegration and reintegration of production clusters in the Ruhr Area', in P. Cooke (ed.) *The Rise of the Rustbelt*, London: UCL Press, pp. 85–102.
Rehfeld, D. (1999) *Produktionscluster*, Munich and Mering: Hampp.
Rehfeld, D., Baumer, D. and Wompel, M. (2000) *Regionalisierte Strukturpolitik als Lernprozess*, Gelsenkirchen: IAT Graue Reihe.
Rehfeld, D. and Wompel, M. (1997) *Künftige Produktionscluster im Raum Köln: Gutachten im Auftrag der Stadtsparkasse Köln*, Gelsenkirchen: IAT Graue Reihe.
Rehfeld, D. and Wompel, M. (1999) *Standort mit Zukunftsprofil: Innovationsschwerpunkte in Dortmund. Eine Untersuchung im Auftrag der Wirtschafts- und Beschäftigungsförderung Dortmund*, Gelsenkirchen: IAT Projektberichte.
Roland Berger (2001) *Neue Wirtschaft: NRW. Kompetenzfelder für das Ruhrgebiet*, Düsseldorf 2001 Studie im Auftrag des Ministeriums für Wirtschaft und Mittelstand, Energie und Verkehr des Landes Nordrhein-Westfalen, Düsseldorf: Roland Berger
Schlieper, A. (1986) *150 Jahre Ruhrgebiet: Ein Kapitel deutscher Wirtschaftsgeschichte*, Düsseldorf: Schwann.
Seufert, W. (1994) *Gesamtwirtschaftliche Position der Medien in Deutschland 1982–1992*, DIW Beiträge zur Strukturförderung Heft 152, Berlin: Duncker & Humboldt.
Stadt Dortmund (2001) *Das Dortmund Projekt*, available on: http://www.dortmund.de
Weber, W. (1990) 'Entfaltung der Industriewirtschaft', in W. Köllmann, H. Korte and W. Weber (eds) *Das Ruhrgebiet im Industriezeitalter*, vol. 2, Düsseldorf: Schwann, pp. 200–319.

10 Regional innovation systems in the less-favoured region of Japan

Abe, S. (1990) 'Rational of Tohoku Intelligent Cosmos Plan', *Technology and Economy*, 279: 27–35.
Abe, S. (1997) 'Regional policies and the re-interpretation of local-regional culture and history', in N. Watanabe (ed.) *The Recovery of Histories in Tohoku*, Tokyo: Kawade Shobo Shinsha.
Abe, S. and NIRA (1994) *Decentralization from the Perspective of Urban Growth and the Future for Wide Area Nucleus Cities*, Research Report 940039, Tokyo: NIRA.
Abe, S. and Study Group of the Province Centre Cities (1995) *The Study of the New Structure of Land and the Province Center Cities*, Sendai: The Study Group of the Province Center Cities.
Acs, Z.J., de la Mothe, J. and Paquet, G. (2000) 'Regional innovation: in search of an enabling strategy', in Z.J. Acs (ed.) *Regional Innovation, Knowledge and Global Change*, London and New York: Pinter.

Aoki, M. (1988) *Information, Incentives and Bargaining in the Japanese Economy*, Cambridge: Cambridge University Press.

Aoki, M. (1997) 'Unintended fit: organizational evolution and government design of institution in Japan', in M. Aoki, H. Kim and H. Okuno-Fujiwara (eds) *The Role of Government in East Asian Economic Development*, Oxford: Clarendon Press.

Archibugi, D., Howells, J. and Michie, J. (eds) (1999) *Innovation Policy in a Global Economy*, Cambridge: Cambridge University Press.

Castells, M. and Hall, P. (1994) *Technopoles of the World*, London: Routledge.

Cooke, P. (2002) *Knowledge Economies*, London: Routledge.

Cooke, P., Uranga, M.G. and Exebarria, G. (1998) 'Regional systems of innovation: an evolutionary perspective', *Environment and Planning A*, 30: 1563–1584.

Dore, R. (1987) *Taking Japan Seriously*, London: Athlone Press.

Dore, R. (2000) *Stock Market Capitalism*, Oxford: Oxford University Press.

Freeman, C. (1987) *Technology Policy and Economic Performance*, London: Pinter.

Fujita, K. (1991) 'A world city and flexible specialization', *International Journal of Urban and Regional Research*, 15: 269–285.

Fujita, K. and Hill, R.C. (1993) *Japanese Cities in the World Economy*, Philadelphia, PA: Temple University Press.

Glasmeier, A.K. (1988) 'The Japanese Technopolis Programme', *International Journal of Urban and Regional Research*, 12: 268–284.

Hilpert, U. (ed.) (1991) *Regional Innovation and Decentralization*, London: Routledge.

Ishida, N. (1996) *Madarao*, Sendai: Kinkodo.

Ito, K. (1998) *The Study of Technopolis Policy*, Tokyo: Nihon Hyoron Sha.

Ito, K., Tanaka, T., Nakano, H. and Suzuki, S. (1995) *Technopolis in Japan*, Tokyo: Nihon Hyoron Sha.

JILC (Japan Industrial Location Center) (1999) *The Course of the Promotion of Technopolis and Brain Location Plans*, Tokyo: JILC.

Keating, M. (1997) 'The political economy of regionalism', in M. Keating and J. Loughlin (eds) *The Political Economy of Regionalism*, London: Frank Cass.

Koestler, A. (1978) *Janus*, London: Hutchinson.

Lash, S. and Urry, J. (1994) *Economies of Signs and Space*, London: Sage.

Markusen, A. (1997) 'Sticky places in slippery space', *Economic Geography*, 72: 293–313.

Massey, D. (1979) 'In what sense a regional problem?', *Regional Studies*, 13(2): 233–243.

Morgan, K. and Nauwelaers, C. (eds) (1999) *Regional Innovation Strategies*, London: The Stationery Office.

Neary, I. (2002) *The State and Politics in Japan*, Cambridge: Polity Press.

Nishizawa, J. (1995) *The Age of Tohoku*, Tokyo: Ushio Shuppan.

Ohmae, K. (1995) *The End of the Nation State*, New York: Free Press.

Okamoto, T. (ed.) (1985) *The Economic Analysis of the Tohoku Region* (Report of research by grant-in-aid for scientific research), Sendai: Tohoku University.

Okamoto, T. (1986) 'Method for comparative regional study', paper presented to the international conference on Comparative Regional Studies, Tohoku University.

Ozawa, T. (1997) 'Japan', in J.H. Dunning (ed.) *Governments, Globalization, and International Business*, Oxford: Oxford University Press.

Park, S.C. (1997) 'The Japanese Technopolis strategy', in J. Simmie (ed.) *Innovation, Networks and Learning Regions?*, London: Jessica Kingsley Publishers.

Porter, M.E., Takeuchi, H. and Sakakibara, M. (2000) *Can Japan Compete?*, Basingstoke: Macmillan Press.

Sakamoto, H., Kasuya, K., Nakamura, S. and Nagasu, I. (eds) (1989) *The Future of Local Regions and Tokyo Problems*, Tokyo: Gyosei.

Samuels, R.J. (1983) *The Politics of Regional Policy in Japan*, Princeton, NJ: Princeton University Press.

Sasao, J. (1991) *The Changes of Industries and their Location*, Tokyo: Taimeido.

Saxenian, A.L. (1994) *Regional Advantage*, Cambridge, MA: Harvard University Press.

Sazanami, H. (1991) 'Structural transformation in Japan', in L. Rodwin and H. Sazanami (eds) *Industrial Change and Regional Economic Transformation*, London: HarperCollins Academic.

Smilor, R.W., Kozmatsky, G. and Gibson, D.V. (1988) *Creating the Technopolis*, Cambridge, MA: Ballinger.

Sternberg, R. (1995) 'Supporting peripheral economies or industrial policy in favour of national growth?', *Environment and Planning C*, 13: 425–439.

Stockwin, J.A.A. (1997) 'The need for reform in Japanese politics', in A. Clesse, T. Inoguchi, E.B. Keehn and J.A.A. Stockwin (eds) *The Vitality of Japan*, London: Macmillan Press.

Stöhr, W. and Pönighaus, R. (1992) 'Toward a data-based evaluation of the Japanese Technopolis policy', *Regional Studies*, 26(7): 605–618.

Yada, T. (ed.) (1990) *The Theory of Regional Structure*, Kyoto: Minerva Shobo.

Yada, T. (1996) *The Land Policy and the Regional Policy*, Tokyo: Taimeido.

Yamazaki, A. (1992) *The Network-Type Location and the Diversionary Policy*, Tokyo: Taimeido.

11 Innovative milieu and co-operation networks: Singapore

Asian Development Bank (1994) *Asian Development Outlook 1994*, Oxford: Oxford University Press.

Aydalot, P. (1985) *High Technology Industry and Innovative Environments*, London: Routledge.

Aydalot, P. (1986) *Milieux Innovateurs en Europe*, Paris: GERMI.

Business Times, Singapore, available online at http://www.business-times.asia1.com.sg.

Business Week, available online at http://www.businessweek.com.

Camagni, R. (ed.) (1991) *Innovation Networks: Spatial Perspectives*, London: Pinter.

Department of Statistics (various years) *Report of the Labour Force Survey*, Singapore: Department of Statistics.

Economic Committee (1986) *Singapore Economy, New Directions*, Singapore: Ministry of Trade and Industry.

Economic Development Board (various years) *Annual Report* (Print and Online) Singapore: EDB.

Economic Planning Committee, Ministry of Trade and Industry (1991) *Strategic Economic Plan (SEP) 1991*, Singapore: Ministry of Trade and Industry.

Hersh, J. (1993) *The USA and the Rise of East Asia since 1945*, London: Macmillan.

IT Focus (various issues) Singapore.

Lakshmanan, T.R. (1995) 'The nature and evolution of knowledge network in Japanese manufacturing', *Regional Science*, 74(1), 63–86.

Lee, H.L. (1995) Unpublished speech to Singapore Economic Forum, Singapore, July.

Lee, K.Y. (1995) Interview. NTUC *News Weekly* (May Day issue).

Lee, K.Y. (1992) Unpublished speech delivered at the University of Mauritius, November.

Low, L. (1993) *Challenge and Response: Thirty Years of Economic Development*, Singapore: Times Academic Press.

Ministry of Environment (1993) *Pollution Control Report*, Singapore: The Ministry of Environment.

Ministry of Manpower (2001) *Report of Labour Force Survey*, Singapore.

Ministry of Trade and Industry (2001) *Economic Survey of Singapore, 2001 and 2002*. Singapore.

Monetary Authority of Singapore (MAS) (various years) *Annual Report*, Singapore: MAS.

National Science and Technology Board (NSTB) (1991) *National Technology Plan 1991*, Singapore: NSTB.

National Science and Technology Board (NSTB) (1994) *Annual Report*, Singapore: NSTB.

National Science and Technology Board (NSTB) (various years) *National Survey of R&D in Singapore*, Singapore: NSTB.

Ng, C.Y., Hirono, R. and Siy, R.Y. (1986) *Technology and Skills in ASEAN*, Singapore: Japan Institute of International Affairs/Institute of SE Asian Studies.

Odaka, K. (1989) *Skills in Asia*, Tokyo: Institute of Developing Economics.

PHP Institute (1995) 'Singapore's dilemma', *Intersect Japan – Asia*, 10(June): 48–50.

Singapore Anti-Pollution Department (1970–72) *Annual Report*, Singapore: Prime Minister's Office.

Singapore Census of Population (various years) *Singapore Census of Population*, Singapore: Department of Statistics.

Singapore Department of Statistics (1993) *Statistical Highlights*, Singapore: Department of Statistics.

Singapore Department of Statistics (various years) *Report on the Census of Industrial Production*, Singapore: Department of Statistics.

Singapore International Chamber of Commerce (1994) *The Investor's Guide to Singapore 1994*, Singapore: Chamber of Commerce.

Sinnakaruppan, R. (1995) Graduation ceremony speech, Institute of Technical Education (ITE). Annual Basic Education Skills Training and Workers' Improvement and Secondary Education Programme, Institute of Technical Education, Singapore.

Straits Times Interactive Singapore.

Today (2002) MediaCorps, Singapore.

World Bank (1993) *The East Asia Miracle*, Washington, DC: The World Bank.

World Competitiveness Report (2000) Switzerland: IMD.

World Competitiveness Yearbook (2000) Switzerland: IMD.

Word Economic Forum (2001) *Global Competitiveness Report 2001/2002*, Geneva: World Economic Forum.

12 Regional innovation support systems in South Korea

Amin, A. and Thrift, N. (1994) 'Living in the global', in A. Amin and N. Thrift (eds) *Globalization, Institutions, and Regional Development in Europe*, Oxford: Oxford University Press, pp. 1–22.

Amin, A. (1999) 'An institutional perspective on regional economic development', *International Journal of Urban and Regional Research*, 23: 365–378.

Atkinson, R.D. (1991) 'Innovation policy making in a federalist system: lessons from the states for U.S. federal innovation policy making', *Research Policy*, 20: 559–577.

Barnes, T.J. (1999) 'Industrial Geography, Institutional Economics and Innis', in T.J. Barnes and M.S. Gertler (eds) *The New Industrial Geography: Regions, Regulation and Institutions*, London: Routledge, pp. 1–20.

Braczyk, H.-J., Cooke, P. and Heidenreich, M. (eds) (1998) *Regional Innovation Systems: The Role of Governances in a Globalized World*, London: UCL Press.

Chung, S. (1999a) 'Korean Innovation Policies for SMEs', *Science and Public Policy*, 26: 70–82.

Chung, S. (1999b) 'Regional innovation systems in Korea', paper prepared for the 3rd International Conference on Technology Policy and Innovation, Austin, USA, 30 August–2 September.

Chung, S. (2001) 'Innovation and regional clustering: a Korean case', paper presented at the Tenth International Conference on Management of Technology, 19–22 March, Lausanne, Switzerland.

Cooke, P. (1992) 'Regional innovation systems: competitive regulation in the New Europe', *Geoforum*, 23: 365–382.

Cooke, P. (1998) 'Introduction', in H.-J. Braczyk, P. Cooke and M. Heidenreich (eds) *Regional Innovation Systems: The Role of Governances in a Globalized World*, London: UCL Press, pp. 2–25.

Cooke, P. and Morgan, K. (1998) *The Associational Economy; Firms, Regions, and Innovation*, Oxford: Oxford University Press.

Cooke, P., Uranga, M.G. and Etxebarria, G. (1998) 'Regional systems of innovation: an evolutionary perspective', *Environment and Planning A*, 30: 1563–1584.

Dodgson, M. and Bessant, J. (1996) *Effective Innovation Policy: A New Approach*, London: International Thomson Business Press.

Edquist, C. (1997) 'Systems of innovation approaches – their emergence and characteristics', in C. Edquist (ed.) *Systems of Innovation: Technologies, Institutions and Organizations*, London: Pinter, pp. 1–35.

Ergas, H. (1987) 'Does technology policy matter?', in B. Guile and H. Brooks (eds) *Technology and Global Industry: Companies and National Policies in the World Economy*, Washington, DC: National Academy Press, pp. 191–245.

Granovetter, M. (1985) 'Economic action and social structure: the problem of embeddedness', *American Journal of Sociology*, 91: 481–510.

Hassink, R. (1996) 'Technology transfer agencies and regional economic development', *European Planning Studies*, 4: 167–184.

Hassink, R. (2000) 'Regional innovation support systems in South Korea and Japan compared', *Zeitschrift für Wirtschaftsgeographie*, 44: 228–245.

Hassink, R. (2001) 'Towards regionally embedded innovation support systems in South Korea? Case-studies from Kyongbuk-Taegu and Kyonggi', *Urban Studies*, 38: 1373–1395.

Hassink, R. and Lagendijk, A. (2001) 'The dilemmas of interregional institutional learning', *Environment and Planning C*, 19: 65–84.

Hong, K. (1997) 'Regional policy in the Republic of Korea', *Regional Studies*, 31: 417–423.

Jessop, B. (1994) 'Post-Fordism and the state', in A. Amin (ed.) *Post-Fordism: A Reader*, Oxford: Blackwell Publishers, pp. 251–279.

Kang, I.-W. (1997) *Endogene Raumentwicklung in Südkorea: Fallstudie Provinz Chungbuk*, Dortmund: Institut für Raumplanung, Dortmunder Beiträge zur Raumplanung (Blaue Reihe), No. 81.

Kim, L. (1997) *Imitation to Innovation: The Dynamics of Korea's Technological Learning*, Boston: Harvard Business School Press.

Kim, L. (2000) 'Korea's national innovation system in transition', in L. Kim and R.R. Nelson (eds) *Technology, Learning and Innovation*, Cambridge: Cambridge University Press, pp. 335–360.

Kim, L. and Nugent, J.B. (1994) *The Republic of Korea's Small and Medium-Size Enterprises and Their Support Systems*, Washington, DC: The World Bank.

Lee, H.J. (2001) 'Institutionalization of knowledge formation and dissemination: the case of Kyonggy Province in Korea', paper presented at the Joint Conference of the IGU Commission on the Dynamics of Economic Spaces and the IGU Study Group on Local Development: Local Development: Issues of Competition, Collaboration and Territoriality, Turin, 10–14 July.

Lee, Y.-S. (2002) 'Business networks and suppliers' locational choice', *Environment and Planning A*, 34: 1001–1020.

Lorenzen, M. (2001) 'Localized learning and policy: academic advice on enhancing regional competitiveness through learning', *European Planning Studies*, 9: 163–185.

Markusen, A., Lee, Y.-S. and Digiovanni, S. (eds) (1999) *Second Tier Cities: Rapid Growth Beyond the Metropolis*, Minneapolis: University of Minnesota Press.

Morgan, K. (1997) 'The learning region: institutions, innovation and regional renewal', *Regional Studies*, 31: 491–503.

Mothe, J. De La and Paquet, G. (eds) (1998) *Local and Regional Systems of Innovation*, Boston: Kluwer Academic Publishers.

Mytelka, L.K. (2000) 'Local systems of innovation in a globalized world economy', *Industry and Innovation*, 7: 15–32.

Nauwelaers, C. and Wintjes, R. (2000) *SME policy and the Regional Dimension of Innovation: Towards a New Paradigm for Innovation Policy?* Maastricht: Maastricht Economic Research Institute on Innovation and Technology.

OECD (1996) *Reviews of National Science and Technology Policy: Republic of Korea*, Paris: OECD.

OECD (2001) *Territorial Review Korea*, Paris: OECD.

Oinas, P. (1997) 'On the socio-spatial embeddedness of business firms', *Erdkunde*, 51: 23–32.

Paquet, G. (1994) 'Technonationalism and meso innovation systems', University of Ottawa: Program of Research in International Management and Economy (draft discussion paper).

Park, J.-K. (1998) 'Creating extrafirm infrastructure of institutions for small and medium-sized businesses', in L.-J. Cho and Y.-H. Kim (eds) *Korea's Choices in Emerging Global Competition and Cooperation*, Seoul: Korea Development Institute, pp. 179–228.

Park, S.O. (2000) 'Innovation systems, networks, and the knowledge-based economy in Korea', in J.H. Dunning (ed.) *Regions, Globalization, and the Knowledge-Based Economy*, Oxford: Oxford University Press, pp. 328–348.

Park, S.O. and Markusen, A. (1999) 'Kumi and Ansan: dissimilar Korean satellite platforms', in A. Markusen, Y.-S. Lee and S. Digiovanni (eds) *Second Tier Cities: Rapid Growth Beyond the Metropolis*, Minneapolis: University of Minnesota Press, pp. 147–162.

Park, S.Y. and Lee W. (2000) 'Regional innovation system built by local agencies: an alternative model of regional development', paper presented at the 2nd International Critical Geography Conference, Taegu, South Korea, 9–13 August.

Porter, M.E. (1990) *The Competitive Advantage of Nations*, London: Macmillan.

Rothwell, R. and M. Dodgson (1992) 'European technology policy evolution: convergence towards SMEs and regional technology transfer', *Technovation*, 12: 223–238.

Schamp, E.W. (2000) *Vernetzte Produktion: Industriegeographie aus institutioneller Perspektive*, Darmstad: Wissenschaftliche Buchgesellschaft.

Suh, J. (2000) *Korea's Innovation System: Challenges and New Policy Agenda*, Maastricht: UNU-INTECH.

Tsipouri, L. (1999) *Up-Grading Knowledge and Diffusing Technology in a Regional Context*, Paris: OECD.

Wessel, K. (1997) 'Südkorea: Technologiepolitik und High-Tech Industrie im Spannungsfeld von Wirtschaftswachstum und ausgleichsorientierter Regionalentwicklung', *Die Erde*, 128: 17–33.

13 Slovenia – a fragmented innovation system?

Andersen, E. and Lundvall, B.-Å. (1988) 'Small national systems of innovation facing technological revolutions: an analytical framework', in C. Freeman and B.-Å. Lundvall (eds) *Small Countries Facing the Technological Revolution*, London: Pinter Publishers, pp. 9–36.

Asheim, B.T. and Isaksen, A. (2002) 'Regional innovation systems: the integration of local "sticky" and global "ubiquitous" knowledge', *The Journal of Technology Transfer*, 27: 77–86.

Braczyk, H.-J., Cooke, P. and Heidenreich, M. (eds) (1998) *Regional Innovation Systems: The Role of Governances in a Globalized World*, London: UCL Press.

Bross, U. and Walter, G.H. (1998) *Development Prospects of the Czech Venture Capital Market: Assessment and Starting Points for Policy Measures*, Stuttgart: Fraunhofer IRB-Verlag.

Cohen, W.M. and Levinthal, D.A. (1990) 'Absorptive capacity: a new perspective on learning and innovation', *Administrative Science Quarterly*, 35: 128–152.

Cooke, P. (1998) 'Introduction: origins of the concept', in H.-J. Braczyk, P. Cooke, and M. Heidenreich (eds) *Regional Innovation Systems: The Role of Governances in a Globalized World,* London: UCL Press, pp. 2–25.

Cooke, P. (2002) 'Regional innovation systems: general findings and some new evidence from biotechnology clusters', *The Journal of Technology Transfer*, 27: 133–145.

Cooke, P., Uranga, M.G. and Etxebarria, G. (1997) 'Regional innovation systems: institutional and organisational dimension', *Research Policy*, 26: 475–491.

Dyker, D.A. and Perrin, J. (1997) 'Technology policy and industrial objectives in the context of economic transition', in D.A. Dyker (ed.) *The Technology of Transition. Science and Technology Policies for Transition Countries*, Budapest: Central European University Press, pp. 3–19.

Edquist, C. (ed.) (1997) *Systems of Innovation: Technologies, Institutions and Organizations*, London: Pinter Publishers.

European Commission (1993) *Science and Technology in Slovenia*, Brussels: European Commission.

European Commission (1999) *Impact of the Enlargement of the European Union Towards the Associated Central and Eastern European Countries on RTD-Innovation and Structural Policies*, Luxembourg: European Commission.

Feldman, M.P. (1994) 'Knowledge complementarity and innovation', *Small Business Economics*, 6: 363–372.

Fritsch, M. (2001) 'Innovation by networking: an economic perspective', in K. Koschatzky, M. Kulicke and A. Zenker (eds) *Innovation Networks. Concepts and Challenges in the European Perspective*, Heidelberg: Physica-Verlag, pp. 25–34.

Fritsch, M., Broeskamp, A. and Schwirten, C. (1996) 'Innovationen in der Sächsischen Industrie – Erste empirische Ergebnisse', Freiberg Working Press 96/13, Freiberg: Technical University Bergakademie Freiberg.

Fritsch, M., Koschatzky, K., Schätzl, L. and Sternberg, R. (1998) 'Regionale Innovationspotentiale und innovative Netzwerke', *Raumforschung und Raumordnung*, 56: 243–252.

Fritsch, M. and Schwirten, C. (1998) 'Öffentliche Forschungseinrichtungen im regionalen Innovationssystem', *Raumforschung und Raumordnung*, 56: 253–263.

Government of Slovenia (2000) *Science & Technology*, Ljubljana: Public Relations and Media Office.

Grabher, G. and Stark, D. (eds) (1997) *Restructuring Networks in Post-Socialism: Legacies, Linkages, and Localities*, Oxford: Oxford University Press.

Harter, S. (1997) *From 'Third Rome' to 'Third Italy'? Economic Networks in Russia*, Research Papers in Russian and East European Studies, Centre for Russian and East European Studies, Birmingham: The University of Birmingham.

IMAD (Institute of Macroeconomic Analysis and Development) (1998) *Slovenian Economic Mirror*, No. 4. Ljubljana: IMAD.

Kline, S.J. and Rosenberg, N. (1986) 'An overview of innovation', in R. Landau and N. Rosenberg (eds) *The Positive Sum Strategy: Harnessing Technology for Economic Growth*, Washington, DC: National Academy Press, pp. 275–305.

Koschatzky, K. (1998) 'Firm innovation and region: the role of space in innovation processes', *International Journal of Innovation Management*, 2: 383–408.

Koschatzky, K. (2002) 'Networking and knowledge transfer between research and industry in transition countries: empirical evidence from the Slovenian innovation survey', *The Journal of Technology Transfer*, 27: 27–38.

Koschatzky, K., Bross, U. and Stanovnik, P. (2001) 'Development and innovation potential in the Slovene manufacturing industry: analysis of an industrial innovation survey', *Technovation*, 21: 311–324.

Koschatzky, K. and Sternberg, R. (2000) 'R&D co-operation in innovation systems: Some lessons from the European Regional Innovation Survey (ERIS)', *European Planning Studies*, 8: 487–501.

Landabaso, M., Oughton, C. and Morgan, K. (2001) 'Innovation networks and regional policy in Europe', in K. Koschatzky, M. Kulicke and A. Zenker (eds)

Innovation Networks: Concepts and Challenges in the European Perspective, Heidelberg: Physica-Verlag, pp. 243–273.

Lundvall, B.-Å. (1988) 'Innovation as an interactive process: from user-producer interaction to the national system of innovation', in G. Dosi, C. Freeman, R. Nelson, G. Silverberg and L. Soete (eds) *Technical Change and Economic Theory*, London: Pinter Publishers, pp. 349–369.

Lundvall, B.-Å. (1992) 'Introduction', in B.-Å Lundvall (ed.) *National Systems of Innovation: Towards a Theory of Innovation and Interactive Learning*, London: Pinter Publishers, pp. 1–19.

Meske, W. (1998) 'Toward new S&T networks: the transformation of actors and activities', in W. Meske, J. Mosoni-Fried, H. Etzkowitz and G. Nesvetailov (eds) *Transforming Science and Technology Systems: The Endless Transition*, Amsterdam: IOS Press, pp. 3–26.

Messner, D. (1995) *Die Netzwerkgesellschaft: Wirtschaftliche Entwicklung und internationale Wettbewerbsfähigkeit als Probleme gesellschaftlicher Steuerung*, Cologne: Weltforum Verlag.

Nelson, R.R. (1993) *National Innovation Systems: A Comparative Analysis*, New York: Oxford University Press.

Pavitt, K. (1984) 'Sectoral patterns of technical change: towards a taxonomy and a theory', *Research Policy*, 13: 343–373.

Radosevic, S. (2001) 'Integration through industrial networks in the wider europe: an assessment based on survey of research', in K. Koschatzky, M. Kulicke and A. Zenker (eds) *Innovation Networks: Concepts and Challenges in the European Perspective*, Heidelberg: Physica-Verlag, pp. 153–174.

Raiser, M. and Sanfey, P. (1998) 'Statistical review', *Economics of Transition*, 6: 241–286.

Reid, S. and Garnsey, E. (1998) 'How do small companies learn? Organisational learning and knowledge management in the high-tech small firm', in High-Technology Small Firms Conference (ed.) *The 6th Annual International Conference at the University of Twente, the Netherlands*, Proceedings Vol. 1, Twente: University of Twente, pp. 391–401.

Revilla Diez, J. (2000) 'The importance of public research institutions in innovative networks – empirical results from the metropolitan innovation systems Barcelona, Stockholm and Vienna', *European Planning Studies*, 8: 451–463.

Špilek, H. (2000) 'Slovenia – some views on the innovation system in Slovenia', in S. Ertel (ed.) *Innovation Systems in the Enlargement Countries*, Seville: IPTS.

Stanič, U., Zabukovec, S. and Oblak, M. (2002) 'The ongoing integrated national and EU actions to enhance the cooperation between academia and SMEs', manuscript, Conference on The Role and Importance of SMEs in the Process of EU Enlargement, Ljubljana, 27–28 June.

Stanovnik, P. (1998) 'The Slovenian science and technology transition', in W. Meske, J. Mosoni-Fried, H. Etzkowitz and G. Nesvetailov (eds) *Transforming Science and Technology Systems: the Endless Transition*, Amsterdam: IOS Press, pp. 98–107.

Sternberg, R. (2000) 'Innovation networks and regional development – evidence from the European Regional Innovation Survey (ERIS): theoretical concepts, methodological approach, empirical basis and introduction to the theme issue', *European Planning Studies*, 8: 389–407.

Storper, M. (1995) 'The resurgence of regional economies, ten years later: the region as a nexus of untraded interdependencies', *European Urban and Regional Studies*, 2: 191–221.

Storper, M. (1997) *The Regional World: Territorial Development in a Global Economy*, New York: Guilford Press.

Walter, G.H. and Bross, U. (1997) 'The Adaptation of German Experiences to building up innovation networks in Central and Eastern Europe', in K. Koschatzky (ed.) *Technology-Based Firms in the Innovation-Process: Management, Financing and Regional Networks*, Heidelberg: Physica-Verlag pp. 263–286.

World Bank (2002) *Slovenia at a Glance*, Washington, DC: World Bank Group.

14 Conclusion

Amin, A. (1999) 'An institutional perspective on regional economic development', *International Journal of Urban and Regional Research*, 23: 365–378.

Amin, A. and Thrift, T. (1992) 'Neo-Marshallian nodes in global networks', *International Journal of Urban and Regional Research*, 16: 571–587.

Amin, A. and Thrift, T. (eds) (1994) *Globalization, Institutions, and Regional Development in Europe*, Oxford: Oxford University Press.

Archibugi, D., Howells, J. and Michie J. (eds) (1999) *Innovation Policy in a Global Economy*, Cambridge: Cambridge University Press.

Archibugi, D. and Michie, J. (1995) 'The globalization of technology: a new taxonomy', *Cambridge Journal of Economics*, 19: 121–140.

Asheim, B.T. and Isaksen, A. (2002) 'Regional innovation systems: the integration of local "sticky" and global "ubiquitous" knowledge', *The Journal of Technology Transfer*, 27: 77–86.

Audretsch, D.B. (1994) 'Marktprozeß und Innovation', in W. Zapf and M. Dierkes (eds) *Institutionenvergleich und Institutionendynamik*, Berlin: WZB-Jahrbuch, pp. 310–326.

Boekholt, P. and Thuriaux, B. (1999) 'Public policies to facilitate clusters: background, rationale and policy practices in international perspective', in *Boosting Innovation: The Cluster Approach*, Paris: OECD, pp. 381–412.

Braczyk, H.-J. and Heidenreich, M. (1998) 'Regional governance structures in a globalized world', in H.-J. Braczyk, P. Cooke and M. Heidenreich (eds) *Regional Innovation Systems*, London: UCL-Press, pp. 414–440.

Castells, M. and Hall, P. (1994) *Technopoles of the World: The Making of Twenty-First-Century Industrial Complexes*, London: Routledge.

Chesbrough, H.W. and Teece, D.J. (1996) 'When is virtual virtuous? Organizing for innovation', *Harvard Business Review* (January–February 1996): 65–73.

Cooke, P. (2002) *Knowledge Economies: Clusters, Learning and Cooperative Advantage*, London: Routledge.

Crouch, C. and Farrell, H. (2002) *Breaking the Path of Institutional Development? Alternatives to the New Determinism*, MPIfG Discussion Paper 02/5, Cologne: Max Planck Institute for the Study of Societies.

Crouch, C., Le Galès, P., Trigilia, C. and Voelzkow, H. (2001) *Local Production Systems in Europe. Rise or Demise?* Oxford: Oxford University Press.

Crouch, C. and Trigilia, C. (2001) 'Conclusions: still local economies in global capitalism?', in C. Crouch, P. Le Galès, C. Trigilia, and H. Voelzkow (eds)

Local Production Systems in Europe. Rise or Demise? Oxford: Oxford University Press, pp. 212–237.

David, P. (1985) 'Clio and the eonomics of QWERTY', *American Economic Review*, 75: 332–337.

Dosi, G. (1982) 'Technological paradigms and technological trajectories: a suggested interpretation of the determinants and directions of technical change', *Research Policy*, 11: 147–162.

Dosi, G. (1988) 'The nature of the innovative process', in G. Dosi, C. Freeman, R. Nelson, G. Silverberg and L. Soete (eds) *Technical Change and Economic Theory*, London: Pinter, pp. 221–238.

Dunning, J.H. (ed.) (2000) *Regions, Globalization, and the Knowledge-Based Economy*, Oxford: Oxford University Press.

Edquist, C. (ed.) (1997) *Systems of Innovation: Technologies, Institutions and Organizations*, London: Pinter.

European Commission (1995) *Green Paper on Innovation*, Brussels: European Commission.

European Commission (2002) *Regions: Statistical Yearbook 2002*, Luxembourg: Office for the Official Publications of the EC.

Faulkner, W. (1994) 'Conceptualizing knowledge used in innovation: a second look at the science-technology distinction and industrial innovation', *Science, Technology, and Human Values* 19(4): 425–458.

Fritsch, M. (2001) 'Cooperation in regional innovation systems', *Regional Studies*, 35, 297–307.

Giddens, A. (1990) *The Consequences of Modernity*, Stanford, CA: Stanford University Press.

Gordon, R. (1995) 'Globalisation, new production systems and the spatial division of labour', in W. Littek and T. Charles (eds) *The New Division of Labour: Emerging Forms of Work Organisation in International Perspective*, Berlin: De Gruyter, pp. 161–207.

Grabher, G. (1993) 'Rediscovering the social in the economics of interfirm relations', in G. Grabher (ed.) *The Embedded Firm: On the Socioeconomics of Industrial Networks*, London: Routledge, pp. 1–31.

Hage, J. and Hollingsworth, J.R. (2000) 'A strategy for the analysis of idea innovation networks and institutions', in *Organization Studies*, 21(5): 971–1004.

Hall, P.A. and Soskice, D. (2001) 'An introduction to varieties of capitalism', in P.A. Hall and D. Soskice (eds) *Varieties of Capitalism: The Institutional Foundations of Comparative Advantage*, Oxford: Oxford University Press, pp. 1–68.

Kenney, M. (ed.) (2000) *Understanding Silicon Valley: The Anatomy of an Entrepreneurial Region*, Stanford, CA: Stanford University Press.

Krauss, G. (2002) *Risiko, Misserfolge und Entwicklungsbrüche junger E-Commerce-Unternehmen in wissensbasierten Wirtschaftsfeldern in Kalifornien*, Stuttgart: Akademie für Technikfolgenabschätzung in Baden-Württemberg.

Lane, C. and Bachmann, R. (eds) (1998) *Trust Within and Between Organizations: Conceptual Issues and Empirical Applications*, New York: Oxford University Press.

Le Galès, P. and Voelzkow, H. (2001) 'Introduction: the governance of local economies', in C. Crouch, P. Le Galès, C. Trigilia, and H. Voelzkow (eds) *Local Production Systems in Europe. Rise or Demise?* Oxford: Oxford University Press, pp. 1–24.

Leslie, S.W. (2000) 'The biggest "angel" of them all: the military and the making of Silicon Valley', in M. Kenney (ed.) *Understanding Silicon Valley: The Anatomy of an Entrepreneurial Region*, Stanford, CA: Stanford University Press, pp. 48–67.

Luhmann, N. (1975) 'Weltgesellschaft', in N. Luhmann *Soziologische Aufklärung 2: Aufsätze zur Theorie der Gesellschaft*, Opladen: Westdeutscher Verlag, pp. 51–71.

Luhmann, N. (1994) *Die Wissenschaft der Gesellschaft*, 2nd edn, Frankfurt: Suhrkamp.

Lundvall, B.-A (ed.) (1992) *National Systems of Innovation: Towards a Theory of Innovation and Interactive Learning*, London: Pinter.

Metcalfe, S. (1995) 'The economic foundations of technology policy: equilibrium and evolutionary perspectives', in P. Stoneman (ed.), *Handbook of the Economics of Innovation and Technological Change*, Oxford: Blackwell Publishers, pp. 409–512.

Nelson, R.R. (ed.) (1993) *National Systems of Innovation: A Comparative Analysis*, Oxford: Oxford University Press.

Nelson, R.R. and Winter, S.G. (1982) *An Evolutionary Theory of Economic Change*, Cambridge, MA: Harvard University Press.

North, D.C. (1990) *Institutions, Institutional Change and Economic Performance*, Cambridge: Cambridge University Press.

Patel, P. and Pavitt, K. (1998) *National Systems of Innovation under Strain: The Internationalisation of Corporate R&D*, Electronic Working Papers Series Paper No 22. Sussex: Science Policy Research Unit.

Piore, M.J. and Sabel, C.F. (1984) *The Second Industrial Divide: Possibilities for Prosperity*, New York: Basic Books.

Powell, W., Koput, K. and Smith-Doerr, L. (1996) 'Interorganizational collaboration and the locus of innovation: networks of learning in biotechnology', *Administrative Science Quarterly*, 116–145.

Rammert, W. (1988) *Das Innovationsdilemma: Technikentwicklung im Unternehmen*, Opladen: Westdeutscher Verlag.

Salais, R. and Storper, M. (1993) *Les mondes de production: Enquête sur l'identité économique de la France*, Paris: Edition de l'Ecole des Hautes Etudes en Sciences Sociales.

Sassen, S. (2000) *Cities in a World Economy*, Thousand Oaks, CA: Sage Press.

Saxenian, A. (1994) *Regional Advantage: Culture and Competition in Silicon Valley and Route 128*, Cambridge, MA: Harvard University Press.

Schumpeter, J.A. (1935) *Theorie der wirtschaftlichen Entwicklung*, 4th edn, Leipzig: Duncker & Humboldt.

Scott, A.J. (1998) *Regions and the World Economy: The Coming Shape of Global Production, Competition, and Political Order*, Oxford: Oxford University Press.

Simmie, J., Sennett, J., Wood, P. and Hart, D. (2002) 'Innovation in Europe: a tale of networks, knowledge and trade in five cities', *Regional Studies*, 36(1): 47–64.

Storper, M. (1997) *The Regional World: Territorial Development in a Global Economy*, London: Guilford Press.

Storper, M. and Scott, A.J. (1995) 'The wealth of regions: market forces and policy imperatives in local and global context', *Futures*, 27(5) June: 505–526.

Tushman, M.L., and Rosenberg, L. (1992) 'Organizational determinants of technological change: toward a sociology of technological evolution', *Research in Organizational Behavior*, 14: 311–347.

Weick, K.E. and Westley, F. (1996) 'Organizational learning: affirming an oxymoron', in S.R. Clegg, C. Hardy and W.R. Nord (eds) *Handbook of Organization Studies*, London: Sage, pp. 440–458.

Winter, S.G. (1984) 'Schumpeterian competition in alternative technological regimes', *Journal of Economic Behavior and Organization*, 5: 287–320.

Zaltman, G., Duncan, R. and Holbek, J. (1973) *Innovations and Organizations*, New York: John Wiley.

Index